BLACKSTONE'S GUIDE

The Equality Act

FOURTH EDITION

CW00923649

The Equality Act 2010

FOURTH EDITION

Edited by
Anthony Robinson, David Ruebain,
and Susie Uppal

OXFORD
UNIVERSITY PRESS

OXFORD
UNIVERSITY PRESS

Great Clarendon Street, Oxford, OX2 6DP,
United Kingdom

Oxford University Press is a department of the University of Oxford.
It furthers the University's objective of excellence in research, scholarship,
and education by publishing worldwide. Oxford is a registered trade mark of
Oxford University Press in the UK and in certain other countries

© Oxford University Press 2021

First Edition published in 2010
Second Edition published in 2012
Third Edition published in 2016
Fourth Edition published in 2021

Impression: 3

Published in the United States of America by Oxford University Press
198 Madison Avenue, New York, NY 10016, United States of America

British Library Cataloguing in Publication Data

Data available

Library of Congress Control Number: 2020951486

ISBN 978–0–19–887087–6

DOI: 10.1093/oso/9780198870876.001.0001

Printed and bound by
CPI Group (UK) Ltd, Croydon, CR0 4YY

Foreword

Equality – you might think it is quite a simple idea but in fact it is very complicated and very controversial. When the law first began to tackle race and sex discrimination in the 1960s and 1970s, the idea of equality was that 'like cases should be treated alike'. Women should be treated the same as men. Blacks should be treated the same as whites. But that also meant that men should be treated the same as women and whites should be treated the same as blacks, despite the historic advantages that men and whites had enjoyed and the historic disadvantages that women and blacks had suffered. A simple enough idea: but even then there were questions. What areas of activity should be covered by the law? And should there be any exceptions? And even in those early days, it was understood that treating everyone in the same way did not always have the same impact on both sexes or all races. So we had the first complication – the concept of indirect discrimination: imposing a requirement which one sex would find harder to meet than the other and which could not be objectively justified. This was a small contribution to levelling the playing field. A much greater contribution to levelling the playing field but introducing complexity came with the Disability Discrimination Act of 1995. Disabled people had sometimes to be treated differently from others if they were to have genuine equality of opportunity. Reasonable adjustments would have to be made. People might be treated better because of their disability but not worse because of it.

Then the range of personal characteristics protected from discrimination was extended further – principally to include sexual orientation, religion or belief, and age. Delicate balances had to be struck: the law had to decide deciding whether a person or body who sincerely believed that they had to treat certain people differently from others should be allowed to do so.

The next question was what to do about securing genuine equality for traditionally excluded or disadvantaged groups? To what extent is it possible to discriminate in their favour in order to bring their level of participation up to that of the traditionally advantaged groups? What is the difference between affirmative action to help bring them on and positive discrimination in their favour? And perhaps the biggest question of all: if we believe in the equal dignity of all human beings we probably also believe in diversity as a good in itself. A diverse body not only looks better than a homogenous one: it is also likely to make better decisions. But to what extent is it permissible to take the benefits of having a diverse team into account in training and recruitment decisions?

Over time we have moved on a little from equality of *treatment*, towards equality of *opportunity*, but we are still a long way from equality of *outcome* – and perhaps we always should be. Readers who are interested in these niceties might like to start with the chapter by Rachel Crasnow QC on 'Redressing the Balance'.

The resulting legislation is enormously complex. The Equality Act 2010 replaced the rag bag of separate, characteristic-based laws with a single law which was meant to be coherent and easy to understand. But it has 218 sections and 28 schedules (one repealed). There are also numerous sets of regulations made under the Act. It is not easy to look up the answer to a simple question by looking at the legislation. This book aims to provide that guide. The fact that it is now in its fourth edition after only ten years since the Act was passed shows what a mammoth task that is. But it also shows how necessary it is.

Brenda Hale

Preface

Although all the editors and some of the chapter authors were previously employed by the Equality and Human Rights Commission, any views expressed are our own and not those of the Commission, and we must take responsibility for the errors. The law is stated as at December 2020.

Anthony Robinson, David Ruebain, and Susie Uppal
November 2020

Acknowledgements

The editors and authors would again like to acknowledge all those who helped to ensure that this legislation became an Act and that its provisions came into force quickly after Royal Assent, at the time making the final version perhaps one of the most impressive domestic equality laws anywhere in the world.

The editors would particularly like to acknowledge and thank John Wadham, our friend and former colleague, who was instrumental in the instigation of this book and was our co-editor in the first three editions. In addition, the editors would like to thank those authors of previous editions who have not been able to help with this one—Sarfraz Khan (Chapter 1), Keith Ashcroft (Chapter 3), Esther Maynard and Brenda Parkes (Chapter 4), Nony Ardill (Chapter 5), and Ulele Burnham (Chapter 8). A special thanks to Andy Redman, Zoe Tustin, and Arokia Anthuvan Rani from Oxford University Press, who have been helpful and supportive to us throughout the draft of this edition. Finally, we are very appreciative of Lady Hale agreeing to give up her time to consider this volume and write the Foreword.

The royalties from this publication are to be paid to the Equal Rights Trust, a charity whose mission is to combat discrimination and promote equality as a fundamental human right and a principle of social justice.

Anthony Robinson, David Ruebain, and Susie Uppal
November 2020

Contents—Summary

Contents—Detailed

8. THE PUBLIC SECTOR EQUALITY DUTY AND THE SOCIO-ECONOMIC DUTY

List of Contributors

EDITORS

Anthony Robinson is an Assistant Director in the Professional Regulation Directorate at the Nursing & Midwifery Council. He set up and is the Managing Partner of the Human Rights & Equalities Consultancy. He was the Director of Casework and Litigation at the EHRC. Prior to this Anthony was the Director of Legal Services at the Commission for Racial Equality. He was one of the founders of Euroneb that became Equinet (the European Network of Equality Bodies). He has published widely on these areas and is a regular conference speaker. Anthony is a CEDR accredited mediator.

David Ruebain is Chief Executive of the Conservatoire for Dance and Drama. Prior to that, he was Chief Executive of the Equality Challenge Unit, a policy and research agency funded to advance equality and diversity in the UK further and higher education sectors. Before that, he was a practising solicitor for 21 years; latterly as Director of Legal Policy at the Equality and Human Rights Commission of Great Britain and before that as a Partner at and founder of the department of Education, Equality and Disability Law at Levenes Solicitors. David is also a Visiting Professor of Law at Birkbeck University of London. He is an ADR Group accredited mediator, a judge on the annual Guardian University Awards, equality adviser to the English FA Premier League, a member of the Diversity and Inclusion Strategic Advisory Board of the Wellcome Trust, and a Fellow of the British American Project. David has published widely and taught nationally and internationally on education, disability, and equality law and has been involved in numerous voluntary organizations, drafting Private Members Bills and in making oral representations to Committees of Parliament. He was a member of the Advisory Group of the Office for Fair Access, a Trustee of Action on Disability and Development International, a Member of the Rights & Justice Committee of the Joseph Rowntree Charitable Trust, a past Chair of the Law Society of England and Wales' Mental Health and Disability Committee, a Board member of Equinet—the European Network of Equality Bodies, a Short Term Expert to a European Union Twinning Project, and an ADR Group Accredited Mediator. David is the winner of RADAR's People of the Year Award for Achievement in the Furtherance of Human Rights of Disabled People in the UK, 2002. He was also shortlisted for the Law Society's Gazette Centenary Award for Lifetime Achievement—Human Rights, in November 2003. In August 2006, David was listed as one of the 25 Most Influential Disabled People in the UK by *Disability Now* Magazine. He was listed in the Disability News Service's 'Influence Index' and is listed in three editions of the Disability Power List.

Susie Uppal is the Chief Executive and Solicitor of the Press Recognition Panel, the independent body set up to ensure that any organization which regulates the press is independent, properly funded and able to protect the public, while recognizing the important role carried out by the press. Susie is a solicitor and was previously Senior Ombudsman at The Legal Ombudsman, Director of Legal Enforcement at the EHRC,(where she led the Commission's work on Judicial Reviews, Inquiries and investigations)and before that Head of

Enforcement for the Gambling Commission. She has also conducted forensic investigations for the Solicitors Regulation Authority, served as an independent member of the Regulatory Affairs Board of the Law Society and was a Commercial Litigation solicitor in private practice for many years. In addition to leading on a number of high profile investigations, inquiries, and actions in domestic courts and European courts Susie has a wealth of experience in building and leading organizations through transformational change.

CONTRIBUTORS

Robin Allen QC is Queen's Counsel and a Recorder; from 2002–2018 he was Head of Cloisters barristers' chambers, and from 2013–2019 he chaired the Bar Council's Equality and Diversity Committee. He has specialized in employment, discrimination, public, and human rights law since the 1970s, working throughout Europe and the UK. He advised the European Commission over the use of Article 13 EC to make the Equality Directives and was also a member of the Government's Human Rights Act Task Force. He has appeared in numerous leading domestic and ECJ equality cases. He is a former special legal adviser to the UK's Disability Rights Commission, a former Chair of the Employment Law Bar Association, and a founder member of the Discrimination Law Association. He has worked with the Equality Authority, the Equality Commission for Northern Ireland, and the EHRC. In 2018 he gave the prestigious Hamlyn Lectures, which were published in 2020 as *Making Comparisons in Equality Law*. His other books include *Employment Law and Human Rights* (with Rachel Crasnow QC and others) and *Family Rights at Work* (also with Rachel Crasnow).

Anna Beale is a barrister at Cloisters chambers who specializes in employment, discrimination, clinical negligence and personal injury law. She has extensive experience of litigating discrimination claims under the Equality Act, including representing many thousands of employees in several of the most high profile public and private sector mass equal pay claims. She is a fee-paid Employment Judge, and a member of the EHRC's panel of counsel. Anna is very familiar with the European aspects of employment and discrimination law, having co-authored a comparative report on Age and Employment for the European Commission in 2011, and conducted seminars for the Commission and the Academy of European Law on equality matters. Anna is also the co-author of *Employment Law and Human Rights* (3rd edn, OUP 2018), a co-editor of *Discrimination in Employment: a claims handbook* (LAG 2013), and a contributor to *Family Rights at Work* (ed Allen and Crasnow, Jordans 2012). In 2017, she was appointed as a member of the Fawcett Society's Sex Discrimination Law Review Panel, which produced a report (published January 2018) advising on the future of sex discrimination law in the UK.

Tom Brown practises as a barrister from Cloisters chambers. He specializes in employment, equality, human rights, and public law. He has worked at the United Nations International Criminal Tribunal for Rwanda, as a Judicial Assistant to the late Lord Bingham of Cornhill, Senior Law Lord, and at the Federal Court of Australia. He has lectured on equality law at the Academy of European Law and written on employment and equality law.

Sophie Buckley is a barrister specializing in employment law and discrimination. She was called to the bar in 1999 and has spent time in private practice, as a Senior Lecturer in employment law at Northumbria University, and as a Senior Lawyer at the EHRC. She currently sits as a fee-paid employment and information rights tribunal judge. She is a door tenant at Dere Street Barristers. Her publications include *Dispute Resolution—The New Law* (co-author), Northumbria Law Press, 2004; *Pearce, McDonald and the new Legislation— three steps forward, two steps back?*(co-author), *J. Civ. Lib.* 08/2 July 2003 67; *Dunnachie—the return of the phoenix?* (co-author), *ELA Bulletin; Equal Pay Update 2007* and *2009, Industrial Relations Law Bulletin.*

Catherine Casserley is a barrister at Cloisters chambers. She specializes in equality, human rights, and employment law. She has particular expertise in disability discrimination law, having worked as Senior Legal Adviser with the Disability Rights Commission (DRC), and in the Equality Act 2010. Having previously been appointed as specialist adviser to the House of Lords Committee on Disability and the Equality Act in 2020 she was appointed as Specialist Adviser to the Women and Equality Committee sub inquiry on disability and Covid-19. She has also developed particular expertise in trans discrimination issues, advising national organizations on strategic and policy issues arising from the legislation. She is on the EHRC panel of counsel, and has been instructed by law centres, individuals, public authorities, and employers and has appeared at all levels up to and including the House of Lords, and Supreme Court on some of the leading discrimination cases. She advises disability organizations and the EHRC on a regular basis on strategic litigation and legal policy issues; she has a predominantly claimant-based practice in non-employment discrimination, including services, public authority functions, particularly the equality duties, premises, and education. She has written and presented widely on discrimination law.

Glynis Craig works as an in-house solicitor as part of Legal Services to the Independent Police Complaints Commission (IPCC). In addition to advising and representing the IPCC in relation to deaths in police custody, deaths or serious injury following police contact, and police disciplinary proceedings, she regularly advises on equality and human rights matters and is the lawyer responsible for developing the IPCC discrimination guidelines. She previously was a senior lawyer at the Equality and Human Rights Commission; dealing mainly with litigation enforcing the Equality Act. Her background is in the Law Centres Federation and she has spent many years as a solicitor in the North West specializing in immigration and asylum law. She is the vice-chair of the St John's Centre, an organization established to promote equality following the Manchester Moss Side riots in 1981.

Rachel Crasnow QC is a leading employment specialist, appointed silk in 2015 and described by Chambers & Partners as 'a determined, gutsy advocate who demonstrates the rare ability to spot subtle points in highly specialised discrimination cases'. Rachel appears at all levels in complex, high-value discrimination complaints as well as worker status, injunctive relief, equal pay, and whistleblowing cases. Her appellate work has recently focused on the securing of judicial pensions for part-time judges in claims worth £2.2 billion to the Treasury following success in the Supreme Court (*O'Brien v MOJ*). She has also sought disability and whistleblowing rights for judges. Rachel has many years of experience in equal pay work in the public and private sector and appeared in the Court of Justice in *Cadman v HSE* on service-based pay scales as a defence to equal pay claims. She has represented thousands of women in local authority and care home equal pay claims. Rachel has led on equality and diversity work for the Bar Council as chair of its legislation committee for many years and was made a Diversity Law Champion in 2018. In September 2015 she gave evidence before the House of Lords Select Committee on the Equality Act regarding access to justice and disability rights. Her publications include *Employment Law and Human Rights* (OUP) 3rd edition 2019 and *Family Rights in Employment Law* (Jordans 2012) (both with Robin Allen QC). Rachel sits as a part-time Police Appeals Tribunal judge and a Recorder and is a trained mediator. She writes and lectures extensively both in the UK and beyond. Her recent positive action work includes writing the Bar Council's positive action guidance for sets of chambers.

Chris Fry is one of the leading Disability Rights lawyers in the UK. He is founder of Fry Law which has been responsible for many high profile successful cases which have shaped the evolution of disability rights, including the only Supreme Court case in goods and services: *Paulley v First Bus*. He is a trusted Media commentator on disability discrimination in a consumer and public law context, speaks regularly at conferences, and is a CEDR accredited mediator. Chris is also co-founder of Disability Rights Advice TV.

Elizabeth George is a specialist employment and discrimination law barrister with more than 20 years' experience. She began her legal career as an employment solicitor at Paddington Law Centre before transferring to the bar in 2005, completing her barrister training with leading employment set, Cloisters. Elizabeth was the first woman, in its one-hundred-year history, to head up the employment and discrimination department at national trade union firm, Pattinson Brewer. She is currently Employed Counsel at human rights firm, Leigh Day. She has a particular interest in and long-standing commitment to using equalities legislation to achieve a fairer workplace for women and is currently acting for acting for hundreds of women store staff in their national group equal pay claim. Elizabeth still conducts her own employment tribunal advocacy (when she has time) and is an experienced trainer and speaker, devising and delivering employment and discrimination law training for ACAS, TUC, employment solicitors, trade unions, and charities.

Karen Jackson is a solicitor and Managing Director of didlaw, a niche discrimination law firm specializing in disability discrimination, other health-related work issues and women's issues in the workplace. Karen is a Chambers & Partners ranked lawyer. didlaw is ranked in the Legal 500 for employee work. Karen is a CEDR accredited mediator and litigates in the Employment Tribunals. Karen founded her firm didlaw in 2008 after being out of work for several years due to heart failure. Her survival is thanks to a successful heart transplant at Royal Papworth Hospital in 2006. A Law Society nominee for Woman Lawyer of the Year, Karen is a LawCare Champion and a former trustee of the Mental Health Foundation. Karen represented the claimant in *Williams v Swansea* which was the first Supreme Court decision on section 15 of the Equality Act in the employment context. Karen is regularly asked to comment on employment and discrimination law issues in the national press and media and has appeared on Panorama, on BBC TV, and radio more widely. She is co-author of *Disability Discrimination, Law & Case Management* published by Law Society Publishing and is a vocal advocate for equality.

Razia Karim is a non-practising solicitor and discrimination law consultant. She was a senior lawyer at the EHRC where she focused on race discrimination, socio-economic, and children's rights. She was also part of the team who worked on the Equality Bill and produced the Commission's Statutory Codes of Practice on the Equality Act 2010. Prior to joining the Commission, she was Head of Legal and European Policy at the Commission for Racial

Equality (CRE) where she led the CRE's programme of work on a single equality act and worked closely with civil servants on the creation of the EHRC. Razia has also worked as a legal specialist to the Justice Select Committee in the House of Commons and as a legal policy officer at JUSTICE, working on miscarriages of justice, discrimination, and human rights. She is a trustee of the Race Equality Foundation which promotes race equality in health, social care, housing, and education and a member of the Citizens' Advice Equality Committee. She currently works as an ombudsman.

Rhodri McDonald is a salaried Employment Judge sitting in the North Western Region. Prior to his appointment to the judiciary he was a Senior Lawyer at the Equality and Human Rights Commission and sat as a fee paid Employment Judge in Wales.

Laura Prince is a barrister at Matrix chambers specializing in employment and discrimination law. Laura is recommended in Chambers and Partners as having particular 'expertise in handling complex TUPE and equal pay matters' and it is stated that 'her calm, intelligent and measured approach to all cases and request for advice is a great legal and commercial asset to any company'. Laura has been involved in over thirty cases at appellate level. Laura's reported cases include *Alemo-Herron v Parkwood Leisure* (CJEU), *Houga v Allen* (Supreme Court, illegality and discrimination), *Okedina v Chile* (Court of Appeal) and *Gallop v Newport* (Court of Appeal, disability discrimination).

Rana Ranjit is a freelance equality and human rights consultant. He has extensive experience in the equality and human rights field, specializing in race equality, working with clients to navigate the legal terrain, to develop and action pragmatic bespoke strategies that strengthen capability creating sustainable business edge. Rana is a Committee member, on the 'Big Baby Project', at Warwick University, which is testing new techniques that may reduce shoulder dystocia during the birthing process, minimizing risk of injury to mother and child. Previously Rana was at the Equality and Human Rights Commission (EHRC), as Programme Head in the Legal department, where he led on the operationalization of the Equality Act 2010, the Equalities Mediation Service, Legal Grants Programme, Human Rights Programme, and the 'Is Britain Fairer?' report. Prior to this, he was at the Commission for Racial Equality, as Head of Employment Policy. Rana has authored 'Racial Discrimination', a chapter in the *Working in the UK: Newcomer's Handbook, 2nd edition*, aimed at advisers, representatives, and advocates.

Peter Reading is an international human rights lawyer who has been working in the field of human rights law and advocacy for 20 years in Australia, the United Kingdom, Europe, Commonwealth countries, and most recently in Hong Kong, China. Since November 2012, Peter has been working at the Equal Opportunities Commission (EOC) in Hong Kong, most recently as Senior Legal Counsel. In his role he has been leading the EOC's advocacy work to modernize all the existing discrimination legislation in Hong Kong relating to sex, disability, race, and family status. He has also been instrumental in work to introduce anti-discrimination legislation relating to LGBTI groups. Previously for 11 years Peter worked in London in a number of human rights roles including at Amnesty International UK; the CRE as Principal Litigation Officer and Head of European and International Legal Policy from 2005 to 2008; the EHRC as a Senior Lawyer and Director of Legal Policy from 2008 to 2012; and at the Commonwealth Secretariat in 2012 as a human rights consultant on Commonwealth projects. In Europe, between 2008 and 2012, Peter was also the Moderator of the Legal Working Group of the Equinet Network of 41 Equality Bodies in Europe, where he was responsible for a number of Equinet's legal reports on equality issues. Peter is a co-author of *Blackstone's Guide to the Equality Act*, (1st–3rd edns, OUP; and *Tort Law and Practice in Hong Kong* (2nd edn, 1st supp 2013, Sweet and Maxwell). Since 2009, Peter has also been a regular speaker at the European Academy of Law in Germany on EU anti-discrimination and human rights law, and since 2015 has been a Member of the Executive Committee of Amnesty International Hong Kong.

Table of Cases

Table of Legislation

1

INTERNATIONAL TREATIES

1

INTRODUCTION AND BACKGROUND

A.	Territorial Application	1.01
B.	History and Sources of Equality Law in the UK	1.03
C.	The Introduction and Passage of the Equality Act 2010	1.19
D.	Structure of the Act	1.36
E.	Brexit and UK Equality Law	1.41

A. TERRITORIAL APPLICATION

The Equality Act 2010 ('the Act') forms part of the law of England and Wales.[1] Apart from **1.01** section 190 (improvements to let dwelling houses) and Part 15 (family property), it also forms part of the law of Scotland.[2] Claims under Part 3 (Services and Public Functions), and those for discrimination on grounds of race, religion, or belief in an entry clearance decision, can be founded on something done outside the UK.[3] There are provisions enabling Welsh and Scottish Ministers to bring devolved law in line with that in England, particularly in relation to the duties on their public sector bodies and cross-border public bodies in respect of their devolved functions.[4] With very minor exceptions, the Act does not apply in Northern Ireland. Equal opportunities and discrimination are among the areas of legislative responsibility transferred to the Northern Ireland Assembly under the Northern Ireland Act 1998.[5] In practice the Act is an important source of ideas for the Northern Ireland Assembly though there are significant differences in equality law there and in Great Britain, for instance, there are as yet no provisions outlawing discrimination on grounds of age in relation to goods, facilities, and services. However these differences are a source of contention and since the last edition of this book a major difference has been eroded. It is now possible to enter into a same-sex marriage in Northern Ireland.[6]

The provisions stating that the Act forms part of the law of England and Wales and **1.02** Scotland do not limit the reach of the Act solely to events that occur in one or more of those places. It is sometimes possible to rely on this law in relation to events that have happened

---

[1] See s. 217(1).
[2] See s. 217(2).
[3] S. 114(5)(b) and s. 29(9).
[4] See e.g. s. 2(4)–(7), ss. 151–5.
[5] Sch. 2.
[6] See Northern Ireland (Executive Formation etc) Act 2019 s. 8 entering into effect from the 13 January 2020.

Robin Allen QC, *Introduction and Background* In: *Blackstone's Guide to the Equality Act 2010*. Fourth Edition. Edited by: Anthony Robinson, David Ruebain, and Susie Uppal, Oxford University Press (2021). © Oxford University Press. DOI: 10.1093/oso/9780198870876.003.0001

geographically elsewhere. The Explanatory Notes to the Act made this intention clear stating[7] that 'As far as territorial application is concerned, in relation to Part 5 (work) and following the precedent of the Employment Rights Act 1996, the Act leaves it to tribunals to determine whether the law applies, depending for example on the connection between the employment relationship and Great Britain.' So, in approaching jurisdiction issues Employment Tribunals will consider cases such as the House of Lords judgment in *Lawson v Serco* [2006] IRLR 289, HL.[8]

It is likely that the Employment Tribunal will accept jurisdiction where an employee is or has been working abroad for the purposes of a business carried on at the employer's establishment in Great Britain if he or she was ordinarily resident in Great Britain either when applying for or being offered the job, or at any time during the employment.[9] Indeed it has been argued that 'Given the close links between EU equality law and the domestic legislation, there is the likelihood that (at least where some or all of the relevant facts relate to events in another Member State) the courts will be reluctant to allow arguments of "no jurisdiction" to frustrate claims by individuals with directly effective rights that otherwise would be arguable.'[10]

B. HISTORY AND SOURCES OF EQUALITY LAW IN THE UK

1. Background

1.03 The development of Equality Law through legislation has taken place in fits and starts over a very long period. Discrimination was endemic against women, slaves, Roman Catholics, Non-Conformists, and Jews for many centuries. Changes can be traced back at least to first enactments for the abolition of slavery and the Catholic Emancipation Acts of the 19th Century.[11] After the abolition of slavery persons of colour working in the British Navy were expressly given an entitlement to equal pay by successive Navy Acts of the 19th Century. By 1918 the Vienna Treaty ending the First World War was able to say when founding the International Labour Organization that there should be equal pay for work of equal value.[12] Various constitutional enactments in the 20th Century relating to Ireland and later Northern Ireland forbade discrimination on the basis of religion and belief.

1.04 However, in broad terms it can be said that modern Equality Law has taken one or more of three routes into UK law:

- by Parliament enacting statutes, following campaigns or lobbying by the sections of society affected and their advocates;

---

[7] See Explanatory Notes at [15].

[8] See also *Bleuse v MBT Transport* [2008] IRLR 264, EAT; *MOD v Wallis and Grocott* [2011] EWCA Civ 231; [2011] 2 CMLR 42; [2011] ICR 617; [2011] Eq LR 388, CA. Note also the approach in *Duncombe v Secretary of State for Children, Schools and Families (No 2)* [2011] UKSC 36; *Ravat v Halliburton Manufacturing & Services Ltd* [2012] UKSC 1; and *British Council v Jeffery* [2018] EWCA Civ 2253.

[9] See for comparison s. 10(1), 10(1A) of the Sex Discrimination Act 1975.

[10] See *Harvey on Industrial Relations* at [103].

[11] See for instance the Roman Catholic Relief Act 1829.

[12] For a discussion of the implementation of this right see R. Allen (2020). *Making Comparisons in Equality Law: Within Gender, Age and Conflicts* (The Hamlyn Lectures). (Cambridge University Press 2020), chapter 2.

- in the case of the public sector duties, as a response to the criticisms of the police and other public services in Sir William Macpherson's report on the death of Stephen Lawrence;[13] and
- by European Union (EU) making primary laws and directives.

Overlaid on these routes there are three other factors that are working their way into the modern jurisprudence and affecting how it develops. These are:

- the provisions of the European Convention on Human Rights, particularly Article 14 which though only operating in a parasitic way through other provisions of the Convention, prohibits discrimination on a wide set of grounds,
- the European Charter of Fundamental Rights which incorporates rights from the European Convention on Human Rights and also economic and social rights found in other international instruments,[14]
- United Nations Conventions such as the Convention on the Rights of Persons with Disabilities 2006 (CRPD),[15] the Convention on the Elimination of All Forms of Discrimination against Women 1979 (CEDAW),[16] and the International Convention on the Elimination of All Forms of Racial Discrimination 1965.[17]

2. Race and Sex Discrimination Law in the 1960s–1970s

The reforming Labour governments of the late 1960s and 1970s first introduced laws to protect certain groups from adverse discrimination. These laws drew on the approaches taken by the United States government in its Equal Pay Act 1963, and Civil Rights Acts 1964 and 1968. Another driver was the law of the European Economic Community (EEC), or 'Common Market', the precursor of the European Union, which the UK applied to join in 1963 and 1967, and finally joined in 1973. The EEC's founding Treaty required Member States to 'maintain the principle that men and women should receive equal pay for equal work'.[18]   1.05

Like the legislation passed by the US Congress, the original UK anti-discrimination statutes related initially to race and then to sex, but here extended additionally to prohibit discrimination on grounds of married status. (Previously, women often had to stop work on marriage, the expectation being that their husbands—who would have higher earning power—should support them, and priority being given to employing men.) The UK Parliament enacted Race Relations Acts in 1965, 1968, and 1976, each statute extending the sectors affected. The Equal Pay Act 1970 and Equal Pay Act (Northern Ireland) 1970 were enacted in the expectation that the UK would be joining the EEC. By the time of the Sex Discrimination Act 1975 (SDA), this had happened. But the UK led the rest of the Community by passing the SDA before the EEC issued its Equal Treatment Directive of 1976.[19]   1.06

---

[13] *The Stephen Lawrence Inquiry* (Cm 4262–1).
[14] See for instance *Benkharbouche v Embassy of Sudan* [2015] EWCA Civ 33; [2016] QB 347; [2015] 3 WLR 301; [2016] 1 All ER 816; [2015] 2 CMLR 20; [2015] ICR 793; [2015] IRLR 301; [2015] HRLR 3; CA.
[15] See <https://www.un.org/development/desa/disabilities/convention-on-the-rights-of-persons-with-disabilities/convention-on-the-rights-of-persons-with-disabilities-2.html>.
[16] See <https://www.ohchr.org/EN/ProfessionalInterest/Pages/CEDAW.aspx>.
[17] See <https://www.ohchr.org/en/professionalinterest/pages/cerd.aspx>.
[18] Now see Art. 157 of the Treaty on the Functioning of the European Union.
[19] 76/207/EEC.

1.07   By the mid-1970s the basic architecture of UK discrimination law was in place:

(a) fundamental concepts including direct and indirect discrimination, victimization, and incitement were defined;

(b) the law extended (though neither equally nor fully) to employment, education, training, and the provision of goods and services;

(c) there existed Commissions (the Equal Opportunities Commission and the Commission for Racial Equality) with responsibilities such as oversight of the legislation in practice, and powers to conduct investigations, fund individuals' legal costs in proceedings, and take enforcement proceedings in their own right.

3. Disability Discrimination

1.08   Perhaps because the campaigns carried out by people with disabilities were so effective, legislation to extend similar protection in relation to disability was introduced to Parliament not by a Labour government, like those that have brought in other equality legislation, but by a Conservative administration. The Disability Discrimination Act 1995 prohibited discrimination according to a pattern similar to that established in the race and sex legislation of the 1970s. Where campaigners initially fell short of their objectives was in getting the government to set up a Commission to oversee the functioning of the law and bring or fund proceedings under it. Only after the election of a Labour administration in 1997 was the Disability Rights Commission created.[20]

1.09   Disability discrimination law does not reproduce the template of other forms of equality law exactly.[21] A departure that was of great practical significance was that the new law addressed the disadvantages suffered by people with disabilities because vehicles, shops, homes, and offices are designed for the majority and are often not accessible for people with particular needs. The Act introduced a requirement for employers[22] and service providers[23] to make 'reasonable adjustments' to alter features of the workplace, shop, office, or other environment that put disabled people at a disadvantage. Campaigners in the USA had succeeded in bringing in similar provisions, in relation to public places, as federal law a few years previously.[24] Such obligations are now part of international human rights norms as can be seen in the CRPD.

4. The Public Sector Duties

1.10   The government's decision to power up discrimination law by the creation of public sector duties (and make other significant changes in the law)[25] was its response to the justice system's failure following the murder of a 19-year-old black student, Stephen Lawrence, while he was waiting for a bus in Eltham, South East London, on 22 April 1993. Known individuals were

---

[20] Disability Rights Commission Act 1999.

[21] See para. 3.18.

[22] Disability Discrimination Act 1995 s. 6.

[23] *ibid*, s. 21.

[24] Americans with Disabilities Act 1990.

[25] For example, Freedom of Information Act 2000 s. 31 (creating rights of subject access to information held by the police); Criminal Justice Act 2003 Part 10 (abolition of double jeopardy rule).

widely suspected of guilt, and of having been motivated solely by racial hostility. But because of mistakes and omissions during the police investigation, no-one was convicted of Stephen's murder until long afterwards.[26]

A campaign by Stephen's friends and family led eventually to the Home Secretary of the time setting up a Public Inquiry, chaired by Sir William Macpherson, which reported in February 1999. The Report made 70 recommendations[27] for changes in policy, practice, and the law. It did not attribute racist attitudes to any of the individuals who investigated the crime, but described the police 'and other institutions countrywide' as 'institutionally racist'.[28]   1.11

Some stakeholders responded to this conclusion by denying and contesting it.[29] Others treated it as a springboard for positive change, aimed at making the police and other public services more representative of, and responsive to, all the communities they serve, rather than only the dominant majority. In particular, the public sector duties can be seen as Parliament putting into effect (at least in respect of the public sector) Macpherson's exhortation: 'It is incumbent upon every institution to examine their policies and the outcome of their policies and practices to guard against disadvantaging any sections of our communities.'[30]   1.12

The 'public sector duties' represent a qualitative change from the law that preceded them. Whereas the statutes prohibiting discriminatory acts imposed a negative duty—not to commit or perform certain acts in relation to an individual, in a range of situations—these provisions say that the public sector bodies must: 1.13

- 'give due regard to the need to eliminate unlawful discrimination and to promote equality of opportunity' (the general duties); and

- carry out defined actions in order to achieve the general duty.

The nature of the 'specific duties' varies according to the form of discrimination being addressed, but includes assessing the impact of policies and procedures on people of different ethnic origins, and publishing equality schemes, produced in consultation with staff and service users.   1.14

Once again the law began to make headway in relation to race, imposing public sector duties in the Race Relations (Amendment) Act 2000. The Disability Discrimination (Amendment) Act 2005, and provisions in the Equality Act 2006, introduced similar requirements in relation to disability and gender respectively. In July 2008 the government announced its intention to create a Single Equality Duty, so that all seven strands of equality law would be contained in one set of general and specific public sector duties. The projected date for that duty to be brought into effect was January 2010, so it became entwined with the implementation of the Equality Act.   1.15

---

[26] See *The Stephen Lawrence Inquiry* (Cm 4262–1); Gary Dobson and David Norris were convicted of his murder on 3 January 2012.

[27] *ibid*, Ch. 47.

[28] *ibid*, Ch. 6.39, Ch. 46.27.

[29] See e.g. Green (ed.), *Institutional Racism and the Police: Fact or Fiction?* (Institute for the Study of Civil Society, August 2000).

[30] *ibid* 46.27.

5. Provisions Entering UK Law as a Result of EU Law

1.16　The UK entered the European Union[31] by becoming a signatory to the Treaty of Rome.[32] Article 189 of that Treaty made a directive of the EU directly binding in each member state, while leaving it to the signatory state to determine the form and means by which the directive would be put into effect within its jurisdiction or jurisdictions.[33] The approach has been continued in Community law up to the present day.[34]

1.17　Over time, the EU Council, or the Council and EU Parliament together, have issued the following:

- directives initially concerning equal pay,[35] and equal treatment in the workplace in respect of gender,[36] eventually combined with others in the Recast Gender Directive;[37]
- a directive in respect of race;[38] and
- a Framework Directive, making overarching provision for equal treatment in the workplace in respect of disability, religion or belief, sexual orientation, and age.[39]

1.18　These directives affected existing principles of UK law, including the definition of indirect discrimination and the burden of proof in proceedings. The Framework Directive compelled the UK Parliament to extend the scope of protection from discrimination earlier than it might otherwise have done. In this way, during the years leading up to the passage of the Equality Act, regulations introduced three new areas of unlawful discrimination:

- discrimination in the workplace on the grounds of religion or belief (the Employment Equality (Religion or Belief) Regulations 2003),[40]
- sexual orientation (the Employment Equality (Sexual Orientation) Regulations 2003),[41] and
- age (the Employment Equality (Age) Regulations 2006 and the Employment Equality (Age) Regulations (Northern Ireland) 2006).[42]

These directives and their domestic implementation changed UK law more than the Equality Act did: by comparison the provisions of the Equality Act are matters of detail.

---

[31] Treaty concerning the Accession of the New Member States to the EEC and the EAEC, Brussels 22 January 1972: Official Journal L2 of 1 January 1973.
[32] Official Journal C340 of 10 November 1997.
[33] The relevant procedure is in the European Communities Act 1972 s. 2(2) and Sch. 2.
[34] See Ch. 12.
[35] 75/117/EEC.
[36] 76/207/EEC.
[37] 2006/54/EC.
[38] 2000/43/EC.
[39] 2000/78/EC.
[40] SI 2003/1660.
[41] SI 2003/1661.
[42] SI 2006/1031 and SR (N.I.) 2006/261.

C. THE INTRODUCTION AND PASSAGE OF THE EQUALITY ACT 2010

1. Consultation on the Policy

The process leading to the introduction of the Equality Bill to Parliament began in February 2005   **1.19**
when the government set up both an Equality Review 'into the causes of persistent discrimination and equality in Britain' and a Discrimination Law Review. One of the aims of the Equality Review was 'to inform both the modernisation of equality legislation towards a Single Equality Act; and the development of the new Commission for Equality and Human Rights'. The Review of Discrimination Law was 'to address long-term concerns about inconsistencies in the current discrimination law framework'. Because of the different ways in which protection from discrimination had come about, the rules varied according to the kind of discrimination being alleged. This Review was given the job of 'considering the fundamental principles of discrimination legislation … and the opportunities for creating a clearer and more streamlined framework of equality legislation which produces better outcomes for those who experience disadvantage … a key priority will be seeking to achieve greater consistency in the protection afforded to different groups …'.

The Labour Party was re-elected in May 2005. Its Manifesto committed it to advances in   **1.20**
workplace equality, to introducing 'a Single Equality Act[43] to modernise and simplify equality legislation', and to establishing the Commission for Equality and Human Rights.[44] Ideas emerging from the Discrimination Law Review and proposals for a Bill that would fulfil the government's Manifesto commitment appeared in the consultation paper, 'A Framework for Fairness: proposals for a Single Equality Bill for Great Britain' in June 2007.

The following October, the new Commission for Equality and Human Rights (EHRC) began   **1.21**
work. Its purpose (in relation to discrimination) is 'to protect, enforce and promote equality across … age, disability, gender, race, religion and belief, sexual orientation and gender reassignment'. The EHRC took over from the three existing Commissions—the Commission for Racial Equality, the Equal Opportunities Commission, and the Disability Rights Commission—and assumed the same role in relation to the other groups. It began work in October 2007 and applied its specialist knowledge, while furthering its purpose as the champion of equality, in discussions with government about the proposals and the Bill.

Also in October 2007, a new government department came into existence: the Government   **1.22**
Equalities Office (GEO). The GEO's responsibility for equality was government-wide, affecting the departments responsible for business, education, employment, and other areas. Responsibility for the Bill passed from the Department for Communities and Local Government to the GEO. The way government engineered the administrative machinery specifically to address these issues shows how much its members believed in using the power of the law and the State to oppose discrimination. The Equality Bill is another manifestation of the same commitment.

The GEO published a series of papers setting out proposals for the Bill and responses to   **1.23**
them.[45] The basic case for legislation was presented as twofold. First, although the position

---

[43] *sic*, although constitutionally a government can only introduce a Bill and it is for Parliament to decide whether it is to be an Act.

[44] Labour Manifesto 2005 p. 112.

[45] *A Framework for Fairness: Proposals for a Single Equality Bill for Great Britain*: GEO June 2007; *Framework for a Fairer Future—the Equality Bill*: June 2008 Cm 7431; *The Equality Bill—Government Response to the*

of some disadvantaged groups was improving, progress was not fast enough. Secondly, the government pointed to the present state of the law, describing it as 'complex and difficult' and referring to 'nine major pieces of discrimination legislation, around 100 statutory instruments and more than 2,500 pages of guidance and statutory codes of practice'.[46] The intention that the Act would not just consolidate and 'declutter' or tidy up the relevant law, but improve the position of disadvantaged people, was apparent throughout the preparation and progress of the Bill. Wherever the rights of different victims of discrimination were uneven, they were to be levelled up, not down.

1.24   The preparation of the Bill had reached an advanced stage when the government published a proposal to introduce an entirely new public sector duty in an area that discrimination law had not previously reached, namely socio-economic disadvantage. This appeared in a wide-ranging consultation paper[47] aimed at nothing less than improving Britain's position as a world economy as global markets recovered from the downturn of autumn 2008. By comparison with most proposals for changes to the law, the new duty's purpose was set out in high-flown terms: 'to firmly engage the public sector in delivery of this ambitious agenda ... to ensure successive generations have the opportunities to realize their potential and improve their position in society, delivering improvements in wealth, wellbeing and ambitions for individuals and their families and ensuring a fairer and more equal society'.[48]

1.25   The intention described in the consultation paper was for the duty to form part of a network of measures designed to produce a more socially mobile, higher-skilled workforce and a more successful economy. The thinking behind the proposals can be traced to evidence from studies showing that more equal societies perform better across a range of measures.[49]

2. The Bill in Parliament: the House of Commons

1.26   The Bill was introduced to the House of Commons on 24 April 2009. From the following 2 June to 7 July, as a stage in the Bill's passage through the Commons, a Public Bill Committee examined it at a level of detail that could not be achieved in the full House. It began with sessions entirely devoted to taking oral evidence from organizations with an interest. These included employers' organizations such as the Confederation of British Industry (CBI); groups representing women and lesbians, gays, bisexuals and transgendered (LGBT); bodies concerned with the operation of the law such as the Arbitration, Conciliation and Advisory Service (ACAS); and faith groups such as the General Synod of the Church of England. Among the first bodies to appear before it was the EHRC. The Committee had also invited written representations, and its members could make use of briefings and draft amendments prepared by lobby and interest groups.

Consultation: July 2008 Cm 7454; *Equality Bill: Assessing the impact of a Multiple Discrimination Provision*: GEO April 2009; *Equality Bill: Making it Work—Policy Proposals for Specific Duties; Equality Bill: Making it Work—Ending Age Discrimination in Services and Public Functions*, and *A Fairer Future—The Equality Bill and other action to make equality a reality*: GEO April 2009.

[46] *A Fairer Future—The Equality Bill and other action to make equality a reality*: GEO April 2009 p. 6.
[47] *New Opportunities White Paper*: January 2009 Cm 7533.
[48] *ibid*, para. 159.
[49] See e.g. Wilkinson and Pickett, *The Spirit Level: Why more equal societies almost always do better* (Allen Lane 2009).

The members of every Public Bill Committee are appointed by the House's Committee of Selection from the membership of the House of Commons, and have to reflect the composition of the House. In this case the Committee, like the House, had a Labour majority. But because the Bill was concerned with equality and discrimination, the positions adopted by members of the Committee on its various provisions often reflected not so much their political affiliations, as their life-histories, backgrounds, values, and deeply-held beliefs. This was a Committee capable of challenging whether the Bill was doing enough for the groups that are subjected to discrimination as well as whether it went too far in their interests. Members included: Diane Abbott (Labour), the first black woman to be elected to the British Parliament; Lynne Featherstone (Liberal Democrat), an active MP with a background in the private sector; Evan Harris, a qualified doctor of medicine with a commitment to secular humanism, who was Honorary President of the Liberal Democrat Campaign for Lesbian and Gay Rights; Mark Harper (Conservative), who was the Opposition's Shadow Minister for the Disabled, and a Roman Catholic; John Mason (SNP), an active and committed Christian from a Baptist congregation in Glasgow; and John Penrose (Conservative), whose background includes working in banking and management consultancy, and who demonstrated a concern with the potential burden regulation can impose on organizations.

1.27

Much of the debate in Committee revolved around whether the government had struck the right balance between competing interests or principles. Should the Bill's list of protected characteristics be longer, so as to include caste, genetic discrimination (such as an hereditary predisposition to a disease or condition), carers, people of indeterminate or third sex, or membership of a disadvantaged socio-economic group; or would this be interference by the State where none has been shown to be necessary? Should the principle of equality be enshrined in an equality guarantee, in the way the Human Rights Act 1998 (HRA) compels interpretation of the law according to Convention principles,[50] or should equality law be restricted to what Parliament has chosen to do? And repeatedly: if it is unlawful for someone to discriminate against LGBT people because of their religious beliefs, does this mean there is a hierarchy of victims of discrimination, with religion and belief having to yield to others?

1.28

Questions like these were posed in relation to several provisions:

1.29

- the exclusion of both sexual orientation and religion from the characteristics fully protected from harassment in the provision of services;[51]

- whether churches should be able to refuse to employ people in roles such as youth workers, or teachers, because of their sexuality;[52]

- whether a faith school would be liable for harassment if a pupil was taught that her homosexual parents were morally at fault and would suffer in the after-life.[53]

The weight to be given to religious beliefs in discrimination law was, and continues to be, an issue at the centre of litigation and policy debate. Prominent cases like *Ladele*,[54] concerning the London registrar who had refused to perform civil partnership ceremonies because she believed them to be contrary to the will of God, and *Eweida*,[55] brought by the member

1.30

---

[50] HRA s. 3(1).
[51] See s. 29(8).
[52] See Sch. 9(2).
[53] See Sch. 22, paras 3 and 4.
[54] *Ladele v Mayor and Burgesses of the London Borough of Islington* [2009] EWCA Civ 1357.
[55] *Eweida v British Airways Plc* [2008] UKEAT 0123/08.

of British Airways staff who was prevented from displaying a crucifix when in uniform, were attempts to rely on the regulations prohibiting discrimination on grounds of religion or belief. There were references to both these cases in the discussions about the Bill in Committee.

1.31   At Committee stage in the Commons none of the Bill's provisions was defeated. The fact that the majority of the Committee, like that of the House, was from the government's party meant that there was unlikely to be a situation in which the government would lose on a division of the Committee and a vote. However, in Committee the Solicitor-General Vera Baird agreed to consider whether several provisions should be amended—all of them technical, procedural, or points that needed to be clarified, rather than significant matters of principle. They were:

- adding certain fire and rescue bodies to the list of those subject to the socio-economic duty;
- clarifying the asymmetric nature of disability discrimination, which is unlawful when practised against someone who has a disability but not against someone who does not;
- making provision to address the concept of disability related discrimination;
- enabling representative actions in tribunals;
- restricting the use of pre-employment questionnaires in recruitment.[56]

3. The Bill in Parliament: the House of Lords

1.32   All Members of the House of Lords are entitled to sit in the Committee stage of a bill, and many did choose to hear the debates on this Bill. Among the peers who proposed, or spoke on, amendments were Lord Alli, the successful media entrepreneur who is also gay and Muslim; Baroness Flather, the first Asian woman to be awarded a peerage; Lord Lester, a practising human rights barrister who has been associated, in various capacities, with most major changes to the law in a liberal direction since the 1960s; Lord Mackay, who served as Lord Chancellor during Margaret Thatcher's and John Major's premierships, and who is a member of a Calvinist church little-known outside the Scottish Highlands and Islands; and Lady O'Cathain, a businesswoman who represents the views of evangelical Christian groups in the House of Lords.

1.33   The government accepted some amendments without the Committee having to vote: to add to the circumstances in which a duty to make a reasonable adjustment arises so that it covers, for instance, producing material in large print;[57] to make it clear that a disabled person does not have to meet the cost of a reasonable adjustment;[58] to extend schools' duties to make reasonable adjustments (in the form of auxiliary aids);[59] to allow members of the clergy not to celebrate the marriage of a person who has undergone gender reassignment;[60] and to provide broadcasters with more protection from claims of discrimination.[61]

1.34   The government did not get its way with the wording of the exemption that allows churches and other religious organizations to discriminate in whom they employ.[62] The provision was controversial—even the Pope, the conservative Benedict XVI, had published a letter to the

---

[56] House of Commons Public Bill Committee on Equality Bill 2008–09 col 746 (7 July 2009).
[57] S. 20(6).
[58] S. 20(7).
[59] Sch. 13.
[60] Sch. 3, Part 6, para. 24(2).
[61] Sch. 3, Part 8.
[62] Sch. 9, Part 1, para.

Catholic bishops of England and Wales saying that they should oppose it 'with missionary zeal'. But in the Commons the Minister for Women and Equality, Harriet Harman, subsequently said that although the government had not achieved the clarification it wanted, the law was nevertheless as it had intended: '... our position has always been that for specifically religious work—as a vicar, priest, rabbi or imam—religious organisations would be exempt from discrimination law. A religious organisation cannot discriminate against gay people when it hires a bookkeeper but it can when hiring a minister of religion ...'.[63]

As the Bill completed its later stages in the Lords—being further refined and amended— 1.35 the context became increasingly urgent. Parliament's five-year term was soon to expire and the government was expected to call an election. Whether the same party would remain in power was highly uncertain (in the event it did not). Although the Bill completed its passage and received Royal Assent during the parliamentary session, there was no time to bring it into effect, in whole or in part. The next government would be able to choose whether to bring its provisions into effect and, if so, when. Moreover, there are over 20 'Henry VIII clauses' (named after the legendarily autocratic Tudor king) in the Act. These are provisions by which a Minister can, using subordinate legislation such as regulations, amend provisions in the Act, even though it is primary legislation.

D. STRUCTURE OF THE ACT

The Act is long, having over 200 sections and 28 Schedules. The provisions are mainly organ- 1.36 ized in a logical series. Nearly half of the text consists of Schedules that expand on, or make exceptions to, the provisions in the main part of the Act. One good way to understand the Act's purposes is to consult the Explanatory Notes published with the Act.[64] These reflect the intentions when the Act was presented for approval and the amendments made thereafter. These notes show that, although not technically a consolidating measure, the Act was intended in many places to build on the existing jurisprudence under previous legislation. In some cases it is made clear that where jurisprudence is thought to have gone wrong the new Act takes a correcting or enlarging approach.

The Act begins with its most novel provisions in Part 1 headed 'Socio-economic 1.37 Inequalities'. This Part has not been brought into force throughout the United Kingdom and at present the English Government has expressed no interest in doing so. Nonetheless it has effect in Scotland and Wales. In Scotland it is called the Fairer Scotland Duty and it came into force in April 2018.[65] The duty will come into force in Wales on 31 March 2021.[66]

Part 2 of the Act, 'Equality: Key Concepts' contains the Act's basic building-blocks, in 1.38 the form of definitions of the *protected characteristics* and the different kinds of *prohibited conduct* (direct and indirect discrimination; the duty to make reasonable adjustments, failure to perform which amounts to discrimination; victimization and harassment). The next five parts (3–7) apply the concepts of prohibited conduct to the protected characteristics in relation to the sectors in which they may occur: Part 3, 'Services and Public Functions'; Part 4,

---

[63] *Hansard* HC, cols 468, 474 (4 February 2010).
[64] See <http://www.legislation.gov.uk/ukpga/2010/15/notes/contents>.
[65] See Equality Act 2010 (Commencement No 13) (Scotland) Order 20187, SSI 2017/403 art. 2.
[66] See <https://gov.wales/socio-economic-duty-overview#section-42134>.

'Premises'; Part 5, 'Work'; Part 6, 'Education'; Part 7, 'Associations'. Parts 5 and 6 are divided into Chapters.

1.39   The following three parts are concerned with the machinery needed to put the Act's provisions into effect. Part 8, 'Prohibited Conduct: Ancillary' neatly puts together the circumstances in which prohibited conduct can occur when the relationship between the parties is not the most usual and straightforward one, such as where there is a third party in the form of an agent or someone instigating an act of discrimination. Part 9, 'Enforcement' covers the jurisdiction of courts and tribunals, as well as the sex equality clauses and rules by which sex discrimination and equal pay law operate (Chapter 4) and the principles that determine how the issues in dispute will be resolved, such as, importantly, the burden of proof (Chapter 5). Part 10, 'Contracts, Etc' deals with the effect of discrimination law on contracts, in the sense of making certain terms void or unenforceable. This Part makes provision for the compromise agreements that record settlements between the parties to discrimination proceedings.

1.40   With Part 11, 'Advancement of Equality' the Act changes gear and deals not with negative prohibitions, but with positive duties on public authorities and the limited circumstances in which positive action is lawful. Part 12, 'Disabled Persons: Transport' contains very practical rules about how taxis, trains, and buses must be accessible to people with disabilities, and will not be able to operate unless they are. Part 13, 'Disability: Miscellaneous' makes similar provision in relation to premises. Part 14, 'General Exceptions' contains the exceptions that apply in all the contexts covered by the Act; the exceptions that relate only to particular sectors, such as the employment provisions or schools, appear among the Schedules. Lastly Part 15, 'General and Miscellaneous' puts together the important but technical provisions that do not concern most people who need to look at the Act: community and devolution matters, amendments, interpretation, commencement, and the like.

E. BREXIT AND UK EQUALITY LAW

1.41   The European Communities Act 1972 has provided the over-arching legal base for the alignment between UK and European Law where Parliament has not otherwise made special provisions in primary legislation to transpose European obligations into domestic law. The effect of the Brexit withdrawal legislation is that the 1972 Act is repealed. This raises the question whether the Equality Act 2010 will be immediately and directly affected. The short answer is that as the Equality Act 2010 was not made under the 1972 Act, but is free-standing primary legislation, and so will not—as legislation—be changed by Brexit. Nonetheless it would be a mistake to think that Brexit changes nothing in relation to the understanding and application of the Equality Act 2010. It is not yet possible to be sure of all the effects that the withdrawal legislation will have but some effects are clear, and some have been anticipated specifically and addressed. As the following chapters of this book will show, on many occasions the interpretation of provisions of the Equality Act 2010 has followed the interpretation of the relevant European legislation to which it is understood to give effect. Sometimes this has been the direct result of the UK court or tribunal holding that judgments of the Court of Justice of the European Union (CJEU) are directly in point, or that the law of the European Union is *acte clair*. In other cases, it has been the result of the CJEU answering specific questions about the interpretation of European law provisions pursuant to the preliminary ruling procedure under Article 267 of the Treaty on the Functioning of the European Union (TFEU). Brexit will bring such references to an end, so judges in courts and tribunals in the UK will have to answer such questions themselves. It is foreseeable that a dialogue may develop between the CJEU's judgments and those in the UK and that could be beneficial. Yet it may also lead to delay if for instance the same point is considered by the CJEU after a UK court has addressed it and if the CJEU reaches a different conclusion, causing an appeal or application for review in the UK. It is too early to say exactly how this kind of problem will be resolved but it seems inevitable that in some cases at least it will lead to uncertainty, delay, and greater cost for litigants.

While the Equality Act 2010 will not be repealed by any of: 1.42

- European Union (Withdrawal Agreement) Act 2020 ('the 2020 Act')

- The Agreement on the withdrawal of the United Kingdom of Great Britain and Northern Ireland from the European Union and the European Atomic Energy Community of 21 November 2019 ('the 2019 Agreement')

- European Union (Withdrawal) (No. 2) Act 2019 ('the 2019/2 Act')

- European Union (Withdrawal) Act 2019 ('the 2019/1 Act')

- European Union (Withdrawal) Act 2018 ('the 2018 Act')

- European Union (Notification of Withdrawal) Act 2017 ('the 2017 Act'),

    some knowledge of these steps to Brexit will definitely be necessary in the future when considering how the Equality Act 2010 is to be interpreted and applied. The following paragraphs give only a short overview of their effect.

The 2017 Act is principally of historic interest now. It gave the Prime Minister the power   1.43
to notify the European Council of the United Kingdom's intention to withdraw from the European Union following the outcome of the Brexit referendum on 23 June 2016. On 2 October 2016 the Prime Minister announced that the Government would commence the formal process of leaving the European Union before the end of March 2017 but did not then notify the exact date. The 2017 Act completed the legislative authority for this to take place.

The 2018 Act contained 25 sections and nine Schedules and was the first major legislative   1.44
attempt to define how UK law would be affected from the point of leaving the European Union. The Government has said that 'Its purpose is to provide a functioning statute book when the UK leaves the EU.'[67] The Act repealed the European Communities Act 1972 on the day the United Kingdom left the European Union with the stated intention of then converting all EU law as it then stood into domestic law, and preserving laws made in the UK to implement EU obligations as they then stood.[68] It also creates temporary powers to make secondary legislation to enable corrections to be made to the laws that would otherwise no longer operate appropriately once the UK has left, so that the domestic legal system continues to function correctly outside the EU. The Act also enabled domestic law to reflect the content of a withdrawal agreement under Article 50 of the Treaty on European Union once the UK left the EU, subject to the prior enactment of a statute by Parliament approving the final terms of withdrawal. A key point is that section 2 has been designed to save EU-derived

---

[67] See the Explanatory Notes to the European Union (Withdrawal) Act 2020 at [6]; see <https://www.legislation.gov.uk/ukpga/2020/1/notes/division/3/index.htm>.

[68] See the Explanatory Notes to the European Union (Withdrawal) Act 2018 at [2]; see <https://www.legislation.gov.uk/ukpga/2018/16/notes/division/2/index.htm>.

domestic legislation and to the extent that the Equality Act 2010 can be said to be such legislation, this is of importance for this book. Section 3 incorporates direct EU regulation.

1.45　　The 2019/1 and 2019/2 Acts were concerned with the extension of the period and process under Article 50 Treaty on European Union for leaving the EU. These two will also now be broadly seen as of historic interest. The 2019 Agreement set out in very great detail how the relationship between the EU and the UK would be unwound, the protections for citizens in the future, and the future more specific relationships.[69]

1.46　　The 2020 Act substantively amended the 2018 Act. One major purpose of the 2020 Act has been to amend the 2018 Act to allow for an effective transition; this is called the 'Implementation Period' which runs from 'Exit day'—the day on which the UK formally leaves the EU (31 January 2020)—until 31 December 2020 'IP completion day'. Section 1 of the 2020 Act amends the 2018 Act to ensure that notwithstanding the repeal of the 1972 Act it effectively remains in force for existing law during the implementation period.[70] The 2020 Act ensures that sections 2 to 4 of the Act 2018 save, and incorporate into domestic law, that EU law which applied in the UK on IP completion day. Section 14 relates to the non-discrimination rights particularly of frontier workers; that is to say those in Northern Ireland and the Republic of Ireland.[71]

1.47　　The effects of EU equality law have been felt within the UK not only as a result of Directives, Regulations, and directly effective provisions of the Lisbon Treaty and predecessor Treaty texts, but also as a result of the application of general principals of equality law recognized as part of the *acquis communautaire*. The extent to which such principles have now become part of UK law and will survive and perhaps be developed after Brexit is completed is not wholly clear. Great care will be needed when relying on those principles to interpret the Equality Act 2010 in the future. The 2018 Act took exception to the Charter of Fundamental Rights of the European Union continuing to have effect in the UK. However, it got around this by stating that the principles which enunciated—as principles of EU law—were to continue to have limited effect. The Explanatory Note to the 2018 Act stated:[72]

> 106 … The Charter did not create new rights, but rather reaffirmed rights and principles which already existed in EU law. By converting the EU *acquis* into UK law, those underlying rights and principles will also be converted into UK law, as provided for in this Act. References to the Charter in the domestic and CJEU case law which is being retained, are to be read as if they referred to the corresponding fundamental rights.

> 107 Given that the Charter did not create any new rights, [section 5(5)] makes clear that, whilst the Charter will not form part of domestic law after exit, this does not remove any underlying fundamental rights or principles which exist, and EU law which is converted will continue to be interpreted in light of those underlying rights and principles.

---

[69] See <https://eur-lex.europa.eu/legal-content/EN/TXT/PDF/?uri=CELEX:12019W/TXT(02)& from=EN>.

[70] See Explanatory Notes to the 2020 Act at [73] and ff.; see <https://www.legislation.gov.uk/ukpga/2020/1/notes/division/21/index.htm>.

[71] See Explanatory Notes to the 2020 Act at [200] and ff.; see <https://www.legislation.gov.uk/ukpga/2020/1/notes/division/34/index.htm>.

[72] See Explanatory Notes to the 2018 Act at [106]–[107]; see <https://www.legislation.gov.uk/ukpga/2018/16/notes/division/21/index.htm>.

2

PROTECTED CHARACTERISTICS

A. INTRODUCTION

One of the objectives of the Equality Act 2010 ('the Act') is to bring together in one place **2.01** all of those characteristics on which it is unlawful to discriminate and to establish a single approach to discrimination, with some exceptions. These 'protected characteristics' are set out in Part 2, Chapter 1 of the Act.

The protected characteristics covered by the Act are: **2.02**

- Age
- Disability
- Gender reassignment
- Marriage and civil partnership
- Race
- Religion or belief
- Sex
- Sexual orientation
- Pregnancy and maternity

Razia Karim, *Protected Characteristics* In: *Blackstone's Guide to the Equality Act 2010.* Fourth Edition. Edited by:
Anthony Robinson, David Ruebain, and Susie Uppal, Oxford University Press (2021). © Oxford University Press.
DOI: 10.1093/oso/9780198870876.003.0002

B. AGE

1. Introduction

2.03   Section 5 of the Act covers the protected characteristic of age. People of all ages are covered, with some exceptions (see Chapter 5 on services, public functions, and transport).

2.04   Section 5 of the Act provides:

(1) In relation to the protected characteristic of age:
  (a) a reference to a person who has a particular protected characteristic is a reference to a person of a particular age group;
  (b) a reference to persons who share a protected characteristic is a reference to persons of the same age group.

(2) A reference to an age group is a reference to a group of persons defined by reference to age, whether by reference to a particular age or a range of ages.

2. Meaning of Age Group

2.05   The Act does not define an age group. An age group refers to a group of people of the same age or people of a range of ages. People who fall into the same age group share the protected characteristic of age.[1] An age group can be wide and would include, for example, 'over forties' or 20-year-olds.[2] It may also be narrow, for example, people in their mid-thirties, or it could be relative, for example, 'older than me' or 'older than us'.[3]

2.06   The concept of age group will usually be grounded in chronological age or ages. There may be features which identify a chronological age group such as age-related terms[4] or reference to a particular period in history which may have more relevance to a particular age group. For example, the term 'digital native' describes a person who has grown up in the digital age, usually someone born after 1980. Age groups can also be linked to factors which have no relationship to chronological age, for example physical appearance.[5]

2.07   There is a flexibility within the definition of age group; for example, a 30-year-old could be described as 'aged 30', 'under 40', '25 to 35', or '30-something'.[6]

2.08   The Act does not specify the age group with which the comparison should be made. Much will depend on the context and circumstances; for example, it could be anyone outside the person's age group.

---

[1] EN para. 36.

[2] See n. 1 above 'Examples'.

[3] Equality and Human Rights Commission (EHRC) Employment and Services, Public Functions and Associations Statutory Codes of Practice (2011).

[4] See *Chief Constable of West Midlands Police & Ors v Harrod & Ors* UKEAT/0189/14/DA. A rule in police pension regulations which allowed police forces to require a police officer to retire once he or she reaches 30 years' service and is entitled to a pension of two-thirds of pensionable pay meant that only those officers over the age of 48 could be forced to retire.

See *Lord Chancellor & Anor v McCloud & Ors* [2018] EWCA Civ 2844. Transitional provisions affecting the pensions of judges and firefighters, which were based on the number of years to retirement, were held to discriminate against younger judges and firefighters.

[5] See n. 3 above.

[6] See n. 3 above.

The Act protects all age groups except those aged 18 and under who do not benefit from the protection in the sphere of goods, facilities, services, and public functions.[7]   2.09

C. DISABILITY

1. Introduction

Section 6 of the Act covers the protected characteristic of disability and establishes who is a disabled person for the purposes of the Act. Supplementary provisions on how to determine who is a disabled person are contained in Schedule 1 Part 1 and in the Equality Act 2010 (Disability) Regulations 2010, which set out conditions that are to be treated, or not treated, as an impairment.   2.10

Statutory guidance on matters to be taken into account in determining questions relating to the definition of disability is also provided in the 'Equality Act 2010 Guidance'.[8] An adjudicating body,[9] which is determining for any purpose of the Act whether a person is a disabled person, must take into account any aspect of this guidance which appears to it to be relevant.[10]   2.11

2. Meaning of Disability and Disabled Person

Only people who have a disability, or who have had a disability in the past, are protected against discrimination. The status of 'non-disabled' is not a protected characteristic for the purposes of the Act. This 'asymmetrical' protection originates in the need to prohibit the historic discrimination against disabled people and, importantly, to allow for reasonable adjustments to be made without which equality for disabled people would be difficult to achieve.   2.12

'Non-disabled' persons are protected from disability discrimination and harassment only where they are perceived to have a disability or are associated with a disabled person;[11] for example, carers of a disabled person, or where they experience some other prohibited conduct, such as victimization (see Chapter 3).   2.13

Section 6 of the Act provides: 2.14

(1) A person (P) has a disability if—
    (a) P has a physical or mental impairment, and
    (b) the impairment has a substantial and long-term adverse effect on P's ability to carry out normal day-to-day activities.

'Impairment' must be given its ordinary and natural meaning.[12] Physical or mental impairment includes sensory impairments such as sight and hearing, or mental impairments   2.15

---

[7] S. 28(1).

[8] The 'Equality Act 2010 Guidance: Guidance on matters to be taken into account in determining questions relating to the definition of disability' (May 2011). Issued by the Secretary of State under s. 6(5).

[9] A court, a tribunal, or a person who may decide a claim relating to a contravention of Part 6 (education) Sch. 1, Part 2, para. 12.

[10] Sch. 1, Part 2, para. 12.

[11] *Colman v Attridge Law* C-303/06. See also *Price v Action-Tec Services Ltd t/a Associated Telecom Solutions* ET/1304312/2011 discriminatory dismissal after time off for husband's leukaemia and *Chief Constable of Norfolk v Coffey* [2019] EWCA Civ 1061 direct discrimination because the claimant was perceived to have a progressive hearing impairment and, thus, a disability under the Equality Act 2010.

[12] *McNichol v Balfour Beatty Rail Maintenance Ltd* [2002] ICR 1498 CA.

such as Asperger's syndrome, autism, dyslexia, and mental illness. In relation to mental illness, the Act follows antecedent legislation by not requiring that mental illness be clinically
recognized.[13]

2.16   The focus of the Act is on the effect of the impairment, not its cause; and so a formal
medical diagnosis for the cause of the impairment is not always necessary, provided there is
evidence of a substantial and long-term adverse effect.[14]

However, in practice, it might be difficult to show that there is an impairment without
some evidence of its cause.

2.17   People with a past disability, which falls within the definition, are protected from discrimination even if they have since recovered (but not in relation to Part 12 (transport) and section
185 (improvements to let dwelling houses)).[15]

2.18   A reference to a person who has a particular protected characteristic is a reference to a
person who has a particular disability and a reference to persons who share a protected characteristic is a reference to persons who have the same disability.[16]

3. Long Term Effect

2.19   What constitutes a long term effect is set out in Schedule 1, Part 1, paragraph 2:

(1) The effect of an impairment is long-term if—
    (a) it has lasted for at least 12 months,[17]
    (b) it is likely to last for at least 12 months, or
    (c) it is likely to last for the rest of the life of the person affected.

(2) If an impairment ceases to have a substantial adverse effect on a person's ability to carry
    out normal day-to-day activities, it is to be treated as continuing to have that effect if
    that effect is likely to recur.

(3) For the purposes of sub-paragraph (2), the likelihood of an effect recurring is to be dis-
    regarded in such circumstances as may be prescribed.

(4) Regulations may prescribe circumstances in which, despite sub-paragraph (1), an effect
    is to be treated as being, or as not being, long-term.

2.20   Effects which are not long term would include loss of mobility due to a broken limb,
which is likely to heal within 12 months, or the effects of temporary infections from which a
person would be likely to recover within 12 months.

2.21   During the Parliamentary passage of the Equality Bill probing amendments were tabled
to remove the requirement for the effect of the impairment to be 'long term'.[18] Of particular
concern was the treatment of short term conditions, such as depression or anxiety orders,
whose effects do not last continuously for 12 months but may recur. The Minister responded

---

[13] *Millar v Inland Revenue Commissioners* [2006] IRLR 112 IH; *Hospice of St Mary of Furness v Howard*
UKEAT/0646/06; [2007] IRLR 944.

[14] *Walker v Sita Information Networking Computing Ltd* EAT/0097/12.

[15] S. 6(4).

[16] S. 6(3).

[17] *Tesco Stores Ltd v Tennant* UKEAT 0167/19/00. There must be a 'long term effect' at the time the alleged
acts of discrimination take place.

[18] HC Deb (Public Bill Committee), 16 June 2009 col. 191.

that where the effect of the impairment is likely to recur then they are to be treated as 'long term' (see below).

As it is, the requirement for the effect of the impairment to be 'long term' is consistent **2.22** with the United Nations Convention on the Rights of Persons with Disabilities.

The duration of the effects of two different, consecutive impairments which each last less **2.23** than 12 months can be aggregated in order to decide whether they were long term, provided the second impairment has developed from the first.[19]

4. Recurring Conditions

If an impairment has had a substantial adverse effect on normal day-to-day activities but that **2.24** effect ceases, the substantial effect is treated as continuing if it is likely to recur. This is so even where there are episodic effects of less than 12 months.

A substantial effect is likely to recur if it 'could well happen'.[20] **2.25**

In Swift v Chief Constable of Wiltshire[21] the EAT affirmed that the approach to recurring **2.26** conditions is to ask:

- Was there at some stage an impairment?
- Did that impairment have a substantial adverse effect on the applicant's ability to carry out normal day-to-day activities?
- Did the impairment cease to have a substantial adverse effect on normal day-to-day activities and if so when?
- What was the substantial adverse effect?
- Is the same substantial adverse effect likely to recur?

It should be noted that it is the 'substantial adverse effect' of the impairment which must **2.27** be likely to recur, not the impairment itself, which may or may not recur. Also, the recurrence of the substantial adverse effect need not last 12 months.

5. Substantial Adverse Effect

A substantial adverse effect is something which is more than a minor or trivial effect.[22] An **2.28** impairment may not directly prevent someone from carrying out one or more normal day-to-day activities, but it may still have a substantial adverse long-term effect on how s/he carries out those activities. For example, where an impairment causes pain or fatigue in performing normal day-to-day activities the person may have the capacity to do something but suffer pain in doing so; or the impairment might make the activity more than usually fatiguing so that the person might not be able to repeat the task over a sustained period of time.[23]

Determining whether an impairment has a substantial adverse effect requires a compari- **2.29** son between the way a person carries out an activity with the impairment and the way s/he

---

[19] *Patel v Oldham MBC* [2010] UKEAT 0225_09_1501.

[20] *SCA Packaging Ltd v Boyle* [2009] UKHL 37.

[21] [2004] UKEAT 0484_03_1802; [2004] IRLR 540.

[22] S. 212(1). See also *Goodwin v The Patent Office* [1998] UKEAT 57_98_2110.

[23] See *Davies v Scottish Courts and Tribunals Service* ET S/4104575/2017. Menopause is not of itself a disability but severe symptoms of menopause may constitute a disability.

would carry out the activity without it. It is not a comparison with the way the activity is carried out by members of the population at large.[24]

2.30 Account should also be taken of where a person avoids doing things which, for example, cause pain, fatigue, or substantial social embarrassment because of a loss of energy and motivation.

6. Disregard for Medical Treatment and Other Measures

2.31 Where a person is taking measures to treat or correct an impairment, and, but for those measures, the impairment would have a substantial adverse effect on the ability to carry out normal day-to-day activities, it is still to be treated as though it does have such an effect. 'Measures' includes medical treatment and the use of a prosthesis or other aid.[25]

2.32 The disregard for medical treatment means that 'hidden' impairments are also included in the definition of disability such as diabetes and epilepsy where they meet all the other requirements of section 6.

2.33 However, the disregard does not apply where the corrective treatment is the wearing of spectacles or contact lenses.[26]

7. Severe Disfigurement

2.34 An impairment which consists of a severe disfigurement is treated as having a substantial adverse effect on the ability of the person concerned to carry out normal day-to-day activities;[27] but it still has to be long term to constitute a disability.

8. Normal Day-to-day Activities

2.35 The Act contains neither a list nor a definition of normal day-to-day activities. The advantage of this approach is that it allows greater flexibility and scope for arguing there is an effect on normal day-to-day activities.

2.36 In *Chacón Navas*,[28] the CJEU applied a broad test by asking whether the impairment 'hinders the full and effective participation of the person concerned in professional life over a long period of time'. The effect of the impairment need not be 'substantial'; and the impairment need not have an effect on a person's ability to carry out normal day-to-day activities. *Paterson* confirms that a normal day-to-day activity could be something which is done only at work and holds that *Chacón Navas* applies to UK law.[29]

2.37 The principle in *Chacón Navas* was reaffirmed in *Sobhi v Commissioner of the Police of the Metropolis* in which the EAT held that a person must be regarded as a disabled person if their condition has a substantial and long-term adverse effect on any activity of theirs which

---

[24] *Paterson v Commissioner of Police* UKEAT/0635/06; [2007] IRLR 763.

[25] Sch. 1, Part 1, para. 5. See *Metroline Travel Ltd v Stoute* UKEAT/0302/14/JOJ. A claimant who could control his type two diabetes by avoiding sugary food and drinks was not disabled (as this was not a medical treatment).

[26] Sch. 1, Part 1, para. 5(3).

[27] *Hutchison 3G UK Ltd v Edwards* UKEAT/0467/13/DM.

[28] Case C-13/05 *Chacón Navas v Eurest Colectividades SA* [2007] All ER (EC) 59.

[29] See n. 24 above.

relates to their effective participation in professional life—in this case a one-off application to become a police constable.[30]

Normal day-to-day activities will continue to include those which are carried out by most people on a regular and frequent basis. These may include: walking, driving, using public transport, cooking, eating, lifting or carrying everyday objects, continence, typing, writing, talking and hearing, reading, taking part in normal social interaction or forming social relationships, nourishing and caring for one's self.   **2.38**

The activity does not need to be done by both sexes to be treated as a normal day-to-day activity. In Ekpe v Commissioner of Police of the Metropolis[31] the EAT held that using hair rollers is a normal day-to-day activity for a woman and therefore a normal day-to-day activity for a person.[32]   **2.39**

Similarly, those activities which are normal for persons who perform a particular skill, professional sport, or other specialized task, for example, a musician or professional footballer, may now be treated as normal day-to-day activities under the ruling in *Chacón Navas*.   **2.40**

9. Certain Medical Conditions

Cancer, HIV infection, and multiple sclerosis are each expressly stated to be a disability under the Act.[33] The advantage of this provision is that these conditions are treated as a disability in their own right, without the need to demonstrate a substantial adverse effect on normal day-to-day activities.[34]   **2.41**

10. Progressive Conditions

Progressive conditions are those which are likely to change, develop, or deteriorate over time. A person who has a progressive condition has a disability if s/he has an impairment which has some effect. That effect does not have to be substantial, but the condition must be likely to result in the impairment having a substantial adverse effect in the future.[35]   **2.42**

11. Deemed Disability

A person who is certified blind, severely sight impaired, or partially sighted by a consultant ophthalmologist is deemed to have a disability under the Equality Act 2010 (Disability) Regulations 2010.[36]   **2.43**

---

[30] *Sobhi v Commissioner of the Police of the Metropolis* UKEAT/0518/12/BA. See also *Banaszczyk v Booker Ltd* UKEAT/0132/15/RN. Work activities that are non-specialized and common across many occupations, in this case lifting, should constitute 'normal day to day activities'. See also *Aderemi v London and South Eastern Railway* UKEAT/2012/0316_12_0612. The focus of a tribunal must necessarily be upon that which a claimant maintains he cannot do as a result of his physical or mental impairment.

[31] [2001] ICR 1084; [2001] IRLR 605.

[32] [2001] IRLR 605 EAT.

[33] Sch. 1, Part 1, para. 6.

[34] *Lofty v Hamis (t/a First Café)* EAT [2018] 1 WLUK 231 A claimant with a pre-cancerous lesion was treated as disabled under Sch. 1, Part 1, para. 6.

[35] Sch. 1, Part 1, para. 8.

[36] S. 7.

12. Genetic Conditions

2.44   A person with a genetic condition has a disability only if the effect of the condition has a substantial and long term adverse effect on P's ability to carry out normal day-to-day activities. A diagnosis of a genetic condition itself is insufficient to bring a person within the meaning of disabled. If the condition is progressive then the provision on progressive conditions applies.

13. Excluded Impairments

2.45   The Equality Act 2010 (Disability) Regulations 2010 states that certain conditions are not to be regarded as impairments for the purposes of the Act. These are:

- addiction to, or dependency on, alcohol, nicotine, or any other substance (other than in consequence of the substance being medically prescribed);
- the condition known as seasonal allergic rhinitis (e.g. hayfever), except where it aggravates the effect of another condition;
- tendency to set fires;
- tendency to steal;
- tendency to physical or sexual abuse of other persons;
- exhibitionism;
- voyeurism.

The exclusions apply to free-standing conditions and where the conditions 'arise as a consequence of, or a manifestation of, an impairment that constitutes a disability for the purposes of the Act.[37]

2.46   This was affirmed in *X v Governing Body of a School*, where the Upper Tribunal held that a disabled pupil's tendency to physical abuse, which arose as a result of her autism, was not to be treated as an impairment for the purposes of the Act.[38]

2.47   The House of Lords Select Committee on the Equality Act 2010 and Disability expressed its concern that the list of exclusions, in particular a tendency to physical abuse, undermined the need to encourage and support schools to make adjustments for children whose disability leads to challenging behaviour.[39] The government responded that it would consult more widely on the merits of changing the regulations but proposals fell by the wayside because of the general election.

2.48   In *C & C v The Governing Body of a School, The Secretary of State for Education (First Interested Party) and The National Autistic Society (Second Interested Party)*,[40] the Upper Tribunal held that, in the context of education, the exclusion in regulation 4(1)(c)—a tendency to physical abuse—violated the European Convention of Human Rights Article 14 (non-discrimination) when read with Protocol 1, Article 2 (right to education).

---

[37] The 'Equality Act 2010 Guidance: Guidance on matters to be taken into account in determining questions relating to the definition of disability' (May 2011).

[38] [2015] UKUT 7 (AAC).

[39] The Equality Act 2010: the impact on disabled people HL Paper 117 24 March 2016.

[40] (SEN) [2018] UKUT 269 (AAC).

D. GENDER REASSIGNMENT

1. Introduction

Section 7 of the Act covers the protected characteristic of gender reassignment and **2.49**
provides that:

(1) A person has the protected characteristic of gender reassignment if the person is proposing to undergo, is undergoing or has undergone a process (or part of a process) for the purpose of reassigning the person's sex by changing physiological or other attributes of sex.

(2) A reference to a transsexual person is a reference to a person who has the protected characteristic of gender reassignment.

(3) In relation to the protected characteristic of gender reassignment—
  (a) a reference to a person who has a particular characteristic is a reference to a transsexual person;
  (b) a reference to persons who share a protected characteristic is a reference to transsexual persons.

2. Meaning of Gender Reassignment

It is not a requirement of the Act for a person actually to be undergoing a medical process **2.50**
to benefit from protection. Instead, the Act shifts the focus to a personal process of moving away from birth sex, to the preferred gender.[41] So, people who choose to dress in their preferred gender continuously or intermittently, or those who wish to present their gender differently to that of their birth are now covered by the Act.

The definition of gender reassignment expands the scope of protection for trans people. **2.51**
This is because the term *'proposing to undergo'* is considered to have a broader meaning than, for example, *'considering undergoing'*.[42] According to the then Solicitor General, 'proposing' can be manifested in various ways; for instance, it can be indicating an intention to reassign gender even if there is no intention to go further than this[43]—this might be evidenced by attending counselling sessions related to the process or informing others of that intention. Alternatively, it could mean dressing or behaving in a way which shows that a person is changing his/her gender; or that a person is living an identity of the opposite sex. In addition, the term will also protect those people who might have started the medical process but decide not to continue with it. This is very important for trans people who choose to discontinue medical treatment for health-related reasons.

Thus, the Act widens the scope of protection for trans people. Those who benefit from **2.52**
its protection are people who have fully transitioned to their preferred gender; those who have started the process of reassignment; those who started the process of reassignment but discontinued it; those who choose to dress differently continuously or intermittently as part

---

[41] See n. 3 above.
[42] An amendment was tabled to replace the term 'proposing' with the term 'considering'. This was withdrawn as it was accepted that the Solicitor General's explanation of 'proposing' provided adequate protection. HC Deb (Public Bill Committee) 16 June 2009 col. 202.
[43] See n. 36 above.

of their desire to live in the opposite gender; and those who make known their intention to reassign their sex.[44] In *Taylor v Jaguar Land Rover Ltd* ET 1304471/2018 the employment tribunal extended protection to non-binary and gender fluid persons. The Services, Public Functions and Association Statutory Code of Practice states that this broad, non-medical definition is particularly important for children as some may reassign their gender while at school while others may be too young to make such a decision.[45]

2.53   A person may also gain protection indirectly through the concept of discrimination by perception. This would mean, for example, that a transvestite who does not meet the definition of gender reassignment would be protected if s/he were perceived as undergoing gender reassignment.

E. MARRIAGE AND CIVIL PARTNERSHIP

1. Introduction

2.54   Section 8 of the Act covers the protected characteristic of marriage and civil partnership and provides that:

(1) A person has the protected characteristic of marriage and civil partnership if the person is married or is a civil partner.

(2) In relation to the protected characteristic of marriage and civil partnership—
    (a) a reference to a person who has a particular characteristic is a reference to a person who is married or is a civil partner;
    (b) a reference to persons who share the protected characteristic is a reference to persons who are married or are civil partners.

2. Meaning of Marriage and Civil Partnership

2.55   To obtain protection a person must be married or in a civil partnership. Marriage includes a union between a man and a woman or a same-sex couple. A married person is a person who is legally married in accordance with the Marriage Act 1949. A civil partner is someone who has been registered as a civil partner under the Civil Partnership Act 2004.[46]

2.56   There is a distinction between cases where the close relationship is the reason for the less favourable treatment and those where the fact of the marriage or civil partnership is the reason for the treatment. In *Hawkins v Atex Group Ltd & Ors* the EAT held that the discrimination must be because the claimant is married, rather than in a close relationship which happens to take the form of marriage. Yet, in the earlier decision in *Dunn v Institute of Cemetery and Crematorium Management*[47] the EAT held that the scope of protection was broad enough to include a person who is discriminated against because s/he is married to a particular person, as opposed to just the mere fact of being married.

---

[44] See n. 3 above.

[45] Para. 2.21.

[46] The Civil Partnership Act 2004 was amended by the Civil Partnership (Opposite-sex Couples) Regulations 2019, SI 2019/1458 to include opposite-sex couples as well as same-sex couples.

[47] [2011] UKEAT 0531. This was decided under the Sex Discrimination Act 1975 s. 3 (discrimination in employment against a married person of either sex on the ground of his or her marital status).

As mentioned above only married people and civil partners are protected. The provision 2.57 is asymmetrical in nature since it only affords protection to people who are married or civil partners but not single people. Because the Act only protects those in formal legally recognized unions it means that a wide group of people are excluded from its protection. These include single people, divorcees, fiancées, 'cohabitees'—people living together as a couple whether as 'husband and wife' or as 'civil partners'—widows, and widowers.[48]

F. RACE

1. Introduction

Section 9 of the Act covers the protected characteristic of race: 2.58

(1) Race includes—
   (a) colour;
   (b) nationality; and
   (c) ethnic or national origins.
(2) In relation to the protected characteristic of race—
   (a) a reference to a person who has a particular protected characteristic is a reference to a person of a particular racial group;
   (b) a reference to persons who share a protected characteristic is a reference to persons of the same racial group.
(3) A racial group is a group of persons defined by reference to race; and a reference to a person's racial group is a reference to a racial group into which the person falls.
(4) The fact that a racial group comprised two or more distinct racial groups does not prevent it from constituting a racial group.

...

2. Meaning of Race

Race includes colour, nationality, and ethnic or national origins,[49] which means a person 2.59 is protected from discrimination if s/he is treated less favourably because of one or more of these attributes. Colour includes white, black, or brown. Nationality is determined by citizenship, although there may be an interface with national origins (see further below). Nationality includes, for example, being a British, Chinese, or an Indian citizen.

---

[48] Parliament debated whether this provision should be repealed or extended to include single people, i.e. those not married or in a civil partnership. It considered that the original purpose behind the provision was no longer a prominent issue; however, if the provision were to be retained, it should be equalized for all groups. The government decided 'on balance' to retain the provision and reject any extension to single people. HC Deb (Public Bill Committee) 16 June 2009 col. 208.

[49] It is interesting to note that the new wording of the Act has changed. Under the Race Relations Act the terms 'racial grounds' and 'racial groups' were defined to include race, colour, nationality, and ethnic or national origin. However, race is no longer used in the Act as a racial ground or group. Presumably this is because race as a characteristic is an outdated and discredited concept which sought to distinguish biological differences.

2.60   'Caste' is not expressly prohibited by the Act although section 9(5)(a)[50] of the Act requires the government to introduce secondary legislation making caste discrimination a form of race discrimination.[51]

2.61   In *Chandok v Tirkey*[52] the EAT held that 'caste' as an autonomous concept did not presently come within section 9(1). However, it went on to find that the definition of 'race' in the Act is not exhaustive and that many of the facts relevant to considering caste in its many forms might be capable of falling within the definition, since the meaning of 'ethnic origins' had a wide and flexible ambit, including characteristics determined by 'descent'.[53]

3. Ethnic Origins

2.62   An ethnic group is regarded as a distinct and separate community by virtue of certain characteristics. In the seminal case of *Mandla v Dowell Lee*,[54] the House of Lords established the features necessary to determine what constitutes an ethnic group. First, the group must have two essential characteristics: a long shared history and a cultural tradition of its own. Secondly, other characteristics may be taken into consideration in deciding whether a group can bring itself within the meaning of an ethnic group. These characteristics include a common language and/or literature, religion, geographical origin/descent, or a sense of being a minority or an oppressed or dominant group. An ethnic group is capable of including converts and people who marry into the group providing they are accepted by members of the group. It is also capable of excluding those who have left the group. Sikhs,[55] Jews,[56] Romany Gypsies,[57] Irish Travellers,[58] and Scottish Travellers[59] have all been held to be ethnic groups. The Scots, Welsh, and English are, however, not an ethnic group.[60]

2.63   Ethnic origins can be closely intertwined with religion. Thus a religious group with a common ethnic origin can bring itself within the ambit of the protected characteristic of race.[61]

---

[50] As amended by the Enterprise and Regulatory Reform Act 2013 s. 97.

[51] In 2013 the Government undertook to carry out a public consultation on how best to prohibit caste discrimination and indicated its intention to introduce a draft Order but it failed to launch its proposed consultation. It has since claimed that the ruling in *Chandok v Tirkey* makes complaints about caste-based discrimination possible under the 'ethnic origins' provision of the Act.

[52] [2014] UKEAT /0190/14.

[53] 'Descent' was raised in *R v Governing Body of JFS and Others* [2009] UKSC 15. It was read into the legislation to comply with human rights law and European law. Not only does the Human Rights Act 1998 prohibit discrimination on the basis of descent in the exercise of Convention rights under Art. 14, but the UN Committee on the Elimination of All Forms of Racial Discrimination has stated that caste discrimination is a form of descent discrimination which is prohibited by the International Convention on the Elimination of Racial Discrimination, to which the UK is a signatory.

[54] [1983] 2 AC 548.

[55] *ibid.*

[56] *Seide v Gillette Industries Ltd* [1980] IRLR 427.

[57] *Commission for Racial Equality v Dutton* [1989] IRLR 8.

[58] *O'Leary v Allied Domecq Inns Ltd* CL 950275 July 2000, Central London County Court.

[59] *MacLennan v Gypsy Traveller Education and Information Project* ET Case No 13272/07.

[60] *Northern Joint Police Board v Power* [1997] IRLR 610; *BBC Scotland v Souster* [2001] IRLR 150.

[61] Although there might be less need for this now that there is specific protection for religion or belief. Before there was legislation prohibiting religion or belief discrimination, the only way in which a religious group could hope to obtain protection against discrimination was to bring itself within the ambit of the race provisions, by showing that a requirement or a condition would have a disproportionate adverse impact on that group as a whole. This was achieved by arguing that the religion was closely tied up with the ethnicity. Consequently, Jews and Sikhs could benefit from the protection under the race provisions but Muslims and Rastafarians could not.

Sikhs and Jews have demonstrated that they are both an ethnic group and a religious group whereas Muslims and Rastafarians have not been able to show that they meet the criteria for an ethnic group.[62]

4. National Origins

As mentioned above, national origins may overlap with nationality. However, the two con- 2.64
cepts can be distinguished since 'nationality' is concerned with membership of a particular nation; and 'national origins' describe a person's connection by birth with a nation.[63] Thus people of Australian national origins may be citizens of the UK, Canada, or Australia. The Scots, Welsh, and English, whilst not being an ethnic group, have been held to be a national group because Great Britain is made up of three distinct nations.[64]

5. Meaning of a Racial Group

A racial group includes a group of people who have or share a colour, ethnic, or national ori- 2.65
gin or nationality. A person may fall into one or more racial groups: for example, a 'Canadian' may be defined by nationality or ethnic or national origin.[65] A racial group can comprise of two or more distinct racial groups: for example, 'British Asians' which would include people who are of Asian national origin and who are British citizens.[66] A racial group could also be 'Black Britons' which would include people who are black and who are British citizens.[67]

Racial groups can be defined negatively and by exclusion: for example, 'non-British' or 2.66
'non-European'.[68]

G. RELIGION OR BELIEF

1. Introduction

Section 10 of the Act covers the protected characteristic of religion or belief. Section 10 2.67
provides that:

(1) Religion means any religion and a reference to religion includes a reference to a lack of
    religion.[69]

---

[62] See *Nyazi v Rymans Ltd* [1988] EAT/6/88 and *Dawkins v Department of the Environment* [1993] IRLR 284.

[63] *Ealing LBC v Race Relations Board* [1972] AC 342.

[64] See n. 52 above.

[65] EN 47–50.

[66] *ibid.*

[67] *ibid.*

[68] *Orphanus v Queen Mary College* [1985] IRLR 349. But note that 'immigration status' will not constitute 'non-British' nationality—see *Taiwo v Olaigbe & Anor and another case* [2016] UKSC 31. The Supreme Court held that nationality and immigration status could not be equated given that non-British nationals may have a secure immigration status here and therefore not be vulnerable in the way that the appellants were.

[69] Only the claimant's religion, belief, or lack of either is protected and not that of the alleged discriminator—see *Gan Menachem Hendon Ltd v Ms Zelda De Groen* UKEAT/0059/18/OO where the claimant was dismissed for cohabiting with her boyfriend, which went against her employer's religious values.

(2) Belief means any religious or philosophical belief and a reference to belief includes a reference to a lack of belief.

(3) In relation to the protected characteristic of religion or belief—

    (a) a reference to a person who has a particular protected characteristic is a reference to a person of a particular religion or belief;

    (b) a reference to persons who share a particular characteristic is a reference to persons who are of the same religion or belief.

2. Meaning of Religion or Belief

2.68   The Act does not define religion or belief explicitly: in essence, it follows the line of Article 9 of the European Convention on Human Rights. In most cases, it will be obvious what is or is not a religion or religious or philosophical belief since these will be in the main the major religions or beliefs such as Christianity, Islam, Judaism, Hinduism, Sikhism, Humanism, Secularism, and Paganism.[70]

2.69   Where the religion is not established, the factors which might be relevant in deciding whether a belief constitutes a religion include such things as a collective act of worship or devotion, a clear structure and belief system, and a profound belief affecting the way of life.

2.70   The Act protects any religion, or religious or philosophical belief and a lack of religion or belief.

3. Meaning of Religion

2.71   'Religion' means any religion and includes religions such as those mentioned above as well as the Baha'i faith, Buddhism, Jainism, Rastafarianism, and Zoroastrianism.[71] This does not mean that a religion has to be mainstream or well known to enjoy the protection of the Act; what matters is that it has a clear structure and belief system. The Act also protects denominations, branches, or sects within religions such as Jehovah's Witnesses and Baptists within Christianity or Orthodox and Masorti Jews within Judaism.

2.72   A lack of religion is also protected by the Act, which means that Atheists benefit from the protection of the Act.

4. Meaning of Belief

2.73   Belief means any religious belief or philosophical belief: it also includes a lack of belief. It is not necessary for a belief to entail any faith or worship of a god or gods.

5. Religious Belief

2.74   Religious belief is not limited to a belief about or adherence to a religion or its central articles of faith. Religious belief can also vary from individual to individual within the same religion and a belief or practice may be protected even where it is not mandated by the religion in

---

[70] Equality and Human Rights Commission (ECHR) Services, Public Functions and Associations Statutory Code of Practice (2011).

[71] EN 53 Examples.

question. For example, some Christians believe that they should wear the cross as a symbol of their faith while others do not;[72] some Jews believe that men should wear the Kippah (skull cap) at all times while others do not; and some Muslims believe that women should cover their entire body and face with the Jilbab[73] and 'Burqa', while others believe that they need only cover their heads with a 'Hijab' and others believe that it is not necessary to cover their heads at all times.

In *Eweida v United Kingdom*[74] the ECtHR held that under article 9 ECHR a religious belief will be a 'manifestation' if it is 'intimately linked to the religion or belief', that is, there is a 'sufficiently close and direct nexus between the act and the underlying belief. Whether or not the act is mandated by a recognised religion is irrelevant.'   2.75

6. Philosophical Belief

Philosophical belief is also protected by the Act and includes beliefs such as Atheism and Secularism.[75]   2.76

The EAT has provided useful guidance on the factors to be taken into consideration in deciding whether a belief is a philosophical belief.[76] To qualify as a philosophical belief: 2.77

- the belief must be genuinely held;
- it must be a belief and not an opinion or viewpoint based on current information;[77]
- it must be a belief as to a weighty and substantial aspect of human life and behaviour;
- it must attain a certain level of cogency, seriousness, cohesion, and importance;
- it must be worthy of respect in a democratic society, not be incompatible with human dignity, and not conflict with the fundamental rights of others.[78]

The following beliefs have been held to be philosophical beliefs after applying these criteria: a belief in the moral imperative to avoid catastrophic climate change;[79] a belief that 'public service broadcasting has the higher purpose of promoting cultural interchange and social cohesion';[80] and a humanist belief in equality and dignity for all people and a belief that to ignore injustice is to be complicit with it.[81]

The Act appears to exclude political belief; however, in *Grainger* the EAT suggests that a belief based on a political philosophy might be brought within the definition of philosophical belief such as the political philosophies of Socialism, Marxism, Communism, or   2.78

---

[72] See *Eweida v British Airways* [2009] IRLR 78.

[73] *R (Begum) v Governors of Denbigh High School* [2006] UKHL 15.

[74] [2013] ECHR 37; [2013] IRLR 231.

[75] In *Holland v Angel Supermarket Ltd & Anor* [2013] ET 3301005-2013 a 'Wiccan' who claimed that she was mocked and later dismissed after switching her shifts to celebrate All Hallows' Eve won her claim of religion or belief discrimination.

[76] *Grainger Plc and Others v Nicholson* [2009] UKEAT/0219/09/ZT.

[77] *McClintock v Department of Constitutional Affairs* [2008] IRLR 29.

[78] EN 52. See also *Regina v Secretary of State for Education and Employment and others (Respondents) ex parte Williamson (Appellant) and others* [2005] UKHL 15; *Forstater v CGD Europe* [2019] 12 WLUK 516—a belief that sex is biologically immutable attained the necessary level of cogency and cohesion but was incompatible with human dignity and the fundamental rights of others.

[79] See n. 76 above.

[80] *Maistry v BBC* [2011] EqLR 549.

[81] *Streatfeild v London Philharmonic Orchestra Ltd* [2012] EqLR 901.

free-market Capitalism.[82] In *The General Municipal and Boilermakers Union v Henderson* the Employment Tribunal found that left-wing democratic socialism is a protected belief for the purposes of the Act.[83] A person with a strong affiliation with a political party and its values may also be protected under the Act: in Olivier v Department of Work and Pensions[84] the Employment Tribunal found that a strong support for, and an interest in, the history and moral tenets of the Labour Party and belief in democratic socialism amounted to more than just an opinion and fell within the definition of 'philosophical belief'.[85]

To enjoy protection of the provision the belief must satisfy the requirements set out in the test. It is not entirely clear whether a person must satisfy all criteria or only some of them to benefit from the protection of the Act although in *Oliver* the tribunal held that the political belief in question satisfied all the criteria.

7. Manifestation of Religion or Belief

2.79 The statutory codes of practice state that 'there is not always a clear line between holding a religion or belief and the manifestation of that religion or belief' and that 'placing limitations on a person's right to manifest their religion or belief may amount to unlawful discrimination; this would usually be indirect discrimination'.[86]

However, *Patmalniece v Secretary of State for Work and Pensions*[87] suggests that less favourable treatment because of the manifestation of a religion or belief may constitute direct discrimination where it is necessarily linked to a characteristic indissociable from the religion or belief.

2.80 By contrast, in *Mackereth v the Department for Work and Pension and Anor*,[88] a Christian doctor who refused to refer to transgender benefits claimants by their chosen pronouns lost his claim for religious discrimination and harassment. The tribunal accepted that the claimant's Christianity was protected under the Equality Act 2010, but it ruled that his conscientious objection to transgenderism was incompatible with human dignity and conflicted with the fundamental rights of others and was not protected under the Equality Act 2010.

H. SEX

1. Introduction

2.81 Section 11 of the Act covers the protected characteristic of sex and provides that:

(a) a reference to a person who has a particular characteristic is a reference to a man or a woman;

---

[82] See n. 76 above.
[83] UKEAT/0073/14/DM.
[84] ET/1701407/2013.
[85] See also *Redfearn v United Kingdom* [2013] IRLR 51 where the ECtHR held that the absence in British law of a remedy for a British National Party councillor, who was dismissed on grounds of affiliation with a political party, was a breach of article 10 ECHR.
[86] Equality and Human Rights Commission (EHRC) Employment Statutory Code of Practice para. 2.61 and Services, Public Functions and Associations Statutory Code of Practice para. 2.54.
[87] [2011] UKSC 11.
[88] ET/1304602/18.

(b) a reference to persons who share a protected characteristic is a reference to persons of the same sex.

2. Meaning of Sex

The provision makes clear that the protected characteristic of sex applies to both men and **2.82** women of any age and so includes boys and girls. It also means that women can share this characteristic with other women and men with other men.[89]

I. SEXUAL ORIENTATION

1. Introduction

Section 12 covers the protected characteristic of sexual orientation. Section 12 provides that: **2.83**

(1) Sexual orientation means a person's sexual orientation towards—
    (a) a person of the same sex,
    (b) persons of the opposite sex, or
    (c) persons of either sex.
(2) In relation to the protected characteristic of sexual orientation—
    (a) a reference to a person who has a particular protected characteristic is a reference to a person who is of a particular sexual orientation;
    (b) a reference to persons who share the protected characteristic is a reference to persons who are of the same sexual orientation.

2. Meaning of Sexual Orientation

Sexual orientation is defined as being a person's sexual orientation towards: a person of the **2.84** same sex; a person of the opposite sex; and persons of either sex. Sexual orientation relates to a person's sexual attraction as well as to their behaviour.[90] People who share a particular sexual orientation means people of the same sexual orientation.[91]

Discrimination because of sexual orientation includes discrimination because someone is **2.85** gay or lesbian, heterosexual ('straight'), or bisexual.

Discrimination based on manifestation of sexual orientation is also covered by the Act. **2.86** This may include such things as a person's appearance, the places s/he visits, or the people s/he associates with.[92]

Anyone who is gay or lesbian, heterosexual, or bisexual is protected. The Act does not **2.87** cover sexual practices, such as celibacy. However, references to a person's sexual practices or a requirement for abstinence might constitute sexual orientation discrimination by perception, indirect discrimination or harassment.

---

[89] EN 54.
[90] Equality and Human Rights Commission (EHRC) para. 2.65 and Services, Public Functions and Associations Statutory Code of Practice para. 2.59.
[91] EN 56.
[92] Equality and Human Rights Commission (EHRC) para. 2.66 and Services, Public Functions and Associations Statutory Code of Practice para. 2.60. See also *English v Sanderson Blinds Ltd* [2008] EWCA Civ 1421.

2.88   Gender reassignment should not be confused with sexual orientation; the two are separate and distinct characteristics. Consequently, trans people are not protected under this provision unless the act of discrimination is because of their sexual orientation.

J. PREGNANCY AND MATERNITY

1. Introduction

2.89   Although not strictly protected characteristics in Part 2, Chapter 1, the Act protects women from discrimination because of their pregnancy or maternity, which includes breastfeeding. Discrimination because of these conditions is a form of prohibited conduct.[93]

2.90   For services, public functions, and associations it is discrimination to treat a woman unfavourably because:

- of either her current or a previous pregnancy;[94]
- she has given birth, and the unfavourable treatment occurs within a period of 26 weeks beginning with the day on which she gave birth; or[95]
- she is breastfeeding, and the unfavourable treatment occurs within a period of 26 weeks beginning with the day on which she gave birth.[96]

2.91   A woman is protected under this section even when the baby is stillborn, so long as she was pregnant for at least 24 weeks before she gave birth.[97]

2.92   Outside of the 26-week period, she may be protected by the sex discrimination provisions.

2.93   For the purposes of work, it is unlawful direct discrimination to treat a woman unfavourably because of her pregnancy or a related illness, or because she is exercising, has exercised, or is seeking or has sought to exercise her right to maternity leave.[98]

2.94   The Act states that such unfavourable treatment during 'the protected period' is unlawful pregnancy and maternity discrimination, and is not treated as direct sex discrimination.[99]

2. The Protected Period

2.95   The protected period starts when a woman becomes pregnant, and its duration depends on her statutory maternity leave entitlements. It will therefore be different for each individual. The maternity leave scheme is set out in Part VIII of the Employment Rights Act 1996 (ERA) and the Maternity and Parental Leave etc Regulations 1999 (MPLR).

2.96   The protected period in relation to a woman's pregnancy ends either:

- if she is entitled to ordinary and additional maternity leave, at the end of the additional maternity leave period, or when she returns to work after giving birth, if that is earlier; or

---

[93] Ss 17 and 18.
[94] S. 17(2).
[95] S. 17(3).
[96] S. 17(4).
[97] S. 17(5).
[98] S. 18(2), (3), (4).
[99] S. 18(7).

- if she is not entitled to maternity leave, for example, because she is not an employee, two weeks after the baby is born.[100]

If a woman experiences unfavourable treatment after the end of the protected period, but which results from a decision made during that period, it is regarded as occurring during the protected period.[101] **2.97**

Otherwise, unfavourable treatment of a woman because of her pregnancy or maternity outside the protected period would be considered as sex discrimination. **2.98**

3. Pregnancy of Hers/Unfavourable Treatment Because of Own Pregnancy

The unfavourable treatment must be because of the woman's own pregnancy and does not extend to association, unlike other protected characteristics.[102] However, it may be sex discrimination because of association with a pregnant woman if a man is treated less favourably because of his partner's pregnancy. **2.99**

4. Surrogacy Discrimination

In *CD v ST*[103] and *Z v A Government Department and the Board of Management of a Community School*,[104] the CJEU clarified that the Pregnant Workers Directive does not require a member state to allow a commissioning mother who has had a baby through a surrogacy arrangement to take maternity leave or its equivalent. Also, a refusal to grant paid leave did not amount to sex and/or disability discrimination. Although the CJEU acknowledged that one of the benefits of maternity leave is to protect the special relationship between a woman and her child over the period which follows pregnancy and childbirth, the main objective of the Pregnant Workers Directive is to protect the health of the mother of the child in the especially vulnerable situation arising from her pregnancy. **2.100**

Consequently, a commissioning mother who has had a baby through a surrogacy arrangement cannot claim pregnancy or maternity discrimination if she is refused maternity leave or pay.[105] **2.101**

---

[100] S. 18(6).

[101] S. 18(7).

[102] In *Kulikaoskas v MacDuff Shellfish* UKEATS/0063/09/BI the EAT confirmed that a man who argued that he was dismissed because of his association with his pregnant partner could not pursue a pregnancy discrimination claim under the Sex Discrimination Act 1975 (SDA 1975). The EAT held that it was clear that neither the Pregnant Workers Directive nor the Equal Treatment Directive requires protection against 'associative' pregnancy discrimination.

[103] Case C-167/12 [2014] EqLR 298. The claimant issued proceedings under the Equality Act 2010 claiming discrimination because of sex and/or pregnancy and maternity.

[104] Case C-363/12 [2014] EqLR 316.

[105] UK parents having children born through surrogacy now have employment protection, leave, and pay (equivalent to maternity rights) under the Children and Families Act 2014.

3

CORE RIGHTS AND DUTIES

A. INTRODUCTION

3.01 This chapter explains the principal concepts of discrimination defined in Part 2 of the Equality Act 2010 ('the Act'). Chapters 4, 5, 6, and 7 describe how and to what extent each form of discrimination is prohibited in the areas of activity covered by the Act.

3.02 In general, discrimination is defined in the same way for each of the protected characteristics. There are important exceptions to this rule, in recognition of the particular needs of certain groups protected by the Act. For example, the distinctive nature of disability discrimination is recognized through the concepts of discrimination arising from disability[1] and the duty to make reasonable adjustments.[2] These are specific forms of discrimination which apply only to disability. Special provisions deal with absences from work because of gender reassignment[3] and specific measures are set out to deal with pregnancy and maternity discrimination.[4]

---

[1] See paras 3.24–3.31.
[2] See paras 3.57–3.69.
[3] See para. 3.32.
[4] See paras 3.33–3.41.

Anna Beale, *Core Rights and Duties* In: *Blackstone's Guide to the Equality Act 2010*. Fourth Edition. Edited by: Anthony Robinson, David Ruebain, and Susie Uppal, Oxford University Press (2021). © Oxford University Press.
DOI: 10.1093/oso/9780198870876.003.0003

B. DIRECT DISCRIMINATION

Direct discrimination is the concept which corresponds most closely to the common understand- **3.03**
ing of discrimination; that is, different treatment of two individuals, where the reason for the
difference in treatment is a protected characteristic. To prohibit direct discrimination is to require
people to be treated in the same way, regardless of race, sex, etc. Section 13(1) provides that 'A
person (A) discriminates against another (B) if, because of a protected characteristic, A treats B less
favourably than A treats or would treat others'. There are, therefore, a number of elements which
claimants must satisfy if they are to establish that they have experienced direct discrimination. To
constitute direct discrimination, the treatment experienced by B must be *different* from that of
another person (often referred to as a 'comparator').[5] The treatment of B must be *less favourable*
than the treatment afforded a comparator.[6] Finally, A's less favourable treatment of B will not
constitute direct discrimination unless the *reason* for the treatment was a protected characteristic.[7]

1. Comparator

Direct discrimination is concerned with distinctions in treatment. Therefore, to show direct **3.04**
discrimination, B may compare his/her treatment with that of another person. That other
person, commonly referred to as a comparator, must, save for the protected characteristic
which forms the basis of the claim, have materially similar circumstances to those of the
claimant.[8] That does not mean that the comparator's circumstances must be the same in all
respects: the question of whether the situation is comparable is one of fact and degree.[9] The
Act states explicitly that for direct disability discrimination, the comparison must be made
with the treatment of a person who, though not disabled, has the same abilities as the disabled claimant.[10] If the protected characteristic is sexual orientation, the fact that one person
is married while another is a civil partner is not a material difference in their circumstances.[11]

The comparator need not be an actual other person. Section 13(1) provides that the treat- **3.05**
ment experienced by B must be less favourable than the way in which A treats *or would treat*
others. The comparator can therefore be hypothetical. B can establish direct discrimination
by showing that if there were another person in similar circumstances, but without B's protected characteristic, that person would be treated more favourably.

The task of showing how a hypothetical comparator would have been treated is not sim- **3.06**
ple.[12] Reference can be made to actual people who, because their circumstances are different

---

[5] See paras 3.04–3.06.
[6] See paras 3.07–3.08.
[7] See paras 3.09–3.12.
[8] S. 23(1).
[9] See *Hewage v Grampian Health Board* [2012] UKSC 37 at paras 21–23 for a discussion of the types of
similarities and differences that may affect comparability.
[10] S. 23(2)(a) and Equality and Human Rights Commission (ECHR), Equality Act 2010 Code of
Practice: Employment Statutory Code of Practice (2011) ('CoP') 3.29.
[11] S. 23(3) and CoP 3.31.
[12] For an explanation of how hypothetical comparators are used in cases of direct discrimination see
Shamoon v Chief Constable of the Royal Ulster Constabulary [2003] UKHL 11. Cases which elucidate concepts
defined in the pre-existing equality enactments are used to elaborate equivalent concepts in the Act, where they
are likely to be interpreted in the same way.

in material ways to those of the claimant, cannot serve as the comparator for the purposes of a claim. The treatment of such people might serve as evidence to show how a hypothetical person in the claimant's circumstances would have been treated. Alternatively, the likely treatment of a hypothetical comparator can be established by focusing on the reason for the treatment experienced by B. Where the reason for the treatment is demonstrably a protected characteristic, it will follow that a hypothetical comparator in the same circumstances, but without that protected characteristic, would have been treated more favourably.[13]

2. Less Favourable Treatment

3.07 Less favourable treatment is a broad concept. Any disadvantage to which B has been subject will constitute less favourable treatment. There is no need for B to have suffered a tangible or material loss.[14] Merely to deprive a person of choice is to subject them to less favourable treatment.[15] However, it is not enough merely to show unreasonable treatment.[16] The treatment must be *less* favourable.

3.08 The Act specifies that racial segregation constitutes less favourable treatment.[17] The Act makes no specific provision in respect of segregation relating to other protected characteristics, but such treatment could amount to less favourable treatment.

3. Causation

3.09 Direct discrimination will not be made out simply because one person was treated less favourably than another. The less favourable treatment complained of will only be direct discrimination under the Act if the reason for it was a protected characteristic. The test of whether less favourable treatment was 'because of' a protected characteristic is an objective test of causation.[18] The question is whether the criterion or fact behind the treatment was a protected characteristic.[19] Where the reason for the treatment is the application of a particular criterion, the precise degree of correlation required between the criterion and the protected characteristic has been the topic of much dispute and the case law still affords no clear answer.[20]

---

[13] *ibid.* See also CoP 3.27.

[14] *Chief Constable of West Yorkshire Police v Khan* [2001] UKHL 48, paras 52–3.

[15] *R v Birmingham City Council ex p Equal Opportunities Commission* [1989] AC 1155.

[16] *Bahl v The Law Society* [2004] IRLR 799.

[17] S. 13(5).

[18] The words 'because of' in s. 13 have the same meaning as the words 'on grounds of', which are used to define direct discrimination in pre-existing anti-discrimination legislation. See *Hansard* HC, vol 494, cols 240–4 (16 June 2009). Case law clarifying the meaning of 'on grounds of' will, therefore, be relevant to understanding the scope of s. 13.

[19] See *R (E) (Respondent) v Governing Body of JFS and the Admissions Appeal Panel of JFS (Appellants) and others* [2009] UKSC 15, para. 13; *R v Birmingham City Council ex p Equal Opportunities Commission* [1989] AC 1155; and *James v Eastleigh Borough Council* [1990] 2 AC 751. Therefore, an employer who treats an employee less favourably because s/he objects to an instruction to discriminate in relation to a protected characteristic will be acting 'because of' that characteristic and thereby subjecting the employee to direct discrimination. See e.g. *Weathersfield Ltd t/a Van & Truck Rentals v Sargent* [1999] ICR 425, CA. See also CoP 3.20.

[20] See e.g. *Bressol v Gouvernement de la Communauté Francaise* (Case C73/08) [2010] 3 CMLR 559; *Regina (E) v Governing Body of JFS and another* [2009] UKSC 19; *Patmalniece v Work and Pensions Secretary* [2011] UKSC 11; *Preddy v Bull* [2013] UKSC 73; *Onu v Akwiwu; Taiwo v Olaigbe* [2016] UKSC 31 (vulnerable immigration status not indissociable from (non-British) nationality); and *Owen v Amec Foster Wheeler Energy*

The 'because of' formulation does not imply a requirement to show motive or intent. **3.10**
Once it is established that the protected characteristic is a cause of the less favourable treatment, the treatment will amount to direct discrimination whether the discriminator had a
benign motive, acted subconsciously, or thought that the treatment was in the best interests
of its recipient.[21]

The protected characteristic need not be the sole, or even the main cause of the less favour- **3.11**
able treatment to satisfy the causation requirement in section 13. The intention behind the
legislation is that there should be no discrimination 'whatsoever' on grounds of a protected
characteristic.[22] Therefore, a protected characteristic need only have had a significant influence, or an influence that is more than trivial, to satisfy the 'because of' test.[23]

(a) Discrimination Because of a Perception or Association

Section 13 does not require that the treatment complained of be connected to the complain- **3.12**
ant's own protected characteristic. The 'because of' formulation is wide enough to allow
claims of direct discrimination where less favourable treatment is based on the claimant's perceived protected characteristic, even where this perception is incorrect.[24] This is likely to be
particularly important in relation to disability and gender reassignment, where the protected
characteristics are defined narrowly and exclude from their scope many who might nevertheless experience discrimination because of incorrect perceptions about them.[25] Paragraphs
3.19 and 3.39 of this chapter deal with claims which require the treatment complained of to
be connected to the complainant's own protected characteristic.

Less favourable treatment of a person because that person is associated with a protected **3.13**
characteristic is also within the scope of the provision. Associative discrimination is considered at paragraphs 3.92–3.95 below.

(b) Shared Protected Characteristics

The Act makes specific provision to clarify that a claim of direct discrimination will not be **3.14**
frustrated where A and B share the protected characteristic which forms the basis of the
claim.[26]

Ltd [2019] EWCA Civ 822 (high medical risk on overseas assignment not indissociable from disability, and
the court noted that the concept of indissociability could not readily be applied in disability discrimination
claims; see para. 78).

[21] See *Birmingham City Council v Equal Opportunities Commission* [1989] 1 AC 1155, *Nagarajan v London
Regional Transport* [2000] 1 AC 50, and *Amnesty International v Ahmed* [2009] IRLR 884. See also CoP 3.14.
[22] See Art. 2(1) of Council Directive 97/80/EC of 15 December 1997 on the burden of proof in cases of
discrimination based on sex (the 'Burden of Proof Directive') and Art. 2(1) of Council Directive 2000/78/EC
of 27 November 2000 establishing a general framework for equal treatment in employment and occupation
(the 'Framework Directive').
[23] See *Nagarajan v London Regional Transport* [2000] 1 AC 50, para. 19 and *Igen Ltd v Wong; Chamberlin
Solicitors v Emokpae; Brunel University v Webster* [2005] EWCA Civ 142.
[24] See *English v Thomas Sanderson Blinds Ltd* [2008] EWCA Civ 1421.
[25] In *Chief Constable of Norfolk Constabulary v Coffey* [2019] EWCA Civ 1061, the Court of Appeal confirmed that there could be a claim for discrimination because of a perceived disability, where the putative
discriminator believed that all the elements of the statutory definition of disability were present, albeit that it
was not necessary that he/she should attach the label 'disability' to them (para. 35). This could include a belief
that all the elements of a progressive condition, within the meaning of para. 8(1) and (2) of Sch. 1 Equality
Act 2010, were present (see paras 50–56).
[26] S. 24(1).

4. Exceptions

3.15 Justification of direct discrimination is not possible under the Act, unless the less favourable treatment is because of age. Treatment which falls within the definition of direct discrimination will be unlawful unless the Act makes specific provision exempting the type of treatment experienced from the scope of its prohibitions. The specific exceptions that apply in each area of activity covered by the Act are discussed in chapters 4–7.

(a) *Age*

3.16 Direct discrimination because of age is treated differently by the Act. Section 13(2) provides that where the protected characteristic is age, if A can show that his/her treatment of B was a proportionate means of achieving a legitimate aim, A does not discriminate by treating B in that way.[27] It is important to note that the circumstances in which direct age discrimination may be so 'justified' are narrower than those which might apply in a case of indirect discrimination. Direct age discrimination may only be justified on the basis of social policy objectives which are distinguishable from purely individual reasons particular to the employer's situation, such as cost reduction or improving competitiveness. The CJEU has recognized two different types of legitimate objective in this context: 'inter-generational fairness' and 'dignity'.[28]

(b) *Positive Action*

3.17 Save in relation to disability,[29] the protection afforded by the notion of direct discrimination is symmetrical. Where the Act prohibits direct discrimination, it requires people to be treated in the same way, regardless of their protected characteristics. More favourable treatment of one person because of a protected characteristic will constitute direct discrimination against others not so treated. Therefore, positive discrimination, that is, more favourable treatment of a person because of a protected characteristic, is generally unlawful under the Act. However, there is a limited exception to this general rule. The Act sets out a narrowly defined concept of 'positive action', which, broadly, allows limited action to overcome disadvantage connected to a protected characteristic.[30]

(c) *Asymmetrical Protection Against Direct Disability Discrimination*

3.18 In relation to most protected characteristics, protection against direct discrimination is 'symmetrical'. For example, both men and women are protected against sex discrimination, and a person is protected against discrimination on religious grounds, whether Christian, Muslim, Atheist, or without belief. However, in recognition of the fact that disabled people must be treated 'more favourably' if they are to have equal access, the Act protects only disabled people against direct discrimination because of disability.[31] It remains, therefore, perfectly lawful to treat a disabled person more favourably than a non-disabled person under the Act.

(d) *Marriage and Civil Partnership*

3.19 Only married people and civil partners are protected against discrimination because of marriage and civil partnership. This means that those outside of a formally recognized

---

[27] This is known as objective justification and is explained further in paras 3.52–3.55.
[28] See *Seldon v Clarkson Wright & Jakes* [2012] UKSC 16 and Chapter 5 at paras 5.02–5.04 for consideration of the test in the context of goods and services.
[29] See para. 3.18 on the asymmetrical nature of disability and s. 13(3) of the Act.
[30] See ss 158 and 159. Chapter 12 explains the concept of positive action in detail.
[31] S. 13(3).

relationship, whether single, cohabiting, divorced, or with another relationship status, are not protected against discrimination because of marriage or civil partnership.[32] Nor are those who are associated with a married person or civil partner and those who are perceived to be married or in a civil partnership. Section 13 does not allow a claim where the reason for the discriminator's treatment is his/her own marriage or civil partnership.

(e) Sex, Pregnancy, and Maternity

As described above, in order to show direct discrimination, the claimant may compare her/his treatment with that of a similarly situated comparator. This element of the test of direct discrimination is problematic if women are to be protected against the negative treatment they often experience because of pregnancy and maternity. There is no appropriate comparator in materially similar circumstances, since a man could never find himself in a similar situation. For this reason the Act contains specific provisions dealing with pregnancy and maternity discrimination and where these apply, a woman must bring a claim under these rather than under section 13.[33] However, even where the specific pregnancy/maternity provisions do not, for whatever reason, apply, and a woman has to bring her claim under section 13, if she has been treated unfavourably on the ground of pregnancy or maternity, she will not need to prove that a man would have been treated differently.[34] Further, the Act specifies that in non-work cases, treating a woman less favourably because she is breastfeeding a baby who is more than six months old constitutes direct sex discrimination.[35]   **3.20**

The prohibition of direct discrimination in section 13 also provides that, where the protected characteristic in question is sex and the claimant is a man, no account shall be taken of more favourable treatment afforded to a woman in connection with pregnancy or childbirth, allowing for limited positive action in respect of pregnant women and new mothers.[36] As the law currently stands, section 13(6)(b) has been held to permit only more favourable treatment that is 'reasonably necessary' to compensate such women for the disadvantages occasioned by their condition.[37]   **3.21**

(f) Religion and Belief

Section 13 does not permit a claim where the reason for the treatment complained of is the religion or belief of the alleged discriminator. The treatment must be because of the actual or perceived religion or belief of the complainant, or a person with whom he or she is associated.[38]   **3.22**

5. Advertising an Intention to Discriminate

A person who advertises an intention to discriminate against people with a particular protected characteristic is likely to dissuade others with that protected characteristic from accessing, for example, that person's service, education facility, or premises. This will, therefore,   **3.23**

---

[32] CoP 3.34.
[33] S. 13(8) and paras 3.33–3.41.
[34] *Commissioner of the City of London Police v Geldart* [2020] ICR 920 at para. 92.
[35] S. 13(6)(a), (7), and (8).
[36] S. 13(6)(b).
[37] *Eversheds Legal Services v De Belin* [2011] ICR 1137.
[38] *Lee v Ashers Baking Co Ltd* [2018] UKSC 49 at paras 40–45; *Gan Menachem Hendon Ltd v De Groen* [2019] ICR 1023 at paras 19–23.

constitute direct discrimination, even if it is not possible to identify an individual who was disadvantaged by the declaration.[39] If an employer advertises an intention to discriminate against people with a particular protected characteristic it will also constitute direct discrimination. However, only those who are eligible to apply for the job could bring a claim.[40] On a connected point, the CJEU has held that no claim for discrimination may be brought under the Framework Directive by an individual who *has* applied for an advertised role, but did so with the purpose of seeking compensation, rather than to obtain the post.[41]

C. DISCRIMINATION ARISING FROM DISABILITY

3.24   The concept of 'discrimination arising from disability' set out in section 15 of the Act replaces and improves upon the concept of 'disability-related discrimination' found in the Disability Discrimination Act 1995 (DDA).[42] Section 15 provides:

(1) A person (A) discriminates against a disabled person (B) if—
   (a) A treats B unfavourably because of something arising in consequence of B's disability, and
   (b) A cannot show that the treatment is a proportionate means of achieving a legitimate aim.
(2) Subsection (1) does not apply if A shows that A did not know, and could not reasonably have been expected to know, that B had the disability.

This form of discrimination addresses unfavourable treatment of a disabled person, where the reason for the treatment is not the disability itself, but something which arises in consequence of the disabled person's disability.

1. Unfavourable Treatment

3.25   The test in section 15 does not require a comparison between the treatment of the disabled person and the treatment of another person. It is irrelevant whether a non-disabled person or a person with a different disability would have been subject to the same treatment in the same circumstances.

3.26   'Unfavourable treatment' is not defined in the Act. Treatment which is advantageous; for example, the award of an early or enhanced pension because a person is or has become disabled, cannot be said to be 'unfavourable' simply because it could have been more advantageous. If treatment cannot reasonably be regarded as in any sense 'unfavourable', it will not be caught by the section.[43] Sometimes it will be clear that the treatment is unfavourable, such as where a disabled person is denied an opportunity or is subject to a loss. However, even

---

[39] Case C-54/07 *Centrum voor gelijkheid van kansen v Firma Feryn NV* [2008] 3 CMLR 22.
[40] CoP 3.32.
[41] Case C/423/15 *Kratzer v R+V Allgemeine Versicherung AG* [2016] ICR 967.
[42] For the problems which arose under the DDA notion of disability-related discrimination, see *London Borough of Lewisham v Malcolm* [2008] UKHL 43.
[43] *Trustees of Swansea University Pension and Assurance Scheme and another v Williams* [2018] UKSC 65 at para. 28.

treatment which a discriminator thinks is in the best interests of the disabled person may still amount to unfavourable treatment.

2. Causation

It is not necessary for there to be a direct causal link between the disabled person's disability and the unfavourable treatment to which s/he was subjected. It is the *thing which arises in consequence* of disability which must be the reason for the treatment. This will include anything which is a result, effect, or outcome of the disability, such as, for example, absence from work, the need to be accompanied by a dog, or behavioural or capability issues.[44]

3.27

3. Justification

A person who otherwise would be liable for discrimination arising from disability can avoid liability if able to show that the treatment was a proportionate means of achieving a legitimate aim.[45]

3.28

4. Knowledge

A person who can show that s/he did not know, and could not reasonably have been expected to know, of the disabled person's disability at the time of the unfavourable treatment will not be found to have discriminated within section 15. However, to establish discrimination arising from disability, it is not necessary to show that disability was on the mind of the discriminator in deciding to subject the disabled person to unfavourable treatment. Nor does the discriminator have to be aware of the causal link between the person's disability and the 'something arising' that resulted in the unfavourable treatment.[46] A person seeking to show his/her reasonable ignorance will have to show both that s/he did not know of the disability and that s/he did all s/he could reasonably have been expected to do to find out whether the person concerned had a disability. In cases where constructive knowledge is relied upon, the court or tribunal must also consider what reasonable enquiries or investigation would have elicited, and if the disability would not then have been revealed, the knowledge requirement will not be met.[47]

3.29

Where a person's agent or employee knows, in that capacity, of the person's disability, the principal will normally be found to have known of it too.[48] However, information given in confidence to an employer's occupational health service will not be attributed to the employer.[49] Conversely, an employer may not rely on an unreasoned opinion from an occupational health service that an employee is not disabled within the meaning of the Act; it must make its own factual judgement on the question, albeit that this may be informed by occupational health advice.[50]

3.30

---

[44] CoP 5.9.

[45] See paras 3.52–3.55 for further discussion of these concepts.

[46] *York City Council v Grosset* [2018] EWCA Civ 1105.

[47] *A Ltd v Z* [2020] ICR 199 at para. 42.

[48] CoP 5.17.

[49] See *Hartman v South Essex Mental Health and Community Care NHS Trust; Best v Staffordshire University; Wheeldon v HSBC Bank Ltd; Grimsby & Scunthorpe Newspapers Ltd; Moore v Welwyn Components Ltd; Melville v Home Office* [2005] EWCA Civ 6.

[50] *Gallop v Newport City Council* [2013] EWCA Civ 1583 at paras 40–44.

5. Relationship with Duty to Make Reasonable Adjustments

3.31   It will be more difficult for a person to justify discrimination arising from disability where s/he has failed to make a reasonable adjustment.[51]

D. GENDER REASSIGNMENT—ABSENCE FROM WORK

3.32   The Act contains a specific provision to deal with absences from work 'because of gender reassignment'.[52] According to section 16, a transsexual person[53] should be treated no less favourably in relation to such absences than s/he would be treated in relation to sickness absence. Section 16 also provides that it is discrimination to treat a transsexual person less favourably in relation to absences because of gender reassignment than in relation to absences for other reasons, unless it is reasonable to do so. A person's absence is 'because of gender reassignment' if it is because the person is proposing to undergo, is undergoing, or has undergone gender reassignment (or part of that process).

E. PREGNANCY AND MATERNITY DISCRIMINATION

3.33   Where a woman is subjected to discriminatory treatment because of pregnancy or maternity the treatment is, of course, inextricably linked to her sex. However, under the Act, pregnancy and maternity discrimination is excluded from the definition of direct sex discrimination[54] and dealt with under separate provisions set out in sections 17 (in relation to non-work situations) and 18 (in relation to work). These distinctive provisions, which do not require a woman's treatment to be compared with that of another person, recognize that the notion of direct discrimination is inadequate to address discrimination linked to pregnancy and maternity. Pregnancy and maternity discrimination cannot be justified.

1. Non-work Cases

3.34   Section 17 defines pregnancy and maternity discrimination for the purposes of those parts of the Act which address discrimination in services and public functions, premises, education, and associations.

3.35   Section 17 provides that it is discrimination to treat a woman unfavourably because of her pregnancy (whether current or previous). It is also discrimination to subject a woman to unfavourable treatment because she has given birth,[55] or because she is breastfeeding,[56] during the 26-week period beginning with the day on which she gives birth. A woman is protected even when the baby is stillborn, so long as she was pregnant for at least 24 weeks

---

[51] CoP 5.21.
[52] S. 16.
[53] 'Transsexual person' remains the terminology used in the legislation.
[54] See ss 13(8), 17(6), and 18(7).
[55] S. 17(3).
[56] S. 17(4).

before she gave birth. Outside of the 26-week period, a woman subject to unfavourable treatment because of pregnancy or maternity may be protected by the prohibition of direct sex discrimination.[57]

A woman is only protected in relation to her own pregnancy, or the birth of her own baby.[58] **3.36**
Section 17 does not, therefore, make it possible for a person to complain of treatment caused by another person's pregnancy or maternity, or because of a perceived pregnancy or maternity. Such cases may, though, constitute direct sex discrimination.[59]

2. Work Cases

For the purposes of Part 5 of the Act (work), during a certain period, known as the protected **3.37**
period, it is unlawful discrimination to treat a woman unfavourably because of her pregnancy or an illness related to it. It is also discrimination to treat a woman unfavourably because she is on compulsory maternity leave or because she is exercising, has exercised, or is seeking or has sought to exercise her right to ordinary or additional maternity leave.[60]

The duration of the protected period depends on the statutory maternity leave entitlements **3.38**
of the woman in question. The protected period starts when a woman becomes pregnant[61] and ends either:

- if she is entitled to ordinary and additional maternity leave, at the end of the additional maternity leave period or when she returns to work after giving birth, if that is earlier; or
- if she is not entitled to maternity leave, two weeks after the end of the pregnancy.[62]

If a woman's unfavourable treatment results from a decision taken during the protected period, the treatment will be treated as having occurred within that period.[63] This is so even if the decision was not implemented until after the period had ended. Otherwise, where a woman is treated unfavourably because of her pregnancy or maternity outside of the protected period, it will fall to be considered as sex discrimination under section 13.[64]

The use of the words 'pregnancy of hers' in section 18(2) excludes the possibility of a per- **3.39**
son complaining under section 18 of unfavourable treatment because of an association with a pregnant woman, or because of being perceived to be pregnant. An argument that Directive 2006/54/EC requires the pregnancy discrimination provisions to be interpreted so as to cover associative discrimination has been rejected by the Scottish EAT.[65] The question was referred to the Court of Justice of the European Union by the Court of Session, but the case settled

---

[57] See ss 13(6)(a) and 17(6).
[58] See para. 3.39 below.
[59] See s. 13 and para. 3.12.
[60] The maternity leave scheme is set out in the Employment Rights Act 1996 (ERA), which defines the rights to compulsory, ordinary, and additional maternity leave, and amplified in the Maternity and Parental Leave etc Regulations 1999 (MAPLE).
[61] Where a woman becomes pregnant through IVF treatment, she will not qualify for protection under this section until the fertilized ova have been transferred into her uterus: Case C-506/06 *Mayr v Bäckerei und Konditorei Gerhard Flockner OHG* [2008] 2 CMLR 27; *Sahota v Home Office* [2010] ICR 772.
[62] S. 18(6).
[63] S. 18(5).
[64] S. 18(7).
[65] *Kulikaoskas v Macduff Shellfish* [2011] ICR 48.

prior to any decision. In any event, such treatment may amount to direct discrimination under section 13.[66]

3. Causation

3.40   As with direct discrimination, the 'because of' wording in sections 17 and 18 is intended to import an objective test of causation into the notion of pregnancy and maternity discrimination. The 'because of' formula does not imply any motivation or intention. The pregnancy/maternity leave need not be the only or even the principal cause of the treatment to satisfy the test, but it should be an effective cause. The fact that a woman is absent on maternity leave when unfavourable treatment happens is insufficient by itself to fulfil that test.[67]

4. Unfavourable Treatment

3.41   Any disadvantageous treatment will constitute 'unfavourable treatment'.[68] It is not necessary to compare a woman's treatment with that of another person to show that it was unfavourable.[69]

F. INDIRECT DISCRIMINATION

3.42   While provisions prohibiting direct discrimination are aimed at achieving formal equality of treatment, those prohibiting indirect discrimination are aimed at bringing about a more substantive result—equality of outcome.[70] Practices which appear neutral as to a person's protected characteristics, and so respect the principle of equality of treatment, may, in practice, have a disproportionately adverse effect on people with a particular protected characteristic.

3.43   The effect of section 19, which defines indirect discrimination, is that where a provision, criterion, or practice places people with a protected characteristic at a particular disadvantage, it will be considered discriminatory unless it can be justified. It provides:

(1) A person (A) discriminates against another (B) if A applies to B a provision, criterion or practice which is discriminatory in relation to a relevant protected characteristic of B's.

(2) For the purposes of subsection (1), a provision, criterion or practice is discriminatory in relation to a relevant protected characteristic of B's if—

    (a) A applies, or would apply, it to persons with whom B does not share the characteristic,

    (b) it puts, or would put, persons with whom B shares the characteristic at a particular disadvantage when compared with persons with whom B does not share it,

---

[66] A Scottish Employment Tribunal has found that s. 13 does cover discrimination because of association with a pregnant woman; see *Gyenes and another v Highland Welcome (UK) Ltd t/a The Star Hotel*, Case No. S/4112392/12, and see CoP 8.16.

[67] *Interserve FM Ltd v Tuleikyte* [2017] IRLR 615 paras 20–21.

[68] See paras 3.07 and 3.26.

[69] Before it became an Act, the Equality Bill was amended by the House of Commons to replace the words 'less favourably' in ss 17 and 18 with the non-comparative 'unfavourably'. See *Hansard* HC (5th Series), col. 278 (16 June 2009).

[70] *R (E) (Respondent) v Governing Body of JFS and the Admissions Appeal Panel of JFS (Appellants) and Others* [2009] UKSC 15, para. 56.

(c) it puts, or would put, B at that disadvantage, and

(d) A cannot show it to be a proportionate means of achieving a legitimate aim.

...

A claim of indirect discrimination will be made out, therefore, if the discriminator applied a provision, criterion, or practice to the claimant and applies or would apply it to persons without the claimant's protected characteristic; but it puts or would put people with the claimant's protected characteristic at a particular disadvantage and puts the claimant at that disadvantage; and the discriminator cannot justify the provision, criterion, or practice. 'Pregnancy and maternity' is not a relevant protected characteristic for the purposes of indirect discrimination.   **3.44**

1. Application of a Provision, Criterion, or Practice

The terms 'provision, criterion, or practice' are not defined in the Act, but should be construed broadly.[71] The terms can overlap and it is not always necessary to identify which of the three applies to the particular policy subject to challenge. The terms include, but are not limited to, policies, procedures, rules, arrangements, requirements, and prerequisites, whether formal or informal, general or particular, mandatory or discretionary.[72] The Court of Appeal has, however, held that all three terms carry the connotation of a state of affairs (whether framed positively or negatively, and however informal), indicating how similar cases are generally treated, or how a similar case would be treated if it occurred again.[73]   **3.45**

The Act allows challenges to provisions, criteria, or practices which have not yet been applied to a person, but which would be indirectly discriminatory if they were applied. This covers situations in which a person is deterred from doing a thing, such as applying for a job, because a policy which would apply if s/he did so would put him/her at a disadvantage.[74]   **3.46**

2. Comparative Disadvantage

There will only be indirect discrimination if the group sharing the claimant's protected characteristic is, or would be, put at a particular disadvantage in comparison with those who do not share the characteristic. When comparing the impact of the provision, criterion, or practice on the two groups, the circumstances of the individuals in one group must not be materially different to those in the other group.[75]   **3.47**

Since the Act envisages hypothetical comparisons, it is not necessary to establish actual disadvantage. Both the advantaged and disadvantaged groups can be hypothetical. Thus, even where an employer's policy has not disadvantaged any other employees with the claimant's   **3.48**

---

[71] See the comments of Lord Walker in *Rutherford and Another v Secretary of State for Trade and Industry (No 2)* [2006] UKHL 19, para. 47 in relation to the definition of indirect discrimination in the Burden of Proof Directive.

[72] See e.g. *British Airways Plc v Starmer* [2005] IRLR 862; and CoP 4.5.

[73] *Ishola v Transport for London* [2020] EWCA Civ 112, para. 38. *Ishola* was a reasonable adjustments case, but the Court of Appeal held that the same interpretation of the terms 'provision, criterion or practice' must apply in both contexts; see para. 27.

[74] See para. 79 of the Explanatory Notes to the Act; and CoP 4.7 and 4.8.

[75] S. 23(1), and see *Gray v Mulberry Co (Design) Ltd* [2019] EWCA Civ 1720 for confirmation that the requirement for group disadvantage remains in domestic law following *Eweida v UK* (2013) 57 EHRR 8, GC.

characteristic, indirect discrimination could be made out if the policy would *normally* disadvantage those sharing the characteristic in question.

3.49   A particular disadvantage can be established in several ways. The disadvantage which would be occasioned to a group sharing a protected characteristic might be common knowledge. For example, it is common knowledge that many more women than men would find it difficult to work full time, because of their caring responsibilities. Statistics or expert opinion will often be used to show the effect of a provision, criterion, or practice.

3.50   The import of the examples given in the Code of Practice[76] is that there is no need to show a causal link between the disadvantage and the protected characteristic to show indirect discrimination. This has now been confirmed by the Supreme Court, overturning two Court of Appeal decisions to contrary effect.[77] If a provision, criterion or practice puts those with a protected characteristic at a particular disadvantage, it is not necessary to prove why it does so.

3.51   It is not enough to show that people who share the claimant's protected characteristic are, or would be, put at a disadvantage. It is also essential to show that the claimant experienced, or would have experienced, that disadvantage.[78]

3. Justification

3.52   Treatment which satisfies the other elements of the definition will constitute indirect discrimination unless the person applying the provision, criterion, or practice can show that it was a proportionate means of achieving a legitimate aim. A person seeking to justify a provision, criterion, or practice cannot do so by relying on generalizations, since any claim of justification will be subject to rigorous scrutiny.[79]

3.53   In order to be legitimate, an aim must not be discriminatory in itself, and must represent a real, objective consideration.[80] Both the CJEU and the Supreme Court have held that states and organizations seeking to justify a provision, criterion, or practice with a discriminatory impact cannot rely on pure cost considerations.[81] However, the position remains that cost may nevertheless be put into the balance along with other justifications.[82] Some domestic authorities[83] have suggested that it is illogical and artificial to draw a bright line between aims solely and partly related to cost, but the prohibition on purely cost-based aims was strongly reinforced by *O'Brien*[84] and was upheld in *Heskett*. However, a narrow

---

[76] See in particular para. 4.11.

[77] *Essop and others v Home Office (UK Border Agency); Naeem v Secretary of State for Justice* [2017] UKSC 27.

[78] CoP 4.23 and *Essop* at paras 31–32.

[79] See e.g. *Osborne Clarke Service v A Purohit* [2009] IRLR 341; and CoP 4.26.

[80] See para. 3.16 above for the slightly different test applicable in claims of direct age discrimination.

[81] Case C-343/92 *De Weerd, nee Roks v Bestuur van de Bedrijfsvereniging voor de Gezondheid* [1994] ECR 1-571 and *Ministry of Justice v O'Brien* [2013] UKSC 6.

[82] The so-called 'cost-plus' approach, exemplified in *Cross and Others v British Airways Plc* [2005] IRLR 423 and *Woodcock v Cumbria Primary Care Trust* [2012] EWCA Civ 330, and recently reaffirmed in *Heskett v Secretary of State for Justice* [2020] EWCA Civ 1487, although Underhill LJ preferred the phraseology that an aim will only be illegitimate if it is *solely* to avoid cost.

[83] See e.g. *Woodcock v Cumbria Primary Care Trust* [2011] ICR 143 (EAT) and *HM Land Registry v Benson* [2012] ICR 627.

[84] See also the Court of Appeal's judgment in *Woodcock v Cumbria Primary Care Trust* [2012] EWCA Civ 330 at paras 66–67.

definition of aims that are 'solely to avoid cost' has been adopted; see in particular *Heskett*, where the Court of Appeal confirmed that an aim of reducing staffing costs to allow an employer to live within its means, or meet externally-imposed budgetary constraints, may be legitimate.[85]

The provision, criterion, or practice must also be proportionate to any legitimate aim iden- 3.54 tified if it is not to constitute indirect discrimination. Consideration of whether a provision, criterion, or practice is proportionate involves a consideration of whether it is appropriate and necessary.[86] Necessary, in this context, has been interpreted by the domestic courts as meaning 'reasonably necessary'. It does not mean that the provision, criterion, or practice must have been the only means of achieving the legitimate aim. But generally, a provision, criterion, or practice will not be necessary if less discriminatory measures could have been taken to pursue the aim.[87] The less discriminatory measures relied upon must, however, be capable of achieving the actual legitimate aim and not some other (albeit similar or related) aim.[88] A provision, criterion, or practice must also, on balance, be appropriate to the achievement of the aim (i.e. it must in fact be an apt means of achieving the aim relied upon[89]), taking into account the severity of the disadvantage caused and the importance of the aim pursued. The closer the provision, criterion, or practice is, in effect, to direct discrimination, the more difficult it will be to justify.[90]

Where the protected characteristic in question is disability, it will be difficult to justify 3.55 an otherwise discriminatory provision, criterion, or practice if the person who applied it has failed to comply with the duty to make reasonable adjustments. Where the person seeking to justify a provision, criterion, or practice is subject to the public sector equality duty, the extent to which that person has complied with the duty will be highly relevant to whether or not otherwise indirectly discriminatory treatment is justified.[91]

4. Motive

Indirect discrimination is unlawful, whether it was intentional or not, and whatever the 3.56 motive of the provision, criterion, or practice. Intention is, however, relevant to remedies available once indirect discrimination has been established.[92]

---

[85] See paras 98–101 of the Court of Appeal's judgment.

[86] The test of objective justification set out in the European Directives which the Act is intended to implement is that the 'provision, criterion or practice is objectively justified by a legitimate aim and the means of achieving that aim are appropriate and necessary'. See e.g. Art. 2(2)(b)(i) of the Framework Directive.

[87] CoP 4.31 and see *Chief Constable of West Yorkshire Police v Homer* [2012] UKSC 15 at para. 25.

[88] See for example *Blackburn v Chief Constable of West Midlands Police* [2009] IRLR 135, CA, where the legitimate aim of rewarding 24/7 working could not be achieved by the less discriminatory means relied upon by the Employment Tribunal.

[89] *Homer* at para. 22, and see Case C-270/16 *Ruiz Conejero v Ferroser Servicios Auxiliares*, [2018] IRLR 372 at paras 45–48.

[90] *Secretary of State for Defence v Elias* [2006] EWCA Civ 1293, para. 161.

[91] *ibid*, para. 179; and Statutory Code of Practice on Services, Public Functions and Associations ('Services CoP') 5.36.

[92] See ss 119(5) and 124(4). For the meaning of 'intention' see *Walker Ltd v Hussain and Others* [1996] IRLR 11.

G. REASONABLE ADJUSTMENTS

3.57　The duty to make reasonable adjustments is a key element of the range of measures intended to eliminate barriers to access and participation for disabled people. Broadly, it requires those caught by the Act's provisions to take reasonable steps to avoid putting disabled people at a substantial disadvantage by changing a provision, criterion, or practice, by removing or modifying physical barriers, and by providing auxiliary aids and services. The duty does not create a cause of action in itself: the Act provides that a failure to comply with the duty is a form of discrimination.

3.58　The main elements of the duty are set out in section 20 of the Act, but it operates differently depending on the context in which it arises, whether in relation to services or public functions, premises, work, education, or associations. A detailed analysis of the nuances of the duty's operation in each field of activity is beyond the scope of this chapter, but the definition in section 20, and the explanation below, should be read subject to the details set out in the Schedule relevant to each Part of the Act.

1. The Limbs of the Duty

3.59　The duty can take three forms:

- The first requirement is, where a provision, criterion, or practice puts a disabled person at a substantial disadvantage in relation to a relevant matter in comparison with non-disabled people, to take reasonable steps to avoid the disadvantage.
- The second requirement is, where a physical feature puts a disabled person at a substantial disadvantage in relation to a relevant matter in comparison with non-disabled people, to take reasonable steps to avoid the disadvantage.
- The third requirement is to take reasonable steps to provide auxiliary aids and services where a disabled person would otherwise be at a substantial disadvantage in relation to a relevant matter in comparison with non-disabled people.

3.60　The terms 'provision', 'criterion', and 'practice' are not defined, but are intended to have the same meaning as that given in the indirect discrimination provisions, and the comments in paragraph 3.45 apply.[93] Physical features are defined in section 20(10) of the Act. An auxiliary aid or service is anything which provides additional support or assistance to a disabled person. This might include the provision of a special piece of equipment, or extra staff to assist the disabled person.[94] What constitutes a 'relevant matter' varies according to the context in which the duty arises. In employment, for example, deciding to whom to offer employment is a relevant matter.[95]

---

[93] See also CoP 6.10.
[94] CoP 6.13.
[95] Sch. 8, para. 5(1).

2. Substantial Disadvantage in Comparison with Persons Who are Not Disabled

3.61 The common threshold for all three requirements is 'substantial disadvantage'. Substantial disadvantage is disadvantage which is more than minor or trivial.[96]

3.62 The disabled person must be disadvantaged in comparison with other persons. However, in the case of reasonable adjustments, the purpose of the comparison is to establish whether the disabled person was put at substantial disadvantage as compared with a non-disabled person, as opposed to being less favourably treated, because of his/her disability. A more general comparative exercise is required in a reasonable adjustments claim than that which is applied in the individual, like-for-like comparison required in cases of direct discrimination.[97] There is no requirement to identify a comparator or comparator group whose circumstances are the same as the disabled person's.[98] Thus, for example, in considering whether a disabled person was placed at a substantial disadvantage by a requirement of regular attendance at work, the appropriate comparator would be a non-disabled colleague, not a non-disabled colleague with a similar sickness absence record.[99] As in the case of indirect discrimination, the comparison exercise does not require separate proof that the substantial disadvantage suffered is caused by the disability.[100]

3. Discharging the Duty

3.63 Those subject to the duty must take 'such steps as it is reasonable to have to take' to avoid the disadvantage or provide the auxiliary aid or service. Whether or not it is reasonable for a particular step to be taken will depend on all the circumstances in an individual case. Paragraph 6.28 of the Employment Code of Practice sets out some of the factors which might be taken into account when deciding what is a reasonable step for an employer to have to take and paragraph 7.30 of the Service, Public Functions and Associations Code of Practice does likewise. The test of reasonableness is an objective one. However, the Act specifies that where the first and third requirements are concerned with the provision of information, it is reasonable to have to ensure that the information in question is provided in an accessible format.[101] Paragraph 6.33 of the Employment Code of Practice gives some examples of the steps it might be reasonable for an employer to have to take to discharge the duty.

3.64 A failure to make reasonable adjustments cannot be justified. Once an adjustment is 'reasonable' a failure to make it will breach the duty and constitute discrimination.

4. The Trigger for the Duty

3.65 In certain fields of activity covered by the Act, including services, public functions, and associations, the duty is anticipatory, in that it requires those subject to the duty to consider, and take action in relation to, the needs of disabled people prior to being faced with an individual

---

[96] See the definition of 'substantial' in s. 212(1).
[97] *Fareham College Corporation v Walters* [2009] IRLR 991; *Griffiths v Secretary of State for Work and Pensions* [2015] EWCA Civ 1265.
[98] CoP 6.16.
[99] *Griffiths* at para. 58.
[100] *Sheikholeslami v The University of Edinburgh* [2018] IRLR 1090 at para. 53.
[101] S. 20(6).

disabled person.[102] The mere existence of a provision, criterion, or practice, or a physical feature which places disabled people at a substantial disadvantage gives rise to the duty. This means that the duty is a continuing and evolving obligation. It applies regardless of whether the person subject to the duty knows that a particular person is disabled.

3.66   In contrast, in other areas of activity covered by the Act, including work, the duty is only triggered when a particular disabled person faces substantial disadvantage. Further, in work situations, the duty only arises where the person who would be required to make adjustments knows, or could reasonably be expected to know, that the disabled person has a disability and is likely to be placed at a substantial disadvantage.[103] In the context of premises, the duty only arises when the person who would be required to make an adjustment receives a request from or on behalf of the disabled person.[104] Later chapters dealing in more detail with the specific areas of activity covered by the Act explain the extent to which the duty is anticipatory in each.

5. Costs

3.67   A person required to make a reasonable adjustment cannot, unless expressly permitted, pass the cost of complying with the duty onto the disabled person in respect of whom the adjustment is made.[105]

6. Binding Obligations which Prevent Alterations

3.68   Where a person is subject to a legal obligation (save an obligation imposed by a tenancy agreement) which prevents the alteration of premises without another's consent, the Act provides that it is always reasonable for that person to have to take steps to obtain that consent, but it is never reasonable for a person to have to make the adjustment before having obtained that consent.[106]

3.69   Leases which would otherwise prevent the tenant from making a reasonable adjustment are deemed to contain a term providing that where alterations are necessary to discharge the duty, consent to those alterations, subject to reasonable conditions, shall not be unreasonably withheld by the landlord.[107] If a person who is required to make a reasonable adjustment fails to request consent to make an alteration from the landlord, that person cannot defend a failure to make reasonable adjustments by relying on a term in a lease which prevents alterations. Where a landlord refuses consent or attaches unreasonable conditions to its consent, the duty holder or disabled person in question may refer the matter to a County Court, or, in Scotland, to a Sheriff Court.[108] Where a court finds that the failure to consent or conditions is/are unreasonable, it may make a declaration, or authorize the duty-holder to make the alterations under a court order. In any legal proceedings relating to a failure to make reasonable adjustments, the duty holder or disabled person may ask the court to direct that the landlord be made a party to the proceedings.[109] Where a court finds that a failure to consent

---

[102] Services CoP 7.20 and 7.21.
[103] Sch. 8, para. 20(1), and see paras 3.29–3.30 above.
[104] Sch. 4, paras 2(6), 3(5), 4(6), and 5(6).
[105] S. 20(7).
[106] Sch. 21, para. 2.
[107] Sch. 21, para. 3.
[108] Sch. 21, para. 4.
[109] Sch. 21, para. 5.

or conditions are unreasonable, it may make a declaration, or authorize the duty-holder to make the alterations, or order the landlord to pay compensation. Where a landlord is ordered to pay compensation, the duty-holder will not be required to do so.[110]

H. HARASSMENT

3.70 The Act contains express protection against 'harassment'.[111] There are three types of harassment:

- harassment related to a protected characteristic;
- sexual harassment; and
- less favourable treatment because of a person's reaction to harassment.

Each of these are dealt with in turn.

1. Harassment Related to a Protected Characteristic

3.71 The first type of harassment concerns unwanted conduct related to a protected characteristic, which has the purpose or effect either of violating a person's dignity or of creating an intimidating, hostile, degrading, humiliating, or offensive environment for a person. This type of harassment applies to all protected characteristics apart from pregnancy and maternity (though unwanted conduct related to pregnancy and maternity will often constitute harassment related to sex) and marriage and civil partnership (although unwanted conduct related to civil partnership will often constitute harassment related to sexual orientation).[112]

(a) *Unwanted Conduct*

3.72 Unwanted conduct can include a wide range of behaviour, including spoken or written words, imagery, physical gestures, etc. In order to constitute harassment, the conduct must be 'unwanted', but a person claiming that s/he has been subject to harassment need not show that s/he expressed objection to the conduct.[113]

(b) *Related to a Protected Characteristic*

3.73 The definition of harassment captures not only conduct which is engaged in because of a protected characteristic, but also any conduct which is connected to a protected characteristic. Conduct which touches on a protected characteristic, even when engaged in for a reason unrelated to that characteristic, will fulfil the 'related to' element of the definition. Conduct need not, therefore, be targeted at a person in order for that person to complain about it. Nor is there a requirement to show comparative less favourable treatment. A person is protected, therefore, against gender-specific or race-specific conduct, even if everyone was treated in the same way regardless of their gender or race, because it will satisfy the 'related to' test.

---

[110] *ibid.*
[111] S. 26.
[112] CoP 7.5.
[113] CoP 7.8.

3.74　The 'related to' formula also provides protection for those who do not themselves have the protected characteristic to which the conduct relates. This captures harassment based on an association or perception (see paragraphs 3.12 above and 3.92–3.95 below), but also where a person finds, for example, an Islamophobic environment offensive even if s/he is not Muslim. Paragraphs 7.9 to 7.10 of the Employment Code give practical examples of the application of the 'related to' formula and paragraphs 8.11 to 8.13 of the Services Code do likewise.

(c) *'Purpose' or 'Effect'*

3.75　To constitute harassment, it is necessary to show that the conduct complained of either had the purpose or had the effect of producing the proscribed consequences. It is not necessary that the conduct should have had both the purpose and effect.

3.76　If conduct is engaged in with the purpose of violating a person's dignity, or of creating an adverse environment, there is no need to show that it did, in fact, have that effect. It is not therefore necessary to inquire into the effect of the conduct on the person(s) against whom it is directed.[114]

3.77　If the conduct has the effect of violating a person's dignity, or of creating, for example, an offensive environment, the person engaging in the conduct will be liable for it even if that was not his/her purpose. However, in considering whether the conduct had the proscribed effect, the court or tribunal must take into account subjective considerations (the claimant's perception) and objective factors (whether it is reasonable for the conduct to have that effect), and the other circumstances of the case.[115]

(d) *The Proscribed Consequences*

3.78　The purpose or effect in question is that of violating a person's dignity or of creating an intimidating, hostile, degrading, humiliating, or offensive environment for a person. Whether conduct does so or is likely to do so is a matter of fact and degree. One incident which is sufficiently serious may amount to harassment.[116]

2. Sexual Harassment

3.79　Sexual harassment is similar to the first type of harassment, save that it is concerned with unwanted conduct 'of a sexual nature', rather than that which is 'related to a protected characteristic'. Therefore, the comments above relating to the concepts of 'unwanted conduct', 'purpose or effect', and the proscribed consequences apply equally to sexual harassment. Conduct of a sexual nature can include sexual advances, touching, sexual jokes or comments, the display of pornographic pictures, or the sending of emails with material of a sexual nature.

3. Less Favourable Treatment Because of a Person's Reaction to Harassment

3.80　A further form of harassment is defined in section 26(3). When a person has experienced harassment related to gender reassignment or sex, or harassment of a sexual nature, and is

---

[114] CoP 7.16.

[115] S. 26(4).

[116] See e.g. *Richmond Pharmacology v Dhaliwal* [2009] IRLR 336.

treated less favourably either because of having rejected the conduct or having submitted to it, that treatment will constitute harassment within section 26(3).

It is irrelevant whether the initial unwanted conduct was carried out by the perpetrator of the less favourable treatment, or another person. **3.81**

4. Relationship with Other Provisions

The provisions prohibiting harassment do not overlap with other provisions outlawing discriminatory detriment, since the Act provides that detriment does not include conduct which amounts to harassment.[117] However, where the harassment provisions do not apply,[118] conduct which might otherwise have been made unlawful by provisions outlawing harassment may still fall within a prohibition of direct discrimination.[119] **3.82**

5. Third Party Harassment

As originally enacted, Part 5 of the Act provided that an employer would also be liable for harassment if it failed, under certain circumstances, to take reasonably practicable steps to prevent third parties from repeatedly harassing an employee.[120] That provision was repealed with effect from 1 October 2013. The domestic courts have decided that neither the Equality Act 2010, nor the relevant EU Directives permit a claim in respect of third party harassment, unless the employer's failure to act was itself unwanted conduct, which had the purpose or effect of violating the claimant's dignity or creating (in whole or in part) the prohibited environment and was also related to the protected characteristic.[121] **3.83**

I. VICTIMIZATION

Unlike the other forms of discrimination described in this chapter, victimization is not concerned with treatment connected to a person's protected characteristics, but rather is intended to protect those who exercise their rights under the Act, or help others to do so. In this way, it aims to make the remedies available under the Act more effective, by ensuring that those who experience discrimination are not intimidated in asserting their rights. Only individuals are protected against victimization.[122] **3.84**

Section 27, which defines victimization, sets out a list of 'protected acts'.[123] It provides that victimization occurs where one person subjects another to a detriment because s/he believes (whether rightly or wrongly) that the person has done, or may do, a protected act.[124] **3.85**

---

[117] S. 212(1).

[118] For example, harassment related to sexual orientation and religion or belief is not made unlawful outside of a work context. Neither is harassment because of gender reassignment made unlawful in education.

[119] S. 212(5).

[120] S. 40.

[121] See *Unite the Union v Nailard* [2018] EWCA Civ 1203 at paras 91–101; *Bessong v Pennine Care NHS Foundation Trust* [2020] ICR 849.

[122] S. 27(4).

[123] See also s. 77(4), which provides that acts connected to discussions about pay are also to be treated as protected acts.

[124] See also paras 3.92–3.95 below for an explanation of the extension to cover associative victimization.

1. Protected Acts

3.86 The list of protected acts is broad. It includes bringing proceedings under the Act, giving evidence or information in connection with such proceedings, making an allegation (whether express or not) that another person has contravened its provisions, and doing any other thing for the purposes of, or in connection with, the Act. The Act specifies that even where a person subjects another to a detriment because of an allegation against a third person, it will constitute victimization.[125] The equal pay provisions provide that a 'relevant pay disclosure', that is, broadly, a discussion about whether there has been pay discrimination (including discrimination linked to characteristics other than sex), should also be treated as a protected act in the context of employment and appointments.[126]

3.87 A person who acts in bad faith to give false evidence or information, or to make false allegations, will not be protected against victimization.[127]

2. Subject to a Detriment

3.88 It is not necessary to carry out a comparison between treatment of a person who claims to have experienced victimization and the treatment of another person in order to show victimization. The legislators have deliberately moved away from the comparative model of victimization which appeared in the pre-existing anti-discrimination enactments. It is enough to show that a person was subject to a detriment. The fact that others would have been treated in the same way had they engaged in similar behaviour, but for reasons unconnected to discrimination, should not defeat a claim of victimization. Nor does section 27 rest on a comparison of the claimant's treatment with the treatment of those who have engaged in no such conduct. Such comparisons will, though, remain useful as evidence indicating the reason for the claimant's treatment.

3.89 The courts have interpreted the notion of 'detriment' in pre-existing equality enactments broadly. The test as to what constitutes a detriment is, to a great extent, subjective. It covers any loss of opportunity which is reasonably valued by the person having experienced it. It is not necessary to show any tangible or material disadvantage.[128] Paragraphs 9.8 and 9.9 of the Employment Code also give guidance on what constitutes a detriment.

3. Causation

3.90 As for direct discrimination, the 'because' formula does not mean that the protected act (or belief) must have *motivated* the discriminator. It need only have *caused* the detrimental treatment.[129] The protected act (or belief) must be an effective cause, but need not be the only cause of the treatment.

3.91 If the alleged discriminator acted because of a belief that the claimant had carried out a protected act, this will satisfy the test, even if the belief was incorrect. Similarly, where the

---

[125] S. 27(2)(d).

[126] S. 77(4).

[127] S. 27(3).

[128] *Chief Constable of West Yorkshire Police v Khan* [2001] UKHL 48, paras 52–3.

[129] See *Nagarajan v London Regional Transport* [2000] 1 AC 501 and *Chief Constable of West Yorkshire Police v Khan* [2001] UKHL 48.

discriminator's actions were caused by a belief that the claimant may do a protected act, victimization will be made out, whether or not the claimant went on to do the act.

J. ASSOCIATIVE DISCRIMINATION

3.92 It has been established for some time that less favourable treatment of a person because that person is associated with a protected characteristic, for example, because the person has a friend or partner with a particular protected characteristic, or carries out work related to a protected characteristic, is within the scope of the Act's provisions on direct discrimination.[130]

3.93 In recent years, the domestic and European courts have held that the concept of associative discrimination may extend beyond direct discrimination. Thus in 2015, the CJEU held that there could be indirect discrimination by association, although the case before it appeared in truth to be a case of direct discrimination.[131] In the UK, a Tribunal has held (with no appeal on this point) that section 27 of the Act must be read so as to cover a person who is victimized because of his/her association with someone who has done a protected act.[132]

3.94 There are, however, limits to the areas in which discrimination by association can occur. There is no requirement on an employer to make reasonable adjustments to accommodate the needs of a disabled third party with whom an employee is associated, as the entire focus of Article 5 of the Framework Directive is upon provisions to be made for disabled applicants or employees themselves.[133]

3.95 No particular degree of association or relationship is required; the question is instead whether the protected characteristic (or the protected act, as the case may be) of the third party was part of the reason for the treatment of the employee.[134] The concept has been applied in a variety of factual situations, including the less favourable treatment of a grocer on the basis that she operated a shop within a predominantly Roma district (race discrimination);[135] less favourable treatment of a limited company by an LLP of which the company was a member because of the age of its sole director;[136] and alleged victimization of an employee because of complaints about race discrimination reportedly made by another member of his union.[137] However, where the reason for the less favourable treatment was disagreement, on the basis of genuinely held religious beliefs, with a slogan supporting gay marriage, the connection with the protected characteristic of sexual orientation was found to be insufficiently close to found a claim of associative discrimination.[138]

---

[130] See in particular Case C-303/06 *Coleman v Attridge Law and another* [2008] ICR 1128.

[131] Case C-83/14 *CHEZ Razpredelenie Bulgaria AD v Komisia za Zashtita ot Diskriminatsia* [2015] IRLR 746 at para. 60. See more explicitly the Opinion of Advocate General Kokott at paras 102–9.

[132] *Thompson v London Central Bus Company* [2016] IRLR 9 at para. 8.

[133] *Hainsworth v Ministry of Defence* [2014] EWCA Civ 763.

[134] *Thompson* [2016] IRLR 9 at para. 24.

[135] *CHEZ* [2015] IRLR 746.

[136] *EAD Solicitors LLP and others v Abrams* [2015] IRLR 978.

[137] *Thompson v London Central Bus Company* [2016] IRLR 9.

[138] *Lee v Ashers Baking Co Ltd.* [2018] UKSC 49.

K. BURDEN OF PROOF

3.96 Proceedings in relation to contraventions of the Act (except for offences) are subject to the rules on burden of proof set out in section 136. That section provides that if there are facts from which a court or tribunal could decide, in the absence of any other explanation, that a person contravened the provision in question, the court or tribunal must hold that the contravention occurred, unless the alleged discriminator shows that there was no contravention.

3.97 Section 136 reflects similar provisions in pre-existing anti-discrimination legislation, which were implemented initially as a result of the Burden of Proof Directive.[139] The Court of Appeal has expressly concluded that the difference in wording between section 136 and the precursor anti-discrimination legislation does not in substance change the law, and thus that the authorities based on that previous wording remain binding.[140]

3.98 Under the Directive, member states are required to take measures to ensure that once the complainant establishes facts from which it might be presumed that there had been discrimination, the burden of proof shifts to the respondent to prove no breach of the principle of equal treatment.[141] The scheme is based on the logic that a complainant can be expected to know, and, therefore, to prove, how s/he was treated by the respondent. But since it is unusual to find direct evidence of discrimination, the claimant would have immense difficulty in showing why the respondent treated him/her in that way. It is reasonable, therefore, to expect the respondent to explain the reason behind the treatment.

3.99 If there are facts from which a court could conclude that there has been an act of unlawful discrimination, the burden of proof shifts to the respondent. Once the burden has shifted, the respondent must show on the balance of probabilities that there was, in fact, no discrimination. If the respondent fails to do so, the court or tribunal is not merely permitted to conclude that the complaint should be upheld, but must do so.

3.100 Generally the court or tribunal will hear all the evidence, including the respondent's explanation, before deciding whether there are facts from which it could conclude that there has been an act of discrimination. In considering what inferences or conclusions could be drawn from the primary facts, the tribunal must assume that there was no adequate explanation for those facts. This does not mean that all evidence from the respondent must be ignored when considering whether a prima facie case was made out; regard should only be had to evidence that undermines the primary facts which are the basis of the claim.[142] If the tribunal is satisfied that the necessary inference can be drawn from the facts, it can then go on to consider whether the respondent has discharged the burden of disproving discrimination.

3.101 However, there are cases in which the court or tribunal might omit express consideration of the first stage of the test, by moving straight to the second stage of the test and concluding that the respondent has discharged the burden on him/her by proving that the treatment was not on the proscribed ground.[143]

---

[139] The Race, Framework, and Gender Goods and Services Directives contain provisions to the same effect in Arts 8, 10, and 9, respectively.

[140] *Ayodele v Citylink Ltd* [2017] EWCA Civ 1913 at para. 106, overruling *Efobi v Royal Mail Group Ltd* [2018] ICR 359.

[141] Art. 4.

[142] See *Laing v Manchester City Council* [2006] IRLR 748, *EB v BA* [2006] IRLR 471, *Hewage v Grampian Health Board* [2012] UKSC 37 at para. 31 and *Ayodele v Citylink Ltd and another* [2017] EWCA Civ 1913 at para. 67.

[143] *Brown v London Borough of Croydon* [2007] EWCA Civ 32.

4

EMPLOYMENT RIGHTS AND DUTIES, STATUTORY OFFICE HOLDERS, AND VOLUNTEERS

A. INTRODUCTION

Part 5 of the Equality Act 2010 ('the Act') prohibits discrimination, harassment, and **4.01** victimization in employment and analogous situations. It contains provisions regarding those who are not strictly employees but who are also protected from discrimination in the course of performing their duties such as police officers, partners, barristers and advocates, and other office holders. Part 5 also contains the Occupational Pension Schemes provisions. Chapter 3 of Part 5 contains the provisions relating to equal pay, pregnancy and maternity pay, restrictions on pay discussions, and gender pay gap information. These provisions relating to equality of pay are dealt with separately in Chapter 11 on Equality of Terms.

The Act consolidates and replaces the previous anti-discrimination legislation which is **4.02** largely replicated in the Act, with some notable amendments which are intended to unify the level of protection across all of the protected characteristics and to resolve any anomalies, for example around disability-related discrimination.

B. EMPLOYMENT

The provisions on employment cover all of the possible stages of an employment rela- **4.03** tionship from the application stage, recruitment and selection, to employment, and post-employment. The chapter covers the various types of employment relationships, work, and analogous relationships. It also covers the exceptions to the prohibition against discrimination in employment.

Elizabeth George and Karen Jackson, *Employment Rights and Duties, Statutory Office Holders, and Volunteers* In: *Blackstone's Guide to the Equality Act 2010*. Fourth Edition. Edited by: Anthony Robinson, David Ruebain, and Susie Uppal, Oxford University Press (2021). © Oxford University Press. DOI: 10.1093/oso/9780198870876.003.0004

1. Applicants for Work and Employees

4.04   Section 39(1) and (3) prohibits an employer discriminating against or victimizing applicants for employment because of any one of the protected characteristics:

(a) in the arrangements they make for deciding to whom to offer employment;

(b) as to the terms on which they offer an applicant employment;

(c) by not offering an applicant employment.

4.05   Section 39(2) and (4) prohibits discrimination and/or victimization by an employer against their employees because of any one of the protected characteristics:

(a) as to the terms of employment;

(b) in how they afford employees access, or by not affording them access, to opportunities for promotion, transfer, or training or for receiving any other benefit, facility, or service;

(c) by dismissing an employee;

(d) by subjecting an employee to any other detriment.

4.06   In addition to the duty not to discriminate, an employer also has a duty to make reasonable adjustments for disabled employees (see section C below and for further detail, Chapter 3).[1] In relation to sex and pregnancy, if the act of discrimination concerns a term or offer of employment relating to pay this will amount to a breach of the equality clause or rule (see Chapter 10). If the act of discrimination does not relate to pay or terms which might invoke the equality clause or rule, this could amount to direct, or pregnancy or maternity discrimination.[2] This is a new provision within the Act.

4.07   As regards dismissals, the Act applies to the termination of employment including the expiry/termination of fixed term contracts and constructive dismissals. Whilst discrimination in these areas was always prohibited, the Act now makes this explicit.

2. Meaning of Employment

4.08   Section 83 defines employment as: employment under a contract of employment, or of apprenticeship or a contract personally to do work. Crown employment and employment as a relevant member of the House of Commons and House of Lords staff are also included in the definition.

4.09   The definition of employment under the Act has a broad meaning compared to unfair dismissal legislation[3] and at common law. The definition applies to employees working under a contract of employment, apprentices,[4] and any person undertaking a contract to do work personally; or where the dominant purpose of the contract is to do work personally in whole

---

[1] S. 39(5).

[2] S. 39(6). See also ss 13 and 18.

[3] Employment Rights Act 1996 (ERA) s. 230; this defines an employee as anyone who has entered into or works under a contract of employment. A 'contract of employment' means a contract of service or apprenticeship. Workers are those who have entered into or who work under a contract of employment or a contract to undertake or perform personally any work or services for a third party.

[4] See Apprenticeships Skills, Children and Learning Act 2009, which puts apprenticeships on a statutory footing.

or in part.[5] It includes agency and contract workers and sometimes even self-employed individuals if they are 'workers'. Where a worker is under a contract to do work personally but can provide a substitute to undertake the work and there is no obligation on the employer to provide work, the worker will not benefit from the protection of the Act.[6] The decision as to whether someone is an employee or a worker will turn on the substance of the relationship not the label attached to it. The law is still unclear in this area despite the recent boom of 'gig economy' cases which seeks to bring clarity to this area.

Although it is not necessary for the employment relationship to be premised solely on the provision of labour for a wage, the contract must contemplate an obligation to perform work or labour *personally* as its dominant purpose. It has been held, for example, that the provision of services by a professional person, constitutes employment[7] and on occasion, but not always, that ordained ministers of a church can be employees.[8] There will however be no employment relationship where the dominant purpose of the contract is to achieve a particular outcome and the obligation to provide personal services is an incidental or secondary consideration,[9] for example, providing publicly funded legal services,[10] or arbitration services.[11] Similarly, there will be no employment relationship where there is no obligation on an individual to actually carry out work if they choose not to do so.[12] The Supreme Court considered the distinction between employees and the self-employed in *Bates van Winkelhof v Clyde & Co LLP* [2014] UKSC 32 and held that an equity partner in an LLP could be a worker for the purposes of section 230(3)(b) ERA 1996 in relation to a whistleblowing claim. Employment status is being addressed at the EU level. 4.10

3. Volunteers

Volunteers are not expressly covered by the Act, which replicates the scope of the former legislation. The government did not consider it necessary to extend protection to volunteers because there was no evidence of 'systematic discrimination'; and further that volunteers could enjoy some protection in respect of the provisions on goods, facilities, and services.[13] The European Council rejected a proposal that volunteers be covered in the Employment Equality Framework Directive 2000/78/EC. The legal status of volunteers and interns is not clear cut partly because there are so many different types of volunteering arrangements. 4.11

---

[5] K. Monaghan, *Blackstone's Guide to the Disability Discrimination Legislation* (Oxford University Press 2005), 240; also see *Mirror Group Newspapers Ltd v Gunning* [1986] ICR 145 and *Pimlico Plumbers Ltd and Mullins v Smith* [2018] UKSC 29.

[6] *Halawi v WDFG UK Ltd (t/a World Duty Free)* [2014] EWCA Civ 1387.

[7] *Kelly v Northern Ireland Housing Executive* [1998] ICR 828, 835–836a: this was a case brought under the Fair Employment (Northern Ireland) Act 1976, which contains similar provisions to the employment provisions in the Race Relations Act 1976 (RRA) and the Sex Discrimination Act 1975 (SDA).

[8] *Percy v Board of National Mission of the Church of Scotland* [2005] UKHL 73. Contrast with *President of the Methodist Conference v Preston* [2013] UKSC 29 in which a majority of the Supreme Court held that a Methodist minister was not an employee. Also, *Trustees of Celestial Church of Christ, Edward Street Parish (A Charity) v Lawson* [2017] EWHC 97 (Ch). Note that it is usual for rabbis to be employees of synagogues.

[9] *Jivrag v Hashwani* [2011] UKSC 40.

[10] *Patterson v Legal Services Commission* [2003] EWCA Civ 1558, where the CA held that a franchise agreement was not employment for the purposes of RRA s. 4 but fell within the qualification body's provisions.

[11] *Jivrag v Hashwani* [2011] UKSC 40.

[12] *Halawi v WDFG UK Ltd (t/a World Duty Free)* [2014] EWCA Civ 1387; *Mingeley v Pennock and Another (Trading as Amber Cars)* [2004] EWCA Civ 328; [2004] ICR 727.

[13] *Hansard* HC, col. 441 (20 August 2009).

4.12   Notwithstanding the government's failure to provide specific protection under the Act, volunteers may still benefit from the Act's protection in some circumstances but much will depend on the nature of the volunteering arrangement. The Supreme Court confirmed in *X v Mid Sussex Citizens Advice Bureau*[14] that a volunteer without a contract was not an employee and has no Equality Act protection. By contrast, in *Migrant Advisory Service v Chaudri*[15] the EAT upheld the first instance tribunal's decision that expenses paid to Mrs Chaudri were in reality pay for work done and she was held to be an employee. She could pursue claims for unfair dismissal and discrimination.

4.13   The Employment Appeal Tribunal (EAT) has held that the 'test which may help in this identification exercise is to consider whether, if the volunteer should decline without prior notice to perform any work for the employer, the latter would have any legal remedy against him; and similarly to consider whether, if the volunteer attends to do work and there is none, they have any legal remedy against the employer'.[16] In other words, if there was a contractual obligation on the organization to provide work and an obligation on the volunteer to do it there might be an employment relationship. On the facts the EAT said that an expectation that work would be done is not the same as an obligation and the volunteer was not an employee.

4.14   Where there is no sanction for not honouring an agreement between the volunteer and the employer, that would suggest there is no intention to create a legal relationship and therefore no employment.[17] For example, if there is no obligation for the volunteer to work a set number of hours and they can only recover genuine expenses incurred, this type of arrangement is unlikely to be protected.[18] On the other hand, where the arrangement requires the volunteer to work a set number of hours each week and to repay the costs of training if they fail to work an agreed maximum number of hours over a set period of time,[19] or the volunteer is entitled to expenses that could not be regarded as genuine expenses,[20] then it is possible that such an arrangement could amount to an employment relationship.

4.15   There have been a number of recent cases in which it has been argued that volunteering amounts to an occupation for the purposes of the Employment Framework Directive and that as such volunteers should benefit from the protection of anti-discrimination legislation. However, the EAT has rejected such argument, holding that 'employment in the Directive requires a material contract between the parties'.[21] The Supreme Court has endorsed the EAT's decision with regards to voluntary activity falling within the meaning of occupation under the Directive. The Court considered that the European Commission, though given the opportunity to include voluntary and unpaid work in Article 3(1) of the Directive, had chosen not to do so when invited to by the European Parliament, indicating a clear intention that voluntary work was outside the scope of the Directive.[22]

4.16   It would seem that the position of volunteers will remain uncertain until the Court of Justice of the European Union (CJEU) can make a judgment on their rights under

---

[14] *X v Mid Sussex Citizens Advice Bureau and others* [2012] UKSC 59 IRLR 76.
[15] *Migrant Advisory Service v Chaudri* [1998] UKEAT 1400_97_2807.
[16] *South East Sheffield Citizens' Advice Bureau v Grayson* [2004] IRLR 353, para. 12.
[17] *ibid*, para. 16.
[18] *Gradwell v Council for Voluntary Service Blackpool, Wyre and Fylde* [1997] COIT 2404314/97.
[19] *Armitage v Relate* [1994] DCLD 26.
[20] *Chaudri v Migrant Advice Service (MAS)* [1997] EAT/1400/97.
[21] *X v Mid Sussex CAB* [2009] UKEAT/0220/08/SM.
[22] *X v Mid Sussex CAB* [2012] UKSC 59.

anti-discrimination law. The opportunity to definitively establish the position of volunteers might not be too far off.

4. Illegality

The meaning of employment in the Act implies a contractual relationship. This does not, however, preclude a claim under the Act where the contract of employment is tainted with illegality and would therefore be unenforceable at common law. This is because the Act is not primarily 'concerned with employees' rights under their contracts of employment[23] '... [but is] ... designed to provide effective relief in respect of discriminatory conduct'.[24] This means a claim under the Act could still succeed even if the contract of employment is tainted with illegality. The courts will first look at whether there is an inextricable link between the complaint of discrimination and the claimant's illegal conduct. If it is not possible to separate out the worker's conduct in perpetuating the illegality from the complaint of discrimination the defence will generally be upheld. However, it is recognized that the inextricable link test can be problematic and can lead to conflicting decisions. Therefore, the courts will also consider wider public policy issues. In doing this, the courts should first consider the public policy on which the defence is founded. Secondly, the court should consider whether there is any other aspect of public policy which may run counter to the defence. **4.17**

The Supreme Court explored the public policy test in the case of *Hounga v Allen*.[25] This was about a young woman who conspired with the Respondent to travel to the UK under a false passport, with the intention of taking up illegal work as an au pair. Ms Hounga, the applicant, was physically and verbally abused by the Respondent, Mrs Allen, who took away her passport and threatened to report her to the police because of her illegal immigration status. Ms Hounga was subsequently dismissed from her employment by Mrs Allen and made a claim of race discrimination. Her claim was upheld at first instance and by the EAT but overturned by the Court of Appeal, on the grounds that she had knowingly participated in the illegality. Ms Hounga appealed. The Supreme Court upheld her appeal. It found that although she had participated in the illegality and that the rationale for the defence, namely, the preservation of the integrity of the legal system was helpful, it hardly existed in Ms Hounga's case. In the court's view, the Respondent's actions in persuading Ms Hounga to come to the UK was tantamount to human trafficking, which the UK was striving to combat and afford protection against. Therefore, Mrs Allen could not be permitted to rely on the defence: '*The public policy in support of the application of that defence, to the extent that it exists at all, should give way to the public policy to which its application is an affront*' [para. 45]. Where the illegality however is not supported by a pressing public policy it is highly likely that the inextricable link test will be applied. **4.18**

A person will not benefit from the protection of the Act if they fraudulently obtained the employment. For example, in the case of *Vakante*[26] an employee who was found to have been instrumental in defrauding his employer by gaining employment in breach of his immigration conditions restricting his right to work in the UK could not rely on the protection of the Race Relations Act 1976. In contrast, in *Hall v Woolston Leisure Centre*,[27] an employee who **4.19**

---

[23] *Rhys-Harper v Relaxion Group Plc* [2001] ICR 1176.
[24] *ibid.*
[25] April [2014] UKSC 47.
[26] *Vakante v Addey and Stanhope School Governing Body* [2002] EWCA Civ 1065; [2004] 4 All ER 1056.
[27] *Hall v Woolston Hall Leisure Centre* [2001] 1 WLR 225.

was merely aware of her employer's failure to deduct tax and national insurance contributions from her wages but played no part in the fraud was entitled to the protection of the Sex Discrimination Act 1975. In *Wijesundera v Heathrow Logistics*[28] the EAT held that the present case was not a *Vakante* situation and applied the principles of *Hall v Woolston Leisure Centre*:[29] the employer could not rely on illegality as a defence. Ms Wijesundera was entitled to bring a claim for sexual harassment even though she was working illegally.

5. Territorial Scope

4.20   Unlike the previous legislation, the Act does not set out the territorial scope for when a claim can be brought in the employment tribunals or the courts.[30] Instead, the Act leaves it to the courts and tribunals to decide the question of jurisdiction by reference to standard employment law.[31] The Court of Appeal found without hesitation in *Hottak*[32] that the territorial reach of the Act is the same as the ERA. It is clear that the tribunals will have jurisdiction where the act of discrimination occurs in Great Britain or where the act takes place outside Great Britain and the company or organization is based in Great Britain. The picture is less clear when the facts become more complex. Cases will be decided on their specific facts with the *Lawson v Serco*[33] principles and other case law being applied as appropriate. The Equality and Human Rights Commission's Employment Statutory Code of Practice states that discrimination protection is afforded where there is a 'sufficiently close link between the employment relationship and Great Britain'.[34] This 'sufficient connection' question was considered at length by the Court of Appeal in *British Council v Jeffrey and Green v SIG Trading Limited*[35]. The Court of Appeal concluded that this is a question of law and fact. In *Hottack*[36] the Court of Appeal held that the High Court were correct to find that the Equality Act did not extend to Afghan interpreters who were employees of the British Government and working with British Forces in Afghanistan.

6. Harassment

4.21   The prohibition against harassment (see Chapter 3) in employment as defined in section 26 of the Act is retained.[37] Section 40 prohibits an employer engaging in unwanted conduct

---

[28] *Wijesundera v (1) Heathrow 3PL Logistics Ltd (Debarred) (2) Mr N Natarajan (Debarred)* UKEAT/0222/13/0152[2013].

[29] *Hall v Woolston Hall Leisure Centre* [2001] 1 WLR 225.

[30] The previous legislation defined employment as being at an establishment in Great Britain; if the work is done wholly or mainly in Great Britain; or the work is done wholly or mainly outside Great Britain but the employer has a place of business at an establishment in Great Britain, the work is done for the purpose of that business at that establishment, and the employee is ordinarily resident in Great Britain when they applied for the job or was offered it or at any time during the course of their employment.

[31] This follows the ERA; see ENs 14 and 15.

[32] *R (Hottak and another) v The Secretary of State for Foreign and Commonwealth Affairs and another* [2015] EWHC 1953 (Admin).

[33] *Serco Limited v Lawson and other cases* [2006] UKHL 3 (Lawson).

[34] Equality and Human Rights Commission, 'Equality Act 2010 Code of Practice: Employment Statutory Code of Practice' (2011) paras 10.70–10.72 ('EHRC Code').

[35] [2018] EWCA Civ 2253.

[36] *Ibid.*

[37] See s. 40.

which violates the dignity of an employee or prospective employee; or creating an intimidating, hostile, degrading, humiliating, or offensive environment for them. It is not only the individual affected by prohibited harassing conduct who would benefit from the protection but another employee who considers that their dignity has been violated as a result of, for example, witnessing such conduct. Employers have a defence if they can show they have taken 'all reasonable' steps to prevent the harassment.

(a) *Third Party Harassment*

Until September 2013 employers were liable if an employee was persistently harassed by a third party (such as a client or supplier) in the course of their employment and certain conditions were met.[38] The provision was known as the 'three strikes rule' because if an employer knew that an employee had been harassed on two previous occasions the employer would be liable for the third incident. This helpful provision was repealed with effect from 1 October 2013, so employers are no longer liable for third party harassment in most circumstances. Subsequent case law has been reluctant to imply the provisions into the employment relationship on the basis that if Parliament had intended for the provisions to apply they would not have been repealed. The general consensus among legal commentators is that this was a useful provision which ought not to have been repealed. An employee may still have a section 13 direct discrimination claim if the harassment is linked to a protected characteristic and if the employee can show that in failing to protect them from third party harassment the employer has treated them less favourably.

4.22

The repeal of the third party harassment provision presents a conundrum for the law. Previously, the House of Lords rejected the concept of third party harassment in the case of *Pearce v Governing Body of Mayfield School*[39] when it concluded that the case of *Burton v De Vere Hotels*[40] was wrongly decided. *Burton* had established the long-standing principle that employers could incur liability for discrimination against employees by a third party where the employer is in a position of control. However, subsequent to the *Pearce* decision and prior to the Equality Act coming into force, the EAT held the harassment provisions in the Race Relations Act (Amendment) Regulations 1976 afforded protection against third party harassment.[41] The High Court reached a similar conclusion in the case of the Equal Opportunities Commission's challenge of the government's transposition of Directive 76/207/EEC (the Equal Treatment Directive).[42]

Whether the current case law on protection against third party harassment will stand in light of the repeal remains to be seen. The Government in its decision to repeal the provision considered that it was not necessary since employees may still find redress 'under existing employment law breach of contract provisions or the Protection from Harassment Act'.[43] However, the case law suggests that the Race Directive and the Equal Treatment Directive both envisage protection against third party harassment. In *Unite the Union v Nailard*[44] the

4.23

---

[38] Previously EqA ss 40(2)–(4) as repealed by Enterprise and Regulatory Reform Act 2013 s. 65.
[39] [2003] ICR 937; [2003] IRLR 512.
[40] [1997] ICR 1.
[41] *Gravell v London Borough of Bexley* UKEAT/0587/06/CEA.
[42] *Equal Opportunities Commission v Secretary of State for Trade and Industry* [2007] EWHC 483 (Admin).
[43] Home Office (Government Equalities Office), 16 October 2012, '*Impact Assessment of removing the provisions in the Equality Act 2010 which makes employers liable for persistent harassment of their employees by third parties over whom the employer has no direct control*'.
[44] *Unite the Union v Nailard* 2019 ICR28, CA.

claimant argued that liability for third party harassment was implicit in the section 26 definition of harassment and was still intact despite its repeal. The Court of Appeal disagreed. The EAT followed *Nailard* in *Bessong v Pennine Care*.[45] The way an employer deals with third party (or any form of) harassment can itself amount to harassment.[46]

(b) *Harassment of a Sexual Nature (Sexual Harassment)*

4.24 Harassment of a sexual nature, i.e. 'sexual harassment' (see Chapter 3), is also unlawful. This applies to behaviour such as requests for sexual favours, lewd jokes, promises, and threats concerning a person's employment conditions in return for sexual favours. The definition is similar to the general section 26(1) definition but the conduct must be 'of a sexual nature' rather than because it is related to a protected characteristic.

(c) *Discrimination because of a Person's Reaction to Harassment of a Sexual Nature or Related to Gender Reassignment or Sex*

4.25 It is also unlawful harassment for an employer to engage in conduct of a sexual nature or related to gender reassignment or sex by treating an employee less favourably because they reject or submit to such conduct (see Chapter 3); these provisions replicate the provisions under the SDA.[47] Thus if a woman objects to sexual harassment by male colleagues and is treated less favourably because of her objection this will constitute unlawful sexual harassment. Similarly, if a transsexual person participates in banter of a sexual nature related to gender assignment and is treated less favourably because they do not object to the banter, this will also amount to unlawful harassment.

7. Post-employment Discrimination and Harassment

4.26 Part 8 of the Act, which covers ancillary prohibited conduct, prohibits discrimination and harassment following the termination of an employment relationship. The discrimination or harassment must arise out of or be closely connected to the employment relationship and the conduct must be such that it would constitute discrimination or harassment if the employment relationship was continuing.[48] The most likely scenario in which post-employment discrimination or harassment might arise is in the provision of references. An employer who refuses or fails to provide a reference for a former employee because of a protected characteristic but would provide references for others in similar circumstances would be acting unlawfully. Post-employment discrimination and harassment can take place many years after the employment relationship has ended and even applies if the employment relationship ended before the coming into force of section 108.

4.27 On a strict reading the provisions on post-employment discrimination and harassment did not appear to apply to victimization in the EqA;[49] Section 108(7) provides that 'conduct is not a contravention of this section in so far as it also amounts to victimisation ...'. In the

---

[45] *Bessong v Pennine Care NHS Foundation Trust* EAT 0247/18.

[46] See for example the Employment Tribunal first instance decisions in *Rose-Brown v Home Office (UKBA)* 2313044/10 and *Owens v Euro Quality Coatings Ltd and ors* 1600238/15.

[47] S. 26(3).

[48] *Relaxion Group Plc (Respondents) v Rhys-Harper (FC) (Appellant), D'Souza (Appellant) v London Borough of Lambeth (Respondents), Jones (Appellant) v 3M Healthcare Limited (Respondents) and three other actions* [2003] UKHL 33.

[49] S. 108(7).

Explanatory Notes, the Government suggests that post-employment victimization would be caught by the section 27 provision on victimization: '… if the treatment which is being challenged constitutes victimisation, it will be dealt with under the victimisation provisions and not under this section'[50] (see further Chapter 3). Curiously there was no evidence that at any stage during the passage of the EqA through Parliament there was any intention to delete the protection. The uncertainty generated around this has now helpfully been resolved by the Court of Appeal in *Jessemey v Rowstock*.[51] A 2011 Employment Tribunal decision in *Taiwo v Olaigbe*[52] took this position but the case was not previously binding. The Court of Appeal decided that the omission of victimization from section 108 was a drafting error rather than a deliberate exclusion. Case law has restored the protection. On appeal, the Court of Appeal confirmed that post-termination victimization is protected and its view is that: '*the failure of the statute to proscribe post- termination victimisation was a drafting error. s108 contained no clear indication of an intention that post- termination victimisation should be lawful*'.

4.28   The duty to make reasonable adjustments also applies post-employment where a failure to make a reasonable adjustment would put a disabled former employee at a substantial disadvantage (see Chapter 3 on prohibited conduct and section C below on the duty to make reasonable adjustments in work). The EHRC Code gives the example of a former worker who has lifetime membership to a social club but who is unable to access the premises due to a physical impairment.[53]

8. Liability for Discrimination in Employment

(a) *Employers and Principals*

4.29   Section 109 imposes liability on employers and principals for acts of discrimination, victimization, and harassment by employees or agents. In the case of an employee, liability will attach to the employer if the employee was acting in the course of employment and/or the unlawful conduct on the part of the employee was within the range of the duties of their job.[54] 'In the course of employment' has a wide application. This might include, for example, an act of discrimination by an employee carried out at an after-work social event organized by the employer[55] or an incident during a business trip overseas but not actually during working time. In the case of an agent, liability will attach to the principal if the agent is acting on the authority of the principal or the agent is carrying out the functions they are authorized to do.[56]

4.30   An employer or principal will be liable regardless of whether or not they were aware of or approved of the employee's or agent's action. Employers may escape liability if they can show that they took 'all reasonable steps' to prevent an employee contravening the Act. While this

---

[50] Equality Act 2010, Explanatory Notes para. 353.

[51] *Jessemey v Rowstock Ltd and another* [2014] EWCA Civ 185.

[52] *Taiwo v Olaigbe and others* ET/2389629/11.

[53] Equality and Human Rights Commission (ECHR), Equality Act 2010 Code of Practice: Employment Statutory Code of Practice (2011) 10.60 example.

[54] *Mr A M Mohamud in substitution for Mr A Mohamud deceased Appellant v Morrisons Supermarkets PLC* [2016] UKSC 11.

[55] *Chief Constable of the Lincolnshire Police v Stubbs* [1999] IRLR 81.

[56] *Lana v Positive Action in Training (Housing) Limited* [2001] IRLR 501 approved by the Supreme Court in *Kemeh v Ministry of Defence* [2014] EWCA Civ 91.

is an important defence for an employer, it will not help if the employer merely shows that there is an equality policy in place.[57] The employer may also have to show the policy has been implemented effectively, for example, that it has been communicated to employees and/or underpinned by training. The defence of 'taking all reasonable steps' places a higher threshold on employers than under the previous legislation. This might mean that an employer should not only provide training on any equality policy they might have in place but also ensure that staff are made aware of the employer's duty and their individual responsibilities under the Act[58]. This reasonable steps defence does not apply to principals.

(b) Employees

4.31 Employees and agents, independent of their employers or principal, may incur liability for their acts of discrimination, victimization, or harassment. Employees, but not agents, are liable whether or not the employer is also found to be liable for the unlawful act; and/or whether or not there is a corresponding claim against the employer.[59] An employee may however avoid liability if they can show they relied on a statement by the employer that the act is lawful; and it is reasonable for the employee to rely on such a statement.[60] For example, an employer tells the human resources (HR) manager to discard applications from applicants with foreign sounding names and advises that it is not unlawful to do so. If the HR manager acts on the employer's instructions in reliance on the statement it is unlikely they will be able to show that it was reasonable to do so. This is because an HR manager could be expected to have a reasonable degree of knowledge of discrimination law.[61]

4.32 It is a criminal offence for an employer to knowingly or recklessly make a statement of the kind referred to above.[62]

(c) Contract Workers

4.33 Section 41(1) and (3) makes it unlawful for a person (a 'principal') to discriminate against, harass, or victimize a person supplied to the principal, but employed by another person, to do work ('contract workers'):

(a) as to the terms on which the principal allows the worker to do the work;

(b) by not allowing the worker to do, or to continue to do the work;

(c) in the way the principal affords the worker access, or by not affording the worker access to opportunities for receiving a benefit, facility, or service; or

(d) by subjecting the worker to any other detriment.

4.34 In order for a contract worker to benefit from the protection of the Act, there must be a contractual relationship between the principal and the supplier of the contract worker.[63] Although, 'there does not need to be a direct contractual relationship between the employer

---

[57] *Baptiste v Westminster Press Ltd t/a Bradford and District Newspapers* [1996] DCLD 30 and *Umerji v Blackburn Borough Council* [1995] DCLD 47.

[58] *Quashie v Yorkshire Ambulance Service NHS Trust* ET/1802401/15.

[59] *Barlow v Stone* UKEAT/0049/12/MAA.

[60] S. 110.

[61] If the employee fails to carry out a discriminatory instruction and is subjected to a detriment as a result the employee would have a claim under the Act; see s. 110.

[62] S. 112(3).

[63] S. 41(5). See *Abbey Life Assurance Co. Ltd v Tansell* [2000] IRLR 387, CA.

and the principal for the protection to apply'.[64] The objective behind the provision, as the Explanatory Notes explain, is to codify the case law in this area while replicating the effect of the provisions in previous legislation.[65] In *Abbey Life Assurance v Tansell*,[66] for example, the Court of Appeal (CA) held that the 'statutory definition [of section 12 of the DDA] only requires the supply of the individual to be "under a contract made with A [the principal]"'.[67] It does not expressly stipulate who is to be the party who contracts with 'A'.

Mr Tansell was the sole shareholder of and an employee of a self-owned company 4.35 (Intelligents Ltd). He obtained contract work with Abbey Life through a specialist employment agency (MHC Consulting Services Limited). MHC had a contract with Abbey Life for the provision of freelance consultants. Mr Tansell's company, Intelligents Ltd, entered into a contract with MHC to provide computer consultancy services for MHC to MHC's client, Abbey Life. There was no contract between Intelligents Ltd or Abbey Life. Mr Tansell's services were terminated when he was diagnosed with diabetes. The CA held that: (a) Abbey Life made the work available to Mr Tansell; (b) Mr Tansell was employed by another legal person, Intelligents Ltd; and (c) Intelligents Ltd supplied Mr Tansell to Abbey Life under a contract made with Abbey Life ('the MHC contract'). Mr Tansell was therefore treated as employed by Intelligents Ltd and could bring his disability discrimination claim.

Problems might arise where an agency worker cannot prove that they were employed by 4.36 the supplier or the principal. To claim against the end-user, i.e. the principal, the agency worker must either be directly employed by the end-user or rely on the contract worker provision. To rely on the contract worker provision, the agency worker needs to be employed by the agency (supplier). In both cases, the agency worker needs to prove that they were employed either in the narrow unfair dismissal sense or in the wider sense under the Act. It is very difficult for an agency worker to prove that they have been employed directly by the end-user. This is because there is not usually a contract of any kind between the agency worker and the end-user.[68] The Court of Appeal has reaffirmed in *Muschett v HM Prison Service*[69] that nothing less than 'necessity' will do in such cases: 'it still remains the law that an employment relationship cannot be created by the mere and unilateral wish of the putative employee'.[70]

As for whether the agency worker can prove they were employed by the supplier on a con- 4.37 tract personally to execute work under the Act, this will turn on the facts of the case. For example, in *Muschett*, M, an agency worker was supplied by Brook Street Agency to work for the HMPS. He undertook work in accordance with the terms of his agency agreement. HMPS terminated M's assignment and he made claims for unfair dismissal and discrimination under the Race Relations Act 1976. The Employment Tribunal found M had a contract for services for temporary workers with Brook Street but was not its employee. It also found that there was no mutuality of obligation between M and HMPS, which the Employment Tribunal said meant that M could not bring himself within the wider definition of employment under the Race Relations Act.[71] The EAT and the CA agreed with the tribunal's decision.

---

[64] EN 148.
[65] EN 148.
[66] [2000] All ER (D) 483.
[67] Mummery LJ.
[68] *Dacas v Brook Street Bureau (UK) Ltd* [2004] ICR 1437; *James v London Borough of Greenwich* [2007] IRLR 168.
[69] [2008] UKEAT/0132/08/LA.
[70] *ibid.*
[71] *ibid.*

4.38   The *Muschett* case neatly illustrates the difficulties for agency workers in bringing dis-
        crimination cases against end-users. In *Bohill v Police Service of Northern Ireland*[72] it was
        held that an agency worker who was never selected for duty could not bring discrimination
        claims, however in *London Borough of Camden v Pegg*[73] the EAT found that an agency worker
        on a long-term assignment was 'employed' for the purposes of bringing a discrimination
        claim. The EAT held that the employment relationship began when the worker accepted the
        assignment. From this point Ms Pegg owed a contractual duty to provide services personally
        and was therefore 'employed' for the purposes of the Act. Any judicial decisions around the
        employment status of agency workers will be very fact specific.

4.39   The retention of the requirement in section 41 for contract workers to be employed by another
        person (whether directly or indirectly) means that the protection for agency workers who are
        deemed not to be employees of their agency remains precarious.[74] In *Bohill* the NICA were
        reluctant to hold that they had no jurisdiction to hear the claims because this deprives workers
        of important protections against discrimination. That is however the current state of the law.

4.40   The duty to make reasonable adjustments for disabled contract workers does apply to
        principals and employment agencies.

9. Discrimination in Other Occupations

4.41   In addition to the provisions on employment, the Act also prohibits discrimination, victimi-
        zation, and harassment in other non-employment work relationships. These include police
        officers, partners, members of limited liability partnerships, office holders, local government
        members, barristers, and pupils of barristers (known as advocates and devils in Scotland).

(a) *Police Officers*

4.42   For the purposes of the Act, police constables and police cadets are deemed employees of
        either the Chief Officer (Chief Constable in Scotland) or the responsible authority, depend-
        ing on who commits the act of discrimination in question.[75] The Act does not define who
        is a police constable but it is likely to include officers holding the rank of police constable,
        sergeants, and inspectors.[76] It would also apply, for example, to police officers of British
        Transport Police.

4.43   A police cadet is defined as a person 'appointed to undergo training with a view to becom-
        ing a constable'.[77]

4.44   The Chief Officer (Chief Constable in Scotland), is in relation to an appointment under
        a relevant Act, the Chief Officer of Police for the police force to which the appointment
        relates; or in relation to any other appointment, the person under whose direction and con-
        trol the body of constables or other persons to which the appointment relates is/are subject;
        in relation to a constable or other person under the direction and control of a Chief Officer
        of Police, that Chief Officer of Police; in relation to any other constable or any other person,
        the person under whose direction and control the constable is subject.

---

[72] [2011] NICA 2.
[73] *London Borough of Camden v Pegg and others* UKEAT/0590/11.
[74] IDS (5 February 2010) *Agency workers vulnerable to end-user discrimination*, News from IDS Brief.
[75] S. 42.
[76] S. 42(2).
[77] S. 43.

The responsible authority means an authority in relation to an appointment under a rel- 4.45
evant Act, the police authority that maintains the police force to which the appointment
relates; in relation to any other appointment, the person by whom a person would be paid;
in relation to a constable or other person under the direction and control of a chief officer of
police, the police authority that maintains the police force; in relation to a constable or any
other person, the person by whom the constable or other person is paid.

The 'relevant Acts' are the Metropolitan Police Act 1829, the City of London Police Act 4.46
1839, and the Police Act 1996 (the Police (Scotland) Act 1967 in Scotland).

In the case of the Serious Organised Crime Agency (SOCA) and the Scottish Police 4.47
Services Authority (SPSA), a constable (including a constable seconded as a member of staff)
is treated as an employee of that Agency or Authority. A constable at the Scottish Crime and
Drugs Enforcement Agency (SCDEA) is treated as an employee of the Director General of
the SCDEA in respect of any act done by the Director General in relation to any constable.

(b) *Partnerships and Limited Liability Partnerships (LLPs)*
Section 44 prohibits discrimination, victimization, and harassment by firms (partnerships) 4.48
or a proposed firm against prospective partners and partners. Section 45 prohibits conduct
referred to above by LLPs against prospective members and members, including those who
are corporations.[78] The situations in which firms and LLPs are covered are the same as those
for employment, for example, from the application stage, recruitment and selection, the
terms on which it offers the person a position as a partner, and during the partnership. The
duty to make reasonable adjustments also applies to a firm or proposed firm and LLPs.

(c) *Barristers and their Clerks*
Section 47 prohibits discrimination, victimization, and harassment by barristers or advocates 4.49
(in Scotland) of pupils and tenants. The duty to make reasonable adjustments also applies
to barristers and advocates. Clerks (or any person carrying out the function of a clerk for a
barrister or advocate) are subject to the same prohibitions and duty. The provision also prohibits discrimination, victimization, and harassment of barristers and advocates by those who
instruct them, for example, solicitors.

(d) *Office-holders*
The Act makes it unlawful to discriminate, victimize or harass those who are or wish to become 4.50
personal or public office-holders. These provisions[79] apply in so far as the other work provisions
do not, meaning that office-holders who are also employees will be protected by the provisions
dealing with employment.[80] The prohibitions apply to both the person who makes the appointment and any person responsible for the act complained of (referred to as a 'relevant person').

(i) *Personal offices.* A personal office-holder is defined as a person who performs a function 4.51
personally as directed by another person and who in return is entitled to payment other than
expenses or compensation for lost income or other benefits.[81] This would include, for example, priests or members of non-executive boards.

---

[78] *EAD Solicitors LLP v Abrahams* [2015] IRLR 978.
[79] Ss. 49 -51
[80] Equality Act 2010, EN para. 168.
[81] S. 49(2); see also EN para. 169.

4.52   The duty to make reasonable adjustments also applies to a person who has the power to make an appointment to a personal office and any relevant person in relation to a personal office.

4.53   (ii) *Public offices.*   A public office is defined as an appointment to an office or post by a government minister, or an office or post which is made on the recommendation or requires the approval of a government minister; or the appointment to an office or post which is made on the recommendation of or requires the approval of the House of Commons, the House of Lords, the National Assembly for Wales, or the Scottish Parliament; or an office or post, which is appointed to by the Lord Chief Justice or the Senior President of Tribunals.[82] The duty to make reasonable adjustments also applies to people who appoint, recommend, or approve a public office.

4.54   A public office includes, for example, commissioners of non-departmental public bodies such as the Commissioners of the Independent Police Complaints Commission who are appointed by the Secretary of State for the Home Department.

4.55   Schedule 6, paragraph 1(1) sets out the posts and offices that are excluded from the definition of a personal or public office. These include an office or post covered by the provisions on employees, contract workers, partnerships, LLPs, barristers, and advocates. Paragraph 2 specifies a list of political offices that are not personal or public offices. The political offices listed include an office of the House of Commons held by a member of that House, an office of the House of Lords held by a member of that House, an office of the Scottish Parliament, and an office of the National Assembly for Wales. Similar provisions apply to an office in local government held by a member of a council or an office of the Greater London Authority held by the Mayor of London. Paragraph 3 specifies that a life peerage[83] or any dignity or honour conferred by the Crown such as an OBE is not a personal or public office.

10. Qualifications Bodies

4.56   Qualifications bodies are bound by the duty not to discriminate against, victimize, or harass those who apply for a relevant qualification or those who hold a relevant qualification. This includes conferring, renewing, or extending a qualification. A relevant qualification is an authorization, qualification, recognition, registration, enrolment, approval, or certification which is needed for or facilitates engagement in a particular trade or profession (section 54).

4.57   A qualifications body is a body or authority which can confer a relevant qualification such as the Solicitors Regulation Authority, the General Medical Council, the Public Carriage Office, or the Legal Services Commission.[84] It also includes a body which awards diplomas to people pursuing a particular trade, for example CORGI registered gas fitters. In *Pemberton v Inwood* [85] the Court of Appeal held that the granting of an extra-parochial ministry licence, was a relevant qualification for the purposes of section 53 and the granting bishop, a 'qualifications body' for these purposes. It does not include a qualifications body under the education provisions of the Act,[86] the governing body, local authority, or trustees of schools,[87] the

---

[82] S. 52 (interpretative provisions and exceptions). Amendment made by the Crime and Courts Act 2013 Sch. 13, para. 50(2).

[83] As defined by the Life Peerages Act 1958.

[84] See n. 10 above.

[85] [2018] EWCA Civ 564.

[86] See s. 96.

[87] See s. 85.

governing body of a further education college,[88] or a body that exercises functions under the Education Acts or the Education (Scotland) Act 1980 (see Chapter 6). Political parties are not qualifications bodies for the purposes of the Act.[89] The employment tribunal does not have jurisdiction to hear complaints of discrimination, victimization or harassment against a qualifications body if a mechanism exists whereby the treatment complained of can be appealed (see Chapter 10). Judicial review is not an appeal for these purposes.[90]

It is not unlawful discrimination for qualifications bodies to apply a competence stand-   4.58
ard[91] to a disabled person provided the application of the competence standard can be justified. They do however have a duty to make reasonable adjustments for disabled people.

11. Employment Service Providers

Section 55 prohibits discrimination against, victimization, or harassment by employment   4.59
service providers of those who apply to use or use their services.
It also places a duty on providers of employment services to make reasonable adjustments for disabled people in broadly the same way that it applies to employers. The key difference is that it is an anticipatory duty, meaning that it is owed to disabled people at large whether they are a known user of the service or not.[92]

The provision of an employment service includes providing or making arrangements   4.60
for vocational training (defined as training for employment or work experience); finding employment for individuals; careers guidance; supplying contract workers; the services of Job-Centre Plus, i.e. finding employment and careers advice; and an assessment related to the conferment of a relevant qualification by a 'qualification body' (see Part 10 above). An employment service does not include the provision of a service, which is provided by way of, or as part of, a trade or profession. For example, the Chartered Institute of Personnel Development is not an employment service provider but a trade organization (see further below). It also excludes training or guidance provided by schools and further and higher education institutions.[93] However, a complaint about discrimination by the provider during a work placement (as opposed to a complaint about the access afforded by the educational institution) will fall under this section.[94]

12. Trade Organizations

Section 57 prohibits trade organizations from discriminating against, victimizing, or harass-   4.61
ing members and prospective members. They are also subject to the duty to make reasonable adjustments for disabled members. The extent of the duty differs depending on whether

---

[88] See s. 91.
[89] *Watt (formerly Carter) (sued on his own on behalf of the other members of the Labour Party) v Ashan* [2007] UKHL 51; *Ali v McDonagh* [2002] ICR 1026.
[90] *General Medical Council v Michalak* [2018] IRLR 60.
[91] Defined as an academic, medical or other standard for the purpose of determining a person's particular level of competence; s. 54(6).
[92] Ss 55(6)(7); See Part 3 of the Act (ss 28–31) and the relevant Schedules that apply to that part for the duty as it applies to the provision of a vocational service.
[93] Such claims must be brought in the County Court under the education provisions of the Act (see Chapter 6).
[94] *Blackwood v Birmingham and Solihull Mental Health NHS Foundation Trust* [2016] EWCA Civ 607.

the disabled person is a prospective member or a member.[95]A trade organization is defined as: an organization of workers, such as a trade union; an organization of employers, such as the Confederation of British Industry; or any other organization whose members carry on a particular trade or profession for the purposes of which the organization exists, such as the Royal Institution of Chartered Surveyors or the Bar Council.

13. Local Authority Members

4.62 Section 58 makes it unlawful for a local authority to discriminate against or victimize its elected members in the way in which it affords them access to facilities such as training or by subjecting them to any other detriment. However, a failure to appoint or elect a member to a local authority post or a committee or sub-committee, or to appoint or nominate a member for an appointment by an authority in the exercise of its appointment powers, will not constitute a detriment (see section 58(4)). The Act also prohibits harassment against a local authority member carrying out official duties. Section 58(6) imposes a duty on local authorities to make reasonable adjustments for disabled members carrying out official business. There is no duty to make reasonable adjustments in relation to prospective members. Section 59 lists the various bodies covered by the term 'local authority'.

14. Pre-employment Enquiries about Disability and Health

4.63 A welcome addition to the equality landscape, section 60 of the Act was designed to complement existing protection for disabled job applicants. It prohibits employers asking questions about health and disability during the job recruitment process except in very narrow circumstances.

4.64 An employer must not make enquiries about health issues before offering work to an applicant or including the applicant in a pool for selection.[96]

4.65 A contravention of the provision is enforceable as an unlawful act by the Equality and Human Rights Commission only, meaning it does not give rise to an individual claim in its own right.[97]

4.66 However, if an individual brings a claim of discrimination in breach of the disability provisions, the employment tribunal is entitled to treat the employer's action in making the enquiry as a fact which would shift the burden of proof (see Chapter 3 on burden of proof).

4.67 An employer will not breach section 60 if the health or disability question is necessary for one or more specified purposes set out in section 60(6).

4.68 The specified purposes are to: establish whether an applicant will be able to comply with a requirement to undergo an interview or other recruitment selection process; establish whether an applicant will be able to carry out an intrinsic part of the work (if reasonable adjustments are made); pursue a positive action programme; determine if an occupational requirement applies; or find out whether an applicant has a particular disability identified as an occupational requirement for the job.

---

[95] Trade organizations are not required to make reasonable adjustments to premises in respect of prospective members. See Sch. 8, paras 2 and 17 of the Act.
[96] S. 60(1)(a)–(b).
[97] S. 60(2).

It is also permissible to make enquiries which are part of a vetting process for national security purposes.[98] **4.69**

Section 60 applies to all job applicants including contract workers, prospective partners, tenants, pupils and the Scottish equivalents, and appointments to personal or public office.[99] **4.70**

C. OCCUPATIONAL PENSION SCHEMES

By virtue of section 61, a non-discrimination rule is implied into all occupational pension schemes in respect of all protected characteristics. This means that trustees, managers of schemes, employers, or an appointor of personal and public offices must not discriminate against, harass, or victimize a person in carrying out any functions relating to the scheme.[100] They are also subject to the duty to make reasonable adjustments. In *McCloud and Ors v Lord Chancellor and Anor*[101] the court held that protections offered to only some members of the judges' and firefighters' schemes, as part of public service pension reforms, directly discriminated against the claimants on ground of age and in breach of the non-discrimination rule. **4.71**

The non-discrimination rule does not apply to 'pension credit members' of the scheme.[102] **4.72**

The provisions contain certain exceptions and limitations to the non-discrimination rule. The rule does not apply:

- to persons entitled to benefits awarded under a divorce settlement or on the termination of a civil partnership;

- to practices, decisions, or actions of employers, trustees, or managers relating to age to be specified in regulations following consultation; or

- if an equality rule applies or would apply but for the fact that the equality rule relates to differences in treatment between men and women for the purposes of a state retirement pension or actuarial factors used to calculate an employer's contribution to an occupational pension scheme (see Chapter 10).

In addition, section 61 does not apply to pension rights and benefits payable for periods of service before the commencement of the section on 1 October 2010. Such rights and benefits will be subject to the previous legislation.[103]

The Act confers an order-making power allowing a Minister to introduce an age exception which would enable employers to maintain or use practices, actions, or decisions relating to contributions to personal pensions.[104] **4.73**

---

[98] S. 60(14).

[99] S. 60(9).

[100] S. 61 applies to the rules and operation of an occupational pension scheme. It will not apply if the complaint concerns the manner in which an employer has afforded access to such a scheme, which is covered by the employment provisions at Chapter 1 of Part 5 of the Act in the usual way.

[101] [2018] EWCA Civ 2844.

[102] As defined by Pensions Act 1995 s. 124.

[103] EN 205.

[104] The relevant order is the Equality Act (Age Exceptions for Pension Schemes) Order 2010, SI 2010/2133.

D. THE DUTY TO MAKE REASONABLE ADJUSTMENTS IN WORK

1. Generally

4.74 The duty to make reasonable adjustments is a key measure to eliminate the barriers to access and participation for disabled people in the work context. It applies to the recruitment stage and during all stages of employment including dismissal. The duty requires those who are caught by the Act's provisions to take reasonable steps to avoid putting disabled people at a disadvantage, by removing or modifying barriers which might do so, and providing auxiliary aids and services.

4.75 Where there is a duty to make adjustments under the provisions of Part 5 of the Act, section 20 defines what is meant by reasonable adjustments in general terms. Section 20 must be read with Schedule 8, which explains in detail how the duty applies to employers and the other bodies, organizations, and individuals specified in Part 5.

4.76 The duty in section 20 to make reasonable adjustments has three requirements. The first requirement concerns changing a provision, criterion, or practice that puts a disabled person at a substantial disadvantage in comparison to a non-disabled person. The second requirement concerns making changes to a physical feature that puts a disabled person at a substantial disadvantage in comparison to a non-disabled person. The third requirement concerns providing auxiliary aids including services for a disabled person without which they would be put at a disadvantage in comparison to a non-disabled person.[105]

4.77 The three requirements apply where an 'interested' disabled employee or job applicant is placed at a substantial disadvantage compared with non-disabled employees or applicants.

4.78 The tables at Schedule 8 define who is an 'interested disabled person' in relation to a particular set of circumstances, described as a 'relevant matter'.

4.79 Depending on the relevant matter in question, the interested disabled person may either be: a person who has notified the employer that the person applying for the employment may be a disabled person; an applicant for employment; or an employee. It does not, however, extend to relatives of disabled people.[106]

4.80 The EHRC Code of Practice outlines the principles and application of the duty to make reasonable adjustments for disabled people in employment.[107] Section 15(4)(b) of the Act obliges an employment tribunal to take the Code into account where relevant.

4.81 The duty has generated a substantial body of case law over the years. More recently, in *J v K*[108] the Court of Appeal confirmed that employment tribunals are, as a matter of general law and fairness, under a duty to make reasonable adjustments to accommodate a disabled party put at a substantial disadvantage by the proceedings. Such adjustments may include permitting a disabled litigant to make an audio recording of proceedings.[109] That an adjustment

---

[105] The duties in s. 20 are covered in greater detail in Chapter 3.

[106] *Hainsworth v Ministry of Defence* [2014] EWCA Civ 763.

[107] Equality and Human Rights Commission (ECHR), Equality Act 2010 Code of Practice: Employment Statutory Code of Practice (2011), Chapter 6.

[108] [2019] EWCA Civ 5.

[109] *Heal v The Chancellor, Master and Scholars of the University Oxford*, UKEAT/0070/19.

need not be completely effective to be reasonable (the 'test of effectiveness') was endorsed by the Court of Appeal in *Griffiths v Secretary of State for Work and Pensions*.[110] In the case of Hainsworth[111] it was argued that Article 5 extended reasonable accommodation to relatives of an employee. The appellant's daughter was disabled and the appellant submitted a formal request to be transferred to a location within the United Kingdom in order to be able to meet the special needs of her daughter. The claim was dismissed on the basis that the duty to make reasonable adjustments relates to disabled employees, prospective employees, and trainees. It would make Article 5 too uncertain if it was applied more widely.

The Court of Appeal has determined that the duty applies to sickness absence policies;[112]   **4.82** and that it is a case of whether it is reasonable for an employer to adjust a policy in a particular circumstance. The correct comparator for a person who has to take sickness absence because of their disability is a non-disabled person who is less likely to suffer periods of sickness absence and is therefore less likely to incur sanctions or risk losing their jobs as a result.[113] The Court of Appeal has highlighted the importance of clearly defining the 'provision, criterion, or practice' when formulating a reasonable adjustment claim.[114] The duty can extend to treating a disabled person more favourably when making any adjustments: in *Redcar & Cleveland PCT v Lonsdale*[115] it required an amendment to the Human Resources Framework to allow an employee who was otherwise unable to apply for a certain higher graded post to do so to avoid redundancy. The duty does not, however, extend to appointing someone to a job they are not qualified to undertake.[116]

2. Application of the Duty to Different Work Contexts

How the duty applies in the wider work areas that fall under Part 5, for example to firms,   **4.83** barristers and their clerks, and qualification bodies, is specified in the Schedule 8 tables.

3. Concurrent Duties to Make Reasonable Adjustments

Where two or more persons are subject to a duty to make reasonable adjustments in relation   **4.84** to the same interested disabled person, each of them must comply with the duty so far as it is reasonable for each of them to do so (Schedule 8, paragraph 2(5)).

4. Contract Workers

An employer ('principal') of a disabled contract worker must comply with all three of the   **4.85** duty's requirements on each occasion when the employee is supplied to the principal to do contract work (Schedule 8, paragraph 5).

---

[110] [2017] ICR 160.
[111] *Hainsworth v Ministry of Defence* [2014] EWCA Civ 763.
[112] *Griffiths v the Secretary of State for Work and Pensions* [2015] EWCA 1265.
[113] *Perratt v The City of Cardiff Council* [2016] UKEAT/0079/16.
[114] *Brangwyn v South Warwickshire NHS Foundation Trust* UKEAT/0125/15/LA.
[115] [2013] UKEAT/0090/12/0905.
[116] *Wade v Sheffield Hallam University* [2013] UKEAT/0194/12/1504.

E. EXCEPTIONS TO THE WORK PROVISIONS

4.86 The Act contains a number of exceptions to the prohibition against unlawful discrimination in work, which are set out in Schedule 9 to the Act. The exceptions can be divided into three broad categories: occupational requirements; age-related exceptions; and general exceptions. These are discussed in more detail below.

1. Occupational Requirements

4.87 Equality law has always recognized that there are circumstances in which it may be necessary for a person with a particular protected characteristic to do a particular job. Thus, the Act permits employers, principals (as defined in section 41), partners, members of an LLP and those with the power to appoint or remove office-holders, or to recommend an appointment to public office to apply an occupational requirement ('OR') to be of a particular protected characteristic for a job in specified circumstances set out below.

4.88 The Act replicates the provisions for genuine occupational requirements that applied to all of the protected characteristics in previous equality legislation. An employer can require that an applicant or employee have a particular protected characteristic if, having regard to the nature or context of the work: it is an occupational requirement; it is a proportionate means of achieving a legitimate aim; and the person to whom the requirement applies does not meet it or, except in relation to sex, the employer is not reasonably satisfied that the person meets it.[117]

4.89 The OR provisions apply to appointments, transfers and promotions, and dismissals. For example, a rape crisis centre could, given the context of the work, lawfully make being a woman an OR for posts as counsellors/advisors to serve the legitimate aim of ensuring that women who use the service feel comfortable relating their experiences of rape. An OR must be a crucial element of the post in question and not one of several important factors. It should not be applied automatically to a job and the need for its application should be regularly assessed.[118]

4.90 In addition there are specific OR provisions for organized religions and organizations with an ethos based on religion, which are discussed further below.

2. Organized Religions

4.91 An organized religion can apply a requirement related to sexual orientation for an employee to be of a particular sex, or not to be transsexual, or not to be married or a civil partner, or not to be married to a person of the same sex if because of the nature or context of the job it is necessary to comply with the doctrines of the religion (the 'compliance principle');[119] or to avoid conflicting with the religious convictions of a significant number of the religion's followers (the 'non-conflict principle').[120]

---

[117] Sch. 9, para. 1(1).
[118] See *Hender v Prospects for People with Living Disabilities* [2007] ET 2902090/06.
[119] Sch. 9, para. 2(5).
[120] Sch. 9, para. 2(6).

For the exception to apply, the relevant employment must be 'for the purposes of an   4.92
organized religion'. The term is not defined in the Act but the High Court in *R (Amicus-MSF
Section) v Secretary of State for Trade and Industry*,[121] concluded that on its proper construction, its confines are narrow. The case was decided under the predecessor legislation but the
language is the same and the court is unlikely to depart from its earlier approach.

However, it should not be interpreted so narrowly as to limit it to employment within a   4.93
religious organization. In *Pemberton v Inwood*[122] a Church of England priest who had sought
employment as a hospital chaplain for an NHS trust, was refused the licence necessary for
him to carry out the role by the bishop, because he had entered into a same-sex marriage. The
Court of Appeal rejected the argument that because the licence was a condition of employment with the Trust, rather than the church, it was not 'employment for the purposes of an
organized religion'. The correct approach is to consider the focus of the employment rather
than the identity of the employer.

Pemberton also confirmed that 'doctrines' for the purposes of paragraph 2(5) should be   4.94
construed to mean 'the teachings and beliefs of the particular religious organization', which
may be wider than what the organization itself expressly labels 'doctrine'.

3. Organizations with an Ethos Based on Religion or Belief

Paragraph 3 of Schedule 9 permits a person with an ethos based on religion or belief to apply   4.95
an OR in relation to work to be of a particular religion or belief, if having regard to that ethos
and to the nature or context of the work: it is an occupational requirement; the requirement
is a proportionate means of achieving a legitimate aim; and the person to whom it is applied
does not meet it or is reasonably believed not to meet it. This specific exception replicates
the general OR exception noted at paragraph 4.87 save that it has the additional hurdle of
showing the existence of a religious ethos that must be related to the nature or the context
of the work.

The religious ethos exception is based on Article 4(2) of Council Directive 200/78/EC   4.96
which was considered by the European Court of Justice in *IR v JQ*.[123] The case concerned
the dismissal of a Roman Catholic doctor from his managerial position at a Catholic hospital
due to his remarriage. In a preliminary ruling the ECJ ruled that adherence to the ethos in
question did not appear to be necessary to the occupational activities undertaken by JQ (the
giving of medical advice and care). It placed reliance on the fact that similar activities were
undertaken by employees who were not Catholics. This narrow construction of the religious
ethos exception is reflected in the limited case law decided under the predecessor provisions
in the Religion or Belief Regulations.[124]

4. Armed Forces

Paragraph 4 of Schedule 9 allows the armed forces to exclude women and 'transsexual' peo-   4.97
ple from service if this is a proportionate means of ensuring the combat effectiveness of the

---

[121] [2007] ICR 1176.
[122] [2018] EWCA Civ 564.
[123] 2019 ICR 417, ECJ.
[124] *Sheridan v Prospects For People With Learning Disabilities and another case* ET 2901366/06; Glasgow City
Council v McNab [2007] IRLR 476.

armed forces. This exception applies only to those combat roles requiring close ground face-to-face combat.[125] In addition, paragraph 9 exempts the armed forces from the work provisions relating to disability and age.

5. Age Exceptions

4.98 There are a number of exceptions to the work provisions relating to age. These include exceptions on length of service, redundancy, life insurance, and childcare.

(a) *Retirement*

4.99 There is no longer a default retirement age exception. It was repealed on 6 April 2011 by the Employment Equality (Repeal of Retirement Age Provisions) Regulations 2011, SI 2011/1069. An employer requiring an employee to retire because they have reached a particular age will need to objectively justify the requirement under section 13(2) of the Act.

(b) *Service-related Benefits*

4.100 Paragraph 10 of Schedule 9 permits employers and others covered by the Part 5 employment provision of the Act to provide different benefits, facilities, and services based on a length of service criterion of no more than five years. Service-related benefits for these purposes includes pay increments, holiday entitlement, access to financial advice, private medical insurance, share options etc. The exception does not apply to service-related termination payments[126] but it does apply to an award of points based on length of service as part of a redundancy selection.[127]

4.101 The criterion can exceed five years only if the employer 'reasonably believes' that it fulfils a 'business need'.[128] Business need is not defined in the Act. The EHRC Statutory Code of Practice states that the test for 'fulfilling a business need' is less onerous than the test for objective justification. It provides that rewarding higher levels of experience, or increasing or maintaining motivation of long-serving staff are examples of a business need for these purposes.[129]

4.102 Length of service can be determined by either the length of time that a person has been working for the employer at or above a certain level; or by the total length of time a person has been working for the employer.[130]

(c) *Redundancy*

4.103 Paragraph 13 of Schedule 9 permits enhanced redundancy payments based on age or length of service to employees who are entitled to a statutory redundancy payment under the ERA, including those who take voluntary redundancy and those who would qualify but for the two year service requirement. The process for calculating enhanced redundancy payments is prescribed in the Act as follows:

- to remove the maximum amount on a week's pay so that the actual weekly pay is used in the calculation;

---

[125] See EN 799.
[126] Para. 10(7).
[127] *Rolls-Royce Plc v Unite the Union* [2009] EWCA Civ 387.
[128] Para. 10(2).
[129] Equality and Human Rights Commission (EHRC), Equality Act 2010 Code of Practice: Employment Statutory Code of Practice (2011).
[130] Para. 10(3).

- to raise the maximum amount on a week's pay, thereby using a higher amount of pay in the calculation; and/or
- to multiply the appropriate amount for each year of employment set out in the statutory formula by a figure of more than one.[131]

Capping or otherwise reducing enhanced redundancy payments by reference to a specified retirement age is not permitted within the exception. Such treatment contravenes the age provisions unless it is objectively justified. The abolition of the default retirement age means that employers can no longer assume such payments would constitute a windfall by way of justification.[132]

(d) *Life Insurance*

Schedule 9, paragraph 14 of the Act allows employers to discriminate because of the pro- 4.104 tected characteristic of age in the provision of insurance and 'related financial services' such as private medical insurance or sickness and accident insurance. Specifically employers can refuse to provide these benefits to employees who have reached the age of 65 (or, if greater, the state pensionable age) even if the employee continues to work beyond that age.

(e) *National Minimum Wage*

The Act permits differential pay as between younger and older workers on the national mini- 4.105 mum wage. It also permits pay differentials between apprentices who qualify for the national minimum wage and those who do not.[133]

(f) *Child Care*

It is not unlawful age discrimination for an employer to provide or make arrangements for 4.106 or facilitate the provision of child care for children of a particular age group (under the age of 17).[134] This might include, for example, the employer providing child care vouchers for an employee's child to attend an after-school club.

6. General Exceptions

In addition to the exceptions for occupational requirements and age, Schedule 9 contains 4.107 further exceptions of a general nature on benefits relating to maternity leave, marital status, provision of services to the public, and insurance contracts.

(a) *Maternity Leave Benefits*

It is not unlawful discrimination for an employer to deny women on maternity leave a 4.108 non-contractual benefit relating to pay, such as bonuses. This exception does not apply to maternity-related pay to which a woman would be entitled as a result of her pregnancy or in respect of times when she is on maternity leave.[135]

---

[131] EHRC, Equality Act 2010 Code of Practice: Employment Statutory Code of Practice (2011).
[132] BAE Systems (Operations) Ltd v McDowell [2018] ICR 214, EAT.
[133] Paras 11 and 12.
[134] Para. 15.
[135] Para. 17.

(b) *Benefits Dependent on Marital Status*

4.109 The Act permits an employer to restrict or provide benefits, facilities, or services to married people (which includes same-sex married people)[136] and people in civil partnerships, for example death in service payments, to the exclusion of single people.[137]

(c) *Provision of Services to the Public*

4.110 Paragraph 19 of Schedule 9 provides that where an employer provides services to the public that it also provides to employees it will not be liable for claims of discrimination or victimization by the employee in relation to those services under the employment provisions of the Act.[138]

4.111 The provision applies to principals, firms, LLPs, and any person who appoints office holders. However, if the employer, LLP, etc. provides a service under the terms and conditions of employment and does so differentially as between employees, or the service is to do with training, the employee will have a claim under the employment provisions.

(d) *Insurance Contracts*

4.112 The Act permits employers who offer their employees an annuity, life insurance policy, or accident insurance policy, to discriminate in relation to gender reassignment, marital or civil partnership status, pregnancy and maternity, and sex where it is reasonable to do so based on actuarial or other reliable data.[139]

---

[136] Amendment made to the Equality Act 2010 by Marriage (Same Sex Couples) Act 2013 Sch. 4, Part 2, para. 17(3).

[137] Para. 18.

[138] The employer will, however, be liable under provisions on goods, services, and public functions (see Chapter 5).

[139] Para. 20.

5

SERVICES, PUBLIC FUNCTIONS, AND TRANSPORT

A. SERVICES AND PUBLIC FUNCTIONS

1. Introduction

This chapter is divided into two sections. It deals with services and public functions in section   **5.01**
A and the transport provisions in section B. Both are covered by Part 3 of the Equality Act 2010
('the Act'), which deals with discrimination in services and public functions. As with other Parts
of the Act, Part 3 consolidates and harmonizes previous legislation. Practitioners familiar with
the predecessor enactments will note that the phrase 'goods, facilities and services' has been
subsumed within the term 'services', and that public functions have been brought within the
same provisions. Transport and the use of transport vehicles were 'services' for the purposes of
the Act. However, some provisions dealing with transport and disability discrimination in rail
services have now become exempt from the Equality Act as Schedule 3, paragraph 34A states
that section 29 does not apply to anything governed by Regulation (EC) No 1371/2007 of the
European Parliament and of the Council of 23 October 2007 on rail passengers' rights and obligations. The Rail Passengers' Rights and Obligations (Exemptions) Regulations 2014, SI 2014/
2793 provided that the exemption to the Rail Regulation would cease on 4 December 2019 and
it has not been renewed.

These are considered separately and in greater detail in section B of this chapter.

Compared to the previous enactments, one of the most significant changes made by the   **5.02**
Act is to introduce a new ban on age discrimination in services and public functions,[1] which
applies to service users aged 18 and over.[2] However, unlike direct discrimination because of
other protected characteristics, age-differentiated treatment is lawful if it can be objectively

---

[1] The Act also introduced a ban on age discrimination in associations under Part 7, which does not exclude
under 18s; see Chapter 11 Part N.

[2] In relation to under 18s, Part 3 of the Act does not apply to the protected characteristic of age: s. 28(1)(a).

Chris Fry, *Services, Public Functions, and Transport* In: *Blackstone's Guide to the Equality Act 2010.* Fourth Edition. Edited
by: Anthony Robinson, David Ruebain, and Susie Uppal, Oxford University Press (2021). © Oxford University Press.
DOI: 10.1093/oso/9780198870876.003.0005

justified under section 13(2) as a proportionate means of achieving a legitimate aim,[3] or if there is a relevant exception.

5.03   Commencement of this ban was delayed; it did not come into effect until 1 October 2012,[4] two years after the bulk of the Act's provisions had been commenced. Exceptions to the ban, which are explained later in this chapter, were introduced simultaneously by the Equality Act 2010 (Age Exceptions) Order 2012[5] under powers provided by sections 197 and 207(4) and (6) of the Act. These age exceptions mainly take effect as amendments to Schedule 3.

5.04   The two-year delay in commencement is partly explained by the extended process of consultation on these age exceptions. The financial services and holiday industries were particularly nervous of age discrimination being outlawed in their sectors, because of the age-based rules embedded in their business practices. In its March 2011 consultation paper,[6] the Government Equalities Office suggested that the draft exceptions would meet the objective justification test for direct discrimination because of age under section 13(2) of the Act;[7] but the Government favoured creating express exceptions in order to provide legal certainty and help avoid court challenges. Whether in practice the application of the exceptions, as enacted, would in all cases satisfy the objective justification test is very much open to debate. As widely anticipated, the order contains no express exceptions for health and social care services; in these sectors, most examples of age-differentiated treatment would need to satisfy the objective justification test under section 13(2).

5.05   The Equality and Human Rights Commission had planned to produce a supplement to its existing statutory Code of Practice on Services, Public Functions and Associations, covering the new ban on age discrimination; it published a draft for consultation in March 2014. The Commission submitted the revised draft to the Government in June 2014 so that it could be approved and laid before Parliament to come into force as Code of Practice. Nearly two years later, the Government still had not decided whether to approve the draft Code, so the Commission has published the text as Technical Guidance.[8]

5.06   Another significant change to Part 3 of the Act was made necessary following the 2011 decision of the Court of Justice of the European Union in the case of *Association Belge des Consommateurs Test-Achats*.[9] This decision established that the EU Gender Directive provision that permits proportionate differences between men and women's insurance premiums

---

[3] In *Seldon v Clarkson Wright and Jakes* [2012] UKSC 16, a case relating to mandatory retirement, taking account of CJEU case law the Supreme Court held that direct age discrimination in employment and occupation only could be justified by reference to social policy objectives of a public interest nature; further, legitimate aims fell into two broad categories: inter-generational fairness and dignity. For age discrimination in services, as there is no relevant EU directive, it is unclear whether or not s. 13(2) should be interpreted using the narrower, *Seldon* approach, or using a wider test—as for indirect discrimination under s. 19. Domestic case law is awaited.

[4] Equality Act 2010 (Commencement No 9) Order 2012, SI 2016/1569.

[5] SI 2012/2466.

[6] Government Equalities Office, March 2011; *Equality Act 2010: Banning Age Discrimination in Services, Public Functions and Associations—a Consultation on Proposed Exceptions to the Ban* (para. 2.12).

[7] Under s. 13(2).

[8] Equality and Human Rights Commission, March 2016. Technical Guidance on age discrimination in services, public functions and associations.

[9] *Association Belge des Consommateurs Test-Achats ASBL and Others v Council* (Case C-236/09, 1 March 2011).

and insurance benefits was unlawful. In response to this decision, regulations[10] made by HM Treasury repealed the insurance exception in paragraph 22 of Schedule 3 relating to sex and gender reassignment and pregnancy and maternity. This is addressed more fully in paragraph 5.107 below.

2. Application of Part 3

Section 28 of the Act defines the scope of Part 3. Thus section 28(1)(a) provides that this Part does not apply to the protected characteristic of age so far as it relates to persons under the age of 18. The view of the government of the time was that protection from age discrimination was not the best way of addressing children's problems. Against this, children's organizations pointed to the UK's obligations under international law to protect children from discrimination.[11]   **5.07**

The second limitation to Part 3, under section 28(1)(b), excludes the protected characteristic of marriage and civil partnership. This reflects the fact that it was in the employment field where women historically needed protection from the 'marriage bar' that operated against them—protection that was later extended to civil partners.   **5.08**

Section 28(2)(a) clarifies that Part 3 does not apply to discrimination, harassment, or victimization that is prohibited by Part 4 (premises), Part 5 (work), or Part 6 (education). For the avoidance of doubt, section 28(2)(b) extends this exclusion to conduct that would be prohibited under these parts but for an express exception. In the case of *Hottak*, it was held that section 28 did not mean that an employment claim outside the territorial reach of Part 5 could be brought under Part 3 instead.[12] By section 28(3), Part 3 does not cover a breach of an equality clause or rule in a person's terms of work, nor does it cover a non-discrimination rule in an occupational pension scheme.   **5.09**

The scope of Part 3 is also limited in relation to harassment. By section 29(8), neither religion or belief nor sexual orientation is a relevant protected characteristic for the prohibition on harassment in providing services or exercising public functions. However, section 212(5) provides that the disapplication of harassment in relation to a protected characteristic does not prevent conduct from amounting to a detriment for the purposes of section 13 (direct discrimination). In this way, conduct that might otherwise have amounted to harassment because of religion or belief or sexual orientation may be dealt with as a form of direct discrimination.[13]   **5.10**

Other limitations to the scope of Part 3 are expressed as exceptions under sections 192, 193, 194, and 195; and Schedules 3, 22, and 23. All these exceptions are dealt with later in this chapter.   **5.11**

---

[10] Equality Act 2010 (Amendment) Regulations 2012, SI 2012 No. 2992.
[11] For example, UN Convention on the Rights of the Child Art. 2.
[12] See *R (on the application of Hottak and another) v (1) Secretary of State for Foreign and Commonwealth Affairs (2) Secretary of State for Defence* [2016] EWCA Civ 438.
[13] See, e.g., *Small v Taylor Edwards*, Case No. A68YM129, Southend County Court, a case where it was held that actions of blowing kisses and other gestures at a gay man which would otherwise have amounted to harassment were direct discrimination, resulting in damages of £7,500 for injury to feelings.

3. What is a Service?

5.12   There is no comprehensive definition of 'service' in the Act, which simply states that a service is something provided to the public, or a section of the public, whether for payment or not. By section 29(1):

A person (a 'service-provider') concerned with the provision of a service to the public or a section of the public (for payment or not) must not discriminate against a person requiring the service …

5.13   Recognizing the need to align the Act with previous legislation, the drafters wisely inserted an interpretation provision (section 31(2)) clarifying that a reference to the provision of a service includes a reference to the provision of *goods or facilities*. Likewise, the inclusion within the definition of service of 'a service in the exercise of a public function' is acknowledged by section 31(3).

5.14   Discrimination legislation that preceded the Act did not offer a definition of the word 'goods'; this term was thought to be non-contentious and was simply given its ordinary meaning. Neither was the term 'services' defined, although all the relevant legislation provided non-exhaustive lists of facilities and services. For example, the following list was set out in the Sex Discrimination Act 1975 (SDA):[14]

(a) access to and use of any place which members of the public or a section of the public are permitted to enter;

(b) accommodation in a hotel, boarding house, or other similar establishment;

(c) facilities by way of banking or insurance or for grants, loans, credit, or finance;

(d) facilities for entertainment, recreation, or refreshment;

(e) facilities for transport or travel;

(f) the services of any profession or trade, or any local or other public authority.

5.15   It can be safely assumed that Part 3 of the Act is intended to cover all these areas. The Statutory Code of Practice on Services, Public Functions and Associations provides an illustrative list that is more extensive:

Among the services which are covered are those provided to the public, or a section of the public, by local authorities, such as toilet facilities; government departments and their agencies; some charities; associations; voluntary organizations; hotels; restaurants; pubs; post offices; banks; building societies; solicitors; accountants; telecommunications organizations; public utilities (such as gas, electricity, and water suppliers); services provided by bus and train operators, railway stations, airports; public parks; sports stadia; leisure centres; advice agencies; theatres; cinemas; hairdressers; shops; market stalls; petrol stations; telesales businesses; hospitals; and clinics.[15]

4. What is a Public Function?

5.16   The distinction between services and public functions is not always an easy one to make. The residual nature of the public function provisions means that they only apply when other provisions of the Act do not. The distinction between services and public functions was

---

[14] SDA s. 29.

[15] Statutory Code of Practice on Services, Public Functions and Associations ('Services CoP'), para. 11.3.

addressed in the case of *R v Entry Clearance Officer ex p Amin*,[16] where Ms Amin claimed that the special voucher scheme allowing entry to the UK for heads of household indirectly discriminated against women. The House of Lords ruled that decisions relating to this scheme did not qualify as 'facilities or services' under section 29 of the SDA as they did not resemble the activities carried out by private bodies. In *Farah v Metropolitan Police*,[17] the Court of Appeal made a distinction between different aspects of policing, some of which came within the meaning of 'services' under section 20 of the Race Relations Act 1976 (RRA), and others which—based on *Amin*—did not. Note however that these cases pre-date the public functions provisions with the Equality Act 2010.

Section 29(6) of the Act makes it clear that a public function does not include a service to   5.17
the public delivered by a public authority:

A person must not, in the exercise of a public function that is not the provision of a service to the public or a section of the public, do anything that constitutes discrimination, harassment or victimization.

The Explanatory Notes to the Act cite law enforcement and revenue raising or collection as   5.18
examples of 'pure' public functions. These are contrasted with public functions that involve the provision of a service—for example, medical treatment on the National Health Service (NHS)—which are covered by the provisions dealing with services.[18] More recently, in the case of *Coll*, it was accepted that the decision where to place approved premises (a type of criminal justice facility) would involve the exercise of a public function within the meaning of section 31(4) of the Act.[19]

The Statutory Code of Practice notes that when performing a public function, a public   5.19
authority will often be acting under a statutory power or duty.[20] It gives examples of the wide variety of actions that may be covered by the term 'public function', including determining frameworks for entitlement to benefits[21] or services; law enforcement; receiving someone into prison or detention; planning control and licensing; enforcement of parking controls, trading standards and environmental health; exercise of statutory powers under mental health and children legislation; regulatory functions; and the investigation of complaints.[22] The Code also observes that whether or not an activity is a *service to the public* or a *public function* will depend on all the circumstances of the case;[23] essentially, however, the Act imposes very similar legal duties on persons exercising public functions as it does on those providing a service.

The meaning of 'public function' of a public authority for the purpose of Part 3 of the Act   5.20
can be compared with the Human Rights Act (HRA) 1998. The latter makes it unlawful for public authorities 'to act in a way that is incompatible with a Convention right' when carrying out their statutory functions; thus, all statutory services provided by public authorities are

---

[16] [1983] 2 AC 818.
[17] [1998] QB 65.
[18] Explanatory Note (EN) 111.
[19] *R (on the application of Coll) (Appellant) v Secretary of State for Justice (Respondent)* [2017] UKSC 40.
[20] Services CoP, para. 11.13.
[21] See *R (on the application of Winder) v Sandwell Metropolitan Borough Council* [2014] EWHC 2617 (Admin), where the court accepted that the operation of the local authority's council tax reduction scheme was a public function for the purposes of s. 29. The scheme's residence test was held to be unlawful, inter alia, because it was indirectly discriminatory.
[22] Services CoP, para. 11.15.
[23] *ibid*, para. 11.17.

covered by the HRA 1998, making it similar in breadth to the public sector equality duty.[24] In relation to public functions performed by bodies *other than* public authorities, Part 3 of the Act aligns more closely with the HRA 1998. Section 31(4) states that a public function is 'a function of a public nature for the purposes of the Human Rights Act 1998.' The HRA 1998, which applies to all public authorities, does not contain a definition of 'function of a public nature', other than to state (in section 6(3)(b)) that a 'public authority' includes any person certain of whose functions are of a public nature. Such persons are often referred to as 'hybrid bodies'.

5.21   The scope of section 6(3)(b) has been held to exclude provision of social care by private care homes under contract with local authorities[25] but to include management and allocation of social housing provided by a registered social landlord.[26] It is unclear whether, in similar circumstances, either type of body would be seen as exercising 'public functions' rather than providing services under Part 3 of the Act.

5. What is Unlawful in Relation to Services?

5.22   As with other Parts of the Act, Part 3 outlaws discrimination, harassment, and victimization in relation to services. The comprehensive drafting of section 29 ensures that the Act has effect at all stages of the service provider's relationship with the user. Section 29(1) prohibits a service provider from discriminating by not providing a service to someone who requires it. For the avoidance of doubt, section 31(6) states that a reference to a person requiring a service should be taken to include a person seeking to obtain or use the service.

5.23   The Act also tackles discrimination by the service provider in the quality of the service or the manner in which it is provided (section 31(7)). In addition, it is unlawful to discriminate in any decision to cease providing the service or by subjecting the user to any other detriment. By section 29(2):

A service-provider (A) must not, in providing the service, discriminate against a person (B)—

 (a) as to the terms on which A provides the service to B;
 (b) by terminating the provision of the service to B;
 (c) by subjecting B to any other detriment.

5.24   As the Statutory Code of Practice points out,[27] these provisions may overlap. Treating a customer—or would-be customer—rudely or offensively could amount to a 'detriment' or, alternatively, could be construed as not providing the service on the terms on which the service is normally provided.

5.25   Similar provisions apply to victimization by a service provider, under section 29(4) and (5); victimization is unlawful whether it is through refusing to provide a service, giving the user a poor quality of service, terminating the service, or subjecting the user to any other detriment. However, if the service user experiences conduct or treatment by the provider amounting to victimization and which takes place after the relationship with the provider has come to an end, this should be dealt with under section 108(7) of the Act, which outlaws

---

[24] See s. 149.
[25] *YL (by her litigation friend the Official Solicitor) v Birmingham City Council and Others* [2007] UKHL 27. Note, however, that the provision of regulated social care that is publicly funded or arranged is now deemed to be a public function under s. 6(3)(b) Human Rights Act 1998, by virtue of s. 73 Care Act 2014.
[26] *Weaver v London Quadrant Housing Trust* [2009] EWCA Civ 235.
[27] Para. 11.20.

discrimination and harassment in the context of relationships that have ended, rather than the victimization provisions.[28]

Protection from harassment in the provision of services is dealt with by section 29(3), which states that a service provider must not harass a person requiring the service, or a person to whom the service is provided. The Act extends protection against harassment to the protected characteristic of disability.　　5.26

Specifically section 26 sets out the definition of harassment. This is a broad concept—in the context of disability employment, it has been held to encompass the suspension of a staff member for failing to undertake a particular course where this was considered to be unwarranted (see *Prospects for People with Learning Difficulties v Harris*[29]); and in services, the treatment of a wheelchair user by implying that she would damage a lift (see *Samuels v Corn Exchange Theatre Company* [30]). Sections 111 and 112 have not been extensively used. Such case law as there is suggests that there must be evidence of inducement, causation instruction (s. 111) and knowledge as well as aiding/assisting (s. 112). There are two cases of particular relevance to s. 112 which are instructive.　　5.27

In *Anyanwu and Ebuzoeme v South Bank Students' Union and South Bank University*,[31] it was held that what is meant by 'aid' in this context is to be decided by asking whether help or assistance was given by the person whose liability is in issue. Although decided under the provisions of the RRA 1976, the decision has equal application in the context of the other protected characteristics, and now under the EqA (given that the wording is broadly the same). Their Lordships, reversing a controversial decision of the CA, held that what is necessary is no more than a relationship of co-operation or collaboration.　　5.28

The scope of the concept of 'knowingly aids' was, however, narrowed following the judgment of the House of Lords in *Hallam v Avery*.[32]　　5.29

The case was concerned with discrimination in the provision of services and it was claimed that the police had aided a council to discriminate against gypsies. The claimants sought damages from the police officers concerned, for knowingly aiding the council to discriminate. The claim failed on the ground that it had to be proved that, with the requisite knowledge or intention, aid was provided. The House of Lords held that on the particular facts the County Court judge had found there was no breach of RRA 1976 section 33(1) because the police officers were neither a party to, nor involved in, the making of the council's decision. The fact that the police officers had been 'helpful' to the council in a general sense was not enough. This would seem to mean that in any case where it is alleged that liability arises under section 33(1), and what is now section 112, the party potentially liable must be shown either to have wanted the discriminatory result to follow, or to have known that the employer would treat or was contemplating treating the victim in a discriminatory way. It will not necessarily be enough if the alleged aider merely suspects that a discriminatory act will be the outcome of his own behaviour, without actually wanting it to come about, far less if it can only be said that he should, as a reasonable person, have realized (but did not) that discrimination would be the result. The House of Lords stopped short of saying that the giving of information to another on which the other relies in doing a discriminatory act could never be enough for　　5.30

---

[28] *Jessemey v Rowstock Limited & Another* [2014] EWCA Civ 185.
[29] UKEAT/0612/11/DMUKEAT/0612/11/DM.
[30] Before District Judge Capon, Case No. B05YM747, Peterborough County Court, 21 November 2019.
[31] [2001] UKHL 14, [2001] IRLR 305, [2001] ICR 391.
[32] [2001] IRLR 312, [2001] ICR 408.

liability under section 33(1). Their Lordships also indicated that their decision in the instant case should be read alongside what had been said in relation to 'aids' and the scope of section 33(1) in *Anyanwu* above (paragraph 5.29).

5.31   As noted above (paragraph 5.10), where the protected characteristic is sexual orientation or religion or belief, there is no protection from harassment (section 29(8)). However, under section 212(5), the Act makes clear that this disapplication of the harassment provisions does not prevent conduct from amounting to a detriment for the purposes of direct discrimination under section 13.

Section 13 prohibits direct discrimination—less favourable treatment because of a protected characteristic.[33]

5.32   Section 15 provides that it is discrimination to treat a disabled person unfavourably because of something arising in consequence of their disability, where it cannot be justified as being a proportionate means of achieving a legitimate aim, unless the service provider did not know or could not reasonably be expected to know that the person was disabled. The knowledge required is of the facts of the service user's disability, rather than knowledge that the person meets the legal definition of a 'disabled person'. The provider has to form their own view, and cannot merely 'rubber stamp' the unreasoned opinion of a medical adviser that the service user is not disabled.[34]

5.33   In relation to public functions, all forms of prohibited conduct are addressed together in section 29(6), which provides that a person exercising a public function must not 'do anything that constitutes discrimination, harassment or victimization'. As with the provision of services, in the exercise of public functions the prohibition of harassment does not apply where the protected characteristic is sexual orientation or religion or belief (section 29(8)).

5.34   Section 17 provides that a woman who is pregnant, has given birth within the previous 26 weeks, or is breastfeeding is protected from discrimination, defined as 'unfavourable treatment', in relation to non-work cases, including services and public functions.

5.35   Section 19 provides for indirect discrimination—where a provision criterion or practice puts those sharing a protected characteristic at a particular disadvantage; and it cannot be justified; and section 20 makes provision for reasonable adjustments.

6. The Duty to Make Reasonable Adjustments

(a) *The Duty to Make Reasonable Adjustments in the Provision of Services*

5.36   Under section 29(7), the duty to make reasonable adjustments applies to both service providers and a person exercising a public function. The principles of the duty to make reasonable adjustments are set out in section 20 of the Act; these are discussed in detail in Chapter 3.

5.37   The nature of the duty is summarized as follows in the Explanatory Notes to the Act:[35]

The duty comprises three requirements which apply where a disabled person is placed at a substantial disadvantage in comparison to non-disabled people. The first requirement covers changing the way things are done (such as changing a practice), the second covers making changes to the built environment (such as providing access to a building), and the third covers providing auxiliary aids and services (such as providing special computer software or providing a different service).

---

[33] See *Mandeep & Anor v Royal Borough of Windsor & Maidenhead* [2019] EWFC B64 where a couple were dismissed as suitable for adoption because of their race.

[34] *Gallop v Newport City Council* [2013] EWCA Civ 1583.

[35] EN 82.

In essence, duty-holders should go beyond merely avoiding discrimination against disabled 5.38
people who face barriers that would place them at a substantial disadvantage. Service providers
and those exercising public functions should take positive steps to ensure that disabled people
can access services in a manner that as closely as possible resembles the access enjoyed by other
members of the public. Failure to make reasonable adjustments is a form of discrimination.

In the context of services and public functions, the duty to make reasonable adjustments is 5.39
modified by Schedule 2, given effect by section 31(9). By paragraph 2(2) of Schedule 2, the
reference in section 20 to a disabled person is a reference to disabled persons generally. The
effect of this change is to make the duty an anticipatory one, requiring service providers and
people exercising public functions to consider in advance what reasonable adjustments disabled people might need, and to keep this under continuous review. Simply reacting whenever
a disabled person wants to use a service would be an inadequate discharge of the duty.

The duty to make reasonable adjustments is further modified by paragraph 2(7) of Schedule 5.40
2. In meeting the duty, service providers are not required to take steps that would fundamentally alter the nature of the service or the nature of the provider's trade or profession.

Under section 20(7), subject to any express provision to the contrary, a service provider or 5.41
person exercising a public function cannot pass on the costs of making a reasonable adjustment by charging the disabled person concerned. However, there is nothing in the Act to
stop the costs of making reasonable adjustments being treated as part of general overheads,
thus being recouped via increased charges to service users in general.

(b) *What Adjustments are 'Reasonable'?*

The provision that adjustments need only be 'reasonable' is not qualified further by the Act. 5.42
What is reasonable will depend on all the circumstances of the case, and will vary according
to the type of service, the nature and size of the service provider, and the resources available
to it, as well as the effect of the disability on the individual concerned.[36] A non-exhaustive list
of factors that should be taken into account is given in the Code of Practice:

• whether taking any particular steps would be effective in overcoming the substantial disadvantage faced by disabled people in accessing the services in question;

• the extent to which it is practicable for the service provider to take the steps;

• the financial and other costs of making the adjustment;

• the extent of any disruption that taking the steps would cause;

• the service provider's financial resources, and the extent of resources already spent on making adjustments;

• the availability of financial or other assistance.[37]

As to how these factors might work in practice, the Code gives some helpful examples to 5.43
illustrate this, which include the following:

• If a disabled customer with severe arthritis has difficulty standing in the queue at a busy
post office, reasonable adjustments might include asking him/her to take a seat and then

---

[36] Services CoP, para. 7.29. See also *Roads v Central Trains Ltd* [2004] EWCA Civ 1541.

[37] Services CoP, para. 7.30. Also see *Plummer v Royal Herbert Freehold Ltd*, Case No. B01CL659, Central
London County Court, 6 June 2018, para. 366. Taking out a loan to fund works can be a reasonable
adjustment.

serving him/her as if s/he had been in the queue; or providing a separate service desk with seating for disabled customers.[38]

- A small retailer has two shops offering the same services in close proximity to each other, one of which is accessible to customers with mobility impairments and offers accessible services. If the retailer is at present constrained by limited resources from making the other shop fully accessible, it is unlikely to be in breach of the Act.[39]

(c) *Making Reasonable Adjustments to Physical Features*

5.44   Section 20(4) of the Act requires reasonable adjustments to be made to physical features to avoid any substantial disadvantage that a disabled person would otherwise face. This duty is further defined by section 20(9) as including removing the feature, altering it, or providing a reasonable means of avoiding it. Schedule 2, paragraph 2(3) qualifies this requirement by allowing a service provider or person exercising public functions, as an alternative, 'to adopt a reasonable alternative method of providing the service or exercising the function'. Under paragraph 2(6), the definition of 'physical feature' includes a feature brought onto premises other than those occupied by the service provider or person exercising public functions.

5.45   The duty of a service provider to make reasonable adjustments to physical features of premises is an objective one as discussed in *Royal Bank of Scotland Plc v Allen*.[40] This case concerned the failure of the bank to make its central Sheffield branch accessible to wheelchair users. At paragraph 47 of the judgment, the Court of Appeal confirmed the sequence of reasoning that should be followed in assessing whether there has been a failure to make reasonable adjustments to a physical feature, as follows:

i) Was the Bank a provider of services within the meaning of section 19(2)? (of the then Disability Discrimination Act)

ii) Did a duty arise under section 21(2) i.e. did the physical feature make it impossible or unreasonably difficult for disabled people, or a class of disabled people, to use the service?

iii) If so, were there reasonable steps that should be taken to remove, alter, provide a reasonable means of avoiding, or a reasonable alternative method of service?

iv) If so, did the Bank take those steps?

v) If not, did the failure to take those steps make it impossible or unreasonably difficult for Mr Allen to use the service?

vi) If the answer to (v) is yes, is the failure to take the steps justified in accordance with section 20(4)?

Note also that the court was prepared to order the bank to make its premises accessible.

5.46   'Provision criterion or practice' (as in section 20(3) of the duty to make reasonable adjustments—known as a 'pcp') has a broad meaning and can include a 'one off' decision—see *British Airways plc v Starmer*[41]—though this has now been tempered by the Court of Appeal's decision in *Ishola v Transport for London*.[42]

5.47   The duty is triggered when the disadvantage is substantial—more than minor or trivial (section 212) compared with the disadvantage to non-disabled people; it does not matter

---

[38] *ibid.*
[39] *ibid,* para. 7.31.
[40] [2009] EWCA Civ 1213.
[41] [2005] IRLR 862.
[42] [2020] EWCA Civ 112.

that the pcp also affects non-disabled people, so long as it 'bites harder' on disabled people (*Griffiths v Secretary of State for Work and Pensions*[43]).

The duty to make adjustments is anticipatory—this is made clear by the reference to 'disabled persons' in Schedule 2, in the statutory Code of Practice produced by the Equality and Human Rights Commission on services ('the Code'—see 7.20 and 7.21)—and from case law—the needs of disabled people must be anticipated in advance (see *Roads v Central Trains Ltd*,[44] discussed at paragraphs 11 to 13, affirmed in subsequent case law e.g., *Finnigan v Chief Constable of Northumbria Police*[45]).   5.48

There does not have to be a guarantee that the adjustment would work, but a 'real prospect' that it will (see *First Group v Paulley*[46]).

(d) *The Duty to Make Reasonable Adjustments in the Exercise of Public Functions*

Schedule 2 also customizes the duty to make reasonable adjustments so that it is more appropriate to people exercising public functions. Recognizing the legal constraints on the performance of public functions, paragraph 2(8) provides that a person exercising such a function is not required to take any step that s/he has no power to take. In addition, clarification is given to the meaning of 'substantial disadvantage' in the context of public functions. By paragraph 2(5), the term includes: 5.49

(a) if a benefit is or may be conferred in the exercise of the function, being placed at a substantial disadvantage in relation to the conferment of the benefit; or

(b) if a person is or may be subjected to a detriment in the exercise of the function, suffering an unreasonably adverse experience when being subjected to the detriment.

This provision is illustrated by an example in the Statutory Code of Practice: 5.50

An ombudsman has a policy that all complaints must be made in writing. This policy places disabled people, for example those with learning disabilities or visual impairments, at a substantial disadvantage in making a complaint. The ombudsman amends the policy to permit disabled people and others who cannot use a written complaints procedure to make their complaint over the telephone. This is likely to be a reasonable step to take.[47]

(e) *Reasonable Adjustments to Premises*

The Act recognizes that service providers and those exercising public functions may be legally prevented (for example, by a mortgage or restrictive covenant) from altering the premises that they occupy without obtaining someone else's consent. Under Schedule 21, paragraph 2, it will always be reasonable for them to seek consent, but never reasonable for them to make alterations without first obtaining the consent that they need. Paragraph 3 makes special provisions for service providers and those exercising public functions who occupy premises under a tenancy. This allows the terms of the tenancy to be overridden in certain circumstances so that consent for reasonable adjustments can be requested. Schedule 21 is discussed in more detail in Chapter 6.   5.51

It should be noted that the Equality Act provides no exemptions for Listed Buildings.

---

[43] [2015] EWCA Civ 1265 at 58.
[44] [2004] EWCA Civ 1541.
[45] [2013] EWCA Civ 1191 at 31.
[46] [2017] UKSC 4.
[47] Services CoP, para. 11.29.

7. Services and Public Functions Exceptions

(a) *Overview*

5.52 The prohibition on discrimination in services and public functions is far from absolute; under the Act, there is a large number of exceptions permitting discrimination in this field, and practitioners cannot afford to treat section 29 as a self-contained provision. The majority of exceptions are legacies from previous discrimination legislation, although the Act presented an opportunity to make some important modifications.

5.53 It may be helpful to consider these exceptions as falling into three broad groups. The first group covers exceptions relating to constitutional or public policy matters, such as functions of government. The second group includes exceptions designed to allow service providers and those exercising public functions to provide, in certain circumstances, a more appropriate service to people who share a protected characteristic—such as single-sex services. In contrast, the policy intention behind the third group is to permit certain services or public functions to continue practices that make them more commercially effective or profitable, an example being the exception allowing insurers to offer differential premiums and benefits to people with certain protected characteristics.

5.54 Some exceptions are only permitted where they satisfy the two-stage 'objective justification' test; that is, they can be shown to be a proportionate means of achieving a legitimate aim. This test, which also applies to other provisions of the Act, is explained in Chapter 3.

5.55 Exceptions to the general prohibition of discrimination in services and public functions should be distinguished from positive action measures that are designed to alleviate disadvantage, meet particular needs, or reduce under-representation among people sharing a protected characteristic. Positive action is discussed in Chapter 11.

5.56 Certain general exceptions apply, not just to Part 3, but to all (or several other) Parts of the Act. These exceptions are covered as a group in subsection (b) below. Subsection (c) deals with the group of exceptions that apply only to services and public functions—that is, where discrimination, harassment, and victimization would otherwise be outlawed by section 29. These are the provisions set out in Schedule 3, given effect by section 31(10).[48]

(b) *General Exceptions*

5.57 (i) *Statutory provisions.* Schedule 22 (given effect by section 191) consolidates general exceptions that have their origin in statutory provisions, replacing the separate exceptions in previous legislation. Under paragraph 1(1), a service provider or person exercising a public function does not contravene Part 3 of the Act by doing something that s/he is obliged to do by some other law. This is expressed as 'a requirement of an enactment' and/or (except for age and sex) 'a relevant requirement or condition imposed by virtue of an enactment'. The exception applies to the protected characteristics of age, disability, religion or belief, sex, and sexual orientation.

5.58 It is immaterial whether the enactment was made before or after the passing of the Act; a reference to an enactment also includes a measure of the General Synod of the Church of England.[49] Schedule 22, paragraph 1(1) also refers to orders or regulations made under an enactment; these may be introduced by a Minister of the Crown, a member of the Scottish Executive, the National Assembly for Wales, a Welsh Minister, or the Counsel General to the Welsh Assembly Government.[50]

---

[48] Sch. 3 exceptions relating to age were introduced separately, by Order-making powers under s. 197.

[49] Sch. 22, para. 1(1)(3).

[50] Sch. 22, para. 1(1)(4).

(ii) *Nationality and residence.* A separate statutory authority exception relating to nation- 5.59 ality and residence is to be found in Schedule 23.[51] Where an obligation is imposed on a person by primary or secondary legislation, ministerial arrangements, or ministerial conditions, Schedule 23, paragraph 1 permits direct discrimination because of nationality, and indirect discrimination because of race based on a criterion relating to the place or length of residence.[52] It is immaterial whether or not the provision in question predates the passing of the Act. An example given in the Explanatory Notes is the provision allowing the NHS to impose charges for hospital treatment on some people who are not ordinarily resident in the UK.

(iii) *National security.* Section 192 sets out a general exception relating to national secu- 5.60 rity, similar to measures in previous discrimination legislation, while extending the exception to age and sexual orientation outside the workplace. It provides as follows:

A person does not contravene this Act only by doing, for the purpose of safeguarding national security, anything that is proportionate to do for that purpose.

Thus, an act done to protect national security is not automatically exempt from the Act; 5.61 the exception must be justified as a proportionate means of achieving the aim of national security. In contrast, Schedule 3, paragraph 5, which removes the security services from the scope of section 29, is subject to no such test. Neither does a proportionality test apply to the power given to the courts by section 117 to exclude claimants from proceedings if this is thought to be expedient in the interests of national security.

(iv) *Charities.* Section 193 provides a general exception for charities. 'Charity' is defined by 5.62 section 194(3) as having the meaning given by the Charities Act 2011 in relation to England and Wales; and, in relation to Scotland, a body entered in the Scottish Charity Register. Section 193(1) permits 'the provision of benefits for people who share a protected characteristic' if the person acts in pursuance of his/her charitable instrument. Arguably, there is a potential ambiguity in section 193(1) as to whether 'benefits' include any benefits to a group of persons, or whether they are limited to benefits that fall within the organization's charitable objectives.

The lawful limitation on provision of benefits is further qualified by section 193(2), and 5.63 must be:

(a) a proportionate means of achieving a legitimate aim, or

(b) for the purpose of preventing or compensating for a disadvantage linked to the protected characteristic.

In *Catholic Care (Diocese of Leeds) v Charity Commission for England and Wales*, it was 5.64 accepted that justification of less favourable treatment because of sexual orientation, using the test under section 193(2), had to be considered by reference to Article 14 of the European Convention on Human Rights. In this long-running case, Catholic Care, a Roman Catholic charity, had challenged the Charity Commission's refusal to allow an amendment to its objects so it could continue refusing adoption services to same-sex couples, in accordance with the doctrines of the Roman Catholic Church. The Upper Tribunal (UT) held that, if the charity could show a significant prospect of more children being placed into adoption by allowing it to discriminate against same-sex couples, then the interests of those children would provide an argument in favour of permitting the amendment to its objects. But the First Tier Tribunal

---

[51] Sch. 23 is given effect by s. 196.
[52] This paragraph replaces a similar exception in RRA 1976 s. 41(2).

had been entitled to find that this prospect had not been established on the facts and, accordingly, had been right to conclude that the charity had failed to show weighty and convincing reasons why it should be permitted to discriminate against same-sex couples.[53]

5.65   The charities exception does not allow colour to be used as the protected characteristic referred to in section 193(1).[54] Where an existing charity has a charitable instrument that defines beneficiaries by reference to colour, the instrument should be read as though the reference were omitted. Thus, under section 193(4), benefits should be provided to the class of people that results from ignoring the reference to colour. If, however, the original class of beneficiaries is defined *only* by reference to colour, then people in general should benefit from the charity.

5.66   By section 193(5), the Act permits established charities that make membership a condition of access to certain benefits, facilities, or services to require members or would-be members to state adherence to, or acceptance of, a particular religion or belief. However, section 193(6) limits this exception to charities that imposed this requirement before 18 May 2005 and have continued to impose it without interruption since that date. It should be noted that the exception for religious organizations under Schedule 23, paragraph 2 is cast somewhat differently, leaving religious charities with a choice as to how access to their services might be lawfully restricted (see section (v) below).

5.67   Section 193(7) has a further exception permitting a person undertaking an activity that promotes or supports a charity to restrict participation to people of one sex. This is a new provision, designed to protect fundraising events such as women-only fun runs and sponsored swims.

5.68   By section 193(8), a charity regulator does not contravene the Act only by exercising a function in relation to a charity in a manner it believes to be 'expedient in the interests of the charity, having regard to the charitable instrument'; a regulator is defined by section 194(5) as the Charity Commission for England and Wales and the Scottish Charity Regulator. This provision gives charity regulators a broad discretion to exercise their functions in the interests of the charity, without this being subject to any proportionality requirement—arguably running against the grain of EU equal treatment principles.

5.69   (v) *Religious organizations.*   Schedule 23 to the Act provides an exception for religious organizations and their ministers with respect to services and public functions, as well as premises and associations. The provision does not apply to organizations whose main purpose is commercial.[55] Under Schedule 23, paragraph 2(1), relevant organizations are those whose purpose is to practise or advance a religion or belief, or teach its principles; enable persons of a religion or belief to receive any benefit or engage in any activity within the framework of that religion or belief; or foster or maintain good relations between persons of different religions or beliefs.

5.70   The exception allows an organization fulfilling this definition, or a person acting on its behalf or under its auspices,[56] to discriminate because of religion or belief or sexual orientation only by restricting the following:

(a) membership of the organization;

(b) participation in activities undertaken by the organization or on its behalf or under its auspices;

---

[53] *Catholic Care (Diocese of Leeds) v Charity Commission for England and Wales* [2012] UKUT 395 (TCC).
[54] S. 194(2).
[55] Sch. 23, para. 2(2).
[56] Sch. 23, para. 2(4).

(c) the provision of goods, facilities, or services in the course of activities undertaken by the organization or on its behalf or under its auspices;

(d) the use or disposal of premises owned or controlled by the organization.[57]

Schedule 23, paragraph 2(5) applies a slightly different exception to a minister, defined as **5.71** a person who performs functions in connection with the particular religion or belief, or holds an office or appointment, or is accredited by the organization. It is not unlawful discrimination because of religion or belief or sexual orientation for a minister to restrict participation in activities carried on in the performance of his/her functions connected with the organization, or in the provision of goods, facilities, or services in the course of performing such activities.

Importantly, both the 'organization' exception and the 'minister' exception are subject to **5.72** further qualification:

- By Schedule 23, paragraph 2(6), a restriction relating to religion or belief must only be imposed because of the purpose of the organization, or to avoid causing offence, on grounds of the religion or belief in question, to people of that religion or belief.

- By Schedule 23, paragraph 2(7), a restriction relating to sexual orientation must only be imposed because it is necessary to comply with the doctrine of the organization, or to avoid conflict with strongly held convictions of the followers of the religion or belief. Strongly held convictions are those held by a significant number of the followers of the religion or belief.[58]

The exception does not apply to sexual orientation discrimination where an organization **5.73** is under a contract with a public authority to provide services or perform a public function on behalf of that authority.[59] An example in the Statutory Code of Practice illustrates this:

A local authority contracts out to a religious organisation the running of a parent and toddler group. The project includes building mutual support among the parents, involving open discussion at fortnightly meetings. A few parents say that they feel uncomfortable discussing personal matters with gay and lesbian parents. The organisation explains that as the council has contracted with them to provide this service they are not permitted to discriminate because of a parent's sexual orientation.[60]

Paragraphs 9A to 9D have now been inserted into Schedule 23, partly in consequence **5.74** of the devolution complexities arising from the same-sex marriage legislation.[61] Paragraph 9A confirms that an organization does not discriminate by refusing to allow premises that it owns or controls to be used to solemnize a Scottish marriage between two people of the same sex, or to register a Scottish civil partnership. Paragraph 9B confirms that a similar exception applies to a person or group of persons who control premises. Paragraph 9C states that an organization does not discriminate by permitting its approved celebrant(s) to refuse to solemnize a same-sex marriage or civil partnership; here, a cross-reference is made to the separate exception for approved celebrants under paragraph 25B, Schedule 3, and the definition of 'approved celebrant' used in that paragraph is also the one used here (see paragraph 9D).

---

[57] Sch. 23, para. 2(3).

[58] Sch. 23, para. 2(9).

[59] Sch. 23, para. 2(10).

[60] Services CoP, para. 13.30.

[61] The new paragraphs were added by the Marriage and Civil Partnership (Scotland) Act 2014 and Civil Partnership 2004 (Consequential Provisions and Modifications) Order 2014/3229.

5.75 (vi) *Communal accommodation.*   Schedule 23, paragraph 3 covers communal accommodation. Paragraph 3(5) and (6) defines this as residential accommodation including dormitories or other shared sleeping accommodation; note that there must be 'reasons of privacy' for the accommodation to be used only by persons of one sex. The effect of paragraph 3 is to create a general exception permitting discrimination because of sex or gender reassignment in the admission to such accommodation or a benefit, facility, or service[62] linked to it,[63] as long as the accommodation is managed as fairly as possible for both men and women.[64] The accommodation provider must consider whether it would be reasonable to expect the accommodation to be altered or extended, and the frequency of demand by persons of one sex as compared to the other sex.[65]

5.76 Reflecting other sections of the Act that require discrimination because of gender reassignment to be objectively justified, when refusing a transsexual person admission to communal accommodation the provider must consider whether this is a proportionate means of achieving a legitimate aim.[66]

5.77 (vii) *Sport.*   The Act recognizes that many competitive activities are organized separately for men and women. Section 195(1) permits this approach for 'gender-affected activity'. A similar exception permits competition organizers to restrict the participation of a transsexual person in gender-affected activity, but only if this is necessary to ensure fair competition or the safety of other competitors.[67]

5.78 Gender-affected activity is defined by section 195(3) as:

.... a sport, game, or other activity of a competitive nature in circumstances in which the physical strength, stamina or physique of average persons of one sex would put them at a disadvantage compared to average persons of the other sex as competitors in events involving the activity.

5.79 However, for child competitors, it will be appropriate to take account of their age and stage of development (section 195(4)).

5.80 A second exception permits organizers to restrict participation in a competitive activity because of nationality, place of birth, or length of residence in a particular place, allowing the selection of participants to represent a country, area, or locality (or a related association).[68] It also applies to selection based on eligibility rules for a particular competition.[69]

5.81 A third exception, set out in section 195(7), applies to anything that would otherwise be age discrimination that is done in relation to 'age-banded' competitive activities. In relation to a person's participation as a competitor, the action taken by the organizer must be necessary to secure fair competition or the safety of competitors; to comply with the rules of a national or international competition; or to increase participation in the activity.

5.82 Section 195(8) defines 'age-banded activity' as a sport, game, or other activity of a competitive nature where physical or mental strength, agility, stamina, physique, mobility, maturity, or manual dexterity of average persons in a particular age group would put them at a disadvantage compared to competitors in another age group taking part in events involving

---

[62] Sch. 23, para. 3(1).
[63] See Sch. 23, para. 3(7) for definition of 'linked to communal accommodation'.
[64] Sch. 23, para. 3(2).
[65] Sch. 23, para. 3(3).
[66] Sch. 23, para. 3(4).
[67] S. 195(2).
[68] S. 195(6)(a).
[69] S. 195(6)(b).

this activity. The Explanatory Note to this section[70] indicates that intellectual activities such as bridge and chess would also be included within the definition. The Technical Guidance on age discrimination in services, public functions, and associations provides the example of a running club that organizes separate races for runners over 50.[71]

(c) Schedule 3 Exceptions

(i) *Constitutional matters.* Part 1 of Schedule 3 deals with constitutional matters, including the armed forces and security services. Section 29 does not apply to functions of Parliament or those exercisable in connection with Parliamentary proceedings;[72] or the preparing, making, or considering of legislation—including legislation using devolved powers of the Scottish Parliament or National Assembly for Wales.[73] This includes specified forms of secondary legislation.[74]   **5.83**

Likewise, there is an exception for judicial functions, including a decision not to commence or continue criminal proceedings or activities relating to such a decision.[75] A judicial function includes functions exercised by a person other than a court or tribunal.[76]   **5.84**

More controversially, Schedule 3, paragraph 4 replicates and extends the exception in the DDA and the SDA for public functions exercised to ensure the 'combat effectiveness' of the armed forces. For this purpose, protection under section 29 is disapplied for age discrimination, disability discrimination, gender reassignment discrimination, and sex discrimination.[77] During the passage of the Bill through Parliament, it was argued strongly by disabled people's organizations that this exception contravened the United Nations Convention on the Rights of Persons with Disabilities, and that at the very least it should have been made subject to an objective justification test. It should be noted that in ratifying the Convention, the UK entered a reservation preserving this exception.   **5.85**

By Schedule 3, paragraph 5, there is a blanket exception removing from the scope of section 29 the Security Service, the Secret Intelligence Service, the Government Communications Headquarters (GCHQ), and any part of the armed forces that is required by the government to assist GCHQ. This exception applies to both services and public functions.   **5.86**

(ii) *Public functions relating to education.* Several exceptions relating to the public functions of local education authorities are set out in Part 2 of Schedule 3. These include provisions allowing authorities to establish faith schools and single-sex schools, and an exception for age discrimination mirroring that which applies to schools under Part 6 of the Act.   **5.87**

By Schedule 3, paragraph 6, in relation to age or religion or belief-related discrimination, section 29 does not apply to local authorities in England and Wales when they are exercising public functions under section 14 of the Education Act 1996, or a function under section 13 of that Act insofar as that relates to a function under section 14. An important effect of this exception is to prevent a local authority being forced to provide schools for pupils of different faiths or no faith, or for particular age groups, in a particular catchment area.   **5.88**

---

[70] See Equality Act 2010 (Age Exceptions) Order 2012, SI 2012/2466, Explanatory Note.
[71] Para. 12.39.
[72] Sch. 3, para. 1.
[73] Sch. 3, para. 2.
[74] Sch. 3, para. 2(3) and para. 3(2)–(5).
[75] Sch. 3, para. 3(1).
[76] Sch. 3, para. 3(2). In relation to exclusion of judicial functions, see *JT v First-tier tribunal & Anor (Criminal Injuries Compensation: reduction and withholding of awards)* [2015] UKUT 478.
[77] Sch. 3, para. 4(2).

5.89   It should be noted that section 14 of the Education Act 1996 requires a local education authority to secure the provision of sufficient schools to provide primary and secondary education for its area, ensuring that schools are both sufficient in number and character. Section 13 of the Education Act 1996 gives a local education authority general responsibility for contributing towards the spiritual, moral, mental, and physical development of the community by securing efficient primary, secondary, and further education to meet the needs of the population of its area. The comparable exception for Scotland is set out in Schedule 3, paragraph 7 to the Equality Act, which cites sections 1, 17, and 50(1) of the Education (Scotland) Act 1980; section 2 of the Standards in Scotland's Schools Act 2000; and sections 4 and 5 of the Education (Additional Support for Learning) (Scotland) Act 2004.

5.90   The setting-up of single-sex schools is protected by Schedule 3, paragraph 8, which disapplies section 29 in relation to sex discrimination to functions connected to the establishment of schools. The exception applies to a local authority (in England and Wales) or to an education authority. However, authorities remain bound by their duties under section 14 of the Education Act 1996 (or section 17 of the Education (Scotland) Act 1980) to provide sufficient school places for both girls and boys.[78] These provisions were considered in the case of *R v Birmingham City Council ex p Equal Opportunities Commission*,[79] where the House of Lords held that the council's provision of more single-sex places for boys than girls amounted to direct discrimination; 'but for' her sex, the relevant girl would have received the same treatment as a boy.

5.91   Schedule 3, paragraph 9 makes an exception to the prohibition on age discrimination for several functions relating to schools. These are: the setting of a school curriculum; admission to a school; transport to or from a school; and the establishment, alteration, or closure of a school. This provision mirrors the exception for schools in Part 6 of the Act in relation to age discrimination, ensuring that age-based policies and practices do not become unlawful when emanating from the functions of education authorities.

5.92   By paragraph 10, when exercising relevant education functions a local authority or education authority's duty to make reasonable adjustments does not include removing or altering any physical features.

5.93   There is no protection from religious or belief-related discrimination where public authorities exercise public functions in relation to faith or non-faith schools. Schedule 3, paragraph 11 sets out a list of areas to which section 29 does not apply for the protected characteristic of religion or belief:

- the curriculum of a school;
- admission to a school with a religious ethos;
- acts of worship (or other religious observance) organized by or on behalf of a school—whether or not as part of the curriculum;
- the responsible (i.e. governing) body of a school with a religious ethos;
- transport to or from school;
- the establishment, alteration, or closure of schools.

5.94   This exception replicates provisions under the Equality Act 2006. As with the age exception under Schedule 3, paragraph 9, it is designed to ensure that decisions covered by a Part 6

---

[78] Sch. 3, para. 8(2).
[79] [1989] IRLR 173, HL.

exception do not become unlawful when carried out by a public authority. Examples of relevant decisions could include a decision to establish, alter, or close a faith school; or to select a person of a particular religion or belief to serve as a school governor.[80]

(iii) *Health and care.* Part 3 of Schedule 3 sets out several exceptions to section 29 that   5.95
are related to health and care:

- A person operating a blood service may reasonably refuse to accept a blood donation because of an assessment of risk to the public or to the blood donor 'based on clinical, epidemiological or other data obtained from a source on which it is reasonable to rely'.[81] A blood service is defined as a service for the collection and distribution of human blood (and blood components) for the purposes of medical services.[82] This exception might be used to decline a blood donation from someone who had been sexually active in a country where there is evidence of a high prevalence of HIV infection, for example.[83]

- A person does not contravene section 29 only by participating in arrangements to take someone else into their own home to care for them as a member of their own family, whether this is for reward or not.[84]

- To remove or reduce a health or safety risk to a pregnant woman, a service provider may refuse to provide a service to her or treat her differently.[85] Refusing to provide a service is lawful if the service provider reasonably believes that to do otherwise would create a risk to the woman's health or safety because of her pregnancy. However, the service provider must also refuse to provide the service to people with other physical conditions for health or safety reasons.[86] Likewise, if the service provider provides (or offers to provide) a service to a pregnant woman on certain conditions, with the aim of removing or reducing a health or safety risk, the different treatment is lawful if people with other physical conditions would be treated the same way.[87]

The exception relating to care in the home would include foster parenting and means, for   5.96
example, that a Muslim family could agree to foster only Muslim children. However, discriminatory treatment by a public authority is not caught by this exception. It was argued in *R (Johns) v Derby City Council* that this could give rise to a tension between the rights of foster parents and the responsibilities of the local authority for making fostering arrangements. However, the point was not explored further as the case was decided on other grounds.[88] The case of *Mander (& Anor) v Royal Borough of Windsor & Maidenhead*[89] covered discrimination in the adoption process. No exception was claimed.

(iv) *Immigration—disability.* Part 4 of Schedule 3 groups together four exceptions relat-   5.97
ing to immigration. Paragraph 16 sets out an exception relating to the protected characteristic of disability. This removes from the scope of section 29 any decision—or action carried

---

[80] See EN 703.
[81] Sch. 3, para. 13(1)(a).
[82] Sch. 3, para. 13(2).
[83] EN 707.
[84] Sch. 3, para. 15.
[85] Sch. 3, para. 14.
[86] Sch. 3, para. 14(1).
[87] Sch. 3, para. 14(2).
[88] *R (Johns) v Derby City Council* [2011] EWHC 375 (Admin).
[89] [2019] EWFC B64.

out for the purposes of a decision—to refuse entry clearance, or refuse, cancel, or vary (or refuse to vary) leave to enter or remain in the UK.[90] The exception only applies if the decision is 'necessary for the public good'[91]—but the scope of the provision is unclear; for example, whether it could extend to cost considerations alone. The government has adopted a similar reservation to the UN Convention on the Rights of Persons with Disabilities, and was criticized for this approach by the Joint Committee on Human Rights.[92]

5.98   It should be noted that this exception applies irrespective of whether the decision is taken in accordance with, or outside, the immigration rules. It also applies to a decision taken, or guidance given, by the Secretary of State in connection with an immigration decision—or any decision that relies on such guidance.[93]

5.99   (v) *Immigration—nationality and ethnic or national origin.*   A second immigration exception relates to the protected characteristic of race. Schedule 3, paragraph 17 preserves the previous exception under RRA 1976, permitting discrimination because of nationality or ethnic or national origin in relation to immigration decisions carried out by a 'relevant person'. A relevant person is a Minister of the Crown, or anyone acting under his/her authority or acting in accordance with immigration legislation or immigration rules.

5.100   Under Schedule 3, paragraph 17(5) relevant enactments are the Immigration Acts; the Special Immigration Appeals Commission Act 1997; a provision under section 2(2) of the European Communities Act 1972 relating to immigration or asylum; and a provision of Community law relating to immigration or asylum. Certain provisions relating to powers of arrest, entry, and search are excluded (Schedule 3, paragraph 17(6)).

5.101   (vi) *Immigration—age.*   A third immigration exception relates to age. Paragraph 15A of Schedule 3 provides an exception to the ban on age discrimination for certain immigration functions; this mirrors the exception relating to nationality and ethnic origins under paragraph 17. It applies to anything done by a Minister of the Crown acting personally or by a person acting under a relevant authorization in accordance with immigration legislation or the immigration rules. Paragraph 15A(5) sets out the relevant enactments, which are identical to those listed in paragraph 17(5) in relation to nationality and ethnic or national origins (see paragraph 5.101 above).

5.102   (vii) *Immigration—religion or belief.*   A fourth exception relates to religion or belief. By paragraph 18, the prohibition on discrimination because of religion or belief in the provision of services and the exercise of public functions does not apply to certain immigration decisions taken in the public interest. Relevant decisions are those taken in accordance with the immigration rules to refuse, or cancel entry clearance or leave to remain in the UK, on the grounds that exclusion is 'conducive to the public good'; or to vary, or refuse to vary, leave to remain in the UK on the grounds that it is 'undesirable to permit the person to remain' in the UK.[94] The Joint Committee on Human Rights expressed doubt about the need for this exception, given the wide scope of other powers to exclude persons whose presence in the UK would not be conducive to the public good.[95]

---

[90] Sch. 3, para. 16(1)–(3).
[91] Sch. 3, para. 16(3).
[92] HRJC, 26th Report 2008–09; *Legislative Scrutiny: the Equality Bill.*
[93] Sch. 3, para. 16(4).
[94] Sch. 3, para. 18(2) and (3).
[95] HRJC, 26th Report 2008–09; *Legislative Scrutiny: the Equality Bill.*

There is a special exception used to exclude from the UK people who hold an office such as **5.103** Minister, or who provide a service connected to a religion or belief. Thus, by paragraph 18(4)–(6), it is not unlawful discrimination because of religion or belief to take a decision in connection with an application for entry clearance or leave to enter or remain in the UK, whether or not taken in accordance with immigration rules, where the grounds of the decision are that:

• the person in question holds an office, or provides a service, connected to a religion or belief;

• the religion or belief is not to be treated in the same way as other religions or beliefs; or

• the exclusion of the person who holds an office is conducive to the public good.

This exception applies not only to individual decisions taken under or outside the **5.104** Immigration Rules, but also to relevant guidance from the Secretary of State, or a decision taken in accordance with such guidance.[96]

(viii) *Exceptions for insurance and other financial services.* Schedule 3, Part 5 contains **5.105** a number of exceptions relating to insurance and other financial services, designed to accommodate current business practices. Insurance business is defined by reference to the Financial Services and Markets Act 2000.[97]

Paragraph 20 clarifies that section 29 does not apply to insurance or a related financial **5.106** service, or to a service connected to a personal pension scheme, if this is arranged by an employer on behalf of the service provider and restricted to employees and their dependants. Thus, were a discrimination claim to arise in connection with one of these so-called 'group schemes', it would need to be brought under Part 5 of the Act relating to work.[98]

Paragraph 20A(1) provides an exception for financial services in relation to direct and **5.107** indirect age discrimination. The exception does not, however, extend to harassment and victimization, which are always unlawful. By paragraph 20A(3), 'financial services' are defined as including a service of a banking, credit, insurance, personal pension, investment, or payment nature. The Government Equalities Office 'quick start' guidance for financial services on the age discrimination ban[99] provides a lengthy, although non-exhaustive, list of products and services that benefit from the financial services exception.

The exception is cast generously and applies to all actions and omissions by financial **5.108** services providers that relate to age—whether defined by age thresholds or a range of ages. However, by paragraph 20A(2), there is a qualification to the exception. The qualification applies when a provider in the financial services sector undertakes a risk assessment based on the customer's age for the purpose of providing a financial service; this is likely to happen when, for example, an insurance company is assessing the level of premium for travel or motor insurance. In this situation, the provider can only rely on the exception in paragraph 20A(1) if the assessment of risk is based on relevant information from a source on which it is reasonable to rely.

While the Act does not elaborate further on what would be 'a source on which it is reasonable **5.109** to rely', the Government Equalities Office guidance suggests that this would include 'any public

---

[96] Sch. 3, para. 18(7).
[97] Sch. 3, paras 21(2) and 23(6).
[98] See EN 720.
[99] Government Equalities Office, September 2012. The Equality Act and age discrimination: what do I need to know? A quick start for financial services.

or private empirical, actuarial, statistical, qualitative research or other material or data such as for-ward looking projections, age related assumptions in changes in life expectancy and health and evidence of costs' and that it can be 'from UK or international sources, based on industry-wide material or data, or firm-specific material or data, or the experience of another firm'. One may also assume that the information should also be current, representative, and credible.

5.110   The Technical Guidance on age discrimination in services, public functions, and associa-tions gives the following example of the operation of the financial services exception:

A 19-year old man in stable, full-time employment applies to a finance company for a short-term car loan. Believing that people under 21 are less reliable, the company only offers him a loan at a significantly higher rate of interest than would be charged to older motorists. This conclusion is not based on an assessment of risk using data or other relevant information relating to the man's age. In these circumstances, charging the higher rate of interest is unlikely to come within the financial services exception and would therefore be unlawful.

5.111   The breadth of the financial services exception for age discrimination allows the industry to lawfully decline insurance cover, particularly to older/younger drivers and older travellers, or to impose higher premiums. When service users are refused cover, a voluntary agree-ment between the Government, the Association of British Insurers, and the British Insurance Brokers' Association[100] obliges the insurance company to refer them to another provider that can assist, or to a signposting service that can identify suitable providers. As well as improv-ing access to insurance, the agreement is designed to improve transparency within this sector.

5.112   Paragraph 21 of Schedule 3 sets out an insurance exception relating to disability. It permits discrimination in insurance business because of disability provided this is done by reference to information that is both relevant to the risk and from a source on which it is reasonable to rely, and provided also that the different treatment is reasonable.[101] It will be noted that this addi-tional 'reasonableness' criterion does not feature in the exception for financial services relating to age. Relevant information is likely to include actuarial or statistical data or a medical report. As noted by the Statutory Code of Practice, insurers cannot rely on untested assumptions, stereotypes, or generalizations about disabled people,[102] nor can they have a general policy of refusing to insure people with particular disabilities or adopt a policy or practice of only offering insurance to disabled people on additional or adverse terms and conditions.[103]

5.113   An insurance exception relating to the protected characteristics of sex, gender reassign-ment, pregnancy, and maternity previously appeared as paragraph 22 of Schedule 3. It per-mitted proportionate differences in insurance premiums and benefits provided they were based on relevant and accurate actuarial and statistical data, published and regularly updated in accordance with guidance issued by the Treasury. However, other than for contracts con-cluded before 21 December 2012, the exception has now been repealed.[104]

5.114   The repeal was a necessary response to the 2011 decision of the Court of Justice of the European Union (CJEU) in the *Test-Achats* case.[105] Here, the CJEU considered the lawfulness

---

[100] HM Government/ABI/BIBA signposting agreement for older customers in respect of motor and travel insurances: <https://d10ou7l0uhgg4f.cloudfront.net/Uploads/449signpostingagreement.pdf>.

[101] Sch. 3, para. 21(1).

[102] Services CoP, para. 13.78.

[103] *ibid*, para. 13.79.

[104] Para. 1, The Equality Act 2010 (Amendment) Regulations 2012, SI 2012/2992.

[105] *Association Belge des Consommateurs Test-Achats ASBL and Others v Council*, Case C-236/09 of 1 March 2011.

of the derogation in the EU Gender Directive on goods and services (2004/113/EC) that allowed Member States to permit exemptions from the rule of unisex insurance premiums and benefits, provided that the relevant actuarial and statistical data was reliable, regularly updated, and available to the public. Although the derogation was due to be reviewed after five years (i.e., by 21 December 2012), the directive was silent as to its maximum duration. This created a risk that the derogation might be allowed to continue indefinitely, contrary to the objective of equal treatment between men and women under Article 8 TFEU. The CJEU therefore ruled that the derogation should be considered invalid with effect from 21 December 2012.

As noted above, the amending Regulations contain a transitional provision that allows the insurance exception for sex, gender reassignment, and pregnancy and maternity to continue to apply to a contract concluded before 21 December 2012.[106] They also require the Treasury to conduct five-yearly reviews of the operation and effect of the Regulations and to decide whether they should be revoked, amended, or remain unchanged.[107]   **5.115**

(ix) *Marriage and civil partnership.*   Paragraph 24 in Part 6 of Schedule 3 preserves an exception provided by the Gender Recognition Act 2004, permitting (but not requiring) a member of the clergy of the Church of England, Church of Wales, or other religions to decline to conduct the marriage of a person who is of an acquired gender or to refuse consent for such a marriage to take place in registered religious premises. The provision also applies in England and Wales to people who may solemnize marriages according to a particular form, rite, or ceremony.[108] Under paragraph 25, a similar exception applies to 'approved celebrants'[109] for marriages and civil partnerships in Scotland.[110]   **5.116**

Part 6A of Schedule 3, relating to the marriage of same-sex couples in England and Wales, was inserted by the Marriage (Same Sex Couples) Act 2013.[111] Here, paragraph 25A provides an exception to protect religious organizations and their officials who do not wish to conduct, or otherwise participate in, a marriage between two people of the same sex—or who refuse consent for the marriage to take place.   **5.117**

Part 6B contains similar provisions relating to Scotland.[112] By paragraph 25B, an approved celebrant does not discriminate by refusing to solemnize a Scottish marriage between two persons of the same sex,[113] or by refusing to register a Scottish civil partnership because it is between two persons of the same sex.[114] Under the same paragraph, there is also an exception for a person refusing to participate in a religious or belief ceremony that is part of—or   **5.118**

---

[106] Para. 3.

[107] Para. 4.

[108] Sch. 3, para. 24.

[109] In relation to marriage, 'approved celebrant' is defined by Sch. 3, para. 25(2) as having the meaning conferred by s. 8(2)(a) of the Marriage (Scotland) Act 1977 as a person who may solemnize a marriage. In relation to civil partnerships, it is defined in para. 25(4) as having the meaning given in s. 94A(4)(a) of the Civil Partnership Act 2004.

[110] As originally enacted para. 25 only related to marriages. It was amended to include Scottish civil partnerships by the Marriage and Civil Partnership (Scotland) Act 2014 and Civil Partnership Act 2004 (Consequential Provisions and Modifications) Order 2014/3229. At the same time, it was moved under a new heading, Schedule 3: 'Part 6ZA: Marriage and Civil Partnership: Scotland'.

[111] S. 2(6) Marriage (Same Sex Couples) Act 2013, brought into force by SI 2014/93.

[112] Inserted by Marriage and Civil Partnership (Scotland) Act 2014 and Civil Partnership Act 2004 (Consequential Provisions and Modifications) Order 2014/3229.

[113] Sch. 3, para. 25B(1).

[114] Sch. 3, para. 25B(2).

connected with—a Scottish marriage or civil partnership between two people of the same sex.[115] Paragraph 25C contains a separate exception for a chaplain who refuses to solemnize a Scottish forces marriage between two people of the same sex.

5.119   Section 202(1) and (2) amends the Civil Partnership Act 2004 to omit the provisions prohibiting use of religious premises for the registration of civil partnerships. For the avoidance of doubt, section 202(4) inserts a new provision into the 2004 Act confirming that there is no obligation on religious organizations to host civil partnerships if they do not wish to do so.

5.120   By a power inserted into the 2004 Act by section 202(3), regulations have been introduced to allow local authorities to approve religious premises for the formalization of civil partnerships.[116] While the detail of these regulations is beyond the scope of this chapter, it should be noted that they require approval to be given by the local authority for any premises to host the registration of civil partnerships. There must be a period of public consultation before approval can be given. Each individual application must demonstrate that it is being made with the consent of the faith group concerned, or clearly state that no consent is required.

5.121   Requirements for the grant of approval of religious premises include that the premises must be regularly available to the public for the formation of civil partnerships. However, this requirement is subject to the exception set out in paragraph 2 of Schedule 23, allowing religious organizations to discriminate because of religion or belief or sexual orientation in certain circumstances.[117]

5.122   The regulations also set out conditions that a local authority must attach to the approval of religious premises for civil partnerships. In contrast to the formalization of civil partnerships in secular premises—which must not be religious in nature—for religious premises this prohibition only applies during the proceedings themselves, but not to their introduction or conclusion.[118]

5.123   (x) *Separate services for the sexes.*   Part 7 of Schedule 3 sets out several exceptions that allow separate, single, or concessionary services to be provided only to persons who share a particular protected characteristic. Paragraph 26 under Part 7 covers services provided separately for persons of each sex or services provided only to persons of one sex. Separate services, including services provided by a person exercising a public function,[119] do not amount to unlawful sex discrimination provided a joint service for both sexes would be less effective and the limited provision would be a proportionate means of achieving a legitimate aim.[120] Providing separate services that are distinct from each other is also permitted, provided—once again—a joint service would be less effective and the limited provision is a proportionate means of achieving a legitimate aim. Additionally, given the extent to which the service is required by one sex, it must not be reasonably practicable to provide the service otherwise than as a separate and different service.[121]

---

[115] Sch. 3, para. 25B(3)(4).

[116] The Marriages and Civil Partnerships (Approved Premises) (Amendment) Regulations 2011, SI 2011/2661 ('the 2011 Regulations'), amending the Marriages and Civil Partnerships (Approved Premises Regulations) 2005, SI 2005/3168 ('the 2005 Regulations').

[117] Schedule 1A to the 2005 Regulations, inserted by reg. 2(16) of (and Sch. 2 to) the 2011 Regulations. See paras 5.62–5.66 above.

[118] Sch. 2A to the 2005 Regulations, inserted by reg. 2(18) of (and Sch. 3 to) the 2011 Regulations.

[119] Sch. 3, para. 26(3).

[120] Sch. 3, para. 26(1).

[121] Sch. 3, para. 26(2).

Likewise, the Act provides an exception permitting single-sex services, including services provided by a person exercising public functions.[122] A single-sex service does not amount to sex discrimination provided it is both a proportionate means of achieving a legitimate aim and one of the following conditions is fulfilled:[123]

- only people of that sex need the service;

- there is a joint service for people of both sexes, but joint provision alone would not be sufficiently effective;

- a joint service would be less effective, but the level of need for the service does not make it reasonably practicable to provide separate services;

- the service is provided at a hospital or another establishment for people needing special care, supervision, or attention;

- the service is likely to be used by more than one person at a time, in circumstances where someone might object to the presence of a person of the opposite sex;

- there is likely to be physical contact between a service user and someone of the opposite sex, and the user might reasonably object to this.

Examples of single-sex services under these provisions could include separate male and female changing rooms or single-sex wards in hospitals.

(xi) *Gender reassignment.* Paragraph 28 contains an exception to the general prohibition on gender reassignment discrimination, in relation to the provision of separate services for people of each sex, or separate services for each sex that are provided differently; or providing a service only to people of one sex. However, the conduct in question must be objectively justified as a proportionate means of achieving a legitimate aim.[124] An example of a lawful use of this exception given in the Explanatory Notes to the Act is that of a group counselling service for female victims of sexual assault; the organizers could exclude transsexual people if they judge that clients would be unlikely to attend the session if a male-to-female transsexual was also there.[125]

(xii) *Services relating to religion.* Part 7 of Schedule 3 also deals with exceptions for services relating to religion. Paragraph 29 provides that it is not unlawful sex discrimination for a minister to provide a service for the purposes of an organized religion to people of one sex, or separate services for each sex, if the limited provision is necessary to comply with the doctrines of the religion, or is necessary to avoid conflict with the strongly held religious convictions of a significant number of the religion's followers. The definition of 'minister' (Schedule 3, paragraph 29(2)) resembles the definition under Schedule 23, paragraph 2(8); the minister must be recognized by a 'relevant organisation', a term defined by Schedule 3, paragraph 29(3). Commercial organizations do not fall within this exception.

Services covered by this exception must be provided at a place that is occupied or used for the purposes of an organized religion—either permanently or for the time being.[126] This exception does not cover acts of worship, as these are not 'services' under the Act. Rather,

5.124

5.125

5.126

5.127

---

[122] Sch. 3, para. 27.
[123] Sch. 3, para. 27(2)–(7).
[124] Sch. 3, para. 28.
[125] EN 749.
[126] Sch. 3, para. 29(1).

it is designed to deal with ancillary issues such as separate seating arrangements in places of worship.[127]

5.128   (xiii) *Services restricted to persons sharing a protected characteristic.*   Paragraph 30 in Part 7 of Schedule 3 covers services generally provided only for persons who share a protected characteristic, which may be permitted by the Act. It is lawful for a service provider who normally provides a service in a particular way to insist on continuing to do so. The service may also be refused to someone who does not share the protected characteristic in question, if the service provider 'reasonably thinks it is impracticable' to provide the services to that person.

5.129   This exception was designed to replicate provisions in the SDA and the Equality Act 2006, extending it to all protected characteristics. Arguably, the policy intention was to permit traditional providers of single characteristic services to continue in operation, rather than extending the exception to new services. The examples used in the Explanatory Notes to the Act[128] are those of an African-Caribbean hairdresser and a Halal butcher.

5.130   An age-specific exception for concessionary services has been inserted as paragraph 30A in Part 7 of Schedule 3. By this exception, it will not be direct or indirect age discrimination for a service provider (or a person exercising a public function) to give a concession to people in a particular age group. Paragraph 30A(2) defines a concession as a benefit, right, or privilege having the effect of making the manner in which the service is provided, or the terms on which it is provided, more favourable than for other members of the public who are not part of the same age group.

5.131   'Benefit', 'right', and 'privilege' are not further defined in the legislation. 'Terms' can be assumed to have the same meaning as in section 29(2), discussed in paragraph 5.23 above. In the absence of any case law, there appears to be no restriction on the form that concessions can take, or the services to which they can be applied. The Government Equalities Office's overview guidance on the age discrimination ban for service providers and customers[129] suggests concessions would include any sort of discount, special arrangement, special offer, etc. open only to people of a particular age group. The guidance gives the examples of retailers offering 10 per cent reductions for over 65s; free or cheaper access for pensioners or younger people to local leisure facilities; and discounted admission for pensioners in museums and theatres.

5.132   Practitioners will note that this exception does not allow discriminatory *refusal* of a service, nor does it apply to harassment or victimization by the service provider. The Technical Guidance on age discrimination in services, public functions, and associations notes that if, because of a concession, a service provider gives such favourable treatment to one age group that a different age group is effectively excluded from receiving this service, should this amount to harassment then it would not be covered by the exception for concessions.[130]

5.133   A further age-specific exception in paragraph 30B of Schedule 3 permits package holidays limited to a particular age group. For the purposes of this exception, a 'relevant holiday service' is defined in paragraph 30B(2) as a holiday service where:

- a service user pays a single price for at least two of the following three elements: travel (even if there is an option for the service user to make separate travel arrangements[131]);

---

[127]   EN 730.

[128]   EN 745.

[129]   Government Equalities Office, 2012. The Equality Act 2010: banning age discrimination in services— an overview for service providers and customers. <https://www.gov.uk/government/uploads/system/uploads/attachment_data/file/85031/age-discrimination-ban.pdf>.

[130]   Para. 10.12.

[131]   Sch. 3, para. 30(B)(4).

accommodation; and/or access to activities or services which form a significant part of the holiday (other than those that are ancillary to travel or accommodation);

- the holiday is for a period of more than 24 hours or includes overnight accommodation;
- the holiday is provided only to people of a certain age group;
- an 'essential feature' of the holiday is bringing together people of that age group in order to facilitate their enjoyment of facilities or services designed with particular regard to that age group.

For the service provider to take advantage of this exception, they must provide a written statement to the service user before the start of the holiday confirming that the holiday service is only being provided to people of that particular age group.[132] **5.134**

The wording of the legislation indicates that a holiday provider would not be able to rely on the exception if they opted to include some older, or younger customers in the—supposedly age restricted—holiday group. Nor does it appear that the exception would apply if the holiday facilities and services were generic in nature, rather than being facilities designed for the target age group. The Technical Guidance on age discrimination in services, public functions, and associations gives the example of a package holiday resort opened exclusively for people over 60, where the facilities on offer have not been tailored for this age group and are in fact identical to facilities in the operator's other resorts. In these circumstances, the operator could not rely on the exception for holiday services.[133] **5.135**

Services that are age restricted by legislation, such as alcohol and cigarettes, are covered by an exception in paragraph 30(C) of Schedule 3. It is not age discrimination for a service provider (or their employee) to refuse to provide a service to a person who appears to be under the age specified in an 'age warning' statement that is displayed on the premises where the age-restricted service is provided, and the person cannot provide satisfactory identification on request.[134] The displayed statement must explain that the service in question will not be provided to anyone who appears to be under the specified age, unless they can provide satisfactory identification when asked to do so.[135] It should be noted that service providers may lawfully adopt an age verification policy that uses an age above that of the statutory minimum, provided this age is made clear in the warning statement; for example, for the sale of alcoholic drinks, many pubs have a policy of asking for age identification from any customer who appears to be younger than 25. **5.136**

Satisfactory identification for this exception is defined in paragraph 30C(4)(b) as meaning a valid document with a photograph of the person, confirming that they have reached the statutory age relating to the service in question. However, if the age-restricted service relates to licensed premises, then a document is only satisfactory if it includes the service user's photograph, date of birth, and a holographic mark, in compliance with section 19A of the Licensing Act 2004.[136] **5.137**

Owners of residential mobile homes located on 'protected sites' (as defined by the Mobile Homes Act 1983) also benefit from an exception to the ban on age discrimination, **5.138**

---

[132] Sch. 3, para. 30(B)(3).
[133] Para. 12.10.
[134] Sch. 3, para. 30C(3).
[135] Sch. 3, para. 30C(2).
[136] Sch. 3, para. 30C(4)(b).

allowing them to impose an age restriction on site occupants: Schedule 3, Part 7, paragraph 30D. This exception applies to either a 'mobile home agreement', meaning an agreement to which the 1983 Act applies; or to a 'mobile home *rental* agreement' which is defined[137] as an agreement entitling someone to reside in a mobile home for a specified period or for successive periods, subject to the payment of money; however, it does not include holiday rentals.

5.139   By this exception, the owner of a protected site may impose an age restriction in one of several ways:

- by entering into a mobile home agreement with someone that entitles only people who have reached a particular age to station and occupy a mobile home on the site;[138]

- by refusing to allow the assignment of a mobile home agreement to anyone who has not reached that age;[139]

- by imposing a requirement in 'park rules' (that is, site rules that residents are obliged to observe because of a term in their agreement) to the effect that mobile homes stationed on the site can only be occupied by people who have reached a particular age;[140]

- by imposing a requirement within a mobile home rental agreement that the mobile home can only be occupied by a person who has reached a particular age;[141]

- by imposing a similar age restriction on the assignment of a mobile home rental agreement.[142]

5.140   If the owner imposes an age restriction in a mobile home agreement or mobile home rental agreement, by paragraph 30D(4) they must provide the person concerned with a written statement setting out the age restriction that applies to the mobile home in question.

5.141   The Government Equalities Office overview guidance[143] points out that this exception cannot be used to impose age restrictions on people visiting the mobile home site, nor does it allow age restrictions to be imposed on services offered on the site once residents or their visitors have been admitted. The guidance also suggests that it would also be open to a site owner normally operating an age restriction to waive this for a younger resident, provided the agreement was not on worse terms.

5.142   (xiv) *Television, radio, and online broadcasting.*   Paragraph 31, at Part 8 of Schedule 3, was created in response to concerns by broadcasters to the perceived 'chilling effect' of the Act on their editorial independence. This provides an exception covering the content of television, radio, and online broadcasting material; section 29 does not apply to the provision of a content service within the meaning of section 32(7) of the Communications Act 2003. However, the exception does not extend to the provision of an electronic communications network,

---

[137] Sch. 3, para. 30D(5).
[138] Sch. 3, para. 30D(1)(a).
[139] Sch. 3, para. 30D(1)(b).
[140] Sch. 3, para. 30D(2).
[141] Sch. 3, para. 30D(3)(a).
[142] Sch. 3, para. 30D(3)(b).
[143] Government Equalities Office, 2012. The Equality Act 2010: banning age discrimination in services—an overview for service providers and customers. <https://www.gov.uk/government/uploads/system/uploads/attachment_data/file/85031/age-discrimination-ban.pdf>.

electronic communications service, or associated facility (each of which has the same meaning as in the Communications Act).

B. TRANSPORT

1. Disability Discrimination and Transport Provision

(a) *Introduction*

As set out above, Part 3 of the Act prohibits discrimination, harassment, and victimization 5.143
in relation to services and public functions. Transport, and the use of transport vehicles, are
services for the purposes of the Act. However, there are specific provisions dealing with transport and disability discrimination. Section 29, which prohibits discrimination, harassment,
and victimization in the provision of goods, facilities, services, and public functions, does not
apply in relation to disability discrimination to land transport unless it falls within one of the
types of vehicle set out in Schedule 3, Part 9. The detail of this is set out below.

Schedule 3 paragraphs 34(1A) and 34 provide that sections 20–2 and section 29 do not apply
to anything that is governed by Regulation (EU) No 181/2011 of the European Parliament
and of the Council of 16 February 2011 concerning the rights of passengers in bus and coach
transport and amending Regulation (EC) No 2006/2004. On that basis, the provisions of
the Regulations relating to ticketing and onboarding of disabled passengers are apparently
exempt from the Equality Act.

Section 29 does not apply to anything governed by Regulation (EC) No 1371/2007 of the
European Parliament and of the Council of 23 October 2007 on rail passengers' rights and
obligations.]

In addition, the extent of the application of the duty to make reasonable adjustments in 5.144
relation to transport vehicles varies depending upon the nature of the vehicle. These variations are detailed below. Part 12 of the Act contains provisions that empower the Secretary
of State to promulgate accessibility regulations for certain vehicles. It also contains provisions
relating to the obligations of drivers of taxis in providing services to assist dog users and
wheelchair users. All these provisions largely replicate those in the Disability Discrimination
Act (DDA).

(b) *Ships and Hovercrafts*

Section 30 of the Act provides that Part 3 prohibitions on discrimination only apply in rela- 5.145
tion to transporting people by ship or hovercraft, or providing services on them, where a
Minister of the Crown has made regulations to such effect. However, this does not exclude
the operation of section 29(6), which prohibits discrimination, harassment, or victimization
in the exercise of a public function which is not the provision of a service (other than in
relation to disability discrimination unless prescribed under regulations).[144] No new regulations have been made but, relevant provisions under the previous enactments continue to
apply.[145]

---

[144] S. 30(2).

[145] See Equality Act 2010 (Commencement No 4, Savings, Consequential, Transitional, Transitory and
Incidental Provisions and Revocation) Order 2010, SI 2010/2317, art. 10 and Schs 1 and 2.

(c) Transport—Application of the Services Provisions

5.146   Section 29 of the Act will only apply, in relation to disability discrimination, to transporting people by land if the vehicle concerned is:[146]

(a) a hire vehicle designed and constructed for the carriage of passengers and comprising no more than eight seats in addition to the driver's seat;

(b) a hire vehicle designed and constructed for the carriage of passengers, comprising more than eight seats in addition to the driver's seat and having a maximum mass not exceeding five tonnes;

(c) a hire vehicle designed and constructed for the carriage of goods and having a maximum mass not exceeding 3.5 tonnes;

(d) a vehicle licensed under section 48 of the Local Government (Miscellaneous Provisions) Act 1976 or section 7 of the Private Hire Vehicles (London) Act 1998 (or under a provision of a local Act corresponding to either of those provisions);

(e) a private hire car (within the meaning of section 23 of the Civil Government (Scotland) Act 1982);

(f) a public service vehicle (within the meaning given by section 1 of the Public Passenger Vehicles Act 1981);

(g) a vehicle built or adapted to carry passengers on a railway or tramway (within the meaning, in each case, of the Transport and Works Act 1992);

(h) a taxi;

(i) a vehicle deployed to transport the driver and passengers of a vehicle that has broken down or has been involved in an accident; or

(j) a vehicle deployed on a system using a mode of guided transport (within the meaning of the Transport and Works Act 1992).

(d) Transport—Reasonable Adjustments

5.147   Schedule 2 to the Act contains provisions relating to the application of the duty to make reasonable adjustments to services and functions. Paragraph 3 makes special provision in relation to transport. A service provider and person exercising a public function must comply with the first, second, and third requirement to make reasonable adjustments contained in section 20.[147]

5.148   However, where a service provider (referred to here as 'A') is concerned with the provision of a service that involves transporting people by land, air, or water, the duty to make adjustments is modified by paragraph 3 of Schedule 2. This reproduces the provisions contained in the Disability Discrimination Act 1995 and in regulations made under it.

5.149   It is never reasonable for A to have to take a step which would:

- involve the alteration or removal of a physical feature of a vehicle used in providing the service;

- affect whether vehicles are provided;

---

[146] Sch. 3, Part 9, para. 34.
[147] Sch. 2, paras 1 and 2(1).

- affect what vehicles are provided;
- affect what happens in the vehicle while someone is travelling in it.[148]

Thus, not only is there no obligation to make physical adjustments, but there is also no obligation to make an accessible vehicle available, nor to do anything in relation to the nature of the vehicle or anything that happens on board the vehicle.

Having set out such a sweeping exception, the Schedule goes on to state that certain vehicles cannot in fact rely upon this exemption. This restriction—other than relating to altering or removing a physical feature—does not apply in relation to the duty to change provisions, criteria, or practices, or to the provision of auxiliary aids or services, if the vehicle concerned is one of those in paragraph 3 of Schedule 2,[149] broadly the same as those listed in paragraph 34 of Schedule 3. Note that particular provisions apply to hire vehicles with no more than eight seats (see paragraph 5.149 below).   **5.150**

Thus all the vehicles listed above at paragraph 5.147 are covered by the anti-discrimination provisions, and transport services must comply with the first and third requirement of the reasonable adjustment duty, i.e. addressing provisions, criteria, or practices, and provision of auxiliary aids and services.   **5.151**

The duty to make reasonable adjustments in relation to public service vehicles was considered by the Supreme Court in the case of *First Group PLC v Paulley*.[150] First Group, a bus operator, had a policy of 'first come first served' to the space designated for wheelchair users. Mr Paulley successfully argued that the policy was a 'provision, criterion or practice' (PCP) which placed the claimant at a 'substantial disadvantage' within the meaning of section 20(3) of the 2010 Act by comparison with non-disabled bus passengers and, in accordance with its duty under section 29(7), there were reasonable adjustments which the defendant could have made which would have eliminated that.   **5.152**

The third requirement, to provide auxiliary aids and services, does not include, in its application to the vehicles above, a device or structure or equipment, the installation, operation, or maintenance of which would necessitate making a permanent alteration to, or which would have a permanent effect on, the internal or external fabric of the vehicle.[151]   **5.153**

There are two types of vehicle that are subject to the second requirement, i.e. the duty to avoid physical features.   **5.154**

The first is a breakdown vehicle, in which case the service provider will not be exempt from the second requirement so far as it relates to adopting a reasonable alternative method of providing the service to disabled persons—this means that it must provide an accessible vehicle, for example, for a wheelchair user should s/he be in need of a breakdown recovery service.[152]   **5.155**

The second is a hire vehicle built to carry no more than eight passengers, in which case for the purposes of the second requirement—the duty to make adjustments to physical features—a part of a vehicle is to be regarded as a physical feature only if it requires alteration in order to facilitate the provision of: **5.156**

---

[148] Sch. 2, para. 3(2).
[149] Sch. 2, para. 3(3).
[150] *FirstGroup Plc v Paulley* [2017] UKSC 4.
[151] Sch. 2, para. 3(8) and (9).
[152] Sch. 2, para. 3(4).

- hand controls to enable a disabled person to operate braking and accelerator systems in the vehicle (fixed seating and in-built electrical systems are not physical features for these purposes);[153] or

- facilities for the stowage of a wheelchair (fixed seating is not a physical feature for these purposes).[154]

5.157　This means that the obligation in relation to hire vehicles is limited to facilities relating to hand controls and facilities for storing wheelchairs.

(e) *Interpretation*

5.158　Paragraph 4 of Schedule 2 provides further interpretations of the types of vehicle to which the duties to make reasonable adjustments apply.

5.159　A 'hire vehicle' is a vehicle hired by way of a trade under a hiring agreement to which section 66 of the Road Traffic Offenders Act 1988 applies.[155]

5.160　A 'taxi' in England and Wales is a vehicle:

(a) licensed under section 37 of the Town Police Clauses Act 1847;

(b) licensed under section 6 of the Metropolitan Public Carriage Act 1869; or

(c) drawn by one or more persons or animals.[156]

5.161　A 'taxi' in Scotland is:

(a) a hire car engaged by arrangements made in a public place between the person to be transported (or someone acting on their behalf) and the driver for a journey starting there and then; or

(b) a vehicle drawn by one or more persons or animals.[157]

(f) *Air Transport*

5.162　Part 9 of Schedule 3 makes specific provisions to exempt air transport from the provisions relating to disability discrimination. Disability discrimination is defined in section 24(2) as meaning direct discrimination (section 13), discrimination arising from disability (section 15), indirect discrimination (section 19), and failure to make reasonable adjustments (section 21).

5.163　Section 29 (the provisions relating to goods, services, and public functions) does not apply in relation to disability discrimination to transporting people by air or a service provided on a vehicle for transporting people by air.[158] In addition, section 29 does not apply to anything governed by Regulation (EC) No 1107/2006 of the European Parliament and the Council of 5 July 2006 concerning the rights of disabled persons and persons with reduced mobility when travelling by air.[159] This Regulation requires assistance to be provided at airports and on

---

[153] Sch. 2, para. 3(6) and (7).
[154] Sch. 2, para. 3(6) and (7).
[155] Sch. 2, para. 4(2).
[156] Sch. 2, para. 4(3).
[157] Sch. 2, para. 4(4).
[158] Sch. 3, para. 33(1).
[159] Sch. 3, para. 33(2).

aircraft, as well as prohibiting disabled people and those with reduced mobility from being refused boarding.[160]

The Air Passenger Rights and Air Travel Organisers' Licensing (Amendment) (EU Exit)   5.164
Regulations 2019 come into effect on Exit Day. Thus any claim for injury to feelings arising out of discrimination on board the plane will have no monetary value. This is because of the 'exclusivity principle' in the Montreal Convention meaning that if a claim is not set out in the Convention it cannot be made. The court considered the issue of compensation for injury to feelings in the air in the case of *Stott v Thomas Cook Tour Operators Limited*.[161] In effect, the above regulations ensure that there are no penalties to air travel service providers for breach.

2. Part 12—Disabled Persons' Transport

Part 12 broadly reproduces Part V of the DDA dealing with provision for: 5.165

- accessibility regulations for taxis, licensing of taxis, and unlawful conduct in relation to wheelchair users;
- assistance dogs in taxis and private hire vehicles;
- accessibility regulations for public service vehicles;
- accessibility regulations for rail vehicles.

Whilst there are regulations already promulgated under the DDA relating to both public   5.166
service vehicles and rail vehicles, there have been none relating to taxi accessibility.[162]

3. Taxi Accessibility

(a) *Generally*

Under section 160 (which is not yet in force), the Secretary of State has the power to make   5.167
regulations (referred to as 'taxi accessibility regulations') for securing that it is possible for disabled people to:

(a) get into and out of taxis in safety;

(b) to do so while in wheelchairs;

(c) to travel in taxis in safety and reasonable comfort;

(d) to do so while in wheelchairs.[163]

The regulations may require a regulated taxi to conform with provisions as to: 5.168

- the size of door opening for the use of passengers;
- the floor area of the passenger compartment (definition as in the taxis accessibility regulations);

---

[160] It was held in *Campbell v Thomas Cook Tour Operations Ltd* ([2014] EWCA Civ 1668) that, notwithstanding Sch. 3, para. 33(2), Regulation 1107/2006 did not displace a tour operator's duty under s. 29 to prevent disability discrimination and make reasonable adjustments for disabled air passengers in respect of airport services in non-Member States.

[161] [2014] UKSC 15.

[162] See e.g. SI 1998/2456 and SI 2000/3215.

[163] S. 160(1).

- the amount of headroom in the passenger compartment;
- the fitting of restraining devices designed to ensure the stability of the wheelchair while the taxi is moving.[164]

5.169   In addition, the regulations may require the driver of a regulated taxi which is plying for hire, or which has been hired, to comply with provisions as to the carrying of ramps or other devices designed to facilitate the loading and unloading of wheelchairs; and, when a disabled person is being carried while in a wheelchair, in regulated taxis, to comply with provisions as to the position in which the wheelchair is to be secured.[165]

5.170   If a driver of a regulated taxi which is plying for hire or has been hired fails to comply with a requirement of the regulations or if the taxi fails to conform with any of the required provisions of the regulations, the driver commits an offence[166] which is punishable on summary conviction, with a fine not exceeding level 3 on the standard scale.[167] A 'regulated taxi' means a taxi to which taxi accessibility regulations apply.[168]

5.171   Examples of how this provision might operate, when brought into effect, are given in the Explanatory Notes:[169]

- It would be an offence for a taxi driver not to comply with a requirement to have a ramp or other device to enable a disabled person in a wheelchair to access the taxi in safety.
- It would be an offence for a taxi driver not to comply with a requirement to ensure the correct position of a wheelchair in the taxi so as to ensure the disabled person can travel in safety.

(b) *Designated Transport Facilities*

5.172   As the Explanatory Notes state,[170] franchise agreements exist between operators of transport facilities (premises which form part of railway stations, airports, ports, and bus stations) and operators of private hire cars, in order to provide services to members of the public so that they can travel from, for example, the mainline station to their destination. Section 161 (which has been commenced insofar as it confers a power to make regulations) allows requirements to be placed on vehicles used under a franchise agreement and their drivers to ensure accessibility for disabled people. This is discussed further below.

5.173   Section 162 (not yet commenced) provides that, in relation to transport facilities in England and Wales, the Secretary of State, and in relation to transport facilities in Scotland, the Scottish Ministers (referred to as the appropriate authority)[171] may make regulations to provide for the application of any taxi provision (with or without modification) to vehicles used for the provision of services under a franchise agreement or the drivers of such vehicles.[172] 'Transport facility' means premises which form part of a port, airport, railway station, or bus station.[173]

---

[164] S. 160(2).
[165] S. 160(3).
[166] S. 160(4).
[167] S. 160(5).
[168] S. 160(6).
[169] EN 532.
[170] EN 538.
[171] S. 162(3).
[172] S. 162(1).
[173] S. 162(3).

A franchise agreement is defined as a contract entered into by the operator of a designated 5.174
transport facility (designated by order made by the appropriate authority),[174] for the provision, by the other party to the contract, of hire car services for members of the public using any part of the facility or which involve vehicles entering any part of the facility.[175]

Section 162(3) sets out further the interpretation provisions for this section: 5.175

- 'hire car' has the meaning specified in regulations made by the appropriate authority;
- 'operator' in relation to a transport facility, means a person who is concerned with the management or operation of the facility;
- 'taxi provision' means a provision of Chapter 1 of Part 12 or regulations made pursuant to section 20(2A) of the Civic Government (Scotland) Act 1982 which applies to taxis or drivers of taxis.

The Secretary of State may exercise a power conferred by this section on the Scottish 5.176
Ministers for the purposes of section 2(2) of the European Communities Act 1972 (implementation of Community obligations).[176]

The Explanatory Notes[177] provide an example of how this section might operate: it could 5.177
be used to make regulations requiring that the vehicles entering, and for use in, an airport must be accessible to wheelchair users to fulfil the terms of a franchise agreement.

(c) *Taxi Licences*
Section 163, yet to be commenced, provides that taxis must conform with the accessibility 5.178
regulations in order to be granted a licence.

Specifically, a licence for a taxi to ply for hire must not be granted unless the vehicle con- 5.179
forms with the provisions of taxi accessibility regulations with which a vehicle is required to conform if it is licensed.[178] This does not apply, however, if a licence is in force in relation to the vehicle at any time during the period of 28 days immediately before the day on which the licence is granted.[179] This means that existing vehicles can still be used as taxis without having to meet the requirements of the accessibility regulations. However, the Secretary of State can, by order, provide for this exemption for preexisting vehicles to cease to have effect on a specified date,[180] and this can be exercised differently for different areas or localities.[181]

(d) *Exemption from Taxi Accessibility Regulations*
Section 164, which has not yet been commenced, allows the Secretary of State to provide 5.180
by regulations for a relevant licensing authority to apply for an order ('an exemption order') exempting the authority from compliance with section 163, i.e. the requirement to ensure that licensed taxis meet the accessibility regulations.[182] The regulations can set out what process an authority must go through to obtain an exemption order.

---

[174] *ibid.*
[175] S. 162(2).
[176] S. 162(4).
[177] EN 542.
[178] S. 163(1).
[179] S. 163(2).
[180] S. 163(3).
[181] S. 163(4).
[182] S. 164(1).

5.181   A 'relevant licensing authority' is an authority responsible for licensing taxis in any area of England and Wales other than the area to which the Metropolitan Public Carriage Act 1869 applies.[183]

Note also that a local authority exercising its public functions in licensing taxis, is also likely to be bound by the Public Sector Equality Duty set out in section 149 of the Equality Act.

5.182   An authority may apply for an exemption order only if it is satisfied that, having regard to the circumstances in its area, it is inappropriate for section 161 to apply; and that the application of that section would result in an unacceptable reduction in the number of taxis in its areas.[184]

5.183   The Secretary of State may make an exemption order in the terms of the application for the order, or in such other terms as s/he thinks appropriate, or refuse the order. Before doing so, however, s/he must consult the Disabled Persons Transport Advisory Committee and such other persons as the Secretary of State thinks appropriate.[185]

5.184   The Secretary of State may by regulations make provision requiring a taxi plying for hire in an area in respect of which an exemption order is in force to conform with provisions of the regulations as to the fitting and use of swivel seats.[186] A 'swivel seat' has the meaning specified in the regulations.[187]

5.185   Explanation of how these provisions may work in practice is given in the Explanatory Notes:[188]

A particular licensing area can apply for an exemption order if it considers that requiring all taxis to comply with the accessibility requirements would mean that licensed taxi drivers in the area would transfer from being hackney carriage drivers to private hire vehicle drivers, because the cost of purchasing accessible taxis would make their business unprofitable. The Secretary of State can agree to make an exemption order but, in doing so, can require a certain number of accessible taxis to be available in the area.

(e) Passengers in Wheelchairs

5.186   Section 165, which makes provisions for taxi passengers in wheelchairs, has come into force only insofar as it relates to the issue of exemption certificates under section 166, considered below. The House of Lords Select Committee on the Equality Act 2010 and Disability has described the Government's reasons for failing to commence the rest of section 165 as 'entirely unconvincing' and has recommended that these provisions (and the remaining provisions of Part 12 of the Act) be 'brought into force forthwith'.[189] In its response to the Select Committee's report, the Government stated that it intended to commence section 165, along with section 167, by the end of 2016.[190] However, at the time of this publication, this has not been put into effect.

---

[183] S. 164(7).
[184] S. 164(3).
[185] S. 164(4).
[186] S. 164(5).
[187] S. 164(7).
[188] EN 543.
[189] House of Lords Select Committee on the Equality Act and Disability, Report of Session 2015/2016: The Equality Act 2010: the impact on disabled people.
[190] Government Response to the House of Lords Select Committee Report on The Equality Act 2010: The impact on disabled people, Cm 9283, July 2016.

(i) *Duties of drivers.* Section 165, when brought fully into effect, will impose duties on the   5.187
driver of a designated taxi that has been hired by or for a disabled person who is in a wheelchair
(or by another person who wishes to be accompanied by a disabled person who is in a wheelchair, or where such a person has indicated that s/he wants to travel in the vehicle).[191] A taxi
or private hire vehicle is designated if it appears on a list maintained under section 167 (list
of wheelchair accessible vehicles), and the passenger means the disabled person concerned.[192]

The driver has the following duties:[193]   5.188

(a) to carry the passenger while in the wheelchair;

(b) not to make any additional charge for doing so;

(c) if the passenger chooses to sit in a passenger seat, to carry the wheelchair;

(d) to take such steps as are necessary to ensure that the passenger is carried in safety and
reasonable comfort;

(e) to give the passenger such mobility assistance as is reasonably required.

Mobility assistance is assistance: 5.189

(a) to enable the passenger to get into or out of the vehicle;

(b) if the passenger wishes to remain in the vehicle, to enable the passenger to get into and
out of the vehicle while in the wheelchair;

(c) to load the passenger's luggage into or out of the vehicle;

(d) if the passenger does not wish to remain in the wheelchair, to load the wheelchair into
or out of the vehicle.[194]

The driver is not required: 5.190

(a) unless the vehicle is of a description specified in regulations made by the Secretary of
State, to carry more than one person in a wheelchair or more than one wheelchair on any
one journey;

(b) to carry a person in circumstances in which it would otherwise be lawful for the driver
to refuse to carry the person.[195]

Where the driver of a designated taxi or a designated private hire vehicle fails to comply   5.191
with a duty imposed on the driver by this section, s/he commits an offence and is liable on
summary conviction to a fine not exceeding level 3 on the standard scale.[196]

The Act provides that it is a defence for a person charged with the offence to show that at   5.192
the time of the alleged offence:

(a) the vehicle conformed to the accessibility requirements which applied to it, but

(b) it would not have been possible for the wheelchair to be carried safely in the vehicle.[197]

---

[191] S. 165(1) and (2).
[192] S. 165(3).
[193] S. 165(4).
[194] S. 165(5).
[195] S. 165(6).
[196] S. 165(8).
[197] S. 165(9).

5.193 The Explanatory Notes provide the following examples of these provisions in practice:[198]

- A person in a wheelchair hires a wheelchair accessible taxi or private hire vehicle. The driver must help the passenger into and out of the vehicle by using a ramp or lift and help the passenger onto the lift or up the ramp. The driver must ensure the wheelchair is correctly positioned in the vehicle and secured so that the passenger travels safely and in reasonable comfort.
- If a passenger in a wheelchair wishes to travel in a passenger seat, the driver must assist the passenger into and out of the vehicle and transport the wheelchair.
- A driver must load a disabled passenger's luggage into and out of the taxi.
- A driver cannot charge a person in a wheelchair more than any other passenger.

5.194 (ii) *Exemption certificates.* Section 166 is in force. By section 166(1), a licensing authority is obliged to issue a person with a certificate exempting him/her from the duties imposed on drivers in relation to passengers with wheelchairs ('an exemption certificate') if satisfied that it is appropriate to do so on medical grounds or on the ground that the person's physical condition makes it impossible or unreasonably difficult for the person to comply with those duties. 'Licensing authority' means the authority responsible in any area for licensing taxis or private hire vehicles in that area.[199] This might, for example, apply to someone whose back condition means that they cannot provide any physical assistance to help a passenger in a wheelchair into and out of a vehicle.

5.195 An exemption certificate is valid for the period specified in the certificate and the driver of a designated private hire vehicle is exempt from the duties imposed by section 165 if s/he has an exemption certificate that is in force and the prescribed notice of the exemption is exhibited on the vehicle in the prescribed manner.[200]

5.196 Like section 165, section 167 is only in force in relation to the issue of exemption certificates under section 166. Sections 165 and 167 are yet to be effected.[201] By section 167, a licensing authority may maintain a list of taxis or private hire vehicles that conform to accessibility requirements that the licensing authority thinks fit.[202] The section makes further provisions relating to inclusion on the list, the issuing and consideration of guidance, and in relation to Scotland.

5.197 'Accessibility requirements' are requirements for securing that it is possible for disabled persons in wheelchairs to get into and out of vehicles in safety, and to travel in vehicles in safety and reasonable comfort, either staying in their wheelchairs or not (depending on which they prefer).[203]

5.198 (iii) *Control of number of licensed taxis: exception.* As noted above, section 161 is not in force other than the power to make regulations. When brought fully into effect, section 161 will prevent a licensing authority (in England or Wales) from refusing to license a wheelchair-accessible vehicle (one in which it is possible for a disabled person to get into and out of, and travel in, safely and in reasonable comfort whilst in a wheelchair) on the grounds of controlling taxi numbers, if the proportion of wheelchair-accessible vehicles operating in the area is smaller than the proportion prescribed in regulations by the Secretary of State.

---

[198] EN 546.
[199] S. 166(6).
[200] S. 166(2) and (4).
[201] See footnotes 177 and 178 above.
[202] S. 167(1) and (2).
[203] S. 167(6).

The provision operates by limiting the power to restrict the numbers of licensed vehicles, contained in section 16 of the Transport Act 1985.[204]

(iv) *Assistance dogs in taxis.* Section 168 (which has been brought into effect) makes specific provision relating to the carriage of assistance dogs—guide dogs, hearing dogs, etc.—in taxis. 5.199

For the purpose of these provisions, an assistance dog means: 5.200

- a dog which has been trained to guide a blind person;
- a dog which has been trained to assist a deaf person;
- a dog which has been trained by a prescribed charity to assist a disabled person who has a disability that consists of epilepsy or affects the person's manual dexterity, physical coordination, or ability to lift, carry, or otherwise move everyday objects;
- a dog of a prescribed category which has been trained to assist a disabled person who has a disability of a prescribed kind.[205]

The driver of a taxi which has been hired by or for a disabled person who is accompanied by an assistance dog, or by another person who wishes to be accompanied by a disabled person with an assistance dog, must carry the disabled person's dog and allow it to remain with that person; and not make any additional charge for doing so.[206] 5.201

If a driver fails to comply with this duty, s/he commits an offence the penalty for which is a fine not exceeding level 3 on the standard scale.[207] 5.202

A taxi means a vehicle which is licensed under section 37 of the Town Police Clauses Act 1847 or section 6 of the Metropolitan Public Carriage Act 1869, and in sections 160 and 163 to 165, also includes a taxi licensed under section 10 of the Civic Government (Scotland) Act 1982, but does not include a vehicle drawn by a horse or other animal.[208] 5.203

(v) *Assistance dogs in private hire vehicles.* Similar provisions to those for taxis and the carriage of assistance dogs are made for private hire vehicles by section 170. Because private hire vehicles are pre-booked, the provisions cover operators as well as drivers. 5.204

The operator of a private hire vehicle (O) commits an offence by failing or refusing to accept a booking for the vehicle: 5.205

- if the booking is requested by or on behalf of a disabled person, or a person who wishes to be accompanied by a disabled person, and
- the reason for the failure or refusal is that the disabled person will be accompanied by an assistance dog.[209]

A private hire vehicle means a vehicle licensed under section 6 of the 1988 Act, section 48 of the 1976 Act, or an equivalent provision of a local enactment.[210] 5.206

O also commits an offence by making an additional charge for carrying an assistance dog which is accompanying a disabled person.[211] 5.207

---

[204] S. 161(2).
[205] S. 173(1).
[206] S. 168(1) and (2).
[207] S. 168(3) and (4).
[208] S. 173(1).
[209] S. 170(1).
[210] S. 170(5).
[211] S. 170(2).

5.208   The driver of a private hire vehicle commits an offence by failing or refusing to carry out a booking accepted by O:

- if the booking is made by or on behalf of a disabled person or a person who wishes to be accompanied by a disabled person, and

- the reason for the failure or refusal is that the disabled person is accompanied by an assistance dog.[212]

5.209   The penalty on summary conviction for these offences is a fine not exceeding level 3 on a standard scale.[213]

5.210   (vi) *Exemption certificates.*   As in relation to the carriage of wheelchair users, there are provisions made for exemption certificates for drivers of both taxis and private hire vehicles in relation to the carriage of guide dogs.

5.211   A licensing authority must issue a person with a certificate exempting him/her from the duties imposed by sections 168 and 170 (i.e. to carry assistance dogs) if satisfied that it is appropriate to do so on medical grounds.[214] For taxis, a licensing authority means in relation to the area in which the Metropolitan Public Carriage Act 1869 applies, Transport for London; and in relation to any other area in England and Wales, the authority responsible for licensing taxis in that area.[215] For private hire vehicles, the licensing authority means the authority responsible for licensing private hire vehicles in that area.[216] A certificate might be issued, for example, where a driver has an allergy to dogs.

5.212   In deciding whether to issue an exemption certificate the authority must have regard, in particular, to the physical characteristics of the taxi or private hire vehicle in which the person drives or those of any kind of taxis/private hire vehicles in relation to which the person requires the certificate.[217] An exemption certificate is valid in respect of a specified vehicle or a specified kind of taxi or private hire vehicle and for the period specified in the certificate.[218]

5.213   If the driver of a taxi or private hire vehicle has an exemption certificate in force in relation to his/her vehicle, and the prescribed notice of the exemption is exhibited on the vehicle in the prescribed manner, s/he is exempt from the duties relating to carriage of guide dogs.[219]

5.214   Drivers can appeal against a decision not to issue an exemption certificate; or against a decision to include a vehicle on the list of vehicles maintained in accordance with section 167.[220]

4. Public Service Vehicles

5.215   Chapter 2 of Part 12 (section 174) sets out the power of the Secretary of State to make regulations (referred to as PSV accessibility regulations) so that disabled people can get on and off regulated public service vehicles in safety and without unreasonable difficulty (and in the case of wheelchair users, to do so whilst remaining in their wheelchairs); and so that they can

---

[212] S. 170(3).
[213] S. 170(4).
[214] Ss 169(1), 171(1).
[215] S. 169(5).
[216] S. 170(5).
[217] Ss 169(2), 171(2).
[218] Ss 169(3), 171(3).
[219] Ss 169(4), 171(4).
[220] S. 172.

travel in such vehicles in safety and reasonable comfort.[221] The Disabled Persons Transport Advisory Committee and such other persons as the Secretary of State thinks fit must be consulted before the regulations are made.[222]

The regulations can make provision as to the construction, use, and maintenance of regulated public service vehicles, including provisions relating to the fitting of equipment to vehicles, equipment to be carried by vehicles, the design of equipment to be fitted to or carried by vehicles, the fitting and use of restraining devices designed to ensure the stability of wheelchairs whilst vehicles are moving, and the position in which wheelchairs are to be secured while vehicles are moving.[223]   5.216

A public service vehicle is a vehicle which is adapted to carry more than eight passengers and which is a public service vehicle for the purposes of the Public Passenger Vehicles Act 1981.[224]   5.217

The Act provides that it is an offence to contravene a provision of the Public Service Vehicles Regulations and using, or causing to be used, a non-compliant public service vehicle.[225]   5.218

As noted below, the Public Service Vehicles Accessibility Regulations previously enabled by the DDA have been saved as though made under the 2010 Act.   5.219

5. Rail Vehicles

Chapter 3 of Part 12 sets out the power of the Secretary of State to make regulations (referred to as rail vehicle accessibility regulations) so that disabled people can get on and off regulated rail vehicles in safety and without unreasonable difficulty (and in the case of wheelchair users, to do so whilst remaining in their wheelchairs); and so that they can travel in such vehicles in safety and reasonable comfort,[226] whilst in their wheelchairs. The Disabled Persons Transport Advisory Committee and such other persons as the Secretary of State thinks fit must be consulted before the regulations are made.[227]   5.220

The regulations can make provision as to the construction, use, and maintenance of regulated rail vehicles, including provision as to the fitting of equipment to vehicles, the equipment to be carried by vehicles, the design or use of equipment to be fitted to or carried by vehicles, the toilet facilities to be provided in vehicles, the location and floor area of the wheelchair accommodation to be provided in vehicles, and assistance to be given to disabled people.[228] Unlike under the Public Service Vehicles Regulations, these provisions require that the Secretary of State exercise the power to make rail vehicle accessibility regulations so that on and after 1 January 2020 every rail vehicle is a regulated rail vehicle.[229]   5.221

Provision is made for the Secretary of State to make exemption orders authorizing the use of a rail vehicle even though it does not conform with the regulations.[230] Regulation 45   5.222

---

[221] S. 174.
[222] S. 174(5).
[223] S. 174(2).
[224] S. 174(3).
[225] S. 175(1).
[226] S. 182.
[227] S. 182(8).
[228] S. 182(2).
[229] S. 182(6).
[230] S. 183(1).

Railways (Interoperability) Regulations 2011 (RIR 2011) prohibited the use of a rail carriage in a trans-European rail system in the UK on or after 1 January 2020 unless it complied with the TSI (Technical Specifications for Interoperability relating to accessibility for person with reduced mobility—Commission Regulation (EU) 1300/2014) or (among other options) a dispensation had been granted under regulation 46. The Secretary of State for Transport granted dispensations under regulation 46(4) of the RIR 2011 to allow inaccessible vehicles to remain in circulation beyond 1 January 2020 deadline, on the basis of widespread non-compliance by train operating companies. At the time of publication it is not known whether further exemptions will be granted beyond December 2020.

5.223   Regulations originally enabled by the DDA relating to both public service vehicles and rail vehicle accessibility remain in force by virtue of savings provisions allowing them to be treated as regulations made under the 2010 Act.[231] Rail vehicles must comply with these regulations by 1 January 2020, whilst double decker buses must be compliant by 1 January 2017, with all coaches compliant by 1 January 2010. Savings provisions ensure that both sets of regulations are to be treated as made under the Equality Act 2010.[232] These regulations will remain in force until such time as new regulations are promulgated.[233]

---

[231] Public Service Vehicles Accessibility Regulations SI 2000/1970 (as amended) and Rail Vehicle Accessibility (Non-Interoperable Rail System) Regulations 2010/432. These regulations remain in force by virtue of Equality Act 2010 (Commencement No 4, Savings, Consequential, Transitional, Transitory and Incidental Provisions and Revocation) Order 2010, SI 2010/2317, Art. 21 and Sch. 7.

[232] See Equality Act 2010 (Commencement No 4, Savings, Consequential, Transitional, Transitory and Incidental Provisions and Revocation) Order 2010, SI 2010/2317, Art. 21 and Sch. 7.

[233] Sch. 20, which now has been repealed, sets out the detail of enforcement for non-compliance with the provisions relating to rail vehicle accessibility provisions.

6

EDUCATION

A. Education	6.01

A. EDUCATION

1. Introduction

Part 6 of the Equality Act sets out what is unlawful conduct in relation to education. Chapter 1 **6.01**
of Part 6 deals with schools; Chapter 2 with further and higher education; and Chapter 3
with general qualifications bodies. At the time of writing, there is no statutory code of practice in relation to either pre-16 education or further and higher education. The Equality and
Human Rights Commission has produced non-statutory guidance, referred to as technical
guidance for schools and for further and higher education.[1] There has been relatively little
case law in the education field, though what there has been has brought either in the First-
tier Tribunal (where disability discrimination cases in schools must be brought) or tended to
focus on race and religious discrimination and has been litigated by way of judicial review. *R
(E) v Governing Body of JFS and the Admissions Appeal Panel of JFS*[2] *and Others* related to the
admissions criteria for children to the Jewish Free School and involved an extensive examination of case law relating to direct and indirect discrimination (see Chapter 2). The conclusion of the Supreme Court, by a majority, was that a matrilineal test (where a child must be
descended from a Jewish mother in order to enter the school) was a test of ethnic origin. By
definition, discrimination that was based upon that test was discrimination on racial grounds
under the Race Relations Act 1976 ('RRA'). The motive of the discriminator for applying
the discriminatory criteria was irrelevant. A person who discriminated on the ground of race,
as defined by the RRA, could not pray in aid the fact that the ground of discrimination was
one mandated by his religion. Under the Equality Act 2010, *G (by his litigation friend) v
Head Teacher and Governors of St Gregory's Catholic College*[3] involved a male pupil challenging
a school's decision that he could not wear his hair in cornrows: this was held to amount to
potential—depending on justification—indirect race discrimination, though a claim of sex
discrimination was dismissed; see also *R (Interim Executive Board of Al-Hijrah School) v HM*

---

[1] <https://www.equalityhumanrights.com/en/advice-and-guidance/equality-act-technical-guidance>.
[2] [2009] UKSC 15.
[3] [2011] EWHC 1452 (Admin).

Catherine Casserley, *Education* In: *Blackstone's Guide to the Equality Act 2010*. Fourth Edition. Edited by:
Anthony Robinson, David Ruebain, and Susie Uppal, Oxford University Press (2021). © Oxford University Press.
DOI: 10.1093/oso/9780198870876.003.0006

Chief Inspector of Education, Children's services and Skills (Secretary of State for Education and others intervening)[4] where the Court of Appeal held that segregation of pupils on the basis of their sex was direct discrimination contrary to section 85(2) of the EqA, with segregation having an adverse impact on the quality and effectiveness of the education given to boys and girls respectively.

2. Schools Scope

6.02 Part 6 of the Act begins by setting out the scope of the schools part. Chapter 1—schools—does not apply to the protected characteristics of age or marriage and civil partnership.[5] In addition, nothing in the chapter applies to anything done in relation to the content of the curriculum.[6]

3. Interpretation

6.03 The schools provisions apply, in England and Wales, to the following:

- a school maintained by a local authority;
- an independent educational institution (in accordance with Chapter 1 of Part 4 of the Education and Skills Act 2008) (other than a special school);
- an alternative provision Academy that is not an independent educational institution;
- a special school which is not maintained by a local authority.

6.04 A school in relation to England and Wales has the meaning given in section 4 of the Education Act 1996.[7]

6.05 In relation to Scotland, the provisions apply to:

- a school managed by an education authority;
- an independent school;
- a school in respect of which the managers are for the time being receiving grants under section 73(c) or (d) of the Education (Scotland) Act 1980.

6.06 A school has the meaning given in section 135(1) of the Education (Scotland) Act 1980. It includes independent educational institutions in England (in accordance with Chapter 1 of Part 4 of the Education and Skills Act 2008).[8]

6.07 The obligations under the Act are placed upon 'responsible bodies'. A 'responsible body' for the purposes of these provisions[9] is:

(a) where the school is a school maintained by a local authority, the local authority, or governing body;

---

[4] [2017] EWCA Civ 1426.
[5] S. 84.
[6] S. 89(2).
[7] Ss 85(7), 89(5), (7), and (8).
[8] Ss 85(8), 89(5), and (8).
[9] S. 85(9).

(b) where it is an independent educational institution, other than a special school, an alternative provision Academy that is not an independent educational institution, or a special school not maintained by the local authority, the proprietor;

(c) if it is a school in Scotland managed by an education authority, the education authority;

(d) if it is an independent school in Scotland, the proprietor;

(e) if it is a school in respect of which the managers are for the time being receiving grants under section 73(c) or (d) of the Education (Scotland) Act 1980, the managers.[10]

Section 85 sets out what is unlawful in relation to schools. It largely replicates provisions under the pre-existing legislation. **6.08**

The Act makes it unlawful for the responsible body of a school to discriminate in relation to admission to a school, in particular: in the arrangements it makes for deciding who is offered admission as a pupil; as to the terms on which it offers to admit the person as a pupil; or by not admitting the person as a pupil.[11] **6.09**

When a person is a pupil at a school, it is unlawful for the responsible body of the school to discriminate against the pupil: in the way it provides education; in the way it affords the pupil access to a benefit, facility or service; by not providing education for the pupil; by not affording the pupil access to a benefit, facility, or service; by excluding the pupil from the school; or by subjecting the pupil to any other detriment.[12] **6.10**

The responsible body of a school is also prohibited from harassing a pupil or anyone who has applied for admission as a pupil.[13] However, the harassment provisions do not apply in relation to gender reassignment, religion or belief, or sexual orientation.[14] This exclusion was the subject of criticism by the Joint Committee on Human Rights[15] and the government resisted attempts during the passage of the Act for the exclusions to be removed. **6.11**

However, although a claim under the education provisions in relation to gender reassignment, sexual orientation, or religion or belief may not be based upon the harassment provisions, it may be possible to bring a claim in relation to conduct which would otherwise amount to harassment under the provisions prohibiting direct discrimination—the Act specifically provides that where the Act disapplies a provision on harassment in relation to a protected characteristic, this does not prevent the conduct amounting to a detriment for the purposes of direct discrimination.[16] **6.12**

Victimization is also prohibited under the schools provisions. The responsible body of a school must not victimize a person: in the arrangements it makes for deciding who is offered admission as a pupil; in the terms on which admission is offered; or by not admitting the person as a pupil.[17] **6.13**

When someone is already a pupil, the responsible body of a school must not victimize him/her in the way in which it provides him/her with education or by not providing it; in the **6.14**

---

[10] There are other consequential interpretive provisions relating to independent educational institutions and special schools, set out in s. 89.

[11] S. 85(1).

[12] S. 85(2).

[13] S. 85(3).

[14] S. 85(10).

[15] See Joint Committee on Human Rights: Legislative Scrutiny: the Equality Bill, 26th Report of Session 2008–2009, 27 October 2009, para. 118.

[16] S. 212(5).

[17] S. 85(4).

way it affords him/her access to a benefit facility or service or by not providing it; by excluding him/her; or by subjecting him/her to any other detriment.[18]

6.15 The definition of victimization is set out in section 27 and has been explained in Chapter 3. However, for the purposes of these provisions, victimization is more broadly defined, so as to protect a pupil or prospective pupil not only where a school takes action against him/her because of their having done something by reference to the Act, etc., but also where such action is taken because of his/her parent or sibling having done or being suspected of having done the act in question.[19]

6.16 There are also consequential additions to the definition of victimization for these purposes whereby giving false information or making a false allegation in good faith is not a protected act in a case where the evidence or information is given, or the allegation is made, by a parent or sibling of the child, and the child has acted in bad faith.[20]

6.17 Additionally, giving false evidence or information, or making a false allegation, in bad faith, is a protected act in a case where the evidence or information is given or the allegation is made by a parent or sibling of the child and the child has acted in good faith.[21] A child for these purposes is a person under 18.[22]

6.18 The Act also provides that the power of the Secretary of State in relation to England to give directions to a responsible body which is in default of its obligations applies in relation to a breach of these provisions of the Act, save in relation to the proprietor of an independent educational institution (other than a special school) or an alternative provision Academy that is not an independent educational institution and, in respect of Scotland, the equivalent provisions do not apply in respect of the proprietor of an independent school.[23]

Provisions to intervene in Wales in respect of breach of an obligation under s.85 are available under Chapter 1 of Part 2 of the School Standards and Organisation (Wales) Act 2013.[24]

4. Disabled Pupils

6.19 Disabled pupils are covered by the provisions set out above. The definition of disability has already been addressed in Chapter 2. However, the exclusion contained in the Equality Act 2010 (Disability) Regulations 2010, SI 2010/2128 at regulation 4 whereby a tendency to physical or sexual abuse of other persons is not to be treated as amounting to an impairment has had particular significance for school pupils. In *Governing Body of X Endowed School v SENDIST and others*,[25] a case involving the exclusion from school of a pupil with ADHD following violent behaviour, the High Court held that the exclusion from protection established by regulation 4(1) was not limited to free-standing conditions but also applied to derivative symptoms from an already protected, non-excluded condition. The reason for the appellant's exclusion was his conduct in assaulting a teacher. That was not a reason relating to

---

[18] S. 85(5).
[19] S. 86(1). A sibling is defined as meaning a brother or sister, a half brother or half sister, or a stepbrother or stepsister—s. 86(5).
[20] S. 86(3).
[21] S. 86(4).
[22] S. 86(5).
[23] S. 87(1). This does not apply in relation to an independent educational institution, other than a special school—s. 87(2).
[24] S. 87(3).
[25] [2009] EWHC 1842 (Admin).

his protected disability but one relating solely to the excluded condition. As a result, he was unable to bring a claim for discrimination in respect of his exclusion. Following *X*, there were a number of other cases that followed the same reasoning.

That changed however with the Upper Tribunal case of *C & C v The Governing Body of*   **6.20** *a School (The Secretary of State for Education) First Interested Party and (the National Autistic Society) Second Interested Party*[26]. L, the appellant (by his mother) has autism anxiety and pathological demand avoidance. A claim was brought on his behalf of discrimination, in the First-tier Tribunal. The claim was concerned with three incidents though the appeal concerned a determination in respect of only one, a fixed term exclusion for 1.5 days as a result of aggressive behaviour, including when he had hit a teaching assistant with a ruler, pulled her hair, punched her, and another time when he hit her with a book. The tribunal found that L generally met the definition in section 6 of the Equality Act 2016; it found however that he had a tendency to physical abuse and as a result of the Equality Act (Disability) Regulations 2010 he was not to be treated as a disabled person because of that tendency. L appealed against that finding, on the basis that the regulations are in breach of Article 2 Protocol 1 (right to education) in conjunction with Article 14 of the European Convention. The appeal was upheld on the basis that the First-tier Tribunal had erred in applying regulation 4(1)(c) to L and treating him as not 'disabled'. This was because applying the regulation to children with an impairment which is more likely to result in physical aggression gave rise to unlawful discrimination contrary to Article 14 ECHR, read with the right to education in Article 2 of the First Protocol. The appeal had been defended by the Secretary of State, who accepted that the issue was within the 'scope or ambit' of Article 2 of the First Protocol and that L had a relevant 'status'. The Secretary of State argued (1) that children such as L were not in an analogous position to other 'disabled' children who did not display a 'tendency to physical abuse' and (2) that in any event the differential impact of the regulations on children such as L was justified. Both these submissions were rejected by the Upper Tribunal. In particular Judge Rowley found that the application of regulation 4(1)(c) to children such as L did not strike a 'fair balance' and was therefore disproportionate. Judge Rowley held that 'the requirement for the protection of the status group's fundamental rights comprehensively outweighed the arguments put forward for the protection of the interests of others' (paragraph 89).

The decision in *C & C* was not appealed and so claimants in the First-tier Tribunal will   **6.21** have the benefit of it. This means that behaviour which might be classified as a tendency to physical violence but which arises out of a disability will no longer be automatically excluded from forming the basis for a disability discrimination claim in the education sphere (and potentially beyond). In addition, it remains the case that where reasonable adjustments have not been made for a disabled child prior to an exclusion which itself is based on a tendency to violence a claim for breach of the duty may be made—in addition to a claim in respect of the exclusion itself (see in respect of the reasonable adjustment duty *C v Governing Body of I School (SEN)*.[27]

There are in respect of education two parts of the Act relating specifically to disabled   **6.22** pupils.

Firstly, Schedule 10 replicates the provisions in the DDA[28] relating to accessibility strate-   **6.23** gies and plans in respect of pupils. Local authorities are required to produce accessibility

---

[26] [2018] UKUT 269.
[27] [2015] UKUT 217 (AAC).
[28] See DDA, s. 28D and s. 28E.

strategies, whilst schools must produce accessibility plans. The requirements of both are similar, and they must not only be produced but also implemented.

6.24   Secondly, the obligation to make reasonable adjustments applies to schools, and its application is set out in Schedule 13.

5. Accessibility Strategies and Plans

6.25   Local authorities in England and Wales must, in relation to schools for which they are the responsible bodies, prepare accessibility strategies and any further strategies that are prescribed in regulations.[29] These provisions do not apply to Scotland.

6.26   The responsible body of a school in England and Wales must prepare an accessibility plan in relation to the school and further such plans at such times as may be prescribed.[30]

6.27   Both an accessibility strategy and a plan must cover the same territory—in the local authority's case for the schools for which it is responsible, rather than for an individual school.

6.28   A strategy/plan is a strategy/plan for, over a prescribed period:[31]

- increasing the extent to which disabled pupils can participate in the schools' curriculums;[32]

- improving the physical environment of the schools for the purpose of increasing the extent to which disabled pupils are able to take advantage of education and benefits, facilities, or services provided or offered by the schools;

- improving the delivery to disabled pupils of information which is readily accessible to pupils who are not disabled, over a prescribed period. The delivery of information must be within a reasonable time and in ways which are determined after taking account of the pupils' disabilities and any preferences expressed by them or their parents.[33]

6. Preparing and Implementing the Strategy

6.29   When preparing the strategy, which must be in writing,[34] the local authority must have regard to: the need to allocate adequate resources for implementing the strategy; any guidance issued by a Minister of the Crown in England and Wales, or by Welsh Ministers in Wales which covers the content of an accessibility strategy; the form in which it is to be produced; and the persons to be consulted in its preparation.[35]

6.30   The strategy must be kept under review during the period to which it relates, and if necessary be revised (with regard had to any guidance as to its review).[36] It must also be implemented.[37]

6.31   If it is asked, a local authority must make a copy of its accessibility strategy available for inspection at such reasonable times as it decides.[38] A local authority in England, and a local

---

[29] Sch. 10, para. 1(1).
[30] Sch. 10, para. 3(1).
[31] Sch. 10, paras 1(2) and 3(2).
[32] 'Disabled pupil' includes a disabled person who may be admitted to the school as a pupil—Sch. 10, para. 6(4).
[33] Sch. 10, paras 1(3) and 3(3).
[34] Sch. 10, para. 1(4).
[35] Sch. 10, para. 2(1)(a) and (b).
[36] Sch. 10, paras 1(5), 2(2).
[37] Sch. 10, para. 1(6).
[38] Sch. 10, para. 2(5).

authority in Wales must, if asked by a Minister of the Crown or the Welsh Ministers respectively, give him/them a copy of its accessibility strategy.[39]

7. Preparing and Implementing the Accessibility Plan

When preparing the plan, which must be in writing,[40] the school's responsible body must keep the plan under review and, if necessary, revise it;[41] and the responsible body must implement its accessibility plan.[42]   **6.32**

The proprietor of an independent educational institution (other than an academy) must make a copy of the school's accessibility plan available for inspection at such reasonable times as the proprietor decides, if asked.[43]   **6.33**

The proprietor of an independent educational institution in England, other than an academy, must give a copy of the schools' accessibility plan to a Minister of the Crown, if asked; the proprietor of an independent school in Wales, other than an academy, must give a copy of the accessibility plan to the Welsh Ministers, if asked.[44]   **6.34**

Appropriate authorities (in England, the Secretary of State, in Wales, the Welsh Ministers) are given the power to issue directions against a responsible body, if they are satisfied that duties under this Schedule are not being discharged, including that the responsible body is acting unreasonably in the discharge of its duties. This power to issue directions also extends to a situation where a responsible body is acting or proposing to act unreasonably in complying with an order given by a tribunal in relation to a finding of disability discrimination in schools (under Schedule 17, paragraph 5).[45]   **6.35**

In addition, an inspection under Part 1 of the Education Act 2005 or Chapter 1 of Part 4 of the Education and Skills Act 2008 (regulation and inspection of independent education provision in England) may extend to the performance by the responsible body of its functions in relation to the preparation, publication, review, revision, and implementation of its accessibility plan.[46]   **6.36**

8. Interpretation

There are various further interpretative provisions contained in Schedule 10.   **6.37**

A responsible body for the purposes of the Schedule means: **6.38**

- in relation to a maintained school or a maintained nursery school, the local authority or governing body;

- in relation to a pupil referral unit, the local authority;

- in relation to an independent educational institution or an alternative provision academy that is not an independent educational institution, the proprietor;

---

[39] Sch. 10, para. 2(7).
[40] Sch. 10, para. 3(4).
[41] Sch. 10, para. 3(5).
[42] Sch. 10, para. 3(6).
[43] Sch. 10, para. 4(3).
[44] Sch. 10, para. 4(4).
[45] Sch. 10, para. 5.
[46] Sch. 10, para. 3(7) and (8).

- in relation to a special school not maintained by a local authority, the proprietor.[47]

6.39   'Governing body' in relation to a maintained school means the body corporate (constituted in accordance with regulations under section 19 of the Education Act 2002, which the school has as a result of that section).[48]

6.40   'Maintained school' has the meaning given in section 20 of the School Standards and Framework Act 1998; and 'maintained nursery school' has the meaning given in section 22 of that Act.[49]

9. Reasonable Adjustments

6.41   The second way in which provision is made for disabled pupils and prospective pupils is in the obligation to make reasonable adjustments. The duty to make reasonable adjustments applies to schools,[50] and Schedule 13 sets out how the duty applies. A responsible body must comply with the first and third requirement in relation to disabled pupils or prospective pupils.[51]

6.42   The relevant matters in respect of which the duty applies is deciding who is offered admission as a pupil, and the provision of education or access to a benefit, facility, or service.

6.43   This means that where a provision, criterion, or practice applied by or on behalf of a responsible body puts disabled pupils (or prospective pupils) at a substantial disadvantage compared with non-disabled people in relation to deciding who is offered admission as a pupil, and/or in the provision of education or access to a benefit facility or service, the school must take reasonable steps to avoid the disadvantage. This might mean, for example, a teacher altering a practice of speaking with their back to the class, so that students with a hearing impairment who lip read can see.

6.44   In addition, where disabled pupils or prospective pupils would be put at a substantial disadvantage compared with non-disabled people in relation to admission as a pupil and/or in the provision of education or access to a benefit facility or service, without the provision of an auxiliary aid or service, the school must take reasonable steps to provide it. This might include, for example, the provision of information in alternative formats.

6.45   The duty to make reasonable adjustments in relation to schools contained in the DDA did not extend to the duty to provide auxiliary aids or services—these were in fact specifically excluded on the basis that special educational needs provision catered for such requirements.[52] Following the publication of the Lamb Inquiry report,[53] however, which recommended the removal of the exclusion of auxiliary aids and services from the duty to make reasonable adjustments, the government accepted the recommendation that this exclusion should be lifted[54] and an amendment was laid to this effect.[55] This was implemented from 1 September

---

[47] Sch. 10, para. 6(5).
[48] Sch. 10, para. 6(6).
[49] Sch. 10, para. 6(7).
[50] S. 85(6).
[51] Sch. 13, para. 2(2).
[52] See discussion of this in Disability Rights Commission (DRC), Code of Practice: Schools, 2002, para. 3.18.
[53] See the Lamb Inquiry: SEN and Parental Confidence, 19 December 2009, recommendation 51.
[54] See Consultation on Auxiliary Aids for Children with Disabilities, 12 September 2011, at <http://www.education.gov.uk/consultations/downloadableDocs/auxiliary%20aids%20consultation%20document%204.doc>.
[55] The amendment was laid by Baroness Royal—see *Hansard* HL, col. 881 (19 January 2010).

2012.[56] Technical guidance is provided by the Equality and Human Rights Commission in respect of it.[57]

The duty to make reasonable adjustments in relation to schools (as with the rest of educa-   6.46
tion, services, and associations) was, under the DDA, anticipatory—it applied to disabled
people at large.[58] There was some doubt initially as to whether the duty to make reasonable
adjustments in the context of education had retained its anticipatory nature, given that there
was no reference in Schedule 13 to 'disabled persons', as there was in Schedule 3 in relation to
services. At report stage on 2 March 2010, the government laid amendments so that the duty
applies to disabled pupils, as opposed to an individual pupil, thus ensuring the anticipatory
nature of the duty.[59]

10. Exceptions

There are a number of exceptions to the schools provisions, which are set out in Schedule   6.47
11. They cover gender issues, relating in particular to single-sex schools, religion- or belief-
related discrimination, and disability discrimination. An overarching provision is contained
in section 89(2), which states that nothing in the education chapter applies to anything
done 'in connection with the curriculum'. Whilst this was at section 50 of the Equality Act
2006 in relation to religion and belief, it has now been extended to apply in relation to all
the protected characteristics. It is unclear, given the broad wording ('in connection with')
to what extent this will limit the scope of the reasonable adjustment duty. It is arguable,
however, that, in relation to the duty to make adjustments, the wording should be given a
narrow interpretation.

(a) *Admission to Single-sex Schools, Single-sex Boarding at Schools, and Single-sex Schools Turning Co-educational*

The admission provisions do not apply, in relation to sex discrimination, to a single-sex   6.48
school.[60] A single-sex school is defined as one which admits pupils of one sex only or, where
it admits a small number of pupils of the opposite sex on an exceptional basis or in relation
to particular courses or classes only.[61]

The admission provisions also do not apply in relation to admission as a boarder to a   6.49
school other than a single-sex school, which has some pupils as boarders and others as non-
boarders and which admits as boarders pupils of one sex only, or where pupils of the opposite
sex are admitted as boarders but their numbers are small compared to the numbers of other
pupils.[62]

The provisions relating to education and benefits facilities and services do not apply in   6.50
relation to boarding facilities at such a school once an individual is a pupil there.[63]

---

[56] See SI 2012/2184.
[57] <https://www.equalityhumanrights.com/en/advice-and-guidance/equality-act-technical-guidance>.
[58] See EHRC Code of Practice for discussion of this concept, as well as the services case of *Roads v Central Trains Ltd* [2004] EWCA Civ 1541.
[59] Sch. 13, para. 2(3)(b), and see *Hansard* HL, col. 1353 (2 March 2010).
[60] Sch. 11, para. 1(1).
[61] Sch. 11, para. 1(2)(b) and (3).
[62] Sch. 11, para. 2(3)(b) and (4), Sch. 11, para. 2(1).
[63] Sch. 11, para. 2(2).

6.51 Where a responsible body of a single-sex school, or a single-sex boarding school, decides to alter its admissions arrangements so that the school will no longer be a single-sex school/boarding school, the body can apply for a transitional exemption order. This is an order which authorizes sex discrimination to be carried out in the arrangements for admission and the refusal of admission because of a person's sex, for a period which is specified in the order. As a result, where a responsible body acting in accordance with a transitional exemption order, or pending the determination of an application for such an order, does not admit a person as a pupil because of the person's sex, it will not be committing an act of unlawful discrimination.[64]

6.52 There are further provisions relating to the powers under which transitional exemption orders may be made and the means by which applications for them may be made contained in Schedule 11.[65] In *R (Interim Executive Board of Al-Hijrah School) v HM Chief Inspector of Education, Children's services and Skills (Secretary of State for Education and others intervening)*[66] the Court of Appeal held that Schedule 11 did not sanction the strict gender separation in a notionally co-educational school practised by the claimant school and that in fact the gender segregation amounted to less favourable treatment because it diminished the quality of education which the girl pupils and boy pupils would receive but for their sex.

(b) *Religious or Belief-related Discrimination*

6.53 The admission provisions and the provisions relating to the provision of education, benefits facilities, and services do not apply in relation to religion or belief to:[67]

- a school designated under section 69(3) of the School Standards and Framework Act 1998 (foundation or voluntary schools with religious character);
- a school (other than an alternative provision Academy) listed in the register of independent schools for England or Wales, if the school's entry in the register records that the school has a religious ethos;
- a school transferred to an education authority under section 16 of the Education (Scotland) Act 1980 (transfer of certain schools to education authorities) which is conducted in the interest of a church or denominational body;
- a school provided by an education authority under section 17(2) of that Act (denominational schools);
- a grant-aided school (within the meaning of that Act) which is conducted in the interest of a church or denominational body;
- a school registered in the register of independent schools for Scotland if the school admits only pupils who belong, or whose parents belong, to one or more particular denominations;
- a school registered in that register if the school is conducted in the interest of a church or denominational body.

6.54 The provisions relating to education, benefits facilities, and services do not apply in relation to anything done in connection with acts of worship or other religious observance organized by or on behalf of a school, whether or not it forms part of the curriculum.[68]

---

[64] Sch. 11, para. 3.
[65] Sch. 11, paras 3 and 4.
[66] [2017] EWCA Civ 1426.
[67] Sch. 11, para. 5.
[68] Sch. 11, para. 6.

This means that faith schools may have admissions criteria which give preference to mem- **6.55** bers of their own religion, and that they can conduct themselves in a way which is compatible with their religious character or ethos. It does not, however, permit them to discriminate because of any other of the protected characteristics, such as sex, race, or sexual orientation. Nor can they discriminate because of religion in other respects, such as by excluding a pupil or subjecting them to any other detriment.

The Explanatory Notes provide examples of how these provisions might operate:[69] **6.56**

- A Muslim school may give priority to Muslim pupils when choosing between applicants for admission (although the Admissions Code will not allow it to refuse to accept pupils of another or no religion unless it is oversubscribed). However, it may not discriminate between pupils on other prohibited grounds, such as by refusing to admit a child of the school's own faith because she is black or a lesbian.

- A Jewish school which provides spiritual instruction or pastoral care from a rabbi is not discriminating unlawfully by not making equivalent provision for pupils from other religious faiths.

- A Roman Catholic school which organizes visits for pupils to sites of particular interest to its own faith, such as a cathedral, is not discriminating unlawfully by not arranging trips to sites of significance to the faiths of other pupils.

- A faith school would be acting unlawfully if it sought to penalize or exclude a pupil because he or she had renounced the faith of the school or joined a different religion or denomination.

(c) Disability Discrimination

An exception is made from the discrimination provisions on admission in relation to dis- **6.57** ability where a permitted form of selection is applied.[70]

A permitted form of selection, in England and Wales, is:[71] **6.58**

- in the case of a maintained school which is not designated as a grammar school under section 104 of the School Standards and Framework Act 1988, a form of selection mentioned in section 99(2) or (4) of that Act;

- in the case of a maintained school which is so designated, its selective admission arrangements (within the meaning of section 104 of that Act);

- in the case of an independent educational institution, arrangements which provide for some or all of its pupils to be selected by reference to general or special ability or aptitude with a view to admitting only pupils of high ability or aptitude.

In relation to Scotland, a permitted form of selection is:[72] **6.59**

- in the case of a school managed by an education authority, arrangements approved by the Scottish Ministers for the selection of pupils for admission;

---

[69] EN 879.
[70] Sch. 11, para. 8(1).
[71] Sch. 11, para. 8(2).
[72] Sch. 11, para. 8(3).

- in the case of an independent school, arrangements which provide for some or all of its pupils to be selected by reference to general or special ability or aptitude with a view to admitting only pupils of high ability or aptitude.

6.60 'Maintained school' has the meaning given in section 22 of the School Standards and Framework Act 1998.[73]

11. Further and Higher Education

(a) *Generally*

6.61 Chapter 2 of Part 6 covers further and higher education, including universities and further education colleges, a 16–19 Academy, as well as certain educational/training recreational facilities provided or secured by the local authority.

6.62 Chapter 2 does not apply to the protected characteristic of marriage and civil partnership. Nor does it apply to anything done in connection with the content of the curriculum.[74]

(b) *What is Unlawful*

6.63 Section 91 sets out what is unlawful in relation to students—and prospective students—in further and higher education. A student is a person for whom education is provided by the institution.[75]

6.64 It is unlawful for the responsible body of an institution to discriminate against a person in the arrangements it makes for deciding who is offered admission as a student; as to the terms on which it offers to admit the person as a student; and/or by not admitting the person as a student.[76]

6.65 When a person is a student at an institution, it is unlawful for the responsible body of the institution to discriminate against him/her in the way it provides education, or by not providing it; in the way it affords the student access to a benefit facility or service or by not affording the student access to a benefit, facility, or service; by excluding the student from the institution; or by subjecting the student to any other detriment.[77]

6.66 One of the facilities that a higher education provider will provide is access to a placement as part of a course. In *Blackwood v Birmingham and Solihull Mental Health NHS Foundation Trust* UKEAT/0130/14/RN it was held by the Employment Appeal Tribunal that the university had the 'power to afford access' to the vocational placement of a student nurse and so her claim for indirect discrimination could not be brought in the employment tribunal but had to be brought in the county court. On appeal this was overturned and it was held that the claim could be brought in the employment tribunal—on an effective construction of the relevant Directives (see [2016] EWCA Civ 607).

6.67 The responsible body is also prohibited from harassing a student, a person who has applied for admission as a student, or a disabled person who holds or has applied for a qualification conferred by the institution.[78] In addition, the responsible body of an institution must not victimize a person in relation to the arrangements made for deciding who is offered

---

[73] Sch. 11, para. 8(4).
[74] S. 94(2).
[75] S. 94(3).
[76] S. 91(1).
[77] S. 91(2).
[78] S. 91(5).

admission as a student; as to the terms on which it offers to admit the person as a student; and by not admitting the person as a student.[79] The responsible body must not victimize a student in the way in which it provides him/her with education or by not providing it; in the way it affords him/her access to a benefit, facility, or service or by not providing it; by excluding him/her; or by subjecting him/her to any other detriment.[80]

The Act also makes it unlawful for a responsible body to discriminate against a disabled   **6.68** person in the arrangements it makes for deciding who to confer a qualification upon, in the terms on which it is prepared to confer such a qualification, or by not conferring a qualification or withdrawing or varying it.[81] These provisions ensure that the provisions specific to disabled people and qualifications contained in the DDA are replicated.[82]

These provisions apply to a university, any other institution within the higher educa-   **6.69** tion sector or within the further education sector[83] in England and Wales, and a 16–19 Academy.[84] The term 'university' includes a university college and a college, school, or hall of a university.[85]

In Scotland, the provisions apply to a university, a designated institution, and a college of   **6.70** further education.

'Responsible body' is defined in section 91(12). The responsible body of a college of further   **6.71** education which is under the management of a board of management, is that board. In the case of any other college of further education, the responsible body is any board of governors of the college or any person responsible for the management of the college, whether or not formally constituted as a governing body or board of governors; for a university, any other institution within the higher education sector, or in the further education sector in England and Wales, it is the governing body; and in respect of a 16–19 Academy, it is the proprietor.

(c) *Disabled Students and Prospective Students*

Disabled students and prospective disabled students are covered by the provisions set out   **6.72** above. In addition, the duty to make reasonable adjustments in relation to disabled students and prospective students applies to further and higher education institutions.[86] The detail of the reasonable adjustment duty is set out in Schedule 13. Two of the cases litigated under the DDA involved a failure to provide a ramp for a graduation ceremony[87] and a failure to make adjustments to enable a disabled student to complete her social work coursework—with injunctive relief as well as damages being awarded in the latter case.[88]

The relevant responsible body must comply with the first, second, and third requirements   **6.73** in relation to prospective or actual disabled students.[89]

---

[79] S. 91(6).

[80] S. 91(7).

[81] S. 91(8).

[82] These provisions were largely contained in the DDA s. 28R. The DRC Code of Practice, Post 16 (2007) covers these provisions in Chapter 11, stating that they apply to non-students.

[83] A reference to an institution within the further or higher education sector is to be construed in accordance with s. 91 of the Further and Higher Education Act 1992 s. 94(5).

[84] S. 94(8).

[85] S. 94(4).

[86] S. 91(6).

[87] *Potter v Canterbury Christchurch University*, Canterbury County Court, Claim No. 5CL14216.

[88] *Nemorin v London Metropolitan University*, Clerkenwell and Shoreditch County Court, Claim No. 9EC08072.

[89] Sch. 13, para. 3(2).

6.74   The relevant matters in respect of which the duty applies are:[90]

- deciding who is offered admission as a student;
- provision of education;
- access to a benefit, facility, or service;
- deciding on whom a qualification is conferred;
- a qualification that is conferred.

6.75   This means that where a provision, criterion, or practice applied by or on behalf of the relevant responsible body places disabled students or prospective students at a substantial disadvantage, compared to non-disabled people, in relation to the relevant matters, set out immediately above, the responsible body must take reasonable steps to avoid the disadvantage.

6.76   Where a physical feature of premises occupied by the responsible body puts disabled students/prospective students at a substantial disadvantage compared to non-disabled people in relation to the matters set out above, the responsible body must take reasonable steps to avoid the disadvantage.

6.77   Finally, where disabled students/prospective students would be put at a substantial disadvantage compared to non-disabled people in relation to the matters set out above, without the provision of an auxiliary aid, the responsible body must take reasonable steps to provide it.

6.78   The duty to make reasonable adjustments is made anticipatory in nature by virtue of Schedule 13, paragraph 3(c)(i) and (ii), which provides that the reference to a disabled person in section 20 is a reference here to disabled persons/students.

6.79   However, this does not apply in relation to the conferment of qualifications on non-students. In relation to these, the duty applies to the individual disabled person (and is thus not anticipatory) in deciding on whom to confer a qualification (where a person is or has notified the responsible body that s/he may be an applicant for the conferment of the qualification); and, in relation to a qualification that a responsible body confers, where the disabled person is an applicant for conferment or a person on whom the qualification is conferred.[91]

6.80   For these purposes, a provision, criterion, or practice does not include the application of a competence standard[92] which is defined as being an academic, medical, or other standard applied for the purpose of determining whether or not a person has a particular level of competence or ability.[93] This means that where a competence standard is applied, it cannot be the subject of a claim based on a failure to make reasonable adjustments, though it may be the basis of a claim for direct discrimination arising from disability or indirect discrimination.

12. Further and Higher Education Courses

(a) *Generally*

6.81   Specific provision is made for further and higher education courses provided by schools and local authorities.

---

[90] Sch. 13, para. 3(4).
[91] Sch. 13, para. 3(c)(iii) and (4).
[92] Sch. 13, para. 4(2).
[93] Sch. 13, para. 4(3).

These provisions apply to:

6.82

- any course of further or higher education secured by a responsible body in England or Wales[94] (in which case the responsible body is the local authority in England and Wales);[95]
- any course of education provided by the governing body of a maintained school under section 80 of the Schools Standards and Framework Act 1998[96] (in which case the responsible body is the governing body);[97]
- any course of further education secured by an education authority in Scotland[98] (the responsible body being an education authority).[99]

'Course' in relation to further education includes each component part of a course (if a person does not have to register separately for the component parts).[100]

6.83

A responsible body is prohibited from discriminating against a person in the arrangements it makes for deciding who is enrolled on the course; as to the terms on which it offers to enrol the person on the course; or by not accepting the person's application for enrolment.[101]

6.84

Enrolment includes registration for a component part of a course.[102]

6.85

Where a person is already enrolled on a course, the responsible body must not discriminate against him/her in the services it provides or offers to provide.[103] 'Services' are services of any description which are provided wholly or mainly for people enrolled on a course to which the section applies.[104]

6.86

In addition, the responsible body must not harass a person who is seeking enrolment on the course, is already enrolled on the course, or is a user of services provided by the body in relation to the course.

6.87

Victimization by the responsible body is prohibited in the arrangements made for deciding who is enrolled on the course; in the terms on which a person is enrolled on the course; by not accepting the person's application for enrolment;[105] or in the services offered, or provided, to a person enrolled on the course.[106]

6.88

(b) The Duty to Make Reasonable Adjustments

The duty to make reasonable adjustments applies in relation to further and higher education courses, and its detail is set out in Schedule 13.[107]

6.89

The responsible body must comply with the first, second, and third requirement[108] in relation to arrangements for enrolling people on a course of further or higher education

6.90

---

[94] S. 92(7)(a).

[95] S. 92(8)(a).

[96] 'Maintained school' has the meaning given in s. 20(7) of the School Standards and Framework Act 1998 s. 92(9).

[97] S. 92(8)(b).

[98] S. 92(7)(c).

[99] S. 92(8)(c).

[100] S. 92(9).

[101] S. 92(1).

[102] S. 92(9).

[103] S. 92(2).

[104] S. 92(9).

[105] S. 92(4).

[106] S. 92(5).

[107] S. 92(6).

[108] Sch. 13, para. 5(2).

secured by the responsible body, and services provided for persons enrolled on the course.[109]

6.91 This means that where a provision, criterion, or practice applied by or on behalf of the responsible body places disabled people at a substantial disadvantage, compared to non-disabled people, in relation to arrangements for enrolling people on a course of further or higher education secured by the body, or in relation to services provided by the responsible body, the responsible body must take reasonable steps to avoid the disadvantage.

6.92 Where a physical feature of premises occupied by the responsible body puts disabled people at a substantial disadvantage compared to non-disabled people in relation to arrangements for enrolling people on a course secured by the body, or in relation to services provided for people on the course, the responsible body must take reasonable steps to avoid the disadvantage.

6.93 Finally, where disabled people would be put at a substantial disadvantage compared to non-disabled people in relation to arrangements for enrolling or services for people enrolled on the course, without the provision of an auxiliary aid, the responsible body must take reasonable steps to provide it.

6.94 There is an exception however where the responsible body is the governing body of a maintained school, in which case it is not required to comply with the second requirement, i.e. the duty to make reasonable adjustments in relation to physical features.[110] This reflects the restriction upon the duty to make reasonable adjustments in relation to schools.

13. Recreational or Training Facilities

(a) *Generally*

6.95 Chapter 2, Part 6 of the Act also contains provisions relating to recreational or training facilities that are provided by local authorities—specifically facilities secured by a local authority in England under section 507A or 507B of the Education Act 1996; facilities secured by a local authority in Wales under section 508 of that Act; and recreational or training facilities provided by an education authority in Scotland.[111] Broadly, these are facilities for recreation and social and physical training for children who have not yet reached the age of 13, and for leisure facilities for those between 13 and 20, and those under 25 with a learning disability. These are generally provided via the youth service, but can include things such as the provision of gym access.

6.96 The provisions replicate the effect of the provisions in the DDA and extend them to the other protected characteristics.

6.97 The provisions do not apply in relation to the protected characteristic of age to those under 18.[112]

6.98 The responsible body (in England and Wales, a local authority, in Scotland, an education authority) must not discriminate against a person in the arrangements it makes for deciding who is provided with the facilities; in the terms on which it offers to provide the facilities; or by not accepting a person's application for the provision of the facilities.[113]

6.99 In addition, the responsible body must not discriminate against a person who is provided with the facilities in the services it provides or offers to provide.[114]

---

[109] Sch. 13, para. 5(4).
[110] Sch. 13, para. 5(2).
[111] S. 93(7).
[112] S. 93(9).
[113] S. 93(1).
[114] S. 93(2).

The responsible body must not harass a person who is seeking to have the facilities provided, is provided with the facilities, or who is a user of services provided in relation to the facilities.[115]   6.100

Victimization in the arrangements the responsible body makes for deciding who is provided with the facilities, in the terms on which it offers to provide the facilities, and in not accepting the person's application for provision of the facilities, is also prohibited.[116] Where a person is provided with facilities, the responsible body must not victimize him/her in the services provided or offered.[117]   6.101

(b) *The Duty to Make Reasonable Adjustments*

The duty to make reasonable adjustments applies in relation to these facilities.[118] The detail of the duty, as with the rest of education, is set out in Schedule 13.   6.102

The responsible body must comply with the first, second, and third requirements,[119] in relation to its arrangements for providing the recreational or training facilities, which are the 'relevant matters' for the purposes of the duty.[120]   6.103

This means that where a provision, criterion, or practice applied by, or on behalf of, the responsible body, places disabled people at a substantial disadvantage compared to non-disabled people in relation to its arrangements for providing the recreational or training facilities, the responsible body must take reasonable steps to avoid the disadvantage.   6.104

Where a physical feature of premises (occupied by the responsible body) puts disabled people at a substantial disadvantage compared to non-disabled people in relation to its arrangements for providing the recreational or training facilities, the responsible body must take reasonable steps to avoid the disadvantage.   6.105

Finally, where disabled people would be put at a substantial disadvantage compared to non-disabled people in relation to its arrangements for providing the recreational or training facilities, without the provision of an auxiliary aid, the responsible body must take reasonable steps to provide it.   6.106

14. Reasonable Adjustments and Education—Generally

There are overarching provisions relating to education and reasonable adjustments.   6.107

Firstly, in deciding whether it is reasonable to have to take a step for the purpose of complying with the duty to make reasonable adjustments, the responsible body must have regard to relevant provisions of a code of practice issued under section 14 of the Equality Act 2006.[121] This does not appear anywhere else in the Act, although in any event, a court or tribunal must take the provisions of the code into account where relevant (sections 14 and 15 of the Equality Act 2006).   6.108

Secondly, where a person has made a confidentiality request which the responsible body is aware of, it will need to have regard to the extent to which making a reasonable adjustment is consistent with the confidentiality request.[122]   6.109

---

[115] S. 93(3).
[116] S. 93(4).
[117] S. 93(5).
[118] S. 93(6).
[119] Sch. 13, para. 6(2).
[120] Sch. 13, para. 6(4).
[121] Sch. 13, para. 7.
[122] Sch. 13, para. 8(2) and (3).

6.110   A confidentiality request, in relation to schools, is a request that the nature or existence of a disabled person's disability be treated as confidential and either the request is made by the person's parent or the responsible body believes that the person has sufficient understanding of the nature and effect of the request.[123]

6.111   In relation to further and higher education institutions, a confidentiality request is a request by a disabled person that the nature or existence of the person's disability be treated as confidential.[124]

15. Exceptions

(a) *Generally*

6.112   Exceptions to the further and higher education provisions are contained in Schedule 12. The exceptions cover single-sex institutions, training, religious ethos, marital status, and child care. They broadly replicate pre-existing provisions.

(b) *Single-sex Institutions*

6.113   The provisions relating to admission do not apply, so far as in relation to sex discrimination, to a single-sex institution.[125]

6.114   A single-sex institution is an institution which admits students of one sex only[126] or which exceptionally admits students of the opposite sex, or their numbers are comparatively small and their admission is confined to particular courses or classes.[127] Such an institution is not prohibited in relation to the provision of education, benefits, facilities, or services from confining students of the same sex to particular courses or classes.[128]

(c) *Transitional Exemption Order*

6.115   Where a responsible body of a single-sex institution decides to alter its admissions arrangements so that it will no longer be a single-sex institution, it can apply for a transitional exemption order.[129]

6.116   This is an order which authorizes sex discrimination by the responsible body of the institution in the arrangements it makes for deciding who is offered admission as a student; and authorizing it not to admit a person as a student because of the person's sex.[130] As a result, the responsible body does not contravene the Act in relation to sex discrimination if in accordance with a transitional exemption order, or pending the determination of an application for one, it does not admit a person as a student because of the person's sex;[131] or if it discriminates in the arrangements it makes for deciding who is offered admission as a student.[132] The process for applying for and making such an order is set out in Schedule 13, paragraph (4)— depending on the nature of the school the process may lie in regulations or in the Schedule.

---

[123] Sch. 13, para. 8(3), (4), and (5).
[124] Sch. 13, para. 8(6).
[125] Sch. 12, para. 1(1).
[126] Sch. 12, para. 1(2)(a).
[127] Sch. 12, para. 1(2)(b) and (3).
[128] Sch. 12, para. 1(4).
[129] Sch. 12, para. 2(1).
[130] Sch. 12, para. 2(2).
[131] Sch. 12, para. 2(4).
[132] Sch. 12, para. 2(5).

(d) *Higher or Further Education Institutions*

A higher or further education institution can treat a person differently based on a pro- **6.117**
tected characteristic in relation to providing training which would help fit him/her for work
which, under exceptions in Schedule 9, Part 1, can lawfully be restricted to people of a
particular race, sex, religion, sexual orientation, or age and for which they would therefore
be ineligible.[133]

(e) *Institutions with a Religious Ethos*

The Act allows the responsible body of an institution which has a religious ethos and is des- **6.118**
ignated by a Minister of the Crown to give preference in admissions to people of a particular
religion or belief in order to preserve the institution's religious ethos (and where the course is
not one of vocational training).[134]

(f) *Benefits Dependent on Marital Status*

An institution will not be discriminating in relation to sexual orientation if it provides access **6.119**
to a benefit, facility, or service (such as residential accommodation) only to married people and
civil partners, to the exclusion of all others.[135]

(g) *Child Care*

A higher or further education institution will not be acting unlawfully if it provides, or makes **6.120**
arrangements for, or facilitates care (which includes supervision) for students' children of a
particular age group.[136] Facilitating child care provision means paying for or subsidizing it,
helping a parent to find a suitable person to provide child care, enabling parents to spend more
time caring for the child, or otherwise assisting the parent with care that s/he provides for the
child.[137] A child is a person who has not reached the age of 17.[138]

(h) *Educational Charities and Endowments*

Schedule 14 contains provisions specific to educational charities and endowments. It provides **6.121**
for trust deeds or other instruments concerning educational charities which restrict available
benefits to a single sex, to be modified by a Minister of the Crown. This cannot be done within
25 years of the trust being created without the consent of the donor, or the donor's or testator's personal representatives. Applicants need to publish particulars of the proposal and invite
representations for the Minister to consider before making the order. This replicates provisions
in section 78 of the Sex Discrimination Act 1975.

According to the Explanatory Notes,[139] this situation is likely to arise when a single-sex **6.122**
school becomes co-educational, and so wants to enable both sexes to benefit from a particular
charity connected with the school.

---

[133] Sch. 12, para. 4.
[134] Sch. 12, para. 5, and see Equality Act 2010 (Designation of Institutions with a Religious Ethos)
(England and Wales) Order 2010, SI 2010/1915.
[135] Sch. 12, para. 6.
[136] Sch. 12, para. 7(1).
[137] Sch. 12, para. 7(2).
[138] Sch. 12, para. 7(3).
[139] EN 889.

6.123   Scottish Ministers are given similar powers in relation to an education endowment to which section 104 of the Education (Scotland) Act 1980 applies and which in any way restricts the benefit of the endowment to persons of one sex.[140]

16. General Qualifications Bodies

(a) *Generally*

6.124   Chapter 3 of Part 6 sets out specific provision for what are termed 'general qualifications bodies'. These are an authority or body which can confer a relevant qualification.[141] A relevant qualification is an authorization, qualification, approval, or certification of such description as prescribed by a Minister of the Crown (for qualifications conferred in England), Welsh Ministers (qualifications conferred in Wales), or Scottish Ministers (qualifications conferred in Scotland).[142] Regulations have been made in respect of all three countries, setting out relevant qualifications. These include, for example, GCSEs.[143] The Explanatory Notes give Edexcel as an example of a qualifications body.[144]

6.125   These provisions replicate those in the DDA,[145] and extend the provisions to cover the other protected characteristics.

6.126   There are other interpretive terms relating to qualifications bodies set out below.

(b) *What is Unlawful*

6.127   A qualifications body must not discriminate against a person in the arrangements it makes for deciding upon whom to confer a relevant qualification; as to the terms on which it is prepared to confer a relevant qualification; or by not conferring a relevant qualification.[146]

6.128   In addition, it must not discriminate against a person upon whom it has conferred a relevant qualification by withdrawing it; varying the terms on which the qualification is held; or by subjecting the person to any other detriment.[147]

6.129   In relation to the conferment of a relevant qualification, a qualifications body must not harass a person who applies for a qualification or who holds it.[148]

6.130   A qualifications body must not victimize a person in the arrangements it makes for deciding upon whom to confer a relevant qualification; as to the terms on which it is prepared to confer such a qualification; or by not conferring it.[149]

6.131   Where a person has had the relevant qualification conferred upon him/her, a qualifications body must not victimize that person by withdrawing the qualification, varying the terms on which it is held, or by subjecting that person to any other detriment.[150]

---

[140] Sch. 14, para. 2.
[141] S. 97(2).
[142] S. 97(3).
[143] See Equality Act 2010 (General Qualifications Bodies Regulator and Relevant Qualifications) Regulations 2010, SI 2010/2245; Equality Act 2010 (General Qualifications Bodies Regulator and Relevant Qualifications) (Wales) Regulations 2010, SI 2010/2217; Equality Act 2010 (Qualifications Body Regulator and Relevant Qualifications) (Scotland) Regulations 2010, SI 2010/315.
[144] EN 330.
[145] DDA s. 31AA.
[146] S. 96(1).
[147] S. 96(2).
[148] S. 96(3).
[149] S. 96(4).
[150] S. 96(5).

Conferring a qualification includes renewing or extending its conferment or authenticating a relevant qualification conferred by another person.[151]   **6.132**

(c) *Limitations of the Provisions*

These provisions do not cover all bodies which might be seen as conferring a general qualification. The Act says that an authority or body is not a qualifications body insofar as it: **6.133**

- is the responsible body of a school to which section 85 applies;
- is the governing body of an institution to which section 91 applies;
- exercises functions under the Education Acts; or
- exercises functions under the Education (Scotland) Act 1980.[152]

(d) *Reasonable Adjustments*

The duty to make reasonable adjustments applies in relation to a qualifications body,[153] subject to an exception in relation to certain specified qualifications. As with the other education provisions, the detail of the application of the duty is set out in Schedule 13.   **6.134**

A qualifications body must comply with the first, second, and third requirements in relation to deciding on whom a qualification is conferred and in relation to a qualification that is conferred, the latter being the 'relevant matters' for the purpose of the duty.[154] As the duty mirrors that in relation to the conferment of qualifications, the duty is not anticipatory, but is owed to an individual disabled person.   **6.135**

This means that where a provision, criterion, or practice applied by or on behalf of the qualifications body places a disabled applicant/person upon whom the qualification is conferred, at a substantial disadvantage compared with non-disabled people in relation to deciding on whom a qualification is conferred and in relation to a qualification that is conferred, the qualifications body must take reasonable steps to avoid the disadvantage. This might include, for example, requiring extra time to be given to a disabled person where there is a time within which an examination must be completed.   **6.136**

Where a physical feature of premises occupied by a qualifications body puts a disabled applicant/person upon whom the qualification is conferred at a substantial disadvantage compared with non-disabled people in relation to deciding on whom a qualification is conferred and in relation to a qualification that is conferred, the responsible body must take reasonable steps to avoid the disadvantage. This might include, for example, putting in a ramp at an examination centre.   **6.137**

Finally, where a disabled applicant/person upon whom the qualification is conferred would be put at a substantial disadvantage compared to non-disabled people, in relation to deciding on whom a qualification is conferred and in relation to a qualification that is conferred, without the provision of an auxiliary aid, the responsible body must take reasonable steps to provide it. This might include, for example, the provision of a British Sign Language interpreter for an oral exam.   **6.138**

The duty only applies, in relation to deciding on whom to confer the qualification, where a person is or has notified the responsible body that s/he may be an applicant for the   **6.139**

---

[151] S. 97(6).
[152] S. 97(4).
[153] S. 96(6).
[154] Sch. 13, para. 9(1) and (2).

conferment of the qualification; and in relation to a qualification that a responsible body confers, it applies to an applicant for conferment or a person on whom the qualification is conferred.[155]

6.140   The Act contains a power[156] for an appropriate regulator (in England, a person prescribed by a Minister of the Crown; in Wales, a person prescribed by the Welsh Ministers; in Scotland a person prescribed by the Scottish Ministers)[157] to specify provisions, criteria, or practices in relation to which the responsible body is not subject to the duty to make reasonable adjustments, or is subject only to such adjustments as are not excluded by the regulator.[158] The regulator prescribed for England is the Office of Qualifications and Examinations; for Wales the Welsh Ministers; and for Scotland the Qualifications Authority. In determining what reasonable adjustments a body must comply with, the appropriate regulator must have regard to:

- the need to minimize the extent to which disabled persons are disadvantaged in attaining the qualification because of their disabilities;
- the need to secure that the qualification gives a reliable indication of the knowledge, skills, and understanding of a person upon whom it is conferred;
- the need to maintain public confidence in the qualification.[159]

6.141   The regulator must consult appropriate people before making such a determination and must publish what adjustments are to be made in the manner prescribed in regulations.[160]

---

[155] Sch. 13, para. 4(1), applied by s. 9(2).

[156] S. 96(7). See also Equality Act 2010 (General Qualifications Bodies Regulator and Relevant Qualifications) Regulations 2010, SI 2010/2245; Equality Act 2010 (General Qualifications Bodies Regulator and Relevant Qualifications) (Wales) Regulations 2010, 2010/2217; Equality Act 2010 (Qualifications Body Regulator and Relevant Qualifications) (Scotland) Regulations 2010, SI 2010/315.

[157] S. 96(10).

[158] S. 96(7).

[159] S. 96(8).

[160] S. 96(9).

7

PREMISES

A. Introduction	7.01
B. Premises	7.02

A. INTRODUCTION

This chapter deals with the provisions relating to premises. Premises do not fall within the   **7.01**
definition of goods, facilities, and services, dealt with in Chapter 5. They are contained in
Part 4 of the Equality Act 2010 ('the Act'). The provisions are heavy in legislative detail and
remain relatively light on case law. There continues to be no statutory Code of Practice in
respect of premises. There have been a number of cases in which reliance has been placed
upon a breach of the equality duties (in conjunction on some occasions with discrimination)
both as a defence to possession proceedings and as a tool for challenging decisions on homelessness. These cases are detailed in Chapter 8, but, broadly, they have held that the equality
duties apply to decisions to take possession proceedings[1] and homelessness applications.[2]

B. PREMISES

1. Generally

Part 4 of the Act sets out what is unlawful in relation to premises. It is concerned with the sale,   **7.02**
leasing, and management of all premises, both residential and commercial. It applies to both the
public and the private sector in their roles relating to the disposal and management of premises.

2. Interpretation of Premises Provisions

Premises and the terms flowing from them are defined in section 38 of the Act and are as follows: **7.03**

- 'premises' are the whole or part of the premises[3]
- reference to disposing of premises includes, in the case of premises subject to a tenancy, a
  reference to assigning the premises, sub-letting them, or parting with possession of them[4]

---

[1] *Barnsley Metropolitan Borough Council v Norton and Others* [2011] EqLR 1167.
[2] *Pieretti v London Borough of Enfield* [2010] EWCA Civ 1104; [2010] EqLR 312.
[3] S. 38(2).
[4] S. 38(3).

Catherine Casserley, *Premises* In: *Blackstone's Guide to the Equality Act 2010*. Fourth Edition. Edited by:
Anthony Robinson, David Ruebain, and Susie Uppal, Oxford University Press (2021). © Oxford University Press.
DOI: 10.1093/oso/9780198870876.003.007

- reference to disposing of premises also includes a reference to granting a right to occupy them[5]
- reference to a tenancy is to a tenancy created (whether before or after the passing of the Act) by a lease or sub-lease, by an agreement for a lease or sub-lease, by a tenancy agreement, or in pursuance of an enactment[6]
- a reference to disposing of an interest in a commonhold unit includes a reference to creating an interest in a commonhold unit[7]
- a reference to commonhold land, a commonhold association, a commonhold community statement, a commonhold unit, or a unit holder is to be construed in accordance with the Commonhold and Leasehold Reform Act 2002[8]

3. Scope of the Provisions

7.04   Part 4 begins by setting out the scope of the premises provisions.[9] They do not apply to the protected characteristics of age and marriage and civil partnership.

7.05   There are also provisions to ensure that there is no overlap between the premises provisions and other parts of the Act. Thus the premises provisions do not apply to discrimination, harassment, or victimization that is prohibited by Part 5 (work), or Part 6 (education), or would be prohibited but for an express exception.[10]

7.06   In addition, the provisions do not apply where the accommodation in issue is generally for the purpose of short stays by individuals who live elsewhere (e.g., the letting of an apartment for a week's holiday—this would be covered by the goods facilities and services provision).[11] This provision did not previously appear in the legislation.[12]

7.07   The provisions also do not apply where the accommodation is for the purpose only of exercising a public function (e.g., the provision of a police station cell) or providing a service to the public or a section of the public (such as accommodation on a hospital ward).[13]

7.08   Further, Part 4 does not apply to a breach of an equality clause or rule, anything that would be a breach of an equality clause or rule but for section 69 or Part 2 of Schedule 7, or a breach of a non-discrimination rule.[14]

---

[5] S. 38(4).
[6] S. 38(6).
[7] S. 38(5).
[8] S. 38(7).
[9] S. 32(1).
[10] S. 32(2).
[11] S. 32(3)(a).
[12] Thus in the disability discrimination case of *Rose v Bouchet* [1999] IRLR 463, in the Sheriff Court, the claim was considered under the premises provisions, although the premises which was the subject of the claim was a flat to be rented purely for the purpose of attending the Edinburgh festival. Such a case would, post Equality Act, be brought under the services provisions—s. 29.
[13] S. 32(3)(b) and (4).
[14] S. 32(5).

4. Disposal and Management of Premises

(a) *Disposal*

Section 33 of the Act prohibits discrimination in the disposal of premises. A person (A) who   7.09
has the right to dispose of premises must not discriminate against another (B) as to the terms
on which A offers to dispose of the premises to B; by not disposing of the premises to B; or
in A's treatment in respect to things done in relation to those seeking premises.[15] The latter
provision would include, for example, the keeping of a local authority waiting list for housing.
Increasingly, the discrimination provisions are being used to challenge housing allocation policies by means of judicial review, in conjunction with the equality duties. Interestingly, however, the unlawful act has not been specified or the claim has been dealt with under the services
or function provisions—see for example *R (on the application of Yilmas Gullu) (Appellant) v
Hillingdon London Borough Council (Respondent) and Equality and Human Rights Commission
(Intervener)*; *R (on the application of Teresa Ward and Ors) (Respondent) v Hillingdon London
Borough Council (Appellant) and Equality and Human Rights Commission (Intervener)* (2019)[16];
or *R (on the application of Z and others) v Hackney Borough Council and Agudas Israel Housing
Association*[17] where direct discrimination in the allocations policy was permitted on the basis
that the reserving of premises for those who were of the Orthodox Jewish faith was positive
action and the provisions at first instance were services and functions.

(i) *Commonhold units.*   This section of the Act also deals with commonhold units—in   7.10
particular, where an interest in a commonhold unit cannot be disposed of unless a particular
person is a party to the disposal. In these circumstances, that person must not discriminate
against a person by not being a party to the disposal.[18]

(ii) *Harassment.*   Harassment is specifically prohibited in relation to premises. A person   7.11
who has the right to dispose of premises must not harass a person who occupies them or
who applies for them in connection with anything done in relation to their occupation or
disposal.[19] However, the harassment provisions do not apply in relation to religion or belief
or sexual orientation.[20] The exclusion of sexual orientation from the harassment provisions in
relation to premises was the subject of criticism by the Joint Committee on Human Rights
in its report on the Equality Bill.[21]

Although a claim under the premises provisions in relation to sexual orientation or reli-   7.12
gion or belief may not be based upon the harassment provisions, it may be possible to bring
a claim in relation to conduct which would otherwise amount to harassment under the provisions prohibiting direct discrimination—the Act specifically provides that where the Act
disapplies a provision on harassment in relation to a protected characteristic, this does not
prevent the conduct amounting to a detriment for the purposes of direct discrimination.[22]

---

[15] S. 33(1).
[16] [2019] EWCA Civ 692 (discrimination found).
[17] [2019] EWCA Civ 1099.
[18] S. 33(2).
[19] S. 33(3).
[20] S. 33(6).
[21] Joint Committee on Human Rights, Legislative Scrutiny, Equality Bill, 26th Report of Session 2008–
2009, at [68].
[22] S. 212(5).

7.13 (iii) *Victimization.* Victimization is also specifically prohibited. A person (A) who has the right to dispose of premises must not victimize another (B) as to the terms on which A offers to dispose of the premises to B; by not disposing of the premises to B; or in A's treatment of B with respect to things done in relation to those seeking premises.[23] Where an interest in a commonhold unit cannot be disposed of unless a particular person is a party to the disposal, that person must not victimize a person by not being a party to the disposal.[24]

(b) *Permission for Disposal*

7.14 There are specific provisions to deal with situations where permission is needed for a disposal of premises—for example, before a sale can be made, or where a landlord's permission is needed for a premises to be let or sub-let.

7.15 A person whose permission is required for the disposal of premises must not discriminate against another by withholding that permission.[25]

7.16 Harassment and victimization are also prohibited in relation to permission to dispose of premises.

7.17 A person whose permission is required for the disposal of premises must not harass a person who applies for permission to dispose of the premises, or to whom the disposal would be made if permission were given.[26] However, the harassment provisions do not apply in relation to religion or belief or sexual orientation.[27] As set out above, at paragraph 7.12, conduct amounting to harassment in relation to religion or belief or sexual orientation may nevertheless amount to direct discrimination.

7.18 The Explanatory Notes (which do not have legal force but provide an illustration of the Act's provisions) provide an example of how these provisions might work:[28]

A disabled tenant seeks permission from his landlord to sublet a room within his flat to help him pay his rent. The landlord tells him that he cannot because he is disabled. This is direct discrimination in permission for disposing of premises.

7.19 A person whose permission is required for the disposal of premises must not victimize another by withholding that permission.[29]

7.20 This section does not apply to anything done in the exercise of a judicial function.[30] This is intended to ensure that where permission to dispose of premises is refused by a court in the context of legal proceedings, it is not an unlawful act under these provisions.[31]

(c) *Management of Premises*

7.21 The provisions also cover management of premises—what happens when an individual is actually an occupant. There is no definition of a manager, or of management, but the term is likely to cover property management agencies, accommodation bureaux, local authorities,

---

[23] S. 33(4).
[24] S. 33(5).
[25] S. 34(1).
[26] S. 34(2).
[27] S. 33(6).
[28] EN 134.
[29] S. 33(3).
[30] S. 34(5).
[31] EN 134.

housing associations, tenant management organizations, estate agents or rent collection services, and the managing agents of commercial premises.[32]

A person (A) who manages premises must not discriminate against a person (B) who occu- 7.22
pies the premises:

(a) in the way A allows B, or does not allow B, to make use of a benefit or facility;

(b) by evicting B (or taking steps for the purpose of securing B's eviction);

(c) by subjecting B to any other detriment.[33]

The wording of the eviction provisions represents a change to previous legislation, which 7.23
referred simply to 'eviction'.[34] 'Steps for the purpose of securing B's eviction' will cover the
complete process—including the issuing of a notice to quit, and the decision to institute and
continue with court proceedings.

Examples given in the Explanatory Notes of how these provisions might operate are as 7.24
follows:[35]

• The manager of a property restricts a tenant's use of a communal garden by setting fixed
  times when she can use the garden because she is undergoing gender reassignment, while
  allowing other tenants unrestricted access to the garden. This would be direct discrimination in the management of premises.

• A manager of a property responds to requests for maintenance issues more slowly or less
  favourably for one tenant than similar requests from other tenants, because the tenant has
  a learning disability. This would be direct discrimination in the management of premises.

A 'benefit or facility' may in fact be a separate service—and fall within section 29 of the 7.25
Equality Act 2010, rather than be a benefit or facility in accordance with the premises provisions. For example, in *Plummer v Royal Herbert Freehold Ltd Central London County Court*.[36]

Mr Plummer, who was a freeholder of a flat in a block of luxury apartments, had the use 7.26
of a leisure centre which was owned by the freeholders and known as the Royal Herbert
Leisure Club. He brought a claim of discrimination when the management company refused
to make adjustments for him and argued that they were providing a service, rather than
premises providers (thus having a more extensive duty to make adjustments). The County
Court found that the management company, Royal Herbert Freehold Ltd, had breached its
duty to make reasonable adjustments under the services provisions of the Equality Act 2010
and that they had indirectly discriminated against Mr Plummer in respect of what works it
undertook. Mr Plummer was awarded £9,000 in damages for injury to feelings, thought to
be the highest award of its kind for such a claim.

The most significant case in which the premises provisions of the Equality Act 2010 7.27
(the EqA) have been examined is the Supreme Court case of *Akerman-Livingstone v Aster*

---

[32] See explanation of who is covered by the premises provisions of the Disability Discrimination Act 1995
(DDA) in the Code of Practice: Rights of Access: Services to the Public, Public Authority Functions, Premises
and Private Clubs, Disability Rights Commission (2006), at 14.18.

[33] S. 35(1).

[34] See *Lewisham London Borough v Malcolm* [2008] UKHL 43 for a discussion of what the term 'eviction'
covered for the purposes of the DDA.

[35] EN 136.

[36] Central London County Court (judgment available at <https://www.equalityhumanrights.com/sites/
default/files/judgment-mr-james-plummer-v-royal-herbert-freehold-ltd.docx>).

Communities Ltd (formerly Flourish Homes Ltd) [2015] UKSC 15 (<https://www.supreme-court.uk/decided-cases/docs/UKSC_2014_0202>). At issue in particular was the test of justification for discrimination under section 15 of the EqA as compared with justification for Article 8 of the Convention.

7.28   The appellant, who has chronic and severe mental ill health, and who there was no dispute met the definition of disability for the purposes of section 6 of the EqA, had been placed in housing association accommodation after being homeless in 2010. The local authority had a duty to provide him with secure accommodation under the Housing Act 1996 but that duty would cease if he refused an offer of suitable accommodation elsewhere. The appellant had refused numerous attempts to find him permanent occupation and so he was notified in April 2011 that the duty had been discharged and they sought possession of his housing association flat.

7.29   The appellant's defence was that the possession order would amount to disability discrimination and breach his rights under the European Convention on Human Rights, Article 8, which was supported by medical evidence of his vulnerability and need for intensive therapy. The Bristol County Court at first instance held that neither defence was arguable; that the same proportionality assessment applied to the defence under section 15 of the EqA as applied to Article 8 and that the defence could be summarily disposed of.

7.30   The appellant was granted permission to appeal on whether the discrimination defence should be treated in the same way as an Article 8 defence. That appeal was dismissed by Cranston J, on the ground that the usual structured approach to proportionality issues in discrimination claims should not apply because of the context, which was the homelessness duties of local authorities. The same reasons, given in Pinnock[37] and Powell,[38] for rejecting the structured approach to an Article 8 defence applied to a discrimination defence.

7.31   A further appeal to the Court of Appeal was also dismissed: [2014] EWCA Civ 1081; [2014] 1 WLR 3980. It was held that the approach to proportionality was the same under the EqA as it was under Article 8 (paragraph 27) and the weight to be given to the interests of a social landlord was no different (paragraph 29). For a tenant to succeed in a disability discrimination case 'he will have to show some considerable hardship which he cannot fairly be asked to bear' (paragraph 37). There was no difference between a social landlord acting on the instructions of a local housing authority and the local housing authority itself (paragraph 46).

7.32   On appeal to the Supreme Court, though the appellant was unsuccessful on his appeal on the facts, he was successful in respect of his arguments as to the approach to be taken to the EqA defence.

7.33   The Court stated that a complaint of disability discrimination under the EqA, section 15, in response to an eviction raises two key questions: (i) whether the eviction is 'because of something arising in consequence of' the complainant's disability; and (ii) whether the landlord can show that the eviction is a proportionate means of achieving a legitimate aim.

7.34   A court considering whether an eviction is proportionate when a defence under Article 8 is raised can assume that an order would meet the legitimate aims of vindicating a local authority's property rights and of enabling the authority to comply with its statutory duties in the allocation and management of the housing stock available to it.

---

[37] *Manchester City Council v Pinnock* [2010] UKSC 45.
[38] *Hounslow v Powell; Leeds v Hall; Birmingham v Frisby* [2011] UKSC 8.

However, the substantive right to equal treatment protected by the EqA is different from and extra to the Article 8 right: it applies to private as well as public landlords; it prohibits discriminatory treatment, for example, by evicting a black person where a white person would not be evicted; and it grants additional rights to disabled people to reasonable adjustments to meet their particular needs. This is consistent with the obligations which the United Kingdom has now undertaken under the United Nations Convention on the Rights of Persons with Disabilities. This defines discrimination on the basis of disability to include the 'denial of reasonable accommodation' (article 2). States Parties are required, not only to prohibit all discrimination on the basis of disability, but also 'In order to promote equality and eliminate discrimination, [to] take all appropriate steps to ensure that reasonable accommodation is provided' (article 5(2) and (3)). By 'reasonable accommodation' is meant adjustment to meet the particular needs of a disabled person.

7.35

The court went on to say that it cannot be taken for granted that the aim of vindicating the landlord's property rights will almost invariably make an eviction proportionate: the protection afforded by section 35(1)(b) EqA is plainly stronger than that given by Article 8 [31, 55–8]. The burden will be on the landlord to show that there were no less drastic means available and that the effect on the occupier was outweighed by the advantages [34]. Summary disposal may still be appropriate, but not in cases where a claim is genuinely disputed on grounds that appear to be substantial, where disclosure or expert evidence might be required [36, 60].

7.36

In the appellant's case, the judge misdirected himself and adopted the wrong approach. He should have undertaken the proportionality assessment in relation to each defence, and he wrongly regarded this exercise as the same for the discrimination defence as for the Article 8 defence.

7.37

The court was in agreement, however, that there was no point in allowing the appeal and remitting it to the county court. The notice to quit that has since been served by the freeholder of the building meant that the respondent was in breach of its legal obligations and left the freeholder unable to proceed with the proposed sale.

7.38

The case set out the correct test to be applied in section 15 cases under the EqA, as well as making clear the supremacy of the EqA defence to that under the Human Rights Act.

7.39

(i) *Harassment and victimization.* Harassment and victimization are also specifically prohibited under the management provisions. A person who manages premises must not, in relation to his/her management, harass a person who occupies them or a person who applies for them.[39] However, for the purposes of harassment in this context also, neither religion or belief nor sexual orientation is a protected characteristic.[40]

7.40

A person (A) who manages premises must not victimize a person (B) who occupies the premises in the way in which A allows, or by not allowing, B to make use of a benefit or facility; by evicting B or taking any steps for the purpose of securing B's eviction; or by subjecting B to any other detriment.[41]

7.41

The Explanatory Notes also contain an example of how the victimization provisions might operate:[42]

7.42

---

[39] S. 35(2).
[40] S. 35(4). And see para. 7.12 for a discussion as to how treatment which might otherwise amount to harassment may nevertheless be made the subject of a claim.
[41] S. 35(3).
[42] EN 136.

A manager of a property refuses to allow a lesbian tenant to use facilities which are available to other tenants, or deliberately neglects to inform her about facilities which are available for the use of other tenants, because she had previously made a claim of discrimination against the manager. This would be victimisation.

5. Reasonable Adjustments

(a) *Generally*

7.43 As explained in Chapter 3, there is a general overarching duty to make reasonable adjustments which is set out in section 20 of the Act. The duty comprises three requirements: the first, to take reasonable steps to avoid substantial disadvantage created by a practice policy or procedure; the second to take reasonable steps to remove, alter, or provide a reasonable means of avoiding substantial disadvantage caused by a physical feature; and the third to take reasonable steps to provide an auxiliary aid or service where, without it, the disabled person would be put at a substantial disadvantage.

7.44 The duty applies in relation to premises,[43] although it is more limited than in other parts of the Act, such as in relation to services and functions, or employment. The duty to make adjustments in relation to premises under the EqA, as with the DDA has been the subject of relatively little reported litigation, with no appellate litigation at all. Two cases were heard at Court of Appeal level under the equivalent DDA provisions. In *Beedles v Guinness Northern Counties Ltd* [2011] EWCA Civ 442 the Court of Appeal held that the words 'enjoy' or 'enjoyment' of premises used in the DDA meant no more than that the tenant should be able to live in his home as any typical tenant would.[44]

7.45 The detail of the application of the duty to make reasonable adjustments in relation to premises is contained in Schedule 4.

7.46 Schedule 21 contains provisions relating to the making of adjustments to physical features which may require permission from another person—such as a superior landlord or a mortgagor.

(b) *Leasehold and Commonhold Premises*

7.47 The duty to make reasonable adjustments applies to:[45]

- a controller of let premises (defined as a person by whom premises are let or a person who manages them)[46]—and let premises includes any premises where there is a right to occupy;
- a controller of premises to let (defined as a person who has premises to let or a person who manages them)[47]—and to let includes sub-letting;
- a commonhold association (this is a reference to the association in its capacity as the person who manages a commonhold unit).[48]

---

[43] S. 36(1).
[44] See also *Dee Thomas-Ashley v Drum Housing Association* [2010] EWCA Civ 265. This case takes a narrow approach to the duty. However, it is doubtful that it would be applicable to the new provisions, given the reduction in the 'trigger' and the slight rephrasing.
[45] S. 36(1).
[46] S. 36(2).
[47] S. 36(3).
[48] S. 36(4).

(c) *Knowledge of the Need for an Adjustment*

7.48 There will be no duty to make reasonable adjustments unless a controller of premises receives a request from or on behalf of the tenant or person entitled to occupy the premises, or by or on behalf of the disabled person who is considering taking a letting of the premises, to take steps to avoid the disadvantage or provide the auxiliary aid.[49] Whilst the DDA required that a request be made for an adjustment, it also specified that the request be one that could reasonably be regarded as a request (see, e.g., section 24C(1)). This aspect of the knowledge requirement is not replicated in the Act. It is doubtful though that this makes a significant difference in practice.

(d) *The Duty to Make Reasonable Adjustments in Relation to Let Premises*

7.49 A controller of premises must comply with the first and third requirements of the duty to make reasonable adjustments[50] in relation to a tenant of the premises or a disabled person who is otherwise entitled to occupy them. The 'relevant matters' for the purposes of the reasonable adjustment duty are the enjoyment of the premises and the use of a benefit or facility, entitlement to which arises as a result of the letting.[51]

7.50 This means that where a provision criterion or practice (including a term of the letting and the terms of an agreement relating to it)[52] of a controller of premises puts a disabled tenant (or a disabled person otherwise entitled to occupy the premises) at a substantial disadvantage compared to non-disabled people in relation to enjoyment of the premises and/or use of a benefit or facility, the controller must take reasonable steps to avoid the disadvantage. This could include, for example, the removal of a policy prohibiting dogs so that a disabled person who needs an assistance dog can acquire one and remain a tenant.

7.51 In addition, where a disabled tenant or a disabled person otherwise entitled to occupy the premises would be put at a substantial disadvantage compared to non-disabled people, in relation to enjoyment of the premises and/or use of a benefit or facility (entitlement to which arises as a result of the letting), without the provision of an auxiliary aid, the controller must take reasonable steps to provide it. This could be, for example, the provision of information in an accessible format, such as the tenancy agreement, for someone with a learning disability or with a visual impairment. The Act provides that auxiliary aids may include certain items, such as an adapted door entry system, which might otherwise be seen as requiring the alteration of physical features—see paragraph 7.69 below.

7.52 The Explanatory Notes provide the following example of how the reasonable adjustment provisions might operate.[53]

A landlord has a normal practice of notifying all tenants of any rent arrears in writing with a follow-up visit if the arrears are not reduced. A disabled person explains to the landlord that he cannot read standard English so would not be aware that he was in arrears. He asks to be notified of any arrears in person or by telephone. The landlord arranges to visit or telephone the learning disabled person to explain when he has any arrears of rent. This personal contact may be a reasonable adjustment for the landlord to make.

---

[49] Sch. 4, paras 2(6), 3(5).
[50] Sch. 4, para. 2(1).
[51] Sch. 4, para. 2(5).
[52] Sch. 4, para. 2(3), (10).
[53] EN 773.

7.53   There are specific provisions relating to tenancy terms prohibiting alterations. Where a term of the letting that prohibits the tenant from making alterations puts the disabled person at a substantial disadvantage (as under section 20(3)) the controller of premises is required to change the term only so far as is necessary to enable the tenant to make alterations to the let premises so as to avoid the disadvantage.[54]

7.54   This particular provision was the subject of one of the few claims under the premises provisions. *Smalies v Clewer Court Residents Ltd*[55] was brought by a couple who had bought the lease of a two-bedroomed residential property in 2014. The lease contained a prohibition on any alteration to the flat. Mrs Poyner-Smailes (PS) has various conditions affecting her health, including Ehlers-Danlos Syndrome, which is characterized by generalized joint hypermobility, joint instability complications, and widespread musculoskeletal pain which give rise to mobility difficulties.

7.55   The couple engaged builders to carry out renovation works to their premises much of which was to make it more suitable for PS. After these works commenced the claimants were served with a notice to stop the works by the defendant as being in contravention of the lease. The claimants brought claims under the Equality Act 2010 for discrimination, harassment, and victimization.

7.56   Of particular importance in this case was the main claim by the claimant in respect of the alteration clause.

7.57   The defendant relied on subparagraph 2(8) of the lease, in submitting that it was not in breach of the duty by refusing to give consent to the works, which provides that,

It is never reasonable for A to have to take a step which would involve the removal or alteration of a physical feature.

7.58   The court dismissed the defendant's argument, holding that the subparagraph did not apply to the duty to amend the alteration clause, and upheld the claimants' claims finding a failure to make adjustments as well as harassment and victimization.

(e) *The Duty to Make Reasonable Adjustments in Relation to Premises to Let*

7.59   A controller of premises to let must comply with the first and third requirements of the duty to make reasonable adjustments,[56] in relation to a disabled person who is considering taking a letting of the premises.[57]

7.60   The 'relevant matter' for the purposes of the reasonable adjustment duty is becoming a tenant of the premises.[58]

7.61   This means that where a provision criterion or practice of a controller of premises puts a disabled person who is considering taking a letting of the premises at a substantial disadvantage compared to non-disabled people in relation to becoming a tenant, the controller must take reasonable steps to avoid the disadvantage.

7.62   Where a disabled person who is considering taking a letting of the premises would be put at a substantial disadvantage compared to non-disabled people in relation to becoming a tenant, without the provision of an auxiliary aid, the controller must take reasonable steps to provide it.

---

[54] Sch. 4, para. 2(7).
[55] Case No. B02BS101, Cardiff County Court, 30 January 2019.
[56] Sch. 4, para. 3(2).
[57] Sch. 4, para. 3(3).
[58] Sch. 4, para. 3(4).

(f) *The Duty in Relation to Commonhold Units*

As with leased premises and premises to let, there will be no duty to make reasonable adjust-   **7.63**
ments unless the commonhold association receives a request from or on behalf of the tenant
or person entitled to occupy the premises to take steps to avoid the disadvantage or provide
the auxiliary aid.[59]

A commonhold association, in its capacity as the person who manages a commonhold   **7.64**
unit, must comply with the first and third requirements of the duty to make reasonable
adjustments[60] in relation to a disabled unit holder, or someone who is otherwise entitled to
occupy it. The 'relevant matters' for the purposes of the reasonable adjustment duty are the
enjoyment of the unit and the use of a benefit or facility, entitlement to which arises as a
result of a term of the commonhold community statement or any other term applicable by
virtue of the transfer of the unit to a unit holder.[61]

This means that where a provision criterion or practice (including a term of the common-   **7.65**
hold community statement or any other term applicable by virtue of the transfer of the unit
to the unit holder[62]) of a commonhold association puts a disabled unit holder, or a disabled
person otherwise entitled to occupy the unit, at a substantial disadvantage compared to non-
disabled people, in relation to enjoyment of the unit and/or use of a benefit or facility, the
commonhold association must take reasonable steps to avoid the disadvantage.

In addition, where a disabled unit holder or a disabled person otherwise entitled to occupy   **7.66**
the unit would be put at a substantial disadvantage compared to non-disabled people in relation to enjoyment of the unit and/or use of a benefit or facility, without the provision of an
auxiliary aid, the commonhold association must take reasonable steps to provide it.

If a term of the commonhold community statement or any other term applicable by virtue of   **7.67**
the transfer of the unit to the unit holder prohibits the tenant from making alterations and puts
the disabled person at a substantial disadvantage compared to non-disabled people (as referred to
in section 20(3)) the commonhold association is required to change the term only so far as is necessary to enable the unit holder to make alternations to the unit so as to avoid the disadvantage.[63]

(g) *Physical Features*

There is no obligation on controllers or commonhold associations to take any step which   **7.68**
would involve the removal or alteration of a physical feature.[64] However, for the purposes
of these provisions, physical features do not include furniture, furnishings, materials, equipment, or other chattels in or on the premises.[65]

In addition, specific provision is made so that certain adjustments, which might other-   **7.69**
wise be excluded as involving the alteration of a physical feature, such as, for example, the
provision of an easy-to-use tap for someone with manual dexterity problems, may have to be
made. The Act says that none of the following is an alteration of a physical feature:

• the replacement or provision of a sign or notice;

• the replacement of a tap or door handle;

---

[59] Sch. 4, para. 4(6).
[60] Sch. 4, para. 4(1) and (2).
[61] Sch. 4, para. 4(5) and (3).
[62] Sch. 4, para. 4(3).
[63] Sch. 4, para. 4(7).
[64] Sch. 4, paras 2(8), 3(6), 4(8).
[65] Sch. 4, paras 2(9), 3(7), 4(8).

- the replacement, provision, or adaptation of a door bell or door entry system;
- changes to the colour of a wall door or any other surface.[66]

(h) *The Duty to Make Reasonable Adjustments in Relation to Common Parts*

7.70   There was, prior to the Act, no obligation upon landlords to make alterations to the physical features of common parts of premises, such as installing a stairlift. In 2005, the government established the Review Group on Common Parts, which published its report on 23 December 2005.[67] It recommended that legislative change should be considered, for example, to require landlords to make adjustments to physical features of common parts, at tenants' expense.

7.71   Schedule 4, paragraph 5 of the Act sets out the duty in relation to common parts. Broadly, it follows the recommendations of the Review Group. The person responsible for common parts must, in the circumstances set out, make alterations to the common parts of premises, but this can be at the expense of the disabled person. The reasonable adjustment provisions do not affect any action that a commonhold association may be required to take under Part 1 of the Commonhold and Leasehold Reform Act 2002.[68]

7.72   Where premises are part of commonhold land the responsible person is the commonhold association; where they are let (and are not part of commonhold land or in Scotland), the responsible person is a person by whom the premises are let.[69]

7.73   The provisions apply specifically in relation to 'common parts' which are defined as being, in relation to let premises (which are not part of commonhold land or in Scotland), the structure and exterior of, and any common facilities within or used in connection with, the building or part of a building which includes the premises. In relation to commonhold land, common parts are every part of the commonhold which is not for the time being a commonhold unit in accordance with the commonhold community statement.[70]

7.74   The Act does not contain any provisions relating to common parts in Scotland, as these are the subject of regulations, though it does set out particular matters which may be prescribed by the regulations.[71]

7.75   The duty to make reasonable adjustments in relation to common parts only arises if a person responsible for common parts receives a request from or on behalf of the disabled person to take steps to avoid the disadvantage and the steps are likely to avoid or reduce the disadvantage.[72]

7.76   The responsible person in relation to common parts must comply with the second requirement to make reasonable adjustments contained in section 20[73] in relation to a disabled person who is a tenant of the premises, a unit holder, or a disabled person who is otherwise entitled to occupy the premises, and who uses or intends to use the premises as his/her only

---

[66] Sch. 4, para. 2(9).

[67] Reference Group on Common Parts: A review of the current position in relation to adjustment of common parts of let residential premises and recommendations for change.

[68] Sch. 4, para. 6(4).

[69] S. 36(5).

[70] S. 36(6).

[71] S. 37 sets out what these regulations may include. On 11 January 2012, the Scottish government issued a consultation on this. Regulations have been made and came into force on 21 February 2020—Relevant Adjustments to Common Parts (Disabled Persons) (Scotland) Regulations 2020, SSI 2020/52.

[72] Sch. 4, para. 5(6).

[73] Sch. 4, para. 5(2).

or main home.[74] It therefore applies only to residential, and not to commercial, premises. The relevant matter for the purposes of the reasonable adjustment duty is the use of the common parts.

7.77   This means that where a physical feature of the common parts[75] puts a disabled tenant, unit holder, or disabled person otherwise entitled to occupy the premises (and who is using or intending to use the premises as his/her only or main home) at a substantial disadvantage in relation to the use of the common parts compared to non-disabled people, the responsible person in relation to common parts must take reasonable steps to avoid the disadvantage.

7.78   There is a specific process set out in Schedule 4 which must be followed where a request has been made for an adjustment to the common parts.

7.79   The person responsible for the common parts (A) must, in deciding whether it is reasonable to make an adjustment, consult all people A thinks would be affected by the adjustment, within a reasonable period of the request being made.[76]

7.80   The Act specifically provides that where A believes that a view is expressed in the consultation which is purely because of the disabled person's disability, A does not have to take notice of this view.[77]

7.81   Following the consultation, if A decides that it is reasonable to take a step in relation to the common parts, A and the disabled person must agree in writing the rights and responsibilities of each of them in relation to the step.[78]

7.82   This agreement must in particular make provision as to the responsibilities of the parties in relation to the costs of any work to be undertaken; other costs arising from the work; and the restoration of the common parts to their former condition if the disabled person stops living in the premises.[79]

7.83   It will always be reasonable before the agreement is made for A to insist that the disabled person pays for the costs of any work and any other cost arising from the work, as well as the costs of any restoration should the disabled person stop living in the premises.[80]

7.84   If an agreement as to reasonable adjustments is made, A's obligations under the agreement become part of A's interest in the common parts and pass on subsequent disposals accordingly[81]—this means that anyone taking over responsibility for the common parts will also be bound by the agreement.

7.85   The Explanatory Notes provide an example of how this obligation might operate in practice:[82]

A landlord is asked by a disabled tenant to install a ramp to give her easier access to the communal entrance door. The landlord must consult all people he thinks would be affected by the ramp and, if he believes that it is reasonable to provide it, he must enter into a written agreement with the disabled person setting out matters such as responsibility for payment for the ramp. The landlord can insist the tenant pays for the cost of making the alteration.

---

[74] Sch. 4, para. 5(4).
[75] Sch. 4, para. 5(3).
[76] Sch. 4, para. 6(1) and (2).
[77] Sch. 4, para. 6(3).
[78] Sch. 4, para. 7(1).
[79] Sch. 4, para. 7(2).
[80] Sch. 4, para. 7(3).
[81] Sch. 4, para. 7(4).
[82] EN 773.

7.86   The common parts provisions have not come into force at the time of writing. The government's position as explained to the House of Lords Select Committee ('the committee') on the Equality Act 2010 and Disability was that it had delayed implementation 'until Scottish Government experience of implementing section 37 was available' and that it was 'currently considering the future of these uncommenced provisions' [page 72, para. 237]. The Committee's final report *The Equality Act 2010: The Impact on Disabled People* (HL Paper 117, published 24 March 2016) called on the government to bring the common parts provisions into force 'forthwith'.

7.87   Subsequently the Women and Equalities Committee published a report on *Building for Equality: Disability and the Built Environment* on 25 April 2017. The government's response was published on 15 March 2018 and in it the government announced that section 36 and Schedule 4 would be brought into force, following further assessment of additional burdens on local authorities. At the time of publication the provision has yet to be brought into force.

7.88   A House of Commons Briefing Paper (No. 3133, 26 March 2018, *Disabled adaptations in leasehold flats and common parts*) provides a full background to the provision.

6. Victimization

7.89   There are specific provisions prohibiting victimization of a tenant or a unit holder because of adjustments required by a disabled member of his/her household. These replicate provisions in the DDA.[83]

7.90   Where an adjustment is required for a disabled person who is lawfully occupying premises or a unit (in relation to let premises, premises to let, or common parts), the person responsible for making the adjustments must not subject the tenant of the premises or the unit holder to a detriment because of costs incurred in complying with the duty to make reasonable adjustments.[84]

7. Improvements to Let Dwelling Houses

7.91   Part 13 of the Act contains provisions relating to improvements to let dwelling houses. These largely reproduce provisions in the DDA.[85] They provide a procedure for a disabled tenant or occupier of rented residential premises to seek consent to make a disability-related improvement to the premises where the lease allows a tenant to make an improvement only with the consent of the landlord. The landlord may not unreasonably withhold consent, but may place reasonable conditions on the consent. A landlord who refuses consent must set out the reasons for that refusal. In deciding whether a refusal or condition is unreasonable, the onus is on the landlord to show that it is not. This section applies to all leases of residential property used as the occupier's or tenant's only or main residence, other than a protected tenancy, a statutory tenancy, or a secure tenancy. That is because similar rights already apply in respect of those tenancies under the Housing Acts 1980 and 1985. In addition, the provisions do not apply if similar provision is already made by the lease.[86]

---

[83] DDA s. 24F.
[84] Sch. 4, para. 5(8).
[85] DDA s. 49G.
[86] S. 190(8).

These provisions are set out below in more detail. 7.92

The provisions relating to improvements to let dwelling houses apply in relation to a lease 7.93
of a dwelling house if each of the following applies:

(a) the tenancy is not a protected tenancy, a statutory tenancy, or a secure tenancy;

(b) the tenant or another person occupying or intending to occupy the premises is a disabled person (D);

(c) D occupies or intends to occupy the premises as D's only or main home;

(d) the tenant is entitled with the consent of the landlord to make improvements to the premises;

(e) the tenant applies to the landlord for consent to make a relevant improvement.[87]

A relevant improvement is an improvement which, having regard to D's disability, is likely 7.94
to facilitate D's enjoyment of the premises.[88]

Where the tenant applies in writing for the consent, and the landlord refuses to give con- 7.95
sent, the landlord must give the tenant a written statement of the reason why the consent
was withheld.[89]

If the landlord neither gives nor refuses to give consent within a reasonable time, or if the 7.96
landlord gives consent subject to an unreasonable condition, consent must be taken to have
been unreasonably withheld.[90]

Where consent is unreasonably withheld, it must be taken to have been given.[91] 7.97

It is for the landlord to show that consent was not unreasonably withheld or that a condi- 7.98
tion imposed was not unreasonable.[92]

If the tenant fails to comply with a reasonable condition imposed by the landlord on the 7.99
making of a relevant improvement, the failure is to be treated as a breach by the tenant of an
obligation of the tenancy.[93]

Section 190(9) sets out various interpretative provisions relating to these provisions: 7.100

- 'improvement' means an alteration in or addition to the premises and includes:
    (a) an addition to or alteration in the landlords' fittings and fixtures;
    (b) an addition or alteration connected with the provision of services to the premises;
    (c) the erection of a wireless or television aerial;
    (d) carrying out external decoration;

- lease includes a sub-lease or other tenancy, and landlord and tenant are to be construed accordingly;

- 'protected tenancy' has the same meaning as in section 1 of the Rent Act 1977;

- 'statutory tenancy' is to be construed in accordance with section 2 of that Act;

- 'secure tenancy' has the same meaning as in section 79 of the Housing Act 1985.

---

[87] S. 190(1).
[88] S. 190(7).
[89] S. 190(2)(a).
[90] Ss 190(2)(b), 193(3).
[91] S. 190(4).
[92] S. 190(5).
[93] S. 190(6).

7.101   The Explanatory Notes provide examples of how these provisions might operate:[94]

A disabled tenant who has mobility problems asks her landlord to consent to the installation of a walk-in shower and a grab rail to help her use the lavatory. Her landlord refuses consent. It would be for the landlord to give reasons for the refusal, and to show that it was not unreasonable.

The landlord consents to the fitting of the grab rail and shower, on condition that their colour matches the other bathroom fittings, and that they must be removed if the disabled person moves out of the property. These might be reasonable conditions, but it is for the landlord to show that they are.

8. Exceptions

7.102   Schedule 5 to the Act contains exceptions to the premises provisions. The exceptions relate to owner occupiers and to what are defined as being 'small premises'. The exceptions also apply differently for certain protected characteristics.

(a) *Private Disposals of Premises by an Owner Occupier*

7.103   Where an owner occupier privately disposes of premises, they are prohibited from discriminating against a person in the disposal of premises only in relation to race.[95]

7.104   In addition, an owner occupier privately disposing of premises is not prohibited from discriminating in giving permission for a disposal of premises in relation to religion or belief or sexual orientation.[96]

7.105   A disposal is a private disposal only if the owner occupier does not use an estate agent for the purpose of disposing of the premises or does not advertise in connection with their disposal.[97] An estate agent is defined as a person who, by way of profession or trade, provides services for the purpose of finding premises for people seeking them or assisting in the disposal of premises.[98]

7.106   The Explanatory Notes provide the following examples of how the exception provisions might operate:[99]

- A homeowner makes it known that she is preparing to sell her flat privately. A work colleague expresses an interest in buying it but she refuses to sell it to him because he is black. That refusal would not be covered by this exception and so would be unlawful.

- A homeowner makes it known socially that he wants to sell his house privately. Various prospective buyers come forward and the homeowner opts to sell it to a fellow Christian. The other prospective buyers cannot claim that they were discriminated against because the homeowner's actions were covered by this exception.

7.107   Where premises are or have been the only principal home of a person by whom they are let, or who has them to let, the duty to make reasonable adjustments does not apply where certain conditions are met. These conditions are:

---

[94] EN 612.

[95] Sch. 5, para. 1(3). An owner occupier is a person who owns an estate or interest in premises and occupies the whole of them—Sch. 5, para. 5.

[96] Sch. 5, para. 1(4).

[97] Sch. 5, para. 1(2).

[98] Sch. 1, para. 5.

[99] EN 782.

- in the case of let premises, since entering into the letting, neither that person nor any other by whom they are let has used a manager for managing the premises[100] (a manager is a person who, by profession or trade, manages let premises);[101]

- in the case of premises to let, neither that person nor any other who has the premises to let uses the services of an estate agent for letting the premises (estate agent is as defined above).[102]

(b) *Small Premises*

There are specific provisions for small premises relating to discrimination in disposal and management of premises.   **7.108**

Small premises are premises in which: **7.109**

(a) the only other people occupying the accommodation are members of the same household;

(b) the premises also include accommodation for at least one other household; the accommodation for each of those other households is let, or available for letting, on a separate tenancy or similar agreement;

(c) the premises are not normally sufficient to accommodate more than two other households.[103]

Premises are also small if they are not normally sufficient to provide residential accommodation for more than six people (in addition to the person concerned with disposal or management of the premises or any relative occupying the premises, and members of the same household).[104]   **7.110**

The exception for small premises means that where certain conditions are met, the prohibition of discrimination in relation to disposal of premises, permission for disposal, and managing of premises applies only in relation to race.[105] Those conditions are that: **7.111**

- the person, or a relative[106] of that person (A) lives, and intends to continue to live, in another part of the premises; and

- the premises include parts (other than storage areas and means of access) shared with residents of the premises who are not members of the same household as A.[107]

The Explanatory Notes provide the following examples of how these exceptions might operate:[108]   **7.112**

---

[100] Sch. 5, para. 2(1).

[101] Sch. 5, para. 2(2).

[102] Sch. 5, para. 3(3) and (4).

[103] Sch. 5, para. 3(3).

[104] Sch. 5, para. 3(4).

[105] Sch. 5, para. 3(2).

[106] 'Relative' means: a spouse or civil partner, unmarried partner, parent or grandparent, child or grandchild (whether or not legitimate), the spouse, civil partner, or unmarried partner of a child or grandchild, brother or sister (whether full blood or half blood). It also means a parent or grandparent, child or grandchild (whether or not legitimate), the spouse, civil partner, or unmarried partner of a child or grandchild, or brother, or sister (whether full blood or half blood) whose relationship arises as a result of marriage or civil partnership: Sch. 5, para. 3(5). A reference to an unmarried partner is a reference to the other member of a couple consisting of two people who are not married to, or civil partners of, each other but are living together as if they were a married couple or civil partners: Sch. 5, para. 3(6).

[107] Sch. 5, para. 3(1).

[108] EN 782.

- A single woman owns a large house in London and lives on the top floor, although the bathroom and toilet facilities are on the first floor. The ground floor is unoccupied and she decides to take in a lodger, sharing the bathroom and toilet facilities. Various prospective tenants apply but she chooses only to let the ground floor to another woman. This would be permissible under this exception.

- A Jewish family own a large house but only live in part of it. They decide to let out an unoccupied floor but any new tenant will have to share kitchen and cooking facilities. The family choose only to let the unoccupied floor to practising Jews as they are concerned that otherwise their facilities for keeping their food kosher may be compromised. This would be permissible under this exception.

7.113   The duty to make reasonable adjustments contained in section 36(1) does not apply if:

- the premises are small premises;

- the relevant person (the controller of premises or the responsible person in relation to the common parts to which the premises relate)[109] or a relative of that person lives and intends to continue living in another part of the premises; and

- the premises include parts (other than storage areas and means of access) shared with residents of the premises who are not members of the same household as the relevant person or their relative.[110]

7.114   'Relative' and 'small premises' have the same meaning as set out above.[111]

---

[109] Sch. 5, para. 4(4).
[110] Sch. 5, para. 4(1).
[111] Sch. 5, para. 4(3).

8

THE PUBLIC SECTOR
EQUALITY DUTY AND THE
SOCIO-ECONOMIC DUTY

A. INTRODUCTION

The public sector equality duty ('PSED') is contained in Part 11 of the Equality Act 2010   **8.01**
('the Act'). Section 149 of the Act consolidates the specific duties in respect of race, gender,
and disability, which were previously contained in separate pieces of primary legislation,[1]
and extends those duties to cover all of the protected characteristics except marriage and civil
partnership (which is protected to a more limited extent).[2]

Section 1 of the Act, which is not currently in force, provides for a public sector duty   **8.02**
relating to socio-economic inequalities. This requires specified public authorities, in the context of strategic decision-making, to have due regard to the desirability of exercising their
functions in a manner designed to reduce inequalities which result from socio-economic
disadvantage.[3]

---

[1] See Race Relations Act 1976 (RRA) s. 71; Sex Discrimination Act 1975 (SDA) s. 76A; and Disability
Discrimination Act 1995 (DDA) s. 49A.

[2] Only strand (1) of the PSED (eliminate discrimination, harassment, victimization, and any other conduct
that is prohibited by or under this act) needs to be complied with in respect of the protected status of marriage
and civil partnership. This is because s. 149(1) refers to 'conduct that is prohibited by or under [the Act]' which
includes discrimination on grounds of marriage and civil partnership. Ss 149(2) and (3) of the Act require
that a public authority (or body exercising public functions) advance equality of opportunity and foster good
relations between persons who share a *relevant* protected characteristic. S. 149(7) of the Act defines a relevant
protected characteristic as including all protected characteristics within the EqA, except for marriage and civil
partnership. See also para. 2.9 of the Equality and Human Rights Commission: *Equality Act 2010: Technical
guidance on the public sector equality duty: England* (technical guidance).

[3] See s. 1(1) of the Act.

Laura Prince, *The Public Sector Equality Duty and the Socio-Economic Duty* In: *Blackstone's Guide to the Equality Act 2010.*
Fourth Edition. Edited by: Anthony Robinson, David Ruebain, and Susie Uppal, Oxford University Press (2021). © Oxford University
Press. DOI: 10.1093/oso/9780198870876.003.0008

B. THE SOCIO-ECONOMIC DUTY

8.03 The government has made it clear that they do not intend to bring this section into force in England.[4] In Scotland and Wales, the position is significantly different:

(a) In Scotland, the socio-economic duty was brought into force on 1 April 2018 (the 'Fairer Scotland Duty').[5]

(b) The Welsh Government has carried out a consultation regarding bringing the socio-economic duty into force in Wales in April 2020.[6] The consultation concluded on 17 January 2020. It is likely that the duty will also be brought into force in Wales in the near future.

C. THE PUBLIC SECTOR EQUALITY DUTY

1. The Aim of the PSED

8.04 The PSED is an important duty; it has been described as an 'integral and important part of the mechanisms for ensuring the fulfilment of the aims of anti-discrimination legislation'.[7] In the Technical Guidance on the PSED[8] the 'broad aim' of the PSED is described as integrating 'consideration of advancement of equality into the day-to-day business of all bodies subject to the duty'.[9] The aims have been similarly described by the courts: In Hurley[10] the aim of the duty was described as bringing 'equality issues into the mainstream of policy consideration'. In *Bracking*[11] the intention of the PSED was described by McCombe LJ as ensuring that 'considerations of equality of opportunity' are 'placed at the centre of formulation of policy by all public authorities, side by side with all other pressing circumstances of whatever magnitude'.[12] More recently in *Adiatu*[13] compliance with the PSED was described as 'an essential preliminary to public decision making'.[14]

---

[4] The initial response of the Conservative Party to the proposed duty was to describe it as creative of class warfare: see <http://news.bbc.co.uk/1/hi/uk_politics/7827032.stm>. The decision not to enforce the duty was announced by the then Minister for Women and Equalities, The Hon Theresa May, in her 'Equality Strategy Speech' (Colin Street Community Centre, London, 17 November 2010).

[5] The Equality Act 2010 (Commencement No 13) (Scotland) Order 2017, SSI 2017/403 and Equality Act 2010 (Authorities subject to the Socio-economic Inequality Duty) Regulations 2018, SSI 2018/101. The power to implement the duty was devolved as part of the Scotland Act 2016.

[6] A More Equal Wales: Commencing the Socio-economic duty (https://gov.wales/sites/default/files/consultations/2020-02/summary-of-responses_2.pdf). The power to implement the duty was devolved under s. 45 of the Wales Act 2017.

[7] R (Elias) v Secretary of State for Defence [2006] EWCA Civ 1293 at 274, quoted in *Bracking and others v Secretary of State for Work and Pensions* ('Bracking') [2013] EWCA Civ 1345 at para. 26.

[8] Equality Act 2010 Technical Guidance on the Public Sector Equality Duty: England, August 2014 ('the Technical Guidance').

[9] At para. 2.10.

[10] [2012] EWHC 201 (Admin) at para. 70 per Elias LJ.

[11] See n. 5 above.

[12] *Bracking* at para. 60.

[13] R (on the application of Adiatu, Independent Workers Union of Great Britain) v HMT [2020] EWHC 1544.

[14] At para. 203.

2. The Statutory Provisions

Section 149(1)–(2) of the Act sets out the PSED and provides that public authorities, and those who exercise public functions, must have 'due regard' to the need to: **8.05**

(a) eliminate discrimination, harassment, victimization, and any other conduct that is prohibited by or under this Act;[15]

(b) advance equality of opportunity between persons who share a relevant protected characteristic and persons who do not share it;

(c) foster good relations between persons who share a relevant protected characteristic and persons who do not share it.[16]

The above are referred to in the Technical Guidance as the 'three aims of the PSED'.[17] **8.06**

Sections 149(3) to (6) provide more details as to how the three aims of the PSED may be met: **8.07**

(3) Having due regard to the need to advance equality of opportunity between persons who share a relevant protected characteristic and persons who do not share it involves having due regard, in particular, to the need to—
   (a) remove or minimize disadvantages suffered by persons who share a relevant protected characteristic that are connected to that characteristic;
   (b) take steps to meet the needs of persons who share a relevant protected characteristic that are different from the needs of persons who do not share it;
   (c) encourage persons who share a relevant protected characteristic to participate in public life or in any other activity in which participation by such persons is disproportionately low.

(4) The steps involved in meeting the needs of disabled persons that are different from the needs of persons who are not disabled include, in particular, steps to take account of disabled persons' disabilities.

(5) Having due regard to the need to foster good relations between persons who share a relevant protected characteristic and persons who do not share it involves having due regard, in particular, to the need to:—
   (a) Tackle prejudice, and
   (b) Promote understanding.

---

[15] The Technical Guidance states that this aim means 'that a body subject to the duty needs to give advance consideration to issues of discrimination before making any policy decisions. This means it should actively examine its current and proposed policy practices to ensure that they are not discriminatory or otherwise unlawful under the Act. The duty requires relevant bodies to tackle the consequences of past decisions which failed to give due regard to the equality aims' (at para. 3.2).

[16] The Technical Guidance gives a working definition of 'good relations' taken from guidance given by the Equality Commission of Northern Ireland: 'the growth of relations and structures that acknowledge the diversity of society, and that seek to promote respect, equity and trust, and embrace diversity in all its forms' (at para. 3.35). The Technical Guidance states that fostering good relations is intended to 'increase integration; reduce the levels of admitted prejudice between people with different protected characteristics; increase understanding of, and reported respect for, difference; increase diversity in civil and political participation (including volunteering) in the relevant community; increase reported confidence and trust in institutions such as the body subject to the duty; lead to a reduction in bullying, harassment, hate crime and violence against those who share a protected characteristic; lead to a reduction in fear of crime both in respect of those who share a protected characteristic and those who do not' (at para. 3.37).

[17] At para. 2.2.

(6) Compliance with the duties in this section may involve treating some persons more favourably than others; but that is not to be taken as permitting conduct that would otherwise be prohibited by or under this Act.

8.08   The Explanatory Notes to the Act offer the following examples of how the PSED could operate in practice:[18]

- The duty could lead a police authority to review its recruitment procedures to ensure they do not unintentionally deter applicants from ethnic minorities, with the aim of eliminating unlawful discrimination.

- The duty could lead a local authority to target training and mentoring schemes at disabled people to enable them to stand as local councillors, with the aim of advancing equality of opportunity for different groups of people who have the same disability, and in particular encouraging their participation in public life.

- The duty could lead a local authority to provide funding for a black women's refuge for victims of domestic violence, with the aim of advancing equality of opportunity for women, and in particular meeting the different needs of women from different racial groups.

- The duty could lead a large government department, in its capacity as an employer, to provide staff with education and guidance, with the aim of fostering good relations between its transsexual staff and its non-transsexual staff.

- The duty could lead a local authority to review its use of internet-only access to council services, or focus on 'Introductions to Information Technology' adult learning courses on older people, with the aim of advancing equality of opportunity, in particular meeting different needs, for older people.

- The duty could lead a school to review its anti-bullying strategy to ensure that it addresses the issue of homophobic bullying, with the aim of fostering good relations, and in particular tackling prejudice against gay and lesbian people.

- The duty could lead a local authority to introduce measures to facilitate understanding and conciliation between Sunni and Shia Muslims living in a particular area, with the aim of fostering good relations between people of different religious beliefs.

3. Who Does the PSED Apply To?

8.09   The PSED applies to public authorities and to those who are not public authorities but carry out public functions (when they are carrying out those functions).

8.10   Public authorities are listed in Schedule 19 of the Act. Section 150(3) of the Act states that a public authority listed in Schedule 19 is subject to the duty in relation to the exercise of all of its functions unless the public authority is only specified in that Schedule in respect of certain specified functions.

8.11   Under Part 1 of Schedule 19, a 'public authority' includes a Minister of the Crown and a Government Department. In *Adiatu*[19] the High Court considered whether primary legislation and subordinate legislation could be subject to challenge because of a failure to comply with the PSED. The High Court held that:

---

[18] See para. 484 of the Equality Act Explanatory Notes.

[19] *R (on the application Adiatu and Independent Workers Union of Great Britain) v HMT* [2020] EWHC 1554.

(i) *Subordinate legislation.* 'it is clear … that the public functions exercised by the Defendant which are covered by s149 include the steps which are taken before delegated legislation is laid before Parliament. … the function of taking those preparatory steps is distinguishable from the function of Parliament, which is to approve and disapprove the rules as laid down. It follows that there is no inconsistency with constitutional principle for Parliament to have decided through s 149, to give the courts a role in reviewing the process followed by a Government Department before laying a statutory instrument before Parliament'.[20]

(ii) *Primary legislation.* 'The making of primary legislation is the quintessential Parliamentary function… it would be a breach of Parliamentary privilege and the constitutional separation of powers for a court to hold that the procedure that led to legislation being enacted was unlawful'.[21]

A 'public function' is defined as 'a function that is a function of a public nature for the purposes of the Human Rights Act 1998'.[22]   **8.12**

Section 153 provides that Regulations can require a public authority listed in Part 1 of Schedule 19 to comply with duties that enable the better performance by the authority of the duty.   **8.13**

4. When Does the PSED Apply?

As set out above, for those who are not public authorities, the PSED only applies when they are carrying out public functions.   **8.14**

For public authorities the PSED applies to *all* of their activities. The 'functions' to which the duty applies are not merely functions which involve the design or formulation of policy; functions can also involve decisions made in individual cases.[23]   **8.15**

The PSED arises 'whenever a decision is taken which may have an impact on matters contained in it'.[24] Once the duty arises, the authority must consciously direct its mind to the section 149 obligations[25] and must analyse its policies or proposed policies 'with the specific statutory consideration in mind'.[26]   **8.16**

---

[20] At para. 220, see also para. 226.

[21] At para. 229.

[22] S. 150(5) of the Act. The Technical Guidance states 'in general terms, a person will be exercising a public function where it is carrying out activities on behalf of the State and which are similar in kind to services that could be performed by private persons' (Appendix A, at A.9). As the law presently stands, a private body might be held to be exercising a public function and thus subject to the general equality duty if in respect of that function some or all of the following factors are present: 'It is publicly funded or has significant reliance on public funding; it is exercising powers of a public nature directly assigned to it by statute; it is taking the place of central or local government; it is providing a public service; it is acting in the public interest; its structures and work are closely linked with that of the delegating or contracting-out state body; there is a close relationship between the private body and any public authority; it is supervised by a state regulatory body; it is exercising coercive powers devolved from the state' (A.11). The EHRC non-statutory guidance sets out a list of factors which should be taken into consideration in deciding whether an organization is exercising a function of a public nature (EHRC: 'The essential guide to the public sector equality duty: England (and non-devolved public authorities in Scotland and Wales)'), January 2014, s. 2.

[23] *Pieretti v London Borough of Enfield* [2010] EWCA Civ 1104, para. 26.

[24] See *R (Watkins-Singh) v GB Aberdare GHS* [2008] ELR 561, para. 97.

[25] *R (Meany) v Harlow District Council* [2009] EWHC 559 (Admin).

[26] *R (Harris) v London Borough of Haringey* [2010] EWCA Civ 703.

8.17   The duty covers steps which a public authority intends to take not those which it *could* have taken.[27]

5. What Does Compliance with the PSED Consist Of?

8.18   The PSED is not 'a duty to achieve results' but a duty 'to have due regard to the need to achieve the goals identified in paras (a) to (c) of section 149(1)'.[28]

8.19   In *R (Brown) v Secretary of State for Work and Pensions*[29] ('*Brown*') a number of general duties referable to the duty to have due regard were identified, these are commonly described as the *Brown* principles:[30]

(1) Those in the public authority who have to take decisions that do or might affect people with a relevant protected characteristic[31] must be made aware of their duty to have 'due regard' to the identified goals;[32]

(2) The 'due regard' duty must be fulfilled before and at the time that a particular policy that will or might affect people with a protected characteristic is being considered by the public authority in question. It involves a conscious approach and state of mind;[33]

(3) The duty must be exercised in substance, with rigour and with an open mind. However, the fact that the public authority has not specifically mentioned the [PSED] in carrying out the particular function where it has to have 'due regard' to the needs set out in the section is not determinative of whether the duty under the statute has been performed;[34]

(4) The duty is non-delegable.[35] In *R (National Association of Health Stores) v Department of Health*[36] the Court of Appeal stated that this means the decision maker cannot be taken to know what his or her officials know or what may have been in the minds of officials proffering advice;

(5) The duty is a continuing one;[37]

(6) It is good practice for those exercising public functions in public authorities to keep an adequate record showing that they had actually considered their disability equality duties and pondered relevant questions.[38] In *R (BAPIO Action Ltd) v Secretary of State for*

---

[27] See *Adiatu* at para. 242: 'The "exercise of the [public authority's] functions" for the purposes of s149(1) consists of the implementation of the measures that the public authority decides upon. In the present case, these were the steps that were taken to change the rule relating to SSP, and to introduce the JRS, in order to combat the effects of the coronavirus pandemic. A public authority must have regard to the equalities implications of the steps that it intends to take. It need not have regard to the equalities implications of other steps, which it is not taking, and is not even considering. Otherwise, the PSED would indeed go on ad infinitum. A public authority would not only have to comply with the PSED in relation to the decision which it takes, but also in relation to the infinite spectrum of other decisions which it might have taken instead'.

[28] See *Hotak v Southwark London Borough Council* [2015] 2 WLR 1341 at para. 73, *Brown* at para. 81, and *Luton Community Housing v Durdana* [2020] EWCA Civ 445 at para. 17.

[29] [2008] EWHC 3158; [2009] PTSR 1506.

[30] The *Brown* principles are expressly referred to in the Technical Guidance (at para. 2.21).

[31] See para. 7.01 above.

[32] *Brown* at para. 90.

[33] *ibid* at para. 91.

[34] *ibid* at paras 92–3.

[35] *ibid* at para. 94.

[36] [2005] EWCA Civ 154.

[37] *Brown* at para. 95.

[38] *ibid* at para. 96.

the Home Department[39] the recording of steps taken by the decision maker in seeking to meet the statutory requirement was described as an important evidential element in the demonstration of the discharge of the duty.

In Bracking[40] the following additional principles were listed by the Court of Appeal: **8.20**

(1) General regard to issues of equality is not the same as having specific regard, by way of conscious approach to the statutory criteria;[41]

(2) Officials reporting to or advising Ministers/other public authority decision makers, on matters material to the discharge of the duty, must not merely tell the Minister/decision maker what he/she wants to hear but they have to be 'rigorous in both enquiring and reporting to them';[42]

(3) Provided the Court is satisfied that there has been a rigorous consideration of the duty, so that there is a proper appreciation of the potential impact of the decision on equality objectives and the desirability of promoting them it is for the decision maker to decide how much weight should be given to the various factors informing the decision;[43]

(4) The duty of due regard requires public authorities to be properly informed before taking a decision. If the relevant material is not available, there will be a duty to acquire it and this will frequently mean some further consultation with appropriate groups is required.[44]

6. Examples of the Types of Issues 'Due Regard' Must be Had to under the PSED

As set out above, the PSED requires public authorities to have due regard to the need to   **8.21** advance equality of opportunity between persons who share a relevant protected characteristic and those who do not having particular regard to the three factors listed above. There can therefore be no exhaustive list of the matters which a public authority need have regard to. However, a quick review of the case law may assist in identifying the types of issues which may be relevant:

(1) The impact of the grant of planning permission to a proposed quarry development on disabled persons (who were alleged to be liable to be severely affected by high levels of dust and fumes);[45]

(2) The impact of the grant of outline planning permission for a redevelopment on existing residents who were elderly and disabled.[46]

(3) The impact of imposing parking restrictions on elderly or disabled people.[47]

---

[39] [2006] EWCA Civ 1293; [2006] IRLR 934; [2006] 1 WLR 3213.
[40] *Bracking*.
[41] At para. 26(6).
[42] At para. 26(7).
[43] Para. 26(8)(i) quoting paras 77–8 of *Hurley* (see n. 8 above).
[44] Para. 26(8)(ii) quoting paras 89–90 of *Hurley*.
[45] *R (on the Application of Isabel Haden) v Shropshire Council v JPE Holding Ltd* [2020] EWHC 23 at para. 76 (although on the facts of *Haden* the High Court found the council had complied with the PSED.
[46] *Buckley v Bath and Somerset Council* [2018] EWHC 1551.
[47] *Anand v Kensington and Chelsea BC* [2019] EWHC 2964. On the facts of *Anand* the Court found that the duty had been complied with.

(4) The impact of the use of Automated Facial Recognition ('AFR') Technology on women and people from ethnic minority groups.[48]

(4) The impact of introducing fees on people bringing or pursuing proceedings in the Employment Tribunal would have on women.[49]

(5) The impact of a housing allocation policy prioritizing housing for people who had been living in the area for ten years would have on non-UK nationals.[50]

(6) The impact of possession proceedings on people suffering from disabilities.[51]

7. How Much Regard is 'Due'?

8.22   As set out above, the duty to have due regard is a duty to have due regard to the need to achieve the goals identified in the Act. It is not a duty to achieve results.[52]

8.23   As a result, a significant amount of the case law on the PSED is concerned with whether the regard which an authority has had towards the identified goals is sufficient to amount to 'due' regard.

8.24   The Courts have defined 'due regard' as being 'regard that is appropriate in all the particular circumstances in which the public authority concerned is carrying out its function as a public authority'.[53] In *Hotak and others v Southwark London Borough Council and others*[54] Lord Neuberger recognized that defining 'due regard' as regard which is 'appropriate in the circumstances' did not provide a particularly helpful guide but stated that it was not 'possible to be more precise or prescriptive, given that the weight and extent of the duty are highly fact-sensitive and dependent on individual judgment'.[55] It is therefore difficult to predict in any given case whether the amount of regard which has been given is 'appropriate' or 'due'.

8.25   As the level of regard which is considered sufficient is fact specific, a decision that may have significant equality impacts is likely to require more careful consideration than one which is likely to have less. For example, in *R (Hajrula) v London Councils*[56] the court stated that the due regard required will be very 'high' where the decision may affect large numbers of vulnerable people, many of whom fall within one or more of the groups protected under the Act.[57] This does not mean, however, that if the impact is statistically small, the regard required will only need to be 'low'. It is the view of the Equality and Human Rights Commission

---

[48] In *R (Bridges) v New South Wales Police* [2019] EWHC 2341 an argument that the police had failed to take this into account was rejected on the ground that there was no evidence that the respondent recognized or ought to have recognized that the software it had licensed might operate in a way that was indirectly discriminatory. The applicant has appealed against this decision. Going forwards the court identified that this was a matter which New South Wales Police may need to take into consideration (see para. 156.)

[49] *R (Unison) v Lord Chancellor* [2016] ICR 1. The Court of Appeal found that the respondent had complied with the PSED in this case. This decision was successfully appealed to the Court of Appeal, although the PSED point was not pursued on appeal.

[50] *R (on the application of Gullu) v Hillingdon LBC* [2019] EWCA Civ 692.

[51] *Forward v Aldwyck Housing Group* [2019] EWHC 24 (QB).

[52] *Durdana* at para.17.

[53] *Brown* at para. 82, *Baker* at para. 31, and *Durdana* at para. 17.

[54] [2015] 2 WLR 1341 ('Hotak').

[55] Hotak at para. 74.

[56] [2011] EWHC 448, paras 58–9.

[57] This statement affirmed in *R(JM and MT) v Isle of Wight Council* at para. 100.

('EHRC') that much will turn on whether the nature and extent of the impact on even a small number of persons is statistically small.

Compliance with the duty to have 'due regard' can only be achieved if the relevant body has a full understanding of the potential equality impacts of their intended actions. As a result, compliance with the duty includes 'taking steps to gather relevant information in order that it can properly take steps to take into account the protected characteristics in the context of the function under consideration'.[58] The technical code describes this as 'ensuring a sound evidence base' and describes 'adequate and accurate equality evidence, properly understood and analysed' as being 'at the root of effective compliance with the general duty'.[59] **8.26**

8. The Weight Given to the PSED Objectives

If the Court is satisfied that the authority has given 'due regard' to the PSED objectives they will not interfere with the amount of weight which has been given to the equality considerations in the decision-making process. As set out by Elias LJ in *Hurley*:[60] **8.27**

78. ... the decision maker must be clear precisely what the equality implications are when he puts them in the balance, and he must recognise the desirability of achieving them, but ultimately it is for him to decide what weight they should be given in the light of all relevant factors.

This point was amplified by Elias LJ in *Bracking*: **8.28**

"Any government, particularly in a time of austerity, is obliged to take invidious decisions which may exceptionally bear harshly on some of the most disadvantaged in society. The PSED does not curb government's powers to take such decisions, but it does require government to confront the anticipated consequences in a conscientious and deliberate way in so far as they impact upon the equality objectives for those with characteristics identified in s 149(7) of the Equality Act 2010".[61]

9. Specific Duties

Pursuant to section 153 of the Act Ministers of the Crown, Welsh, or Scottish Ministers have the power to impose specific duties upon certain identified Schedule 19 public authorities by regulation. It is important to note that the specific duties do *not* apply to all Schedule 19 bodies but only to the further group of Schedule 19 bodies specified in the Equality Act (Specific Duties and Public Authorities) Regulations 2017, SI 2017/353[62] ('the Specific Duties Regulations'). **8.29**

These require: **8.30**

(1) Listed public authorities with 150 or more employees to publish "equality information" to demonstrate their compliance with the PSED' annually;[63]

---

[58] *Brown* at para. 85.

[59] At para. 5.17.

[60] *R (on the application of Hurley) v Secretary of State for Business Innovation and Skills* [2012] EWHC 201; [2012] EqLR 447.

[61] *Bracking*, per Elias LJ at para. 74.

[62] These regulations replaced the Equality Act 2010 (Specific Duties) Regulations 2011, SI 2011/2260.

[63] Reg. 4 of the Specific Duties Regulations. 'Equality information' is defined as: 'The information that you hold (or will collect) about people with protected characteristics, and the impact of your decisions and policies on them' (Appendix 3 of The essential guide to the public sector equality duty (non-statutory guidance published by the EHRC).

(2) Listed public authorities to publish specific and measurable equality objectives annually.[64]

(3) Listed public authorities with 250 or more employees are required to publish gender pay gap information.[65]

8.31   The specific duties therefore require listed public authorities to be transparent about their compliance with the PSED. The purpose of the specific duties is set out in the Explanatory Note to the regulations. This states that 'the purpose of the duties is to enable the better performance by the authority of the public sector equality duty imposed by section 149(1) of the Equality Act 2010 (c 15) ("the Act"). That section requires public authorities to have due regard, in the exercise of their functions, to [the three equality aims]'.

8.32   Individuals cannot enforce the specific duties. However, if a listed statutory authority has failed to comply with the specific duties a court can take this into account when deciding whether they have failed to comply with the section 149 general PSED.

10. The Relevance of Non-statutory Guidance

8.33   Following the 'Review of the Public Sector Equality Duty: Report of the Independent Steering Group' produced by the Government Equality Office in September 2013, the EHRC updated its guidance on the PSED in 2014.[66]

8.34   Where a public authority does not follow such guidance, it must spell out its reasons clearly, logically, and convincingly.[67] The most important guidance is the 'Technical Guidance'.[68] The EHRC describes this guidance as providing 'an authoritative, comprehensive and technical guide to the detail of the law'.[69] In addition to the technical guidance:

(a) Guidance for England (and non-devolved bodies in Scotland and Wales) includes:

- 'The essential guide to the public sector equality duty', updated July 2014;
- 'Meeting the Equality Duty in Policy and Decision-Making', updated October 2014;
- 'Engagement and the equality duty', updated July 2014;
- 'Equality Objectives and Strategic Equality Plans: A Guide for Listed Public Authorities in Wales', updated October 2014;
- 'Equality information and the equality duty: A Guide for Public Authorities', updated July 2014;
- 'A law about making things better for people from different groups, Easy Read guide to the public sector equality duty', March 2012;

---

[64] Regulation 5 of the Specific Duties Regulations.

[65] Regulation 3 of the Specific Duties Regulations.

[66] <https://www.equalityhumanrights.com/en/advice-and-guidance/public-sector-equality-duty-guidance>.

[67] See in particular Lord Bingham at paras 20–1 and Lord Hope at para. 69 in *Munjaz* and see reference to *Munjaz* in *R (Kaur and Shah) v London Borough of Ealing* [2008] EWHC 2062 (Admin), para. 22. See also on the status of a statutory code or guidance *R v Islington LBC ex p Rixon* (1996) 1 CCLR 119, 123 (any departure from statutory guidance 'must be for good reason, articulated in the course of some identifiable decision making process') and *R v Tameside MBC ex p J* [2000] 1 FLR 942, 951 (guidance issued under s. 7 of the Local Authority Social Services Act 1970 'a helpful aid to the way the legislation is intended to be implemented, and it should not be departed from without good reason').

[68] The EHRC has published discrete 'Technical Guidance' for England, Scotland, and Wales.

[69] 'Technical Guidance on the Public Sector Equality Duty: England', August 2014, p. 5.

- 'Public Sector Equality Duty Guidance for Schools in England', updated July 2014;
- 'Buying better outcomes: Mainstreaming equality considerations in procurement: a guide for public authorities in England', March 2013;
- Collecting information on gender identity, updated 28 May 2012;
- Public Sector Equality Duty and Data Protection, March 2015.

11. Territorial Scope of the PSED

In *R (Mohammed Rafi Hottak and AL) v the Secretary of State for Foreign and Commonwealth Affairs and the Secretary of State for Defence*[70] the High Court considered the territorial scope of section 149 and concluded that section 149 was not limited to Great Britain but is limited only by the territorial scope of the other substantive provisions of the Act: **8.35**

the scheme of s 149 is to apply the PSED by reference to the functions of the relevant body. In the formulation of policy it does not matter, in my view that the policy may have an impact wholly or partly outside Great Britain. The territorial limitations implicit in s 149(1)(a) follow the application of the substantive parts of the act but otherwise there are no territorial limitations.

12. Exceptions

Schedule 18 of the Act sets out a number of exceptional situations where the PSED does not apply. These include: **8.36**

(1) Exclusions, in respect of the protected characteristic of age, in relation to various circumstances involving children such as the provision of education and the provision of accommodation under the Children Act 1989;[71]

(2) Exclusions in respect of immigration and nationality functions but only in respect of the protected characteristics of age, nationality, or ethnic origin or religion or belief;[72]

(3) Exclusion of the exercise of judicial functions;[73]

(4) Various exemptions, under sections 4 and 5 of Schedule 18, in respect of a number of bodies and functions including the House of Commons and Secret Intelligence Service. In *Adiatu* the High Court held that this exception did not extend to cover the process followed by a government department *before* laying a statutory instrument before Parliament.[74]

13. Enforcement of PSED

Section 156 of the Act prevents private law claims from being brought in respect of any failure to perform the duty. Alleged breaches of the general PSED are enforceable by way of judicial review proceedings. The specific duties can only be challenged by the EHRC.[75]   **8.37**

---

[70] [2015] EWHC 1953.

[71] Sch. 18 at para. 1.

[72] Sch. 18 at para. 2.

[73] Sch. 18 at para. 3.

[74] See para. 222.

[75] S. 32 Equality Act 2006.

14. Remedy for Breach of the General PSED Duty

8.38   If an applicant for judicial review establishes a breach of the general PSED the impact of that breach will, in many cases, lead to the courts quashing the decision of the public authority. This is particularly so in cases where the PSED has been breached in the implementation of policies which have a wide impact.

8.39   In *Hurley*[76] (an application to quash Regulations raising fees for university students), Elias LJ stated 'It will be a very rare case, I suspect, where a substantial breach of PSEDs would not lead to the quashing of a relevant decision'.[77]

8.40   However, context is important, and not every decision made without consideration of the PSED will be quashed by the courts. This was recognized by McCombe LJ in *Powell*:[78]

> 44. In my judgment, the previous decisions of the courts on the present subject of the application and working of the PSED, as on all subjects, have to be taken in their context. The impact of the PSED is universal in application to the functions of public authorities, but its application will differ from case to case, depending upon the function being exercised and the facts of the case. The cases to which we have been referred on this appeal have ranged across a wide field, from a Ministerial decision to close a national fund supporting independent living by disabled persons (*Bracking*) through to individual decisions in housing cases such as the present. One must be careful not to read the judgments (including *Bracking*) as though they were statutes. The decision of a Minister on a matter of national policy will engage very different considerations from that of a local authority official considering whether or not to take any particular step in ongoing proceedings seeking to recover possession of a unit of social housing[79]

8.41   In housing cases, it is now well established that the court will not dismiss a claim for possession, where a breach of s. 149 is relied on by way of defence, if it is satisfied that it is *highly likely* that the outcome would not have been substantially different had no breach of the duty occurred.[80] In *Aldwyck* Longmore LJ rejected 'the proposition that, as a general rule, if there is a breach of the PSED, any decision taken after such breach must necessarily be quashed or set aside or even the proposition that there is only a narrow category of cases in which that consequence will not follow'[81] and added:

> 24. These decisions cannot be applied indiscriminately to cases in which a decision is made affecting an individual tenant of a social or local authority landlord as recognized by McCombe LJ himself in *Powell* ... (para 44):

> "In the context therefore of a typical possession action the court, while having regard to the importance of the PSED, will also have available to it the facts of the particular dispute and be able to assess the consequence of any breach of the duty more easily than in the context of a wide-ranging ministerial decision... Rather than acting as some sort of mentor the court should, in deciding the consequence of a breach of PSED, look closely at the facts of the particular case and, if on the facts it is highly likely that the decision would not have been substantially different if the breach of duty

---

[76] *R (Hurley) v Secretary of State for Business, Innovation and Skills* [2012] HRLR 13.
[77] At para. 99.
[78] *Powell v Dacorum Borough Council* [2019] EWCA 23.
[79] *Powell* at para. 44. See also similar comments made in *Durdana* at para. 18.
[80] *Aldwyck Housing Group Ltd v Forward* [2019] EWCA Civ 1334 at para. 25 and *Durdana* at para. 29.
[81] At para. 21.

had not occurred, there will (subject to any other relevant considerations) be no need to quash the decision. If, however, it is not highly likely, a quashing order may be made"[82]

The specific duties can only be challenged by the EHRC though.

15. Other Implications of a Failure to Comply with the PSED

A failure to comply with the PSED or the specific duties may be taken into account by a court or tribunal when they are determining whether or not justiciable acts of discrimination have occurred under the EqA.[83]   8.42

---

[82] See also *Durdana* at para. 32 where the court holds that the trial judge applied the wrong test when she asked herself not whether it was highly likely that on a proper consideration of the relevant factors the respondent would have made the same decision, but rather whether such a conclusion was inevitable.

[83] S. 136(2) EqA.

9

PUBLIC PROCUREMENT
AND TRANSPARENCY IN
THE PRIVATE SECTOR

A. INTRODUCTION

9.01   This chapter begins by considering public procurement in the context of equality duties. The United Kingdom government has not used the Act's regulation-making powers to impose specific statutory public procurement equality duties in England, but the Welsh and Scottish Ministers have made such regulations. It is argued below that equality considerations are nonetheless relevant considerations in a public authority's public procurement decisions as part of the general public sector equality duty in section 149 of the Equality Act 2010 ('the Act'). The extent to which equality can (and should) be taken into account in the public procurement process is also, therefore, relevant to private undertakings which might wish to tender for the provision of goods or services to public authorities.

9.02   This chapter then addresses the provisions in the Act intended to improve transparency in the private sector by prohibiting clauses which prevent employees discussing their pay.

9.03   The Act introduced, in section 78, a power to make regulations which would impose a requirement on businesses to report on gender pay differences. The Welsh and Scottish Ministers have made regulations which, in Wales, require public authorities to publish information about the relationship between protected characteristics, jobs, and pay, and, in Scotland, require a listed authority to publish information on the percentage difference among its employees between men's average hourly pay and women's average hourly pay. Meanwhile, the Equality Act 2010 (Gender Pay Gap Information) Regulations 2017[1]

---

[1] SI 2017/172.

Tom Brown, *Public Procurement and Transparency in the Private Sector* In: *Blackstone's Guide to the Equality Act 2010*. Fourth Edition. Edited by: Anthony Robinson, David Ruebain, and Susie Uppal, Oxford University Press (2021). © Oxford University Press. DOI: 10.1093/oso/9780198870876.003.0009

extended gender pay gap reporting obligations to all 'relevant employers' with effect from 6 April 2017.

B. FURTHERING EQUALITY IN PUBLIC PROCUREMENT THROUGH THE GENERAL EQUALITY DUTY

The Government Equalities Office, amongst others, has noted that the public sector spends many billions of pounds every year buying goods and services.[2] The buying power of the public sector therefore affords a lever to encourage best practice within the private sector by awarding public contracts to private undertakings that are able to satisfy equality-related criteria. This could put pressure on businesses to demonstrate their commitment to equality in order to further their economic effectiveness without involving further legal regulation of business. 9.04

The point was made by Harriet Harman MP at the time that the White Paper on the Equality Bill was published:[3] 9.05

... the public sector will lead by example. But 80 per cent. of people are employed in the private sector and the pay gap there is double that of the public sector. We must also have progress on fairness in the private sector, and we will ensure that in five ways.

Given that 30 per cent. of companies do £160 billion-worth of business with the public sector, we will consider how public procurement can be used to deliver transparency and change....

We expect business will increasingly regard reporting on progress on equality as an important part of explaining to investors, employees and others the prospects for those companies. We will review progress on transparency and its contribution to the achievement of equality outcomes in the light of that, and consider within the next five years the use of existing legislation for greater transparency in company reporting on equality.

The Act introduced, in section 155, a regulation-making power by which specific equality-related duties could be imposed on public authorities in relation to their public procurement functions. Section 155 was brought into force on 18 January 2011, but in the UK as a whole (and in England), no regulations relevant to public procurement have been made under it. Regulations have been made for Scotland and Wales. Nonetheless, there are compelling grounds to argue that, as a matter of general EU law, a public authority may take the promotion of equality into account in exercising its public procurement functions, notwithstanding the current absence of a specific statutory duty. Moreover, there are good grounds to argue that the general *ability* of a public authority to use public procurement decisions to eliminate discrimination and advance equality, and the *duty* on a public authority to have due regard to the need to eliminate discrimination and advance equality, mean that an authority should, as a statutory duty under section 149, have due regard to advancing equality and eliminating discrimination through its public procurement decisions. 9.06

The view of the last Labour government, which passed the Act in 2010, was that public authorities were under an obligation, as part of the public sector equality duties which existed 9.07

---

[2] Government Equalities Office Press Release, 'Equality Duty: Consultation Launched—Procurement and Gender Pay Reports—Key Elements', 11 June 2009.
[3] *Hansard* HC, col. 500 (26 June 2008).

before the Act was passed, to take equality into consideration as part of their procurement processes (see Chapter 8.

9.08   However, no legal provisions specifically directed to equality considerations in public procurement existed (although guidance on the obligations to promote equality in public procurement under the race, disability, and gender equality duties had been published by the former equality commissions). The belief of the Government Equalities Office was that equality was not being used in public procurement as frequently or consistently as it could. The Act therefore provides the means to impose specific duties on public bodies that are also contracting authorities in relation to their public procurement activities (subject to exceptions for purchases which fall outside the scope of the EC Public Sector Directive).[4]

1. The Possibility under the Act for a Specific Public Procurement Equality Duty

9.09   The Act does not itself contain comprehensive provision for the scope of a specific equality duty directed to public procurement. Instead, it contains a regulation-making power which has only been exercised in relation to Wales and Scotland.

9.10   Section 155(2) empowers a Minister of the Crown to make regulations which impose duties on a public authority which is a contracting authority within the meaning of Council Directive 2014/24/EU ('the Public Sector Directive') in the exercise of its functions regulated by the Public Sector Directive. The Public Sector Directive (also known as the 'Public Contracts Directive') repeals and replaces Council Directive 2004/18/EC and, correspondingly, with effect from 18 April 2016, the definition of the Public Procurement Directive in section 155(3) of the Act substitutes Council Directive 2014/24/EU for Council Directive 2004/18/EC. The Public Procurement (Amendment etc.) (EU Exit) Regulations 2019, SI 2019/560 will substitute references to the Public Sector Directive with references to the Public Contracts Regulations 2015, SI 2015/102 or, in Scotland, the Public Contracts (Scotland) Regulations 2015, SSI 2015/446 with effect from IP completion day (currently 31 December 2020).

9.11   Article 2(1) of the Public Sector Directive defines contracting authorities as the state, regional, or local authorities, bodies governed by public law, or associations formed by one or more such authorities, or bodies.

9.12   A body governed by public law is defined as any body established for the specific purpose of meeting needs in the general interest, not having an industrial or commercial character; having legal personality; and financed for the most part by the state, regional, or local authorities or other bodies governed by public law or subject to management supervision by those bodies or having an administrative, managerial, or supervisory board, more than half of whose members are appointed by the state, regional, or local authorities or by other bodies governed by public law. Annex I to the Public Sector Directive contains a list of central government authorities.

9.13   Section 155(2) does not extend to bodies subject to Council Directive 2014/25/EU, on procurement by entities operating in the water, energy, transport, and postal services, which repeals Council Directive 2004/17/EC, or to the new Council Directive 2014/23/EU on the award of concession contracts.

---

[4] The applicability of the Directive depends on financial thresholds, set out in Art. 4 of the Public Sector Directive in Euros.

Accordingly, whilst any body which is a public authority for the purposes of section 150, **9.14** and so subject to the section 149 public sector equality duty, has, according to previous government policy, long been required to take equality into consideration in its procurement process, any specific duty would apply to the class of public authorities as defined by the Public Sector Directive. The Public Contracts Regulations 2015/102 set out, in Schedule 1, a list of central government authorities reflecting Annex I to the Public Sector Directive.

2. The Proposed Scope of the Specific Public Procurement Duty

The Government Equalities Office January 2010 policy statement on the Equality Bill, **9.15** 'Making it work: Policy proposals for specific duties', proposed that the specific duties would require public bodies which were also contracting authorities to:[5]

- address how they will ensure that equality factors are considered as part of their public procurement activities to help contribute to the delivery of their equality objectives;

- consider using equality-related award criteria, where they are relevant to the subject matter of the contract and are proportionate; and

- consider incorporating equality-related contract conditions where they relate to the performance of the contract and are proportionate.

In the absence of specific public procurement equality regulations, these examples are **9.16** nonetheless illustrative of how a public body may—and arguably should—use its public procurement responsibilities to promote equality and eliminate discrimination.

3. EU Control of Public Procurement

Unless and until there is specific legislation regulating public procurement and equality in **9.17** England, the pre-existing EU law on public procurement will continue to govern public procurement decisions, and, notwithstanding the introduction of regulations in Scotland and Wales, EU law continues to have primacy.

The European Union (EU) has long controlled public procurement, essentially because of **9.18** the significance of public procurement in securing (or, if abused, restricting) the free movement of goods and services and freedom of establishment within the EC and in particular the prevention of discrimination between providers in different countries (see Articles 34, 56, and 63 of the Treaty on the Functioning of the European Union (TFEU)); in promoting competition; and because of the importance of transparency and objectivity where large sums of public money are at stake.

In the absence of regulation, public authorities within Member States, advertently or inad- **9.19** vertently, could undermine competition or the principle of non-discrimination, by including factors in the procurement process that impede the ability of undertakings to be considered for, or awarded, a contract. This could happen at any stage of the procurement process: when selecting preferred bidders, when selecting contractors, or in provisions regulating the conduct of the contract.

---

[5] 'Making it work: Policy proposals for specific duties', Government Equalities Office, 2010, p. 24, para. 5.2; p. 27, para. 5.11.

4. Award Criteria for Public Contracts

9.20   Article 67(1) of the Public Sector Directive provides that contracting authorities shall base the award of public contracts on the most economically advantageous tender.

9.21   Article 67(2) provides that the most economically advantageous tender shall be identified on the basis of the price or cost, using a cost-effectiveness approach, such as life-cycle costing, and *may* include the best price-quality ratio, which shall be assessed on the basis of criteria, including qualitative, environmental, and/or social aspects, linked to the subject-matter of the public contract in question.

9.22   The express reference in Article 67(2) to 'social aspects' is an innovation in the latest Public Sector Directive. Also significant is preamble 98 to the Directive which provides that:

> Contract performance conditions might also be intended to favour the implementation of measures for the promotion of equality of women and men at work, the increased participation of women in the labour market and the reconciliation of work and private life, the protection of the environment or animal welfare and, to comply in substance with fundamental International Labour Organisation (ILO) Conventions, and to recruit more disadvantaged persons than are required under national legislation.

9.23   However, this does not allow social aspects to take unfettered priority, and, critically, such social aspects must be linked to the subject-matter of the contract in question. This reflects developments in the jurisprudence of the CJEU on social criteria in public procurement.

5. ECJ Case Law on Using Social Criteria in Public Procurement

9.24   In *Beentjes v Netherlands*,[6] a Dutch court referred to the European Court of Justice (ECJ) for a preliminary ruling the question whether and to what extent a contracting authority could reject a tender because the tenderer was unable to employ long-term unemployed people.

9.25   The ECJ held that an inability by the tenderer to comply with such a criterion did not equate to a lack of specific experience for the work to be carried out (which would disqualify a tenderer). However, a condition relating to the employment of long term unemployed persons was compatible with the Procurement Directive if it had no direct or indirect discriminatory effect on tenderers from other Member States of the Community and was mentioned in the contract notice. *Beentjes* was decided by reference to an earlier-still version of the Public Sector Directive. The decision made plain that social criteria were permissible criteria to take into account in assessing economic advantageousness, provided the criteria were explicitly mentioned and did not directly or indirectly discriminate against a tenderer in a manner incompatible with EC law.

9.26   Given the EU-wide basis for so much UK equality legislation in council directives which apply to all Member States in the field of employment and occupation,[7] tendering criteria referable to workplace-related equality standards which an undertaking must in any event comply

---

[6] Case 31/87 [1988] ECR 4635.

[7] For example Council Directive 2000/43/EC implementing the principle of equal treatment between persons irrespective of racial or ethnic origin; Council Directive 2000/78/EC establishing a general framework for equal treatment in employment and occupation; Council Directive 2004/113/EC implementing the principle of equal treatment between men and women in the access to and supply of goods and services; and Directive 2006/54/EC of the European Parliament and of the Council on the implementation of the principle of equal opportunities and equal treatment of men and women in matters of employment and occupation.

with in its country of residence are unlikely to subject the undertaking to direct or indirect discrimination in the tendering process, provided at least that they make allowance for the fact that EC equality legislation may have been enacted in different ways in different Member States and may have been 'gold-plated' in some. Difficulties might arise where, for example, a particular Member State has domestic legislation which imposes more stringent equality standards if, as a result, tenderers from that Member State are more readily able to comply with a particular equality-based criterion. More significantly, difficulties might arise in respect of equality criteria related to goods, facilities, and services, for example, where there is no pan-EU minimum standard and where standards of legal protection do in fact vary significantly.

The ECJ returned to the question in enforcement proceedings brought by the European Commission under ex-Article 226 EC (Article 258, TFEU) against France in relation to the award of a public works contract in *Commission v France*.[8]   **9.27**

The Commission argued that an award criterion relating to employment linked to a local project to combat unemployment infringed Article 30 of Directive 93/37/EC (which mirrors Article 53 of the Public Sector Directive). The ECJ dismissed the Commission's application, citing *Beentjes* and ruling that using as a criterion a condition linked to a campaign against unemployment was not precluded, provided that that condition was consistent with all the fundamental principles of Community law, in particular the principle of non-discrimination flowing from the provisions on the right of establishment and the freedom to provide services. Further, such a criterion had to be applied in conformity with the procedural rules of the Procurement Directives; it must be expressly mentioned in the contract notice so that contractors could become aware of its existence. The Court rejected the Commission's argument that *Beentjes* only concerned a condition of performance of the contract and not a criterion for the award of the contract. The condition relating to the employment of long term unemployed persons, in *Beentjes*, had been used as the basis for rejecting a tender, and therefore necessarily constituted a criterion for the award of the contract.   **9.28**

Partly in response to this ruling, the European Commission published a new Interpretative Communication on the Community Law Applicable to Public Procurement and the Possibilities for Integrating Social Considerations into Public Procurement.[9] Some passages from that publication illustrate the ways in which equality considerations might inform the procurement process:[10]   **9.29**

At [the] selection [stage], a contracting authority can require references concerning tenderers' experience and know-how. It may, for example, verify the composition and management of the personnel of the enterprise, ... in order to ensure that it has the capability, in terms of staff qualifications and resources, to properly perform the contract.

This example would allow a contracting authority to seek references concerning the handling of complaints of discrimination or harassment in past contracts (especially complaints from past service users, or clients, or where the contractor's staff would be working alongside the contracting authority's staff or in customer-facing roles).   **9.30**

---

[8]   Case C-225/98 [2000] ECR I-7445.

[9]   [2001] OJ C333/27. See also the European Commission's *Interpretative Communication on the Community law applicable to public procurement and the possibilities for integrating environmental considerations into public procurement*, Brussels, 4 July 2001, COM(2001) 274 final.

[10]   *Interpretative Communication on the Community Law Applicable to Public Procurement and the Possibilities for Integrating Social Considerations into Public Procurement* [2001] OJ C333/27, s. 1.3.2.

9.31   The Interpretative Communication suggests that:[11]

> If a contract requires specific know-how in the 'social' field, specific experience may be used as a criterion as regards technical capability and knowledge in proving the suitability of candidates.

9.32   Where the subject matter of a contract being put out to tender engages a contracting authority's statutory equality duties, it may be legitimate to use experience as a criterion, provided that this is not in itself indirectly discriminatory. For example, if a contractor and/or its staff do not have knowledge and experience of the existence and significance of the statutory equality duties and obligations, this may impede a public authority's ability to avoid breaches of its obligations. However, if contractors from outside the UK were less able to demonstrate knowledge and experience of UK-specific obligations, this could be indirectly discriminatory and therefore objectionable.

9.33   After the publication of the *Interpretative Communication*, the ECJ considered the validity of an environmental award criterion in *Concordia Bus Finland Oy Ab v Helsingin kaupunki and HKL-Bussiliikenne*.[12] A Finnish public authority awarded a bus contract to a company that could provide low-emission buses. The predecessor to Article 53(1)(a) of the Public Sector Directive, Article 36(1) of Directive 92/50/EEC, did not expressly allow environmental criteria to be taken into account in determining economic advantageousness. The ECJ held, nonetheless, that the criteria for assessing the most economically advantageous tender need not necessarily be of a purely economic nature and that the environmental characteristics of a tender could properly be taken into account. The ECJ gave particular weight to the provision of ex-Article 6 EC (now Article 11 of the TFEU) that environmental requirements must be integrated into the implementation of Community policies and activities. Environmental characteristics were expressly added to the list of possible criteria in Article 53(1) of the Public Sector Directive when it replaced Article 36(1). However the comments of the ECJ in *Concordia Bus* are of wider application, and have relevance to the scope of the public procurement equality duty.

9.34   In *Concordia Bus* the ECJ said at paragraph 55:

> … Article 36(1)(a) cannot be interpreted as meaning that each of the award criteria used by the contracting authority to identify the economically most advantageous tender must necessarily be of a purely economic nature. It cannot be excluded that factors which are not purely economic may influence the value of a tender from the point of view of the contracting authority. That conclusion is also supported by the wording of the provision, which expressly refers to the criterion of the aesthetic characteristics of a tender.

9.35   It is submitted that award criteria based on a public authority's equality duties (and the extent to which a contractor can assist a public authority to fulfill its equality duties) may be similarly economically advantageous and, to the extent that they are, they are permissible under EC law.

9.36   The ECJ's reliance on ex-Article 6 EC (Article 11, TFEU) in *Concordia Bus* is significant. Article 11 provides that environmental protection requirements must be integrated into the definition and implementation of the EU policies and activities. Article 10 of the TFEU creates, for the first time, an equivalent provision in respect of equality: in defining and implementing its policies and activities, the EU shall aim to combat discrimination based on

---

[11] *ibid.*
[12] Case C-513/99 [2002] ECR I-7213.

sex, racial or ethnic origin, religion or belief, disability, age, or sexual orientation. By analogy with *Concordia Bus*, award criteria which seek to combat discrimination cannot be excluded as lacking economic advantageousness.

The scope of using award criteria not of a purely economic nature was defined further in **9.37** *Wienstrom v Republik Österreich*.[13] Austria invited tenders for an electricity supplier, estimating that it would require around 22.5 GWh of electricity per year. Its invitation to tender said that the award would go to the most economically advantageous tender in accordance with criteria including the impact of the services on the environment. The invitation provided that, in relation to the environmental criterion, only the amount of energy that could be supplied from renewable energy in excess of 22.5 GWh would be taken into account. Weinstrom, an unsuccessful tenderer, challenged the legality of this criterion.

The ECJ reaffirmed the principles it had set out in the *Concordia Bus*. There was no **9.38** infringement of EC law even if the award criterion did not help to increase the amount of renewable energy produced.[14] However, on the facts, the environmental award criterion applied by Austria did not relate to the service which was the subject matter of the contract. An award criterion which only concerned the amount of renewable electricity in excess of the tenderer's expected annual consumption could not be regarded as linked to the subject matter of the contract. The criterion concerned, in effect, the electricity that Austria would not be using, not the electricity that it was buying. Such a criterion was liable to confer an advantage on suppliers with larger production or supply capacities and thereby result in unjustified discrimination against those who could nonetheless meet the requirements of the contract. That would distort competition.

In *Commission v Netherlands*,[15] the Dutch province of Noord-Holland wished to enter **9.39** into a new contract for the distribution of coffee. It wished to purchase organic and fairtrade produce, with the aim of promoting sustainable consumption. In the opinion of Advocate General Kokott, these were legitimate factors to be taken into account, and given priority, in considering economic advantageousness.[16] However, as in *Wienstrom*, they could be taken into account only to the extent of a prospective supplier's performance of the contract subject to tender. The supplier's wider purchasing policy could not legitimately be taken into account.[17] The CJEU concluded that promotion of environmental protection, through organic farming, and promoting the interests of small-scale producers in developing countries while maintaining trade relations with them which took into account producers' needs, through fair trade, were environmental and social characteristics, linked to the subject matter of the contract, which could be taken into account in assessing economic advantageousness, even though they were not related to the intrinsic characteristic of the product. However, it was impermissible for Noord-Holland to require certification by specific organic and fairtrade bodies. And a requirement that suppliers fulfil criteria of 'sustainable purchasing and socially responsible business' were not matters of technical or professional ability which Noord-Holland could specify, because they were not linked to the subject matter of the contract in question and were, in any event, too vague for a tenderer to know how to demonstrate satisfaction of the criteria.

---

[13] Case C-448/01 [2003] ECR I-14527.
[14] *ibid*, para. 53.
[15] Case C-368/10.
[16] *ibid*, para. 150.
[17] *ibid*, para. 152.

9.40   So, whilst award criteria which are not of a purely economic nature are not excluded by the Directive, the way in which they are imposed, and the extent to which they actually relate to works, goods, or services being purchased, is critical.

6. Article 70 of the Public Sector Directive

9.41   Article 70 provides that contracting authorities may lay down special conditions relating to the performance of a contract provided that these are linked to the subject-matter of the contract and indicated in the call for competition or in the procurement documents. Such conditions may include economic, innovation-related, environmental, social, or employment-related considerations. This must have been intended to do more than just codify the ECJ decisions in *Concordia Bus* and *Wienstrom* because those cases were not concerned with the performance of a contract but with its subject matter and the criteria for the award of the contract in the first place.

9.42   The European Commission provided guidance on how special conditions relating to social considerations might be included in the procurement process at the stage of executing a contract in its 2001 *Interpretative Communication*:[18]

One way to encourage the pursuit of social objectives is in the application of contractual clauses or of conditions for execution of the contract, provided that they are implemented in compliance with Community law and, in particular, that it does not discriminate directly or indirectly against tenderers from other Member States.

Contracting authorities can impose contractual clauses relating to the manner in which a contract will be executed. The execution phase of public procurement contracts is not currently regulated by the public procurement directives.

However, the clauses or conditions regarding execution of the contract must comply with Community law and, in particular, not discriminate directly or indirectly against non-national tenderers.

In addition, such clauses or conditions must be implemented in compliance with all the procedural rules in the directives, and in particular with the rules on advertising of tenders. They should not be (disguised) technical specifications. They should not have any bearing on the assessment of the suitability of tenderers on the basis of their economic, financial and technical capacity, or on the award criteria. Indeed, 'the contract condition should be independent of the assessment of the bidders' capacity to carry out the work or of award criteria.'

Transparency must also be ensured by mentioning such conditions in the contract notice, so they are known to all candidates or tenderers.

Finally, a public procurement contract should, in any event, be executed in compliance with all applicable rules, including those in the social and health fields.

Contract conditions are obligations which must be accepted by the successful tenderer and which relate to the performance of the contract. It is therefore sufficient, in principle, for tenderers to undertake, when submitting their bids, to meet such conditions if the contract is awarded to them. A bid from a tenderer who has not accepted such conditions would not comply with the contract documents and could not therefore be accepted. However, the contract conditions need not be met at the time of submitting the tender.

---

[18]   N. 12 above, s. 1.6.

Contracting authorities have a wide range of possibilities for determining the contractual clauses on social considerations.

Listed below are some examples of additional specific conditions which a contracting authority might impose on the successful tenderer while complying with the requirements set out above, and which allow social objectives to be taken into account:

– the obligation to recruit unemployed persons, and in particular long-term unemployed persons, or to set up training programmes for the unemployed or for young people during the performance of the contract,

– the obligation to implement, during the execution of the contract, measures that are designed to promote equality between men and women or ethnic or racial diversity,[19]

– the obligation to comply with the substance of the provisions of the ILO core conventions during the execution of the contract, in so far as these provisions have not already been implemented in national law,

– the obligation to recruit, for the execution of the contract, a number of disabled persons over and above what is laid down by the national legislation in the Member State where the contract is executed or in the Member State of the successful tenderer.

It should be noted that it would appear more difficult to envisage contractual clauses relating to the manner in which supply contracts are executed, since the imposition of clauses requiring changes to the organisation, structure or policy of an undertaking established on the territory of another Member State might be considered discriminatory or to constitute an unjustified restriction of trade.

9.43 Support for the use of public procurement to further gender equality can be found in the European Commission's 2010 guide, *Buying Social—A Guide to Taking Account of Social Considerations in Public Procurement*, which makes specific reference to the gender equality duty under the Equality Act 2006 as a tool for promoting gender equality through public procurement.[20]

9.44 There seems, therefore, to be consensus between the legislative and executive arms of the EU that contractual terms may require a contractor to assist a public authority by complying with measures designed to promote equality between men and women or in relation to ethnic and racial diversity. Examples, approved by the Commission in *Buying Social*, of contractual conditions requiring compliance with core ILO conventions would arguably bring anti-discrimination and equal pay considerations into play as well, and other protected grounds.[21]

---

[19] The Commission gives, as an example in the case of services contracts, establishing a policy aimed at promoting ethnic and racial diversity in the workplace, through instructions given to the persons in charge of recruitment, promotion, or staff training. It might also involve the appointment by the contractor of a person responsible for implementing such a policy in the workplace: see endnote 67 to the *Interpretative Communication*.

[20] *Buying Social—A Guide to Taking Account of Social Considerations in Public Procurement* (2010), p. 15.

[21] See the ILO Convention concerning Discrimination in Respect of Employment and Occupation 1958 and the Convention concerning Equal Remuneration for Men and Women Workers for Work of Equal Value 1951, both considered 'fundamental' conventions. The obligation to comply with the substance of ILO conventions would in any event merely complement an undertaking's equal pay obligations to its employees under Art. 157 of the Treaty of Rome, as amended by the Lisbon Treaty (ex-Art. 141 EC).

9.45   This matter has been considered recently by Advocate General Mengozzi on a reference to the CJEU from the Oberlandesgericht (Higher Regional Court) in Germany, in *RegioPost GmbH & Co KG v Stadt Landau*.[22] The question was whether a contracting authority could require tenderers to undertake to pay a local statutory minimum hourly wage to the workers who would do the work which was the subject matter of the contract. In its contract notice, Stadt Landau in der Pfalz stated that the successful tenderer must comply with the law of Rhineland-Palatinate on payment of the minimum wage in the award of public contracts. The law in question applied only to public contracts. The question was whether this was contrary to EU law on public procurement. The Advocate General observed that what is now Article 70 of the Public Sector Directive allowed contracting authorities to lay down special conditions, including employment conditions, for the performance of a contract. A condition as to minimum pay could create an additional economic burden for those operating outside of the area which would amount to a prima facie restriction on the freedom to provide services guaranteed by Article 56 TFEU. However, since Article 70 of the Public Sector Directive authorizes Member States to require suppliers to comply with special conditions, Member States must be empowered to adopt laws, or regulations laying down employment conditions, such as rates of pay, for the benefit of workers providing services under those contracts: if any condition had to be of universal application, it would no longer be special. Such a condition must, however, comply with principles of transparency and non-discrimination. The CJEU agreed.

7. Exclusion from Consideration: Serious Professional Misconduct

9.46   Article 57 of the Public Sector Directive sets out an exhaustive list of circumstances in which a candidate or tenderer must or may be excluded from a procurement procedure because of its personal situation.

9.47   These include (Article 57(4)(c)) where the contracting authority can demonstrate by appropriate means that the economic operator is guilty of grave professional misconduct, which renders his integrity questionable. In such circumstances, contracting authorities may exclude or may be required by a Member State to exclude such an economic operator from participation. Member States must specify by law or regulation, the implementing conditions for this provision, and the period of exclusion is limited to three years: Article 57(7).

9.48   The concept of professional misconduct is not defined; whilst it is a concept which has been considered by the ECJ in the context of free movement of people and services, it has not been comprehensively defined or considered in the context of breaches of the principle of equal treatment. It seems that it is not intended to have an autonomous European law definition.[23]

9.49   Notably, preamble 43 to Council Directive 2004/18, which permitted breaches of EU-derived workplace equality legislation which had been the subject of a final judgment to be considered an offence concerning the professional conduct of the economic operator concerned or grave misconduct has not been included in the new Public Sector Directive. However, it remains arguable that grave professional misconduct might include at least

---

[22] Case C115/14.

[23] See Case C-226/04 *La Cascina Soc. Coop. arl v Ministero Della Difesa* [2006] ECR I-1347 for an example of another undefined expression which has been held therefore to be a matter for Member States to define (in that case, the expression 'has not fulfilled obligations').

breaches of equality legislation. This was the view of the Office for Government Commerce (OGC) in its publication, *Make Equality Count*.[24] And this was the view of the Commission in its 2001 *Interpretative Communication* at section 1.3.1.[25] The Commission states that it is for Member States to define the concept of grave professional misconduct in their national legislation and to determine whether non-compliance with certain social obligations constitutes grave professional misconduct.[26]

8. Putting the Procurement Equality Duty into Practice

Where a contracting authority invites tenders for goods or services which are themselves   9.50
designed to meet a need that furthers the principle of equal treatment (such as services for
disabled people, or victims of domestic violence, or translation services for those whose first
language is not English), then reducing inequality would be at the heart of the contract.
Award criteria and contract conditions connected to the subject matter of the contract, which
reflect that the contracting authority is procuring goods or services to further equality, would
undoubtedly be permissible. The CJEU's decision in the *RegioPost* case (above), provided
important clarification of the limits on special contract conditions.

The legitimacy of award criteria that are not of a purely economic nature has not yet been   9.51
tested in relation to equality-based criteria. The question in each case will be how much
are they linked to the subject matter of the contract. The closer the link, the greater their
proportionality, and, provided they are applied in a transparent and non-discriminatory
manner, the greater the likelihood that they will be immune from challenge. The existence
of the statutory equality duties on public authorities provides a degree of linkage with
the performance of a contract. This will be especially true, for example, when a prospective contractor's workers will work side-by-side with a contracting authority's staff or in
customer-facing roles.

In situations where the performance of a function through the supply of works, goods, or   9.52
services from contractors will impact on an authority's compliance with its equality duties
and with any matters identified as relevant to promoting equality, ensuring that a tenderer is
able to provide a high standard of awareness and appreciation of the need for equal treatment
will be linked to the subject matter of the contract. By definition, equality duties ought (subject to the statutory exceptions in Schedule 18 to the Act) to be generally applicable, affecting
all of the functions of a public authority specified in Schedule 19. A tender that demonstrates
the highest standard of commitment to promoting equal treatment, at least to the extent that

---

[24] See p. 14, col. 2.

[25] 'Circumstances can thus be envisaged in which tenderers who have not complied with social legislation can be excluded from public procurement procedures, where such non-compliance is deemed to constitute grave professional misconduct or an offence having a bearing on its professional conduct. These exclusion clauses can also include, for example, non-compliance with provisions on equality of treatment, [...] or with provisions in favour of certain categories of persons (36). A contracting authority may, for example, exclude a tenderer from its Member State who has not introduced an equal opportunities policy as required by the national legislation of the Member State where the contracting authority is established, provided that non-compliance with such legislation constitutes grave misconduct in the Member State in question.'

[26] 'Grave professional misconduct is a concept that is not yet defined by European legislation or case law. It is thus for the Member States to define this concept in their national legislation and to determine whether non-compliance with certain social obligations constitutes grave professional misconduct': *Interpretative Communication*, n. 13 above, s. 1.3.1.

it assists a public authority to comply with, and further, its statutory equality duties, will thus succeed on this aspect of economic advantageousness. The award criterion would be linked to the subject matter of the contract, because having due regard to equality and the promotion of equal treatment is to be mainstreamed into the contracting authority's duties and priorities. Other evaluation criteria, and the weighting to be given to each criterion, will remain relevant in determining economic advantageousness overall.

9.53   In January 2013, the government issued a Procurement Policy Note on Public Procurement and the Public Sector Equality Duty (which remains in force),[27] reminding central government departments of their legal obligations under the Public Sector Equality Duty when conducting public procurement activities. This suggests that the government sees equality considerations in public procurement as more than merely optional.

9.54   The Equality and Human Rights Commission has published a helpful guide for public authorities in England: *Buying better outcomes: Mainstreaming equality considerations in procurement.*[28]

9. The Equality Act (Statutory Duties) (Wales) Regulations 2011

9.55   The Welsh Ministers, pursuant to section 153(2) of the Act, have made regulations, the Equality Act (Statutory Duties) (Wales) Regulations 2011, SI 2011/1064, which impose a specific public procurement duty. With effect from 6 April 2011, where an authority which is a contracting authority proposes to enter into a relevant agreement on the basis of an offer which is the most economically advantageous, it must have due regard to whether the award criteria should include considerations relevant to its performance of the general equality duty: regulation 18(1). Where a contracting authority proposes to stipulate conditions relating to the performance of a relevant agreement, it must have due regard to whether the conditions should include considerations relevant to the performance of its general equality duty: regulation 18(2).

10. The Equality Act 2010 (Specific Duties) (Scotland) Regulations 2012/162

9.56   Meanwhile, the Scottish Ministers, also acting under section 153(2), made the Equality Act 2010 (Specific Duties) (Scotland) Regulations 2012/162, which came into force on 27 May 2012.

9.57   Regulation 9(1) and (2) of the Scottish Regulations mirror the provisions of regulation 18(1) and (2) of the Welsh Regulations, above. However, Regulation 9(3) imposes an express proportionality requirement which the Welsh Regulations lack: nothing in regulation 9 imposes any requirement on a contracting authority where in all the circumstances such a requirement would not be related, and proportionate, to the subject matter of the public contract.

9.58   The Equality and Human Rights Commission has issued a helpful guide for public authorities in Scotland on procurement and the public sector equality duty.

---

[27] <https://www.gov.uk/government/publications/procurement-policy-note-01-13-public-sector-equality-duty>.

[28] <https://www.equalityhumanrights.com/en/advice-and-guidance/guidance-public-sector-procurement>.

C. EMPLOYMENT DATA IN THE PUBLIC SECTOR

In its policy statement on the Equality Bill,[29] the Labour government proposed introducing **9.59** a specific duty requiring public bodies with 150 or more employees to publish annually their organizational employment data in relation to:

- the overall median gender pay gap (i.e., the percentage difference between male and female permanent employees' median hourly pay, excluding overtime and including part-time workers, with no weighting of employees related to the number of hours worked);
- the percentage of the workforce of:
  - people from ethnic minority groups;
  - people with disabilities.

The objectives would have been to enable public authorities to identify problem areas, **9.60** and enable third parties to benchmark public bodies and hold poor performers to account.

The devolved administrations in Wales and Scotland have introduced legislation requiring **9.61** the collection and publication of employment equality data.

1. Wales

In Wales, regulation 9(1) to (4) of the Equality Act 2010 (Statutory Duties) (Wales) **9.62** Regulations 2011 requires an authority to collect and publish information showing:

- the number of people employed by the authority on 31 March each year; and
- the number of people employed by the authority on that date broken down by:
  - job;
  - grade;
  - pay;
  - contract type; and
  - working pattern.
- the number, during the year ending on 31 March, of:
  - people who have applied externally for employment with the authority;
  - the authority's employees who:
    - have changed, or who applied to change, position (including the number who were successful in their application);
    - applied for training (including the number who were successful in their application);
    - completed the training;
    - were or are the maker or subject of a grievance;
    - were or are the subject of disciplinary proceedings;
    - left the employment of the authority.

---

[29] 'Making it work: Policy proposals for specific duties', Government Equalities Office, 2010, pp. 20–3.

9.63   The numbers of people sharing a protected characteristic must be identified in relation to each break down, other than those relating to job, grade, pay, contract type, and working pattern. In relation to those five factors, the numbers of employees who are men and women must be identified. However, the regulation cannot be used to require any person to provide information to an authority (regulation 9(5)), so an authority cannot insist on employees (or prospective employees: regulation 9(6))) disclosing details of their sexual orientation, (dis)ability, or religion or belief, for example.

2. Scotland

9.64   The Equality Act 2010 (Specific Duties) (Scotland) Regulations 2012 impose a duty on listed authorities to take steps to gather information on the composition, recruitment, development, and retention of the authority's employees with respect to age, disability, gender reassignment, pregnancy, maternity, race, religion, belief, sex, and sexual orientation and publish biennially a report including an annual breakdown of that information and details of the progress that the authority has made in gathering and using that information to enable it to better perform the general equality duty (regulation 6).

9.65   With effect from 18 March 2016, regulation 6A requires the Scottish Ministers to take steps to gather information on the relevant protected characteristics of members of certain authorities and prove that information to the authority in question. Each such authority is required to include in its biennial report details of the number of men and women who have been members of the authority in the period covered by the report and the way in which information provided by the Scottish Ministers has been and will be used towards there being diversity among the authority's members in respect of age, disability, gender reassignment, pregnancy, maternity, race, religion, belief, sex, and sexual orientation.

9.66   Regulation 7 requires authorities with at least twenty employees to publish information on the percentage difference between the mean average hourly pay (excluding overtime) of its male and female employees. The deadline for publication varies from authority to authority and is regulated by regulation 8A.

9.67   Regulation 8 requires authorities with at least twenty employees to publish a statement specifying occupational segregation, and the authority's policy on equal pay, between: men and women, disabled and non-disabled employees, and people in a minority racial group and those in a majority racial group, in particular grades and occupations. 'Racial group' for these purposes is defined by reference to section 9 of the Act, and therefore, there may need to be multiple breakdowns addressing separately colour, nationality, ethnic origins, national origins, and (on the making of regulations to that effect) caste.

9.68   An authority must, so far as is practicable, comply with its duty to publish information by employing an existing means of public performance reporting. It must in any event publish in a manner that makes the information accessible to the public: regulation 10.

3. England and the United Kingdom

9.69   The Equality Act 2010 (Specific Duties and Public Authorities) Regulations 2017[30] require 'relevant public authorities' (meaning those listed in Schedule 2 to the regulations which have

---

[30] SI 2017/353.

250 or more employees on the snapshot date) to publish gender pay gap information. The kinds of information that must be reported are essentially the same as for private employers under the Equality Act 2010 (Gender Pay Gap Information) Regulations 2017,[31] discussed in more detail below, but the snapshot date is 31 March, rather than 5 April. The public authorities listed in Schedule 2 include the armed forces, the police, regulators, ministers and government departments, NHS trusts, and the BBC, whose gender pay reporting led to several equal pay challenges.

D. TRANSPARENCY IN THE PRIVATE SECTOR

1. Discussing Terms and Conditions of Employment with Colleagues

Prior to the Act, there was no express provision which rendered void a term or condition in a contract of employment which kept the terms under which an employee was employed confidential to that employee. Preventing discussions between employees as to their terms and conditions, and in particular any terms relating to pay, impedes the discovery of pay inequalities linked to gender. Whilst the well-established questionnaire procedure, now set out in section 138 of the Act, has long provided a means for obtaining information about pay levels, there is no compulsion to the procedure—employers can and do fail to respond—and the process can be long-winded (a respondent has eight weeks to respond: section 138(4)) and formal, and is not widely understood and used by non-lawyers.   **9.70**

Employers have also hidden behind the shield of data protection legislation, although such arguments by employers are not always well-founded. A comprehensive consideration of the impact of data protection legislation on access to information, and the non-statutory questionnaire procedure is beyond the scope of this chapter, but they are provisions that should be borne in mind by questioners and respondents where data protection arguments are raised.   **9.71**

By contrast, little could be more straightforward than allowing for discussion between two or more work colleagues about their respective levels of pay. If the colleagues are doing the same work, but discussions reveal that they receive different pay (and are of different genders), this could well provide the basis for sending a statutory questionnaire, or bringing a complaint.   **9.72**

Section 77(1) and (2) of the Equality Act 2010 provide that a term of a person's work that purports to prevent or restrict the person (P) from disclosing or seeking to disclose information about the terms of P's work or from seeking the disclosure of information from a colleague about the terms of the colleague's work is unenforceable against P insofar as P makes or seeks to make a 'relevant pay disclosure', or seeks a relevant pay disclosure from the colleague.   **9.73**

The 'terms of a person's work' are the terms in the contract under which the person works or, in the case of an office holder, the terms of the person's appointment to that office: section 80(2). The Act does not distinguish between express and implied terms and written or unwritten terms.   **9.74**

Section 83(2) defines employment to include workers, apprentices, and Crown employees. The provisions apply to members of the armed forces: section 83(3).   **9.75**

A 'relevant pay disclosure' is defined as a disclosure made for the purpose of enabling the person who makes it, or the person to whom it is made, to find out whether or to what extent   **9.76**

---

[31] SI 2017/172.

there is, in relation to the work in question, a connection between pay and having (or not having) a particular protected characteristic: section 77(3).

9.77 The Act does not make express provision for the situation where A and B (a man and a woman) are each entitled by their contracts of employment to a bonus, determination of which is entirely discretionary and where there is a contractual prohibition on discussing bonuses awarded. The contractual terms are the same for the man and the woman, but there may be concerns that the amounts awarded by way of a bonus—in the exercise of the employer's discretion—are different and related to sex. Would an enquiry by the woman of the man about the level of his bonus be for the purpose of enabling the person to find out whether or to what extent there is, in relation to the work in question, a connection between pay and sex? Section 77(1) and (2) render void contractual prohibitions on communication of information about terms of work, not about how the employer has exercised its discretion pursuant to a broad contractual discretion. However, the wording of section 77(3) is broad, applying to disclosures made in the context of finding out in relation to the work a connection between pay and a protected characteristic. The Act is unhelpfully ambiguous on the question whether Parliament intended discussions about discretionary bonuses to be protected, notwithstanding a contractual prohibition to the contrary.

9.78 The Equality Bill originally defined 'colleague' for the purposes of section 77, but later amendments to the Bill mean that colleague is now not defined in the Act, except that a colleague includes a former colleague: section 77(2). Accordingly, the question whether someone is a colleague is a question of fact.

9.79 The statutory definition of colleague is not limited—or at least not necessarily limited—by reference to the same job title, or grade, or general type of work. Nor could it be if it was to be effective in exposing discriminatory pay differentials where, for example, the work is similar, but the grading is different. It seems to allow for discussion between workers who might not colloquially be considered colleagues, for example people who do not know each other or do not work at all with each other, and for people in a line-management relationship to one another.

9.80 The protection of section 77 appears to be afforded only where, objectively viewed, the conditions for protection are met. So if, for example, two people believe that they are colleagues, or believe that they are having a relevant pay discussion but in fact they are not, then they would seem to lack protection. There are no provisions which allow for reasonable belief in a particular state of affairs or good faith.

9.81 Being involved in a relevant pay discussion is also treated as a protected act for the purposes of the prohibitions on victimization contained in section 27 and section 39(3) and (4) (employment), section 49(5) and (8) (personal office), and section 50(5) and (9) (public office).

2. Gender Pay Gap Information

9.82 Section 78 of the Act provided that regulations might require employers to publish information relating to the pay of employees for the purpose of showing whether there are differences in the pay of men and women. Section 78 does not apply to employers with fewer than 250 employees, government departments, the armed forces, or public authorities specified in Schedule 19 to the Act. Its focus, therefore, is the private and voluntary sectors, in distinction to the Welsh and Scottish regulations. Section 78 was not brought into force by the coalition government. But section 147 of the Small Business, Enterprise and Employment Act 2015 required the Secretary of State to make regulations under section 78 no later than 12 months after the passing of the 2015 Act.

The Equality Act 2010 (Gender Pay Gap Information) Regulations 2017[32] came into force **9.83** on 6 April 2017, nearly two years after the passing of the 2015 Act (section 147 of the Small Business, Enterprise and Employment Act 2015 was not brought into force).

They apply to 'relevant employers', employing 250 or more relevant employees: regula- **9.84** tion 1. The regulations do not have an express territorial extent, but logically share the territorial extent of the Act, which applies to Great Britain. The regulations therefore apply to employees working in Scotland and Wales, as well as England, and they may apply to employees who do not work invariably within Great Britain. The armed forces, government departments, and employers who are public authorities within Schedule 19 to the Act are not relevant employers for the purposes of the regulations (and their statutory duties arise under the Equality Act 2010 (Specific Duties and Public Authorities) Regulations 2017[33]). 'Employees' do not include partners in firms (including limited liability partnerships), to the extent defined by regulation 1(4).

'Ordinary pay' is defined by regulation 3 to include basic pay, paid leave, pay for piece- **9.85** work, allowances and shift premia, but excludes overtime pay, benefits in kind, redundancy and termination pay, and pay in lieu of leave. Pay is to be calculated gross. Regulation 4 defines bonus pay as remuneration (whether in money or specified alternative forms) which relates to profit sharing, productivity, performance, incentive or commission (but excludes ordinary pay, overtime, and payments on termination of employment).

Within 12 months of 5 April 2017, and that date each year thereafter (the 'snapshot date'), **9.86** relevant employers must publish the difference in mean and median hourly pay between male and female relevant employees in the pay period (that is, the period in respect of which the employer pays the employee, be it weekly, fortnightly, monthly, etc.) within which 5 April (the snapshot date) falls: regulations 2(1)(a)–(b), 5(2). The difference in mean bonus pay between relevant male and female employees in the 12 months ending with 5 April must also be published: regulations 2(1)(c)—(d), 10, 11. So must the proportion of male and female relevant employees who received bonus pay (regulations 2(1)(e), 12) and the number of male and female relevant employees employed by the relevant employer in quartile pay bands, from lowest pay to highest pay (regulations 2(1)(f), 13). Regulations 6 and 7 make provision for how pay is to be calculated and expressed.

The information must be accompanied by a signed written statement from a director, LLP **9.87** member, partner, or senior employee (according to the nature of the employer), confirming that the information is accurate: regulation 14(1). It must be published on the employer's website and uploaded on a website designated by the Secretary of State: regulation 15.

The Secretary of State is required to review the regulations not later than five years after **9.88** they come into force and set out the conclusions of each review in a report which considers the objectives of the regulations, the extent to which they are achieved and whether they could be achieved through reduced regulation.

Significantly, there is no sanction for non-compliance with the regulations: the govern- **9.89** ment has expressed the hope that naming and shaming those employers who fail to comply will be sufficient deterrence, and its current guidance notes the ability of the Equality and

---

[32] SI 2017/172.
[33] SI 2017/353.

Human Rights Commission to take action in relation to employers who fail to comply under section 20 of the Equality Act 2006.

9.90   Also significant is the difference between equal pay and a lack of gender pay differential. The assessment of gender pay differentials is concerned as much with occupational gender pay segregation as with equal pay: an employer may provide equal pay but have a substantial gender pay gap, if women tend to be employed in low-value jobs and men in high-value jobs, for example. Conversely, an employer with no gender pay gap whatsoever may nonetheless be failing to provide equal pay to some or many of its employees if mean and median averages disguise a lack of equal pay for like work or work of equal value, for example. So, companies reporting small or no gender pay gaps are not thereby confirming that they are providing equal pay to men and women. The detail that employers are required to provide, however, for example, bonus comparisons and the gender of employees by pay quartile are likely, in practice, to reveal some information about the extent to which an employer is providing equal pay and about occupational gender-pay segregation.

9.91   Notably lacking from the 2017 Regulations are any provisions—equivalent to those in the Welsh and Scottish Regulations—which require publication of information about protected characteristics other than sex. The Equality and Human Rights Commission has produced recommendations on measuring and reporting on disability and ethnicity pay gaps.[34]

3. Equal Pay Audits

9.92   There are now, however, limited powers for an employer which has been found to have breached the principle of equal pay to be ordered to carry out an audit. Pursuant to the Equality Act (Equal Pay Audits) Regulations 2014, where, in respect a complaint presented to an Employment Tribunal from 1 October 2014, the tribunal finds that there has been an equal pay breach, it must order the employer to carry out an audit: regulation 2. But the tribunal must not order the respondent to carry out an audit if the information that would be included in such an audit is already available from an audit carried out in the three years preceding the tribunal's judgment, or it is clear without an audit whether any action is required to avoid equal pay breaches, or the breach which the tribunal has found gives no reason to think that there may be other breaches, or the disadvantages of an audit would outweigh its benefits: regulation 3. There are further exemptions, even if these considerations are not met for businesses with fewer than ten employees and new businesses (started within 12 months of the date of the tribunal complaint).

E. CONCLUSION

9.93   After a slow start, the Act's provisions addressing public procurement and transparency in the public *and* private sectors have begun to take shape. It remains to be seen how employers and public authorities engage with the duties on them to provide information, and take steps to comply with the duties on them to eliminate discrimination and, in the case of public authorities, advance equality.

---

[34] <https://www.equalityhumanrights.com/en/publication-download/measuring-and-reporting-disability-and-ethnicity-pay-gaps>.

10

ENFORCEMENT

Part 9 of the Equality Act 2010 ('the Act') sets out the procedure for seeking redress for contraventions of the Act. The Act deals separately with the civil courts procedure in relation to the provision of services, exercise of public functions, disposal and management of premises, education (other than in relation to disability) and associations, and the procedure of the employment tribunal in relation to work and equal pay. **10.01**

Although Part 9 does not deal with the enforcement powers of the Equality and Human Rights Commission which are set out in Part 1 of the Equality Act 2006, these are summarized for completeness. Part 10 is also included in respect of the enforcement of discriminatory terms in contracts and agreements. **10.02**

A. THE CIVIL COURTS

1. Jurisdiction

Section 114 sets out the jurisdiction of the county court, or sheriff court in Scotland, to determine claims in relation to services and public functions, premises, education, and associations. When a claim under section 114 of the 2010 Act is commenced, the claimant must give notice of the commencement of the proceedings to the Equality and Human Rights Commission and file a copy of that notice with the court. In the event of non-compliance with this requirement the court will consider whether any order should be made or any step taken; but any such order or step should not involve any sanction (including any stay, dismissal or striking out) or costs penalty or other costs order against the claimant.[1] **10.03**

There is a presumption that a county court judge or sheriff will appoint a lay assessor to assist the court in all discrimination cases. Lay assessors are experienced in matters concerning **10.04**

---

[1] Civil Procedure Rules, Practice Direction—Proceedings under enactments relating to equality.

Glynis Craig, *Enforcement* In: *Blackstone's Guide to the Equality Act 2010.* Fourth Edition. Edited by: Anthony Robinson, David Ruebain, and Susie Uppal, Oxford University Press (2021). © Oxford University Press.
DOI: 10.1093/oso/9780198870876.003.0010

discrimination and assist the judge in making findings of fact.[2] The judge or sheriff can also decide not to appoint an assessor if there are good reasons not to do so. The Explanatory Notes[3] to the Act suggested that such good reasons could include the judge's own experience of discrimination law, the nature of the case, and the wishes of the claimant.

10.05   This jurisdiction is however not exclusive. Under the Act it is clear that there are some sections which can only be enforced by the Equality and Human Rights Commission.[4] There may also be a question of jurisdiction in applications for judicial review which raise Equality Act arguments. While it is clear that the administrative court can deal with breaches of section 149 Public Sector Equality Duty the courts have been called upon to determine whether section 29 discrimination in the provision of services claims can be determined by judicial review. The Court of Appeal considered the issue in *Hamnett v Essex County Council.*[5] Here the claimant sought to challenge a road traffic order on the basis that it breached the Equality Act 2010 section 29 in relation to parking for disabled drivers. The Road Traffic Regulation Act 1984 Schedule 9 provided for High Court jurisdiction by way of statutory review. The Court of Appeal held that the claim had to be made to the county court under the procedure set out in the Equality Act. Insofar as the provisions in the respect of section 29 claims, they were to be regarded as having been impliedly repealed by the 2010 Act. The principle of implied repeal does not operate in reverse. In *Summers v London Borough Richmond upon Thames,*[6] it was held that the provisions of later legislation were taken to have impliedly repealed the provisions of an ouster clause in earlier legislation, could operate in reverse. Therefore the High Court did not have jurisdiction to determine whether exemptions contained in a Public Spaces Protection Order made under the Anti-social Behaviour, Crime and Policing Act 2014, which applied to disabled persons, were discriminatory under section 29 of the Equality Act 2010 as this was for the county court to determine.

10.06   Where discrimination is raised as part of immigration proceedings or could be so raised, section 115 provides that such claims should be dealt with in the immigration procedure and cannot be brought under the Equality Act.[7] These refer to claims of discrimination in cases regarding whether persons should be allowed to enter or remain in the UK. Where a finding of discrimination is made in immigration proceedings, that finding is binding in any subsequent proceedings brought in the civil courts under section 113 of the Act in respect of compensation. It does not matter that the discriminatory act took place outside of the UK. For example, if an entry clearance officer working in a British post abroad refuses an application for a visa to enter the UK on the grounds that the applicant is disabled, redress would be through an appeal to the First Tier Tribunal (Immigration and Asylum Chamber) sitting in the UK. The Tribunal cannot award compensation but if a finding of discrimination is made the appellant can then bring proceedings for compensation in the county or sheriff court and that court will be bound by the Tribunal finding that discrimination has occurred.

10.07   In a similar way there is a separate procedure in education cases regarding disability. These should be dealt with under the SENDIST[8] procedure and not under the Act. There are

---

[2] See Civil Procedure Rule 35.15. For the role of lay assessors see *Ahmed v University of Oxford* [2002] EWCA Civ 1907. For the experience required of lay assessors see *Cary v Commissioner of the Metropolis* [2014] EWCA Civ 987.

[3] Explanatory Note (EN) 384.

[4] S. 113(2).

[5] [2017] EWCA Civ 6.

[6] [2018] EWHC 782 (Admin).

[7] Including appeals, and reviews under s. 2D and 2E of the Special Immigration Appeals Commission Act 1997.

[8] Special Educational Needs Tribunal established by the Education Act 1993 and consolidated by the Education Act 1996.

separate tribunals for England, Wales, and Scotland. Cases involving disability discrimination in education in Scotland which are heard by the Additional Support Needs Tribunals (Scotland). Schedule 17 to the Act sets out in detail the enforcement procedure in relation to pupils with disabilities. The Upper Tribunal has provided much needed guidance on how disability claims should be registered in *F v Responsible Body of School W* [2020] UKUT 112 (AAC) Where a reasonable adjustment claim could be relevant to the proportionality of the respondent's actions this should not preclude a free standing reasonable adjustments claim. The Upper Tribunal was of the view that guidance should be provided in discrimination cases with multiple heads of claim to avoid being screened out cases or parts of cases. It cautioned against bringing disability discrimination cases to an unduly early end.

Section 117 makes provision for the civil courts rules to permit the use of closed material procedures to safeguard national security where necessary.[9] This can enable the court to exclude a claimant, pursuer, representative, or assessor from all or part of the proceedings. The court can permit anyone so excluded to make a statement to the court before the proceedings or relevant part of the proceedings begin and a special advocate can be appointed to represent the interests of an excluded person. Such appointments are made by the Attorney General in England and Wales and the Advocate General for Scotland. **10.08**

2. Time Limits in the Civil Courts

A claim in the county or sheriff court brought under the Act must be issued within six months less one day of the alleged unlawful act having taken place. The time limit is not usually extended by exercising the right to a grievance or appeal process. If the unlawful act relates to a decision, the time runs from the date the decision is made, which may be earlier than the date it is communicated. This can be extended where the judge or sheriff finds it just and equitable to do so. The term 'just and equitable' is a familiar one used by the county and sheriff courts in other types of claims such as negligence and personal injury. The court will therefore consider the prejudice to the parties in extending the time limit in the light of all the circumstances, including: **10.09**

- the length of and reasons for the delay, including health reasons;
- the likely effect of the delay on the cogency of the evidence;
- the extent to which the respondent has cooperated with requests for information;
- how quickly the claimant acted on becoming aware of the grounds for claim, including obtaining appropriate advice;[10] and
- an assessment of the strength of the case.[11]

There are some exceptions to the general six-month rule.

The period is automatically extended to nine months where a case has been presented to the students complaints scheme within six months in the case of qualifying bodies or the claim has been referred to conciliation under arrangement by the Equality and Human Rights Commission. **10.10**

If a decision is made in an immigration case that there has been a breach of Part 3 in relation to services and public functions, the six months begins to run from the day after the expiry of the period during which proceedings in the county or sheriff court were excluded **10.11**

---

[9] See Justice and Security Act 2013, Part 2.
[10] *British Coal Corporation v Keeble* [1977] IRLR 336, EAT.
[11] *Hutchinson v Westward Television* [1977] IRLR 69, EAT.

by section 114(2). This will be the date on which the immigration tribunal decided that a breach of Part 3 has occurred and an appeal can no longer be brought.

10.12   Section 140A and 140AA also permits time to be extended where there is ongoing mediation of cross-border disputes falling within European Directive 2008/52/EC.

10.13   Discriminatory conduct extending over a period of time may be treated as a single continuing act. The conduct should be part of a series and be similar to one another. There should be necessary connection between the acts in the three-month period and those falling outside of the period. In the case of such continuing discrimination, section 118(6) 'conduct extending over a period is to be treated as done at the end of the period' (section 118(6)(a)). Therefore, the six-month time limit begins to run at the end of the period of the discriminatory conduct.[12]

10.14   Where there is a failure to act, the six-month time limit will run from the date when the decision not to act was made. This is taken to be, in the absence of evidence to the contrary, either the date when the person does something which is inconsistent with doing the act in question or at the end of the period when it would have been reasonable to act.

3. Remedies in the Civil Courts

10.15   The county and sheriff courts can grant any remedy which the High Court has the power to grant in tort, or judicial review proceedings, such as compensation (including injury to feelings), injunctions, and declarations. In determining whether any particular losses are recoverable the test to be applied is whether such losses are caused by (or arise naturally and directly from) the discrimination found proved.

10.16   Where there is a finding of indirect discrimination and the respondent proves that the discrimination was unintentional the judge must not award damages without considering all other alternative remedies such as a declaration or injunction.

10.17   In granting remedies other than compensation or a declaration the court must be satisfied that in doing so it will not prejudice any criminal matter.

B. EMPLOYMENT TRIBUNALS

1. Jurisdiction in the Employment Tribunal

10.18   Section 120 sets out the jurisdiction of the employment tribunals. The employment tribunal hears claims relating to work including those brought in respect of employment that has ended, and instructing, causing, or inducing discrimination or aiding contraventions in a work setting.

10.19   Section 120(7) provides that the employment tribunal does not have jurisdiction to hear claims relating to a contravention of Part 5 (work) where the act complained about may, by virtue of an enactment, be subject to an appeal or proceedings in the nature of an appeal.

10.20   In *Michalak v General Medical Council*,[13] the Supreme Court considered section 120(7) as to whether the availability of judicial review proceedings in respect of decisions or actions of the General Medical Council excluded the jurisdiction of the employment tribunal. The

---

[12] See *Commissioner of Police of the Metropolis v Hendricks* [2002] EWCA Civ 1686.
[13] [2017] UKSC 71.

court considered whether judicial review could properly be described as 'proceedings in the nature of an appeal' and whether it was available 'by virtue of an enactment'. It held that judicial review of such decisions did not constitute proceedings in the nature of an appeal, nor was it a remedy provided by reason of an enactment. Discrimination claims brought by professionals against their regulators must therefore be brought in the employment tribunal, even where judicial review is available as a remedy, unless there exists a separate statutory appeal process.

10.21 It can also determine an application for a declaration in respect of the non-discrimination rule as it applies to occupational pensions[14] or non-discrimination rule cases referred to it by the civil courts under section 122. The non-discrimination rule requires that every occupational pension scheme (see Chapter 4) is to have a rule read into it prohibiting 'a responsible person' from discriminating against, harassing, or victimizing a member or a person who could become a member of the scheme. In hearing complaints about a breach of the non-discrimination rule the employer is to be treated as a party and has the right to appear and to be heard.

10.22 The employment tribunal does not have jurisdiction to hear those cases which are subject to appeal or appeal-type proceedings in respect of qualification bodies.

10.23 Members of the armed forces must not bring a complaint before the employment tribunal without first utilizing the armed forces internal complaints procedure. The employment tribunal is therefore expressly precluded from hearing complaints relating to acts done when the complainant was a member of the armed forces, unless a service complaint has been made about the matter and has not been withdrawn. Such a complaint is treated as withdrawn if has not been referred to the Defence Council and the complainant does not apply for such a referral. A complaint made under the old redress procedures is also treated as withdrawn if not submitted to the Defence Council. A complainant does not have to wait until a complaint has been resolved internally before bringing a claim in the employment tribunal. The requirement is to raise the complaint internally and not withdraw.

10.24 Section 122 contains a provision to allow the civil courts to refer cases to the employment tribunal if the case, or part of the case, concerns a claim or counter-claim in respect of a non-discrimination in the operation of a pension scheme if the court decides that the matter could more conveniently be dealt with by an employment tribunal. The case can be referred and the claim or counter-claim struck out. Where a question relating to the non-discrimination rule arises in the course of civil proceedings the court can either of its own motion or on application by a party stay or sist the proceedings to refer the question for determination by the employment tribunal.

2. Time Limits in the Employment Tribunal

10.25 Proceedings in the employment tribunal must usually be issued within three months of the alleged discriminatory conduct taking place or within such other period as the employment tribunal considers just and equitable.

10.26 There are some exceptions. In armed forces cases the period is extended to six months to reflect the requirement first to utilize the internal complaints procedure; again, this six-month period can be extended where the employment tribunal considers it just and equitable to do so.

---

[14] S. 61.

10.27   In the case of continuing discrimination the three-month time limit begins to run at the end of the period of the discriminatory conduct. Where there is a failure to act, the three-month time limit will run from the date when the decision not to act was made. This is taken to be, in the absence of evidence to the contrary, either the date when the person does something which is inconsistent with doing the act in question or at the end of the period when it would have been reasonable to act. An employer's duty to make reasonable adjustments for disability under section 20 begins when it could take steps to avoid the relevant disadvantage. This is distinct from section 123(4), under which, for the purpose of the three-month time limit for bringing proceedings, the failure to comply with the reasonable adjustments duty was treated as occurring on the expiry of the period in which the employer might reasonably have been expected to make the adjustments. If time began to run then, an employee could be prejudiced as the employer might do nothing while three months passed. The relevant period is to be assessed from the employee's point of view.[15]

10.28   Time is also extended where there is ongoing cross-border mediation.

10.29   Generally a claim cannot be brought in the Employment Tribunal without notice first being given to the Advisory, Conciliation and Arbitration Service (ACAS) in order to attempt early conciliation.[16] From the day after ACAS has been notified the limitation period will be paused for up to one month to allow for conciliation. This can be extended for a further 14 days if agreed by the parties. Where either party does not wish to conciliate, or where conciliation is unsuccessful, the parties will be issued with an early conciliation certificate and unique number as evidence that the procedure was followed. The unique number will be required in order to lodge a claim in the employment tribunal.

10.30   There is no fee payable to bring a claim in the Employment Tribunal, the previous fees regime having been ruled unlawful.[17]

3. Remedies in the Employment Tribunal

10.31   The employment tribunal has the power to order compensation (including compensation for injury to feelings), make a declaration as to the parties' rights, and/or make a recommendation. Where there is a finding of indirect discrimination the tribunal must only order the payment of compensation after it has first considered making a declaration or recommendation.

10.32   The amount of compensation to be awarded is in line with the power of the High Court or Court of Session in tort cases.

10.33   The employment tribunal has the power to make recommendations only in respect of reducing the negative impact on an individual claimant, the power to make recommendations to benefit the wider workforce was repealed by the Deregulation Act 2015.

10.34   Where the employment tribunal finds there has been a breach in the provision governing eligibility for membership, or terms of membership, of an occupational pension scheme, the tribunal has additional powers to make a declaration of entitlement to membership and specify the terms or the right to terms of membership without discrimination. Such an order can be retrospective. Compensation in such occupational pension cases is limited to injury to feelings or compensation awarded as a consequence of the respondent's failure to follow a recommendation made under section 124(7).

---

[15] *Abertawe Bro Morgannwg University Local Health Board v Morgan* [2018] EWCA Civ 640.

[16] Employment Tribunals Act 1996 s. 18(1)(e).

[17] *R (on the application of Unison) v Lord Chancellor* [2017] UKSC 51.

C. EQUALITY OF TERMS (EQUAL PAY)

Part 9, Chapter 4 of the Act sets out the jurisdiction of the employment tribunal to hear complaints relating to a breach of an equality clause or rule. This includes equality in the rules of occupational pension schemes and terms relating to pregnancy and maternity. It includes cases stayed or sisted by the civil courts and referred to the employment tribunal under section 128(2). However there is no corresponding power for the employment tribunal to stay proceedings in order to effect a transfer to the civil courts.[18] As with other provisions where the complaint arises during service with the armed forces, the internal service complaints procedure must be utilized before bringing the complaint to an employment tribunal.   **10.35**

1. Time Limits

Section 129 replaces similar provisions in the preceding legislation but clarifies the time limits in which claims may be brought and sets out factors which indicate the ability to bring a claim. These are set out in table format. Other than armed forces cases the type of case is set out in the first column of the table and the corresponding time limit in the second column. A distinction is drawn between standard and non-standard cases.   **10.36**

Standard cases are defined in section 130(2) as those which do not relate to stable work, concealment, incapacity, or a joint concealment and incapacity case. The time limit for standard cases is six months from the date on which the employment ended (nine months in army cases).   **10.37**

A stable work case is one where the proceedings relate to a period during which there was a stable working relationship between the complainant and the responsible person—including time after the terms of work had expired. This allows for a series of fixed and short term contracts and breaks between contracts to be treated as a continuous single contract. The time limit of six months runs from the date that the stable relationship ends.   **10.38**

A concealment case is one where an employer or trustee/manager of an occupational pension scheme deliberately conceals relevant information from the complainant. The six-month time limit runs from the time that the complainant discovered, or could with reasonable diligence have discovered, the information.   **10.39**

In an incapacity case the six months starts to run from the day the incapacity ends. An incapacity case is defined in section 130(9) as being one where the complainant had an incapacity during the usual six-month limitation period.   **10.40**

Equal pay claims can be brought in either the civil courts or in the employment tribunal. Under section 128 the civil courts have the discretion to strike out or transfer claims which could be more conveniently determined by an employment tribunal. The Court of Appeal has recently considered the effect of this in regard to claims which could have been brought more conveniently in the employment tribunal but are now time barred. The Court of Appeal held that in exercising discretion as to whether to strike out or transfer, the expiry of the employment tribunal time limit will be of considerable weight in most circumstances and will only be relevant to exercise of discretion in exceptional cases.[19]   **10.41**

---

[18] *Asda Stores Ltd v Brierley* [2016] EWCA Civ 566.
[19] *Abdullah and Others v Birmingham City Council* [2011] EWCA Civ 1412.

2. Assessment of Work of Equal Value

10.42   Where a question of whether work of a claimant and a comparator is of equal value arises before an employment tribunal the tribunal may require a member of a panel of independent experts to prepare a report. The members of the panel will be designated by ACAS but cannot be ACAS members, officers, or staff. Unless the requirement for a report is withdrawn the tribunal must not determine the question of equal value until it has received the report. If the tribunal withdraws the request for a report it can request the expert to provide it with specified documents or any other information that will assist in reaching a decision.

10.43   If there has been a job evaluation study[20] finding that the work is not of equal value the tribunal must follow this decision unless it has reasonable grounds for suspecting that evaluation contained in the study is discriminatory on the grounds of sex or is otherwise unreliable.

3. Remedies in Non-pension Cases

10.44   Where there is a finding of a breach of the equality clause in a non-pension case the court or employment tribunal can make a declaration as to the rights of the parties and can order compensation by way of arrears of pay or damages. The period used for calculating arrears varies according to the type of case and there are different provisions for Scotland and England and Wales.

10.45   In a standard case in England and Wales the arrears period is six years from the day on which the proceedings were issued; in Scotland this is five years. In a non-standard case in England and Wales the arrears period goes back to the date on which the breach first occurred.

4. Remedies in Pension Cases

10.46   Where there is a finding that there has been a breach of an equality rule or equality clause in respect of occupational pension scheme membership or rights the court or employment tribunal can make a declaration as to the rights of the parties. Damages or compensation are not available unless the claim is for arrears brought by a pension member.

10.47   Where a declaration is made that a complainant should be admitted to a pension scheme it may specify a date from which the complainant is entitled to membership. This date cannot be before 8 April 1976. This reflects the legal position following the judgment of the European Court in *Defrenne v Sabena*,[21] in which it was held that that principle of equal pay was directly effective but could not be applied to periods of service before the judgment.

10.48   If a declaration is made as to rights which would have accrued under the pension scheme the date specified by the tribunal cannot be before 17 May 1990. Again, this follows a judgment of the European Court in the case of *Barber v Guardian Royal Exchange Insurance Group*.[22] If such a declaration as to rights to terms of the scheme is made the employer must provide the necessary resources to secure those rights for the complainant. The complainant should not have to make up contributions. In *Copple and Others v Littlewoods Plc* the Court of Appeal upheld the EAT's decision that in a claim regarding access to a non-compulsory

---

[20] The meaning of 'job evaluation study' is set out in s. 80(5).

[21] Case 43/75, [1976] ECR 455.

[22] [1990] ECR I-1889.

occupational pension scheme, a claimant is not entitled to a declaration as of right. In this case, the finding was that the women concerned would not have joined the scheme even had they been entitled to do so. Refusing to give a declaration was compatible with EU law as to do so where no loss was suffered would have been to treat the claimants more favourably than, for example, a full-timer who had chosen not to join the scheme.

The court and tribunal can order compensation or damages only in claims for arrears   **10.49**
brought by pension members. Such payments will be limited to the arrears period set out in section 134(5) and (6).

D. CRIMINAL OFFENCES

Although proceedings in relation to discrimination will usually be conducted in the civil   **10.50**
courts and employment tribunals the Act does create some criminal offences in respect of certain prohibited conduct.

Section 112 makes it unlawful to help someone to carry out an act that is known to be   **10.51**
unlawful under the Act. There is a defence if that person reasonably believed that s/he was acting lawfully; however, it is a criminal offence to knowingly or recklessly make a false statement about the lawfulness of doing something under the Act. This is punishable by a fine of up to £5,000.

E. CONTRACTS AND OTHER AGREEMENTS

Part 10 of the Act deals with terms in contracts, compromise agreements, and collective   **10.52**
agreements. Terms which amount to unlawful discrimination, harassment, or victimization are unenforceable or void. This does not apply to contracts modified by an equality clause in respect of equal pay or treatment that would contravene the requirements of the public sector duties (the latter being enforceable only by the Equality and Human Rights Commission).

Section 142(2) applies to disability alone and covers the enforceability of terms of non-   **10.53**
contractual agreements relating to the provision of employment services as set out in section 56(2)(a) to (e) or group insurance arrangements for employees. These terms are referred to in this section as 'relevant non-contractual terms' and include matters such as provision of and arrangements for training and guidance (see Chapter 11).

A complaint must make an application to the county or sheriff court for an order for such   **10.54**
a term to be removed or modified. The order can make provisions in respect of a period prior to the order being made. Section 143 requires that a person bringing such action must have an interest in the contract or agreement containing the term. The court will not make an order unless every person affected by it has been given notice of the application and had the opportunity to make representations.

A discriminatory contract term, or relevant non-contractual term in respect of disability   **10.55**
which purports to exclude any of the provisions of the Act or secondary legislation under it, is also unenforceable. This does not apply to negotiated agreements such as contracts settling claims or complaints through conciliation or qualifying compromise agreements.

Terms of collective agreements and rules of undertakings are also unenforceable if con-   **10.56**
trary to the Act. Only a qualifying person who will be affected by the term in the future and

discriminated against can bring proceedings. The definitions of qualifying persons are set out in table form in section 146(5). Such applications are dealt with by the employment tribunal.

F. MISCELLANEOUS

1. Burden of Proof

10.57 Where there is a claim of discrimination, harassment, victimization, or equality of terms, the burden of proof lies initially with the claimant. Once the claimant has established facts which, in the absence of any other explanation, indicate that a breach has occurred the burden of proof shifts to the respondent to show that there was no breach. This applies in cases before the employment tribunal, the Asylum and Immigration Tribunal, the Special Immigration Appeals Commission, the First-tier Tribunal, the Special Educational Needs Tribunal for Wales and the First-tier Tribunal for Scotland Health and Education Chamber.

2. Obtaining Information, etc.

10.58 As enacted, section 138 provided a mechanism by which a person could obtain further information to determine if an unlawful act has occurred by way of a form of questionnaire prescribed by a Minister of the Crown or in some other form. An adverse inference could be drawn from a failure to answer or providing an evasive answer. Following consultation this provision was repealed in 2014.

10.59 Although the statutory questionnaire process has been repealed there is nothing to prevent claimants requesting information. ACAS has produced a good practice guide as to how this can be put into practice in employment cases.[23]

3. Interest

10.60 Section 139 empowers a Minister of the Crown to make regulations enabling the employment tribunal to add interest to awards of compensation and to set out how such interest should be calculated. The current Employment Tribunals (Interest) Order (Amendment) Order 2013 provides that that interest on an unpaid award accrues from the day after the relevant decision day, but no interest shall be payable if the full amount of the award is paid within 14 days after the relevant decision day.

4. Equal Pay Audits

10.61 Section 139A allows for regulations to be made requiring an employment tribunal to order a respondent to carry out an equal pay audit. The Equality Act 2010 (Equal Pay Audits) Regulations came into force on 1 October 2014 and require the employment tribunal to order that an audit take place where there has been a finding of an equal pay breach. The audit once completed must be provided to the tribunal for a decision on the papers as to

---

[23] <http://www.acas.org.uk/media/pdf/m/p/Asking-and-responding-to-questions-of-discrimination-in-the-workplace.pdf>.

whether it has complied with the order. Thereafter the respondent will be required to publish the audit.

An audit involves the publication of relevant gender pay information. It must identify any **10.62** differences in pay between men and women and the reasons for those differences; include the reasons for any potential equal pay breach identified by the audit; and set out the employer's plan to avoid breaches occurring or continuing. An employer that fails to carry out an audit when required to do can be liable for a penalty of up to £5,000.

5. Conduct Giving Rise to Separate Proceedings

The employment tribunal and civil courts can transfer proceedings to one another where the **10.63** same conduct has given rise to proceedings for a contravention of section 111 (instructing, causing, or inducing discrimination) and at least one other claim. An employment tribunal or civil court cannot make a decision about such a case which is inconsistent with an earlier decision about the same conduct. The Explanatory Notes give the example of an employee who has discriminated against a customer on the instruction of the employer. The employee may bring a claim in the employment tribunal and the customer in the civil courts. Given that both sets of proceedings arise from the same conduct a transfer can take place to allow the cases to be dealt with together.

6. Enforcement by the Equality and Human Rights Commission

The Equality and Human Rights Commission ('the Commission') is the non-departmental **10.64** public body for England, Wales and, in part, Scotland tasked with monitoring the implementation of, and compliance with, the equality and human rights statutes and promoting positive social change through the exercise of its statutory powers. The Commission commenced operation on 1 October 2007. Each of the former equality commissions (the Commission for Racial Equality, the Equal Opportunities Commission, and the Disability Rights Commission) were dissolved and replaced by the Commission.

In order to fulfil its statutory duties, the Commission has been given a wide range of **10.65** enforcement powers as set out in its enabling statute, the Equality Act 2006. The Commission is also listed as a statutory regulator and subject to the regulators' statutory code of practice.[24] The Commission is also responsible for producing the non-statutory guidance and codes of practice to accompany the Equality Act 2010.

The enforcement powers of the Commission include: investigations, unlawful act notices, **10.66** action plans, agreements, applications to court, legal assistance, judicial review and other legal proceedings, public sector duties, assessment and compliance notices.

The Commission's investigation and assessment powers allow it to require any person to **10.67** give oral or written evidence or to produce documents.

Under section 16 of the Equality Act 2006, the Commission has the power to conduct an **10.68** inquiry into any matter relating to its duties in respect of equality and human rights. Such inquiries tend to be thematic or sectoral.

Inquiries enable the Commission to gather evidence and report on equality or human **10.69** rights issues within one sector, or particular equality or human rights issues that are common

---

[24] Legislative and Regulatory Reform (Regulatory Functions) Order 2007, SI 2007/3544.

to a range of organizations or more than one sector. Inquiries also empower the Commission to make recommendations to bring about change.

10.70   Before conducting an inquiry the Commission must publish the terms of reference in a way that it will be brought to the attention of those who are subject to the inquiry or who may be interested in the inquiry. If a specific person is to be subject to the inquiry, that person will also receive a copy of the terms of reference.

10.71   The Commission is obliged to publish a report of the findings of any inquiry. If the inquiry leads to comments being made against a specific individual, those subject to the inquiry will be provided with a draft copy of the report and will have 28 days to write to the Commission with any comments. The Commission will consider those representations before finalizing and publishing the report.

10.72   Inquiries are precluded from making findings that someone has committed an act in breach of the Equality Act 2010; however, the Commission has a power to investigate unlawful acts under section 20 of the Equality Act 2006 and can suspend an inquiry in order to do so.

10.73   The power to investigate arises if the Commission suspects that an unlawful act has been committed. An unlawful act is one that is contrary to the provisions of the Equality Act 2010. If during the course of an investigation the Commission is satisfied that a person has committed an unlawful act, it can serve an unlawful act notice and require him/her to prepare an action plan for the purpose of avoiding repetition or continuation of the unlawful act and recommend actions to be taken for the purpose.[25] The Commission has the power to enforce the provision of and compliance with an action plan through the county or sheriff court.

10.74   Where the Commission thinks a person has committed an unlawful act it can also enter into an agreement[26] whereby the Commission will not take further enforcement action on the basis of an undertaking being given not to commit the unlawful act of a specified kind and to take, or refrain from taking, specified action, including the preparation of an action plan. The Commission can also apply for an injunction to restrain the commission of unlawful acts or to ensure compliance with an agreement.[27] It is immaterial that the Commission knows or suspects that a person may be affected by an unlawful act or its application.[28]

10.75   The Commission can also provide legal assistance, legal representation, and any other form of assistance.[29] The Commission can only provide such assistance to individuals in respect of actions brought under the Equality Act 2010 and does not have the power to provide assistance on purely human rights grounds.

10.76   The Commission can also institute or intervene in any proceedings which are relevant to a matter in connection with which the Commission has a function.[30] To date the Commission has used this power extensively in respect of public interest cases which raise issues beyond any personal interests of the parties in the matter and affect identifiable sectors of the public or disadvantaged groups. The Commission uses this power to seek to clarify or challenge important questions of law; involving serious matters of public policy or general public concern and/or concerning systematic default or abuse by a public body.

---

[25] Equality Act 2006 s. 21(4).
[26] ibid, s. 23.
[27] ibid, s. 24.
[28] ibid, s. 24A(2).
[29] ibid, s. 28.
[30] ibid, s. 30.

The Commission can bring judicial review proceedings in its own name without having to be the victim of the decision or action by a public authority.[31]   **10.77**

The Commission can apply to the relevant court for injunctions to restrain a body from committing unlawful acts if it thinks that a person is likely to commit such an act.[32] For example the Commission has used this power in respect of the British National Party, who were injuncted to discontinue using membership criteria which discriminated on the grounds of race.   **10.78**

The Commission also has responsibility for enforcing the public sector duties which are dealt with in Chapter 8. The Commission can assess the extent to which a public authority has complied with its duties or the manner in which it has complied with its duties. The Commission does not have to suspect that there has been any breach of the public duty before carrying out an assessment.[33]   **10.79**

Before conducting an assessment, the Commission will list the terms of reference. The Commission will ask for comments on the terms of reference and take these into account. Once the terms of reference are finalized they will be published. The Commission will also publish a report at the end of the assessment. Assessments are also a way in which the Commission can obtain evidence for further enforcement action to secure compliance as well as identifying areas of best practice in the performance of the duties.   **10.80**

Where the Commission thinks that a public authority has not complied with a public sector duty, it has the power to serve a compliance notice[34] for breach of public sector equality duty. The notice may require compliance with the duty or provide an opportunity for the written proposal to show the steps that will be taken to ensure compliance. This written information must be produced to the Commission within 28 days of receipt of the compliance notice. A notice may also require further information to be produced to the Commission for the purposes of assessing compliance. A person who receives a compliance notice must comply with it. Failure to comply can result in the Commission applying to the relevant court for an order requiring compliance.   **10.81**

Section 60(1) of the Act prevents enquires being made about health prior to making a decision to offer employment. This is enforceable only by the Commission. Section 60(6) does set out some circumstances where enquiries about health are permitted, but if questions are raised outside these the Commission can use its enforcement powers under the 2006 Act; for example it can investigate an organization where it appears that such inquiries are being made routinely.   **10.82**

7. Territoriality

The Act does not set out its general territorial scope. Section 29(9) provides for the prohibitions in respect of the provision of services or the exercise of public functions to apply in relation to race and religion or belief to decisions on the grant of entry clearance. Such decisions are usually made by Foreign and Commonwealth Office staff at British posts abroad. The Act also creates powers to specify territorial application, for example in relation to ships and hovercraft (sections 30 and 81) and offshore work (section 82).   **10.83**

---

[31] See, e.g., *R (EHRC) v Secretary of State for Justice and Another* [2010] EWHC 147 (Admin).
[32] Equality Act 2006 s. 24.
[33] *ibid*, s. 31.
[34] *ibid*, s. 32.

10.84   Other than this the Act leaves it to the judiciary to decide if the Act applies. In respect of Part 5, Work, the Explanatory Notes[35] state that the Act follows the Employment Rights Act 1996 and leaves it to the employment tribunal to decide if the Act applies. It therefore appears that the tribunal will follow the precedents already decided under the 1996 Act.

10.85   In the Supreme Court, *Duncombe v Secretary of State for Children, Schools and Families*[36] confirms that this remains a matter of applying the principles in *Lawson v Serco Ltd.*[37] Ordinarily the test will be to look at whether the claimant was actually working in the Great Britain at the time of dismissal. Those who have an employer based in Great Britain but who work abroad, for example peripatetic employees such as airline staff or those living and working in a military base or enclave abroad, may also be within the jurisdiction, depending on the facts. The general principle approved in *Duncombe* is that the employee must show a closer connection with Great Britain and with British employment law than any other system of law.[38]

10.86   Devolution issues in respect of Scotland and Wales are set out fully in the Explanatory Notes to the Act in notes 16–18.

---

[35] EN 15.
[36] [2011] UKSC 36. Followed in *British Council v Jeffery* [2018] EWCA Civ 2253.
[37] [2006] UKHL 3.
[38] See Lady Hale at para. 8.

11

EQUALITY OF TERMS

A. INTRODUCTION

Part 5, Chapter 3 of the Equality Act 2010 ('the Act') deals with equality in contractual **11.01** terms and conditions of employment[1] and occupational pension scheme rules.[2] It deals with all aspects of equal pay law, i.e. the rules requiring that men and women doing equal work should have equal contractual and pension benefits. The equality of terms provisions closely reflect those in the repealed Equal Pay Act 1970 (EqPA) and sections 62–6 of the Pensions Act 1995 which the Act replaced. The vast majority of the substantial case law under those previous pieces of legislation will continue to be relevant under the Act.

The equality of terms provisions are divided into four sections: **11.02**

- The first section[3] deals with sex equality, i.e. equality of contractual terms (through a 'sex equality clause') and pension terms (through a 'sex equality rule') between men and women doing equal work. This is what is commonly referred to as equal pay law.

- The second section[4] deals with pregnancy and maternity equality, covering equality in a woman's contractual terms (through a 'maternity equality clause') and pension rights (through a 'maternity equality rule') both during and after her maternity leave.

- The third section[5] deals with disclosure of information about pay. It makes contractual terms prohibiting pay disclosures unenforceable in some circumstances and enables the making of regulations requiring employers to publish gender pay information.

- The fourth section[6] sets out key definitions and exceptions.

---

[1] The definition of employment in s. 83 applies to all of Part 5 (Work).
[2] Referred to in the Act and this chapter as 'equality of terms'.
[3] Ss 64–71.
[4] Ss 72–6.
[5] Ss 77–8.
[6] Ss 79–80.

Rhodri McDonald and Sophie Buckley, *Equality of Terms* In: *Blackstone's Guide to the Equality Act 2010*. Fourth Edition.
Edited by: Anthony Robinson, David Ruebain, and Susie Uppal, Oxford University Press (2021). © Oxford University Press.
DOI: 10.1093/oso/9780198870876.003.0011

11.03   This chapter deals with the first, second, and fourth sections. The third section on disclosing and publishing pay information is dealt with in Chapter 9, 'Public Procurement and Transparency in the Private Sector'. Enforcement is dealt with in Chapter 10, 'Enforcement'.

11.04   Although the sex equality and maternity equality sections of the Act use similar terminology and share the mechanism of implied contractual terms to require parity of pay and pension rights, there are fundamental differences between them, not least that there can be no male comparator for a woman who is or has been on maternity leave.[7] While the sex equality provisions focus on ensuring equality of pay and pensions for equal work with an actual comparator of the opposite sex, the provisions relating to maternity equality focus on eliminating unfavourable treatment in relation to a woman's contractual terms and pension rights arising out of taking maternity leave.

11.05   This chapter begins by briefly setting these provisions in context, addressing their relationship with discrimination law and EU law. It then deals with the sex equality clause (contract terms) and sex equality rule (pensions). The chapter finishes with consideration of the maternity equality clause and maternity equality rule.

B. EQUALITY OF TERMS IN CONTEXT

1. Equality of Terms and Discrimination Law

11.06   The law on equality of terms has traditionally been considered part of discrimination law. The courts have said that the equal pay provisions should be read as a 'harmonious whole' with the legislation outlawing sex discrimination.[8] However, the legislative provisions on equality of terms and sex discrimination have always been mutually exclusive. The Act preserves this position so that a matter that falls within the scope of the equality of terms provisions cannot also give rise to a claim of sex discrimination[9] or pregnancy or maternity discrimination.[10]

11.07   The difference is one of nature and scope. By nature, a discrimination claim, for example, under section 13 of the Act, is a claim for compensation for the commission of a statutory tort. In contrast, an equality of terms claim is a claim for breach of contract terms modified by a sex equality clause or pension scheme rules modified by a sex equality rule.[11] This can be seen both in the remedies available (e.g., non-economic loss such as injury to feelings is not recoverable as damages for breach of a sex equality clause)[12] and in the different procedures

---

[7] In *Ali v Capita Customer Management Ltd, Hextall v Leicestershire Police* [2020] ICR 87 the Court of Appeal held that a male employee could bring an equality of terms claim using a female colleague who had taken maternity leave as a comparator. He claimed that his shared parental leave pay should be paid at the enhanced rate at which she was paid maternity pay. The claim failed because of the exception in Sch. 7, para. 2 of the Act which provides that a sex equality clause has no effect in relation to terms affording special treatment to women in connection with pregnancy or childbirth.

[8] *Shields v E Coombes Holdings Limited* [1978] IRLR 263, per Orr LJ.

[9] S. 70. See *BMC Software Ltd v Shaikh* [2017] IRLR 1074, EAT (overturned on other grounds on appeal). There is a limited exception to this mutual exclusivity as explained in paras 11.08 and 11.32 below.

[10] S. 76. See *The Commissioner of the City of London Police v Geldart* [2019] UKEAT/0032/19 (permission to appeal to the Court of Appeal granted April 2020).

[11] See *BMC Software Ltd v Shaikh* [2017] IRLR 1074, EAT (overturned on other grounds on appeal) and *Graysons Restaurants Ltd v Jones* [2019] IRLR 649, CA.

[12] *Newcastle City Council v Allan and Others; Degnan and Others v Redcar and Cleveland BC* [2005] IRLR 504, EAT. That case was decided under the EqPA but the relevant provisions of the EqPA have been replaced by similar wording at s. 132.

and time limits which apply to such claims (e.g., it is possible to issue an equality of terms claim either in the employment tribunal or in the civil courts).[13] Claims under the equality of terms provisions are limited to discrimination in pension scheme rules[14] or in 'terms', i.e. contractual terms.[15] This means that non-contractual terms, such as a purely discretionary bonus not regulated by the contract of employment, are outside the scope of the equality of terms provisions.[16]

Unlike under previous legislation the Act allows a claim of direct or dual[17] direct discrimination to be brought in relation to a term of a person's work that relates to pay where a sex equality clause or rule has no effect.[18]   **11.08**

2. Equality of Terms and European Law

The influence of European law has been particularly strong in equal pay. Domestic law has had   **11.09** to be compatible with the equal pay principle in Article 157 of the Treaty on the Functioning of the European Union[19] and with the provisions of the Equal Pay Directive,[20] now incorporated in the Recast Directive.[21] Decisions of the Court of Justice of the European Union (CJEU) on compatibility with Article 157 form a significant proportion of the relevant case law.[22] The implications of the European Union (Withdrawal) Act 2018 are considered in detail in Chapter 13.

C. THE SEX EQUALITY PROVISIONS

In this section a claim relying on the sex equality *clause* is referred to as a contract terms claim   **11.10** and a claim relying on the sex equality *rule* is referred to as a pension claim.

1. When Do the Sex Equality Provisions Apply?

The sex equality provisions (sections 64–71) apply where a person (A) is employed on work   **11.11** or where a person (A) holding a personal or public office does work that is equal to the work that a comparator of the opposite sex (B) does.[23] Section 64(2) explicitly states that references to the work that B does are not restricted to work done contemporaneously with the work done by A. This is intended to allow comparisons with predecessors as required by EU law, but is on its face wide enough to allow comparisons with successors.[24]

---

[13] S. 127(9). See the Supreme Court case of *Abdulla v Birmingham City Council* [2013] IRLR 38 on EqPA claims brought in the civil courts.

[14] See *The Lord Chancellor & Anor v McCloud & Ors* [2019] IRLR 477, para. 167.

[15] S. 80(2)(a) and (b).

[16] See e.g., *Hosso v European Credit Management Ltd* [2011] EWCA Civ 1589.

[17] The dual discrimination provisions in the Act have not been brought into force.

[18] S. 71, see para. 11.32 below.

[19] Previously Art. 141 of the Treaty of Rome (as amended by the Treaty of Amsterdam), originally Art. 119 of the unamended Treaty of Rome.

[20] Council Directive 75/117/EEC.

[21] Council Directive 2006/54/EC.

[22] See e.g., *Asda Stores Ltd v Brierley* [2019] IRLR 335 referred to in paras 11.38–11.40 below.

[23] S. 64. Employment is defined in s. 83(2) and public and personal office in s. 83(8).

[24] See *Macarthys Ltd v Smith* [1980] ECR 1275 ECJ on predecessors. It is suggested that a comparison with an actual successor would be permitted under the Act despite the decision (under the EqPA) of the

2. Effect of a Sex Equality Clause or Rule

(a) *Effect of a Sex Equality Clause—Contract Claims*

11.12   The effect of a sex equality clause is that:

- any term of the claimant's terms that is less favourable than a corresponding term of the comparator's is modified so that it is no less favourable (section 66(2)(a));
- if the claimant does not have a term which corresponds to a beneficial term of the comparator's, the claimant's terms are modified so as to include such a term (section 66(2)(b)).[25]

11.13   Once an equality clause applies the modified term will continue to apply until the claimant's contract is validly varied or terminated. This means, for example, that a claimant's entitlement to pay at a higher rate is not lost if the comparator is promoted or his pay is reduced after the equality clause takes effect.[26]

11.14   Comparison is on a term-by-term basis and not of the total pay actually received, even if the claimant's remuneration package is overall more favourable than her comparator's.[27] The emphasis is on the reality of the contractual provisions in the circumstances of the particular case and it is a question of fact whether a discrete term exists. An employer cannot lump together discrete terms like basic pay, bonus and other benefits and say that overall the pay is the same. Equally, a claimant cannot subdivide a discrete term into one or more parts in order to complain about one of those parts.[28]

11.15   In cases of work rated as equivalent within section 65(1)(b) the equality clause applies to all the comparator's work terms regardless of whether or not they were determined by the rating of the work (section 66(4)).

11.16   A sex equality clause can modify a term relating to membership of or rights under an occupational pension scheme only insofar as a sex equality rule would have effect in relation to the term (section 66(3)). This is meant to ensure consistency between the provisions of section 66 and sections 67 and 68. The Explanatory Notes explain that this would allow action to be taken against an employer as it could against a trustee in relation to relevant pension rights to ensure, for example, that a defence that operates in relation to one, will operate in relation to the other.[29]

Employment Appeal Tribunal (EAT) in *Walton Centre for Neurology and Neurosurgery NHS Trust v Bewley* [2008] IRLR 588, EAT. The EAT rejected an argument that EU law required the EqPA to be interpreted to allow such a comparison. Under the Act, a claimant would not need to rely on EU law, because the natural meaning of the section would allow such a comparison.

[25] See Explanatory Note (EN) 226 for an example: 'A male employee's contract includes a term that he can use his employer's car for private purposes. His female comparator who does equal work does not benefit from this term. A sex equality clause will have the effect of including in her contract a term corresponding to that of her male comparator.'

[26] See *Reading Borough Council v James* [2018] IRLR 790, EAT.

[27] *Hayward v Cammel Laird Ship Builders Limited* [1988] AC 894; *St Helens and Knowsley Hospitals NHS Trust v Brownbill and Others* [2011] IRLR 815. Although see *Degnan and Others v Redcar and Cleveland BC* [2005] IRLR 504 for a case where on the particular facts it was appropriate because of features of artificiality and historical anomaly which tended to disguise the reality to treat 'bonus plus basic pay' as one term.

[28] See *McNeil & Ors v HM Revenue & Customs* [2018] IRLR 398, EAT at paras 52–54 approved by the Court of Appeal at [2019] IRLR 915.

[29] See para. 11.54 below on the need for consistency of approach to the material factor defence in claims under s. 66 and under s. 67.

(b) *Effect of a Sex Equality Rule—Pension Claims*[30]

The effect of a sex equality rule is that: **11.17**

- a relevant term which is less favourable to the claimant than it is to the comparator is modified so as to be not less favourable (section 67(2)(a));

- if a term confers a relevant discretion capable of being exercised in a way that would be less favourable to the claimant than to the comparator, the term is modified so as to prevent the exercise of the discretion in that way (section 67(2)(b)).

A term is 'relevant' if it is one on which persons become members of the scheme or   **11.18** on which members are treated (section 67(3)). A term is also covered 'as it has effect for the benefit of dependants of members' (section 67(5)) so that, for example, terms relating to a survivor's pension payable to dependants on the death of the pensioner will be a 'relevant term'.

A discretion is 'relevant' if its exercise in relation to the scheme is capable of affecting   **11.19** the way in which persons become members of the scheme or the way in which members are treated (section 67(4)). A discretion is also covered if it is capable of affecting the way a member is treated 'as it has effect for the benefit of dependants of members' (section 67(6)).

Some of the provisions[31] relating to sex equality rules use the term 'a relevant matter',   **11.20** which section 67(8) defines as including:

- a relevant term;[32]

- a term conferring a relevant discretion;[33]

- the exercise of a relevant discretion in relation to an occupational scheme.

3. What Must the Claimant Establish?

To establish that a sex equality clause or rule potentially applies the claimant needs to: **11.21**

- establish that the claim relates to 'terms' (contract terms claim) or an occupational pension scheme (pension claim);

- show that none of the exceptions apply;[34]

- if his/her claim is a pension claim, show that it is not precluded by the rules on retrospectivity;[35]

- identify a comparator of the opposite sex;

- show that his/her work is equal to the comparator's;

- point to less favourable or absent term(s) compared with terms of the comparator's contract or terms of appointment (contract terms claim) or point to a 'relevant term' in the pension scheme that is less favourable to him/her than the comparator or a term conferring

---

[30] For an example of the complexity involved in achieving equalization in the context of pension claims see *Lloyds Banking Group Pensions Trustees Ltd v Lloyds Bank Plc & Ors* [2018] EWHC 2839.

[31] S. 69(4), s. 67(7) and Sch. 7: see paras 11.42, 11.53, and 11.56 below, respectively.

[32] See para. 11.18 above.

[33] See para. 11.19 above.

[34] S. 80(8) and Sch. 7, discussed at paras 11.55–11.56 below.

[35] S. 67(9) and (10), discussed at paras 11.57–11.58 below.

a 'relevant discretion' capable of being exercised in a way that would be less favourable to him/her than to the comparator (pension claim).

11.22   If the claimant can do this, the sex equality clause or rule will have effect unless the 'responsible person' (contract terms claim)[36] or the trustee or manager of the scheme (pension claim) establishes a material factor defence under section 69(1) or (4), respectively.[37]

4. Equal Work

11.23   Under section 65(1), A's work is equal to that of B if it is like B's work, rated as equivalent to B's work, or is of equal value to B's work. The extensive authorities on the interpretation of these terms remain relevant and will not be set out here.[38]

(a) *Like Work*

11.24   A's work is like B's work if their work is the same or broadly similar, and any differences are not of practical importance in relation to the terms of their work (section 65(2)).[39]

11.25   Section 65(3) provides that when making a comparison for the purposes of like work it is necessary to have regard to:

(a) the frequency with which differences between their work occur in practice, and

(b) the nature and extent of the differences.

11.26   The focus on what happens in practice means that a difference in the requirements of the contract that has never in fact been observed is likely to be irrelevant.

(b) *Work Rated as Equivalent*

11.27   A's work is rated as equivalent to B's work if a job evaluation study gives an equal value to their jobs in terms of the demands made on a worker, or would have done were the evaluation not made on a sex-specific system (section 65(4)). A sex-specific system is one which, for the purposes of one or more of the demands made of the worker, sets different values for men and women (section 65(5)).

11.28   A job evaluation study is:

a study undertaken with a view to evaluating, in terms of the demands made on a person by reference to factors such as effort, skill and decision-making, the jobs to be done—
(a) by some or all of the workers in an undertaking or group of undertakings, or
(b) in the case of armed forces, by some or all of the members of the armed forces.[40]

11.29   In the case of Crown employment, 'undertaking' will usually mean the relevant government department.[41]

---

[36] Defined in s. 80(4).
[37] See paras 11.44–11.54 below.
[38] According to the Explanatory Notes, this clause is designed to 'replicate the substance of definitions contained in the Equal Pay Act 1970 (EqPA)': EN 221.
[39] See *Capper Pass v Lawton* [1977] ICR 83 and *Eaton v Nuttall* [1977] ICR 272 on the interpretation of the equivalent provisions in the EqPA (repealed).
[40] S. 80(5).
[41] S. 80(6), adopting the definition in Employment Rights Act 1996 (ERA) s. 191(4).

(c) *Work of Equal Value*

A's work is of equal value to B's work if it is neither like B's work nor rated as equivalent to B's work, but nevertheless equal in terms of the demands made on A by reference to factors such as effort, skill, and decision-making (section 65(6)). As a result of EU law, an equal value claim can also be made out where the claimant's work is of greater value than that of his/her comparator.[42] However, the remedy will still be parity with the comparator's terms, and will not be adjusted to reflect the greater value of the claimant's work.[43]   11.30

Where A's work has been given a different value from B's by a job evaluation study, a tribunal must decide that their work is not of equal value unless it has reasonable grounds for deciding that the evaluation contained in the study was based on a system that discriminates because of sex or is otherwise unreliable.[44] The impact of a job evaluation study on a claim for equal value is considered in *Redcar and Cleveland BC v Bainbridge (No. 2)*[45] and *Hovell v Ashford and St Peter's Hospital NHS Trust.*[46]   11.31

5. Comparator

The Act requires an actual rather than a hypothetical comparator before a sex equality clause or rule can operate. However, where there is no actual comparator, section 71 allows a claim of direct discrimination on grounds of sex to be brought in relation to contractual pay where an equality clause would not operate because there is no comparator doing equal work.[47]   11.32

The Explanatory Notes to section 71 give the following example: 11.33

An employer tells a female employee 'I would pay you more if you were a man' or tells a black female employee 'I would pay you more if you were a white man'. In the absence of any male comparator the woman cannot bring a claim for breach of an equality clause but she can bring a claim of direct sex discrimination or dual discrimination[48] (combining sex and race) against the employer.[49]

This is a significant change from the previous position. Under the Sex Discrimination Act 1975 (SDA) a claim could not be brought in relation to contractual pay. It also reduces the impact of the inability to use a hypothetical comparator when claiming under the equality of terms provisions. The breadth of this change is arguably restricted by the requirement for there to be no material difference in circumstances between the claimant and his/her comparator (whether real or hypothetical) in discrimination claims. This is likely to prevent   11.34

---

[42] Case 157/86 *Murphy v Bord Telecom Eireann* [1988] IRLR 267, ECJ. In *Redcar and Cleveland BC v Bainbridge* [2007] IRLR 984 the Court of Appeal confirmed this also applies to work rated as equivalent cases.

[43] *Evesham v North Hertfordshire Health Authority and Another* [2000] ICR 612.

[44] S. 131(5) and (6). 'Discriminates because of sex' is defined at s. 131(7). For an example of such a challenge and discussion of the onus of proof see *Armstrong & Ors (HBJ Claimants) v Glasgow City Council* [2017] IRLR 993, CSIH.

[45] [2008] IRLR 776, CA.

[46] [2009] IRLR 734, CA.

[47] See *BMC Software Ltd v Shaikh* [2017] IRLR 1074, EAT (overturned on other grounds on appeal). The Court of Appeal in *Ali v Capita Customer Management Ltd, Hextall v Leicestershire Police* [2020] ICR 87 at para. 18 took the view that s. 71 applied more broadly to 'save direct discrimination claims which would otherwise be excluded by the operation of s.70, e.g. a claim which would have succeeded were it not for the exception in Schedule, para 2. of the Act'.

[48] The dual discrimination provisions in the Act have not been brought into force.

[49] EN 246.

the use of a comparator working for a different employer as an actual comparator in a claim of direct discrimination as defined in section 13 or section 14.[50] However, it might well be possible to rely on evidence of the contractual terms of someone with a different employer to inform the tribunal's conclusions on the likely terms of the hypothetical comparator in the same employment as the claimant. There is no equivalent provision allowing an indirect discrimination claim in relation to contractual pay.[51]

11.35   The definition of 'comparator' in section 79 varies depending on the status of the person making the claim.

(a) *Employment Claims*

11.36   Where the claimant is an employee, his/her comparator must be employed by the same employer or an associated employer (section 79(3)(a) and (4)(a)). Employers are associated employers if one is a company of which the other has control, directly or indirectly, or if both are companies of which a third person has control, directly or indirectly (section 79(9)).[52]

11.37   If they work at different establishments, common terms must apply at both establishments either generally or for employees of the claimant's class and for employees of the comparator's class (section 79(4)(c)).[53] The focus at this stage is on commonality between establishments and there is no need to compare the terms of the claimant with those of her comparator.[54] If work is not done at an establishment, it is treated as done at the establishment with which it has the closest connection (section 80(3)).

11.38   The question of what amounts to common terms and conditions has been considered in a number of cases under the EA and the similar provisions in the EqPA.[55] It includes but is not limited to cases where the establishments are covered by a single collective agreement. In the ordinary case, section 79(4) will have to be construed so far as possible to allow an employee to compare herself with any employee of the same employer, because under Article 157 the question is whether there is a single source responsible for the difference in pay.[56]

11.39   There is no need for each class of employee to be employed at each establishment: it is sufficient that common terms *would* apply if that class of employee worked at the other establishment. Nor does it have to be feasible that the comparator would or might perform their job at the other establishment.[57]

---

[50] Under s. 23 on a comparison of cases there must be no material difference between the circumstances relating to each case.

[51] The government's justification for this is interesting. See e.g., the debates at the House of Lords Committee stage: *Hansard* HL, cols 943 et seq. (19 January 2010).

[52] 'Company' is to be given its ordinary meaning and is not restricted to a limited company under the Companies Act 2006, to include, e.g., a limited liability partnership, see *Glasgow City Council and others v Unison and others* [2014] CSIH 27.

[53] As interpreted by *Asda Stores Ltd v Brierley and ors* [2019] EWCA Civ 44. Note that permission to appeal to the Supreme Court was granted in July 2019.

[54] *Asda Stores Ltd v Brierley and ors* [2019] EWCA Civ 44.

[55] See, in particular, *Asda Stores Ltd v Brierley and ors* [2019] EWCA Civ 44. For cases on the equivalent provisions in the EqPA (repealed) see e.g., *North Yorkshire County Council v Ratcliffe* [1994] IRLR 342, CA; *South Tyneside MBC v Anderson and Others* [2007] IRLR 715.

[56] *North and ors v Dumfries and Galloway Council* [2013] UKSC 45; *Asda Stores v Brierley and ors* [2019] EWCA Civ 44; cf. *Robertson v Defra* [2005] ICR 750. The single source test does not impose an additional hurdle on claimants: *North Cumbria Acute Hospitals NHS Trust v Potter* [2009] IRLR 176; *Beddoes and ors v Birmingham City Council* [2011] EqLR 838.

[57] *North and others v Dumfries and Galloway Council* [2013] UKSC 45 applying *British Coal Corporation v Smith and others* [1996] ICR 515.

Where the claimant and his/her comparator do not work for the same or an associated **11.40**
employer, a comparison might still be possible if there is a single source responsible for the
difference in pay because of Article 157.[58]

(b) *Claims by Office Holders*
Where the claimant is a personal or public office holder, a comparator is another office **11.41**
holder whom the same person is responsible for paying (section 79(5)). A person holding
the office of constable is treated as holding a personal office for the purpose of determining
who can be that person's comparator (section 79(8) and EN 280). Section 79 also sets out
the appropriate comparator for staff of the House of Commons or Lords (section 79(6)
and (7)).

(c) *Comparators in Pension Claims*
In the context of the sex equality rule (pensions claims), the Act expressly states that since **11.42**
an equality rule operates only in relation to differences in sex, where the difference in treatment arising from a relevant matter[59] is attributable to family, marital, or civil partnership
status, the appropriate comparator is a person of the opposite sex with the same status.[60] For
example, a sex equality rule will apply where a married man receives better pension benefits
than a married woman, but not where a married man receives better pension benefits than a
civil partner, whether male or female.[61] Discrimination on grounds of sexual orientation will
instead fall to be considered under the Act's provisions relating to non-discrimination rules
in pension schemes.[62]

6. Terms

Equality of terms applies to all terms of the contract, not just those relating to pay. Under **11.43**
section 80(2) the terms of a person's work are:

- for an employee, the terms in the person's contract of employment, contract of apprenticeship, or contract to do work personally;

- for a personal or public office holder, the terms of the person's appointment to the office.

7. Material Factor Defence

(a) *Material Factor Defence in Contract Claims*
Even if the claimant has shown that an equality clause applies, it will not operate where the **11.44**
defence of material factor in section 69(1) is made out. The defence is made out if the responsible person (usually the employer, but defined in section 80(4)) shows that the difference in

---

[58] At least in like work and work rated as equivalent claims. In *Asda Stores v Brierley* [2018] ICR 387 (EAT)
Kerr J concluded at para. 37 that s. 157 also had direct effect in equal value claims. This is likely to be an issue
in the appeal to the Supreme Court.
[59] Defined in s. 67(8): see para. 11.20 above.
[60] S. 67(7) as amended.
[61] The appropriate comparator for a man in a same-sex marriage is a woman in a same-sex marriage rather
than a man married to a woman: s. 67(7)(b).
[62] S. 61. See, for example, *Walker v Innospec* [2017] IRLR 928.

terms is because of a material factor which is neither directly nor indirectly discriminatory.[63] The factor has to be material to the difference between the claimant and his/her comparator's case. 'Material' is not defined in the Act but has been held to mean 'significant and relevant'.[64]

11.45   It is for the responsible person to prove that reliance on the factor does not involve treating the claimant less favourably because of his/her sex (section 69(1)(a)). If they do so, then the defence is made out unless the claimant shows that the factor is one which is potentially indirectly discriminatory because it puts the claimant A and persons of the same sex and doing equal work with A at a particular disadvantage when compared with persons of the opposite sex doing equal work to them (section 69(2)).[65] A common example is differences in terms because of part-time working. Although ostensibly gender neutral, pay practices which treat part-time workers less favourably will put more women than men at a disadvantage because more women work part time.[66]

11.46   Indirect discrimination has a broader meaning in equality of terms cases than under section 19, not being limited to cases where a provision, criterion, or practice (PCP) has been applied. It also includes what is often referred to as '*Enderby* type' indirect discrimination[67] or, more memorably, 'tainting by numbers',[68] 'where two groups of employees doing work of equal value receive different pay and there is a sufficiently substantial disparity in the gender break-down of the two groups'.[69] A tribunal should not adopt a formulaic and technical approach in deciding whether a factor is tainted with sex discrimination.[70] A tribunal should adopt a common approach to assessing whether there is prima facie discrimination whether it is a PCP or an *Enderby* case.[71]

11.47   If a factor is shown to be potentially indirectly discriminatory, then the burden passes to the responsible person. They will have a defence if they can show the factor is a proportionate means of achieving a legitimate aim. This is the same test of objective justification which applies to indirect discrimination under section 19. The Court of Appeal in *Armstrong v Newcastle upon Tyne NHS Hospital Trust*[72] held that the need to provide such objective justification did not arise if the responsible person could show that the difference in pay was not attributable to the difference in sex. That 'Armstrong defence' can no longer be regarded as

---

[63] See *BMC Software Ltd v Shaikh* [2017] IRLR 1074, EAT (overturned on other grounds on appeal) at paras 88–89 and *Calmac Ferries Ltd v Wallace and McKillop* [2014] ICR 453, at paras 4–8.

[64] *Rainey v Greater Glasgow Health Board* [1987] IRLR 26, HL.

[65] See *McNeil & Ors v Revenue & Customs* [2019] IRLR 915, CA on the meaning of 'particular disadvantage' and the importance of providing evidence of disadvantage in terms of the pay received by men and women in the pool for comparison.

[66] For example, *Bilka-Kaufhaus GmbH v Weber von Hartz* [1996] IRLR 216, ECJ.

[67] First recognized by the European Court of Justice in *Enderby v Frenchay Health Authority* [1993] IRLR 591.

[68] Attributed to Christopher Jeans QC (see n. 6 of the EAT's decision in *Bury MBC v Hamilton and Others; Sunderland City Council v Brennan and Others* [2011] IRLR 358).

[69] *ibid*, at para. 16, per Underhill P giving the judgment of the EAT. *Bury* contains a useful explanation of the structured analysis to be adopted in equal pay cases. The Court of Appeal in *McNeil & Ors v Revenue & Customs* [2019] IRLR 915, CA (paras 20–24) emphasized that while 'far more' people in the protected group must suffer disadvantage the extent of the disadvantage does not need to be 'serious' or 'particularly significant', e.g., the fact that the difference between the average pay of women and men is lower than 3 per cent will not necessarily exclude a case of prima facie indirect discrimination.

[70] *Ministry of Defence v Armstrong* [2004] IRLR 672, EAT; adopted by the Court of Appeal in *Redcar and Cleveland BC v Bainbridge and Others* [2008] IRLR 776.

[71] *McNeil & Ors v Revenue & Customs* [2019] IRLR 915, CA at para. 17.

[72] [2006] IRLR 124, CA.

good law following the Supreme Court's decision in *Essop v Home Office (UK Border Agency); Naeem v Secretary of State for Justice.*[73]

There is a significant body of case law dealing with indirect pay discrimination and objective justification, both at domestic and European level[74] and the equal pay provisions of the Recast Directive[75] also expressly apply the concepts of direct and indirect discrimination to sex equality in pay.[76]   **11.48**

There is no definitive list of factors which will potentially provide a defence under section 69, because the factor put forward must be examined in the context of the particular circumstance of each case. Examples of factors relied on by employers to defeat equal pay claims include length of service,[77] differences arising from the operation of TUPE,[78] and market forces.[79]   **11.49**

The Explanatory Notes[80] explain that this provision 'incorporates the effect of EC law in respect of objective justification of indirectly discriminatory factors' and give examples of when the defence will be made out and when not: **11.50**

An employer introduces a bonus payment to encourage staff doing the same work to work a new night shift to maximise production. Only a small number of female staff can work at night and the bonus payments go almost entirely to male employees. Despite the disparate effect on the female employees, the employer's aim is legitimate and the payment of a bonus to night workers is a proportionate way of achieving it.

A firm of accountants structures employees' pay on the basis of success in building relationships with clients (including at after hours client functions). Because of domestic responsibilities, fewer women than men can maintain regular client contact and women's pay is much lower. The employer is unable to show the way it rewards client relationship building is proportionate, taking into account the disadvantage to women employees.

The long term objective of reducing inequality between men and women's terms of work is always to be regarded as a legitimate aim (section 69(3)). This could be relevant where, for example, an employer decides to implement equality of terms by equalizing down, removing a bonus paid predominantly to male workers. In a number of cases an employer has put in place a pay protection scheme to address the impact of that reduction on the predominantly male group affected.[81] That pay protection perpetuates the indirect pay discrimination in the short term but could be lawful as a means of achieving the long term aim in section 69(3), so long as the means for achieving that aim are proportionate. The Court of Appeal has made   **11.51**

---

[73] [2017] UKSC 27, [2017] IRLR 558. See *McNeil & Ors v HM Revenue & Customs* [2018] IRLR 398, EAT at paras 69–71. Even prior to *Essop* Pill LJ in *Gibson v Sheffield City Council* [2010] EWCA Civ 63, found *Armstrong* 'difficult to reconcile' with earlier authorities but regarded it as binding on him as did the Court of Appeal in *Bury MBC v Hamilton; Sunderland City Council v Brennan* [2012] IRLR 507.

[74] For example, *Enderby v Frenchay HA and Secretary of State for Health* [1993] IRLR 591, ECJ.

[75] Council Directive 2006/54/EC.

[76] *ibid*, Art. 4.

[77] For example, *Cadman v HSE* [2006] IRLR 969, ECJ, and, more recently *McNeil & Ors v Revenue & Customs* [2019] IRLR 915, CA.

[78] *Skills Development Scotland Co Ltd v Buchanan and Another* [2011] UKEATS/0042/10/BI.

[79] *Rainey v Greater Glasgow Health Board* [1987] IRLR 26, HL.

[80] EN 240.

[81] See, e.g., *Audit Commission v Haq* [2013] IRLR 206, Court of Appeal. That case was considered under the EqPA rather than the Equality Act.

it clear that in this sort of circumstance, a great deal is required of the employer in showing that the means are proportionate.[82]

11.52   The EqPA required that the material factor be 'genuine'. The Explanatory Notes to section 69[83] say that this has not been repeated in the Act because 'the adverb added nothing to the meaning of the requirement'.

(b) Material Factor Defence in Pension Claims

11.53   The defence of material factor in section 69(4) is made out in pension claims where the trustees or managers of an occupational pension scheme show that the difference in the effect of a relevant matter[84] on the claimant and the comparator is because of a material factor which is not the difference of sex.

11.54   Unlike the material factor defence to a claim that a sex equality *clause* applies, section 69(4) does not expressly set out the need to objectively justify a factor as being a proportionate means of achieving a legitimate aim where it is shown to have a disparate impact on one sex or the other. However, in *The Lord Chancellor & Anor v McCloud & Ors*[85] the Court of Appeal confirmed that the scope of the defences are the same. If a factor is indirectly discriminatory in its effect the section 69(4) defence will only be established if it can be objectively justified.

8. Exceptions to the Effect of a Sex Equality Clause or Rule[86]

11.55   A sex equality clause (contract terms claims) does not have effect in relation to any terms of work affected by compliance with laws regulating the employment of women or their appointment to public or personal office[87] or in relation to terms of work affording special treatment to women in connection with pregnancy and childbirth.[88]

11.56   A sex equality rule (pension claims) does not have effect in relation to a relevant matter[89] where:

- differences in pension entitlements are attributable to the difference in retirement benefits;[90]

- differences between an employer's contributions or benefits paid to men and women are attributable to the application of actuarial factors which differ for men and women.[91]

---

[82] *Redcar and Cleveland BC v Bainbridge and Others* [2008] IRLR 776 and *Haq* (above). See also *Glasgow City Council v Unison Claimants* [2017] IRLR 739, Court of Session (Inner House).

[83] EN 239.

[84] Defined in s. 67(8): see para. 11.20 above.

[85] [2019] IRLR 477, paras 188–189.

[86] Sch. 7 and see also the Equality Act 2010 (Sex Equality Rule) (Exceptions) Regulations 2010, SI 2010/2132.

[87] Sch. 7 para. 1.

[88] Sch. 7 para. 2. For an example of the application of Sch. 7, para. 2 see *Ali v Capita Customer Management Ltd, Hextall v Leicestershire Police* [2020] ICR 87, CA.

[89] Defined in s. 67(8): see para. 11.20 above.

[90] Sch. 7, para. 4. 'Retirement benefits' are defined in Sch. 7, para. 4(3) as amended from 6 April 2016 by the Pensions Act 2014 (Consequential and Supplementary Amendments) Order 2016/224.

[91] Sch. 7, para. 5. The government removed the equivalent 'actuarial exemption' for goods and services in Sch. 3, para. 22 of the Act following the ruling in Case C-236/09 *Association Belge des Consommateurs Test-Achats ASBL v Conseil des ministres* [2011] 2 CMLR 38 that sex-based actuarial factors were unlawful in the insurance context.

9. Sex Equality Rule—Limits on Retrospectivity

The Act preserves the limits on the retrospective reach of a sex equality rule (pension claims). Specifically: **11.57**

- in relation to the terms on which persons become members of an occupational pension scheme, a sex equality rule does not apply to pensionable service before 8 April 1976;[92]

- in relation to the terms on which members of an occupational pension scheme are treated, the sex equality rule does not apply to pensionable service before 17 May 1990.[93]

These dates derive from cases in which the ECJ decided, respectively, that Article 157 was directly applicable[94] and that occupational pensions were pay[95] for the purposes of Article 157.[96] In both cases, it was decided that the effect of the rulings should not be retrospective.[97]   **11.58**

D. MATERNITY EQUALITY

Sections 72 to 76 deal with pregnancy and maternity equality. Although the devices used to achieve this are a 'maternity equality clause' and (in the case of equality in pension schemes) a 'maternity equality rule', they have little in common with the sex equality clause and sex equality rule in section 64 and section 66 respectively and require no comparator.   **11.59**

1. Equality in Pay: Maternity Equality Clause

Section 73(1) provides that if the terms of a woman's work do not, by whatever means, include a maternity equality clause, they are to be treated as including one. In the case of a term relating to membership of or rights under an occupational pension scheme, a maternity equality clause only has such effect as a maternity equality rule would have (section 73(3)).   **11.60**

(a) *Exceptions*

A maternity equality clause will not have effect in relation to any terms of work affected by compliance with laws regulating the employment of women or their appointment to public or personal office.[98]   **11.61**

---

[92] S. 67(9).

[93] S. 67(10).

[94] Case 43/75 *Defrenne v Sabena* [1976] ECR 455.

[95] ECJ decision in Case 262/88 *Barber v Guardian Royal Exchange Insurance Group* [1990] IRLR 240.

[96] Known as Art. 119 of the Treaty of Rome when the decisions were made.

[97] The reasons for these limits on retrospectivity (and their exceptional nature) were considered by the Supreme Court in *Walker v Innospec* [2017] IRLR 928 and by the CJEU in *O'Brien v Ministry of Justice* [2019] IRLR 185. Their exceptional nature means they do not provide a general rule against retrospectivity in other contexts, e.g., in a claim for a pension for a same-sex spouse (*Innospec*) or a part-time worker (*O'Brien*). For limits on retrospectively 'levelling down' see *Safeway Ltd v Newton and another* [2019] IRLR 1090, CJEU.

[98] Sch. 7, para. 1.

(b) *Effect*

11.62 A maternity equality clause has the effect of modifying a term of a woman's work that provides for maternity-related pay to be calculated by reference to her pay at a particular time, to provide for maternity-related pay to be subject to an increase if three conditions are satisfied:

- after the particular time but before the end of the protected period her pay increases, or would have done if she had not been on maternity leave;
- her maternity-related pay is neither what her pay would have been if she had not been on maternity leave nor the difference between the amount of statutory maternity pay and what her pay would have been had she not been on maternity leave;
- the terms of work do not provide for the maternity-related pay to be subject to the relevant increase (section 74(1)–(5)).

11.63 In addition, under section 74(6), a term of work that provides for pay within section 74(7) but does not provide for her to be given the pay in circumstances in which she would have been given it had she not been on maternity leave, is modified so as to provide for her to be given it in circumstances in which it would normally be given. Section 74(7) covers:

- pay (including pay by way of bonus) in respect of times before the woman is on maternity leave;
- pay by way of bonus in respect of times when she is on compulsory maternity leave; and
- pay by way of bonus in respect of times after the end of the protected period.

11.64 The Explanatory Notes[99] give a couple of useful examples:

Early in her maternity leave, a woman receiving maternity-related pay becomes entitled to an increase of pay. If her terms of employment do not already provide for the increase to be reflected in her maternity-related pay, the employer must recalculate her maternity pay to take account of the increment.

A woman becomes entitled to a contractual bonus for work she undertook before she went on maternity leave. The employer cannot delay payment of the bonus and must pay it to her when it would have been paid had she not been on maternity leave.

11.65 Under section 74(8) if a term of the woman's work provides for pay after the end of the protected period but does not provide for it to be subject to an increase to which it would have been subject had she not been on maternity leave, it is modified so as to provide for it to be subject to the increase.

11.66 Maternity-related pay is defined in section 74(9) as pay, other than statutory maternity pay, to which a woman is entitled as a result of being pregnant or in respect of times when she is on maternity leave.

11.67 'Protected period' is defined in section 18(6). It begins when the pregnancy begins, and ends—if a woman has the right to ordinary and additional maternity leave—either when the woman returns to work or at the end of the additional maternity leave period. If a woman does not have the right to ordinary and additional maternity leave it ends two weeks after the end of the pregnancy.

---

[99] EN 256.

2. Equality in Pensions—Maternity Equality Rule

(a) *When it Applies*

If it does not include one, an occupational pension scheme is deemed to include a maternity equality rule.[100]   **11.68**

(b) *Effect*

The effect of the maternity equality rule is that: **11.69**

- terms relating to membership of the scheme, accrual of rights under the scheme, and the determination of the amount of benefit payable under the scheme have to treat time when a woman is on maternity leave as they treat time when she is not;[101]
- where a term confers a discretion capable of affecting membership of the scheme, accrual of rights under the scheme, and the determination of the amount of benefit payable under the scheme, that term is modified so that the discretion cannot be exercised in a way which treats time when a woman is on maternity leave differently from time when she is not.[102]

A maternity equality rule does not mean that a woman's pension contributions while she is on maternity leave have to be the same as when she is not. All it requires is that her contributions while on maternity leave are calculated by reference to the amount she is paid in respect of maternity leave.[103]   **11.70**

Where a maternity equality rule does apply, the relevant pregnancy and maternity discrimination provisions do not.[104]   **11.71**

(c) *Limitations on Application*

Where a woman is on maternity leave but not being paid by the employer, there are limits on how and when the maternity equality rule provisions apply.   **11.72**

- Where a woman is on ordinary maternity leave,[105] the provisions only apply in a case where the expected week of childbirth began on or after 6 April 2003.[106]
- Where a woman is on additional maternity leave,[107] the provisions do not apply to accrual of rights under the scheme in any case and only apply for other purposes where the expected week of childbirth began on or after 5 October 2008.[108]

Receiving Statutory Maternity Pay from the employer counts as 'being paid', so these limitations do not apply in such cases.[109]   **11.73**

---

[100] S. 75(1).
[101] S. 75(3) and (5).
[102] S. 75(4) and (6).
[103] S. 75(7).
[104] S. 76.
[105] S. 213(5).
[106] S. 75(8).
[107] S. 213(7).
[108] S. 75(9).
[109] S. 75(10)(b).

12

REDRESSING THE BALANCE: POSITIVE ACTION, QUOTAS, POLITICAL SHORTLISTS, AND ASSOCIATIONS

A. INTRODUCTION

12.01 This chapter is concerned with positive action to secure full equality in practice. It will discuss when it is permissible to take positive action in relation to equality issues. It will consider the specific issue of all-women shortlists for elected positions. It does not discuss the equality duties on public authorities (see Chapter 8) although it must be borne in mind that these duties may well cause a public authority to use these provisions. The key provisions in the Equality Act 2010 are in Chapter 2 Positive Action, which is in Part 11 Advancement of

Rachel Crasnow QC, *Redressing the Balance: Positive Action, Quotas, Political Shortlists, and Associations* In: *Blackstone's Guide to the Equality Act 2010*. Fourth Edition. Edited by: Anthony Robinson, David Ruebain, and Susie Uppal, Oxford University Press (2021). © Oxford University Press. DOI: 10.1093/oso/9780198870876.003.0012

Equality. Section 158 concerns Positive Action in general and section 159 concerns specifically Positive Action: Recruitment and Promotion. These sections intersect with other provisions of the Act, for instance those in which certain otherwise discriminatory conduct is rendered permissible by occupational requirements or because it is otherwise justified. These provisions all reflect core ideas in the centre of the equal treatment principle.

Thus it has long been recognized that simply affording the same treatment to different **12.02** people without consideration of the context in which the treatment takes place can easily perpetuate disadvantage since not everyone starts from the same position. This is perhaps most obvious in the context of disability and it is in relation to this ground that the most far reaching positive action steps have been permitted so far.[1] However this recognition has led to specific provisions across domestic law that has enabled some more limited positive action to be taken in relation to other grounds. It is also in part a basis for the development of protection against indirect discrimination.

These steps are all concerned with 'full equality in practice' which is now an explicit aim of **12.03** European equality law and continues to be part of our domestic law as well. It was introduced first in relation to gender as an amendment to the equal pay provisions of the EC Treaty by the Treaty of Amsterdam, as Article 141(4) EC (which is now Article 157(4) of the Treaty on the Functioning of the European Union (TFEU).

It is now also found in the Race Directive,[2] the Employment Equality Framework **12.04** Directive,[3] the Gender Goods and Services Directive,[4] and the Re-cast Sex Equality Directive[5] which replaced and strengthened the old Equal Treatment Directive. While the European Social Charter contains no explicit provision for positive action, even in its revised 1996 form, the Charter on Fundamental Rights provides by Article 23 that:

equality between women and men must be ensured in all areas, including employment, work and pay. The principle of equality shall not prevent the maintenance or adoption of measures providing for specific advantages in favour of the under-represented sex.

This provision will need to be borne in mind in addressing any case or legislation which emanates from Europe.

The aim of full equality in practice closely relates to the principle of equal treatment. It **12.05** has long been recognized that to achieve full equality in practice, disadvantaged groups may require different treatment because they are not similarly situated.[6] In European law the principle of equal treatment prohibits different situations from being treated in the same way

---

[1] See the discussion in the House of Lords in *Archibald v Fife Council* [2004] IRLR 651, paras 57–60 and in the CJEU in *Coleman v Attridge Law* [2008] IRLR 722, para. 42. See also the UN Convention on the Rights of Persons with Disabilities.

[2] See Art. 5 of Council Directive 2000/43/EC of 29 June 2000 implementing the principle of equal treatment between persons irrespective of racial or ethnic origin.

[3] See Art. 7 of Council Directive 2000/78/EC of 27 November 2000 establishing a general framework for equal treatment in employment and occupation.

[4] See Art. 6 of Council Directive 2004/113/EC of 13 December 2004 implementing the principle of equal treatment between men and women in the access to and supply of goods and services.

[5] Art. 3 of Directive 2006/54/EC of the European Parliament and of the Council of 5 July 2006 on the implementation of the principle of equal opportunities and equal treatment of men and women in matters of employment and occupation (recast).

[6] See, for instance, the opinion of AG Sharpston in Case C-427/06 *Birgit Bartsch v Bosch und Siemens Hausgeräte (BSH) Altersfürsorge GmbH* [2008] ECR I-7245, citing Aristotle's Nicomachean Ethics, V.3. 1131a10-b15 and Politics, III.9.1280 a8-15, III. 12. 1282b18-23.

just as much as it prohibits the same situations from being treated differently. The difficulty lies in determining when situations are not the same and to what extent different treatment is justified.[7] One limiting factor may be the point at which it can no longer be said that there is equality of opportunity. However even this limit may be set aside where it is shown that special measures are necessary to remedy past disadvantage.

12.06   As will be further explained later in the chapter, the Labour government did not seek to eradicate disadvantage or dismantle inequality by means of transformative equality provisions, when bringing forward the Bill that became the Equality Act 2010. Rather it was committed to extending the power to take positive action, as far as it was possible to go while still legislating consistently with European and international law.[8] It did this chiefly via legislation which enabled proportionate encouragement to improve chances to succeed. So, it is important first to understand the legal constraints under European Law as these have underpinned the approach that has been taken in the Equality Act 2010.

B. WHAT POSITIVE ACTION IS PERMITTED BY EUROPEAN LAW?

12.07   This chapter aims to clarify what positive action is permitted in the United Kingdom and what is not. This is by no means straightforward, but there is no doubt that the starting point remains European law which is itself relatively limited and lacks a fully worked out set of principles. The case law of the Court of Justice of the European Union (CJEU) concerns a range of contexts. Nonetheless the lack of clarity remains as Advocate General Bobek noted in 2018 in his Opinion in *Cresco Investigation GmbH v Markus Achatzi,*[9] saying:[10]

… the debate as to whether positive action is a (temporary) derogation from the principle of equality or whether it is in fact an inherent component of a truly substantive vision of equality is far from settled.

12.08   The case is interesting also as giving some indication of the range of arguments for positive action that are sometimes advanced and how that is to be controlled. The case concerned the grant of days off for certain religious groups based on less favourable treatment many years ago. The Advocate General rejected the Austrian Government's argument in favour of this measure as follows:[11]

106. …the Austrian Government advanced that the measures could be interpreted as falling within a notion of positive action in the sense of having been adopted to compensate for less favourable treatment in the past. According to the Austrian Government's written pleadings, members of the four churches, unlike the Catholic majority, did not have a right to a day off to celebrate their most important religious festival of the year and had suffered that situation for many years before it was requested and granted in the 1950s.

---

[7] See *ibid* at [44].

[8] See Explanatory Notes (EN) 531 to the Bill which, while noting that there 'are existing positive action provisions in current legislation, [and that] these apply to different protected characteristics in different ways and in some cases are specific about the types of action they permit', added that the Bill 'extends what is possible to the extent permitted by European law'. This is repeated in EN 525 and 529 to the Act.

[9] Case C-193/17 *Cresco Investigation GmbH v Markus Achatzi* ECLI:EU:C:2019:43.

[10] See ECLI:EU:C:2018:614 at [105].

[11] See paras [106]–[111].

107. True, 'positive action' has no clear definition in legislation or the case-law. Thus, there is no prima facie limitation on what might fall under that notion, both substantively and temporally. On that level, it could be indeed suggested that the intention to 'compensate for disadvantages linked to any of the grounds referred to in Article 1' might also include the desire to compensate for (even centuries) of past religious persecution.

108. That being said, I confess that simply from a chronological point of view, it does seem rather questionable whether a measure adopted in the 1950s was really conceived of as 'positive action' in the sense of a much more contemporary notion, first appearing, certainly within EU law, only decades later. Such prescience borders on the miraculous.

109. However, lack of definitional specificity and chronology aside, there are two compelling reasons why I consider that the indemnity cannot in any event constitute 'positive action'.

110. First, the measure targets a very specific group, thus again opening up the already discussed issue of its selectivity and second-level discrimination. Measures were not adopted to ensure full equality of all groups which have been disadvantaged in general in the past or, more specifically, do not have a holiday for an important festival, unlike the Catholic majority.

111. Second, any measure alleged to fall within the scope of positive action must in any event comply with the principle of proportionality... Although the Court's case-law on the application of the concept of positive action in the context of secondary law does not present the analysis in terms of proportionality, it is clear that the Court scrutinises measures to establish whether they are necessary to neutralise perceived disadvantage ... the relevant national law measures cannot in any event be considered as proportionate ...

The Court agreed, and also dismissed these arguments. The next year, in his Opinion in 12.09
WA v Instituto Nacional de la Seguridad Social, Advocate General Bobek returned to this theme, again noting how it remained unresolved:[12]

... whether Article 157(4) TFEU is limited to the sphere of 'equal pay' or has a broader scope of application ... [and]... what kind of measures can be considered as covered by this provision ...

Several CJEU cases concern the early stages of parenthood in which legislative provisions 12.10 have given rights to women but not to men. The issue in short is that up to a point, it is obvious that in the period immediately after birth, women should not be considered in a comparable position to men, just as they are not to be considered in a comparable position when pregnant, yet at some point that ceases to be true and such measures are no longer justified.[13]

The most significant CJEU case discussing what positive action measures are permissible 12.11 remains its 2004 judgment in *Serge Briheche v Ministre de l'Intérieur, Ministre de l'Éducation Nationale and Ministre de la Justice*.[14] That case considered the effects of earlier decisions about parenting at a later stage in life. Both the judgment of the Court, and the Advocate

[12] Case C-450/18 *WA v Instituto Nacional de la Seguridad Social*, ECLI:EU:C:2019:696 at [83]. See also the discussion of this case by the Supreme Court in *Z & Anor, R (on the application of) v Hackney London Borough Council & Anor (Rev 1)* [2020] UKSC 40 and at 12.103 below.
[13] For instance it has been recognized that statutory maternity leave provides women with time (1) to prepare for and cope with the later stages of pregnancy, (2) to recuperate from the pregnancy, (3) to recuperate from the effects of childbirth, (4) to develop the special relationship between the mother and the newborn child, (5) to breastfeed the newborn child (recommended for a period of six months by the World Health Organization), and (6) to care for the newborn child: see *Ali v Capita Customer Management Ltd (Rev 2)* [2019] IRLR 695, [2019] 4 All ER 918, [2019] EWCA Civ 900, [2020] ICR 87 at [64].
[14] Case C-319/2003 [2004] ECR I-8807, ECLI:EU:C:2004:574.

General's Opinion, provide a good review of the prior case law and also explain the present thinking of the CJEU. In *Briheche* the CJEU had to consider whether a French law, which prohibited recruitment to employment in the Civil Service for anyone aged over 45, unless the applicant was a widow or an unmarried man with child care responsibilities, was unlawful positive action. As the Recast Sex Equality Directive had not yet been enacted, the CJEU first reviewed the weaker provisions of Article 2(4) of the Equal Treatment Directive.[15] However it then considered the nature of the obligation of 'full equality in practice' in Article 141(4) EC and held that whilst this provision and Article 2(4) looked beyond formal equality to substantive equality, it was not possible to say how far this goal could be achieved where positive action for a woman might create a claim of unlawful discrimination by a man. The CJEU went on to hold that the French provision in question was *not* consistent with the limits to permissible positive action as the *automatic and unconditional disapplication* of the relevant conditions to certain women was insufficient on the facts to justify the step taken.[16]

12.12   Reference should also be made to Advocate General Maduro's Opinion in *Briheche* which seeks to provide a comprehensive statement at that point as to the CJEU case law concerning what is permitted and what not. [17] In particular Advocate General Maduro considered whether positive action measures under European law could be extended by looking at compensatory forms of positive discrimination on equality of opportunities, rather than on equality of results (which in the form of quotas and set targets has been deemed disproportionate to date).[18]

12.13   In 2009, in *Roca Álvarez*,[19] the CJEU gave its next significant judgment. In this case the Court ruled against a national measure (known colloquially as 'breastfeeding leave'), that provided that female employees who were mothers could take leave during the first nine months following the child's birth, whereas male employees who were fathers were not so entitled, unless the child's mother was also an employed person. The CJEU stated:

33. As the Court has consistently held, Article 2(4) of Directive 76/207 is specifically and exclusively designed to authorize measures which, although discriminatory in appearance, are in fact intended to eliminate or reduce actual instances of inequality which may exist in society. That provision thus authorizes national measures relating to access to employment, including promotion, which give a specific advantage to women with a view to improving their ability to compete on the labour market and to pursue a career on an equal footing with men (see Case C-450/93 *Kalanke* [1995] ECR I-3051, paragraphs 18 and 19; Case C-409/95 *Marschall* [1997] ECR I-6363, paragraphs 26 and 27; Case C-158/97 *Badeck and Others* [2000] ECR I-1875, paragraph 19; and *Lommers*, paragraph 32).

34. The aim of Article 2(4) is to achieve substantive, rather than formal, equality by reducing de facto inequalities which may arise in society and, thus, in accordance with Article 157(4) TFEU, to prevent or compensate for disadvantages in the professional career of the relevant persons (see, to that effect, *Kalanke*, paragraph 19; Case C-407/98 *Abrahamsson and Anderson* [2000] ECR I-5539, paragraph 48; and Case C-319/03 *Briheche* [2004] ECR I-8807, paragraph 25).

---

[15] See Council Directive 76/207/EEC of 9 February 1976 on the implementation of the principle of equal treatment for men and women as regards access to employment, vocational training and promotion, and working conditions which was replaced with strengthened positive action provisions by Directive 2006/54/EC.

[16] See the judgment in *Briheche* at [27]–[28].

[17] The reference for the Opinion is ECLI:EU:C:2004:398.

[18] See *Briheche*, Opinion at [48]–[51].

[19] Case C-104/09 EU:C:2010:561.

In 2015, in *Maïstrellis v Ypourgos Dikaiosynis, Diafaneias kai Anthropinon Diakaiomaton*[20] **12.14** the CJEU returned to the issue and applied the principles it had developed in the cases cited above, though without direct reference to them. In this case a father successfully challenged a Greek provision concerning parental leave for fathers where such leave was made conditional upon having an employed spouse or partner. The Court noted that an objective of the Parental Leave Directive[21] was to encourage new fathers to become involved with early childcare and was not purely targeted at encouraging mothers to return to work.

This objective of achieving substantive equality goes hand in hand with the positive action **12.15** measures in sections 158 and 159 which are considered below at Part F.

C. INTERNATIONAL EQUALITY LAW

The adoption of positive action provisions is allowed under a number of international human **12.16** rights instruments, in particular the International Convention on the Elimination of All Forms of Racial Discrimination 1969 (ICERD),[22] the Convention on the Elimination of All Forms of Discrimination against Women 1979 (CEDAW)[23] and the International Covenant on Civil and Political Rights 1976 (ICCPR).[24] The UN Convention on the Rights of Persons with Disabilities of the 13th December 2006 is also based on the obligations to take action to secure full equality in practice for disabled persons. Practitioners should note that under Article 2.2 ICERD State Parties 'shall take ... concrete measures ... for the purpose of guaranteeing ... full and equal enjoyment of human rights and fundamental freedoms'. Further to these UN human rights provisions there is similar provision for special measures under some Council of Europe treaties,[25] in particular Article 4 of the Framework Convention on the Protection of National Minorities.[26]

Very few cases before the European Court of Human Rights (ECtHR) touch directly upon **12.17** positive action in the sense discussed above, although of course many consider the positive obligations of states to protect human rights.[27] In an advisory Opinion the Court held it was not appropriate for the Council of Europe to reject a list of judges nominated by a state on the basis that it did not contain any women.[28] In a more recent judgment, also concerning parental rights, in *Markin v Russia*[29] the ECtHR decided that the denial of three years' parental leave to a male member of military personnel on the basis that, under Russian law, such leave could only be granted to female personnel amounted to a violation of his right not to be discriminated against under Articles 14 and 8 of the European Convention on Human Rights. The Court stated at [141]:

---

[20] Case C-222/14, EU:C:2015:473.
[21] Council Directive 2010/18/EU of 8 March 2010 implementing the revised Framework Agreement on parental leave concluded by BUSINESSEUROPE, UEAPME, CEEP and ETUC and repealing Directive 96/34/EC (Text with EEA relevance).
[22] See Arts. 1(4) and 2(2).
[23] See Art. 4(1).
[24] See Arts. 25 and 26.
[25] The European Convention on Human Rights (ECHR) is discussed below at part M.
[26] See <http://conventions.coe.int/Treaty/EN/Treaties/Html/157.htm>.
[27] See for instance *Dzhurayev v Russia* (2013) 57 EHRR 22.
[28] See *Advisory Opinion on Certain Legal Questions Concerning the Lists of Candidates Submitted with a View to the Election of Judges to the European Court of Human Rights* (2009) 49 EHRR 33.
[29] (2013) 56 EHRR 8.

... that the [Russian] Government's reference to positive discrimination is misconceived. The difference treatment of servicemen and servicewomen as regards entitlement to parental leave is clearly not intended to correct the disadvantaged position of women in society or 'factual inequalities' between men and women. The Court agrees with the applicant and the third party that such difference has the effect of perpetuating gender stereotypes and is disadvantageous both to women's careers and to men's family life.

D. GENUINE OCCUPATIONAL REQUIREMENTS

12.18   The law on positive action must be contrasted with that relating to genuine occupational requirements (GORs), whereby if the sex, race, religion, or age of an employee or applicant is genuinely deemed essential for the post in question, what would otherwise be unlawful discrimination is rendered lawful.[30] Such provisions are not aimed at enhancing opportunities for disadvantaged groups, as positive action measures are, but instead allow a defence to discriminatory acts where the essential nature of the job calls for a specific characteristic such as age, race, religion, or sex for reasons including physiology, authenticity, privacy, or decency. It is important to emphasize that they are strictly defined in the legislation and carefully scrutinized by the courts to avoid stereotypes in the workplace (such as 'only women are suitable to work with babies in nurseries') being erroneously legitimated under these provisions.

12.19   It has increasingly been contested whether the exclusion of trans people from single-sex groups either in workplace or services scenarios is or can be a GOR. Whether it is discriminatory to refuse access to trans people in such contexts remains unsettled.

12.20   Schedule 9 to the Equality Act 2010 allows employers to stipulate that a post is only open to individuals with a particular protected characteristic, where this constitutes a GOR. This provision appears to have reduced the protection afforded to transgender people, as the Gender Recognition Act 2004 had previously ensured employers could no longer rely on an occupational requirement for an employee not to be transsexual where that employee held a Gender Recognition Certificate (GRC).

12.21   The guidance is also arguably regressive in relation to situations where other service users might complain about, for example, the presence of a trans woman in a single-sex group. Thus the Explanatory Notes to the 2010 Act[31] gives as an example of a lawful occupational requirement:

A counsellor working with victims of rape might have to be a woman and not a transsexual person, even if she has a Gender Recognition Certificate, in order to avoid causing them further distress.

12.22   This statement is arguably too categorical in failing to acknowledge that a GOR must be proportionate and that it would be inadequate for a provider of services to *assume* female victims of sexual assault would necessarily object to a trans woman attending group counselling sessions. Moreover the Equality and Human Rights Commission advises that service providers must treat transgender people 'according to the gender role in which they present'.[32] The level of interference with the rights of the trans service-user might also be affected by the existence of a gender recognition certificate.

---

[30] See Sch. 9, Part 1 to the 2010 Act.
[31] At [789].
[32] See Chapter 13 of the EHRC's Statutory Code of Practice, 'Services, public functions and associations'.

The debate concerning trans women's use of women's single-sex services and the exceptions **12.23** in the Equality Act which permit services providers to exclude people who are biologically male from such services even if they have a GRC continues and requires a legislated resolution. Some gender critical feminists contend that trans women who have much of their life experience as a male, are not able to participate in some single-sex events; others argue that on self-declaring as a woman, the common associated disadvantages suffered by women (from underrepresentation in senior management to studying STEM subjects at A level) spring into existence. The key to lawful participation in single-sex services under section 158 is to assess 'disadvantage' in a proportionate way (see *Z v Hackney LBC*[33] adopting *Coll*[34] below).

Furthermore until clarification is provided on trans people and single-sex spaces, it would **12.24** be prudent to ensure that any exclusion action taken against the presence of trans people in single-sex groups was proportionate to the fullest extent.

E. THE POSITION UP TO THE EQUALITY ACT 2010

It is important to understand that the 2010 Act was meant to increase the possibilities for **12.25** positive action compared with earlier legislation. Prior to the new Act, UK domestic law was much more limited and essentially only permitted training and encouragement to be offered on a limited and targeted basis to under-represented groups.[35] This kind of action enhanced access to job and service opportunities, but the law did not permit selection for substantive benefits such as recruitment or promotion to take place, merely because of under-representation.

The last positive action provision enacted before the 2010 Act was regulation 29(1) of the **12.26** Employment Equality (Age) Regulations 2006,[36] which said:

29. Exceptions for positive action
(1) Nothing in Part 2 or 3 shall render unlawful any act done in or in connection with—
    (a) affording persons of a particular age or age group access to facilities for training which would help fit them for particular work; or
    (b) encouraging persons of a particular age or age group to take advantage of opportunities for doing particular work;

where it reasonably appears to the person doing the act that it prevents or compensates for disadvantages linked to age suffered by persons of that age or age group doing that work or likely to take up that work ...

Under the 2006 Regulations all persons providing the positive action needed to show was that it 'reasonably appeared' to them that the action was appropriate. Some idea of the extent to which this was seen at the time as being progressive can be seen by drawing a contrast with earlier provisions, such as sections 37 and 38 of the Race Relations Act 1976 (RRA), which required a more statistical basis for the positive action. Under the RRA it had to be shown that at any time in the last year at the workplace in question there were no, or only a small proportion of workers of the relevant racial group in relation

---

[33] See the Supreme Court judgment [2020] UKSC 40.
[34] *R (on the application of Coll) v Secretary of State for Justice* [2017] UKSC 40, [2017] 1 WLR 2093.
[35] See, e.g., Race Relations Act 1976 (RRA) ss. 35–8 and Sex Discrimination Act 1975 (SDA) s. 47.
[36] Employment Equality (Age) Regulations 2006, SI 2006/1031.

to the local population or to the entire workforce.[37] The 2010 Act repealed all the earlier provisions and replaced them with the new provisions discussed below in part F. Now it can be said that while the 2010 Act was built on this earlier approach to positive action it permits a broader range of action; training and encouragement will no longer simply be the primary means to achieve a level playing field and other initiatives to influence decisions may be taken under the Act.

F. POSITIVE ACTION IN THE EQUALITY ACT 2010

12.27   Chapter 2 in Part 11 of the Act contains the key positive action provisions.[38] There are two sections which permit positive action though in neither case do they override other statutory provisions.[39] Section 158 covers positive action generally but does not apply when section 159, which covers positive action at work, applies.[40] Section 158 also does not apply when section 104 applies; that section applies to the selection of candidates for political parties and is discussed below. This chapter will consider the specific provisions first before considering the general provisions. Section 158 came into force on 1 October 2010 and section 159 on 6 April 2011.

G. POSITIVE ACTION IN RELATION TO WORK: RECRUITMENT OR PROMOTION

12.28   Section 159 applies specifically in the work context covered by Part 5 of the Act. It is inevitable that the section will give rise to a number of questions of interpretation, which could undermine its utility. It is also inevitable that, since it is a permissive provision and does not impose any obligations, such questions have deterred employers from putting it to use. This is unfortunate, because if a little time is taken to understand it, employers should have more confidence in their ability to use this provision effectively.

1. The Type of Permissible Action

12.29   The kind of action which the legislation contemplates is preferential appointments on specified grounds. This was a radical development from the previous provisions outlined above. The limits and context in which such appointments are likely to be permissible are developed further below.

12.30   Section 159 is concerned solely with the substantive benefits of recruitment or promotion and does not extend more widely than that, though these concepts are widely defined. It can be seen below that section 159(1) defines the basis on which positive action can be taken and in section 159(4) sets out the limits to that action:

---

[37] Section 38(2)(a) and (b) of the RRA.
[38] See EN at [519]–[529].
[39] See ss. 158(6) and 159(3).
[40] See s. 158(4).

159. Positive action: recruitment and promotion

(1) This section applies if a person (P) reasonably thinks that—

    (a) persons who share a protected characteristic suffer a disadvantage connected to the characteristic, or

    (b) participation in an activity by persons who share a protected characteristic is disproportionately low.

(2) Part 5 (work) does not prohibit P from taking action within subsection (3) with the aim of enabling or encouraging persons who share the protected characteristic to—

    (a) overcome or minimise that disadvantage, or

    (b) participate in that activity.

(3) That action is treating a person (A) more favourably in connection with recruitment or promotion than another person (B) because A has the protected characteristic but B does not.

(4) But subsection (2) applies only if—

    (a) A is as qualified as B to be recruited or promoted,

    (b) P does not have a policy of treating persons who share the protected characteristic more favourably in connection with recruitment or promotion than persons who do not share it, and

    (c) taking the action in question is a proportionate means of achieving the aim referred to in subsection (2).

2. What Do 'Disadvantage' and 'Disproportionately Low' Mean?

The basis which must be established for action under this section has similarities with that in **12.31** the Age Regulations. The section does not specifically require a statistical analysis, provided there is a reasonable basis to conclude that there is a connection between a protected characteristic and disadvantage, or the fact of disproportionately low participation.

In those circumstances it enables positive action, with the aim of enabling or encouraging **12.32** persons who share the protected characteristic to overcome or minimize that disadvantage, or participate in the relevant activity. Subject to limitations, this can include more favourable treatment of those who have a specific protected characteristic.

Two questions arise: is it necessary to prove that the disadvantage is generally recognized **12.33** and related to that (a causation issue): how does an employer go about proving that a disadvantage is connected to a characteristic? In the public sector, equality auditing under the equality duties is likely to provide an answer. However, it is clear that the legislation expects other employers as well to be aware of the diversity of their workforce and to wish to address any apparent deficiencies.

In the second part of section 159(1) it is necessary to consider how to determine whether **12.34** participation is disproportionately low. For instance, it might be that the proportion of older people working in the fashion industry is disproportionately low compared to those in the population at large, but would such a generalized comparison be sufficient for the positive action (in the form of the proposed selection) to be legitimate? Unfortunately, the Explanatory Notes to the Act do not seek to answer these questions. Clearly some evidence is vital—without it the measure cannot be shown to be adequate or proportionate to the aim pursued.

Some answers to these questions can be obtained by reference to the case law of the CJEU. **12.35** For instance in Germany the 1990 Bremen Act on Equal Treatment for Men and Women in the Public Service provided that women who are 'under-represented' could be given priority over men for public sector appointments if they had the same qualifications. The legislation stated that there was under-representation if:

women do not make up at least half of the staff in the individual pay, remuneration and salary brackets in the relevant personnel group within a department.

Since the Bremen scheme had given unconditional preference to the under-represented candidate, the CJEU decided it was unlawful on grounds of lack of proportionality. However, the Court did not criticize the German legislation's approach to under-representation.[41]

12.36   Nevertheless it is not certain whether merely rough inequality between the proportions would be sufficient. Such statistics might be unreliable by reason of the numbers, or the time frame, which they represent. They may simply show random events and not disadvantage. The better view is that the level of participation needs to be shown to be low when compared with other groups or with the expected level of participation. Practitioners should also note that section 159 makes the test more subjective than the requirement under the said German legislation by providing: 'if a person P (who is the person who will take the positive action) reasonably thinks that ...'. However, whether the UK courts will demand hard statistical data seems doubtful, but will have to be tested.

12.37   A further question is whether the under-representation must be specific to the workforce and community, locally or nationally? Again, a proportionate consideration of the context will be necessary. Under-representation in a certain employment market is unlikely to justify positive action measures in a different area. On the other hand, the geographical spread of a labour market for some work may be quite large, and it may be wrong to look at it on too narrow a basis.

3. There Must Not be a Policy to Discriminate

12.38   It might seem that the Act expects section 159 to be used relatively rarely and that it is concerned essentially with a tie-break context. This is because there cannot be a *policy* of treating persons who share the protected characteristic more favourably in connection with recruitment or promotion than persons who do not share it. However, the prohibition on having a policy to prefer persons having a particular protected characteristic does not have quite that effect. The purpose of this prohibition is to ensure that whenever the section is applied there is a *specific* consideration of the candidates for recruitment and promotion and their competitors.[42] Thus an unthinking purported application of section 159 is likely to be unlawful.

4. 'As qualified as'

12.39   Secondly, candidates in respect of whom employers can take positive action must be equally suitable for the job. It is quite clear, for instance, that under this provision a woman cannot be given an automatic preference over a man simply by reason of her gender.[43]

12.40   The consequence of this is that there must be an objective selection process that assesses specific skills, qualifications, and abilities, but does this mean that candidates have to be

---

[41] Case C-450/93 *Kalanke v Freie Hansestadt Bremen* [1995] ECR I-3051.

[42] EN 526 states 'each case must be considered on its merits'.

[43] See Case C-158/97 *Badeck v Landesanwalt beim Staatsgerichtshof des Landes Hessen* [2000] IRLR 432, ECJ.

qualified or suitable in *exactly* the same way before a choice based on under-representation is legitimate? The present view is probably not. The Act uses the phrase 'as qualified as' and it was suggested by the government in 2009 that whilst this does not authorize in any way the use of quotas, it will cover situations where candidates meet the minimum qualifications or the particular requirements for the post, in contrast to a scenario where the applications in question are *identical* in their qualifications, skills, and abilities. Thus even if a candidate from a protected group had some weaknesses in areas where his/her competitor was strong, if those related to desirable rather than essential aspects of the job specification, s/he may be considered as qualified for the post. Not all recruitment exercises divide the desired characteristics of the post into necessary and preferred. So the answer to this question may require a more specific examination as to how important the skills in question are for the job.

There are no fixed rules as to how such an assessment must operate. The Explanatory Note   **12.41** to the Act states[44] that the section allows 'the maximum flexibility to address disadvantage and under-representation where candidates are as good as each other'. While it seems inevitable that some litigation will arise from the use of positive action measures in recruitment exercises, it is also certain that the more demonstrably objective an assessment of the candidates has been, the less open to challenge the ultimate selection will be.

For instance, it would normally be straightforward to assess the qualifications required for   **12.42** the post of a legal secretary; by contrast, there would be a high degree of subjectivity in the value judgement involved in determining who is qualified to be a senior partner or even to perform a management role. So, the meaning of the word 'qualified' will surely be the subject of future debate and will require to be developed by either Codes of Practice, or possibly judicial determination.

It is certain that under existing legislation and EU law automatic preferences or quotas   **12.43** will be unlawful if they do not include the requisite exercise in proportionality by prioritizing under-represented groups in an unconditional fashion. Hence the Swedish Equality Act 1991 which permitted employers to appoint a member of one sex over the other (even though the appointee was the worse candidate) where the appointment served to promise equality between men and women in the workplace, was held to be held unlawful by the CJEU in *Abrahamsson v Fogelqvist*.[45]

However, the CJEU has not made this condition for positive action impossibly difficult   **12.44** to meet. In *Abrahamsson* the CJEU ruled that Article 2 of the Equal Treatment Directive did not preclude granting a preference to a candidate belonging to the under-represented group (here women), over a competitor of the opposite sex:

… provided that the candidates possess equivalent or substantially equivalent merits and the candidatures are subjected to an objective assessment which takes account of [*all their*] specific personal situations. (Emphasis added)

Thus, so as long as there is a substantive degree of objective assessment, EU law does not demand that candidates be *identically* qualified for a tie-break to be permitted.

The House of Lords added an amendment to section 159 to make it explicit that:[46]   **12.45**

---

[44] See [528].
[45] Case C-407/98 [2000] IRLR 732.
[46] Hansard HL, col. 658 (9 February 2010).

... any positive action measure taken in recruitment and promotion has to be a proportionate means of achieving the aims set out in subsection (2), that is helping people overcome a disadvantage or participate in an activity.

A proportionality requirement is also added to section 104.

12.46   Fortunately the sections in the Act are not the only basis upon which employers need operate. The Codes of Practice issued by the Equality and Human Rights Commission (see Chapter 8) should provide practical assistance in relation to the issues discussed above. Also the Government Equalities Office published a 'quick start guide' to using positive action in recruitment and promotion in 2011.[47] This contains useful guidance on a variety of relevant issues including the meaning of 'equal merit'. When establishing whether the individuals are of equal merit, the Equalities Office advise that employers should do three things:

(a) establish a set of criteria against which candidates will be assessed in the course of their job application;

(b) be aware of indirect discrimination within the criteria selected, for example unjustifiable requirement for shift working in circumstances where this could put women bearing the burden of childcare at a disproportionate disadvantage;

(c) ensure that the candidates are of equal merit in relation to the particular position being applied for. Their specific skill-base or experience may be more relevant to one post than another.

12.47   The Equalities Office quick start guide gives a useful example of legitimate positive action under section 159:

A health and fitness club is faced with making a choice between two applicants for a job as the manager of a leisure facility. One, a woman, has recently completed a Leisure Management Foundation Degree course but has little practical experience. The other candidate is a man who has no formal qualifications but has several years' experience of working in leisure centres. Having interviewed both candidates, the employer decides that both could do the job to the same standard but in different ways as each would bring a different set of skills and experiences to the job. Therefore, because the candidates are of equal merit the manager could voluntarily use the positive action provisions when choosing between the candidates and opt to employ the man because all of the other senior positions at the leisure complex were held by women.

12.48   However, three scenarios where positive action would not be legitimate under section 159 are set out in these practical examples in the quick start guide:

• A local authority wishes to diversify its workforce and undertakes a large recruitment exercise. In an attempt to create a large pool of 'qualified' people from which it can cherry-pick those with the relevant protected characteristics to make its workforce more diverse, it sets a very low pass mark for the assessment to make sure that a lot of people pass. Picking someone with a particular protected characteristic from the pool in preference to someone who achieved a higher score and was clearly better qualified for the job but didn't have a targeted protected characteristic would not be allowed by the positive action provisions and would be likely to be unlawful discrimination.

---

[47] See <http://www.equalities.gov.uk>.

- A call centre wishes to diversify the ethnicity of its workforce as it is aware that it is currently predominantly white despite being based in an area with a large Indian population. After interview the top two candidates are both white—but in a bid to create greater diversity the company appoints the third placed candidate because he is Indian. This would be positive discrimination so would be unlawful.

- A department store employs nine senior managers but only two of them are women. When a vacancy arises it seeks to address this under-representation by only interviewing women applicants, regardless of whether they meet the criteria for the post. This would be positive discrimination so would be unlawful.

Such examples of a lack of proportionality demonstrate the importance of thinking through objectives and alternatives before putting positive action into place. In particular it must be remembered that an employer must not have a general policy of treating people with the relevant protected characteristic more favourably in connection with recruitment.   12.49

Possible models as to how the assessment process for positive action should take place are available from other jurisdictions. For example, in *Badeck v Landesanwalt beim Staatsgerichtshof des Landes Hessen*,[48] the German state of Hesse utilized an innovative means of assessing skills and abilities of candidates in under-represented fields. The national legislation included the provision that: 12.50

When qualifications are assessed, capabilities and experience which have been acquired by looking after children or persons requiring care in the domestic sector (family work) are to be taken into account, in so far as they are of importance for the suitability, performance and capability of applicants ... Part-time work, leave and delays in completing training as a result of looking after children ... must not have a negative effect on official assessment and not adversely affect progress in employment ... Seniority, age and the date of last promotion may be taken into account only in so far as they are of importance for the suitability, performance and capability of applicants.

This approach was also considered by the European Free Trade Association Court in *EFTA Surveillance Authority v Kingdom of Norway*[49] where the Court stated that: 12.51

.giving weight to the possibility that in numerous academic disciplines female life experience may be relevant to the determination of the suitability and capability for, and performance in, higher academic positions, could enhance the equality of men and women.

Such an approach to the objective assessment of candidates could have a significant impact on the under-representation of women in management posts in the UK in the future, should employers embrace these voluntary measures. Barriers to equal opportunity experienced by black and ethnic minority communities might also start to be overcome with an innovation that recognizes more fully the value of different backgrounds. Whilst most of the CJEU case law to date in this area has been concerned with gender imbalance, it is expected that the positive action measures legitimized by the Act will be particularly useful in attempts to create greater race equality in the workforce. They may also be important in securing greater intergenerational fairness.   12.52

The ACAS guidance to the Equality Act[50] includes an explanation of the positive action provisions in the Act and provides examples of their usage, including: 12.53

---

[48] Case C-158/97 [2000] IRLR 432 ECJ.
[49] Case E-1/02 [2003] IRLR 318.
[50] *Equality and Discrimination: understand the basics*; August 2015.

... *taking 'positive action'*

A national retailer finds out that despite employing a diverse workforce at junior management level, only three of 55 senior managers are female. Research indicates that many of the female employees are put off from applying for promotion because of an apparent 'all-male environment' and that this is losing the business a wealth of experience and creativity.

The company sets up a programme of training and development for female staff where they can develop management skills and gain an understanding of how senior management operates through a mentoring scheme. Over the next 12 months, the proportion of female applicants and appointments increase, and a new campaign spearheaded by the newly-promoted staff brings an increase in sales.

... *taking 'positive action' in recruitment*

A high school, where almost half of the pupils are from a minority ethnic group and none of the ten existing department heads are from a minority community, is recruiting for a new department head.

In the job advertisement, the school says it would welcome applications from qualified candidates from minority ethnic groups as they are under-represented in senior staff positions at the school. All 80 staff at the school are trained to put into practice its equality policies, and deal with any bullying and harassment.

In the recruitment process, all the candidates are scored against a range of job-relevant questions in interviews. The interview panel also objectively assess the experience and qualifications of each candidate. At the end of a rigorous and well-documented selection process, the two best candidates have equal scores. The interview panel has robust documentary evidence to prove the two candidates are equally qualified for the role.

Both are women and one is black. The head of the school thinks it important that its senior leadership reflects the local population and the school, and so decides to appoint the black candidate. This may be lawful under the Equality Act.

12.54 Most of the explanations of section 159 in published guidance (as with the ACAS examples above) take the low-risk approach of requiring identical qualifications and merit rather than the minimum threshold standard discussed above at paragraphs 3.04–3.05. It may be useful to note when arguing against the suggestion that 'as qualified as' means 'the same', that the term 'equally qualified' was specifically rejected during the consultation leading up to the Equality Act due to a concern that this would mean the provision was solely about the quality of qualifications. Professor Simonetta Mandredi has said that the notion of being 'as qualified as' has similarities to the well understood concept of 'equal value' and the established jurisprudence on that concept should aid the use of this tiebreak for employers.[51]

H. THE PROGRESS OF THE POSITIVE ACTION PROVISIONS WITHIN THE EQA 2010

12.55 Despite the hesitant stance taken to these provisions so far, it has been said that without mandatory employer duties to use them and enforcement from the EHRC and the Tribunal

---

[51] Simonetta Manfredi, 'Increasing Gender Diversity in Senior Roles in HE: Who is Afraid of Positive Action?' (2017) 7(2) *Administrative Sciences*, 19.

Service, the utility of sections 158 and 159 will be extremely limited.[52] Debates over accusations of watering-down merit continue, despite some arguing that the detriment of temporary stigma being preferable to ongoing disadvantage experienced if under-representation is not counted by proactive measures.[53]

It is right that there has been little substantive development since the provisions com-   12.56
menced. There are a range of reasons why employers appear not to be embracing the permissive positive action provisions. Dr Chantal Davies and Professor Muriel Robison suggest that:[54]

… the potential risks of introducing a viable positive action initiative, in light of possible legal challenge for "reverse discrimination" from an unsuccessful candidate (e.g., in a tie-break situation), may be considered overly burdensome.

In the only Employment Tribunal consideration of the 'tiebreak' provision, *Furlong v Chief Constable of Cheshire Police*,[55] a white, heterosexual male unsuccessful applicant to the Cheshire Police Service brought claims of direct discrimination on grounds of sex, race, and sexual orientation. The force's policy was to treat all candidates who passed the various recruitment stages (whether they passed with flying colours, or just scraped by) as being equally qualified for the job. They then prioritized BAME (Black, Asian, and minority ethnic) candidates. When the number of successful candidates exceeded the number of vacancies some successful candidates including the claimant were placed on a reserve list. The claimant brought a claim challenging the reliance on section 159 and complaining of direct discrimination contrary to section 13 of the Equality Act 2010. The Tribunal held that the force's reliance on section 159 failed for three reasons. It had wrongly deemed all candidates who had passed the recruitment process as being 'of equal merit' rather than acknowledging different scoring; it was wrong to simply appoint all candidates from under-represented groups; and before commencing this 'radical programme' the police force ought to have waited to assess its earlier diversity and inclusion programmes. Thus adopting a blanket approach was disproportionate and amounted to a policy which is outlawed by section 159(4)(b).

1. Positive Action Initiatives

Various initiatives have been taken since the coming into force of the Equality Act. These   12.57
suggest that a range of organizations are tussling with the concept of positive action, if not utilizing tie-break provisions. These commonly take the form of outreach programmes, however the Judicial Appointments Commission (JAC)'s recent decision to rely upon section 159 shows a different approach to positive action measures (see below at paragraph 12.59).

The previous edition of this book noted various examples of positive action in workplaces   12.58
pursuant to both sections 158 and 159, including:

- Unions trying to encourage employers to engage with positive action initiatives; for instance ASLEF has noted that

---

[52] Lois Thwaites, 'The British Equality Framework is Incapable of Achieving Equality in the Workforce' (2014) 2(1) *NELR* 164.
[53] Mike Noon, 'The Shackled Runner: Time to Rethink Positive Discrimination?' (2010) 24(4) *Work, Employment and Society* 728.
[54] <http://www.chester.ac.uk/fred/research/positive-action>.
[55] [2019] 2 WLUK 725 Liverpool Employment Tribunal 14 February 2019 (2405577/18).

There are a number of train operating companies which have taken advantage of positive action initiatives to try to encourage women and BAEM [black and ethnic minorities] people to apply. These initiatives have included adverts which are designed to present companies as inclusive and welcoming; adverts targeted specifically at women and placed where women are likely to read them; events and open days to encourage women and BAEM people to apply; ensuring that interview panels are trained in preventing bias and internal recruitment strategies which means recruiting from a more diverse pool.

Given that background, we gave some consideration to what steps ASLEF as a union could take to try to increase diversity amongst train drivers. Clearly, the buck stops with the train and freight operating companies themselves who are responsible for recruitment. However, there are a number of initiatives which ASLEF can consider, such as raising awareness of the importance of equality and diversity issues among staff and membership, encouraging more women and BEM members to be active within the union and considering whether ASLEF could support a limited form of part-time working. We have recommended too that ASLEF work in partnership with the train and freight operating companies to support any positive action initiatives which they may be encouraged to implement. Consideration can also be given to whether those governmental and quasi-governmental organisations operating in the rail industry can be called to account for the steps they have implemented to comply with the Public Sector Equality Duty.

- A coaching programme for black and minority ethnic teachers seeks to redress the under-representation of BAME teachers at a senior level. The National Union of Teachers and a coaching organization (Integrity Coaching) ran a programme to increase the number of black and minority ethnic teachers in senior leadership positions in schools.[56]

- The Bank of England Ethnic Minority Network securing engagement from senior management and heads of functions and agreed specific actions with the executive committee of the Bank in order to engage and empower its ethnic minority staff. This will encapsulate ventures including a scholarship programme to financially support three BAME students through university, a new mentoring scheme to support progression for employees and new line management guidance on moderating pay and bonus payments.[57]

- A bursary from a trust set up by the late Judge Jeremy McMullen QC to encourage able female students from disadvantaged and/or under-represented backgrounds with the potential to be successful barristers to make a more informed choice about a career at the Bar by providing award winners with experience of what a career at the Bar involves through work experience and marshalling opportunities. Notably eligibility criteria includes having little or no family history of higher education, having parents with a non-professional education and having completed their secondary education at state school.[58]

- Encouraging greater diversity in broadcasting: when giving evidence to the House of Lords Communications Committee as part of its inquiry into the BBC Charter, the Campaign for Broadcasting Equality (CBE) called for removal of the sweeping exemption for BBC activities such as production, casting, and editorial policy from the public sector equality duty. It also called on the BBC to 'set a quota of 12% BAME employment on its top 10 radio and television programmes and its leading news and current affairs programmes by 2017'. Notably a quota is distinct from a target and according to EHRC guidance on

---

[56] Equal Opportunities Review (EOR) 22/01/2016 Issue 265 (<http://www.eordirect.co.uk/>).
[57] EOR 22/01/2016 Issue 265.
[58] <https://www.justgiving.com/JeremyMcMullen>.

diversity in broadcasting is controversial since 'any steps taken in recruitment or promotion in order to fulfil a quota would run the risk of being unlawful if they went beyond the positive action permitted by the Act'.[59] (The BBC also used to run a Journalism Talent Pool to help increase the diversity of its workforce.)

- The development by HMRC (HM Revenue and Customs) of their 'embrace' programme, which supports and develops talented BAME employees in order to provide them with equal opportunity in recruitment and promotion.[60]

- The measures taken by the Barclays Group to engage with and recruit from the broadest graduate BAME talent pool possible.[61]

- Education charity Teach First's move to embed inclusive processes into its graduate recruitment practices and to attract more diverse talent onto its Leadership Development Programme.[62]

- The Chartered Institute of Library and Information Professionals (CILIP) Encompass scheme which uses positive action to encourage those from BAME communities to develop and choose a career in library and information work.[63]

- The Metropolitan Police Service have introduced a positive action talent development programme to nurture BAME junior officers into senior leadership roles.[64]

More recent initiatives include:

- The Inns of Court provide outreach measures which fall under section 158 including mentoring frameworks[65] and Inner Temple's Pegasus Access and Support Scheme (PASS)[66] and work experience opportunities. The Bar Placement Scheme[67] enables students to spend three days shadowing a barrister along with attending talks and receiving advocacy training from the Inns of Court, if they fulfil specific social mobility criteria. Bursaries may be offered as part of a work experience package, for example to cover the costs of living in London during a week of work experience.

Other legal schemes which seek to utilize section 158 appear to be increasing in number.

- In 2017 Leigh Day Solicitors used the Equality Act for a 'time-limited' period and advertised solicitor apprenticeships for six black students of Afro-Caribbean or African heritage who had completed A Levels in London to a good grade level. The law firm said it needed to tackle the problem it has had attracting African and Afro-Caribbean applicants via its ordinary processes. Having failed to attract a much more diverse group of trainees and specifically including African and Afro-Caribbean applicants, leading to a complete imbalance internally in comparison to the London population, the firm used the Equality Act for a one-off positive action to try to address that balance. Interestingly whilst the firm

---

[59] EOR 21/11/2015 Issue 263.
[60] EOR Carole Foster 2015.
[61] *ibid.*
[62] EOR Carole Foster 2013.
[63] EOR Carole Foster 2010.
[64] EOR Carole Foster 2013.
[65] See <https://www.socialmobility.org.uk/>.
[66] <https://www.innertemple.org.uk/becoming-a-barrister/how-to-get-involved/pass/>.
[67] <https://www.barcouncil.org.uk/becoming-a-barrister/school-students/bar-placement-scheme.html>.

believed the EqA allowed employers to 'correct an imbalance' it acknowledged that this use of it was untested.[68]

- The Freshfields Stephen Lawrence Scholarship Scheme[69] is designed to address under-representation in large commercial law firms and other City institutions of black men from less privileged backgrounds. Their scheme is aimed at first-year law students, and some other students at a small group of universities. It provides the opportunity to work with lawyers and other professionals from Freshfields, Goldman Sachs and the Bank of England. Scholars also receive interview coaching, mentoring, a contribution towards study-related costs, and the opportunity to apply for a training contract at Freshfields. Between 2013 and 2018, more than 320 undergraduates have competed for scholarships, and 55 have been awarded.

- The Freshfields Scholarship which includes the opportunity to apply for a training contract at Freshfields raises the question as to whether an opportunity for a student from, for example, a BAME background, to be guaranteed a first round pupillage interview in a barristers' chambers if they had performed well on an assessed mini-pupillage set up specifically for BAME students would be lawful? One barristers chambers who is doing this for social mobility purposes has devised objectives[70] which would fall under section 158. Such measures should not deprive candidates who are shortlisted for interview in the normal way of interview opportunities. Given that pupillages are often well-funded, the question of additional funding from chambers to cover costs in pupillage does not often arise; however there are examples of funding being offered given to students from specific under-represented groups for example the Stormzy Scholarship at Cambridge University.[71]

12.59   The JAC announced in July 2014 they were intending to use the 'equal merit provision' in recruitment exercises to seek to ensure diversity within the judiciary. This followed a report in 2014 by Sir Geoffrey Bindman QC and Karon Monaghan QC entitled 'Judicial Diversity: Accelerating Change'[72] which endorsed the use of quotas to increase the numbers of women in the UK judiciary. Bindman and Monaghan suggested that this would be lawful as long as quotas did not bar men from entering the judiciary and applied a proportionate approach. Subsequently the Judicial College working with the Bar Council, Law Society and CILEX, and JAC have developed a positive action programme for those who are thinking about applying to become judges called PAJE (Pre-Application Judicial Education).[73]

12.60   The academics Professors Kate Malleson and Colm O'Cinneide wrote in response in a November 2014 article for the Constitution Unit:

judicial selection (at least in respect of appointments below the level of the Supreme Court) comes within the scope of EU law, then the legality of the quota system will depend on whether the CJEU adheres to the restrictive approach it adopted in *Kalanke* and *Abrahamsson*, or whether it adopts a looser, more accommodating standard of review as it did in *Lommers*. Given the particular context of the judicial appointments process and the growing trend across Europe to adopt positive action

---

[68]   See <https://www.lawgazette.co.uk/news-focus/news-focus-thinking-positive-on-race/5101527.article>.
[69]   <https://www.freshfields.com/en-gb/about-us/responsible-business/freshfields_stephen_lawrence_scholarship/>.
[70]   See <https://www.newsquarechambers.co.uk/join-us/social-mobility-mini-pupillage>.
[71]   <https://www.undergraduate.study.cam.ac.uk/stormzy-scholarship>.
[72]   <https://jac.judiciary.gov.uk/news/judicial-diversity-report>.
[73]   See   <https://www.judiciary.uk/about-the-judiciary/who-are-the-judiciary/diversity/pre-application-judicial-education-programme-paje/>.

measures to promote greater diversity in public institutions it is likely that gender and BAME quotas for judicial selection in the UK, if carefully designed, will be lawful under EU law.[74]

The debate continues with the fear of implications for the judiciary if there were any widespread perception that appointments were not based solely on merit, but were subject to some additional consideration such as the application of a quota, seeming to win out over the urgency of changing the status quo or the question of whether a proportionate quota system could actually operate lawfully. 12.61

I. POSITIVE ACTION AND THE QUOTAS DEBATE

There is an ongoing debate as to whether quotas to promote female non-executive board members are lawful under EU law. 12.62

In November 2012 the European Commission took action to break the glass ceiling which appears to prevent female talent from top positions in Europe's biggest companies. The Commission proposed legislation with the aim of attaining a 40 per cent objective of the under-represented sex in non-executive board-member positions in publicly listed companies (excepting small and medium enterprises). At that point in time across Europe boards were made up of 85 per cent of non-executive board members and 91.1 per cent of executive board members men, with women making up 15 per cent and 8.9 per cent respectively. 12.63

In October 2013 the Women's Rights and Gender Equality and Legal Affairs committees of the Commission backed draft rules on board members proposed by the Commission (which provided EU-listed companies must aim to ensure, by 2020, that at least 40 per cent of their non-executive board members are women, so as to promote gender equality in economic decision making). 12.64

Some concerns were raised as to potential breaches of the substantive principle of subsidiarity as well as procedure obligations. In particular it was queried whether the Commission had provided sufficient qualitative or quantitative substantiation of the necessity for action at EU level, given that a number of Member States had already taken measures to increase the presence of women on corporate boards (amounting to a failure on behalf of the Commission to comply with essential procedural requirements in Article 5 of Protocol (No 2)).[75] 12.65

Some critics raised the question of legal competence[76] or argued that gender quotas were contrary to CJEU equal treatment jurisprudence. The Commission headed down this risk arguing that its legal authority arose from key CJEU decisions which had interpreted the Equal Treatment Directive. It reminded critics that Article 4(1) of the proposed Directive required Member States to 'ensure that listed companies in whose boards members of the underrepresented sex hold less than 40 per cent of the non-executive director positions make the appointments to those positions *on the basis of a comparative analysis of the qualifications of each candidate,* by applying pre-established, clear, neutrally formulated and unambiguous criteria, …' [emphasis added].[77] 12.66

---

[74] <https://constitution-unit.com/2014/11/14/are-quotas-for-judicial-appointments-lawful-under-eu-law/>.
[75] <http://www.parliament.uk/business/committees/committees-a-z/lords-select/eu---internal-market-sub-committee-b/inquiries/parliament-2010/women-on-boards/>.
[76] See commentary in <www.fljs.org/sites/www.fljs.org/files/publications/Suk.pdf>.
[77] <eur-lex.europa.eu › EUROPA › EU law and publications › EUR-Lex>.

12.67   This suggests that as with section 159, the draft Directive's gender balance rule could easily be avoided or bypassed, from having to define 'equal qualifications' for board positions along with the question of subjective judgement. It may be the very wording within the draft Directive ensuring its lawfulness also reduces the scope of its effectiveness.

12.68   The Commission's proposed Directive was amended and adopted by the European Parliament in November 2013. One revision was to widen the class of those who could complain that the 40 per cent quota had not been met. Another was to require sanctions for a failure to adopt specified transparent procedures, along with a civil liability regime where non-compliant companies would need to prove compliance with transparency rules and objective justifications for choosing a candidate of the over-represented sex (albeit not an imposition of a sanction on a company for a failure to achieve gender balance on its board).

12.69   Under this draft Directive 2012/0299 unsuccessful candidates would be able to request information on selection criteria relating to non-executive board positions, on the company's comparative assessment of the candidates for the job, and on the company's reasons for selecting candidates. Also companies would have to publish information on gender composition of their boards, and submit yearly progress reports describing measures used and proposed in order to reach the 40 per cent target. Companies failing to meet this target would be required to explain why, to set out measures already taken and clarify steps planned for the future.

12.70   Despite some ongoing discussions as to the wording of the Directive, no timetable has been reached for a final draft or implementation.[78]

12.71   Presently in terms of soft measures, the Companies Act 2006 (Strategic Report and Directors Report) Regulations 2013 imposes a requirement on certain companies to publish an annual report containing information about the gender composition of their boards.

12.72   In relation to current guidance, the EHRC's guidance of August 2018 entitled 'Appointments to Boards and Equality Law' includes these views on shortlisting:[79]

> Where there is no predetermination to draw up an all-women shortlist and an objective and consistent assessment of all candidates demonstrates that the best qualified candidates are all women, an all-women shortlist will be lawful. We do not believe that it is lawful to address under-representation by longlisting or shortlisting only female candidates to the detriment of male candidates. There has been no case law clearly confirming that a decision to use all women shortlists or longlists during a recruitment exercise is a lawful form of positive action under domestic or European equality law. The conditions currently attached by the CJEU to lawful positive action considerably constrain a company's ability to use such measures in accordance with the law, though it is possible judicial interpretation of equality law could develop over time to broaden the concept of lawful positive action.

> A policy or practice of giving automatic and unconditional preference to women over qualified male candidates will amount to unlawful direct sex discrimination.

12.73   Since 2017 mandatory gender pay gap reporting for private and voluntary sector employers in England, Scotland, and Wales with at least 250 employees is required. This did not progress the discussion on quotas which remained inactive at an EU and UK level. The lack of appetite for the introduction of quotas (whether mandatory or voluntary) in the UK has been overtaken by an emphasis on genuine cultural change facilitating equal opportunities in

---

[78] See <http://eur-lex.europa.eu/legal-content/EN/TXT/?uri=consil:ST_14343_2015_INIT> for a 30 November 2015 update from the President of the EU Council.

[79] <www.equalityhumanrights.com>.

the workforce via flexible working, shared parental leave and access to affordable early years childcare. After several years of this process being stalled, in 2020 attempts were made to revive plans for mandatory quotas of women on company boards, with the EU Commission announcing a five-year Gender Equality Strategy.[80] Its 2019 study showed that the rate of increase for EU women holding non-executive director positions had slowed since 2015. As the Commission's 2012 plan to set a EU wide quota for women on boards was blocked by the UK's coalition Government it might be thought that the departure of the UK from the EU would aid the progress of the law on mandatory quotas. However, it seems that the views of individual member states have not changed despite the efforts of the Commission to persuade them, led by Věra Jourová, the EU commissioner for values and transparency.

J. POSITIVE ACTION IN RELATION TO POLITICAL PARTIES

By section 104 of the Act positive action is permitted (short of shortlisting on a particular protected characteristic) in the process of selection of candidates for election. This, and the next sections, are discussed in the Explanatory Notes (EN) at [344]–[348]. Only in relation to sex does the Act permit shortlisting criteria that are specifically linked to a protected characteristic: see section 104(7). This section therefore continues the effect of the Sex Discrimination (Election Candidates) Act 2002. In all other cases EN 345 notes that there can be reserved places on the shortlists for those having a protected characteristic, such as race or disability, etc.   **12.74**

Additionally the Act contains a new sunset clause for single-sex shortlists. Section 105 limits the effect of section 104(7) and the 2002 Act so as to permit single-sex shortlists to be lawful up to 2030 by which time it is to be hoped they will no longer be necessary.   **12.75**

The House of Lords added an amendment to section 104 containing a proportionality test for positive action taken in the selection of candidates for relevant elections. This aims to clarify that the only action permitted is that which is a proportionate means of achieving the objective of reducing inequality in the party's representation. This does not apply to women-only shortlists.   **12.76**

The EHRC gives the following practical examples[81] of positive action steps which a political party can take with regard to selection arrangements: **12.77**

- encourage prospective candidates with a particular protected characteristic to come forward, for example, by holding an event just for them or writing just to members who share the under-represented protected characteristic,

- increase candidates' prospects of being selected, for example, by giving public speaking training only to people with the under-represented protected characteristic,

- identify suitable candidates, for example, by reducing the time people with the under-represented protected characteristic have to have been party members to be allowed to stand for election, or

- decide how a final shortlist will be chosen, for example, by reserving places on a shortlist for people with the under-represented protected characteristic, or having a shortlist made

---

[80] <https://ec.europa.eu/commission/presscorner/detail/en/ip_20_358>.
[81] See <http://www.equalityhumanrights.com/advice-and-guidance/service-users-guidance/parliaments-politicians-and-political-parties/how-equality-law-applies-to-political-parties/>.

up only of people who share the under-represented protected characteristic, although this only applies to disability and sex.

12.78 Challenges are certainly conceivable to the use of section 104 in such circumstances and the EHRC provides an example of this on its website:[82]

A political party looks at the proportion of people with different protected characteristics representing the party on a local council. It sees that it has no councillors of Chinese origin, despite there being a large local Chinese population and a significant number of party members from that population. It decides to reserve half the places on the shortlist in the electoral area with the highest population of people of Chinese origin for people of that origin. A senior figure in the party writes to all the members known to be of Chinese origin and invites them to seek selection.

A party member who is not of Chinese origin and wants to stand for election complains of race discrimination when she is not shortlisted. She will not succeed, provided the party can show that the steps it has taken are lawful, in other words that they genuinely address under-representation and are proportionate.

However, if the party member believed she had been discriminated against because of her sex, for example, because she had been asked questions about her plans for having children at an interview which would be deciding who to shortlist, she would still be able to challenge this alleged sex discrimination.

K. POLITICAL SHORTLISTS

12.79 As noted, section 105 of the Act will extend the permission for political parties to use women-only shortlists for election candidates to 2030 with the aim of providing full equality by then.[83] This exception to the norm of treating candidates equally had been due to expire in 2015 and the government consulted about whether to extend this. More than 90 per cent of respondents agreed this was important to do until a gender balance was achieved in Parliament. There are now (in 2020) 220 women Members of the House of Commons; at 34 per cent, this is an all-time high. Yet it still means that the UK's women are under-represented as they make up 51 per cent of the population.

12.80 In 2016 Rosie Campbell and Sarah Childs drew attention to the importance of all-women shortlists in securing an increase in the number of women elected, stating:

In terms of the representation of women in politics, 2015 saw an increase in the percentage of women in the House of Commons from 22–29%. ... the overall increase was largely driven by the Labour Party and the SNP who increased the percentage of women among their MPs from 35–43% and 17–36% respectively. The Labour Party delivered this increase through their continued use of all-women shortlists.[84]

---

[82] *ibid.*

[83] In March 2016 a Commons Briefing paper Report SN05057 on *All-women shortlists* surveyed steps taken over recent years to bring this goal to fruition; see <http://researchbriefings.files.parliament.uk/documents/SN05057/SN05057.pdf>. For updates see *51% of Labour MPs are women. What now for all-women shortlists?* <https://labourlist.org/2019/12/51-of-labour-mps-are-women-what-now-for-all-women-shortlists/>.

[84] See fn 47 on page 16 of HC Briefing Report SN05057: Rosie Campbell and Sarah Childs, 'All Aboard the Pink Battle Bus? Women Voters, Women's Issues, Candidates and Party Leaders', in Andrew Geddes and Jonathan Tonge (eds), *Britain Votes 2015*, 2015, pp. 221–3. A similar commentary on the results of the 2010 General Election can be found in: Rosie Campbell and Sarah Childs, '"Wags", "Wives" and "Mothers" ... But

The Conservative initiative Women2Win uses soft law options to encourage more females   **12.81**
to be selected to fight winnable seats such as holding weekly training sessions for candidates, one-on-one mentoring, mock hustings, and financial support for female candidates' campaigns.[85] On 20 July 2016 Theresa May taunted the Labour Party during her first Prime Minister's Questions as Prime Minister for their all-women shortlists, quipping that the Conservatives had come up with an all-women shortlist 'without being required to do so'.[86]

The Scottish National Party launched an initiative in March 2015 to select more female   **12.82**
candidates at elections. Proposed measures included: In any constituency where more than one candidate is nominated, at least one of those candidates must be female, where any incumbent SNP constituency MSP announces their intention to stand down, the NEC may direct that an all-women shortlist should be submitted, and the NEC being given authority to nominal female candidates to balance the number of male and female candidates being submitted for regional list rankings.[87]

These initiatives demonstrate the importance to which enhancing the proportion of female   **12.83**
politicians has across the political sphere. The preference for voluntary means of achieving this objective, has been repeated in other areas of public life such as the judiciary and company boards, at least, until very recently.

The proportion of BAME MPs though growing remains lower than in the UK's popula-   **12.84**
tion,[88] so it may be asked why there has been no decision to legislate for black- and ethnic-minority-only shortlists, or indeed for other candidates beyond gender. One reason appears to be the complexity of simply legitimizing non-white shortlists for the purpose of increasing the representation of people from ethnic minority groups. The Commission for Racial Equality (CRE) has stated[89] that:

… the low representation of people from minority ethnic groups as councillors or MPs was a more complex issue than might be presumed. … the activities of political parties generally should be brought within the scope of discrimination law; … various measures were already available to political parties to encourage increased representation, such as mentoring or shadowing, and that these did not require new or additional measures, just commitment and leadership.

The CRE and other bodies had questioned how a black and minority ethnic group would   **12.85**
be defined for the purpose of a shortlist, and so, rather than agreeing with the suggestion of the introduction of legislation permitting black- and ethnic-minority-only shortlists, they have recommended the adoption of a full programme of positive action.[90]

However, in 2020 the new leader of the Labour Party Sir Keir Starmer called for legislative reform in order to permit all-BAME shortlists,[91] but the Conservative government said

what about Women Politicians?', in Andrew Geddes and Jonathan Tonge (eds), *Britain Votes 2010* (2010), pp. 185–6.

[85] <http://www.women2win.com/news/new-conservative-women-mps-%E2%80%93-selected-merit-slaying-big-beasts>.

[86] <http://www.huffingtonpost.co.uk/entry/pmqs-watch-as-theresa-may-mocks-labour-over-all-women-shortlists>.

[87] 'SNP conference: party backs new gender balance rules', BBC News, 29 March 2015.

[88] See <https://www.bbc.co.uk/news/election-2019-50808536>.

[89] Para. 5.31 of the Government's Response to the Consultation 2008 at <http://www.equalities.gov.uk>.

[90] *ibid*.

[91] <https://www.telegraph.co.uk/politics/2020/02/04/sir-keir-starmer-calls-all-bame-shortlists-proposes-major-reforms/>.

it had no plans to introduce such legislation during that parliament. Nonetheless it may be that no reform would be needed to achieve such a shortlist, if section 104(4) of the Equality Act 2010 is used. EN 338 explains the purpose of this section as follows:

A political party cannot shortlist only black or Asian candidates for a local government by-election. However, if Asians are under-represented amongst a party's elected councillors on a particular Council, the party could choose to reserve a specific number of seats for Asian candidates on a by-election shortlist.

There is no prohibition on proportionate earmarking of seats for candidates with a particular protected characteristic as long as the shortlist is not reserved 100 per cent for that group (such as an All-Disability Shortlist). Other suggestions made by Starmer regarding enhancing the ethnic makeup of MPs would be well within the scope of section 158 measures, such as new bursaries for candidates from under-represented backgrounds, and a new 'Labour Party College' to equip such candidates with political, campaigning, and leadership skills.[92]

12.86   There are however other positive action measures within the boundaries set by the Act that could allow political parties to enhance non-white participation in the democratic process. These include setting targets for increasing the proportion of politicians and staff from under-represented groups and running mentoring and leadership programmes. Moreover, the existence of the as yet dormant section 106 has the potential to impose monitoring duties on political parties to publish diversity information so far as possible.

12.87   Section 106 of the Act gives ministers power to make regulations requiring political parties to publish data relating to the background of party candidates seeking selection. Since this provision has not been brought into force, alternatives to legislation have been raised. However, to date, a voluntary approach to the publication of diversity data has not taken place. This was despite a commitment prior to the 2015 election from the three main political parties, to undertake such publications in order to enhance the transparency of party-political candidate selection.

12.88   In recent years a contentious issue has arisen with all-women shortlists and the inclusion of trans women. Some feel that since it is lawful for political parties to restrict the selection of election candidates to only those who share the protected characteristic of the female sex, such shortlists ought to exclude 'legal' males from all women shortlists, including those who self-identify as transgender women, because they are not legally female. The Labour Party has stated that it is operating within the provisions of the Equality Act where it has determined that its all-women shortlists are open to all women, including self-identifying trans women[93] (as are its women's officers and minimum quotas for women in the Party). In 2018 some Labour party supporters resigned from their membership, claiming that without a gender recognition certificate 'any man can simply claim to be a woman' and get onto the shortlist.[94] This dispute is part of the larger debate which relies upon biological sex as opposed to self-identification as part of maintaining women only services, facilities and spaces (see above at paragraph 12.23).

---

[92] <https://keirstarmer.com/plans/reformandunite/>.
[93] <https://labour.org.uk/about/how-we-work/nec-statement-women-shortlists-womens-officers-minimum-quotas-women/>.
[94] <https://www.mayday4women.com/2018/05/01/womens-mass-resignation-labour/>.

L. POSITIVE ACTION WHEN NEITHER SECTION 159 NOR SECTION 104 APPLIES

In circumstances where neither section 159 nor 104 apply then section 158 is potentially   **12.89**
engaged. This section is discussed in the EN 519–525. Section 158 says:

158. Positive action: general

  (1) This section applies if a person (P) reasonably thinks that—
    (a) persons who share a protected characteristic suffer a disadvantage connected to the characteristic,
    (b) persons who share a protected characteristic have needs that are different from the needs of persons who do not share it, or
    (c) participation in an activity by persons who share a protected characteristic is disproportionately low.
  (2) This Act does not prohibit P from taking any action which is a proportionate means of achieving the aim of—
    (a) enabling or encouraging persons who share the protected characteristic to overcome or minimise that disadvantage,
    (b) meeting those needs, or
    (c) enabling or encouraging persons who share the protected characteristic to participate in that activity.
  (3) Regulations may specify action, or descriptions of action, to which subsection (2) does not apply …

These provisions are very similar to those in section 159 and it is to be assumed that they   **12.90**
will be interpreted in a similar way. Whilst this section largely examines their use in the non-employment context, it is important to note they will be relevant in relation to aspects of employment such as training (see the various examples at paragraph 12.58 above).

Section 158 extends the scope for positive action in all areas covered by the Act. The pre-   **12.91**
requisites are that the body applying the measure must reasonably think one of three factors:

(a) that those who share a protected characteristic suffer a disadvantage connected to the characteristic,

(b) that those who share a protected characteristic have needs that are different from the needs of persons who do not share it, or

(c) that participation in an activity by persons who share a protected characteristic is disproportionately low.

As to how to ensure that these factors are present, the following example from the   **12.92**
Government Equalities Office quick start guide provides a useful tool:

A DIY chain begins planning a new recruitment programme. In considering how to create a more diverse workforce the company realises that it does not keep detailed records on the personal details of its employees. However, the Area Manager is able to demonstrate that it is reasonable for him to think that there are a disproportionately low number of women in the workforce from his knowledge of who works for him and by consulting with his local branch managers. The employer could decide to use positive action in aiming to address the number of women in the workforce. Taking positive action based on that information would usually be lawful.

12.93   The width of scope permitted can be seen from the broad spectrum of permitted aims set out in section 158(2):

(a) enabling or encouraging persons who share the protected characteristic to overcome or minimize that disadvantage,

(b) meeting those needs, or

(c) enabling or encouraging persons who share the protected characteristic to participate in that activity.

12.94   Measures will only be legitimate if they are a proportionate means of achieving the aims set out above. Proportionality under section 158 will be applied in the same way as it will be for recruitment questions under section 159: see the discussion above at paragraph 12.07 and following. The EN noted in relation to section 158:

> 520. The extent to which it is proportionate to take positive action measures which may result in people not having the relevant characteristic being treated less favourably will depend, among other things, on the seriousness of the relevant disadvantage, the extremity of need or under-representation and the availability of other means of countering them. This provision will need to be interpreted in accordance with European law which limits the extent to which the kind of action it permits will be allowed.[95]

12.95   The breadth of possible measures permitted under section 158 could be extremely wide, as the disparate examples in the EN show:

> 525 ... Having identified that its white male pupils are underperforming at maths, a school could run supplementary maths classes exclusively for them.

> An NHS Primary Care Trust identifies that lesbians are less likely to be aware that they are at risk of cervical cancer and less likely to access health services such as national screening programmes. It is also aware that those who do not have children do not know that they are at an increased risk of breast cancer. Knowing this it could decide to establish local awareness campaigns for lesbians on the importance of cancer screening.[96]

12.96   A key challenge in relation to the measures provided in section 158 is how to make these provisions work. Professor de Schutter has commented that this may be difficult:[97]

> ... The identification of general criteria would be all the more difficult if, as in the cases of the allocation of scholarships or social housing illustrate, social goods have to be distributed according to a combination of criteria (need, family situation and academic merit as regards scholarships, for example; need, family situation and date of application in the case of social housing), rather than according to one single metric.

12.97   It is plain that reliance on an objective assessment of qualifications or merit (or standard criteria in goods and services cases) could serve only to maintain the status quo rather than challenging negative stereotypes that have led to under-representation in the first place.

12.98   In the *Badeck* and *EFTA v Norway* cases (above at paragraphs 12.39 and 12.50 respectively), the CJEU looked afresh at the life skills that had been developed outside the workplace and revisited the supposedly neutral concept of merit. So, also in non-employment

---

[95] See <http://www.opsi.gov.uk/acts/acts2010>.

[96] *ibid.*

[97] See de Schutter, *Non-Discrimination Law* (Hart Publishing 2007), p. 824.

cases, criteria such as academic qualifications for scholarship applications should be carefully examined to ensure they are not tainted by past obstacles to equal opportunities in education. A similar approach could be taken across the full range of non-employment benefits.

Likewise when service providers take positive action measures to redress the balance of ethnic minorities in a housing application, proximity to the proposed site might not be a neutral factor to take into account, if data demonstrate that a particular ethnic group is historically unlikely to be able to afford to live in a certain postal district. A service provider may not refuse to provide a service to a person for a discriminatory reason (e.g. ethnicity) pursuant to sections 13, 19, and 29 Equality Act 2010, save where positive action is taken to alleviate disadvantage. 12.99

R (Z and another) v London Borough of Hackney and another [2019] EWCA Civ 1099 [2019] HLR 44 is the main concerning positive action in housing provision. In this case the Court of Appeal permitted a Housing Association to avoid liability for direct discrimination, on the basis that the action it had taken was positive action taken to alleviate disadvantage, increase representation or meet the needs of persons who shared a protected characteristic, and so was within section 158. 12.100

The case concerned the policy of a charity called the Agudas Israel Housing Association (AIHA). AIAHA was a registered smaller private provider of social housing, owning property in parts of Hackney inhabited by members of the Orthodox Jewish (Haredi) community. It did not make a particularly large contribution to the housing needs of Hackney; AIHA's properties made up only 1 per cent of the overall 47,000 units let through Hackney. Its policy was to allocate its properties only to members of the Orthodox Jewish community. 'Z', a single mother of four, and her three-year-old son brought a challenge to this policy. They had been assessed by the London Borough of Hackney (Hackney) as being at the highest level of priority need for rehousing, yet when suitable AIHA-owned properties became available they were not offered to Z and her family. The case was defended on the basis that either section 158 or the charitable exception under section 193[98] Equality Act 2010 applied. The Court of Appeal upheld the Divisional Court's decision that AIHA was justified in taking section 158 'positive action' and thus that the refusal was lawful. It held that whilst AIHA's arrangements for allocating housing amounted to direct religious discrimination (since non-members seeking housing experienced less favourable treatment), such treatment was lawful because Haredi members suffered real and substantial disadvantages and had different needs to people who did not share the protected characteristic of their religion. 12.101

The Court of Appeal considered the proportionality assessments required by sections 158(2) (and 193(2)(b)). Its analysis will be a useful template for future decision-making. It found any disadvantage to non-Orthodox Jews was tiny, given the size of AIHA's housing stock which made up only 1 per cent of Hackney's total available accommodation. The housing policy was proportional[99] because: 12.102

- The scale of the disadvantage to non-Haredi members was minuscule;
- The needs of the Haredi members linked to the relevant protected characteristic were many and compelling; and

---

[98] This provision permits charities to restrict the provision of benefits to persons who share the same protected characteristics provided they act in pursuance of their charitable instrument and the provision of the benefits is either a proportionate means of achieving a legitimate aim or to prevent or compensate for a disadvantage linked to the protected characteristic.

[99] Applying *R (on the application of Coll) v Secretary of State for Justice* [2017] UKSC 40.

- As the allocation of properties to non-Haredi members would fundamentally undermine AIHA's charitable objectives there was no more limited way of achieving the legitimate aim.

12.103 Practitioners need to note the Supreme Court appeal judgment's proportionality assessment would be likely to be different where a service provider such as a Housing Association has less limited resources and enjoys a large market share of the resources in question. Further, because Z conceded that the provisions of the section were indeed met including disadvantage, the Court of Appeal judgment did not provide any guidance on the *scope* of section 158. Inevitably, the concession regarding 'disadvantage' reduced the force of Z's case on lack of proportionality. But nonetheless this judgment from the Supreme Court may enable service providers and employers to be more confident in using these positive action provisions (see further https://www.cloisters.com/positive-action-aiha/).

12.104 Other reasons for the sluggish take-up of positive action initiatives in the workplace are described by academic specialist Professor Chantel Davies at paragraph 7 of her Executive Summary to her paper *Equality At Work: Positive Action in Gender Segregated Apprenticeships*:[100]

Reasons given for non-use, included fear of the best person not being recruited, fear of legal liability for 'reverse discrimination' and a belief that inclusive rather than preference-based practice was a more appropriate and effective means of addressing gender disparity. Similarly, many participants likened the fear of 'getting it wrong' to a lack of clarity and guidance around legislation and definitions of positive action. Equally, some felt that positive action denigrates the principle of merit and concern was also expressed that targeted individuals themselves may not wish to have preferential initiatives applied to them.

12.105 So those using section 158 measures need to have confidence to use them flexibly, yet within the law. Another example of positive action in the provision of public services concerns the under-representation of religious Jewish or Muslim women in their use of local sports centres. The fact-specific details of each case are crucial. Here, factors such as demonstrating a previous use of, or interest in, the swimming pool, should not be taken into account without an appreciation of a possible antipathy to mixed swimming sessions.

12.106 Accordingly fixed criteria in the area of access to, or provision of, goods and services, may not assist in leading to substantive equality. Even in the most commonly visited field of gender equality at work, the concept of factors such as *qualifications* will need to be 'unpacked' in order to affect more than superficial change.

12.107 There is an obvious link between positive action measures and the public sector equality duty (section 149). Whilst this provision now covers all protected characteristics apart from marriage and civil partnership (section 149(7)) it has also been weakened to focus only on setting equality objectives and the publication of equality data (see sections 3 and 2 of the Equality Act (Specific Duties) Regulations 2011). The problem with failing to implement the public sector duty regarding socio-economic inequalities is that individuals who are disadvantaged by poverty are left unprotected by transformative measures.

---

[100] <https://www.youngwomenstrust.org/positive-action>.

M. GENDER AND ETHNIC PAY REPORTING

The Equality Act 2010 (Gender Pay Gap Information) Regulations 2017 aim to encour- **12.108**
age employers to audit pay across different workplace groups and ideally take responsibility for equality, whilst also providing individuals with valuable information of use in
enforcing their rights. By requiring mandatory pay audits (which must be undertaken by
private and voluntary-sector organizations with 250 or more employees) the UK has to
some extent extended transformative equality to the private sector. These organizations
have been mandated to collate and report gender pay gap data and submitted the first
reports by April 2018.[101] The public nature of the reports is intended to place pressure on
organizations who fail to narrow the gender pay gap going forward. One way of doing
this is of course by utilizing section 158 positive action measures, but the provisions operate best as part of an overriding toolkit to address diversity issues across work (as well as
services provision).

The only obligation is upon employers to publish their gender pay information rather than **12.109**
to publish an action plan for reducing the gap. Those report employers who do publish any
narrative (the EHRC says it is about half of all who report) generally do so in a broad-brush
fashion with little detail about future remedial measures. The EHRC research[102] also states
that only two employers out of the sample of 440 organizations were intending to utilize section 158 to achieve their action plans and there were no plans to use the tie-breakers under
section 159. As emphasized earlier in this chapter, in order to feel confident about using
positive action measures as part of remedial action, employers have to feel confident about
the lawful remit of such measures.

However some of the action proposed or already underway to reduce the gender pay gap **12.110**
is clearly reliant on section 158 and 159 even if it is not explicitly stated as such, as the following examples make clear:

• Price Waterhouse Cooper reported a 43.8 per cent mean gender pay gap in 2018. It
  decided to ban all-male shortlists for roles in the UK in an attempt to increase the number
  of women in senior roles. They also announced plans to ban all-male interview panels and
  also set a 50:50 gender target across all roles.[103]
• In 2018, TSB announced it would use a 50:50 gender shortlist for candidates to replace
  former CEO, Paul Pester. It also confirmed that gender-balanced shortlisting had already
  been used for external recruitment at senior levels for two years and this was to be extended
  to all roles within the business. When this target was not met by the end of 2019 senior
  figures were penalized with bonus cuts. Sam Smethers, then chief executive of the women's
  campaign group the Fawcett Society, said:

---

[101] Due to the Coronavirus outbreak, the Government Equalities Office (GEO) and the Equality and
Human Rights Commission (EHRC) decided on 24 March 2020 to suspend enforcement of the gender
pay gap deadlines for the reporting year 2019/20, meaning there is no expectation on employers to report
their data for that year: <https://www.gov.uk/government/news/employers-do-not-have-to-report-gender-
pay-gaps>.
[102] <https://www.equalityhumanrights.com/sites/default/files/closing-the-gender-pay-gap_0.pdf>.
[103] <https://www.bbc.co.uk/news/business-44353536>.

TSB have clearly found it more challenging to hit their 2020 target than they anticipated. The precise reasons are unclear in this case, but we know that it can take time to progress gender equality, particularly at senior levels. This is why we argue for interventions such as positive action and proportionate progression to speed up change.[104]

- Another example of a time-bound gender target is where Channel 4 has set a goal of having a 50:50 gender balance in its top earners by 2023 (currently 66:33).[105]

12.111   It is not surprising that after the 2017 Gender Pay Gap Regulations came into force attention would turn to ethnic pay gaps. The Government held an ethnicity pay gap consultation in 2018 which closed in January 2019. The EHRC said in January 2019 in its *Response to the consultation on ethnicity pay reporting* (EPG):

The Gender Pay Gap Reporting Regulations (GPGR, 2017) have driven an important national debate on fairness at work. The meaning and causes of pay gaps, as well as the potential solutions, are now better understood than ever. This new awareness has created the context and infrastructure for progressive employers to begin to take action reducing a range of workplace inequalities, and we welcome the greater focus on barriers faced by ethnic minorities.[106]

12.112   No further steps have been taken by government since that consultation closed and to date, ethnicity pay gap reporting remains optional. A number of organizations from the Greater London Authority (GLA) to Price Waterhouse Cooper have disclosed their EPG data voluntarily. The pressure emanating from bodies such as the Confederation of British Industry in 2020 for firms to voluntarily disclose the difference in average pay for different ethnic groups as soon as possible, suggests that such reporting is likely to become compulsory in the future alongside gender pay gap reporting.

12.113   Mandatory reporting is expected to facilitate employers' identification of key barriers to closing the ethnicity pay gap and will have the associated benefits of enhanced monitoring of diversity measures, reporting on diversity policies, and positive action measures addressing this pay gap. Existing initiatives include the 2018 Race at Work Charter developed by the Government in partnership with Business in the Community (BITC) to tackle ethnic disparities in the workplace. The Charter contains measures for organizations to take, towards tackling recruitment and progression barriers for BAME staff. The five principle actions are:

1. Appointing an executive sponsor for race;
2. Capturing ethnicity data and publicizing progress;
3. Commitment at board level to zero tolerance of harassment and bullying;
4. Making clear that supporting equality in the workplace is the responsibility of all leaders and managers; and
5. Taking action that supports minority ethnic career progression.

---

[104] <https://www.theguardian.com/business/2019/dec/03/tsb-bonuses-to-be-docked-for-failure-to-meet-gender-balance-targets>.

[105] <https://assets-corporate.channel4.com/_flysystem/s3/2019-11/Channel%20Four%20Television%20Corporation%20Pay%20Report%202019.pdf>.

[106] <https://www.equalityhumanrights.com/sites/default/files/consultation-response-ethnicity-pay-reporting-accessible-january-2019.pdf>.

It is too early to identify the correlation between signing the Charter and the quality of reporting on boardroom ethnic diversity. Until data is actually gathered, action plans are meaningless. Simply starting by learning more about the make-up of the workplace would enable employers to understand which sections of their workforce are disadvantaged and under-represented and thereby enable a strong evidence base from which recruitment retention and progression can be augmented for such groups by constructive means including positive action measures. 12.114

Gathering ethnicity data will be a challenge in itself for many employers. It is important that workplaces are aware of General Data Protection Regulation (GDPR) restrictions since data on ethnicity amounts to personal data; but the GDPR doesn't prevent the collection of ethnicity data. Crucially, employees need to trust both that the data they provide is confidential and that it is sought for constructive purposes—above all—to assess and reduce existing disadvantage. We have already identified some of the difficulties of taking lawful action under section 158. They are mirrored to some degree when facing the task of gathering ethnicity pay data. The EHRC summarized a key challenge in its Consultation response where it stated: 12.115

Data that is not based on Census categories risks resulting in a binary White versus Ethnic Minority classification, which risks masking the often significant range of barriers and outcomes faced by different groups, such as by Bangladeshi as opposed to Indian men, or by British as opposed to foreign-born ethnic minorities. This may not provide the evidence required as the basis for effective action to drive reductions in pay gaps.[107]

Just as the drive to reduce the GPG must bear in mind the availability of early years childcare along with flexible working, addressing the EPG involves identifying factors beyond the ability of workplaces to tackle in many respects, as the EHRC has noted: 12.116

We should also note that many of the causes of ethnicity pay gaps are beyond the direct control of employers. These include differences in subject and career choices, education attainment and access to apprenticeships, and the uneven distribution of economic activity and job opportunities across Britain. We reiterate our recommendation for Government leadership in a holistic approach to tackling these issues and, ultimately, workplace inequalities for ethnic minorities.[108]

The impetus or drive to improve the status quo can be spurred on by all kinds of events. Following the death of George Floyd in May 2020 at the hands of US police officers, the Black Lives Matters movement called for steps to be taken to address structural and longstanding ethnic disadvantage internationally. In relation to the perceived lack of empowerment in the UK, this has reignited the debate between quotas and targets and the limits of the Equality Act's positive action measures. Whether pronouncements will be matched by change on a voluntary or mandated level remains to be seen but many organizations took up the opportunity to review policies and to utilize positive action measures especially with recruitment. 12.117

---

[107] https://www.equalityhumanrights.com/sites/default/files/consultation-response-ethnicity-pay-reporting-accessible-january-2019.pdf

[108] <https://www.equalityhumanrights.com/sites/default/files/consultation-response-ethnicity-pay-reporting-accessible-january-2019.pdf>.

N. POSITIVE ACTION AND HUMAN RIGHTS: TEMPORARY MEASURES

12.118   In any case in which positive action is taken there is always a question as to how long the action can be maintained. The jurisprudence of the ECHR recognizes that positive action may be necessary but also establishes that is ought to be time limited. The ECHR permits the treatment of groups differently to ameliorate the inequalities between them.[109] This will be essentially a political assessment although there are obvious limits. It should be noted that both the International Convention on the Elimination of All Forms of Racial Discrimination 1969 (ICERD) and the Convention on the Elimination of All Forms of Discrimination against Women 1979 (CEDAW) indicate that positive action should not be continued after the objectives for which they were taken have been achieved.

12.119   Accordingly in *Hooper v Secretary of State for Work and Pensions*,[110] the House of Lords debated the question of the duration of special treatment for a particular group and said (at paragraph 32):

> Once it is accepted that older widows were historically an economically disadvantaged class which merited special treatment but were gradually becoming less disadvantaged, the question of the precise moment at which such special treatment is no longer justified becomes a social and political question within the competence of Parliament.

12.120   Under Article 14 of the ECHR, the question of phasing out positive action measures is a key element of the concept of proportionality. Member States are given a broad margin of appreciation as to the moment when such measures are no longer justified. Yet if the aim of positive action is a move towards greater equality, the suspension of temporary measures before the action in question is operating effectively would be inappropriate, just as their suspension when real change has been effected will be necessary.

12.121   The ECHR Code gives the example of a time limited measure in relation to enhancing participation in sport: see paragraph 10.23 EHRC Services Code:

> Figures from competition records show that fewer women than men compete as judo players and this is because of their low participation in the sport. A national judo organisation considers two options to meet its aim of increasing women's participation in judo. One option is to stage a major event with prize money for women twice the prize money for men. A second option is, for six months, to mount a major publicity campaign combined with the promotion of a discounted training programme for women judo players only.

> The first option is unlikely to be a proportionate means of achieving greater participation by women; it would discriminate against male judo players and would not meet the appropriate and necessary test since it would only benefit women already active as judo players.

> The second option is more likely to be a proportionate way to meet their aim. Although it would involve less favourable treatment of men (both in terms of more limited promotion of men within the sport and exclusions from discounted training fees) this action could meet the appropriate and

---

[109] See e.g. *Belgian Linguistic Case (No. 2)* (1968) 1 EHRR 252, 284, para. 10 and *Willis v UK* no. 36042/97 2002.

[110] [2005] UKHL 29; [2005] 1 WLR 1681.

necessary test since it is likely to be effective in attracting more women to the sport, and the less favourable treatment of men would be short-term.

The ethics of single-sex literary prizes has been long contested but awards that cater for single 12.122 protected characteristics can be lawful measures by which to alleviate disadvantage pursuant to section 158. The EHRC Services Code gives the example of 'a leading publisher of scientific publications establishes a literary prize for a female scientist. This will raise the profile of women currently working in science and encourage girls to consider it as a career.' In circumstances where 'Research indicates that women in Britain experience significant disadvantages in pursuing successful careers in science subjects as reflected in their low participation in the profession, their lower status within it, and fewer contributions to publications' (paragraph 10.11) the measure can have as its objective raising the profile of the protected group in question. The lack of visible role models in itself can be evidence of under-representation amounting to 'disadvantage' under section 158, and the ways this can be identified can be from data from monitoring or surveys, from complaints such as those in petitions, exit interviews, or online comments.

For a recent example of how a literary prize for BAME unpublished female writers was 12.123 justified, the organizers of the SI Leeds Literary Prize declared:

Why is the Prize only for Black and Asian women? ... Women writers of Black & Asian backgrounds are disproportionately under-represented in bestseller lists and in the writing industry – a disadvantage linked to their minority status. In 2010 not a single writer defined as Black or Asian entered the Nielsen Bookdata bestseller list. Over ten years of records we identified only 4 Black and Asian women writers who reside in the UK, and 14 overall. We believe the Prize is justifiable under the terms of Positive Action in the 2010 Equality Act, on the basis that: Black and Asian women writers suffer a disadvantage linked to their race and gender, and have a disproportionately low level of participation in the UK writing industry, the action we are taking encourages this group to overcome this disadvantage and encourages participation and the prize is a proportionate response to the issue.[111]

However in contrast there is no requirement under the Equality Act for an 'association' 12.124 catering for a protected group to demonstrate such disadvantage in order to be lawful under Schedule 16 to the Act, as we explain below. A men's fiction prize may be unlawful, a men's running club will probably not be.

O. ASSOCIATIONS

Legislation prior to 2010 prohibited associations from discriminating against existing or 12.125 potential members on grounds of race, disability, and sexual orientation. Yet clubs which were genuinely private were able to have discriminatory membership categories and prices between men and women. This state of affairs provoked much concern for many years leading up to the Bill, as can be seen from the following comments made in a debate on the issue on 16 January 2001 following the Carlton Club's decision not to grant women members equal access:

... if a West End club, a golf club or indeed a working man's club were to exclude people from membership or access to membership because they were black, Jewish or had some kind of

---

[111] <https://www.sileedsliteraryprize.com/faqs/>.

disability there would be a public outcry. It would of course be illegal. Is it not even more offensive that private clubs are able to discriminate against people solely because they are women?[112]

12.126   With the Equality Act came stricter controls. Section 101 of the Act extends protection against discrimination by associations to protect the characteristics of gender, age, religion or belief, pregnancy and maternity, and gender reassignment.

12.127   Examples are given by the government in EN 337 that a gentlemen's club will be guilty of direct discrimination when it charges a person a higher subscription because he is a Muslim. Further, a private members' golf club is not permitted to allow its female members to play golf only on certain days in contrast to the men who can play whenever they wish.

12.128   The same protection is given to guests of members of private clubs under section 102. So an association unlawfully discriminates if it refuses to invite the disabled wife of a member to attend an annual dinner, simply because she is a wheelchair user.

12.129   The exception to this rule in Schedule 16 to the Act permits associations to restrict membership to those who share protected characteristics; so that for example religious clubs, gay associations, and same-sex clubs will still be permitted even though they select members according to, for example, gender or sexual orientation or nationality.[113]

Paragraph 1 to the Schedule provides:

(1) An association does not contravene section 101(1) by restricting membership to persons who share a protected characteristic.

(2) An association that restricts membership to persons who share a protected characteristic does not breach section 101(3) by restricting the access by associates to a benefit, facility or service to such persons as share the characteristic.

(3) An association that restricts membership to persons who share a protected characteristic does not breach section 102(1) by inviting as guests, or by permitting to be invited as guests, only such persons as share the characteristic.

12.130   However, an association may not restrict membership to people of a particular colour: see paragraph 1(4) of Schedule 16. The government stated in its Response to the Consultation on the Equality Bill that this exception must not provide an excuse for people to set up clubs just so as to exclude particular vulnerable groups of people and that it should be for a real positive benefit rather than for purposes of segregation (paragraph 13.12). Thus an association could be set up only for retired women or only for retired African-Caribbean women, but it could not be an association for retired black women as this would be based on colour.[114]

12.131   The EHRC Services Code at paragraph 12.46 provides an example of a permitted membership condition based on national origins not colour. The constitution of an association called the Black Jazz Players Club states that all members must have national origins in Africa or the Caribbean. It is unlawful for an association to say that it will only accept black people as members. However, despite the use of 'black' in its name, the restrictions on membership of this particular association are based on national origins and not colour, and so these restrictions would be lawful.

---

[112] Lord Faulkner of Worcester HL Deb cols 1032–4 (16 January 2001); cited in V Keter's 2009 paper, 'Sex Discrimination in Private Clubs' at <http://www.parliament.uk/commons/lib/research/briefings/snbt-01081.pdf>.

[113] See also Article 16 of the Gender Goods and Services Directive.

[114] Equality Act 2010, Sch. 16, para. 1(3).

It is lawful to restrict membership to more than one protected characteristic at a time in accordance with Schedule 16, but associations are subject to the usual anti-discrimination provisions of the Equality Act, thus a women's association must not refuse to accept Muslim women as members (see paragraph 12.49, EHRC Services Code). But an association for Christian women can bar women of beliefs other than Christianity as well as men whether they are Christian, or of any other belief (page 20, EHRC Guide). Neither do the exceptions apply to associations which are political parties.   **12.132**

Despite the exemption, single-sex establishments remain a divisive issue. Notably in 2016 the EHRC Scottish Commissioner called the decision by the Muirfield golf club to continue not to allow women golfers to join the club, as legal but not desirable. In September 2020 a businesswoman, Emily Bendell, sued the Garrick club in London—which had been a gentlemen's club since 1831—not on the basis that it as a single-sex association was unlawful in how it determined its membership, but because it offers services to customers (such as a restaurant and guest rooms) it is bound under section 29 Equality Act to offer its services in a non-discriminatory way. Can an organization be a service provider as well as an association? Certainly the rigour of the Equality Act's positive action measures do not apply to the exemptions that apply to associations under current law.   **12.133**

13

INTERNATIONAL OBLIGATIONS AND THE HUMAN RIGHTS ACT

A. INTRODUCTION

13.01   The preceding chapters have analysed how the provisions of the Equality Act 2010 ('the Act') operate. However, the Act does not and cannot operate in isolation. The Act has a direct relationship with the UK's international human rights obligations at regional and global levels in the European Union[1] (EU), the Council of Europe, and the United Nations (UN). It is vital to the understanding, interpretation, and application of the Act to appreciate how it interacts with: EU equality and human rights law, before and after the UK ceasing its membership of the European Union (Brexit); the European Convention on Human Rights (ECHR) and the Human Rights Act 1998 (HRA) which implements the ECHR; and the key United Nations Conventions which relate to issues of equality of particular groups.

13.02   The UK's membership of the EU ended on 31 January 2020. This will have a fundamental effect on the application of EU equality and human rights law to the Act. In general terms, after the implementation period for ending the UK's membership, the UK is no longer bound by EU law and the Act is no longer required to be interpreted consistently with EU equality and human rights law. This represents a major and arguably backward step in protections from discrimination in the UK. The UK's membership of the EU has been instrumental both to the development of EU equality and human rights law, as well as the introduction and interpretation of UK equality laws over the last thirty years. It is essential to understand what has been the previous position regarding the effect of EU equality and human rights law on the Act, and what is its effect after the implementation period, which ended on 31 December 2020.

13.03   The UK government is also a Member State of the Council of Europe, the intergovernmental European body that developed the ECHR and to which the UK government is a party. It should be noted, that the UK's departure from the EU does not in any way effect its

---

[1] The European Union is a European intergovernmental body consisting of 27 Member States.

Peter Reading, *International Obligations and the Human Rights Act* In: *Blackstone's Guide to the Equality Act 2010*. Fourth Edition. Edited by: Anthony Robinson, David Ruebain, and Susie Uppal, Oxford University Press (2021). © Oxford University Press. DOI: 10.1093/oso/9780198870876.003.0013

membership of the Council of Europe, or being a party to the ECHR. The ECHR has been implemented into the UK's domestic law by the enactment of the HRA. Under the HRA, as a piece of primary legislation the Act must be interpreted in a manner consistent with the rights and freedoms contained in the ECHR. In addition, a number of the rights and freedoms protected under the HRA have a direct relationship with notions of equality and non-discrimination. This will be of particular significance where consideration is being given as to whether a discrimination claim or a human rights claim is brought, or both.

Finally, the UK government is a Member State of the UN global intergovernmental body and a party to the key UN international Conventions relating to human rights. A number of these Conventions contain provisions relating to discrimination and the protection of the human rights of particular groups. The Act is one means by which the UK government gives effect to its obligations under those UN Conventions and several of them provide an alternative means of bringing claims of breaches of human rights in the UN system.   **13.04**

This chapter analyses these issues in three parts. Part B analyses the previous and current effect after Brexit of EU equality and human rights law on the Act, Part C analyses the interaction between the ECHR, the HRA, and the Act. Part D analyses the relationship between the UK government's obligations under the key UN Conventions and the Act.   **13.05**

B. BREXIT AND THE FUTURE EFFECT OF EUROPEAN UNION LAW

1. Ending the Role of EU Law

In the last edition of this publication, it highlighted the crucial role EU law and its institutions have played in advancing the rights to equality and non-discrimination as well as other human rights for everyone in the EU including the UK. Brexit not only meant the end of a 45-year relationship, but also meant immense legal changes since the UK is no longer required to comply with EU laws applying to Member States. These profound changes also apply in the field of EU equality and human rights law, which previously have had a significant positive impact on the development of UK equality law.   **13.06**

EU law has had a direct impact on the development and application of domestic equality legislation in the UK in four key ways. First, the EU has the power to legislate in the field of equality law, and all Member States must implement those laws. Secondly, the implementation of those laws in the UK has been instrumental in the strengthening and harmonizing of protection from discrimination. Thirdly, domestic courts and tribunals had to interpret and apply domestic legislation consistently with EU law and principles of interpretation. Fourthly, the Court of Justice of the European Union (CJEU) played a vital role in the interpretation of EU law and the manner in which it was implemented into domestic law. For example, domestic courts could make references to the CJEU by the preliminary ruling procedure to determine how EU law in the field of equality and other human rights should be interpreted and, often as a result, whether domestic law implementing the EU law complied with EU law.   **13.07**

The UK Government has said that it is committed to ensuring that the protections in the Act will continue to apply after the UK left the EU.[2] The Government's stated intention   **13.08**

---

[2] Para. 8, Equality Analysis European Union (Withdrawal) Bill, Department for Exiting the European Union, July 2017 <https://assets.publishing.service.gov.uk/government/uploads/system/uploads/attachment_data/file/629244/European_Union__Withdrawal__Bill_equality_analysis.pdf>.

is that there will be continuity in protections from discrimination by preserving existing domestic equality legislation which implements EU obligations, and converting EU law as it applies in the UK into domestic law.[3]

13.09   However, by leaving the EU the UK Government is no longer required to comply with EU law or the CJEU. This not only ends the interdependency between the positive development of EU and UK equality law, but also opens up the possibility of future regression of UK equality law below EU requirements.

13.10   In practice the effect of EU law on the Act will either end, or be substantially limited in scope because of the UK's departure from the EU. In order to be able to apply and interpret the Act, it is essential to understand the legal effect of the UK no longer being subject to EU equality and human rights laws. Below the following points are examined: the existing EU laws, principles and institutions relating to equality law; and what is the legal effect of Brexit on the Act in terms of its operation and interpretation.

2. The Existing EU Laws, Principles, and Institutions

13.11   This section analyses the EU legal framework relating to equality and other human rights which consist of: the EU Treaties; the Equality Directives; the EU Charter of Fundamental Rights ('the Charter'); principles on the implementation and interpretation of EU law; and the role of the CJEU.

(a) *The EU Treaties*

13.12   The Treaty of the European Union (TEU) and the Treaty on the Functioning of the European Union (TFEU)[4] embed provisions relating to equality and other human rights into the powers and functions of the EU institutions in a number of ways.[5] The powers and functions relating to equality and other human rights were amended and enhanced by the ratification of the Lisbon Treaty, which entered into force on 1 December 2009 and made significant changes to the constitutional framework of the EU.[6]

13.13   (i) *The TEU* The TEU sets out the aims and objectives of the EU. It places the rights to equality and other human rights at the heart of the EU, stating that:

The Union is founded on the values of respect for human dignity, freedom, democracy, equality, the rule of law and respect for human rights, including the rights of persons belonging to minorities. These values are common to the Member States in a society in which pluralism, non-discrimination, tolerance, justice, solidarity and equality between women and men prevail.[7]

13.14   In addition, the TEU includes a provision that the Union 'shall combat social exclusion and discrimination, and shall promote social justice and protection, equality between women and men, solidarity between generations and protection of the rights of the child'.[8]

---

[3] *ibid* para. 3.
[4] Formerly the Treaty of the European Community.
[5] Consolidated Version of the Treaty of the European Union, OJ C115/13, 9 May 2008; Consolidated Version of the Treaty of the Functioning of the European Union, OJ C115/47, 9 May 2008.
[6] OJ C306/50, 17 December 2007. The Lisbon Treaty entered into force on 1 December 2009.
[7] *ibid*, TEU Art. 2.
[8] TEU Art. 3(3) (formerly Art. 2 TEC).

The TEU also has the effect of incorporating the Charter into the legal order of the TEU   **13.15**
and the TFEU such that it has binding effect and the same status as the two Treaties. The
effect of the Charter in relation to equality is discussed below in section 2(c).

(ii) *The TFEU*   The TFEU organizes the functioning and the areas of competence of the   **13.16**
EU. A new Part Two of the TFEU was created which concerns non-discrimination and rights
associated with citizenship of the EU. Article 19[9] provides the power to take action to combat
discrimination:

1. Without prejudice to the other provisions of the Treaties and within the limits of the powers
conferred by them upon the Union, the Council, acting unanimously in accordance with a special
legislative procedure and after obtaining the consent of the European Parliament, may take appropriate action to combat discrimination based on sex, racial or ethnic origin, religion or belief,
disability, age or sexual orientation.

Article 19 was introduced in 1997[10] and has had a significant impact in the development   **13.17**
of equality legislation in the EU. A number of directives have been agreed to combat discrimination and promote equality ('the Equality Directives'), and their implementation in the
UK has expanded protection from discrimination. This is discussed below in section 2(b).

There are also specific provisions relating to eliminating gender discrimination and pro-   **13.18**
moting gender equality. Unlike other protected characteristics, gender equality was a feature
of the original Treaty of Rome 1957 by requiring equal pay for men and women and this
requirement is maintained in Article 157 of the TFEU.[11] In addition, there is a requirement
to mainstream gender equality into all its policies and activities. Article 8[12] states that the
Union 'shall aim to eliminate inequalities, and promote equality, between men and women'.

Finally, the Lisbon Treaty introduced a new provision relating to eliminating discrimi-   **13.19**
nation. Article 10 of the TFEU states that in 'defining and implementing its policies and
activities, the Union shall aim to combat discrimination based on sex, racial or ethnic origin,
religion or belief, disability, age or sexual orientation'. The provision highlights the movement of the EU towards strengthening provisions on the mainstreaming of equality into the
work of the EU institutions across all protected characteristics. For example, equality impact
assessments of the effect of EU legislation or policies may become increasingly important.

(b) *Equality Directives*

The introduction of Article 19 of the TFEU in 1997 had a significant impact on the develop-   **13.20**
ment of equality law in the UK. In relation to the characteristics protected from discrimination under the Act, the Equality Directives have either required significant amendments to
domestic legislation (where there was already domestic law), or have necessitated the introduction of completely new domestic law in that field.[13]

(i) *Gender Directives.*   Prior to the introduction of Article 19, Article 157 of the TFEU   **13.21**
provided the competence for the introduction of the Gender Directives. The Equal Pay
Directive relating to equal pay of men and women was agreed in 1975.[14] The Equal Treatment

---

[9] Formerly Art. 13 TEC.
[10] Introduced by the Treaty of Amsterdam.
[11] Formerly Art. 119 of the Treaty of Rome.
[12] Formerly Art. 3(2) TEC.
[13] For example, there was no domestic discrimination law in relation to religion or belief, sexual orientation,
or age prior to the implementation of the Framework Directive 2000/78/EC.
[14] Directive 75/117/EEC.

Directive was agreed in 1976 and prohibited discrimination on grounds of gender in access to employment, vocational training and promotion, and working conditions.[15]

13.22   All of the key Gender Directives relating to equality between men and women in employment and occupation have been consolidated and amended by the Recast Gender Directive.[16] This provides for protection from direct and indirect discrimination (including in pay and occupational social security schemes), harassment, sexual harassment, and victimization. It also includes a gender mainstreaming provision, which requires Member States to 'actively take into account the objective of equality between men and women when formulating and implementing laws, regulations, administrative provisions, policies and activities' in areas provided for in the Directive.

13.23   In addition, the Pregnant Workers Directive[17] provides measures to promote the equality of pregnant women at work, including provisions addressing maternity leave, time off for ante-natal care, risk assessments, and prohibiting dismissal. The European Commission had proposed to amend the Pregnant Workers Directive to improve and harmonize the provisions protecting pregnant women and those who have given birth and are breastfeeding.[18] However, the proposals have not been agreed by the EU, and at a meeting of the Council of Ministers in 2011 it was decided not to proceed with the proposals.[19] It is therefore not clear whether the proposal will be agreed in the future.

13.24   In December 2004, a new Gender Directive was agreed which provides protection from gender discrimination in the field of goods and services.[20] This applies to all persons (whether public or private sectors) who provide goods or services to the public, so long as they are offered outside the field of private and family life.[21] Importantly, however, the Directive does not extend competence to the fields of media and advertising or education.[22] In addition, unlike the Race Directive discussed below, the Gender Directive does not provide for protection from discrimination in relation to social protection including social security and healthcare (where healthcare would not come within the provision of a service) and social advantages. It is also not clear whether it covers housing as, unlike the Race Directive, there is no express reference to housing.

13.25   (ii) *Race Directive.*   The Race Directive[23] was agreed in 2000. It provides protection from discrimination based on racial or ethnic origin.[24] The Race Directive, similarly to all the other Equality Directives, prohibits direct and indirect discrimination, harassment, and victimization.

---

[15] Directive 76/207/EEC.

[16] Directive 2006/54/EC consolidates seven directives: Directive 75/117/EEC on equal pay; Directive 76/207/EEC on equal treatment in employment; Directive 2002/73/EC which amended Directive 76/207/EEC; Directive 86/378/EEC on equal treatment of men and women in occupational social security schemes; Directive 96/97/EC amending Directive 86/378/EEC; Directive 97/80/EC on the burden of proof in sex discrimination cases; and Directive 98/52/EC on the extension of Directive 97/80/EC to the UK.

[17] Directive 92/85/EEC.

[18] Proposal for a Directive of the European Parliament and of the Council amending Council Directive 92/85/EEC on the introduction of measures to encourage improvements in the safety and health at work of pregnant workers and workers who have recently given birth or are breastfeeding, COM(2008) 600/4.

[19] Council of Ministers of the EU, Press Release 17943/11, 1 and 2 December 2011.

[20] Directive 2004/113/EC implementing the principle of equal treatment between men and women in the access to and supply of goods and services.

[21] Art. 3(1).

[22] Art. 3(3).

[23] Directive 2000/43/EC.

[24] It does not provide for protection based on colour, national origins, or nationality. The nationality exception exists in order that the Directive does not interfere with the immigration policy of Member States.

However, it provides protection in the broadest range of fields: employment and related areas, social protection including social security and healthcare, social advantages, education, and access to and supply of goods and services which are available to the public including housing.

The Race Directive contains an exception for discrimination based on genuine occupa- **13.26** tional requirements[25] and, as for the other Equality Directives, for positive action measures.[26]

The Race Directive also importantly required for the first time that Member States des- **13.27** ignate 'a body or bodies for the promotion of equal treatment' with competence: to provide independent assistance to victims of discrimination in pursuing their complaints of discrimination; to conduct independent surveys concerning discrimination; and to publish independent reports making recommendations on any issue relating to such discrimination.[27] This provision was unique, as the original Gender Directives[28] contained no such provision. Significantly this requirement was mirrored in the Recast Gender Directive and the Gender Goods and Services Directive, but the designation of a body or bodies for the promotion of equal treatment was not required by the Framework Directive.

(iii) *Framework Directive.* The Framework Directive[29] was agreed in 2000, only five **13.28** months after the Race Directive. It provides for protection from discrimination in employment and related fields across four characteristics of disability, religion or belief, sexual orientation, and age. The Directive had a significant impact on the development of British equality law as previously there was no domestic protection from discrimination in employment on grounds of religion or belief, sexual orientation, and age.

The protection from discrimination is similar in scope to race and gender, prohibiting **13.29** direct and indirect discrimination, harassment, and victimization. In addition, in relation to disability there is a requirement on employers to make reasonable adjustments to enable disabled persons to have access to, participate in, or advance in employment and training unless such measures would propose a disproportionate burden on employers.[30]

It is important to note that unlike other protected characteristics, direct age discrimina- **13.30** tion can be justified under the Directive. This recognizes that in certain circumstances it is reasonable to treat persons differently on grounds of age, whether they are younger or older persons. Article 6 provides that differences of treatment on grounds of age will not constitute discrimination if they are 'objectively and reasonably justified by a legitimate aim, including legitimate employment policy, labour market and vocational training objectives, and if the means of achieving that aim are appropriate and necessary'.[31]

Examples of what may constitute lawful differences of treatment are: setting of special **13.31** conditions on access to employment and vocational training, employment, and occupation; the fixing of minimum conditions of age, professional experience, or seniority in service for access to employment or to certain advantages linked to employment; and the fixing of a maximum age for recruitment which is based on the training requirements of the post in question or the need for a reasonable period of employment before retirement.[32]

---

[25] Art. 4 and see further Chapter 4.
[26] Art. 5 and see further Chapter 12.
[27] Art. 13.
[28] The Equal Treatment Directive and the Equal Pay Directive.
[29] 2000/78/EC.
[30] Art. 5.
[31] Art. 6(1).
[32] Art. 7.

13.32   The Framework Directive contains other important exceptions. For example, the Directive contains an exception similar to exceptions under the articles of the ECHR relating to public security, the prevention of crime, and the protection of the rights of others.[33] There are also exceptions relating to the armed forces permitting Member States to determine that the Directive does not apply to age and disability discrimination in the armed forces[34] and exceptions relating to genuine occupational requirements.[35] These include an exception for religious organizations and 'other public or private organisations the ethos of which is based on religion or belief'. It permits these organizations to employ persons of a particular religion or belief where a person's religion or belief constitutes a genuine occupational requirement, so long as it does not justify discrimination on another ground.[36]

13.33   (iv) *Proposed Goods and Services Directive.*   In 2008 the European Commission proposed a new Equality Directive that would expand and harmonize protection from discrimination on grounds of disability, religion or belief, sexual orientation, and age.[37] This is intended to expand on the protection provided in the Framework Directive and ensure that those characteristics have the same or similar levels of protection as race and gender in relation to the provision of goods and services.

13.34   The proposed directive seeks to prohibit discrimination in both the public and private sectors in relation to: social protection, including social security and healthcare; social advantages; education; and access to and supply of goods and other services which are available to the public, including housing.[38] The proposed scope of protection is therefore very similar to the Race Directive. Unfortunately, to date it has not been possible for the European Council to secure unanimous agreement of all Member States to the proposal.

(c) *EU Charter of Fundamental Rights*

13.35   The enhanced status of the Charter indicates that equality and protection of human rights are primary goals of the EU. The Charter was agreed by the EU in December 2000,[39] although it did not become a legally binding instrument until the Lisbon Treaty came into force on 1 December 2009.

13.36   The Charter provides a human rights framework for the development and implementation of EU law (including Equality Directives) that is similar to the ECHR. The Charter indicates that insofar as the rights correspond to rights in the ECHR, the meaning and scope of those rights shall be the same.[40] The effect of the Charter is that where EU law is developed and implemented, the Charter must be complied with by the EU institutions, and the Member States implementing the EU law.[41] It does not, however, create any new powers or tasks for the EU.[42]

---

[33] Art. 2(5).

[34] Art. 3(4).

[35] Art. 4(1) and (2).

[36] Art. 4(2).

[37] Proposal for a Council Directive on implementing the principle of equal treatment between persons irrespective of religion or belief, disability, age or sexual orientation, COM(2008) 426 final, 2 July 2008.

[38] Draft Art. 3(1).

[39] [2000] OJ C364, 18 December 2000.

[40] Art. 52.

[41] Art. 51(1).

[42] Art. 51(2).

Chapter III of the Charter is dedicated to issues of equality. Article 21 provides a free- 13.37
standing right to non-discrimination in the implementation of EU law on 'any ground such
as sex, race, colour, ethnic or social origin, genetic features, language, religion or belief, political or any other opinion, membership of a national minority, property, birth, disability, age
or sexual orientation'. Of note, this is broader in scope than the grounds for which the EU
can legislate against discrimination under Article 19 of the TFEU and similar in some ways
to Article 14 of the ECHR.[43]

In addition, Chapter III contains a number of other significant provisions on equality; for 13.38
example, it provides that:

- everyone is equal before the law;[44]
- children shall have the right to such protection and care as is necessary for their well-being;[45]
- the EU recognizes and respects the rights of the elderly to lead a life of dignity and independence and to participate in social and cultural life;[46]
- the EU recognizes and respects the right of persons with disabilities to benefit from measures designed to ensure their independence, social and occupational integration, and participation in the life of the community.[47]

The Charter has been referred to and relied on in a number of decisions of the CJEU, 13.39
some of which relate to issues of equality of particular groups.[48] The UK and Polish governments signed a protocol to the Charter which relates to its interpretation and application
in those Member States.[49] Some argued that the protocol constituted an 'opt-out' from the
Charter altogether, while others argued that it is an interpretive instrument that clarifies the
effect of the Charter but does not change its applicability in the UK. The effect of the protocol was clarified in a preliminary ruling decision of the CJEU in *NS v Secretary of State for
the Home Department*.[50] The case concerned the application of the EU system of transferring
asylum seekers to the Member State responsible for determining their asylum application.[51]
At issue was whether an asylum seeker in the UK should be returned to the EU Member
State where he entered the EU (in this case, Greece) and whether the conditions in Greece
were compliant with the Charter. Several organizations including the Equality and Human
Rights Commission and Amnesty International intervened at domestic level and before the

---

[43] The scope of protection from discrimination under Art. 21 is similar to Art. 14 of the ECHR: e.g.
although sexual orientation and disability are not expressly referred to in Art. 14, case law has interpreted that
those characteristics are within the scope of 'other status' under Art. 14. However, the Art. 21 provision is
broader in the sense that it provides a free-standing right to non-discrimination in the implementation of EU
law, whereas Art. 14 is only engaged where the facts come within the ambit of a substantive right.
[44] Art. 20.
[45] Art. 24.
[46] Art. 26.
[47] Art. 26. The European Union also recently ratified the United Nations Convention on the Rights of
Disabled Persons (CRPD) on 23 December 2010. This means that the EU institutions and Member States
must comply with the CRPD in developing and implementing all EU law and policies.
[48] For example, Case C-176/08 *Hasan and Others*, 2 March 2010 concerning the rights of asylum seekers to seek asylum; Case C-403/09 *Deticek*, 23 December 2009 concerning the rights of children in custody
disputes of parents.
[49] Protocol 7, On the Application of the Charter of Fundamental Rights to Poland and the United
Kingdom.
[50] Case C-411/10, 21 December 2011.
[51] The system is set out in Regulation No 343/2003.

CJEU to argue that the Charter has full effect in the UK. The CJEU agreed and the decision therefore was an important precedent for all cases in the UK where the Charter was referred to or relied on in some way.

(d) *Principles on the Implementation and Interpretation of EU Law*

13.40 There are a number of principles relating to the implementation, interpretation, and applica- tion of EU law that have been relevant to the interpretation and application of the Act and previous UK equality laws. It should be noted that these principles no longer apply, or only have limited effect after the implementation period for the departure of the UK from the EU which ended on 31 December 2020.

13.41 Firstly, the UK has given domestic effect to its obligations arising out of the TEU and the TFEU in UK law by section 2 of the European Communities Act 1972 (ECA). Section 2(1) states that all obligations and rights arising from or by the Treaties 'are without further enact- ment to be given legal effect ... shall be recognised and available in law, and enforced ...'.

13.42 By section 2(2) a Minister may make regulations to implement community obligations, and this has been done in the case of the Equality Directives by a series of regulations. The Act also contains a new provision which enables the government to amend the Act in an area not within the scope of the Equality Directives, but which the government considers is an appropriate field to harmonize protection.[52]

13.43 The Equality Directives all specify and require the transposition of the provisions of the Directives by a particular date. If a directive is not transposed into domestic law within that timeframe, the European Commission may commence proceedings against the Member State.[53] Such proceedings have been brought against a number of Member States in relation to several of the Equality Directives.[54]

13.44 Secondly, domestic legislation which gives effect to EU law must be construed purposively, so as to give it a meaning consistent with EU law, insofar as is possible.[55] This is the case whether or not the domestic legislation was passed before or after the coming into force of the relevant EU law. As a result the Act must be interpreted consistently with all the Equality Directives.

13.45 Thirdly, the principle of non-discrimination has been recognized as a general principle of EU law.[56] National courts must therefore need to give effect to this principle, even where the date for the transposition of the specific measure in the field of equality has not yet expired.[57]

13.46 Fourthly, EU law must be interpreted consistently with human rights obligations of Member States under the Charter and the ECHR.[58] Article 6(2) of the TEU requires the EU to accede to the ECHR and, according to Article 6(3) of the TEU, fundamental rights as guaranteed by the ECHR constitute general principles of EU law. The CJEU has repeatedly

---

[52] Ss 203 and 204. For example, the Explanatory Notes refer to introducing harmonizing provisions relat- ing to colour and nationality which are not within the scope of the Race Directive 2000/43/EC.

[53] Art. 258 TFEU.

[54] For example, in February 2005, the ECJ ruled against Finland and Luxembourg for their failure to trans- pose the provisions of the Race Directive 2000/43/EC in time.

[55] Case C-106/89 *Marleasing SA v LA Commercial Internacional de Alimentacion* [1990] ECR I-4135.

[56] *Mangold v Helm* [2006] IRLR 143; Case C-555/07 *Seda Kucukdeveci v Swedex GmbH & Co* [2010] All ER (D) 126 (Feb).

[57] *Mangold v Helm* [2006] IRLR 143, para. 76.

[58] The accession of the EU to the ECHR is yet to be agreed. A draft agreement on the accession was pro- posed in April 2013. However, in December 2014 the CJEU decided that draft agreement was not compatible with EU law in a number of respects: Opinion 2/13, 18 December 2014.

held that fundamental rights form part of the traditions of the European Community and will be taken into account in interpreting its laws.[59]

Fifthly, often EU law has direct effect. This means that it has binding force in Member   **13.47**
States whether or not action has been taken by a Member State to implement it. The TFEU may have direct effect where the provisions are precise and unconditional. For example, Articles 157 and 45[60] require equal pay for men and women and require free movement of workers, respectively. They have been held to be directly effective,[61] whereas Article 19 is not as it only empowers the EU to take action.

Directives provide Member States with discretion as to the means by which they achieve   **13.48**
the aims of the directive, but they are *binding* as to the result to be achieved.[62] Consequently, provisions of directives that are 'sufficiently clear, precise and unconditional' may have direct effect. Where it is not possible to interpret legislation consistently with a directly effective provision of a directive, the incompatible domestic provision must be disapplied in any proceedings against the State. This has powerful ramifications, as the principle goes further than the mechanisms in the HRA. The Act only permits a declaration of incompatibility where legislation cannot be read consistently with a Convention right.[63] There have been a number of examples of the disapplication of domestic law in the field of domestic equality legislation.[64]

(e) *The CJEU and the Preliminary Ruling Procedure*

The CJEU has the following functions: reviewing the legality of the acts of the institutions   **13.49**
of the European Union; ensuring that the Member States comply with obligations under the EU Treaties; and interpreting EU law at the request of the national courts and tribunals. The CJEU therefore constitutes the judicial authority of the European Union and, in cooperation with the courts and tribunals of the Member States, it ensures the uniform application and interpretation of EU law.[65]

The judgments of the CJEU have sometimes extended or clarified the scope of protection   **13.50**
from discrimination under the Equality Directives. National courts are obliged to give effect to judgments of the CJEU, and to disapply any national laws that conflict with the requirements of EU law.

Article 267 of the TFEU[66] provides an extremely important procedure by which the CJEU   **13.51**
can make a preliminary ruling on the proper interpretation of EU law, following a reference by a national court. A reference can be made whenever the decisions on the questions referred to the CJEU are 'necessary to enable it to give judgment'.

---

[59] For example, Case C-222/84 *Johnston v Chief Constable of the Royal Ulster Constabulary* [1986] ECR 1651, para. 18; Case C-260/89 *Elliniki Radiophonia Tileorass-AE v Pliroforissis and Kouvelas* [1991] ECR I-2925.

[60] Formerly Arts 141 and 39.

[61] Case 43/75 *Defrenne (No. 2)* [1976] ECR 455 and Case 170/84 *Bilka-Kaufhaus GmbH v Weber von Hartz* [1986] ECR 1607 on the direct effect of Art. 157; Case 41/74 *Van Duyn v Home Office* [1974] ECR 1337 on the direct effect of Art. 39.

[62] Art. 288 TFEU, formerly Art. 249.

[63] HRA s. 4.

[64] Case C-271/91 *Marshall v Southampton and South West Area Health Authority II* [1993] ECR I-4367; *Bossa v Nordstress Ltd* [1998] ICR 694; *Alabaster v Barclays Bank plc (formerly Woolwich plc) and Secretary of State for Social Security (No. 2)* [2005] EWCA Civ 508.

[65] Court of Justice of the European Union website: <https://curia.europa.eu/jcms/jcms/Jo2_6999/en/>.

[66] Formerly Art. 234.

13.52   This procedure is important as it enables parties to proceedings to seek a reference to the CJEU in order to determine whether domestic law, practice, and remedies are compliant with the Equality Directives. If they are not, the domestic courts are required to interpret the domestic legislation consistently with the meaning of a provision provided by the CJEU, or if they cannot do so, disapply the domestic law.

13.53   A number of decisions have been relevant to the scope of protection and interpretation of the Act, or previous UK equality laws.

13.54   (i) *Gender Reassignment Discrimination as a Form of Sex Discrimination*   *P v S and Cornwall County Council*[67] related to a situation in which a transgender woman was dismissed from her job because she was transitioning. The employment tribunal in the UK decided that it was unclear whether the Sex Discrimination Act (SDA), as originally drafted, was in breach of the EU's Equal Treatment Directive,[68] by excluding gender reassignment as part of the SDA. The tribunal in the UK made a reference to the CJEU to ask whether the Directive applied in the case of transgender people; if that was the case, the SDA would need to be amended. The CJEU ruled that under the Equal Treatment Directive, sex discrimination does include less favourable treatment relating to a person undergoing gender reassignment. As a consequence, the UK was obliged to change the law through the Sex Discrimination (Gender Reassignment) Regulations 1999.

13.55   (ii) *Discrimination by Association*   Several decisions have considered the issue of discrimination by association. In *Coleman*[69] the CJEU was referred questions by an employment tribunal on the proper interpretation of the provisions of the Framework Directive.[70] Ms Coleman was the carer of her disabled son and brought a claim of direct disability discrimination and harassment against her employer. She was not herself disabled. The reference was made to determine whether the scope of the Directive was wide enough to provide protection from direct discrimination or harassment where the person claiming discrimination is not disabled but is associated in some way with a disabled person. This was an issue, as the Disability Discrimination Act 1995 (DDA) did not provide for protection from associative disability discrimination in such circumstances. The Grand Chamber held that the intention of the Directive is to provide protection from all forms of disability discrimination and that it would undermine the purpose of the Directive if discrimination by association was not prohibited.

13.56   On return to the Employment Appeal Tribunal, the provisions of the DDA were interpreted in such a way as to include a prohibition on discrimination by association.[71] Further, the formulation of direct discrimination and harassment in the Act[72] has been constructed in a manner which is wide enough and intended to encompass discrimination by association and perception, other than for the protected characteristics of marriage or civil partnership. This is explicitly recognized in the Explanatory Notes to the Act.[73]

13.57   The more recent decision of the Grand Chamber in *CHEZ Razpredelenie Bulgaria AD v Komisia za zashtita ot diskriminatsia*[74] concerned claimed direct and indirect racial

---

[67] Case C-13/94 *P v S and Cornwall County Council* [1996] ECR I-2146.
[68] Directive 76/207/EEC.
[69] Case C-303/06 *Coleman v Attridge Law* [2008] ECR I-5603.
[70] Directive 2000/78/EC.
[71] UKEAT/0071/09/JOJ.
[72] Ss 13 and 26.
[73] EN 63 and 94; see <http://www.opsi.gov.uk/acts/acts2010/en/ukpgaen_20100015_en.pdf.>
[74] Case C-83/14, 16 July 2015.

discrimination by association in Bulgaria in relation to the provision of services. The discrimination by association concerned a Bulgarian woman of Bulgarian ethnic origin that claimed she was discriminated against by a company's policy regarding the installation of electricity meters in an area inhabited mainly by people of Roma ethnic origin. The Grand Chamber decided that the meaning of indirect race discrimination under the Race Directive 2000/43/EC included indirect race discrimination by association.

The decision has direct implications for the interpretation and application of the Act. The current provisions are such that discrimination by association can only apply in situations of direct discrimination or harassment. The definition of indirect discrimination in section 19 of the Act requires the complainant to have the same characteristic (e.g., race, religion, or sexual orientation) as the disadvantaged group. As a result of the *CHEZ* decision, it is therefore arguable the indirect discrimination provisions of the Act must be interpreted consistently with the relevant provisions of the Race Directive and other Equality Directives, by permitting claims of indirect discrimination by association. 13.58

(iii) *Sex Discrimination Relating to Insurance* Another preliminary ruling decision by the CJEU that relates to a reference from the Belgian courts had a direct effect on the Act by requiring its amendment. In *Association belge des Consommateurs Test-Achats ASBL*[75] a reference was made from the Belgium constitutional court to the CJEU on the interpretation of the exception in the Gender Directive on goods and services concerning insurance.[76] Article 5(2) permitted differences in the insurance premiums and benefits between men and women where the use of sex is a 'determining factor in the assessment of risk based on relevant and accurate actuarial and statistical data'.[77] The claimant argued that the provision in the Belgian national law that implemented Directive 2004/113/EC and provided for an exception pursuant to Article 5(2) was contrary to the principle of equality between men and women. Importantly, the Court relied on Articles 21 and 23 of the Charter of Fundamental Rights, which state that any discrimination based on sex is prohibited and that equality between men and women must be ensured in all areas. The CJEU held that Article 5(2) was incompatible with Articles 21 and 23 of the Charter and that Article 5(2) would be invalid at the expiry of the transition period (21 December 2012). The decision was significant, as it demonstrates the interaction between EU equality law and the Charter, as EU equality law must be compatible with the Charter. 13.59

In December 2012 the UK government made amendments to the Act to implement the decision. Amendments were made by repealing the exception in paragraph 22 of Schedule 3 to the Act permitting differences in insurance premiums and benefits between men and women.[78] The effect of the amendment only applies to contracts entered after 21 December 2012. 13.60

(iv) *Discrimination Against Women having Children by Surrogacy* The CJEU made two decisions relating to the interpretation of several of the Equality Directives and the right 13.61

---

[75] Case C-236/09, 1 March 2011.

[76] Directive 2004/113/EC implementing the principle of equal treatment between men and women in the access to and supply of goods and services.

[77] Such differences in treatment were permitted where the Member States decided before 21 December 2007 to permit differences in premiums and benefits and as those Member States ensured that accurate data concerning the use of sex as a determining actuarial factor are compiled, published, and regularly updated: Art. 5(2). Member States were also required to review their decision five years after 21 December 2007.

[78] Equality Act 2010 (Amendment) Regulations 2012, which came into force on 21 December 2012.

to maternity leave of women who have children by surrogacy.[79] In the *CD* decision, a female employee who became a mother by a surrogacy arrangement was refused maternity leave by her employee. The mother claimed sex and/or pregnancy discrimination under the Act before an employment tribunal. A reference was made to the CJEU to determine whether a refusal of maternity leave in such circumstances could be discrimination on grounds of pregnancy under the Pregnant Workers Directive 92/85, or on the grounds of sex of the Recast Gender Directive 2006/54. The Grand Chamber held that the Pregnant Workers Directive does not apply to mothers unless they are themselves pregnant and therefore that Member States are not required to grant maternity leave to such workers. The Grand Chamber also found that such treatment did not constitute direct or indirect sex discrimination under the Recast Gender Directive as men would be treated in the same way as women seeking paid leave equivalent to maternity leave. In the *Z* decision involving surrogacy in Ireland, the Grand Chamber held for similar reasons there was no sex discrimination under the Recast Gender Directive. In addition, in relation to a claim that the refusal to provide maternity leave was disability discrimination under the Framework Directive 2000/78, the Court decided that the fact that the mother could not herself give birth because of a medical condition was not a disability within the meaning the Framework Directive. This was because it did not hinder her ability to participate in employment on an equal basis with other workers.

13.62 It should be noted that in Britain, the possible discrimination against parents who have children by surrogacy were addressed in the Children and Families Act 2014.[80] The Act provides equal employment protection, leave, and pay (equivalent to maternity rights) to British parents having children born through surrogacy, whether or not the parents are in a heterosexual or same-sex relationship.

3. The Future Effect of EU Law on the Act

13.63 In simple terms, after the end of the implementation period for the departure of the UK from the EU on 31 December 2020, the application and interpretation of the Act no longer needs to comply with EU law. This could have a number of practical effects on the advancement of UK equality law which are discussed below. This section examines the legal requirements of Brexit and its implications for the Act; the future status of the CJEU and its case law; and the legal effect of no longer being a party to the Charter.

(a) *Legal Requirements and Effects of Brexit*

13.64 The legislation setting out the terms of the UK's withdraw from the EU is the EU (Withdrawal) Act 2018 as amended by the EU (Withdrawal Agreement) Act 2020 (EUWA).[81] The main legal elements of the withdrawal are set out below.

13.65 The EUWA firstly repealed the European Communities Act 1972 by which the UK acceded to the three European Communities (the predecessor to the EU) and which set out the legal effect of EU law in the UK.[82] The repeal of the European Communities Act, and

---

[79] *CD v ST* Case C-167/12 and *Z v A Government Department, The Board of Management of a community school* C-363/12, 18 March 2014.

[80] The Act came into force on 5 April 2015.

[81] EU (Withdrawal) Act 2018, including amendments by the EU (Withdrawal Agreement) Act 2020, <https://www.legislation.gov.uk/ukpga/2018/16/contents>.

[82] *ibid*, s. 1.

the day on which the UK ceased to be a member of the EU ('exit day'), was on 31 January 2020.[83] However, it should be noted that the EUWA provided for an implementation period of the withdrawal for the EU and the implementation period completion day ('IP completion day') was on 31 December 2020.[84] The EUWA also provides that the implementation period could not have been extended beyond 31 December 2020.[85]

During the implementation period the UK remained bound by nearly all EU law, and   **13.66** during that period the European Communities Act 1972 remained in effect, subject to certain modifications.[86] This for example meant that until 31 December 2020, the EU Equality Directives continued to apply to the UK and the interpretation of any EU derived UK law such as the Act.[87]

After the end of the implementation period, laws derived from the EU such as the Act   **13.67** continue to be part of UK law.[88] This is consistent with the Government's position that it remains committed to maintaining the current levels of protection from discrimination after the UK left the EU. However, after the implementation period there is nothing that legally prevents the UK Government from amending the Act in any way which is no longer consistent with previous obligations under EU law. There are no non-regression clauses in the EUWA to prevent the possibility of such regression, despite the previous recommendations by key stakeholders, such as the UK parliament Women and Equalities Committee:

The Government should include a clause … that explicitly commits to maintaining the current levels of equalities protection when EU law is transposed in UK law …[89]

There are concerns that a future Government may amend the Act to weaken protections   **13.68** from discrimination or related provisions. One issue which has been raised by some stakeholders as a possible area for amendment is limiting the amount of compensation that can be awarded under the Act. Currently such limitations exist in relation to unfair dismissal compensation awards, however because of the UK's membership of the EU and obligations under the relevant Equality Directives, no such limitation could previously be made for discrimination claims.[90]

(b) *The Future Status of the CJEU and its Case Law*

The UK's departure from the EU as stated previously, ended the role of the CJEU in terms of   **13.69** the application and interpretation of the Act. This is for several reasons: first, the UK courts are no longer required to apply CJEU decisions in relation to the interpretation of the Act

---

[83] The exit day of the UK from the EU was agreed to be extended to 31 January 2020 by The European Union (Withdrawal) Act 2018 (Exit Day) (Amendment) (No 3) Regulations 2019, SI 2019/1423 <https://www.legislation.gov.uk/uksi/2019/1423/made>.

[84] EU (Withdrawal) Act 2018 s. 1A(6).

[85] *ibid*, s. 15A.

[86] *ibid*, s. 1A.

[87] *ibid*, s. 1B.

[88] *ibid*, s. 2.

[89] House of Commons Women and Equalities Committee, UK Parliament, 'Ensuring strong equalities legislation after the EU exit', Seventh report of session 2016–17, p. 27 <https://publications.parliament.uk/pa/cm201617/cmselect/cmwomeq/799/799.pdf>.

[90] See for example 'Brexit and disability discrimination under Equality Act 2010' (31 January 2020) *Stammeringlaw* 14–15 <https://www.stammeringlaw.org.uk/disability-equality-law/european-union-human-rights-un/eu/brexit/>.

after the end of the implementation period on 31 December 2020; and secondly, it is no longer possible to make a reference from UK courts to the CJEU on the proper interpretation of UK equality law.

13.70   The EUWA states that UK courts and tribunals are not bound by any principles laid down or decisions by the CJEU after the implementation period.[91] However, UK courts and tribunals will generally be required to continue to apply and follow CJEU decisions made before the end of the implementation period.

13.71   The EUWA also sets out the way in which UK courts must now apply EU law. The EUWA provides that in interpreting 'retained EU law' (which includes the Act implementing EU law), the UK courts must follow relevant decisions made before IP completion day (i.e. before 31 December 2020) by the CJEU, or by UK courts on EU law.[92] This will only be subject to three exceptions: the Supreme Court need not follow CJEU decisions in certain cases; where regulations allow other UK courts to depart from EU case law; or so far as the law has been modified after IP completion day.[93]

13.72   In relation to the Supreme Court, it can depart from EU court decisions made before the end of the implementation period where it would depart from its own decisions.[94] The Supreme Court normally treats its former decisions as binding, but may depart from them when it appears right to do so. Lower courts would follow any new decision of the Supreme Court.

13.73   In relation to possible regulations allowing other courts and tribunals to depart from pre-IP completion day EU case law, it remains to be seen what the regulations will say. It is possible for example that they may only allow appeal courts to depart from it, so that lower courts can only do so to allow the judgment of an appeal court. Or the regulations might say that only certain appeal courts can depart from it, which may or may not include the Employment Appeal Tribunal. The regulations will need to be examined once they are introduced.

13.74   In addition to UK courts having to follow CJEU decisions made before the IP completion day, they will also be required to follow 'retained general principles of EU law'.[95] Examples of such principles include: proportionality, fundamental rights, non-retroactivity, equality before the law, and non-discrimination and equality between men and women.[96] However, there is no right of action in domestic law after the end of the implementation period based on a failure to comply with any of the general principles of EU law, and after the end of that period a court cannot quash or disapply any enactment or other rule of law because it is incompatible with any of the general principles of EU law.[97]

13.75   In relation to CJEU decisions made after IP completion day, UK courts and tribunals are no longer bound by them, but 'may have regard to' them so far as they are 'relevant to a matter before the court or tribunal'.[98] It is concerning that the legislation does not set

---

[91] EU (Withdrawal) Act 2018 s. 6(1)(a).

[92] *ibid*, s. 6(3).

[93] *ibid*, s. 6(4)–(7).

[94] *ibid*, s. 6(5).

[95] *ibid*, s. 6(7).

[96] Equality Analysis, European Union (Withdrawal) Bill, Department for Exiting the European Union, July 2017, para. 21, <https://assets.publishing.service.gov.uk/government/uploads/system/uploads/attachment_data/file/629244/European_Union__Withdrawal__Bill_equality_analysis.pdf>.

[97] EU (Withdrawal) Act 2018 Sch. 1, para. 3.

[98] *ibid*, s. 6(2).

out any guiding principles as to the relevant circumstances in which UK courts may refer to CJEU decisions in the future. Relevant UK parliament committees which examined the human rights implications of Brexit, both recommended that the UK Government should provide in legislation or statutory guidance, explanations of when and how future CJEU case law should be applied on issues of equality and other human rights.[99]

Finally, UK courts are no longer able to refer any case to the CJEU requesting an interpretation of any UK equality or related laws.[100] As discussed previously in this chapter, the CJEU has played an important role in interpreting EU equality law and UK equality law over the years which has led to significant improvements in protections from discrimination. As a result, this marks an important regression in the UK system for promoting and protecting everyone's rights to equality and non-discrimination in Britain. **13.76**

(c) *The Charter of Fundamental Rights*

The Charter no longer has effect in UK law, since the exit day of 31 January 2020.[101] However decisions by the CJEU and the UK courts relating to the interpretation and application of the Charter made before exit day will continue to have effect.[102] **13.77**

The UK Government has argued that the Charter did not create any new human rights, it merely catalogued the rights that already existed in EU law. And as a result, it has further argued that there will be no reduction in human rights protections in the UK, and that there will be no impact on the Act by the Charter no longer applying to the UK.[103] **13.78**

This position has been challenged by a number of stakeholders working in the field of equality and other human rights. For example, the Equality and Human Rights Commission (EHRC) has stated that in its view, the fact that the Charter will no longer apply to the UK will definitely result in a reduction of human rights protections.[104] The EHRC published a legal opinion it obtained on the issues, which in summary advised: **13.79**

- the Charter has created valuable new human rights in UK laws in the context of issues of UK equality law;
- the human rights conferred by the Charter are not all comprehensively reflected in other aspects of domestic law such as the Human Rights Act (HRA) and the common law; and

---

[99] House of Commons Women and Equalities Committee, UK Parliament, 'Ensuring strong equalities legislation after the EU exit', Seventh report of session 2016–17, para. 60 <https://publications.parliament.uk/pa/cm201617/cmselect/cmwomeq/799/799.pdf>; Joint Committee on Human Rights, 'The human rights implications of Brexit', Fifth report of session 2016–17, para. 93 <https://publications.parliament.uk/pa/jt201617/jtselect/jtrights/695/695.pdf>.

[100] EU (Withdrawal) Act 2018 s. 6(1)(b).

[101] *ibid*, s. 5(4).

[102] *ibid*, s. 5(5).

[103] Equality Analysis, European Union (Withdrawal) Bill, Department for Exiting the European Union, July 2017, pp. 4–5, <https://assets.publishing.service.gov.uk/government/uploads/system/uploads/attachment_data/file/629244/European_Union__Withdrawal__Bill_equality_analysis.pdf>.

[104] Equality and Human Rights Commission, 'Brexit and the EU Charter of Fundamental Rights', last updated 18 January 2018, <https://www.equalityhumanrights.com/en/what-are-human-rights/how-are-your-rights-protected/what-charter-fundamental-rights-european-union-0>.

- as a result there will be significant gaps in human rights protections in the UK, given the Charter is not being implemented into UK domestic law in any way.[105]

13.80   A UK case which illustrates the beneficial and added legal effect the Charter had in relation to discrimination claims, is the Court of Appeal case of *Benkharbouche and Anor v Embassy of the Republic of Sudan*.[106] The decision highlighted how the Charter added to the existing human rights protections in the UK in two respects: the fact that the right to an effective remedy under Article 47 of the Charter is broader than the right to a fair hearing under Article 6 of the ECHR; and where domestic UK laws do not comply with the Charter, the UK courts must disapply the domestic law.

13.81   The two cases involve employment claims brought by two employees of the Embassy of Sudan and the Embassy of Libya who were dismissed. The claims include aspects within the scope of the EU in relation to alleged breaches of the Working Time Regulations 1998 and racial discrimination. The embassies argued that the effect of the State Immunity Act 1978 was that no employment claims could be brought in UK courts against the States of Sudan or Libya.

13.82   The Court of Appeal decided that the relevant provisions of the State Immunity Act infringed Article 6 of the ECHR concerning the right to a public hearing and to access courts to determine civil claims. Further the provisions also infringed the right to an effective remedy under Article 47 of the Charter. There were however differences between the Article 6 ECHR rights and Article 47 Charter rights. The right to an effective remedy may encompass procedural obstacles, such as restrictions on the availability of compensation, which are not within the ambit of Article 6.

13.83   The court decided that the right to an effective remedy is a general principle of EU law and as a result Article 47 has direct horizontal effect. The court therefore decided to disapply the effect of the relevant provisions of the State Immunity Act and allow the claims within the scope of EU law including for racial discrimination. The Court of Appeal decision was upheld by the Supreme Court on appeal by the Government.[107] This can be contrasted with the claim under the HRA, where only a declaration of incompatibility could be and was made. The requirement on UK courts to disapply domestic law which is incompatible with the Charter, is a much stronger enforcement mechanism than declarations of incompatibility under the HRA.

13.84   Some other areas where it has been argued the Charter creates additional human rights are: Articles 20 and 21 of the Charter create free-standing rights to equality, which can be contrasted with Article 14 of the ECHR which is more limited in application since it only applies when another ECHR right is engaged, the right to dignity in Article 1, and the rights of the child in Article 24 of the Charter.[108]

---

[105] European Union (Withdrawal) Bill: EU Charter of Fundamental Rights, Opinion, Jason Coppel QC, 5 January 2018, <https://www.equalityhumanrights.com/sites/default/files/eu-withdrawal-bill-legal-advice-jason-coppel-qc.pdf>.

[106] [2015] EWCA Civ 33.

[107] Benkharbouche v Secretary of State for Foreign and Commonwealth Affairs [2017] UKSC 62.

[108] European Union (Withdrawal) Bill: EU Charter of Fundamental Rights, Opinion, Jason Coppel QC, 5 January 2018, pp. 10–11, <https://www.equalityhumanrights.com/sites/default/files/eu-withdrawal-bill-legal-advice-jason-coppel-qc.pdf>.

C. THE EUROPEAN CONVENTION ON HUMAN RIGHTS AND THE HUMAN RIGHTS ACT

1. The European Convention on Human Rights

In the aftermath of the Second World War, European countries decided to create a new   **13.85**
European intergovernmental organization to help to promote democracy and human rights
and to prevent the atrocities perpetrated during the war from reoccurring. The Council of
Europe was founded in 1949 and in 1950 it adopted the European Convention on Human
Rights (ECHR), which protects primarily civil and political rights. The UK government
was one of the first to ratify the ECHR in 1951, which came into force in 1953. It now
provides human rights protection to over 800 million people in 47 Member States and is
often described as the most successful human rights Convention in the world. As stated
previously in this chapter, the UK's departure from the EU does not in any way affect the
UK Government's membership of the Council of Europe, or its ratification of the ECHR.

2. The Relationship between the Equality Act and the Human Rights Act

The Human Rights Act 1998 (HRA) came into force on 2 October 2000 and sought to   **13.86**
'bring rights home' in the sense of implementing into domestic law most of the rights and
freedoms protected under the ECHR. Although the UK government ratified the ECHR
in 1951, the enactment of the HRA enabled persons in the UK for the first time to bring
a human rights claim in UK domestic courts. This also overcame the problem of the delays
and expenses of only being able to bring a claim in the European Court of Human Rights.

The HRA is the UK's Bill of Rights as it satisfies the key criteria: it is a legal instrument   **13.87**
which is binding on government and enshrines a set of fundamental human rights, and it
provides a right to redress in the event of violations.[109] The HRA also provides the rights with
certain constitutional effect by the creation of a number of mechanisms and obligations: the
obligation to interpret all primary and secondary legislation compatibly with the ECHR
rights so far as it is possible to do so (section 3); the ability of courts to make declarations
of incompatibility of legislation with ECHR rights (section 4); the obligation on public
authorities not to breach a person's ECHR rights (section 6); and the requirement on the
Minister with responsibility for a Bill introduced to Parliament to make a statement of the
Bill's compatibility with ECHR rights (section 19).

The HRA and the rights that it protects have a relationship with the Act in several ways.   **13.88**
Firstly, from a general perspective, like all primary legislation, the Act must be interpreted by
the courts (and others, such as public authorities) compatibly with ECHR rights so far as is
possible to do so. In addition, the government is required pursuant to section 19 of the HRA
to make a statement of the compatibility of the Equality Bill with ECHR rights when it is
introduced to Parliament. Secondly, a number of rights under the ECHR have a close and

---

[109] This was recognized by the then Home Secretary, Jack Straw, when the Human Rights Act entered into
force. See, e.g., a speech he delivered to the Institute of Public Policy Research on 13 January 2000. It has
also been recognized internationally. For example, on the first page of his leading textbook on Bills of Rights,
Philip Alston identifies the UK's Human Rights Act as a Bill of Rights: *Promoting Human Rights Through Bills
of Rights—Comparative Perspectives* (Clarenden Press 2000), p. 1.

sometimes overlapping relationship with issues of discrimination law. For example, Articles 3, 8, 9, and 14 raise issues of the right to dignity and respect in treatment, personal identity, and the manifestation of that identity, and the right to non-discrimination in the enjoyment of those rights. Thirdly, the relationship between ECHR rights and the Act has implications for bringing proceedings for a breach of the Act, as in a number of situations it may also be possible to bring a claim of a breach of ECHR rights under the HRA. The following section examines how several of the substantive ECHR rights and Article 14 are relevant to issues of equality law.

3. Significance of ECHR Rights for Equality Law

13.89 All the substantive ECHR rights are relevant to equality law since Article 14 requires that the enjoyment of all the rights and freedoms must be 'secured without discrimination on any grounds'. However, there are several rights and freedoms that have particular links with notions of equality and the enjoyment of rights by particular groups. The most important of these are Articles 3, 8, 9, and 14. Articles 3, 8, and 9 are discussed below and Article 14 is discussed in section 4 below.

(a) *Article 3*

13.90 Article 3 requires that no one shall be subjected to torture or to inhuman or degrading treatment. Article 3 is an absolute right in that its breach can never be justified and the right can never be derogated from. Treatment has been held to be inhuman or degrading 'if, to a seriously detrimental extent, it denies the most basic needs of any human being. As in all article 3 cases, the treatment to be proscribed, must achieve a minimum standard of severity, and ... in a context ... not involving the deliberate infliction of pain or suffering, the threshold is a high one.'[110]

13.91 Article 3, in terms of the right not to be subjected to inhuman or degrading treatment, is relevant to issues of equality in a number of situations, such as the treatment of asylum seekers,[111] the detention and treatment of disabled and older persons, as well as the treatment of children.[112] It links to key concepts of equality in terms of being treated with dignity and respect, and the prohibition on discrimination in the provision of services in Part 3 of the Act (see Chapter 5).

13.92 In relation to the treatment of asylum seekers, the House of Lords held in *Limbuela* that denying them basic support such as shelter and food may, in certain circumstances, constitute inhuman or degrading treatment.[113]

13.93 In *Price* the European Court of Human Rights (ECtHR) held that the detention of a severely disabled person in conditions where she was dangerously cold, risks developing sores because her bed was too hard or unreachable, and was unable to go to the toilet or keep clean without the greatest of difficulty constituted degrading treatment. This was despite the absence of any intention to subject her to degrading treatment. As a result, Article 3 may

---

[110] *R v Secretary of State for the Home Department ex p Limbuela, R v Secretary of State for the Home Department ex p Tesema (Conjoined appeals)* [2005] UKHL 66, para. 7.

[111] *ibid.*

[112] *Price v UK* (2002) 34 EHRR 53.

[113] *Limbuela* (n. 114 above). The Court held that the Nationality, Immigration and Asylum Act 2002 s. 55 violated Art. 3.

therefore be engaged in situations where persons are detained for mental health reasons and the treatment of disabled or older persons in hospitals and care homes.[114]

In relation to the detention of children in secure training centres, the Court of Appeal held in *R* **13.94** *(C) v Secretary of State for Justice*[115] that restraining rules that permitted children to be restrained by staff for 'good order and discipline' and included very painful rib and thumb 'distractions', breached Article 3 and the Article 8 right to private life. The rules were quashed by the Court of Appeal.

(b) *Article 8*

In the context of the treatment of gypsies and travellers, it has been said that the overarch- **13.95** ing aim of Article 8 is to protect 'rights of central importance to the individual's identity, self-determination, physical and moral integrity, maintenance of relationships with others and a settled and secure place in the community'.[116] Article 8 consists of four elements: private life, family life, home, and correspondence. The first three have particular links to notions of equality and non-discrimination. These rights are qualified and can be limited for reasons such as public safety, to prevent disorder or crime, or for the rights and protection of others.[117]

(i) *Private life* The right to private life is a broad concept which has been held to include **13.96** personal identity, integrity, as well as personal autonomy in the sense of being able to conduct one's life as one chooses.[118] This has clear links to situations of inequality, as any state measures differentiating between people on grounds of personal status (such as the protected characteristics of gender reassignment, sexual orientation, or race) or lifestyle will fall within the ambit of private life, and therefore be required to be justified by the state.

Sexuality has been held to be a 'most intimate aspect' of an individual's private life.[119] **13.97** Differences in treatment based on sexual orientation 'require particularly serious reasons by way of justification'.[120] A number of cases have found breaches of private life based on a person's sexual orientation. The ECtHR held in *Smith and Grady v UK* that the investigation by the Ministry of Defence into the sexual orientation of members of the services and their subsequent discharge were 'especially grave' interferences with private life.[121] In *EB v France*, the ECtHR found a violation of Articles 8 and 14 where a homosexual woman in a long term relationship was refused approval to adopt a baby.[122] In relation to gender identity, the ECtHR held in *Goodwin v UK* that the UK had failed to comply with its positive obligation to ensure the right to private life of the applicant (a post-operative male-to-female transsexual), by not providing legal recognition to her gender reassignment.[123] This led to the enactment of the Gender Recognition Act 2004.

More recently, the issue of the right to private life of transgender people was examined in **13.98** the case of *R(TT) v Registrar General*.[124] It involved a claim by a transgender male who had

---

[114] *Price* (n. 116 above). See e.g., *YL (by her litigation friend the Official Solicitor) (FC) v Birmingham City Council and Others* [2007] UKHL 27.
[115] [2008] EWCA Civ 882.
[116] *Connors v UK* (2005) 40 EHRR 9, para. 82.
[117] Art. 8(2).
[118] *Pretty v UK* (1998) 26 EHRR 241, para. 32.
[119] *Dudgeon v UK* (1981) 4 EHRR 149.
[120] *Karner v Austria* (2003) 14 BHRC 674, para. 37; *Dudgeon v UK* (n. 123 above), para. 41.
[121] (2000) 29 EHRR 548.
[122] (2008) 47 EHRR 21.
[123] (2002) 35 EHRR 447.
[124] [2019] EWHC 2384 (Fam).

undergone gender transition from a female to a male, and was legally recognized as a male in a Gender Recognition Certificate. He subsequently gave birth to a child and wished to be legally recognized as either the 'father' or 'parent' of the child. The registrar required that he be registered as the child's 'mother'. The claimant argued that it was a breach of his Article 8 right to private life to not be recognized either as the 'father' or 'parent'. However the Family Division of the High Court held that, although there was an interference with his private life, such interference was proportionate and justified to ensure there was a consistent and coherent scheme for the registration of birth, which always records the person who gave birth to a child as the 'mother'.

13.99   (ii) *Family life*   Formal unions such as marriage clearly constitute family life, but the jurisprudence has expanded the scope of family life to non-formal relationships, such as de facto relationships.

13.100   Homosexual[125] and transsexual[126] unions have previously been held by the ECtHR not to be protected by family life, although, as discussed above, these may be protected under the right to private life. Domestically, the courts have also adopted a narrow view. In *Secretary of State for Work and Pensions v M*,[127] the House of Lords held that on the present state of Strasbourg jurisprudence, homosexual relationships do not fall within the scope of the right to family life. The position in relation to homosexual relationships has more recently changed, however, as a result of the decision of *Schalk and Kopf v Austria*.[128] The ECtHR held for the first time that same-sex relationships do fall within the scope of family life. The claimants were a same-sex couple who brought proceedings in Austria arguing that the fact they were unable to marry or have some form of similar union was in breach of their rights under Articles 12, 8, and 14. The Court unanimously held that there was no breach of the Article 12 right to marriage as that right under the ECHR is only available to heterosexual couples. In relation to the Articles 8 and 14 claims, the majority of the Court (4 to 3) held that there had been no breach of the Article 8 right to family life or the Article 14 right to non-discrimination in the enjoyment of that right. Although it was noted that there was a growing trend of some form of recognition of same-sex relationships, there was currently no majority of Member States to provide such recognition. Given the strong minority view that there had been a breach of Articles 8 and 14 and the increasing formal recognition of same-sex relationships across Europe, it is likely that this issue will be revisited by the ECtHR in the future.

13.101   (iii) *Home*   The House of Lords has held that a person's home constitutes the place where a person 'lives and to which he returns and which forms the centre of his existence'.[129] The right to a home is relevant to Part 4 of the Act, which relates to discrimination and reasonable adjustments for premises (see Chapter 6).

13.102   The right to respect for the home is of particular relevance to the protected characteristics of disability and race in the context of the treatment of gypsies and travellers. For example, in relation to disability the Court of Appeal found that respect for the home obliged a health authority to act fairly in removing a disabled resident from a care home after it promised she would remain there for life.[130]

---

[125] *S v UK* (1986) 47 DR 274.
[126] *X v UK* (1997) 24 EHRR 143.
[127] [2006] UKHL 11.
[128] (Application No. 30141/04) 24 June 2010.
[129] *London Borough of Harrow v Qazi* [2004] 1 AC 983, para. 8, per Lord Bingham.
[130] *R v North and East Devon District Health Authority ex p Coughlan* [2001] QB 213.

In relation to gypsies and travellers, a crucial issue they face is the limited number of   **13.103**
authorized sites across Britain. This inhibits their ability to maintain a travelling lifestyle. As
many are forced to camp on unauthorized sites and in certain circumstances are evicted, this
raises possible breaches of the right to a home. Two key decisions in the ECtHR relating to
the Article 8 right to a home of gypsies and travellers are *Buckley v UK*[131] and *Chapman v
UK*.[132] The Court expressly recognized that the vulnerable position of gypsies and travellers as
a minority racial group means special consideration should be given to their needs and their
different lifestyles both in the relevant regulatory planning framework for providing sites
and in arriving at decisions in particular cases.[133] Further to that extent, there is a positive
obligation on the state to 'facilitate the Gypsy way of life'.[134] However, the ECtHR has also
indicated that in relation to such planning policies and decisions on sites for gypsies, the state
has a wide margin of appreciation and in practice it is often difficult to establish a breach of
Article 8 in such circumstances.[135]

(c) *Article 9*

Article 9 relates to religious freedom and consists of two elements. First, by Article 9(1) it   **13.104**
provides an absolute right to hold a religion or belief. Secondly, by Article 9(2) it provides a
right to manifest that religion or belief. However, this is a qualified right that can be limited
where the limitation is prescribed in law and is necessary in a democratic society in the interests of public safety, for the protection of public order, health, or morals, or for the protection
of the rights and freedoms of others. Article 9 links to the provisions in the Act prohibiting
religious or racial discrimination, both in employment (see Chapter 4) and the provision of
services, including education (see Chapters 5 and 6). It also is relevant in some situations to
the issue of the balance between the right to freedom of religion, and the protections from
sexual orientation or gender identity discrimination under the Act.

Article 9 jurisprudence has influenced the development of the discrimination law relating   **13.105**
to religion or belief in several ways. First, it has influenced the understanding of the scope of
religious and other beliefs protected. Secondly, it has impacted on the test for whether any
indirect discrimination on grounds of religion or belief is justified, as that test is analogous to
the test of justification under Article 9(2).

Article 9 protects mainstream religious faiths such as Christianity, Islam, Judaism, and   **13.106**
Buddhism. It protects non-religious belief such as atheism and agnosticism[136] and certain
philosophical beliefs such as pacifism[137] and veganism.[138] It does not protect political beliefs,
although this is protected under the Article 10 right to freedom of expression.

In relation to Article 9(2), the ECtHR and domestic courts have, for a number of reasons,   **13.107**
previously taken a narrow approach to manifestations of religious belief and not often found
a breach of that right. Firstly, there must be a direct connection between the belief and its
manifestation such that the act of manifestation is 'intimately linked' to the belief.[139] Secondly,

---

[131] (1996) 23 EHRR 101.
[132] (2001) 33 EHRR 399.
[133] See *Buckley* (n. 135 above), paras 76, 80, and 84.
[134] See *Chapman* (n. 136 above), para. 96.
[135] See *Buckley* (n. 135 above), para. 75 and *Chapman* (n. 136 above), para. 92.
[136] *Kokkinakis v Greece* (1994) 17 EHRR 397.
[137] *Arrowsmith v UK* (1987) 19 DR 5.
[138] *H v UK* (1993) 16 EHRR CD 44.
[139] *R (Williamson) v Secretary of State for Education and Employment* [2005] UKHL 15.

the courts have often been unwilling to recognize that there has been any interference with the manifestation of a belief. For example, in *Karaduman v Turkey*, a woman challenged a refusal to let her graduate from university unless she was photographed without her headscarf. The Commission found that the woman had chosen to pursue higher education in a secular university and submitted to its rules so there was no interference established.[140] A crucial factor in the reasoning of a number of decisions is the extent of choice a person has in continuing to manifest his/her belief, for example by moving school or changing employment. Thirdly, even if an interference is established, the court often finds that the interference is justified.

13.108   Justification for an interference with the right to manifest a religion or belief can take a number of forms, such as the need to promote a secular society[141] and the need for dress codes in schools to promote religious harmony.[142] In the *Begum* case, it was held that the refusal to permit a student to wear the jilbab was a proportionate response to a legitimate aim of protecting the rights and freedoms of others. A crucial factor was the care with which the school had designed the uniform policy responding to a range of religious identities and permitting a range of dress for Muslims, including the shalwar kameeze and headscarf.

13.109   It is, however, to be noted that there is possibly a divergence in approaches emerging between discrimination law and the jurisprudence relating to Article 9. In *R (Watkins-Singh) v Governing Body of Aberdare Girls' High School*[143] a girl brought a discrimination claim under the Race Relations Act 1976, alleging that the school had discriminated against her for refusing to allow her to wear the Sikh 'kara' bangle. The court found that there had been indirect race discrimination and that it was not justified.[144]

13.110   The relationship between Article 9 and the prohibition on religious discrimination under the Equality Act 2010 was reconsidered in four significant British cases before the ECtHR.[145] These involved two categories of cases. The cases of *Eweida v British Airways Plc*[146] and *Chaplin v Royal Devon and Exeter Trust*[147] concerned employment dress codes that prohibited the external display of crosses. Both claims failed in the UK courts, in respect of direct and indirect religious discrimination and claimed breaches of Article 9. Before the ECtHR, in *Eweida* the court found a breach of Article 9, but in *Chaplin* it found no breach. In *Eweida* the court decided that it was a disproportionate interference with the claimant's Article 9 rights by refusing her wearing a Christian cross externally while working as a flight attendant. The court took a broader approach than previously on Article 9 in two respects. Firstly, it held that the visible wearing of a cross or other manifestation does not need to be a mandatory requirement of a religion in order to be protected. Secondly, it held the fact that an employee can change employment should not be determinative as to whether there was an interference with Article 9 rights, but a factor in deciding whether policies were proportionate. This broader approach to issues of interference with manifesting a religion or belief is of

---

[140] (1993) 74 DR 93.

[141] *Sahin v Turkey* (2005) 41 EHRR 8.

[142] *R (SB) v Governors of Denbigh High School* [2006] UKHL 15 ('the *Begum* case').

[143] [2008] EWHC 1865 (Admin).

[144] It should also be borne in mind that a significant factor in the decision was that the defendant had failed to comply with its race equality duty under the Race Relations Act 1976, s. 71. S. 149 provides a new equality duty which includes the characteristics of race and religion or belief.

[145] *Eweida v UK* (Application No. 48420/10); *Chaplin v UK* (Application No. 59842/10); *Ladele v UK* (Application No. 51671/10); and *McFarlane v UK* (Application No. 36516/10).

[146] [2010] EWCA Civ 80.

[147] [2010] ET 1702886/2009.

direct relevance to the future interpretation and application of the indirect religious discrimination provisions in the Act. Issues of justification for indirect discrimination will need to be
applied consistently with the approach under Article 9.

The second category of cases of *Ladele v London Borough of Islington*[148] and *McFarlane*   13.111
v Relate Avon Ltd[149] concerned employees who refused to perform services (conducting
civil partnerships in the case of *Ladele* and providing relationship counselling in the case of
McFarlane) to same-sex couples. In both cases claims of indirect religious discrimination and
breaches of Articles 9 and 14 failed in the UK courts. The indirect religious discrimination
against Ladele was held to be justified: requiring her to conduct civil partnerships served a
legitimate aim of a public authority preventing discrimination and in the circumstances it
was proportionate. In relation to the case of *McFarlane* it was also held that it was justified to
require a relationship counsellor to provide those services without discrimination on grounds
of sexual orientation. The ECtHR held in relation to both *Ladele* and *McFarlane* that there
had been no breach of Articles 9 and 14 as an interference with the right to manifest their
religion was justified to protect persons from discrimination on grounds of sexual orientation. The decisions highlight the balance that should be drawn between freedom of religion
and protecting other groups from discrimination. They reiterate the principles that where
services are provided to the public, the right to manifest your religion can be restricted to
prevent discrimination on grounds of sexual orientation.

A more recent decision by the Court of Appeal, has examined the extremely difficult issues   13.112
concerning rights of a transgender woman to have access to her children, in the context of
Article 9 rights of the other family members who sought to deny such access. The case of *M
(Children)* involved a transgender woman who had, prior to her gender transition, fathered five
children.[150] The claimant was ostracized by her ultra orthodox Jewish community, and because
she was transgender, her children faced ostracism by the community if they had direct contact
with her. The Court of Appeal allowed her appeal against the lower court's decision to deny her
access to her children on the basis of family law, but the court also made important observations
on the limits of the Article 9 right to manifest your religious beliefs. In particular it observed
that a restriction on the Jewish community's right to manifest their religion by denying access
of the children to the claimant was justified. This is because such a restriction on the Article 9
right had a legitimate aim of protecting the children's rights to have access to their parent.[151]

4. Article 14: The Right to Non-discrimination

(a) *The Developing Importance of Article 14*

The right to equality and non-discrimination is a fundamental human right recognized in   13.113
many international human rights treaties[152] and equality of treatment has been recognized
as 'one of the building blocks of democracy'.[153] Article 14 seeks to ensure that all persons are

---

[148] [2009] EWCA Civ 1357.
[149] [2010] EWCA Civ 880.
[150] [2017] EWFC 4.
[151] *ibid*, paras 130–135.
[152] For example, Art. 26 of the International Covenant on Civil and Political Rights, Art. 2(1) of the
Convention on the Elimination of Racial Discrimination, Art. 2 of the Convention on the Elimination of
Discrimination Against Women, Art. 5 of the Convention on the Rights of Persons with Disabilities.
[153] Per Lord Hoffmann in *Matadeen v Pointu* [1999] AC 98, PC.

able to enjoy the rights under the ECHR without discrimination. As a result, Article 14 is a key provision of the ECHR and, given its links with domestic discrimination law, it is vital to appreciate how it interacts with discrimination law.

13.114 It should be recognized that the importance of Article 14 has evolved and enhanced over time. For a considerable period the case law in the ECtHR on Article 14 was undeveloped and provided a narrow interpretation of certain concepts of discrimination, such as indirect discrimination. One of the reasons for this was that in the past the ECtHR took the approach that if it found a breach of a substantive right, it was unnecessary to go on to consider whether there had been a breach of Article 14. In *Airey v Ireland* the court found that where a violation of a substantive provision is found, further examination of Article 14 is 'not generally required' unless 'a clear inequality of treatment in the enjoyment of the rights in question is a fundamental aspect of the case'.[154] In *Dudgeon v UK* the ECtHR went further, stating that examining Article 14 once a violation of a substantive provision had been found served 'no useful purpose'.[155] As a result, although the Court found a breach of Article 8 in respect of private life, it found it unnecessary to consider whether there was discrimination on grounds of sexual orientation. This approach has been criticized by a number of judges and commentators.[156]

13.115 More recently the ECtHR has taken a more expansive and progressive approach to the consideration of Article 14 claims generally and to its interpretation of concepts of discrimination.[157] In the landmark decision *DH v Czech Republic*, the Grand Chamber substantially broadened the interpretation of indirect discrimination before the ECtHR and relied on the EU Equality Directives in analysing discrimination concepts. This constitutes a movement towards further harmonization of discrimination concepts between the EU and the ECHR.[158]

(b) *The Scope of Article 14*

13.116 Article 14 does not provide a free-standing guarantee of equal treatment but rather that the enjoyment of other ECHR rights shall be secured without discrimination.[159] Although Protocol 12 of the ECHR does provide a free-standing prohibition on discrimination, this is yet to be signed or ratified by the UK government. Article 14 is only engaged when the facts of a case come within the ambit of another Convention right, although it is not necessary to establish a breach of another Convention right.[160] This is an important difference from the manner in which domestic and EU discrimination law is constructed.[161]

13.117 Although the effect of Article 14 is circumscribed by the engagement of other Convention rights, it is wider in scope than UK domestic discrimination provisions in the Act as it prohibits discrimination against a much broader range of groups. Article 14 states that the rights shall be secured without discrimination 'on any ground such as sex, race, colour, language, religion, political or other opinion, national or social origin, association with a national minority, property, birth or other status'.

---

[154] (1979) 2 EHRR 305.
[155] (1981) 4 EHRR 149, para. 69.
[156] For example, in *Dudgeon*, dissenting opinion of Matscher J.
[157] *Stec v UK* (2005) 41 EHRR SE295 and *DH v Czech Republic* (2007) 23 BHRC 526.
[158] *ibid.*
[159] Art. 14 is more limited, e.g., than Art. 26 of the International Convention on Civil and Political Rights.
[160] *Abdulaziz, Cabales and Balkndali v UK* (1985) 7 EHRR 471.
[161] Although Art. 21 of the EU Charter of Fundamental Rights does provide a free-standing right to non-discrimination which will apply in the implementation of EU law.

'Other status' has been held to cover a number of characteristics such as nationality,[162]   **13.118**
immigration status,[163] sexual orientation,[164] disability,[165] and being homeless.[166]

Domestic courts in a number of cases have equated the term 'other status' with 'personal   **13.119**
characteristics' and that any distinction must relate to a characteristic intrinsic to the person concerned, as opposed to historical facts.[167] This approach has been criticized in some
jurisdictions. However, a more fluid approach was taken by Lord Walker in the *RJM* House
of Lords decision concerning homelessness as a status under Article 14. Lord Walker stated
that 'personal characteristics' is not a precise expression and that the key issue was 'the more
peripheral or debateable any suggested personal characteristic is, the less likely it is to come
within the most sensitive area where discrimination is particularly difficult to justify'.[168]

(c) *Direct and Indirect Discrimination*

Discrimination occurs where there is both discriminatory treatment of individuals in 'rel-   **13.120**
evantly similar' or analogous situations, and there is no objective or reasonable justification
for the distinction in treatment.

Article 14 is different from domestic discrimination concepts in a number of ways. First,   **13.121**
unlike domestic discrimination law and EU equality law, the terms of Article 14 do not
expressly provide for both direct and indirect discrimination being unlawful. However, case
law has clearly established that Article 14 is broad enough to encompass both direct and indirect discrimination. As a result, this may require not only that persons in the same situations
are treated equally (direct discrimination), but also to situations 'where States without an
objective and reasonable justification fail to treat differently persons whose situations are significantly different' (indirect discrimination).[169] Secondly, Article 14—unlike most domestic
discrimination law—permits direct discrimination to be justified, although in practice such
discrimination will be very difficult to justify in relation to certain suspect classes (see paragraphs 13.99 to 13.102 on justification).

A number of decisions have found that no Article 14 issue is raised as the facts of the case   **13.122**
establish no comparator in an analogous situation.[170] However, more recent domestic cases
on Article 14 have begun to stress that the selection of a comparator is only part of a 'framework' of useful analysis, and that it is not a barrier to asking the overarching question, namely
whether two cases are sufficiently similar to require a court to ask itself whether the difference
in treatment is nonetheless justified.[171]

In relation to indirect discrimination, the ECtHR provided an in-depth and progressive   **13.123**
analysis of the necessary elements. In *DH v Czech Republic* (paragraph 13.90), the Grand
Chamber considered whether the disproportionate placing of Roma children in 'special
schools' with a reduced curriculum was in breach of Article 2 of Protocol 1 (right to an
education) and Article 14. The case was significant in a number of respects: it re-affirmed the

---

[162] *Gaygusuz v Austria* (1996) 23 EHRR 364.
[163] *A v Secretary of State for the Home Department* [2005] 2 AC 68.
[164] *Ghaidan v Godin-Mendoza* [2004] UKHL 30.
[165] *Glor v Switzerland* (Application No. 13444/04) 30 April 2009.
[166] *R (RJM) v Secretary of State for Work and Pensions* [2008] UKHL 63.
[167] *R (Marper) v Chief Constable of South Yorkshire* [2004] 1 WLR 2196.
[168] *RJM* (n. 170 above), para. 5, per Lord Walker.
[169] *Thlimmenos v Greece* (2000) 31 EHRR 411.
[170] *Van der Mussele v Belgium* (1983) 6 EHRR 163.
[171] *R (Carson) v Secretary of State for Work and Pensions* [2005] UKHL 37.

concept that indirect discrimination may occur where a neutral policy had a disproportionate impact on a particular group; it held that the use of statistical data is prima facie evidence of indirect discrimination; and it held that there is a shift in burden of proof where a claimant establishes evidence of discrimination. In relation to statistics, the Court relied on statistics of the over-representation of Roma children in such schools without analysing the facts of the individual cases of the 18 Roma children applicants. In relation to the burden of proof, the Grand Chamber held that where an applicant proves facts indicating that a policy is discriminatory, the burden of proof shifts to the state to show that the difference in treatment was not discriminatory. The decision therefore brings the ECtHR jurisprudence closer into line with domestic and EU law concepts of discrimination.

(d) *Justification*

13.124 Under Article 14, discrimination can be justified in a similar manner as under the Act, where it is for a legitimate aim and the means used to achieve that aim are proportionate and necessary.[172]

13.125 In accessing justification, the ECtHR affords states a certain 'margin of appreciation' in accessing whether or not and to what extent differences in treatment are justified. Discrimination based on certain 'suspect classes', in particular, sex, race, nationality, religion, and sexual orientation, will be subject to particularly rigorous scrutiny and will require 'very weighty reasons' if they are to be held as justified.[173]

13.126 In relation to disability, the ECtHR has more recently found violations of Article 14 in relation to the differential treatment of disabled persons in a variety of situations such as the right to private and family life, education, and property.[174] Of particular note is the fact that the ECtHR has interpreted the prohibition on discrimination under Article 14 as including a failure to provide reasonable accommodation for disabled people, consistent with the obligations under the United Nations Convention on the Rights of Persons with Disabilities (CRPD). For example, the recently decided *Cam* case concerned a refusal to enrol the claimant as a student in the Turkish National Music Academy because she was blind. The ECtHR decided that there had been a violation of Article 14 and the right to education under Article 2 of Protocol 1 of the ECHR for failure to provide reasonable accommodation. This highlights the similar and increasingly consistent approaches to disability discrimination under the ECHR, the Act, and the CRPD.

13.127 Recently the ECtHR decided the case of *JD and A v United Kingdom*[175] which examined justifications for disability and sex discrimination in the context of reduced housing benefits for social housing. The two claimants respectively claimed disability and sex discrimination under Article 14 and Article 1 of Protocol 1 which provides the right to property. The Supreme Court had dismissed both the claims. The ECtHR held that the reduction in housing benefit in relation to people with disabilities was justified. However, in relation to the second claim of sex discrimination, the court noted that the housing benefit was provided for the specific purpose to protect women from serious cases of domestic violence, and enable them to stay in suitable homes for that purpose. The reduction in housing benefit which

---

[172] *Ghaidan v Godin-Mendoza* [2004] UKHL 30.

[173] *R (Carson) v Secretary of State for Work and Pensions* [2006] 1 AC 173, para. 16, per Lord Hoffmann.

[174] *Glor v Switzerland* (Application No. 13444/04) 30 April 2009, *Cam v Turkey* (Application No. 51500/08) 23 February 2016, and *Guberina v Croatia* (Application No. 23682/13) 22 March 2016.

[175] *JD and A v United Kingdom* (Application Nos. 32949/17 and 34614/17) 24 October 2019.

aimed at incentivizing them to leave those homes was therefore not justified, and there was a violation of Article 14 in conjunction with Article 1 Protocol 1.

In relation to age, Member States are provided a wide margin of appreciation and it has **13.128** not been held by the ECtHR to be a suspect class requiring very weighty reasons to justify discrimination.[176] The House of Lords has also held that discrimination on grounds of old age 'may be a contemporary example of a borderline case' where it is difficult to categorize as suspect or not.[177] The fact that, in relation to EU law, it is accepted that even direct discrimination on grounds of age can be justified in appropriate circumstances, may mean it is less likely that age will be treated as a suspect class.[178]

D. THE UNITED NATIONS CONVENTIONS

The final key international influence over the protected groups in the Act is the United **13.129** Nations and the international human rights obligations under key Conventions. The United Nations is an intergovernmental body that was established in 1945 after the Second World War to replace the League of Nations. It has similar goals to the Council of Europe in terms of promoting democracy and the protection of human rights, but has global membership. There are currently 193 Member States from around the world, including the UK.

Human rights have been promoted within the organization and around the world by a series **13.130** of declarations, covenants, and conventions. In 1948 the UN General Assembly signed the Universal Declaration of Human Rights which calls on all Member States to provide a common standard of human rights protections for everyone. This also led to the development of a series of covenants and conventions protecting particular types of human rights or particular groups. There are seven key documents: the International Covenant on Civil and Political Rights 1966 (ICCPR), the International Covenant on Economic, Social and Cultural Rights 1966 (ICESCR), the Convention Against Torture 1984 (CAT), the Convention on the Elimination of All Forms of Racial Discrimination 1966 (CERD), the Convention on the Elimination of All Forms of Discrimination Against Women 1979 (CEDAW), the Convention on the Rights of the Child 1989 (CRC), and the Convention on the Rights of Persons with Disabilities 2006 (CRPD). The UK government has ratified and is a party to all of these documents, which means that it is bound by them in international law. They are not, however, binding in domestic law (unlike, for example, the ECHR), as they have not been directly incorporated.

The Conventions relating to the rights of particular groups (CERD, CEDAW, CRC, and **13.131** CRPD) are relevant to the Act in a number of different respects. First, the Act is one means by which the UK government gives effect to its obligations under the Conventions. For example, the Conventions all require states parties to prohibit discrimination against the groups in a number of contexts which link to the sectors in which discrimination is prohibited under the Act.[179] The provisions in the Act may come under scrutiny by the United Nations committees that periodically examine state parties' compliance with the Conventions. For

---

[176] *Schwizgebel v Switzerland* (Application No. 24724/94).

[177] *R (Carson) v Secretary of State for Work and Pensions* [2006] 1 AC 173, para. 17, per Lord Hoffmann.

[178] See the Framework Directive 2000/78/EC in relation to employment and the Proposed Goods and Services Directive.

[179] For example, Art. 2 of the CERD; Art. 2 of the CEDAW; Art. 2 of the CRC; and Arts 4 and 5 of the CRPD.

example, in the most recent examination of the UK government's compliance under the CERD, the UN Committee recommended that the exception permitting racial discrimination in immigration functions be repealed for non-compliance with the CERD.[180] Finally, a number of the Conventions have individual petition mechanisms which permit individuals to bring claims before the relevant UN Committee where it is argued that their rights have been breached under the Conventions.[181] The UK government has agreed the individual petition mechanism in relation to the CEDAW and the CRPD, but not the CERD. This mechanism does, however, have its limitations as it is only available where all domestic and other international remedies have been exhausted, and there is no entitlement to a remedy, given that the UN Committees do not have the status of courts. Nevertheless, the individual petition mechanism may provide individuals with possible alternative measures to seek access to justice on claims relating to the Act or the HRA, once those claims have been determined domestically or internationally.

13.132   Although the Conventions are not binding in domestic law, where appropriate they have been applied in the interpretation of both claims of discrimination under the Act, and claims under the HRA, for example of breaches of the right to non-discrimination in the enjoyment of other rights under Article 14 of the ECHR.

13.133   In the context of claims of disability discrimination under the Act the CRPD has been referred to and relied on in different contexts. For example in relation to evictions of disabled tenants in social housing, the CRPD was relied on by the Supreme Court in explaining the differences between the test for disability discrimination under the Act and the right to respect for the home under the HRA and Article 8 of the ECHR.[182] Lady Hale who delivered the leading judgment, referred to the fact that the provisions of the Act provide rights to be protected from disability discrimination, including the distinct obligation to be provided reasonable accommodation by social landlords, consistent with obligations of reasonable accommodation under the CRPD.[183]

13.134   The relevance and application of the CRC has also been examined in detail by the Supreme Court in an HRA claim concerning caps to welfare benefits for claimants in non-working households.[184] The relevant legislation was challenged on the basis that it unjustifiably discriminated between men and women contrary to Article 14 of the ECHR, read with Article 1 of Protocol 1 in relation to the right to property. The legislation was argued to not only discriminate against women, but also to adversely affect the children of the families. A key issue was the extent to which the CRC was relevant in interpreting the rights under the ECHR and in particular the Article 3(1) obligation to take into account the best interests of children in all matters affecting children. The Supreme Court confirmed that, consistent with case law of the ECtHR,[185] the obligations under Article 3(1) of the CRC should be considered in interpreting the obligations under the ECHR where it is relevant to the particular rights in question.

---

[180] UN Committee on the Elimination of all Racial Discrimination, Concluding Observations, CERD/C/GBR/CO/18–20, 14 September 2011, para. 16.

[181] Currently the individual petition mechanism exists in relation to the CERD, CEDAW, and CRPD. An individual petition mechanism for the CRC was agreed by the UN General Assembly on 19 December 2011 and will enter into force once 10 UN Member States have ratified it.

[182] *Akerman-Livingstone v Aster Communities Limited (formerly Flourish Homes Limited)* [2015] UKSC 15.

[183] *ibid*, paras 25 and 26.

[184] *R (on the application of SG and others) v Secretary for Work and Pensions* [2015] UKSC 16.

[185] For example, *Demir v Turkey* (2008) 48 EHRR 1272.

Equality Act 2010 (as amended)[1]

An Act to make provision to require Ministers of the Crown and others when making strategic decisions about the exercise of their functions to have regard to the desirability of reducing socio-economic inequalities; to reform and harmonise equality law and restate the greater part of the enactments relating to discrimination and harassment related to certain personal characteristics; to enable certain employers to be required to publish information about the differences in pay between male and female employees; to prohibit victimisation in certain circumstances; to require the exercise of certain functions to be with regard to the need to eliminate discrimination and other prohibited conduct; to enable duties to be imposed in relation to the exercise of public procurement functions; to increase equality of opportunity; to amend the law relating to rights and responsibilities in family relationships; and for connected purposes.

[8th April 2010]

BE IT ENACTED by the Queen's most Excellent Majesty, by and with the advice and consent of the Lords Spiritual and Temporal, and Commons, in this present

Parliament assembled, and by the authority of the same, as follows:—

PART 1
SOCIO-ECONOMIC INEQUALITIES

1 Public sector duty regarding socio-economic inequalities

(1)   An authority to which this section applies must, when making decisions of a strategic nature about how to exercise its functions, have due regard to the desirability of exercising them in a way that is designed to reduce the inequalities of outcome which result from socio-economic disadvantage.

(2)   In deciding how to fulfil a duty to which it is subject under subsection (1), an authority must take into account any guidance issued [in accordance with subsection (2A)][2].

[(2A) The guidance to be taken into account under subsection (2) is—

    (a)   in the case of a duty imposed on an authority in relation to devolved Scottish functions, guidance issued by the Scottish Ministers;

    [(aa) in the case of a duty imposed on an authority in relation to devolved Welsh functions, guidance issued by the Welsh Ministers;][3]

    (b)   in any other case, guidance issued by a Minister of the Crown.][4]

---

[1] We have endeavoured to amend the Act with any changes that were available up to May 2020.
[2] Substituted by Scotland Act 2016.
[3] Inserted by Wales Act 2017.
[4] Inserted by Scotland Act 2016.

[England and Wales]

(3)   The authorities to which this section applies are—

      (a) a Minister of the Crown;

      (b) a government department other than the Security Service, the Secret Intelligence Service or the Government Communications Headquarters;

      (c) a county council or district council in England;

      (d) the Greater London Authority;

      (e) a London borough council;

      (f) the Common Council of the City of London in its capacity as a local authority;

      (g) the Council of the Isles of Scilly;

    (h)–(i) [...][5]

      (j) [...][6]

      (k) a [police and crime commissioner][7] established for an area in England.

[Scotland]

[(3)   The authorities to which this section applies are—

      (a) the Scottish Ministers;

      (b) Food Standards Scotland;

      (c) Keeper of the Registers of Scotland;

      (d) National Records of Scotland;

      (e) Revenue Scotland;

      (f) Scottish Courts and Tribunals Service;

      (g) a council constituted under section 2 of the Local Government etc. (Scotland) Act 1994;

      (h) an integration joint board established under section 9(2) of the Public Bodies (Joint Working) (Scotland) Act 2014;

      (i) a Health Board constituted under section 2(1)(a) of the National Health Service (Scotland) Act 1978;

      (j) a Special Health Board constituted under section 2(1)(b) of that Act;

      (k) Scottish Police Authority;

      (l) Highlands and Islands Enterprise;

    (m) Scottish Enterprise.][8]

(4)–(5) [...][9]

    (6) The reference to inequalities in subsection (1) does not include any inequalities experienced by a person as a result of being a person subject to immigration control within the meaning given by section 115(9) of the Immigration and Asylum Act 1999.

2 Power to amend section 1

(1) A Minister of the Crown may by regulations amend section 1 so as to—

    (a) add a public authority to the authorities that are subject to the duty under subsection (1) of that section;

    (b) remove an authority from those that are subject to the duty;

---

   [5] Repealed by Health and Social Care Act 2012.

   [6] Repealed by Public Bodies Act 2011.

   [7] Substituted by Police Reform and Social Responsibility Act 2011.

   [8] Substituted by Equality Act 2010 (Authorities subject to the Socioeconomic Inequality Duty) (Scotland) Regulations 2018, SI 2018/101.

   [9] Repealed by Deregulation Act 2015.

(c) make the duty apply, in the case of a particular authority, only in relation to certain functions that it has;

(d) in the case of an authority to which the application of the duty is already restricted to certain functions, remove or alter the restriction.

(2) In subsection (1) 'public authority' means an authority that has functions of a public nature.

(3) Provision made under subsection (1) may not impose a duty on an authority in relation to any devolved Scottish functions or devolved Welsh functions.

(4) The Scottish Ministers or the Welsh Ministers may by regulations amend section 1 so as to—

(a) add a relevant authority to the authorities that are subject to the duty under subsection (1) of that section;

(b) remove a relevant authority from those that are subject to the duty;

(c) make the duty apply, in the case of a particular relevant authority, only in relation to certain functions that it has;

(d) in the case of a relevant authority to which the application of the duty is already restricted to certain functions, remove or alter the restriction.

(5) For the purposes of the power conferred by subsection (4) on the Scottish Ministers, 'relevant authority' means an authority whose functions—

(a) are exercisable only in or as regards Scotland,

(b) are wholly or mainly devolved Scottish functions, and

(c) correspond or are similar to those of an authority for the time being specified in section 1(3).

(6) For the purposes of the power conferred by subsection (4) on the Welsh Ministers, 'relevant authority' means [a devolved Welsh authority (within the meaning given by section 157A of the Government of Wales Act 2006) whose functions correspond][10] or are similar to those of an authority for the time being specified in subsection (3) of section 1 or referred to in subsection (4) of that section.

(7) [...][11]

(8) Regulations under this section may make any amendments of section 1 that appear to the Minister or Ministers to be necessary or expedient in consequence of provision made under subsection (1) or (as the case may be) subsection (4).

(9)–(10) [...][12]

(11) For the purposes of this [Part][13]—

(a) a function is a devolved Scottish function if it is exercisable in or as regards Scotland and it does not relate to reserved matters (within the meaning of the Scotland Act 1998) [.]

(b) [...][14]

3 Enforcement

A failure in respect of a performance of a duty under section 1 does not confer a cause of action at private law.

---

[10] Substituted by Wales Act 2017.
[11] Repealed by Wales Act 2017.
[12] Repealed by Wales Act 2017.
[13] Substituted by Scotland Act 2016.
[14] Repealed by Wales Act 2017.

PART 2
EQUALITY: KEY CONCEPTS

CHAPTER 1
PROTECTED CHARACTERISTICS

4 The protected characteristics

The following characteristics are protected characteristics—
age;
disability;
gender reassignment;
marriage and civil partnership;
pregnancy and maternity;
race;
religion or belief;
sex;
sexual orientation.

5 Age

(1) In relation to the protected characteristic of age—
 (a) a reference to a person who has a particular protected characteristic is a reference to a person of a particular age group;
 (b) a reference to persons who share a protected characteristic is a reference to persons of the same age group.
(2) A reference to an age group is a reference to a group of persons defined by reference to age, whether by reference to a particular age or to a range of ages.

6 Disability

(1) A person (P) has a disability if—
 (a) P has a physical or mental impairment, and
 (b) the impairment has a substantial and long-term adverse effect on P's ability to carry out normal day-to-day activities.
(2) A reference to a disabled person is a reference to a person who has a disability.
(3) In relation to the protected characteristic of disability—
 (a) a reference to a person who has a particular protected characteristic is a reference to a person who has a particular disability;
 (b) a reference to persons who share a protected characteristic is a reference to persons who have the same disability.
(4) This Act (except Part 12 and section 190) applies in relation to a person who has had a disability as it applies in relation to a person who has the disability; accordingly (except in that Part and that section)—
 (a) a reference (however expressed) to a person who has a disability includes a reference to a person who has had the disability, and
 (b) a reference (however expressed) to a person who does not have a disability includes a reference to a person who has not had the disability.

(5) A Minister of the Crown may issue guidance about matters to be taken into account in deciding any question for the purposes of subsection (1).

(6) Schedule 1 (disability: supplementary provision) has effect.

7 Gender reassignment

(1) A person has the protected characteristic of gender reassignment if the person is proposing to undergo, is undergoing or has undergone a process (or part of a process) for the purpose of reassigning the person's sex by changing physiological or other attributes of sex.

(2) A reference to a transsexual person is a reference to a person who has the protected characteristic of gender reassignment.

(3) In relation to the protected characteristic of gender reassignment—

(a) a reference to a person who has a particular protected characteristic is a reference to a transsexual person;

(b) a reference to persons who share a protected characteristic is a reference to transsexual persons.

8 Marriage and civil partnership

(1) A person has the protected characteristic of marriage and civil partnership if the person is married or is a civil partner.

(2) In relation to the protected characteristic of marriage and civil partnership—

(a) a reference to a person who has a particular protected characteristic is a reference to a person who is married or is a civil partner;

(b) a reference to persons who share a protected characteristic is a reference to persons who are married or are civil partners.

9 Race

(1) Race includes—

(a) colour;

(b) nationality;

(c) ethnic or national origins.

(2) In relation to the protected characteristic of race—

(a) a reference to a person who has a particular protected characteristic is a reference to a person of a particular racial group;

(b) a reference to persons who share a protected characteristic is a reference to persons of the same racial group.

(3) A racial group is a group of persons defined by reference to race; and a reference to a person's racial group is a reference to a racial group into which the person falls.

(4) The fact that a racial group comprises two or more distinct racial groups does not prevent it from constituting a particular racial group.

(5) A Minister of the Crown [...][15]—

(a) [must by order][16] amend this section so as to provide for caste to be an aspect of race;

(b) [may by order][17] amend this Act so as to provide for an exception to a provision of this Act to apply, or not to apply, to caste or to apply, or not to apply, to caste in specified circumstances.

---

[15] Repealed by Enterprise and Regulatory Reform Act 2013.

[16] Inserted by Enterprise and Regulatory Reform Act 2013.

[17] Inserted by Enterprise and Regulatory Reform Act 2013.

(6) The power under section 207(4)(b), in its application to subsection (5), includes power to amend this Act.

10 Religion or belief

(1) Religion means any religion and a reference to religion includes a reference to a lack of religion.

(2) Belief means any religious or philosophical belief and a reference to belief includes a reference to a lack of belief.

(3) In relation to the protected characteristic of religion or belief—

    (a) a reference to a person who has a particular protected characteristic is a reference to a person of a particular religion or belief;

    (b) a reference to persons who share a protected characteristic is a reference to persons who are of the same religion or belief.

11 Sex

In relation to the protected characteristic of sex—

(a) a reference to a person who has a particular protected characteristic is a reference to a man or to a woman;

(b) a reference to persons who share a protected characteristic is a reference to persons of the same sex.

12 Sexual orientation

(1) Sexual orientation means a person's sexual orientation towards—

    (a) persons of the same sex,

    (b) persons of the opposite sex, or

    (c) persons of either sex.

(2) In relation to the protected characteristic of sexual orientation—

    (a) a reference to a person who has a particular protected characteristic is a reference to a person who is of a particular sexual orientation;

    (b) a reference to persons who share a protected characteristic is a reference to persons who are of the same sexual orientation.

CHAPTER 2
PROHIBITED CONDUCT

Discrimination

13 Direct discrimination

(1) A person (A) discriminates against another (B) if, because of a protected characteristic, A treats B less favourably than A treats or would treat others.

(2) If the protected characteristic is age, A does not discriminate against B if A can show A's treatment of B to be a proportionate means of achieving a legitimate aim.

(3) If the protected characteristic is disability, and B is not a disabled person, A does not discriminate against B only because A treats or would treat disabled persons more favourably than A treats B.

(4) If the protected characteristic is marriage and civil partnership, this section applies to a contravention of Part 5 (work) only if the treatment is because it is B who is married or a civil partner.

(5) If the protected characteristic is race, less favourable treatment includes segregating B from others.

(6) If the protected characteristic is sex—
   (a) less favourable treatment of a woman includes less favourable treatment of her because she is breast-feeding;
   (b) in a case where B is a man, no account is to be taken of special treatment afforded to a woman in connection with pregnancy or childbirth.

(7) Subsection (6)(a) does not apply for the purposes of Part 5 (work).

(8) This section is subject to sections 17(6) and 18(7).

14 Combined discrimination: dual characteristics

(1) A person (A) discriminates against another (B) if, because of a combination of two relevant protected characteristics, A treats B less favourably than A treats or would treat a person who does not share either of those characteristics.

(2) The relevant protected characteristics are—
   (a) age;
   (b) disability;
   (c) gender reassignment;
   (d) race;
   (e) religion or belief;
   (f) sex;
   (g) sexual orientation.

(3) For the purposes of establishing a contravention of this Act by virtue of subsection (1), B need not show that A's treatment of B is direct discrimination because of each of the characteristics in the combination (taken separately).

(4) But B cannot establish a contravention of this Act by virtue of subsection (1) if, in reliance on another provision of this Act or any other enactment, A shows that A's treatment of B is not direct discrimination because of either or both of the characteristics in the combination.

(5) Subsection (1) does not apply to a combination of characteristics that includes disability in circumstances where, if a claim of direct discrimination because of disability were to be brought, it would come within section 116 (special educational needs).

(6) A Minister of the Crown may by order amend this section so as to—
   (a) make further provision about circumstances in which B can, or in which B cannot, establish a contravention of this Act by virtue of subsection (1);
   (b) specify other circumstances in which subsection (1) does not apply.

(7) The references to direct discrimination are to a contravention of this Act by virtue of section 13.

15 Discrimination arising from disability

(1) A person (A) discriminates against a disabled person (B) if—
   (a) A treats B unfavourably because of something arising in consequence of B's disability, and
   (b) A cannot show that the treatment is a proportionate means of achieving a legitimate aim.

(2) Subsection (1) does not apply if A shows that A did not know, and could not reasonably have been expected to know, that B had the disability.

16 Gender reassignment discrimination: cases of absence from work

(1) This section has effect for the purposes of the application of Part 5 (work) to the protected characteristic of gender reassignment.

(2) A person (A) discriminates against a transsexual person (B) if, in relation to an absence of B's that is because of gender reassignment, A treats B less favourably than A would treat B if—

  (a) B's absence was because of sickness or injury, or

  (b) B's absence was for some other reason and it is not reasonable for B to be treated less favourably.

(3) A person's absence is because of gender reassignment if it is because the person is proposing to undergo, is undergoing or has undergone the process (or part of the process) mentioned in section 7(1).

17 Pregnancy and maternity discrimination: non-work cases

(1) This section has effect for the purposes of the application to the protected characteristic of pregnancy and maternity of—

  (a) Part 3 (services and public functions);

  (b) Part 4 (premises);

  (c) Part 6 (education);

  (d) Part 7 (associations).

(2) A person (A) discriminates against a woman if A treats her unfavourably because of a pregnancy of hers.

(3) A person (A) discriminates against a woman if, in the period of 26 weeks beginning with the day on which she gives birth, A treats her unfavourably because she has given birth.

(4) The reference in subsection (3) to treating a woman unfavourably because she has given birth includes, in particular, a reference to treating her unfavourably because she is breastfeeding.

(5) For the purposes of this section, the day on which a woman gives birth is the day on which—

  (a) she gives birth to a living child, or

  (b) she gives birth to a dead child (more than 24 weeks of the pregnancy having passed).

(6) Section 13, so far as relating to sex discrimination, does not apply to anything done in relation to a woman in so far as—

  (a) it is for the reason mentioned in subsection (2), or

  (b) it is in the period, and for the reason, mentioned in subsection (3).

18 Pregnancy and maternity discrimination: work cases

(1) This section has effect for the purposes of the application of Part 5 (work) to the protected characteristic of pregnancy and maternity.

(2) A person (A) discriminates against a woman if, in the protected period in relation to a pregnancy of hers, A treats her unfavourably—

  (a) because of the pregnancy, or

  (b) because of illness suffered by her as a result of it.

(3) A person (A) discriminates against a woman if A treats her unfavourably because she is on compulsory maternity leave.

(4) A person (A) discriminates against a woman if A treats her unfavourably because she is exercising or seeking to exercise, or has exercised or sought to exercise, the right to ordinary or additional maternity leave.

(5) For the purposes of subsection (2), if the treatment of a woman is in implementation of a decision taken in the protected period, the treatment is to be regarded as occurring in that period (even if the implementation is not until after the end of that period).

(6) The protected period, in relation to a woman's pregnancy, begins when the pregnancy begins, and ends—
  (a) if she has the right to ordinary and additional maternity leave, at the end of the additional maternity leave period or (if earlier) when she returns to work after the pregnancy;
  (b) if she does not have that right, at the end of the period of 2 weeks beginning with the end of the pregnancy.
(7) Section 13, so far as relating to sex discrimination, does not apply to treatment of a woman in so far as—
  (a) it is in the protected period in relation to her and is for a reason mentioned in paragraph (a) or (b) of subsection (2), or
  (b) it is for a reason mentioned in subsection (3) or (4).

19 Indirect discrimination

(1) A person (A) discriminates against another (B) if A applies to B a provision, criterion or practice which is discriminatory in relation to a relevant protected characteristic of B's.
(2) For the purposes of subsection (1), a provision, criterion or practice is discriminatory in relation to a relevant protected characteristic of B's if—
  (a) A applies, or would apply, it to persons with whom B does not share the characteristic,
  (b) it puts, or would put, persons with whom B shares the characteristic at a particular disadvantage when compared with persons with whom B does not share it,
  (c) it puts, or would put, B at that disadvantage, and
  (d) A cannot show it to be a proportionate means of achieving a legitimate aim.
(3) The relevant protected characteristics are—
  age;
  disability;
  gender reassignment;
  marriage and civil partnership;
  race;
  religion or belief;
  sex;
  sexual orientation.

Adjustments for disabled persons

20 Duty to make adjustments

(1) Where this Act imposes a duty to make reasonable adjustments on a person, this section, sections 21 and 22 and the applicable Schedule apply; and for those purposes, a person on whom the duty is imposed is referred to as A.
(2) The duty comprises the following three requirements.
(3) The first requirement is a requirement, where a provision, criterion or practice of A's puts a disabled person at a substantial disadvantage in relation to a relevant matter in comparison with persons who are not disabled, to take such steps as it is reasonable to have to take to avoid the disadvantage.
(4) The second requirement is a requirement, where a physical feature puts a disabled person at a substantial disadvantage in relation to a relevant matter in comparison with persons who are not disabled, to take such steps as it is reasonable to have to take to avoid the disadvantage.

(5) The third requirement is a requirement, where a disabled person would, but for the provision of an auxiliary aid, be put at a substantial disadvantage in relation to a relevant matter in comparison with persons who are not disabled, to take such steps as it is reasonable to have to take to provide the auxiliary aid.

(6) Where the first or third requirement relates to the provision of information, the steps which it is reasonable for A to have to take include steps for ensuring that in the circumstances concerned the information is provided in an accessible format.

(7) A person (A) who is subject to a duty to make reasonable adjustments is not (subject to express provision to the contrary) entitled to require a disabled person, in relation to whom A is required to comply with the duty, to pay to any extent A's costs of complying with the duty.

(8) A reference in section 21 or 22 or an applicable Schedule to the first, second or third requirement is to be construed in accordance with this section.

(9) In relation to the second requirement, a reference in this section or an applicable Schedule to avoiding a substantial disadvantage includes a reference to—

  (a) removing the physical feature in question,

  (b) altering it, or

  (c) providing a reasonable means of avoiding it.

(10) A reference in this section, section 21 or 22 or an applicable Schedule (apart from paragraphs 2 to 4 of Schedule 4) to a physical feature is a reference to—

  (a) a feature arising from the design or construction of a building,

  (b) a feature of an approach to, exit from or access to a building,

  (c) a fixture or fitting, or furniture, furnishings, materials, equipment or other chattels, in or on premises, or

  (d) any other physical element or quality.

(11) A reference in this section, section 21 or 22 or an applicable Schedule to an auxiliary aid includes a reference to an auxiliary service.

(12) A reference in this section or an applicable Schedule to chattels is to be read, in relation to Scotland, as a reference to moveable property.

(13) The applicable Schedule is, in relation to the Part of this Act specified in the first column of the Table, the Schedule specified in the second column.

21 Failure to comply with duty

(1) A failure to comply with the first, second or third requirement is a failure to comply with a duty to make reasonable adjustments.

(2) A discriminates against a disabled person if A fails to comply with that duty in relation to that person.

Part of this Act	Applicable Schedule
Part 3 (services and public functions)	Schedule 2
Part 4 (premises)	Schedule 4
Part 5 (work)	Schedule 8
Part 6 (education)	Schedule 13
Part 7 (associations)	Schedule 15
Each of the Parts mentioned above	Schedule 21

(3) A provision of an applicable Schedule which imposes a duty to comply with the first, second or third requirement applies only for the purpose of establishing whether A has contravened

this Act by virtue of subsection (2); a failure to comply is, accordingly, not actionable by virtue of another provision of this Act or otherwise.

22 Regulations

(1) Regulations may prescribe—
   (a) matters to be taken into account in deciding whether it is reasonable for A to take a step for the purposes of a prescribed provision of an applicable Schedule;
   (b) descriptions of persons to whom the first, second or third requirement does not apply.

(2) Regulations may make provision as to—
   (a) circumstances in which it is, or in which it is not, reasonable for a person of a prescribed description to have to take steps of a prescribed description;
   (b) what is, or what is not, a provision, criterion or practice;
   (c) things which are, or which are not, to be treated as physical features;
   (d) things which are, or which are not, to be treated as alterations of physical features;
   (e) things which are, or which are not, to be treated as auxiliary aids.

(3) Provision made by virtue of this section may amend an applicable Schedule.

Discrimination: supplementary

23 Comparison by reference to circumstances

(1) On a comparison of cases for the purposes of section 13, 14, or 19 there must be no material difference between the circumstances relating to each case.
   (a) The circumstances relating to a case include a person's abilities if—
   (b) on a comparison for the purposes of section 13, the protected characteristic is disability;

(2) on a comparison for the purposes of section 14, one of the protected characteristics in the combination is disability.

(3) If the protected characteristic is sexual orientation, the fact that one person (whether or not the person referred to as B) is a civil partner while another is married [...][18] is not a material difference between the circumstances relating to each case.

[(4) If the protected characteristic is sexual orientation, the fact that one person (whether or not the person referred to as B) is married to [, or the civil partner of,][19] a person of the same sex while another is married to [, or the civil partner of,][20] a person of the opposite sex is not a material difference between the circumstances relating to each case.][21]

24 Irrelevance of alleged discriminator's characteristics

(1) For the purpose of establishing a contravention of this Act by virtue of section 13(1), it does not matter whether A has the protected characteristic.

(2) For the purpose of establishing a contravention of this Act by virtue of section 14(1), it does not matter—
   (a) whether A has one of the protected characteristics in the combination;
   (b) whether A has both.

---

[18] Repealed by Civil Partnership (Opposite-sex couples) Regulations 2019, SI 2019/1458.
[19] Inserted by Civil Partnership (Opposite-sex couples) Regulations 2019, SI 2019/1458.
[20] Inserted by Civil Partnership (Opposite-sex couples) Regulations 2019, SI 2019/1458.
[21] Inserted by Marriage (Same Sex Couples) Act 2013.

25 **References to particular strands of discrimination**

(1) Age discrimination is—
    (a) discrimination within section 13 because of age;
    (b) discrimination within section 19 where the relevant protected characteristic is age.

(2) Disability discrimination is—
    (a) discrimination within section 13 because of disability;
    (b) discrimination within section 15;
    (c) discrimination within section 19 where the relevant protected characteristic is disability;
    (d) discrimination within section 21.

(3) Gender reassignment discrimination is—
    (a) discrimination within section 13 because of gender reassignment;
    (b) discrimination within section 16;
    (c) discrimination within section 19 where the relevant protected characteristic is gender reassignment.

(4) Marriage and civil partnership discrimination is—
    (a) discrimination within section 13 because of marriage and civil partnership;
    (b) discrimination within section 19 where the relevant protected characteristic is marriage and civil partnership.

(5) Pregnancy and maternity discrimination is discrimination within section 17 or 18.

(6) Race discrimination is—
    (a) discrimination within section 13 because of race;
    (b) discrimination within section 19 where the relevant protected characteristic is race.

(7) Religious or belief-related discrimination is—
    (a) discrimination within section 13 because of religion or belief;
    (b) discrimination within section 19 where the relevant protected characteristic is religion or belief.

(8) Sex discrimination is—
    (a) discrimination within section 13 because of sex;
    (b) discrimination within section 19 where the relevant protected characteristic is sex.

(9) Sexual orientation discrimination is—
    (a) discrimination within section 13 because of sexual orientation;
    (b) discrimination within section 19 where the relevant protected characteristic is sexual orientation.

Other prohibited conduct

26 **Harassment**

(1) A person (A) harasses another (B) if—
    (a) A engages in unwanted conduct related to a relevant protected characteristic, and
    (b) the conduct has the purpose or effect of—
        (i) violating B's dignity, or
        (ii) creating an intimidating, hostile, degrading, humiliating or offensive environment for B.

(2) A also harasses B if—
    (a) A engages in unwanted conduct of a sexual nature, and
    (b) the conduct has the purpose or effect referred to in subsection (1)(b).

(3) A also harasses B if—
    (a) A or another person engages in unwanted conduct of a sexual nature or that is related to gender reassignment or sex,

(b) the conduct has the purpose or effect referred to in subsection (1)(b), and

(c) because of B's rejection of or submission to the conduct, A treats B less favourably than A would treat B if B had not rejected or submitted to the conduct.

(4) In deciding whether conduct has the effect referred to in subsection (1)(b), each of the following must be taken into account—

(a) the perception of B;

(b) the other circumstances of the case;

(c) whether it is reasonable for the conduct to have that effect.

(5) The relevant protected characteristics are—

age;

disability;

gender reassignment;

race;

religion or belief;

sex;

sexual orientation.

27 Victimisation

(1) A person (A) victimises another person (B) if A subjects B to a detriment because—

(a) B does a protected act, or

(b) A believes that B has done, or may do, a protected act.

(2) Each of the following is a protected act—

(a) bringing proceedings under this Act;

(b) giving evidence or information in connection with proceedings under this Act;

(c) doing any other thing for the purposes of or in connection with this Act;

(d) making an allegation (whether or not express) that A or another person has contravened this Act.

(3) Giving false evidence or information, or making a false allegation, is not a protected act if the evidence or information is given, or the allegation is made, in bad faith.

(4) This section applies only where the person subjected to a detriment is an individual.

(5) The reference to contravening this Act includes a reference to committing a breach of an equality clause or rule.

PART 3

SERVICES AND PUBLIC FUNCTIONS

Preliminary

28 Application of this Part

(1) This Part does not apply to the protected characteristic of—

(a) age, so far as relating to persons who have not attained the age of 18;

(b) marriage and civil partnership.

(2) This Part does not apply to discrimination, harassment or victimisation—

(a) that is prohibited by Part 4 (premises), 5 (work) or 6 (education), or

(b) that would be so prohibited but for an express exception.

(3) This Part does not apply to—

(a) a breach of an equality clause or rule;

(b) anything that would be a breach of an equality clause or rule but for section 69 or Part 2 of Schedule 7;

(c) a breach of a non-discrimination rule.

Provision of services, etc.

29 Provision of services, etc.

(1) A person (a 'service-provider') concerned with the provision of a service to the public or a section of the public (for payment or not) must not discriminate against a person requiring the service by not providing the person with the service.

(2) A service-provider (A) must not, in providing the service, discriminate against a person (B)—
  (a) as to the terms on which A provides the service to B;
  (b) by terminating the provision of the service to B;
  (c) by subjecting B to any other detriment.

(3) A service-provider must not, in relation to the provision of the service, harass—
  (a) a person requiring the service, or
  (b) a person to whom the service-provider provides the service.

(4) A service-provider must not victimise a person requiring the service by not providing the person with the service.

(5) A service-provider (A) must not, in providing the service, victimise a person (B)—
  (a) as to the terms on which A provides the service to B;
  (b) by terminating the provision of the service to B;
  (c) by subjecting B to any other detriment.

(6) A person must not, in the exercise of a public function that is not the provision of a service to the public or a section of the public, do anything that constitutes discrimination, harassment or victimisation.

(7) A duty to make reasonable adjustments applies to—
  (a) a service-provider (and see also section 55(7));
  (b) a person who exercises a public function that is not the provision of a service to the public or a section of the public.

(8) In the application of section 26 for the purposes of subsection (3), and subsection (6) as it relates to harassment, neither of the following is a relevant protected characteristic—
  (a) religion or belief;
  (b) sexual orientation.

(9) In the application of this section, so far as relating to race or religion or belief, to the granting of entry clearance (within the meaning of the Immigration Act 1971), it does not matter whether an act is done within or outside the United Kingdom.

(10) Subsection (9) does not affect the application of any other provision of this Act to conduct outside England and Wales or Scotland.

Supplementary

30 Ships and hovercraft

(1) This Part (subject to subsection (2)) applies only in such circumstances as are prescribed in relation to—
  (a) transporting people by ship or hovercraft;
  (b) a service provided on a ship or hovercraft.

(2) Section 29(6) applies in relation to the matters referred to in paragraphs (a) and (b) of sub-section (1); but in so far as it relates to disability discrimination, section 29(6) applies to those matters only in such circumstances as are prescribed.

(3) It does not matter whether the ship or hovercraft is within or outside the United Kingdom.

(4) 'Ship' has the same meaning as in the Merchant Shipping Act 1995.

(5) 'Hovercraft' has the same meaning as in the Hovercraft Act 1968.

(6) Nothing in this section affects the application of any other provision of this Act to conduct outside England and Wales or Scotland.

31 Interpretation and exceptions

(1) This section applies for the purposes of this Part.

(2) A reference to the provision of a service includes a reference to the provision of goods or facilities.

(3) A reference to the provision of a service includes a reference to the provision of a service in the exercise of a public function.

(4) A public function is a function that is a function of a public nature for the purposes of the Human Rights Act 1998.

(5) Where an employer arranges for another person to provide a service only to the employer's employees—
   (a) the employer is not to be regarded as the service-provider, but
   (b) the employees are to be regarded as a section of the public.

(6) A reference to a person requiring a service includes a reference to a person who is seeking to obtain or use the service.

(7) A reference to a service-provider not providing a person with a service includes a reference to—
   (a) the service-provider not providing the person with a service of the quality that the service-provider usually provides to the public (or the section of it which includes the person), or
   (b) the service-provider not providing the person with the service in the manner in which, or on the terms on which, the service-provider usually provides the service to the public (or the section of it which includes the person).

(8) In relation to the provision of a service by either House of Parliament, the service-provider is the Corporate Officer of the House concerned; and if the service involves access to, or use of, a place in the Palace of Westminster which members of the public are allowed to enter, both Corporate Officers are jointly the service-provider.

(9) Schedule 2 (reasonable adjustments) has effect.

(10) Schedule 3 (exceptions) has effect.

PART 4
PREMISES

Preliminary

32 Application of this Part

(1) This Part does not apply to the following protected characteristics—
   (a) age;
   (b) marriage and civil partnership.

(2) This Part does not apply to discrimination, harassment or victimisation—
  (a) that is prohibited by Part 5 (work) or Part 6 (education), or
  (b) that would be so prohibited but for an express exception.
(3) This Part does not apply to the provision of accommodation if the provision—
  (a) is generally for the purpose of short stays by individuals who live elsewhere, or
  (b) is for the purpose only of exercising a public function or providing a service to the public or a section of the public.
(4) The reference to the exercise of a public function, and the reference to the provision of a service, are to be construed in accordance with Part 3.
(5) This Part does not apply to—
  (a) a breach of an equality clause or rule;
  (b) anything that would be a breach of an equality clause or rule but for section 69 or Part 2 of Schedule 7;
  (c) a breach of a non-discrimination rule.

Disposal and management

33 Disposals, etc.

(1) A person (A) who has the right to dispose of premises must not discriminate against another (B)—
  (a) as to the terms on which A offers to dispose of the premises to B;
  (b) by not disposing of the premises to B;
  (c) in A's treatment of B with respect to things done in relation to persons seeking premises.
(2) Where an interest in a commonhold unit cannot be disposed of unless a particular person is a party to the disposal, that person must not discriminate against a person by not being a party to the disposal.
(3) A person who has the right to dispose of premises must not, in connection with anything done in relation to their occupation or disposal, harass—
  (a) a person who occupies them;
  (b) a person who applies for them.
(4) A person (A) who has the right to dispose of premises must not victimise another (B)—
  (a) as to the terms on which A offers to dispose of the premises to B;
  (b) by not disposing of the premises to B;
  (c) in A's treatment of B with respect to things done in relation to persons seeking premises.
(5) Where an interest in a commonhold unit cannot be disposed of unless a particular person is a party to the disposal, that person must not victimise a person by not being a party to the disposal.
(6) In the application of section 26 for the purposes of subsection (3), neither of the following is a relevant protected characteristic—
  (a) religion or belief;
  (b) sexual orientation.

34 Permission for disposal

(1) A person whose permission is required for the disposal of premises must not discriminate against another by not giving permission for the disposal of the premises to the other.
(2) A person whose permission is required for the disposal of premises must not, in relation to an application for permission to dispose of the premises, harass a person—
  (a) who applies for permission to dispose of the premises, or
  (b) to whom the disposal would be made if permission were given.

(3) A person whose permission is required for the disposal of premises must not victimise another by not giving permission for the disposal of the premises to the other.

(4) In the application of section 26 for the purposes of subsection (2), neither of the following is a relevant protected characteristic—

    (a) religion or belief;

    (b) sexual orientation.

(5) This section does not apply to anything done in the exercise of a judicial function.

35 Management

(1) A person (A) who manages premises must not discriminate against a person (B) who occupies the premises—

    (a) in the way in which A allows B, or by not allowing B, to make use of a benefit or facility;

    (b) by evicting B (or taking steps for the purpose of securing B's eviction);

    (c) by subjecting B to any other detriment.

(2) A person who manages premises must not, in relation to their management, harass—

    (a) a person who occupies them;

    (b) a person who applies for them.

(3) A person (A) who manages premises must not victimise a person (B) who occupies the premises—

    (a) in the way in which A allows B, or by not allowing B, to make use of a benefit or facility;

    (b) by evicting B (or taking steps for the purpose of securing B's eviction);

    (c) by subjecting B to any other detriment.

(4) In the application of section 26 for the purposes of subsection (2), neither of the following is a relevant protected characteristic—

    (a) religion or belief;

    (b) sexual orientation.

Reasonable adjustments

36 Leasehold and commonhold premises and common parts

(1) A duty to make reasonable adjustments applies to—

    (a) a controller of let premises;

    (b) a controller of premises to let;

    (c) a commonhold association;

    (d) a responsible person in relation to common parts.

(2) A controller of let premises is—

    (a) a person by whom premises are let, or

    (b) a person who manages them.

(3) A controller of premises to let is—

    (a) a person who has premises to let, or

    (b) a person who manages them.

(4) The reference in subsection (1)(c) to a commonhold association is a reference to the association in its capacity as the person who manages a commonhold unit.

(5) A responsible person in relation to common parts is—

    (a) where the premises to which the common parts relate are let (and are not part of commonhold land or in Scotland), a person by whom the premises are let;

    (b) where the premises to which the common parts relate are part of commonhold land, the commonhold association.

(6) Common parts are—
- (a) in relation to let premises (which are not part of commonhold land or in Scotland), the structure and exterior of, and any common facilities within or used in connection with, the building or part of a building which includes the premises;
- (b) in relation to commonhold land, every part of the commonhold which is not for the time being a commonhold unit in accordance with the commonhold community statement.

(7) A reference to letting includes a reference to sub-letting; and for the purposes of subsection (1)(a) and (b), a reference to let premises includes premises subject to a right to occupy.

(8) This section does not apply to premises of such description as may be prescribed.

37 Adjustments to common parts in Scotland

(1) The Scottish Ministers may by regulations provide that a disabled person is entitled to make relevant adjustments to common parts in relation to premises in Scotland.

(2) The reference in subsection (1) to a disabled person is a reference to a disabled person who—
- (a) is a tenant of the premises,
- (b) is an owner of the premises, or
- (c) is otherwise entitled to occupy the premises, and uses or intends to use the premises as the person's only or main home.

(3) Before making regulations under subsection (1), the Scottish Ministers must consult a Minister of the Crown.

(4) Regulations under subsection (1) may, in particular—
- (a) prescribe things which are, or which are not, to be treated as relevant adjustments;
- (b) prescribe circumstances in which the consent of an owner of the common parts is required before a disabled person may make an adjustment;
- (c) provide that the consent to adjustments is not to be withheld unreasonably;
- (d) prescribe matters to be taken into account, or to be disregarded, in deciding whether it is reasonable to consent to adjustments;
- (e) prescribe circumstances in which consent to adjustments is to be taken to be withheld;
- (f) make provision about the imposition of conditions on consent to adjustments;
- (g) make provision as to circumstances in which the sheriff may make an order authorising a disabled person to carry out adjustments;
- (h) make provision about the responsibility for costs arising (directly or indirectly) from an adjustment;
- (i) make provision about the reinstatement of the common parts to the condition they were in before an adjustment was made;
- (j) make provision about the giving of notice to the owners of the common parts and other persons;
- (k) make provision about agreements between a disabled person and an owner of the common parts;
- (l) make provision about the registration of information in the Land Register of Scotland or the recording of documents in the Register of Sasines relating to an entitlement of a disabled person or an obligation on an owner of the common parts;
- (m) make provision about the effect of such registration or recording;
- (n) make provision about who is to be treated as being, or as not being, a person entitled to occupy premises otherwise than as tenant or owner.

(5) In this section—
'common parts' means, in relation to premises, the structure and exterior of, and any common facilities within or used in connection with, the building or part of a building which includes

the premises but only in so far as the structure, exterior and common facilities are not solely owned by the owner of the premises; 'relevant adjustments' means, in relation to a disabled person, alterations or additions which are likely to avoid a substantial disadvantage to which the disabled person is put in using the common parts in comparison with persons who are not disabled.

Supplementary

38 Interpretation and exceptions

(1) This section applies for the purposes of this Part.

(2) A reference to premises is a reference to the whole or part of the premises.

(3) A reference to disposing of premises includes, in the case of premises subject to a tenancy, a reference to—

(a) assigning the premises,

(b) sub-letting them, or

(c) parting with possession of them.

(4) A reference to disposing of premises also includes a reference to granting a right to occupy them.

(5) A reference to disposing of an interest in a commonhold unit includes a reference to creating an interest in a commonhold unit.

(6) A reference to a tenancy is to a tenancy created (whether before or after the passing of this Act)—

(a) by a lease or sub-lease,

(b) by an agreement for a lease or sub-lease,

(c) by a tenancy agreement, or

(d) in pursuance of an enactment, and a reference to a tenant is to be construed accordingly.

(7) A reference to commonhold land, a commonhold association, a commonhold community statement, a commonhold unit or a unit-holder is to be construed in accordance with the Commonhold and Leasehold Reform Act 2002.

(8) Schedule 4 (reasonable adjustments) has effect.

(9) Schedule 5 (exceptions) has effect.

PART 5
WORK

CHAPTER 1
EMPLOYMENT, ETC.

Employees

39 Employees and applicants

(1) An employer (A) must not discriminate against a person (B)—

(a) in the arrangements A makes for deciding to whom to offer employment;

(b) as to the terms on which A offers B employment;

(c) by not offering B employment.

(2) An employer (A) must not discriminate against an employee of A's (B)—

(a) as to B's terms of employment;

    (b) in the way A affords B access, or by not affording B access, to opportunities for promotion, transfer or training or for receiving any other benefit, facility or service;

    (c) by dismissing B;

    (d) by subjecting B to any other detriment.

(3) An employer (A) must not victimise a person (B)—

    (a) in the arrangements A makes for deciding to whom to offer employment;

    (b) as to the terms on which A offers B employment;

    (c) by not offering B employment.

(4) An employer (A) must not victimise an employee of A's (B)—

    (a) as to B's terms of employment;

    (b) in the way A affords B access, or by not affording B access, to opportunities for promotion, transfer or training or for any other benefit, facility or service;

    (c) by dismissing B;

    (d) by subjecting B to any other detriment.

(5) A duty to make reasonable adjustments applies to an employer.

(6) Subsection (1)(b), so far as relating to sex or pregnancy and maternity, does not apply to a term that relates to pay—

    (a) unless, were B to accept the offer, an equality clause or rule would have effect in relation to the term, or

    (b) if paragraph (a) does not apply, except in so far as making an offer on terms including that term amounts to a contravention of subsection (1)(b) by virtue of section 13, 14 or 18.

(7) In subsections (2)(c) and (4)(c), the reference to dismissing B includes a reference to the termination of B's employment—

    (a) by the expiry of a period (including a period expiring by reference to an event or circumstance);

    (b) by an act of B's (including giving notice) in circumstances such that B is entitled, because of A's conduct, to terminate the employment without notice.

(8) Subsection (7)(a) does not apply if, immediately after the termination, the employment is renewed on the same terms.

40 Employees and applicants: harassment

    (1)   An employer (A) must not, in relation to employment by A, harass a person (B)—

        (a) who is an employee of A's;

        (b) who has applied to A for employment.

(2)–(4)   […][22]

41 Contract workers

(1) A principal must not discriminate against a contract worker—

    (a) as to the terms on which the principal allows the worker to do the work;

    (b) by not allowing the worker to do, or to continue to do, the work;

    (c) in the way the principal affords the worker access, or by not affording the worker access, to opportunities for receiving a benefit, facility or service;

    (d) by subjecting the worker to any other detriment.

(2) A principal must not, in relation to contract work, harass a contract worker.

(3) A principal must not victimise a contract worker—

    (a) as to the terms on which the principal allows the worker to do the work;

---

[22] Repealed by Enterprise and Regulatory Reform Act 2013.

(b) by not allowing the worker to do, or to continue to do, the work;

(c) in the way the principal affords the worker access, or by not affording the worker access, to opportunities for receiving a benefit, facility or service;

(d) by subjecting the worker to any other detriment.

(4) A duty to make reasonable adjustments applies to a principal (as well as to the employer of a contract worker).

(5) A 'principal' is a person who makes work available for an individual who is—

(a) employed by another person, and

(b) supplied by that other person in furtherance of a contract to which the principal is a party (whether or not that other person is a party to it).

(6) 'Contract work' is work such as is mentioned in subsection (5).

(7) A 'contract worker' is an individual supplied to a principal in furtherance of a contract such as is mentioned in subsection (5)(b).

Police officers

42 Identity of employer

(1) For the purposes of this Part, holding the office of constable is to be treated as employment—

(a) by the chief officer, in respect of any act done by the chief officer in relation to a constable or appointment to the office of constable;

(b) by the responsible authority, in respect of any act done by the authority in relation to a constable or appointment to the office of constable.

(2) For the purposes of this Part, holding an appointment as a police cadet is to be treated as employment—

(a) by the chief officer, in respect of any act done by the chief officer in relation to a police cadet or appointment as one;

(b) by the responsible authority, in respect of any act done by the authority in relation to a police cadet or appointment as one.

(3) Subsection (1) does not apply to service with the Civil Nuclear Constabulary (as to which, see section 55(2) of the Energy Act 2004).

(4) Subsection (1) does not apply to a constable at [NCA][23] [or SPA][24].

(5) A constable at [NCA][25] or [SPA][26] is to be treated as employed by it, in respect of any act done by it in relation to the constable.

(6) […][27]

43 Interpretation

(1) This section applies for the purposes of section 42.

(2) 'Chief officer' means—

(a) in relation to an appointment under a relevant Act, the chief officer of police for the police force to which the appointment relates;

---

[23] Substituted by Crime and Courts Act 2013.

[24] Substituted by Police and Fire Reform (Scotland) Act 2012 (Consequential Provisions and Modifications) Order 2013, SI 2013/602.

[25] Substituted by Crime and Courts Act 2013.

[26] Substituted by Police and Fire Reform (Scotland) Act 2012 (Consequential Provisions and Modifications) Order 2013, SI 2013/602.

[27] Repealed by Police and Fire Reform (Scotland) Act 2012 (Consequential Provisions and Modifications) Order 2013, SI 2013/602.

   (b) in relation to any other appointment, the person under whose direction and control the body of constables or other persons to which the appointment relates is;

   (c) in relation to a constable or other person under the direction and control of a chief officer of police, that chief officer of police;

   (d) in relation to any other constable or any other person, the person under whose direction and control the constable or other person is.

(3) 'Responsible authority' means—

   (a) in relation to an appointment under a relevant Act, the [local policing body or police authority][28] that maintains the police force to which the appointment relates;

   (b) in relation to any other appointment, the person by whom a person would (if appointed) be paid;

   (c) in relation to a constable or other person under the direction and control of a chief officer of police, the [local policing body or police authority][29] that maintains the police force for which that chief officer is the chief officer of police;

   (d) in relation to any other constable or any other person, the person by whom the constable or other person is paid.

(4) 'Police cadet' means a person appointed to undergo training with a view to becoming a constable.

[(5) 'NCA' means the National Crime Agency; and a reference to a constable at
NCA is a reference to a constable seconded to it to serve as an NCA officer.][30]

[(5A)'SPA' means the Scottish Police Authority; and a reference to a constable at SPA is a reference to a constable serving as a member of its staff by virtue of paragraph 7(1) of Schedule 1 to the Police and Fire Reform (Scotland) Act 2012.][31]

(6) [...][32]

(7) [...][33]

(8) For the purposes of this section, the relevant Acts are—

   (a) the Metropolitan Police Act 1829;

   (b) the City of London Police Act 1839;

   (c) the [Police and Fire Reform (Scotland) Act 2012][34];

   [(d) the Police Reform and Social Responsibility Act 2011.][35]

[(9) Subsections (2) and (3) apply in relation to Scotland as follows—

   (a) a reference to a police authority includes a reference to the Scottish Police Authority;

   (b) a reference to a police force includes a reference to the Police Service of Scotland; and

   (c) a reference to a chief officer of police includes a reference to the chief constable of the Police Service of Scotland.][36]

---

[28] Substituted by Police Reform and Social Responsibility Act 2011.

[29] Substituted by Police Reform and Social Responsibility Act 2011.

[30] Substituted by Crime and Courts Act 2013.

[31] Substituted by Police and Fire Reform (Scotland) Act 2012 (Consequential Provisions and Modifications) Order 2013, SI 2013/602.

[32] Repealed by Police and Fire Reform (Scotland) Act 2012 (Consequential Provisions and Modifications) Order 2013, SI 2013/602.

[33] Repealed by Police and Fire Reform (Scotland) Act 2012 (Consequential Provisions and Modifications) Order 2013, SI 2013/602.

[34] Substituted by Police and Fire Reform (Scotland) Act 2012 (Consequential Provisions and Modifications) Order 2013, SI 2013/602.

[35] Substituted by Police Reform and Social Responsibility Act 2011.

[36] Substituted by Police and Fire Reform (Scotland) Act 2012 (Consequential Provisions and Modifications) Order 2013, SI 2013/602.

Partners

44 Partnerships

(1) A firm or proposed firm must not discriminate against a person—
    (a) in the arrangements it makes for deciding to whom to offer a position as a partner;
    (b) as to the terms on which it offers the person a position as a partner;
    (c) by not offering the person a position as a partner.

(2) A firm (A) must not discriminate against a partner (B)—
    (a) as to the terms on which B is a partner;
    (b) in the way A affords B access, or by not affording B access, to opportunities for promotion, transfer or training or for receiving any other benefit, facility or service;
    (c) by expelling B;
    (d) by subjecting B to any other detriment.

(3) A firm must not, in relation to a position as a partner, harass—
    (a) a partner;
    (b) a person who has applied for the position.

(4) A proposed firm must not, in relation to a position as a partner, harass a person who has applied for the position.

(5) A firm or proposed firm must not victimise a person—
    (a) in the arrangements it makes for deciding to whom to offer a position as a partner;
    (b) as to the terms on which it offers the person a position as a partner;
    (c) by not offering the person a position as a partner.

(6) A firm (A) must not victimise a partner (B)—
    (a) as to the terms on which B is a partner;
    (b) in the way A affords B access, or by not affording B access, to opportunities for promotion, transfer or training or for receiving any other benefit, facility or service;
    (c) by expelling B;
    (d) by subjecting B to any other detriment.

(7) A duty to make reasonable adjustments applies to—
    (a) a firm;
    (b) a proposed firm.

(8) In the application of this section to a limited partnership within the meaning of the Limited Partnerships Act 1907, 'partner' means a general partner within the meaning of that Act.

45 Limited liability partnerships

(1) An LLP or proposed LLP must not discriminate against a person—
    (a) in the arrangements it makes for deciding to whom to offer a position as a member;
    (b) as to the terms on which it offers the person a position as a member;
    (c) by not offering the person a position as a member.

(2) An LLP (A) must not discriminate against a member (B)—
    (a) as to the terms on which B is a member;
    (b) in the way A affords B access, or by not affording B access, to opportunities for promotion, transfer or training or for receiving any other benefit, facility or service;
    (c) by expelling B;
    (d) by subjecting B to any other detriment.

(3) An LLP must not, in relation to a position as a member, harass—
    (a) a member;
    (b) a person who has applied for the position.

(4) A proposed LLP must not, in relation to a position as a member, harass a person who has applied for the position.

(5) An LLP or proposed LLP must not victimise a person—

(a) in the arrangements it makes for deciding to whom to offer a position as a member;

(b) as to the terms on which it offers the person a position as a member;

(c) by not offering the person a position as a member.

(6) An LLP (A) must not victimise a member (B)—

(a) as to the terms on which B is a member;

(b) in the way A affords B access, or by not affording B access, to opportunities for promotion, transfer or training or for receiving any other benefit, facility or service;

(c) by expelling B;

(d) by subjecting B to any other detriment.

(7) A duty to make reasonable adjustments applies to—

(a) an LLP;

(b) a proposed LLP.

46 Interpretation

(1) This section applies for the purposes of sections 44 and 45.

(2) 'Partnership' and 'firm' have the same meaning as in the Partnership Act 1890.

(3) 'Proposed firm' means persons proposing to form themselves into a partnership.

(4) 'LLP' means a limited liability partnership (within the meaning of the Limited Liability Partnerships Act 2000).

(5) 'Proposed LLP' means persons proposing to incorporate an LLP with themselves as members.

(6) A reference to expelling a partner of a firm or a member of an LLP includes a reference to the termination of the person's position as such—

(a) by the expiry of a period (including a period expiring by reference to an event or circumstance);

(b) by an act of the person (including giving notice) in circumstances such that the person is entitled, because of the conduct of other partners or members, to terminate the position without notice;

(c) (in the case of a partner of a firm) as a result of the dissolution of the partnership.

(7) Subsection (6)(a) and (c) does not apply if, immediately after the termination, the position is renewed on the same terms.

The Bar

47 Barristers

(1) A barrister (A) must not discriminate against a person (B)—

(a) in the arrangements A makes for deciding to whom to offer a pupillage or tenancy;

(b) as to the terms on which A offers B a pupillage or tenancy;

(c) by not offering B a pupillage or tenancy.

(2) A barrister (A) must not discriminate against a person (B) who is a pupil or tenant—

(a) as to the terms on which B is a pupil or tenant;

(b) in the way A affords B access, or by not affording B access, to opportunities for training or gaining experience or for receiving any other benefit, facility or service;

(c) by terminating the pupillage;

(d) by subjecting B to pressure to leave chambers;

(e) by subjecting B to any other detriment.

(3) A barrister must not, in relation to a pupillage or tenancy, harass—
 (a) the pupil or tenant;
 (b) a person who has applied for the pupillage or tenancy.
(4) A barrister (A) must not victimise a person (B)—
 (a) in the arrangements A makes for deciding to whom to offer a pupillage or tenancy;
 (b) as to the terms on which A offers B a pupillage or tenancy;
 (c) by not offering B a pupillage or tenancy.
(5) A barrister (A) must not victimise a person (B) who is a pupil or tenant—
 (a) as to the terms on which B is a pupil or tenant;
 (b) in the way A affords B access, or by not affording B access, to opportunities for training or gaining experience or for receiving any other benefit, facility or service;
 (c) by terminating the pupillage;
 (d) by subjecting B to pressure to leave chambers;
 (e) by subjecting B to any other detriment.
(6) A person must not, in relation to instructing a barrister—
 (a) discriminate against a barrister by subjecting the barrister to a detriment;
 (b) harass the barrister;
 (c) victimise the barrister.
(7) A duty to make reasonable adjustments applies to a barrister.
(8) The preceding provisions of this section (apart from subsection (6)) apply in relation to a barrister's clerk as they apply in relation to a barrister; and for that purpose the reference to a barrister's clerk includes a reference to a person who carries out the functions of a barrister's clerk.
(9) A reference to a tenant includes a reference to a barrister who is permitted to work in chambers (including as a squatter or door tenant); and a reference to a tenancy is to be construed accordingly.

48 Advocates

(1) An advocate (A) must not discriminate against a person (B)—
 (a) in the arrangements A makes for deciding who to take as A's devil or to whom to offer membership of a stable;
 (b) as to the terms on which A offers to take B as A's devil or offers B membership of a stable;
 (c) by not offering to take B as A's devil or not offering B membership of a stable.
(2) An advocate (A) must not discriminate against a person (B) who is a devil or a member of a stable—
 (a) as to the terms on which B is a devil or a member of the stable;
 (b) in the way A affords B access, or by not affording B access, to opportunities for training or gaining experience or for receiving any other benefit, facility or service;
 (c) by terminating A's relationship with B (where B is a devil);
 (d) by subjecting B to pressure to leave the stable;
 (e) by subjecting B to any other detriment.
(3) An advocate must not, in relation to a relationship with a devil or membership of a stable, harass—
 (a) a devil or member;
 (b) a person who has applied to be taken as the advocate's devil or to become a member of the stable.
(4) An advocate (A) must not victimise a person (B)—
 (a) in the arrangements A makes for deciding who to take as A's devil or to whom to offer membership of a stable;

    (b) as to the terms on which A offers to take B as A's devil or offers B membership of a stable;

    (c) by not offering to take B as A's devil or not offering B membership of a stable.

(5) An advocate (A) must not victimise a person (B) who is a devil or a member of a stable—

    (a) as to the terms on which B is a devil or a member of the stable;

    (b) in the way A affords B access, or by not affording B access, to opportunities for training or gaining experience or for receiving any other benefit, facility or service;

    (c) by terminating A's relationship with B (where B is a devil);

    (d) by subjecting B to pressure to leave the stable;

    (e) by subjecting B to any other detriment.

(6) A person must not, in relation to instructing an advocate—

    (a) discriminate against the advocate by subjecting the advocate to a detriment;

    (b) harass the advocate;

    (c) victimise the advocate.

(7) A duty to make reasonable adjustments applies to an advocate.

(8) This section (apart from subsection (6)) applies in relation to an advocate's clerk as it applies in relation to an advocate; and for that purpose the reference to an advocate's clerk includes a reference to a person who carries out the functions of an advocate's clerk.

(9) 'Advocate' means a practising member of the Faculty of Advocates.

Office-holders

49 Personal offices: appointments, etc.

(1) This section applies in relation to personal offices.

(2) A personal office is an office or post—

    (a) to which a person is appointed to discharge a function personally under the direction of another person, and

    (b) in respect of which an appointed person is entitled to remuneration.

(3) A person (A) who has the power to make an appointment to a personal office must not discriminate against a person (B)—

    (a) in the arrangements A makes for deciding to whom to offer the appointment;

    (b) as to the terms on which A offers B the appointment;

    (c) by not offering B the appointment.

(4) A person who has the power to make an appointment to a personal office must not, in relation to the office, harass a person seeking, or being considered for, the appointment.

(5) A person (A) who has the power to make an appointment to a personal office must not victimise a person (B)—

    (a) in the arrangements A makes for deciding to whom to offer the appointment;

    (b) as to the terms on which A offers B the appointment;

    (c) by not offering B the appointment.

(6) A person (A) who is a relevant person in relation to a personal office must not discriminate against a person (B) appointed to the office—

    (a) as to the terms of B's appointment;

    (b) in the way A affords B access, or by not affording B access, to opportunities for promotion, transfer or training or for receiving any other benefit, facility or service;

    (c) by terminating B's appointment;

    (d) by subjecting B to any other detriment.

(7) A relevant person in relation to a personal office must not, in relation to that office, harass a person appointed to it.

(8) A person (A) who is a relevant person in relation to a personal office must not victimise a person (B) appointed to the office—

(a) as to the terms of B's appointment;

(b) in the way A affords B access, or by not affording B access, to opportunities for promotion, transfer or training or for receiving any other benefit, facility or service;

(c) by terminating B's appointment;

(d) by subjecting B to any other detriment.

(9) A duty to make reasonable adjustments applies to—

(a) a person who has the power to make an appointment to a personal office;

(b) a relevant person in relation to a personal office.

(10) For the purposes of subsection (2)(a), a person is to be regarded as discharging functions personally under the direction of another person if that other person is entitled to direct the person as to when and where to discharge the functions.

(11) For the purposes of subsection (2)(b), a person is not to be regarded as entitled to remuneration merely because the person is entitled to payments—

(a) in respect of expenses incurred by the person in discharging the functions of the office or post, or

(b) by way of compensation for the loss of income or benefits the person would or might have received had the person not been discharging the functions of the office or post.

(12) Subsection (3)(b), so far as relating to sex or pregnancy and maternity, does not apply to a term that relates to pay—

(a) unless, were B to accept the offer, an equality clause or rule would have effect in relation to the term, or

(b) if paragraph (a) does not apply, except in so far as making an offer on terms including that term amounts to a contravention of subsection (3)(b) by virtue of section 13, 14 or 18.

50 Public offices: appointments, etc.

(1) This section and section 51 apply in relation to public offices.

(2) A public office is—

(a) an office or post, appointment to which is made by a member of the executive;

(b) an office or post, appointment to which is made on the recommendation of, or subject to the approval of, a member of the executive;

(c) an office or post, appointment to which is made on the recommendation of, or subject to the approval of, the House of Commons, the House of Lords, the National Assembly for Wales or the Scottish Parliament [;]

[(d) an office or post, appointment to which is made by the Lord Chief Justice or the Senior President of Tribunals.][37]

(3) A person (A) who has the power to make an appointment to a public office within subsection (2)(a) [, (b) or (d)][38] must not discriminate against a person (B)—

(a) in the arrangements A makes for deciding to whom to offer the appointment;

(b) as to the terms on which A offers B the appointment;

(c) by not offering B the appointment.

(4) A person who has the power to make an appointment to a public office within sub-section (2) (a) [, (b) or (d)][39] must not, in relation to the office, harass a person seeking, or being considered for, the appointment.

---

[37] Inserted by Crime and Courts Act 2013.

[38] Substituted by Crime and Courts Act 2013.

[39] Substituted by Crime and Courts Act 2013.

(5) A person (A) who has the power to make an appointment to a public office within subsection (2)(a) [, (b) or (d)]⁴⁰ must not victimise a person (B)—

    (a) in the arrangements A makes for deciding to whom to offer the appointment;

    (b) as to the terms on which A offers B the appointment;

    (c) by not offering B the appointment.

(6) A person (A) who is a relevant person in relation to a public office within subsection (2)(a) [, (b) or (d)]⁴¹ must not discriminate against a person (B) appointed to the office—

    (a) as to B's terms of appointment;

    (b) in the way A affords B access, or by not affording B access, to opportunities for promotion, transfer or training or for receiving any other benefit, facility or service;

    (c) by terminating the appointment;

    (d) by subjecting B to any other detriment.

(7) A person (A) who is a relevant person in relation to a public office within subsection (2)(c) must not discriminate against a person (B) appointed to the office—

    (a) as to B's terms of appointment;

    (b) in the way A affords B access, or by not affording B access, to opportunities for promotion, transfer or training or for receiving any other benefit, facility or service;

    (c) by subjecting B to any other detriment (other than by terminating the appointment).

(8) A relevant person in relation to a public office must not, in relation to that office, harass a person appointed to it.

(9) A person (A) who is a relevant person in relation to a public office within subsection (2)(a) [, (b) or (d)]⁴² must not victimise a person (B) appointed to the office—

    (a) as to B's terms of appointment;

    (b) in the way A affords B access, or by not affording B access, to opportunities for promotion, transfer or training or for receiving any other benefit, facility or service;

    (c) by terminating the appointment;

    (d) by subjecting B to any other detriment.

(10) A person (A) who is a relevant person in relation to a public office within subsection (2)(c) must not victimise a person (B) appointed to the office—

    (a) as to B's terms of appointment;

    (b) in the way A affords B access, or by not affording B access, to opportunities for promotion, transfer or training or for receiving any other benefit, facility or service;

    (c) by subjecting B to any other detriment (other than by terminating the appointment).

(11) A duty to make reasonable adjustments applies to—

    (a) a relevant person in relation to a public office;

    (b) a person who has the power to make an appointment to a public office within subsection (2)(a) [, (b) or (d)]⁴³.

(12) Subsection (3)(b), so far as relating to sex or pregnancy and maternity, does not apply to a term that relates to pay—

    (a) unless, were B to accept the offer, an equality clause or rule would have effect in relation to the term, or

    (b) if paragraph (a) does not apply, except in so far as making an offer on terms including that term amounts to a contravention of subsection (3)(b) by virtue of section 13, 14 or 18.

---

⁴⁰ Substituted by Crime and Courts Act 2013.
⁴¹ Substituted by Crime and Courts Act 2013.
⁴² Substituted by Crime and Courts Act 2013.
⁴³ Substituted by Crime and Courts Act 2013.

51 Public offices: recommendations for appointments, etc.

(1) A person (A) who has the power to make a recommendation for or give approval to an appointment to a public office within section 50(2)(a) [, (b) or (d)][44], must not discriminate against a person (B)—

    (a) in the arrangements A makes for deciding who to recommend for appointment or to whose appointment to give approval;

    (b) by not recommending B for appointment to the office;

    (c) by making a negative recommendation of B for appointment to the office;

    (d) by not giving approval to the appointment of B to the office.

(2) A person who has the power to make a recommendation for or give approval to an appointment to a public office within section 50(2)(a) [, (b) or (d)][45]must not, in relation to the office, harass a person seeking or being considered for the recommendation or approval.

(3) A person (A) who has the power to make a recommendation for or give approval to an appointment to a public office within section 50(2)(a) [, (b) or (d)][46], must not victimise a person (B)—

    (a) in the arrangements A makes for deciding who to recommend for appointment or to whose appointment to give approval;

    (b) by not recommending B for appointment to the office;

    (c) by making a negative recommendation of B for appointment to the office;

    (d) by not giving approval to the appointment of B to the office.

(4) A duty to make reasonable adjustments applies to a person who has the power to make a recommendation for or give approval to an appointment to a public office within section 50(2)(a) [, (b) or (d)][47].

(5) A reference in this section to a person who has the power to make a recommendation for or give approval to an appointment to a public office within section 50(2)(a) [or (d)][48] is a reference only to a relevant body which has that power; and for that purpose 'relevant body' means a body established—

    (a) by or in pursuance of an enactment, or

    (b) by a member of the executive.

52 Interpretation and exceptions

(1) This section applies for the purposes of sections 49 to 51.

(2) 'Personal office' has the meaning given in section 49.

(3) 'Public office' has the meaning given in section 50.

(4) An office or post which is both a personal office and a public office is to be treated as being a public office only.

(5) Appointment to an office or post does not include election to it.

(6) 'Relevant person', in relation to an office, means the person who, in relation to a matter specified in the first column of the table, is specified in the second column (but a reference to a relevant person does not in any case include the House of Commons, the House of Lords, the National Assembly for Wales or the Scottish Parliament).

---

[44] Substituted by Crime and Courts Act 2013.

[45] Substituted by Crime and Courts Act 2013.

[46] Substituted by Crime and Courts Act 2013.

[47] Substituted by Crime and Courts Act 2013.

[48] Inserted by Crime and Courts Act 2013.

Matter	Relevant person
A term of appointment	The person who has the power to set the term.
Access to an opportunity	The person who has the power to afford access to the opportunity (or, if there is no such person, the person who has the power to make the appointment).
Terminating an appointment	The person who has the power to terminate the appointment.
Subjecting an appointee to any other detriment	The person who has the power in relation to the matter to which the conduct in question relates (or, if there is no such person, the person who has the power to make the appointment).
Harassing an appointee	The person who has the power in relation to the matter to which the conduct in question relates.

(7) A reference to terminating a person's appointment includes a reference to termination of the appointment—

    (a) by the expiry of a period (including a period expiring by reference to an event or circumstance);

    (b) by an act of the person (including giving notice) in circumstances such that the person is entitled, because of the relevant person's conduct, to terminate the appointment without notice.

(8) Subsection (7)(a) does not apply if, immediately after the termination, the appointment is renewed on the same terms.

(9) Schedule 6 (excluded offices) has effect.

Qualifications

53 Qualifications bodies

(1) A qualifications body (A) must not discriminate against a person (B)–

    (a) in the arrangements A makes for deciding upon whom to confer a relevant qualification;

    (b) as to the terms on which it is prepared to confer a relevant qualification on B;

    (c) by not conferring a relevant qualification on B.

(2) A qualifications body (A) must not discriminate against a person (B) upon whom A has conferred a relevant qualification—

    (a) by withdrawing the qualification from B;

    (b) by varying the terms on which B holds the qualification;

    (c) by subjecting B to any other detriment.

(3) A qualifications body must not, in relation to conferment by it of a relevant qualification, harass—

    (a) a person who holds the qualification, or

    (b) a person who applies for it.

(4) A qualifications body (A) must not victimise a person (B)—

    (a) in the arrangements A makes for deciding upon whom to confer a relevant qualification;

    (b) as to the terms on which it is prepared to confer a relevant qualification on B;

    (c) by not conferring a relevant qualification on B.

(5) A qualifications body (A) must not victimise a person (B) upon whom A has conferred a relevant qualification—

    (a) by withdrawing the qualification from B;

    (b) by varying the terms on which B holds the qualification;

    (c) by subjecting B to any other detriment.

(6) A duty to make reasonable adjustments applies to a qualifications body.

(7) The application by a qualifications body of a competence standard to a disabled person is not disability discrimination unless it is discrimination by virtue of section 19.

54 Interpretation

(1) This section applies for the purposes of section 53.

(2) A qualifications body is an authority or body which can confer a relevant qualification.

(3) A relevant qualification is an authorisation, qualification, recognition, registration, enrolment, approval or certification which is needed for, or facilitates engagement in, a particular trade or profession.

(4) An authority or body is not a qualifications body in so far as—

    (a) it can confer a qualification to which section 96 applies,

    (b) it is the responsible body of a school to which section 85 applies,

    (c) it is the governing body of an institution to which section 91 applies,

    (d) it exercises functions under the Education Acts, or

    (e) it exercises functions under the Education (Scotland) Act 1980.

(5) A reference to conferring a relevant qualification includes a reference to renewing or extending the conferment of a relevant qualification.

(6) A competence standard is an academic, medical or other standard applied for the purpose of determining whether or not a person has a particular level of competence or ability.

Employment services

55 Employment service-providers

(1) A person (an 'employment service-provider') concerned with the provision of an employment service must not discriminate against a person—

    (a) in the arrangements the service-provider makes for selecting persons to whom to provide, or to whom to offer to provide, the service;

    (b) as to the terms on which the service-provider offers to provide the service to the person;

    (c) by not offering to provide the service to the person.

(2) An employment service-provider (A) must not, in relation to the provision of an employment service, discriminate against a person (B)—

    (a) as to the terms on which A provides the service to B;

    (b) by not providing the service to B;

    (c) by terminating the provision of the service to B;

    (d) by subjecting B to any other detriment.

(3) An employment service-provider must not, in relation to the provision of an employment service, harass—

    (a) a person who asks the service-provider to provide the service;

    (b) a person for whom the service-provider provides the service.

(4) An employment service-provider (A) must not victimise a person (B)—

    (a) in the arrangements A makes for selecting persons to whom to provide, or to whom to offer to provide, the service;

    (b) as to the terms on which A offers to provide the service to B;

    (c) by not offering to provide the service to B.

(5) An employment service-provider (A) must not, in relation to the provision of an employment service, victimise a person (B)—

    (a) as to the terms on which A provides the service to B;

    (b) by not providing the service to B;

    (c) by terminating the provision of the service to B;

    (d) by subjecting B to any other detriment.

(6) A duty to make reasonable adjustments applies to an employment service provider, except in relation to the provision of a vocational service.

(7) The duty imposed by section 29(7)(a) applies to a person concerned with the provision of a vocational service; but a failure to comply with that duty in relation to the provision of a vocational service is a contravention of this Part for the purposes of Part 9 (enforcement).

56 Interpretation

(1) This section applies for the purposes of section 55.

(2) The provision of an employment service includes—

    (a) the provision of vocational training;

    (b) the provision of vocational guidance;

    (c) making arrangements for the provision of vocational training or vocational guidance;

    (d) the provision of a service for finding employment for persons;

    (e) the provision of a service for supplying employers with persons to do work;

    (f) the provision of a service in pursuance of arrangements made under section 2 of the Employment and Training Act 1973 (functions of the Secretary of State relating to employment);

    (g) the provision of a service in pursuance of arrangements made or a direction given under section 10 of that Act (careers services);

    (h) the exercise of a function in pursuance of arrangements made under section 2(3) of the Enterprise and New Towns (Scotland) Act 1990 (functions of Scottish Enterprise, etc. relating to employment);

    (i) an assessment related to the conferment of a relevant qualification within the meaning of section 53 above (except in so far as the assessment is by the qualifications body which confers the qualification).

(3) This section does not apply in relation to training or guidance in so far as it is training or guidance in relation to which another provision of this Part applies.

(4) This section does not apply in relation to training or guidance for pupils of a school to which section 85 applies in so far as it is training or guidance to which the responsible body of the school has power to afford access (whether as the responsible body of that school or as the responsible body of any other school at which the training or guidance is provided).

(5) This section does not apply in relation to training or guidance for students of an institution to which section 91 applies in so far as it is training or guidance to which the governing body of the institution has power to afford access.

(6) 'Vocational training' means—

    (a) training for employment, or

    (b) work experience (including work experience the duration of which is not agreed until after it begins).

(7) A reference to the provision of a vocational service is a reference to the provision of an employment service within subsection (2)(a) to (d) (or an employment service within subsection (2)(f) or (g) in so far as it is also an employment service within subsection (2)(a) to (d)); and for that purpose—

    (a) the references to an employment service within subsection (2)(a) do not include a reference to vocational training within the meaning given by subsection (6)(b), and

    (b) the references to an employment service within subsection (2)(d) also include a reference to a service for assisting persons to retain employment.

(8) A reference to training includes a reference to facilities for training.

Trade organisations

57 Trade organisations

(1) A trade organisation (A) must not discriminate against a person (B)—
    (a) in the arrangements A makes for deciding to whom to offer membership of the organisation;
    (b) as to the terms on which it is prepared to admit B as a member;
    (c) by not accepting B's application for membership.
(2) A trade organisation (A) must not discriminate against a member (B)—
    (a) in the way it affords B access, or by not affording B access, to opportunities for receiving a benefit, facility or service;
    (b) by depriving B of membership;
    (c) by varying the terms on which B is a member;
    (d) by subjecting B to any other detriment.
(3) A trade organisation must not, in relation to membership of it, harass—
    (a) a member, or
    (b) an applicant for membership.
(4) A trade organisation (A) must not victimise a person (B)—
    (a) in the arrangements A makes for deciding to whom to offer membership of the organisation;
    (b) as to the terms on which it is prepared to admit B as a member;
    (c) by not accepting B's application for membership.
(5) A trade organisation (A) must not victimise a member (B)—
    (a) in the way it affords B access, or by not affording B access, to opportunities for receiving a benefit, facility or service;
    (b) by depriving B of membership;
    (c) by varying the terms on which B is a member;
    (d) by subjecting B to any other detriment.
(6) A duty to make reasonable adjustments applies to a trade organisation.
(7) A trade organisation is—
    (a) an organisation of workers,
    (b) an organisation of employers, or
    (c) any other organisation whose members carry on a particular trade or profession for the purposes of which the organisation exists.

Local authority members

58 Official business of members

(1) A local authority must not discriminate against a member of the authority in relation to the member's carrying out of official business—
    (a) in the way the authority affords the member access, or by not affording the member access, to opportunities for training or for receiving any other facility;
    (b) by subjecting the member to any other detriment.
(2) A local authority must not, in relation to a member's carrying out of official business, harass the member.
(3) A local authority must not victimise a member of the authority in relation to the member's carrying out of official business—
    (a) in the way the authority affords the member access, or by not affording the member access, to opportunities for training or for receiving any other facility;
    (b) by subjecting the member to any other detriment.

321

(4) A member of a local authority is not subjected to a detriment for the purposes of subsection (1)(b) or (3)(b) only because the member is—
   (a) not appointed or elected to an office of the authority,
   (b) not appointed or elected to, or to an office of, a committee or subcommittee of the authority, or
   (c) not appointed or nominated in exercise of an appointment power of the authority.

(5) In subsection (4)(c), an appointment power of a local authority is a power of the authority, or of a group of bodies including the authority, to make—
   (a) appointments to a body;
   (b) nominations for appointment to a body.

(6) A duty to make reasonable adjustments applies to a local authority.

59 Interpretation

(1) This section applies for the purposes of section 58.

(2) 'Local authority' means—
   (a) a county council in England;
   (b) a district council in England;
   (c) the Greater London Authority;
   (d) a London borough council;
   (e) the Common Council of the City of London;
   (f) the Council of the Isles of Scilly;
   (g) a parish council in England;
   (h) a county council in Wales;
   (i) a community council in Wales;
   (j) a county borough council in Wales;
   (k) a council constituted under section 2 of the Local Government etc. (Scotland) Act 1994;
   (l) a community council in Scotland.

(3) A Minister of the Crown may by order amend subsection (2) so as to add, vary or omit a reference to a body which exercises functions that have been conferred on a local authority within paragraph (a) to (l).

(4) A reference to the carrying-out of official business by a person who is a member of a local authority is a reference to the doing of anything by the person—
   (a) as a member of the authority,
   (b) as a member of a body to which the person is appointed by, or appointed following nomination by, the authority or a group of bodies including the authority, or
   (c) as a member of any other public body.

(5) 'Member', in relation to the Greater London Authority, means—
   (a) the Mayor of London;
   (b) a member of the London Assembly.

Recruitment

60 Enquiries about disability and health

(1) A person (A) to whom an application for work is made must not ask about the health of the applicant (B)—
   (a) before offering work to B, or
   (b) where A is not in a position to offer work to B, before including B in a pool of applicants from whom A intends (when in a position to do so) to select a person to whom to offer work.

(2) A contravention of subsection (1) (or a contravention of section 111 or 112 that relates to a contravention of subsection (1)) is enforceable as an unlawful act under Part 1 of the Equality Act 2006 (and, by virtue of section 120(8), is enforceable only by the Commission under that Part).

(3) A does not contravene a relevant disability provision merely by asking about B's health; but A's conduct in reliance on information given in response may be a contravention of a relevant disability provision.

(4) Subsection (5) applies if B brings proceedings before an employment tribunal on a complaint that A's conduct in reliance on information given in response to a question about B's health is a contravention of a relevant disability provision.

(5) In the application of section 136 to the proceedings, the particulars of the complaint are to be treated for the purposes of subsection (2) of that section as facts from which the tribunal could decide that A contravened the provision.

(6) This section does not apply to a question that A asks in so far as asking the question is necessary for the purpose of—

    (a) establishing whether B will be able to comply with a requirement to undergo an assessment or establishing whether a duty to make reasonable adjustments is or will be imposed on A in relation to B in connection with a requirement to undergo an assessment,

    (b) establishing whether B will be able to carry out a function that is intrinsic to the work concerned,

    (c) monitoring diversity in the range of persons applying to A for work,

    (d) taking action to which section 158 would apply if references in that section to persons who share (or do not share) a protected characteristic were references to disabled persons (or persons who are not disabled) and the reference to the characteristic were a reference to disability, or

    (e) if A applies in relation to the work a requirement to have a particular disability, establishing whether B has that disability.

(7) In subsection (6)(b), where A reasonably believes that a duty to make reasonable adjustments would be imposed on A in relation to B in connection with the work, the reference to a function that is intrinsic to the work is to be read as a reference to a function that would be intrinsic to the work once A complied with the duty.

(8) Subsection (6)(e) applies only if A shows that, having regard to the nature or context of the work—

    (a) the requirement is an occupational requirement, and

    (b) the application of the requirement is a proportionate means of achieving a legitimate aim.

(9) 'Work' means employment, contract work, a position as a partner, a position as a member of an LLP, a pupillage or tenancy, being taken as a devil, membership of a stable, an appointment to a personal or public office, or the provision of an employment service; and the references in subsection (1) to offering a person work are, in relation to contract work, to be read as references to allowing a person to do the work.

(10) A reference to offering work is a reference to making a conditional or unconditional offer of work (and, in relation to contract work, is a reference to allowing a person to do the work subject to fulfilment of one or more conditions).

(11) The following, so far as relating to discrimination within section 13 because of disability, are relevant disability provisions—

    (a) section 39(1)(a) or (c);

    (b) section 41(1)(b);

    (c) section 44(1)(a) or (c);

    (d) section 45(1)(a) or (c);

(e) section 47(1)(a) or (c);
(f) section 48(1)(a) or (c);
(g) section 49(3)(a) or (c);
(h) section 50(3)(a) or (c);
(i) section 51(1);
(j) section 55(1)(a) or (c).

(12) An assessment is an interview or other process designed to give an indication of a person's suitability for the work concerned.

(13) For the purposes of this section, whether or not a person has a disability is to be regarded as an aspect of that person's health.

(14) This section does not apply to anything done for the purpose of vetting applicants for work for reasons of national security.

CHAPTER 2
OCCUPATIONAL PENSION SCHEMES

61 Non-discrimination rule

(1) An occupational pension scheme must be taken to include a non-discrimination rule.

(2) A non-discrimination rule is a provision by virtue of which a responsible person (A)—
   (a) must not discriminate against another person (B) in carrying out any of A's functions in relation to the scheme;
   (b) must not, in relation to the scheme, harass B;
   (c) must not, in relation to the scheme, victimise B.

(3) The provisions of an occupational pension scheme have effect subject to the non-discrimination rule.

(4) The following are responsible persons—
   (a) the trustees or managers of the scheme;
   (b) an employer whose employees are, or may be, members of the scheme;
   (c) a person exercising an appointing function in relation to an office the holder of which is, or may be, a member of the scheme.

(5) A non-discrimination rule does not apply in relation to a person who is a pension credit member of a scheme.

(6) An appointing function is any of the following—
   (a) the function of appointing a person;
   (b) the function of terminating a person's appointment;
   (c) the function of recommending a person for appointment;
   (d) the function of approving an appointment.

(7) A breach of a non-discrimination rule is a contravention of this Part for the purposes of Part 9 (enforcement).

(8) It is not a breach of a non-discrimination rule for the employer or the trustees or managers of a scheme to maintain or use in relation to the scheme rules, practices, actions or decisions relating to age which are of a description specified by order by a Minister of the Crown.

(9) An order authorising the use of rules, practices, actions or decisions which are not in use before the order comes into force must not be made unless the Minister consults such persons as the Minister thinks appropriate.

(10) A non-discrimination rule does not have effect in relation to an occupational pension scheme in so far as an equality rule has effect in relation to it (or would have effect in relation to it but for Part 2 of Schedule 7).

(11) A duty to make reasonable adjustments applies to a responsible person.

62 Non-discrimination alterations

(1) This section applies if the trustees or managers of an occupational pension scheme do not have power to make non-discrimination alterations to the scheme.

(2) This section also applies if the trustees or managers of an occupational pension scheme have power to make non-discrimination alterations to the scheme but the procedure for doing so—
   (a) is liable to be unduly complex or protracted, or
   (b) involves obtaining consents which cannot be obtained or which can be obtained only with undue delay or difficulty.

(3) The trustees or managers may by resolution make non-discrimination alterations to the scheme.

(4) Non-discrimination alterations may have effect in relation to a period before the date on which they are made.

(5) Non-discrimination alterations to an occupational pension scheme are such alterations to the scheme as may be required for the provisions of the scheme to have the effect that they have in consequence of section 61(3).

63 Communications

(1) In their application to communications the following provisions apply in relation to a disabled person who is a pension credit member of an occupational pension scheme as they apply in relation to a disabled person who is a deferred member or pensioner member of the scheme—
   (a) section 61;
   (b) section 120;
   (c) section 126;
   (d) paragraph 19 of Schedule 8 (and such other provisions of that Schedule as apply for the purposes of that paragraph).

(2) Communications include—
   (a) the provision of information;
   (b) the operation of a dispute resolution procedure.

CHAPTER 3
EQUALITY OF TERMS

Sex equality

64 Relevant types of work

(1) Sections 66 to 70 apply where—
   (a) a person (A) is employed on work that is equal to the work that a comparator of the opposite sex (B) does;
   (b) a person (A) holding a personal or public office does work that is equal to the work that a comparator of the opposite sex (B) does.

(2) The references in subsection (1) to the work that B does are not restricted to work done contemporaneously with the work done by A.

65 Equal work

(1) For the purposes of this Chapter, A's work is equal to that of B if it is—
    (a) like B's work,
    (b) rated as equivalent to B's work, or
    (c) of equal value to B's work.

(2) A's work is like B's work if—
    (a) A's work and B's work are the same or broadly similar, and
    (b) such differences as there are between their work are not of practical importance in relation to the terms of their work.

(3) So on a comparison of one person's work with another's for the purposes of subsection (2), it is necessary to have regard to—
    (a) the frequency with which differences between their work occur in practice, and
    (b) the nature and extent of the differences.

(4) A's work is rated as equivalent to B's work if a job evaluation study—
    (a) gives an equal value to A's job and B's job in terms of the demands made on a worker, or
    (b) would give an equal value to A's job and B's job in those terms were the evaluation not made on a sex-specific system.

(5) A system is sex-specific if, for the purposes of one or more of the demands made on a worker, it sets values for men different from those it sets for women.

(6) A's work is of equal value to B's work if it is—
    (a) neither like B's work nor rated as equivalent to B's work, but
    (b) nevertheless equal to B's work in terms of the demands made on A by reference to factors such as effort, skill and decision-making.

66 Sex equality clause

(1) If the terms of A's work do not (by whatever means) include a sex equality clause, they are to be treated as including one.

(2) A sex equality clause is a provision that has the following effect—
    (a) if a term of A's is less favourable to A than a corresponding term of B's is to B, A's term is modified so as not to be less favourable;
    (b) if A does not have a term which corresponds to a term of B's that benefits B, A's terms are modified so as to include such a term.

(3) Subsection (2)(a) applies to a term of A's relating to membership of or rights under an occupational pension scheme only in so far as a sex equality rule would have effect in relation to the term.

(4) In the case of work within section 65(1)(b), a reference in subsection (2) above to a term includes a reference to such terms (if any) as have not been determined by the rating of the work (as well as those that have).

67 Sex equality rule

(1) If an occupational pension scheme does not include a sex equality rule, it is to be treated as including one.

(2) A sex equality rule is a provision that has the following effect—
    (a) if a relevant term is less favourable to A than it is to B, the term is modified so as not to be less favourable;
    (b) if a term confers a relevant discretion capable of being exercised in a way that would be less favourable to A than to B, the term is modified so as to prevent the exercise of the discretion in that way.

(3) A term is relevant if it is—
    (a) a term on which persons become members of the scheme, or
    (b) a term on which members of the scheme are treated.

(4) A discretion is relevant if its exercise in relation to the scheme is capable of affecting—
    (a) the way in which persons become members of the scheme, or
    (b) the way in which members of the scheme are treated.

(5) The reference in subsection (3)(b) to a term on which members of a scheme are treated includes a reference to the term as it has effect for the benefit of dependants of members.

(6) The reference in subsection (4)(b) to the way in which members of a scheme are treated includes a reference to the way in which they are treated as the scheme has effect for the benefit of dependants of members.

[(7) If the effect of a relevant matter on a person (A) differs according to the effect it has on a person of the same sex as A, according to whether A is married, in a civil partnership, or for some other reason due to A's family status, a comparison for the purposes of this section of the effect of that matter on persons of the opposite sex must be with a person of the opposite sex to A who is in the same position as A and in particular—
    (a) where A is married to [, or the civil partner of,][49] someone of the opposite sex, A is to be compared to a person of the opposite sex to A ('B') where B is married to [or (as the case may be) the civil partner of][50] someone of the opposite sex to B;
    [(b) where A is married to, or the civil partner of, someone of the same sex, A is to be compared to B where B is married to or (as the case may be) the civil partner of someone of the same sex as B.][51]][52]

(8) A relevant matter is—
    (a) a relevant term;
    (b) a term conferring a relevant discretion;
    (c) the exercise of a relevant discretion in relation to an occupational pension scheme.

(9) This section, so far as relating to the terms on which persons become members of an occupational pension scheme, does not have effect in relation to pensionable service before 8 April 1976.

(10) This section, so far as relating to the terms on which members of an occupational pension scheme are treated, does not have effect in relation to pensionable service before 17 May 1990.

68 Sex equality rule: consequential alteration of schemes

(1) This section applies if the trustees or managers of an occupational pension scheme do not have power to make sex equality alterations to the scheme.

(2) This section also applies if the trustees or managers of an occupational pension scheme have power to make sex equality alterations to the scheme but the procedure for doing so—
    (a) is liable to be unduly complex or protracted, or

---

[49] Inserted by Civil Partnership (Opposite-sex couples) Regulations 2019, SI 2019/1458.
[50] Inserted by Civil Partnership (Opposite-sex couples) Regulations 2019, SI 2019/1458.
[51] Substituted by Civil Partnership (Opposite-sex couples) Regulations 2019, SI 2019/1458.
[52] Substituted by— a) Marriage (Same Sex Couples) Act 2013 (Consequential and Contrary Provisions and Scotland) Order 2014, SI 2014/560. b) Marriage and Civil Partnership (Scotland) Act 2014 and Civil Partnership Act 2004 (Consequential Provisions and Modifications) Order 2014, SI 2014/3229.

(b) involves obtaining consents which cannot be obtained or which can be obtained only with undue delay or difficulty.

(3) The trustees or managers may by resolution make sex equality alterations to the scheme.

(4) Sex equality alterations may have effect in relation to a period before the date on which they are made.

(5) Sex equality alterations to an occupational pension scheme are such alterations to the scheme as may be required to secure conformity with a sex equality rule.

69 Defence of material factor

(1) The sex equality clause in A's terms has no effect in relation to a difference between A's terms and B's terms if the responsible person shows that the difference is because of a material factor reliance on which—

(a) does not involve treating A less favourably because of A's sex than the responsible person treats B, and

(b) if the factor is within subsection (2), is a proportionate means of achieving a legitimate aim. (2) A factor is within this subsection if A shows that, as a result of the factor, A and persons of the same sex doing work equal to A's are put at a particular disadvantage when compared with persons of the opposite sex doing work equal to A's.

(3) For the purposes of subsection (1), the long-term objective of reducing inequality between men's and women's terms of work is always to be regarded as a legitimate aim.

(4) A sex equality rule has no effect in relation to a difference between A and B in the effect of a relevant matter if the trustees or managers of the scheme in question show that the difference is because of a material factor which is not the difference of sex.

(5) 'Relevant matter' has the meaning given in section 67.

(6) For the purposes of this section, a factor is not material unless it is a material difference between A's case and B's.

70 Exclusion of sex discrimination provisions

(1) The relevant sex discrimination provision has no effect in relation to a term of A's that—

(a) is modified by, or included by virtue of, a sex equality clause or rule, or

(b) would be so modified or included but for section 69 or Part 2 of Schedule 7.

(2) Neither of the following is sex discrimination for the purposes of the relevant sex discrimination provision—

(a) the inclusion in A's terms of a term that is less favourable as referred to in section 66(2)(a);

(b) the failure to include in A's terms a corresponding term as referred to in section 66(2)(b).

(3) The relevant sex discrimination provision is, in relation to work of a description given in the first column of the table, the provision referred to in the second column so far as relating to sex.

Description of work	Provision
Employment	Section 39(2)
Appointment to a personal office	Section 49(6)
Appointment to a public office	Section 50(6)

71 Sex discrimination in relation to contractual pay

(1) This section applies in relation to a term of a person's work—

(a) that relates to pay, but

(b) in relation to which a sex equality clause or rule has no effect.

(2) The relevant sex discrimination provision (as defined by section 70) has no effect in relation to the term except in so far as treatment of the person amounts to a contravention of the provision by virtue of section 13 or 14.

Pregnancy and maternity equality

72 Relevant types of work

Sections 73 to 76 apply where a woman—
(a) is employed, or
(b) holds a personal or public office.

73 Maternity equality clause

(1) If the terms of the woman's work do not (by whatever means) include a maternity equality clause, they are to be treated as including one.
(2) A maternity equality clause is a provision that, in relation to the terms of the woman's work, has the effect referred to in section 74(1), (6) and (8).
(3) In the case of a term relating to membership of or rights under an occupational pension scheme, a maternity equality clause has only such effect as a maternity equality rule would have.

74 Maternity equality clause: pay

(1) A term of the woman's work that provides for maternity-related pay to be calculated by reference to her pay at a particular time is, if each of the following three conditions is satisfied, modified as mentioned in subsection (5).
(2) The first condition is that, after the time referred to in subsection (1) but before the end of the protected period—
(a) her pay increases, or
(b) it would have increased had she not been on maternity leave.
(3) The second condition is that the maternity-related pay is not—
(a) what her pay would have been had she not been on maternity leave, or
(b) the difference between the amount of statutory maternity pay to which she is entitled and what her pay would have been had she not been on maternity leave.
(4) The third condition is that the terms of her work do not provide for the maternity-related pay to be subject to—
(a) an increase as mentioned in subsection (2)(a), or
(b) an increase that would have occurred as mentioned in subsection (2)(b).
(5) The modification referred to in subsection (1) is a modification to provide for the maternity-related pay to be subject to—
(a) any increase as mentioned in subsection (2)(a), or
(b) any increase that would have occurred as mentioned in subsection (2)(b).
(6) A term of her work that—
(a) provides for pay within subsection (7), but
(b) does not provide for her to be given the pay in circumstances in which she would have been given it had she not been on maternity leave, is modified so as to provide for her to be given it in circumstances in which it would normally be given.
(7) Pay is within this subsection if it is—
(a) pay (including pay by way of bonus) in respect of times before the woman is on maternity leave,

(b) pay by way of bonus in respect of times when she is on compulsory maternity leave, or

(c) pay by way of bonus in respect of times after the end of the protected period.

(8) A term of the woman's work that—

    (a) provides for pay after the end of the protected period, but

    (b) does not provide for it to be subject to an increase to which it would have been subject had she not been on maternity leave, is modified so as to provide for it to be subject to the increase.

(9) Maternity-related pay is pay (other than statutory maternity pay) to which a woman is entitled—

    (a) as a result of being pregnant, or

    (b) in respect of times when she is on maternity leave.

(10) A reference to the protected period is to be construed in accordance with section 18.

75 Maternity equality rule

(1) If an occupational pension scheme does not include a maternity equality rule, it is to be treated as including one.

(2) A maternity equality rule is a provision that has the effect set out in subsections (3) and (4).

(3) If a relevant term does not treat time when the woman is on maternity leave as it treats time when she is not, the term is modified so as to treat time when she is on maternity leave as time when she is not.

(4) If a term confers a relevant discretion capable of being exercised so that time when she is on maternity leave is treated differently from time when she is not, the term is modified so as not to allow the discretion to be exercised in that way.

(5) A term is relevant if it is—

    (a) a term relating to membership of the scheme,

    (b) a term relating to the accrual of rights under the scheme, or

    (c) a term providing for the determination of the amount of a benefit payable under the scheme.

(6) A discretion is relevant if its exercise is capable of affecting—

    (a) membership of the scheme,

    (b) the accrual of rights under the scheme, or

    (c) the determination of the amount of a benefit payable under the scheme.

(7) This section does not require the woman's contributions to the scheme in respect of time when she is on maternity leave to be determined otherwise than by reference to the amount she is paid in respect of that time.

(8) This section, so far as relating to time when she is on ordinary maternity leave but is not being paid by her employer, applies only in a case where the expected week of childbirth began on or after 6 April 2003.

(9) This section, so far as relating to time when she is on additional maternity leave but is not being paid by her employer—

    (a) does not apply to the accrual of rights under the scheme in any case;

    (b) applies for other purposes only in a case where the expected week of childbirth began on or after 5 October 2008.

(10) In this section—

    (a) a reference to being on maternity leave includes a reference to having been on maternity leave, and

(b) a reference to being paid by the employer includes a reference to receiving statutory maternity pay from the employer.

76 Exclusion of pregnancy and maternity discrimination provisions

(1) The relevant pregnancy and maternity discrimination provision has no effect in relation to a term of the woman's work that is modified by a maternity equality clause or rule.

[(1A) The relevant pregnancy and maternity discrimination provision has no effect in relation to a term of the woman's work—

(a) that relates to pay, but

(b) in relation to which a maternity equality clause or rule has no effect.][53]

(2) The inclusion in the woman's terms of a term that requires modification by virtue of section 73(2) or (3) is not pregnancy and maternity discrimination for the purposes of the relevant pregnancy and maternity discrimination provision.

(3) The relevant pregnancy and maternity discrimination provision is, in relation to a description of work given in the first column of the table, the provision referred to in the second column so far as relating to pregnancy and maternity.

Description of work	Provision
Employment	Section 39(2)
Appointment to a personal office	Section 49(6)
Appointment to a public office	Section 50(6)

Disclosure of information

77 Discussions about pay

(1) A term of a person's work that purports to prevent or restrict the person (P) from disclosing or seeking to disclose information about the terms of P's work is unenforceable against P in so far as P makes or seeks to make a relevant pay disclosure.

(2) A term of a person's work that purports to prevent or restrict the person (P) from seeking disclosure of information from a colleague about the terms of the colleague's work is unenforceable against P in so far as P seeks a relevant pay disclosure from the colleague; and 'colleague' includes a former colleague in relation to the work in question.

(3) A disclosure is a relevant pay disclosure if made for the purpose of enabling the person who makes it, or the person to whom it is made, to find out whether or to what extent there is, in relation to the work in question, a connection between pay and having (or not having) a particular protected characteristic.

(4) The following are to be treated as protected acts for the purposes of the relevant victimisation provision—

(a) seeking a disclosure that would be a relevant pay disclosure;

(b) making or seeking to make a relevant pay disclosure;

(c) receiving information disclosed in a relevant pay disclosure.

(5) The relevant victimisation provision is, in relation to a description of work specified in the first column of the table, section 27 so far as it applies for the purposes of a provision mentioned in the second column.

---

[53] Inserted by Equality Act 2010 (Amendment) Order 2010, SI 2010/2622.

Description of work	Provision by virtue of which section 27 has effect
Employment	Section 39(3) or (4)
Appointment to a personal office	Section 49(5) or (8)
Appointment to a public office	Section 50(5) or (9)

78 Gender pay gap information

(1) Regulations may require employers to publish information relating to the pay of employees for the purpose of showing whether, by reference to factors of such description as is prescribed, there are differences in the pay of male and female employees.

(2) This section does not apply to—

    (a) an employer who has fewer than 250 employees;

    (b) a person specified in Schedule 19;

    (c) a government department or part of the armed forces not specified in that Schedule.

(3) The regulations may prescribe—

    (a) descriptions of employer;

    (b) descriptions of employee;

    (c) how to calculate the number of employees that an employer has;

    (d) descriptions of information;

    (e) the time at which information is to be published;

    (f) the form and manner in which it is to be published.

(4) Regulations under subsection (3)(e) may not require an employer, after the first publication of information, to publish information more frequently than at intervals of 12 months.

(5) The regulations may make provision for a failure to comply with the regulations—

    (a) to be an offence punishable on summary conviction by a fine not exceeding level 5 on the standard scale;

    (b) to be enforced, otherwise than as an offence, by such means as are prescribed.

(6) The reference to a failure to comply with the regulations includes a reference to a failure by a person acting on behalf of an employer.

Supplementary

79 Comparators

(1) This section applies for the purposes of this Chapter.

(2) If A is employed, B is a comparator if subsection (3) or (4) applies.

(3) This subsection applies if—

    (a) B is employed by A's employer or by an associate of A's employer, and

    (b) A and B work at the same establishment.

(4) This subsection applies if—

    (a) B is employed by A's employer or an associate of A's employer,

    (b) B works at an establishment other than the one at which A works, and

    (c) common terms apply at the establishments (either generally or as between A and B).

(5) If A holds a personal or public office, B is a comparator if—

    (a) B holds a personal or public office, and

    (b) the person responsible for paying A is also responsible for paying B.

(6) If A is a relevant member of the House of Commons staff, B is a comparator if—

    (a) B is employed by the person who is A's employer under subsection (6) of section 195 of the Employment Rights Act 1996, or

(b) if subsection (7) of that section applies in A's case, B is employed by the person who is A's employer under that subsection.

(7) If A is a relevant member of the House of Lords staff, B is a comparator if B is also a relevant member of the House of Lords staff.

(8) Section 42 does not apply to this Chapter; accordingly, for the purposes of this Chapter only, holding the office of constable is to be treated as holding a personal office.

(9) For the purposes of this section, employers are associated if—

(a) one is a company of which the other (directly or indirectly) has control, or

(b) both are companies of which a third person (directly or indirectly) has control.

80 Interpretation and exceptions

(1) This section applies for the purposes of this Chapter.

(2) The terms of a person's work are—

(a) if the person is employed, the terms of the person's employment that are in the person's contract of employment, contract of apprenticeship or contract to do work personally;

(b) if the person holds a personal or public office, the terms of the person's appointment to the office.

(3) If work is not done at an establishment, it is to be treated as done at the establishment with which it has the closest connection.

(4) A person (P) is the responsible person in relation to another person if—

(a) P is the other's employer;

(b) P is responsible for paying remuneration in respect of a personal or public office that the other holds.

(5) A job evaluation study is a study undertaken with a view to evaluating, in terms of the demands made on a person by reference to factors such as effort, skill and decision-making, the jobs to be done—

(a) by some or all of the workers in an undertaking or group of undertakings, or

(b) in the case of the armed forces, by some or all of the members of the armed forces.

(6) In the case of Crown employment, the reference in subsection (5)(a) to an undertaking is to be construed in accordance with section 191(4) of the Employment Rights Act 1996.

(7) [...][54]

(8) Schedule 7 (exceptions) has effect.

CHAPTER 4
SUPPLEMENTARY

81 Ships and hovercraft

(1) This Part applies in relation to—

(a) work on ships,

(b) work on hovercraft, and

(c) seafarers, only in such circumstances as are prescribed.

(2) For the purposes of this section, it does not matter whether employment arises or work is carried out within or outside the United Kingdom.

---

[54] Repealed by— a) Marriage (Same Sex Couples) Act 2013 (Consequential and Contrary Provisions and Scotland) Order 2014, SI 2014/560. b) Marriage and Civil Partnership (Scotland) Act 2014 and Civil Partnership Act 2004 (Consequential Provisions and Modifications) Order 2014, SI 2014/3229.

(3) 'Ship' has the same meaning as in the Merchant Shipping Act 1995.

(4) 'Hovercraft' has the same meaning as in the Hovercraft Act 1968.

(5) 'Seafarer' means a person employed or engaged in any capacity on board a ship or hovercraft.

(6) Nothing in this section affects the application of any other provision of this Act to conduct outside England and Wales or Scotland.

82 Offshore work

(1) Her Majesty may by Order in Council provide that in the case of persons in offshore work—
  (a) specified provisions of this Part apply (with or without modification);
  (b) Northern Ireland legislation making provision for purposes corresponding to any of the purposes of this Part applies (with or without modification).

(2) The Order may—
  (a) provide for these provisions, as applied by the Order, to apply to individuals (whether or not British citizens) and bodies corporate (whether or not incorporated under the law of a part of the United Kingdom), whether or not such application affects activities outside the United Kingdom;
  (b) make provision for conferring jurisdiction on a specified court or class of court or on employment tribunals in respect of offences, causes of action or other matters arising in connection with offshore work;
  (c) exclude from the operation of section 3 of the Territorial Waters Jurisdiction Act 1878 (consents required for prosecutions) proceedings for offences under the provisions mentioned in subsection (1) in connection with offshore work;
  (d) provide that such proceedings must not be brought without such consent as may be required by the Order.

(3) 'Offshore work' is work for the purposes of—
  (a) activities in the territorial sea adjacent to the United Kingdom,
  (b) activities such as are mentioned in subsection (2) of section 11 of the Petroleum Act 1998 in waters within subsection (8)(b) or (c) of that section, or
  (c) activities mentioned in paragraphs (a) and (b) of section 87(1) of the Energy Act 2004 in waters to which that section applies.

(4) Work includes employment, contract work, a position as a partner or as a member of an LLP, or an appointment to a personal or public office.

(5) Northern Ireland legislation includes an enactment contained in, or in an instrument under, an Act that forms part of the law of Northern Ireland.

(6) In the application to Northern Ireland of subsection (2)(b), the reference to employment tribunals is to be read as a reference to industrial tribunals.

(7) Nothing in this section affects the application of any other provision of this Act to conduct outside England and Wales or Scotland.

83 Interpretation and exceptions

(1) This section applies for the purposes of this Part.

(2) 'Employment' means—
  (a) employment under a contract of employment, a contract of apprenticeship or a contract personally to do work;
  (b) Crown employment;
  (c) employment as a relevant member of the House of Commons staff;
  (d) employment as a relevant member of the House of Lords staff.

(3) This Part applies to service in the armed forces as it applies to employment by a private person; and for that purpose—
  (a) references to terms of employment, or to a contract of employment, are to be read as including references to terms of service;
  (b) references to associated employers are to be ignored.
(4) A reference to an employer or an employee, or to employing or being employed, is (subject to section 212(11)) to be read with subsections (2) and (3); and a reference to an employer also includes a reference to a person who has no employees but is seeking to employ one or more other persons.
(5) 'Relevant member of the House of Commons staff' has the meaning given in section 195 of the Employment Rights Act 1996; and such a member of staff is an employee of—
  (a) the person who is the employer of that member under subsection (6) of that section, or
  (b) if subsection (7) of that section applies in the case of that member, the person who is the employer of that member under that subsection.
(6) 'Relevant member of the House of Lords staff' has the meaning given in section 194 of that Act (which provides that such a member of staff is an employee of the Corporate Officer of the House of Lords).
(7) In the case of a person in Crown employment, or in employment as a relevant member of the House of Commons staff, a reference to the person's dismissal is a reference to the termination of the person's employment.
(8) A reference to a personal or public office, or to an appointment to a personal or public office, is to be construed in accordance with section 52.
(9) 'Crown employment' has the meaning given in section 191 of the Employment Rights Act 1996.
(10) Schedule 8 (reasonable adjustments) has effect.
(11) Schedule 9 (exceptions) has effect.

PART 6
EDUCATION

CHAPTER 1
SCHOOLS

84 Application of this Chapter

This Chapter does not apply to the following protected characteristics—
(a) age;
(b) marriage and civil partnership.

85 Pupils: admission and treatment, etc.

(1) The responsible body of a school to which this section applies must not discriminate against a person—
  (a) in the arrangements it makes for deciding who is offered admission as a pupil;
  (b) as to the terms on which it offers to admit the person as a pupil;
  (c) by not admitting the person as a pupil.

(2) The responsible body of such a school must not discriminate against a pupil—
- (a) in the way it provides education for the pupil;
- (b) in the way it affords the pupil access to a benefit, facility or service;
- (c) by not providing education for the pupil;
- (d) by not affording the pupil access to a benefit, facility or service;
- (e) by excluding the pupil from the school;
- (f) by subjecting the pupil to any other detriment.

(3) The responsible body of such a school must not harass—
- (a) a pupil;
- (b) a person who has applied for admission as a pupil.

(4) The responsible body of such a school must not victimise a person—
- (a) in the arrangements it makes for deciding who is offered admission as a pupil;
- (b) as to the terms on which it offers to admit the person as a pupil;
- (c) by not admitting the person as a pupil.

(5) The responsible body of such a school must not victimise a pupil—
- (a) in the way it provides education for the pupil;
- (b) in the way it affords the pupil access to a benefit, facility or service;
- (c) by not providing education for the pupil;
- (d) by not affording the pupil access to a benefit, facility or service;
- (e) by excluding the pupil from the school;
- (f) by subjecting the pupil to any other detriment.

(6) A duty to make reasonable adjustments applies to the responsible body of such a school.

(7) In relation to England and Wales, this section applies to—
- (a) a school maintained by a local authority;
- (b) an independent educational institution (other than a special school);
- [(ba) an alternative provision Academy that is not an independent educational institution;][55]
- (c) a special school (not maintained by a local authority).

(8) In relation to Scotland, this section applies to—
- (a) a school managed by an education authority;
- (b) an independent school;
- (c) a school in respect of which the managers are for the time being receiving grants under section 73(c) or (d) of the Education (Scotland) Act 1980.

(9) The responsible body of a school to which this section applies is—
- (a) if the school is within subsection (7)(a), the local authority or governing body;
- (b) if it is within subsection (7)(b) [, (ba)][56] or (c), the proprietor;
- (c) if it is within subsection (8)(a), the education authority;
- (d) if it is within subsection (8)(b), the proprietor;
- (e) if it is within subsection (8)(c), the managers.

(10) In the application of section 26 for the purposes of subsection (3), none of the following is a relevant protected characteristic—
- (a) gender reassignment;
- (b) religion or belief;
- (c) sexual orientation.

---

[55] Inserted by Alternative Provision Academies (Consequential Amendments to Acts) (England) Order 2012, SI 2012/976.

[56] Inserted by Alternative Provision Academies (Consequential Amendments to Acts) (England) Order 2012, SI 2012/976.

86 Victimisation of pupils, etc. for conduct of parents, etc.

(1) This section applies for the purposes of section 27 in its application to section 85(4) or (5).

(2) The references to B in paragraphs (a) and (b) of subsection (1) of section 27 include a reference to a parent or sibling of the child in question.

(3) Giving false evidence or information, or making a false allegation, in good faith is not a protected act in a case where—

(a) the evidence or information is given, or the allegation is made, by a parent or sibling of the child, and

(b) the child has acted in bad faith.

(4) Giving false evidence or information, or making a false allegation, in bad faith, is a protected act in a case where—

(a) the evidence or information is given, or the allegation is made, by a parent or sibling of the child, and

(b) the child has acted in good faith.

(5) In this section—

'child' means a person who has not attained the age of 18;

'sibling' means a brother or sister, a half-brother or half-sister, or a stepbrother or stepsister.

87 [Application of enforcement powers under education legislation][57]

[(A1) Subsections (1) and (2) do not apply in the case of a school in Wales.][58]

(1) Sections 496 and 497 of the Education Act 1996 [and section 70 of the Education (Scotland) Act 1980][59] (powers to give directions where responsible body of school in default of obligations, etc.) apply to the performance of a duty under section 85.

(2) But neither of sections 496 and 497 of [the Education Act 1996][60] applies to the performance of a duty under that section by the proprietor of an independent educational institution (other than a special school) [or an alternative provision Academy that is not an independent educational institution][61] [; and section 70 of the Education (Scotland) Act 1980 does not apply to the performance of a duty under that section by the proprietor of an independent school].[62]

[(3) In the case of a school in Wales—

(a) Chapter 1 of Part 2 of the School Standards and Organisation (Wales) Act 2013 ('the 2013 Act') (intervention in conduct of maintained schools) applies to the performance of a duty under section 85, but as if—

(i) the only relevant grounds for intervention were grounds 5 and 6 in section 2 of that Act, and

(ii) sections 3 to 9 and 12 to 16 of that Act did not apply;

---

[57] Substituted by Equality Act 2010 (Consequential Amendments, Saving and Supplementary Provisions) Order 2010, SI 2010/2279.

[58] Inserted by School Standards and Organisation (Wales) Act 2013.

[59] Inserted by Equality Act 2010 (Consequential Amendments, Saving and Supplementary Provisions) Order 2010, SI 2010/2279.

[60] Substituted by Equality Act 2010 (Consequential Amendments, Saving and Supplementary Provisions) Order 2010, SI 2010/2279.

[61] Inserted by Alternative Provision Academies (Consequential Amendments to Acts) (England) Order 2012, SI 2012/976.

[62] Inserted by Equality Act 2010 (Consequential Amendments, Saving and Supplementary Provisions) Order 2010, SI 2010/2279.

(b) Chapter 2 of Part 2 of the 2013 Act (intervention in local authorities) applies to the performance of a duty under section 85, but as if—
  (i) the only relevant grounds for intervention were grounds 1 and 2 in section 21 of that Act, and
  (ii) sections 24 to 27 of that Act did not apply.
(4) But neither of Chapters 1 and 2 of Part 2 of the 2013 Act applies to the performance of a duty under section 85 by the proprietor of an independent educational institution (other than a special school).][63]

88 Disabled pupils: accessibility

Schedule 10 (accessibility) has effect.

89 Interpretation and exceptions

(1) This section applies for the purposes of this Chapter.
(2) Nothing in this Chapter applies to anything done in connection with the content of the curriculum.
(3) 'Pupil'—
  (a) in relation to England and Wales, has the meaning given in section 3(1) of the Education Act 1996;
  (b) in relation to Scotland, has the meaning given in section 135(1) of the Education (Scotland) Act 1980.
(4) 'Proprietor'—
  (a) in relation to a school in England and Wales, has the meaning given in section 579(1) of the Education Act 1996;
  (b) in relation to a school in Scotland, has the meaning given in section 135(1) of the Education (Scotland) Act 1980.
(5) 'School'—
  (a) in relation to England and Wales, has the meaning given in section 4 of the Education Act 1996;
  (b) in relation to Scotland, has the meaning given in section 135(1) of the Education (Scotland) Act 1980.
(6) A reference to a school includes a reference to an independent educational institution in England; and a reference to an independent educational institution in England is to be construed in accordance with Chapter 1 of Part 4 of the Education and Skills Act 2008.
(7) A reference to an independent educational institution is a reference to—
  (a) an independent educational institution in England, or
  (b) an independent school in Wales.
(8) 'Independent school'—
  (a) in relation to Wales, has the meaning given in section 463 of the Education Act 1996;
  (b) in relation to Scotland, has the meaning given in section 135(1) of the Education (Scotland) Act 1980.
(9) 'Special school' has the meaning given in section 337 of the Education Act 1996.
(10) 'Local authority' means—
  (a) in relation to England, an English local authority within the meaning of section 162 of the Education and Inspections Act 2006;
  (b) in relation to Wales, a Welsh local authority within the meaning of that section.

---

[63] Inserted by School Standards and Organisation (Wales) Act 2013.

(11) 'Education authority', in relation to Scotland, has the meaning given in section 135(1) of the Education (Scotland) Act 1980.

(12) Schedule 11 (exceptions) has effect.

CHAPTER 2
FURTHER AND HIGHER EDUCATION

90 Application of this Chapter

This Chapter does not apply to the protected characteristic of marriage and civil partnership.

91 Students: admission and treatment, etc.

(1) The responsible body of an institution to which this section applies must not discriminate against a person—

(a) in the arrangements it makes for deciding who is offered admission as a student;

(b) as to the terms on which it offers to admit the person as a student;

(c) by not admitting the person as a student.

(2) The responsible body of such an institution must not discriminate against a student—

(a) in the way it provides education for the student;

(b) in the way it affords the student access to a benefit, facility or service;

(c) by not providing education for the student;

(d) by not affording the student access to a benefit, facility or service;

(e) by excluding the student;

(f) by subjecting the student to any other detriment.

(3) The responsible body of such an institution must not discriminate against a disabled person—

(a) in the arrangements it makes for deciding upon whom to confer a qualification;

(b) as to the terms on which it is prepared to confer a qualification on the person;

(c) by not conferring a qualification on the person;

(d) by withdrawing a qualification from the person or varying the terms on which the person holds it.

(4) Subsection (3) applies only to disability discrimination.

(5) The responsible body of such an institution must not harass—

(a) a student;

(b) a person who has applied for admission as a student;

(c) a disabled person who holds or has applied for a qualification conferred by the institution.

(6) The responsible body of such an institution must not victimise a person—

(a) in the arrangements it makes for deciding who is offered admission as a student;

(b) as to the terms on which it offers to admit the person as a student;

(c) by not admitting the person as a student.

(7) The responsible body of such an institution must not victimise a student—

(a) in the way it provides education for the student;

(b) in the way it affords the student access to a benefit, facility or service;

(c) by not providing education for the student;

(d) by not affording the student access to a benefit, facility or service;

(e) by excluding the student;

(f) by subjecting the student to any other detriment.

(8) The responsible body of such an institution must not victimise a disabled person—

(a) in the arrangements it makes for deciding upon whom to confer a qualification;

(b) as to the terms on which it is prepared to confer a qualification on the person;

(c) by not conferring a qualification on the person;

(d) by withdrawing a qualification from the person or varying the terms on which the person holds it.

(9) A duty to make reasonable adjustments applies to the responsible body of such an institution.

(10) In relation to England and Wales, this section applies to—

(a) a university;

(b) any other institution within the higher education sector;

(c) an institution within the further education sector [;]

[(d) a 16 to 19 Academy.][64]

(11) In relation to Scotland, this section applies to—

(a) a university;

(b) a designated institution;

(c) a college of further education.

(12) A responsible body is—

(a) in the case of an institution within subsection (10)(a), (b) or (c), the governing body;

[(aa) in the case of an institution within subsection (10)(d), the proprietor (within the meaning of the Education Act 1996);][65]

(b) in the case of an institution within subsection (11)(a) or (b), the governing body;

(c) in the case of a college of further education under the management of a board of management, the board of management;

(d) in the case of any other college of further education, any board of governors of the college or any person responsible for the management of the college, whether or not formally constituted as a governing body or board of governors.

92 Further and higher education courses

(1) The responsible body in relation to a course to which this section applies must not discriminate against a person—

(a) in the arrangements it makes for deciding who is enrolled on the course;

(b) as to the terms on which it offers to enrol the person on the course;

(c) by not accepting the person's application for enrolment.

(2) The responsible body in relation to such a course must not discriminate against a person who is enrolled on the course in the services it provides or offers to provide.

(3) The responsible body in relation to such a course must not harass a person who—

(a) seeks enrolment on the course;

(b) is enrolled on the course;

(c) is a user of services provided by the body in relation to the course.

(4) The responsible body in relation to such a course must not victimise a person—

(a) in the arrangements it makes for deciding who is enrolled on the course;

(b) as to the terms on which it offers to enrol the person on the course;

(c) by not accepting the person's application for enrolment.

(5) The responsible body in relation to such a course must not victimise a person who is enrolled on the course in the services it provides or offers to provide.

(6) A duty to make reasonable adjustments applies to the responsible body.

(7) This section applies to—

(a) a course of further or higher education secured by a responsible body in England or Wales;

---

[64] Inserted by Education Act 2011.
[65] Inserted by Education Act 2011.

   (b) a course of education provided by the governing body of a maintained school under section 80 of the School Standards and Framework Act 1998;

   (c) a course of further education secured by an education authority in Scotland.

(8) A responsible body is—

   (a) a local authority in England or Wales, for the purposes of subsection (7)(a);

   (b) the governing body of a maintained school, for the purposes of subsection (7)(b);

   (c) an education authority in Scotland, for the purposes of subsection (7)(c).

(9) In this section—

'course', in relation to further education, includes each component part of a course if there is no requirement imposed on persons registered for a component part of the course to register for another component part of the course;

'enrolment' includes registration for a component part of a course;

'maintained school' has the meaning given in section 20(7) of the School Standards and Framework Act 1998;

'services' means services of any description which are provided wholly or mainly for persons enrolled on a course to which this section applies.

93 Recreational or training facilities

(1) The responsible body in relation to facilities to which this section applies must not discriminate against a person—

   (a) in the arrangements it makes for deciding who is provided with the facilities;

   (b) as to the terms on which it offers to provide the facilities to the person;

   (c) by not accepting the person's application for provision of the facilities.

(2) The responsible body in relation to such facilities must not discriminate against a person who is provided with the facilities in the services it provides or offers to provide.

(3) The responsible body in relation to such facilities must not harass a person who—

   (a) seeks to have the facilities provided;

   (b) is provided with the facilities;

   (c) is a user of services provided by the body in relation to the facilities.

(4) The responsible body in relation to such facilities must not victimise a person—

   (a) in the arrangements it makes for deciding who is provided with the facilities;

   (b) as to the terms on which it offers to provide the facilities to the person;

   (c) by not accepting the person's application for provision of the facilities.

(5) The responsible body in relation to such facilities must not victimise a person who is provided with the facilities in the services it provides or offers to provide.

(6) A duty to make reasonable adjustments applies to the responsible body.

(7) This section applies to—

   (a) facilities secured by a local authority in England under section 507A or 507B of the Education Act 1996;

   (b) facilities secured by a local authority in Wales under section 508 of that Act;

   (c) recreational or training facilities provided by an education authority in Scotland.

(8) A responsible body is—

   (a) a local authority in England, for the purposes of subsection (7)(a);

   (b) a local authority in Wales, for the purposes of subsection (7)(b);

   (c) an education authority in Scotland, for the purposes of subsection (7)(c).

(9) This section does not apply to the protected characteristic of age, so far as relating to persons who have not attained the age of 18.

94 Interpretation and exceptions

(1) This section applies for the purposes of this Chapter.

(2) Nothing in this Chapter applies to anything done in connection with the content of the curriculum.

(3) A reference to a student, in relation to an institution, is a reference to a person for whom education is provided by the institution.

(4) A reference to a university includes a reference to a university college and a college, school or hall of a university.

(5) A reference to an institution within the further or higher education sector is to be construed in accordance with section 91 of the Further and Higher Education Act 1992.

(6) 'Further education'—
    (a) in relation to England and Wales, has the meaning given in section 2 of the Education Act 1996;
    (b) in relation to Scotland, has the meaning given in section 1(3) of the Further and Higher Education (Scotland) Act 1992.

(7) 'Higher education'—
    (a) in relation to England and Wales, means education provided by means of a course of a description mentioned in Schedule 6 to the Education Reform Act 1988;
    (b) in relation to Scotland, has the meaning given in section 38 of the Further and Higher Education (Scotland) Act 1992.

(8) 'College of further education' has the meaning given in section 36 of the Further and Higher Education (Scotland) Act 1992.

(9) 'Designated institution' has the meaning given in section 44 of that Act.

(10) 'Local authority' means—
    (a) in relation to England, an English local authority within the meaning of section 162 of the Education and Inspections Act 2006;
    (b) in relation to Wales, a Welsh local authority within the meaning of that section.

(11) 'Education authority' has the meaning given by section 135(1) of the Education (Scotland) Act 1980.

[(11A) A reference to conferring a qualification includes a reference—
    (a) to renewing or extending the conferment of a qualification;
    (b) to authenticating a qualification conferred by another person.][66]

(12) Schedule 12 (exceptions) has effect.

CHAPTER 3
GENERAL QUALIFICATIONS BODIES

95 Application of this Chapter

This Chapter does not apply to the protected characteristic of marriage and civil partnership.

96 Qualifications bodies

(1) A qualifications body (A) must not discriminate against a person (B)—
    (a) in the arrangements A makes for deciding upon whom to confer a relevant qualification;
    (b) as to the terms on which it is prepared to confer a relevant qualification on B;
    (c) by not conferring a relevant qualification on B.

---

[66] Inserted by Equality Act 2010 (Consequential Amendments, Saving and Supplementary Provisions) Order 2010, SI 2010/2279.

(2) A qualifications body (A) must not discriminate against a person (B) upon whom A has conferred a relevant qualification—

   (a) by withdrawing the qualification from B;

   (b) by varying the terms on which B holds the qualification;

   (c) by subjecting B to any other detriment.

(3) A qualifications body must not, in relation to conferment by it of a relevant qualification, harass—

   (a) a person who holds the qualification, or

   (b) a person who applies for it.

(4) A qualifications body (A) must not victimise a person (B)—

   (a) in the arrangements A makes for deciding upon whom to confer a relevant qualification;

   (b) as to the terms on which it is prepared to confer a relevant qualification on B;

   (c) by not conferring a relevant qualification on B.

(5) A qualifications body (A) must not victimise a person (B) upon whom A has conferred a relevant qualification—

   (a) by withdrawing the qualification from B;

   (b) by varying the terms on which B holds the qualification;

   (c) by subjecting B to any other detriment.

(6) A duty to make reasonable adjustments applies to a qualifications body.

(7) Subsection (6) does not apply to the body in so far as the appropriate regulator specifies provisions, criteria or practices in relation to which the body—

   (a) is not subject to a duty to make reasonable adjustments;

   (b) is subject to a duty to make reasonable adjustments, but in relation to which such adjustments as the regulator specifies should not be made.

(8) For the purposes of subsection (7) the appropriate regulator must have regard to—

   (a) the need to minimise the extent to which disabled persons are disadvantaged in attaining the qualification because of their disabilities;

   (b) the need to secure that the qualification gives a reliable indication of the knowledge, skills and understanding of a person upon whom it is conferred;

   (c) the need to maintain public confidence in the qualification.

(9) The appropriate regulator—

   (a) must not specify any matter for the purposes of subsection (7) unless it has consulted such persons as it thinks appropriate;

   (b) must publish matters so specified (including the date from which they are to have effect) in such manner as is prescribed.

(10) The appropriate regulator is—

   (a) in relation to a qualifications body that confers qualifications in England, a person prescribed by a Minister of the Crown;

   (b) in relation to a qualifications body that confers qualifications in Wales, a person prescribed by the Welsh Ministers;

   (c) in relation to a qualifications body that confers qualifications in Scotland, a person prescribed by the Scottish Ministers.

(11) For the purposes of subsection (10), a qualification is conferred in a part of Great Britain if there are, or may reasonably be expected to be, persons seeking to obtain the qualification who are or will be assessed for those purposes wholly or mainly in that part.

97 Interpretation

(1) This section applies for the purposes of section 96.

(2) A qualifications body is an authority or body which can confer a relevant qualification.

(3) A relevant qualification is an authorisation, qualification, approval or certification of such description as may be prescribed—

    (a) in relation to conferments in England, by a Minister of the Crown;

    (b) in relation to conferments in Wales, by the Welsh Ministers;

    (c) in relation to conferments in Scotland, by the Scottish Ministers.

(4) An authority or body is not a qualifications body in so far as—

    (a) it is the responsible body of a school to which section 85 applies,

    (b) it is the governing body of an institution to which section 91 applies,

    (c) it exercises functions under the Education Acts, or

    (d) it exercises functions under the Education (Scotland) Act 1980.

(5) A qualifications body does not include an authority or body of such description, or in such circumstances, as may be prescribed.

(6) A reference to conferring a relevant qualification includes a reference—

    (a) to renewing or extending the conferment of a relevant qualification;

    (b) to authenticating a relevant qualification conferred by another person.

(7) A reference in section 96(8), (10) or (11) to a qualification is a reference to a relevant qualification.

(8) Subsection (11) of section 96 applies for the purposes of subsection (3) of this section as it applies for the purposes of subsection (10) of that section.

CHAPTER 4
MISCELLANEOUS

98 Reasonable adjustments

Schedule 13 (reasonable adjustments) has effect.

99 Educational charities and endowments

Schedule 14 (educational charities and endowments) has effect.

PART 7
ASSOCIATIONS

Preliminary

100 Application of this Part

(1) This Part does not apply to the protected characteristic of marriage and civil partnership.

(2) This Part does not apply to discrimination, harassment or victimisation—

    (a) that is prohibited by Part 3 (services and public functions), Part 4 (premises), Part 5 (work) or Part 6 (education), or

    (b) that would be so prohibited but for an express exception.

Membership, etc.

101 Members and associates

(1) An association (A) must not discriminate against a person (B)—

    (a) in the arrangements A makes for deciding who to admit to membership;

    (b) as to the terms on which A is prepared to admit B to membership;

    (c) by not accepting B's application for membership.

(2) An association (A) must not discriminate against a member (B)—
  (a) in the way A affords B access, or by not affording B access, to a benefit, facility or service;
  (b) by depriving B of membership;
  (c) by varying B's terms of membership;
  (d) by subjecting B to any other detriment.
(3) An association (A) must not discriminate against an associate (B)—
  (a) in the way A affords B access, or by not affording B access, to a benefit, facility or service;
  (b) by depriving B of B's rights as an associate;
  (c) by varying B's rights as an associate;
  (d) by subjecting B to any other detriment.
(4) An association must not harass—
  (a) a member;
  (b) a person seeking to become a member;
  (c) an associate.
(5) An association (A) must not victimise a person (B)—
  (a) in the arrangements A makes for deciding who to admit to membership;
  (b) as to the terms on which A is prepared to admit B to membership;
  (c) by not accepting B's application for membership.
(6) An association (A) must not victimise a member (B)—
  (a) in the way A affords B access, or by not affording B access, to a benefit, facility or service;
  (b) by depriving B of membership;
  (c) by varying B's terms of membership;
  (d) by subjecting B to any other detriment.
(7) An association (A) must not victimise an associate (B)—
  (a) in the way A affords B access, or by not affording B access, to a benefit, facility or service;
  (b) by depriving B of B's rights as an associate;
  (c) by varying B's rights as an associate;
  (d) by subjecting B to any other detriment.

102 Guests

(1) An association (A) must not discriminate against a person (B)—
  (a) in the arrangements A makes for deciding who to invite, or who to permit to be invited, as a guest;
  (b) as to the terms on which A is prepared to invite B, or to permit B to be invited, as a guest;
  (c) by not inviting B, or not permitting B to be invited, as a guest.
(2) An association (A) must not discriminate against a guest (B) invited by A or with A's permission (whether express or implied)—
  (a) in the way A affords B access, or by not affording B access, to a benefit, facility or service;
  (b) by subjecting B to any other detriment.
(3) An association must not harass—
  (a) a guest;
  (b) a person seeking to be a guest.
(4) An association (A) must not victimise a person (B)—
  (a) in the arrangements A makes for deciding who to invite, or who to permit to be invited, as a guest;
  (b) as to the terms on which A is prepared to invite B, or to permit B to be invited, as a guest;
  (c) by not inviting B, or not permitting B to be invited, as a guest.

(5) An association (A) must not victimise a guest (B) invited by A or with A's permission (whether express or implied)—

    (a) in the way A affords B access, or by not affording B access, to a benefit, facility or service;

    (b) by subjecting B to any other detriment.

103 Sections 101 and 102: further provision

(1) A duty to make reasonable adjustments applies to an association.

(2) In the application of section 26 for the purposes of section 101(4) or 102(3), neither of the following is a relevant protected characteristic—

    (a) religion or belief;

    (b) sexual orientation.

Special provision for political parties

104 Selection of candidates

(1) This section applies to an association which is a registered political party.

(2) A person does not contravene this Part only by acting in accordance with selection arrangements.

(3) Selection arrangements are arrangements—

    (a) which the party makes for regulating the selection of its candidates in a relevant election,

    (b) the purpose of which is to reduce inequality in the party's representation in the body concerned, and

    (c) which, subject to subsection (7), are a proportionate means of achieving that purpose.

(4) The reference in subsection (3)(b) to inequality in a party's representation in a body is a reference to inequality between—

    (a) the number of the party's candidates elected to be members of the body who share a protected characteristic, and

    (b) the number of the party's candidates so elected who do not share that characteristic.

(5) For the purposes of subsection (4), persons share the protected characteristic of disability if they are disabled persons (and section 6(3)(b) is accordingly to be ignored).

(6) Selection arrangements do not include short-listing only such persons as have a particular protected characteristic.

(7) But subsection (6) does not apply to the protected characteristic of sex; and subsection (3)(c) does not apply to short-listing in reliance on this subsection.

(8) The following elections are relevant elections—

    (a) Parliamentary Elections;

    (b) elections to the European Parliament;

    (c) elections to the Scottish Parliament;

    (d) elections to the National Assembly for Wales;

    (e) local government elections within the meaning of section 191, 203 or 204 of the Representation of the People Act 1983 (excluding elections for the Mayor of London).

105 Time-limited provision

(1) Section 104(7) and the words ', subject to subsection (7),' in section 104(3)(c) are repealed at the end of 2030 unless an order is made under subsection (2).

(2) At any time before the end of 2030, a Minister of the Crown may by order provide that subsection (1) is to have effect with the substitution of a later time for that for the time being specified there.

(3) In section 3 of the Sex Discrimination (Election Candidates) Act 2002 (expiry of that Act), in subsection (1) for '2015' substitute '2030'.

(4) The substitution made by subsection (3) does not affect the power to substitute a later time by order under section 3 of that Act.

106 Information about diversity in range of candidates, etc.

(1) This section applies to an association which is a registered political party.

(2) If the party had candidates at a relevant election, the party must, in accordance with regulations, publish information relating to protected characteristics of persons who come within a description prescribed in the regulations in accordance with subsection (3).

(3) One or more of the following descriptions may be prescribed for the purposes of subsection (2)—
   (a) successful applicants for nomination as a candidate at the relevant election;
   (b) unsuccessful applicants for nomination as a candidate at that election;
   (c) candidates elected at that election;
   (d) candidates who are not elected at that election.

(4) The duty imposed by subsection (2) applies only in so far as it is possible to publish information in a manner that ensures that no person to whom the information relates can be identified from that information.

(5) The following elections are relevant elections—
   (a) Parliamentary Elections;
   (b) elections to the European Parliament;
   (c) elections to the Scottish Parliament;
   (d) elections to the National Assembly for Wales.

(6) This section does not apply to the following protected characteristics—
   (a) marriage and civil partnership;
   (b) pregnancy and maternity.

(7) The regulations may provide that the information to be published—
   (a) must (subject to subsection (6)) relate to all protected characteristics or only to such as are prescribed;
   (b) must include a statement, in respect of each protected characteristic to which the information relates, of the proportion that the number of persons who provided the information to the party bears to the number of persons who were asked to provide it.

(8) Regulations under this section may prescribe—
   (a) descriptions of information;
   (b) descriptions of political party to which the duty is to apply;
   (c) the time at which information is to be published;
   (d) the form and manner in which information is to be published;
   (e) the period for which information is to be published.

(9) Provision by virtue of subsection (8)(b) may, in particular, provide that the duty imposed by subsection (2) does not apply to a party which had candidates in fewer constituencies in the election concerned than a prescribed number.

(10) Regulations under this section—
   (a) may provide that the duty imposed by subsection (2) applies only to such relevant elections as are prescribed;
   (b) may provide that a by-election or other election to fill a vacancy is not to be treated as a relevant election or is to be so treated only to a prescribed extent;
   (c) may amend this section so as to provide for the duty imposed by subsection (2) to apply in the case of additional descriptions of election.

(11) Nothing in this section authorises a political party to require a person to provide information to it.

347

Supplementary

107 Interpretation and exceptions

(1) This section applies for the purposes of this Part.

(2) An 'association' is an association of persons—

    (a) which has at least 25 members, and

    (b) admission to membership of which is regulated by the association's rules and involves a process of selection.

(3) A Minister of the Crown may by order amend subsection (2)(a) so as to substitute a different number for that for the time being specified there.

(4) It does not matter—

    (a) whether an association is incorporated;

    (b) whether its activities are carried on for profit.

(5) Membership is membership of any description; and a reference to a member is to be construed accordingly.

(6) A person is an 'associate', in relation to an association, if the person—

    (a) is not a member of the association, but

    (b) in accordance with the association's rules, has some or all of the rights as a member as a result of being a member of another association.

(7) A reference to a registered political party is a reference to a party registered in the Great Britain register under Part 2 of the Political Parties, Elections and Referendums Act 2000.

(8) Schedule 15 (reasonable adjustments) has effect.

(9) Schedule 16 (exceptions) has effect.

PART 8
PROHIBITED CONDUCT: ANCILLARY

108 Relationships that have ended

(1) A person (A) must not discriminate against another (B) if—

    (a) the discrimination arises out of and is closely connected to a relationship which used to exist between them, and

    (b) conduct of a description constituting the discrimination would, if it occurred during the relationship, contravene this Act.

(2) A person (A) must not harass another (B) if—

    (a) the harassment arises out of and is closely connected to a relationship which used to exist between them, and

    (b) conduct of a description constituting the harassment would, if it occurred during the relationship, contravene this Act.

(3) It does not matter whether the relationship ends before or after the commencement of this section.

(4) A duty to make reasonable adjustments applies to A [if B is][67] placed at a substantial disadvantage as mentioned in section 20.

(5) For the purposes of subsection (4), sections 20, 21 and 22 and the applicable Schedules are to be construed as if the relationship had not ended.

---

[67] Substituted by Equality Act 2010 (Consequential Amendments, Saving and Supplementary Provisions) Order 2010, SI 2010/2279.

(6) For the purposes of Part 9 (enforcement), a contravention of this section relates to the Part of this Act that would have been contravened if the relationship had not ended.

(7) But conduct is not a contravention of this section in so far as it also amounts to victimisation of B by A.

109 Liability of employers and principals

(1) Anything done by a person (A) in the course of A's employment must be treated as also done by the employer.

(2) Anything done by an agent for a principal, with the authority of the principal, must be treated as also done by the principal.

(3) It does not matter whether that thing is done with the employer's or principal's knowledge or approval.

(4) In proceedings against A's employer (B) in respect of anything alleged to have been done by A in the course of A's employment it is a defence for B to show that B took all reasonable steps to prevent A—

(a) from doing that thing, or

(b) from doing anything of that description.

(5) This section does not apply to offences under this Act (other than offences under Part 12 (disabled persons: transport)).

110 Liability of employees and agents

(1) A person (A) contravenes this section if—

(a) A is an employee or agent,

(b) A does something which, by virtue of section 109(1) or (2), is treated as having been done by A's employer or principal (as the case may be), and

(c) the doing of that thing by A amounts to a contravention of this Act by the employer or principal (as the case may be).

(2) It does not matter whether, in any proceedings, the employer is found not to have contravened this Act by virtue of section 109(4).

(3) A does not contravene this section if—

(a) A relies on a statement by the employer or principal that doing that thing is not a contravention of this Act, and

(b) it is reasonable for A to do so.

(4) A person (B) commits an offence if B knowingly or recklessly makes a statement mentioned in subsection (3)(a) which is false or misleading in a material respect.

(5) A person guilty of an offence under subsection (4) is liable on summary conviction to a fine not exceeding level 5 on the standard scale.

[(5A) A does not contravene this section if A—

(a) does not conduct a relevant marriage,

(b) is not present at, does not carry out, or does not otherwise participate in, a relevant marriage, or

(c) does not consent to a relevant marriage being conducted,

for the reason that the marriage is the marriage of a same sex couple.

(5B) Subsection (5A) applies to A only if A is within the meaning of 'person' for the purposes of section 2 of the Marriage (Same Sex Couples) Act 2013; and other expressions used in subsection (5A) and section 2 of that Act have the same meanings in that subsection as in that section.][68]

---

[68] Inserted by Marriage (Same Sex Couples) Act 2013.

[(5BA) If A is a protected person, A does not contravene this section if A—
  (a) does not allow religious premises to be used as the place at which two people register as civil partners of each other under Part 2 of the Civil Partnership Act 2004 ('the 2004 Act'), or
  (b) does not provide, arrange, facilitate or participate in, or is not present at—
      (i) an occasion during which two people register as civil partners of each other on religious premises under Part 2 of the 2004 Act, or
      (ii) a ceremony or event in England or Wales to mark the formation of a civil partnership,
  for the reason that the person does not wish to do things of that sort in relation to civil partnerships generally, or those between two people of the same sex, or those between two people of the opposite sex.
(5BB) In subsection (5BA)—
  'protected person' has the meaning given by section 30ZA(2) of the 2004 Act;
  'religious premises' has the meaning given by section 6A(3C) of the 2004 Act.][69]
[(5C) A does not contravene this section by refusing to solemnise a relevant Scottish marriage for the reason that the marriage is the marriage of two persons of the same sex.
(5D) A does not contravene this section by refusing to register a relevant Scottish civil partnership for the reason that the civil partnership is between two persons of the same sex.
(5E) Subsections (5C) and (5D) apply only if A is an approved celebrant.
(5F) Expressions used in subsections (5C) to (5E) have the same meaning as in paragraph 25B of Schedule 3.
(5G) A chaplain does not contravene this section by refusing to solemnise a relevant Scottish forces marriage for the reason that the marriage is the marriage of two persons of the same sex.
(5H) Expressions used in subsection (5G) have the same meaning as in paragraph 25C of Schedule 3.][70]
  (6) Part 9 (enforcement) applies to a contravention of this section by A as if it were the contravention mentioned in subsection (1)(c).
  (7) The reference in subsection (1)(c) to a contravention of this Act does not include a reference to disability discrimination in contravention of Chapter 1 of Part 6 (schools).

111 Instructing, causing or inducing contraventions

  (1) A person (A) must not instruct another (B) to do in relation to a third person (C) anything which contravenes Part 3, 4, 5, 6 or 7 or section 108(1) or (2) or 112(1) (a basic contravention).
  (2) A person (A) must not cause another (B) to do in relation to a third person (C) anything which is a basic contravention.
  (3) A person (A) must not induce another (B) to do in relation to a third person (C) anything which is a basic contravention.
  (4) For the purposes of subsection (3), inducement may be direct or indirect.
  (5) Proceedings for a contravention of this section may be brought—
      (a) by B, if B is subjected to a detriment as a result of A's conduct;
      (b) by C, if C is subjected to a detriment as a result of A's conduct;
      (c) by the Commission.

---

[69] Inserted by Civil Partnership (Opposite-sex couples) Regulations 2019, SI 2019/1458.
[70] Inserted by Marriage and Civil Partnership (Scotland) Act 2014 and Civil Partnership Act 2004 (Consequential Provisions and Modifications) Order 2014, SI 2014/3229.

(6) For the purposes of subsection (5), it does not matter whether—
    (a) the basic contravention occurs;
    (b) any other proceedings are, or may be, brought in relation to A's conduct.
(7) This section does not apply unless the relationship between A and B is such that A is in a position to commit a basic contravention in relation to B.
(8) A reference in this section to causing or inducing a person to do something includes a reference to attempting to cause or induce the person to do it.
(9) For the purposes of Part 9 (enforcement), a contravention of this section is to be treated as relating—
    (a) in a case within subsection (5)(a), to the Part of this Act which, because of the relationship between A and B, A is in a position to contravene in relation to B;
    (b) in a case within subsection (5)(b), to the Part of this Act which, because of the relationship between B and C, B is in a position to contravene in relation to C.

112 Aiding contraventions

(1) A person (A) must not knowingly help another (B) to do anything which contravenes Part 3, 4, 5, 6 or 7 or section 108(1) or (2) or 111 (a basic contravention).
(2) It is not a contravention of subsection (1) if—
    (a) A relies on a statement by B that the act for which the help is given does not contravene this Act, and
    (b) it is reasonable for A to do so.
(3) B commits an offence if B knowingly or recklessly makes a statement mentioned in subsection (2)(a) which is false or misleading in a material respect.
(4) A person guilty of an offence under subsection (3) is liable on summary conviction to a fine not exceeding level 5 on the standard scale.
(5) For the purposes of Part 9 (enforcement), a contravention of this section is to be treated as relating to the provision of this Act to which the basic contravention relates.
(6) The reference in subsection (1) to a basic contravention does not include a reference to disability discrimination in contravention of Chapter 1 of Part 6 (schools).

PART 9
ENFORCEMENT

CHAPTER 1
INTRODUCTORY

113 Proceedings

(1) Proceedings relating to a contravention of this Act must be brought in accordance with this Part.
(2) Subsection (1) does not apply to proceedings under Part 1 of the Equality Act 2006.
(3) Subsection (1) does not prevent—
    (a) a claim for judicial review;
    (b) proceedings under the Immigration Acts;
    (c) proceedings under the Special Immigration Appeals Commission Act 1997;
    (d) in Scotland, an application to the supervisory jurisdiction of the Court of Session.
(4) This section is subject to any express provision of this Act conferring jurisdiction on a court or tribunal.

(5) The reference to a contravention of this Act includes a reference to a breach of an equality clause or rule.

(6) Chapters 2 and 3 do not apply to proceedings relating to an equality clause or rule except in so far as Chapter 4 provides for that.

(7) This section does not apply to—

    (a) proceedings for an offence under this Act;

    (b) proceedings relating to a penalty under Part 12 (disabled persons: transport).

CHAPTER 2
CIVIL COURTS

114 Jurisdiction

(1) [The county court]⁷¹ or, in Scotland, the sheriff has jurisdiction to determine a claim relating to—

    (a) a contravention of Part 3 (services and public functions);

    (b) a contravention of Part 4 (premises);

    (c) a contravention of Part 6 (education);

    (d) a contravention of Part 7 (associations);

    (e) a contravention of section 108, 111 or 112 that relates to Part 3, 4, 6 or 7.

(2) Subsection (1)(a) does not apply to a claim within section 115.

(3) Subsection (1)(c) does not apply to a claim within section 116.

(4) Subsection (1)(d) does not apply to a contravention of section 106.

(5) For the purposes of proceedings on a claim within subsection (1)(a)—

    (a) a decision in proceedings on a claim mentioned in section 115(1) that an act is a contravention of Part 3 is binding;

    (b) it does not matter whether the act occurs outside the United Kingdom.

(6) The county court or sheriff—

    (a) must not grant an interim injunction or interdict unless satisfied that no criminal matter would be prejudiced by doing so;

    (b) must grant an application to stay or sist proceedings under subsection (1) on grounds of prejudice to a criminal matter unless satisfied the matter will not be prejudiced.

(7) In proceedings in England and Wales on a claim within subsection (1), the power under section 63(1) of the County Courts Act 1984 (appointment of assessors) must be exercised unless the judge is satisfied that there are good reasons for not doing so.

(8) In proceedings in Scotland on a claim within subsection (1), the power under rule 44.3 of Schedule 1 to the Sheriff Court (Scotland) Act 1907 (appointment of assessors) must be exercised unless the sheriff is satisfied that there are good reasons for not doing so.

(9) The remuneration of an assessor appointed by virtue of subsection (8) is to be at a rate determined by the Lord President of the Court of Session.

115 Immigration cases

(1) A claim is within this section if it relates to the act of an immigration authority in taking a relevant decision and—

    (a) the question whether the act is a contravention of Part 3 has been or could be raised on an appeal which is pending, or could be brought, under the immigration provisions, or

---

⁷¹ Substituted by Crime and Courts Act 2013.

(b) it has been decided on an appeal under those provisions that the act is not a contravention of Part 3.

(2) The relevant decision is not—
    (a) subject to challenge in proceedings on a claim within section 114(1)(a), or
    (b) affected by the decision of a court in such proceedings.

(3) For the purposes of subsection (1)(a) a power to grant permission to appeal out of time must be ignored.

(4) Each of the following is an immigration authority—
    (a) the Secretary of State;
    (b) an immigration officer;
    (c) a person responsible for the grant or refusal of entry clearance (within the meaning of section 33(1) of the Immigration Act 1971).

(5) The immigration provisions are—
    (a) the Special Immigration Appeals Commission Act 1997, or
    (b) Part 5 of the Nationality, Immigration and Asylum Act 2002.

(6) A relevant decision is—
    (a) a decision under the Immigration Acts relating to the entitlement of a person to enter or remain in the United Kingdom;
    (b) a decision on an appeal under the immigration provisions relating to a decision within paragraph (a).

(7) An appeal is pending if it is pending for the purposes of section 104 of the Nationality, Immigration and Asylum Act 2002 or (as the case may be) for the purposes of that section as it is applied by section 2(2)(j) of the Special Immigration Appeals Commission Act 1997.

[(8) This section applies in relation to reviews under section 2D [and 2E][72] of the Special Immigration Appeals Commission Act 1997 as it applies in relation to appeals under the immigration provisions.][73]

116 Education cases

(1) A claim is within this section if it may be made to—
    (a) the First-tier Tribunal in accordance with Part 2 of Schedule 17,
    (b) the Special Educational Needs Tribunal for Wales in accordance with Part 2 of that Schedule, or
    (c) [the First-tier Tribunal for Scotland Health and Education Chamber][74] in accordance with Part 3 of that Schedule.

(2) A claim is also within this section if it must be made in accordance with appeal arrangements within the meaning of Part 4 of that Schedule.

(3) Schedule 17 (disabled pupils: enforcement) has effect.

117 National security

(1) Rules of court may, in relation to proceedings on a claim within section 114, confer power as mentioned in subsections (2) to (4); but a power so conferred is exercisable only if the court thinks it expedient to do so in the interests of national security.

(2) The rules may confer power to exclude from all or part of the proceedings—
    (a) the claimant or pursuer;

---

[72] Inserted by Immigration Act 2014.
[73] Inserted by Justice and Security Act 2013.
[74] Substituted by First-tier Tribunal for Scotland (Transfer of Functions of the Additional Support Needs Tribunals for Scotland) Regulations 2018, SI 2018/4.

    (b) a representative of the claimant or pursuer;

    (c) an assessor.

(3) The rules may confer power to permit a claimant, pursuer or representative who has been excluded to make a statement to the court before the commencement of the proceedings, or part of the proceedings, to which the exclusion relates.

(4) The rules may confer power to take steps to keep secret all or part of the reasons for the court's decision.

(5) The Attorney General or, in Scotland, the Advocate General for Scotland may appoint a person to represent the interests of a claimant or pursuer in, or in any part of, proceedings to which an exclusion by virtue of subsection (2)(a) or (b) relates.

(6) A person (P) may be appointed under subsection (5) only if—

    (a) in relation to proceedings in England and Wales, P is a person who, for the purposes of the Legal Services Act 2007, is an authorised person in relation to an activity which constitutes the exercise of a right of audience or the conduct of litigation;

    (b) in relation to proceedings in Scotland, P is an advocate or qualified to practice as a solicitor in Scotland.

(7) P is not responsible to the person whose interests P is appointed to represent.

118 Time limits

(1) [Subject to [sections 140A and 140AA][75]][76] [p]roceedings on a claim within section 114 may not be brought after the end of—

    (a) the period of 6 months starting with the date of the act to which the claim relates, or

    (b) such other period as the county court or sheriff thinks just and equitable.

(2) If subsection (3) [...][77] applies, subsection (1)(a) has effect as if for '6 months' there were substituted '9 months'.

(3) This subsection applies if—

    (a) the claim relates to the act of a qualifying institution, and

    (b) a complaint relating to the act is referred under the student complaints scheme before the end of the period of 6 months starting with the date of the act.

(4) [...][78]

(5) If it has been decided under the immigration provisions that the act of an immigration authority in taking a relevant decision is a contravention of Part 3 (services and public functions), subsection (1) has effect as if for paragraph (a) there were substituted—

    '(a) the period of 6 months starting with the day after the expiry of the period during which, as a result of section 114(2), proceedings could not be brought in reliance on section 114(1)(a);'.

(6) For the purposes of this section—

    (a) conduct extending over a period is to be treated as done at the end of the period;

    (b) failure to do something is to be treated as occurring when the person in question decided on it.

(7) In the absence of evidence to the contrary, a person (P) is to be taken to decide on failure to do something—

---

[75] Substituted by Alternative Dispute Resolution for Consumer Disputes (Amendment) Regulations 2015, SI 2015/1392.

[76] Inserted by Cross-Border Mediation (EU Directive) Regulations 2011, SI 2011/1133.

[77] Repealed by Enterprise and Regulatory Reform Act 2013.

[78] Repealed by Enterprise and Regulatory Reform Act 2013.

(a) when P does an act inconsistent with doing it, or

(b) if P does no inconsistent act, on the expiry of the period in which P might reasonably have been expected to do it.

(8) In this section—

'immigration authority', 'immigration provisions' and 'relevant decision' each have the meaning given in section 115;

'qualifying institution' has the meaning given in section 11 of the Higher Education Act 2004 [, and includes an institution which is treated as continuing to be a qualifying institution for the purposes of Part 2 of that Act (see section 20A(2) of that Act)][79];

'the student complaints scheme' means a scheme for the review of qualifying complaints (within the meaning of section 12 of that Act) that is provided by the designated operator (within the meaning of section 13(5)(b) of that Act).

119 Remedies

(1) This section applies if [the county court][80] or the sheriff finds that there has been a contravention of a provision referred to in section 114(1).

(2) The county court has power to grant any remedy which could be granted by the High Court—
(a) in proceedings in tort;
(b) on a claim for judicial review.

(3) The sheriff has power to make any order which could be made by the Court of Session—
(a) in proceedings for reparation;
(b) on a petition for judicial review.

(4) An award of damages may include compensation for injured feelings (whether or not it includes compensation on any other basis).

(5) Subsection (6) applies if the county court or sheriff—
(a) finds that a contravention of a provision referred to in section 114(1) is established by virtue of section 19, but
(b) is satisfied that the provision, criterion or practice was not applied with the intention of discriminating against the claimant or pursuer.

(6) The county court or sheriff must not make an award of damages unless it first considers whether to make any other disposal.

(7) The county court or sheriff must not grant a remedy other than an award of damages or the making of a declaration unless satisfied that no criminal matter would be prejudiced by doing so.

CHAPTER 3
EMPLOYMENT TRIBUNALS

120 Jurisdiction

(1) An employment tribunal has, subject to section 121, jurisdiction to determine a complaint relating to—
(a) a contravention of Part 5 (work);
(b) a contravention of section 108, 111 or 112 that relates to Part 5.

---

[79] Inserted by Higher Education and Research Act 2017.
[80] Substituted by Crime and Courts Act 2013.

(2) An employment tribunal has jurisdiction to determine an application by a responsible person (as defined by section 61) for a declaration as to the rights of that person and a worker in relation to a dispute about the effect of a non-discrimination rule.

(3) An employment tribunal also has jurisdiction to determine an application by the trustees or managers of an occupational pension scheme for a declaration as to their rights and those of a member in relation to a dispute about the effect of a non-discrimination rule.

(4) An employment tribunal also has jurisdiction to determine a question that—
  (a) relates to a non-discrimination rule, and
  (b) is referred to the tribunal by virtue of section 122.

(5) In proceedings before an employment tribunal on a complaint relating to a breach of a nondiscrimination rule, the employer—
  (a) is to be treated as a party, and
  (b) is accordingly entitled to appear and be heard.

(6) Nothing in this section affects such jurisdiction as the High Court, [the county court][81], the Court of Session or the sheriff has in relation to a non-discrimination rule.

(7) Subsection (1)(a) does not apply to a contravention of section 53 in so far as the act complained of may, by virtue of an enactment, be subject to an appeal or proceedings in the nature of an appeal.

(8) In subsection (1), the references to Part 5 do not include a reference to section 60(1).

121 Armed forces cases

(1) Section 120(1) does not apply to a complaint relating to an act done when the complainant was serving as a member of the armed forces unless—
  (a) the complainant has made a service complaint about the matter, and
  (b) the complaint has not been withdrawn.

[(2) Where the complaint is dealt with by a person or panel appointed by the Defence Council by virtue of section 340C(1)(a) of the 2006 Act, it is to be treated for the purposes of subsection (1)(b) as withdrawn if—
  (a) the period allowed in accordance with service complaints regulations for bringing an appeal against the person's or panel's decision expires, and
  (b) either—
    (i) the complainant does not apply to the Service Complaints Ombudsman for a review by virtue of section 340D(6) of the 2006 Act (review of decision that appeal brought out of time cannot proceed), or
    (ii) the complainant does apply for such a review and the Ombudsman decides that an appeal against the person's or panel's decision cannot be proceeded with.][82]

(3)–(4) [...][83]

(5) The making of a complaint to an employment tribunal in reliance on subsection (1) does not affect the continuation of [the procedures set out in service complaints regulations.][84]

[(6) In this section—
  'the 2006 Act' means the Armed Forces Act 2006;
  'service complaints regulations' means regulations made under section 340B(1) of the 2006 Act.][85]

---

[81] Substituted by Crime and Courts Act 2013.
[82] Substituted by Armed Forces (Service Complaints and Financial Assistance) Act 2015.
[83] Repealed by Armed Forces (Service Complaints and Financial Assistance) Act 2015.
[84] Substituted by Armed Forces (Service Complaints and Financial Assistance) Act 2015.
[85] Inserted by Armed Forces (Service Complaints and Financial Assistance) Act 2015.

122 References by court to tribunal, etc.

(1) If it appears to a court in which proceedings are pending that a claim or counter-claim relating to a non-discrimination rule could more conveniently be determined by an employment tribunal, the court may strike out the claim or counter-claim.

(2) If in proceedings before a court a question arises about a non-discrimination rule, the court may (whether or not on an application by a party to the proceedings)—

(a) refer the question, or direct that it be referred by a party to the proceedings, to an employment tribunal for determination, and

(b) stay or sist the proceedings in the meantime.

123 Time limits

(1) [Subject to [sections 140A and 140B][86]][87] [p]roceedings on a complaint within section 120 may not be brought after the end of—

(a) the period of 3 months starting with the date of the act to which the complaint relates, or

(b) such other period as the employment tribunal thinks just and equitable.

(2) Proceedings may not be brought in reliance on section 121(1) after the end of—

(a) the period of 6 months starting with the date of the act to which the proceedings relate, or

(b) such other period as the employment tribunal thinks just and equitable.

(3) For the purposes of this section—

(a) conduct extending over a period is to be treated as done at the end of the period;

(b) failure to do something is to be treated as occurring when the person in question decided on it.

(4) In the absence of evidence to the contrary, a person (P) is to be taken to decide on failure to do something—

(a) when P does an act inconsistent with doing it, or

(b) if P does no inconsistent act, on the expiry of the period in which P might reasonably have been expected to do it.

124 Remedies: general

(1) This section applies if an employment tribunal finds that there has been a contravention of a provision referred to in section 120(1).

(2) The tribunal may—

(a) make a declaration as to the rights of the complainant and the respondent in relation to the matters to which the proceedings relate;

(b) order the respondent to pay compensation to the complainant;

(c) make an appropriate recommendation.

(3) An appropriate recommendation is a recommendation that within a specified period the respondent takes specified steps for the purpose of obviating or reducing the adverse effect [on the complainant][88] of any matter to which the proceedings relate [.]

(a)–(b) […][89]

(4) Subsection (5) applies if the tribunal—

(a) finds that a contravention is established by virtue of section 19, but

(b) is satisfied that the provision, criterion or practice was not applied with the intention of discriminating against the complainant.

---

[86] Substituted by Enterprise and Regulatory Reform Act 2013.
[87] Inserted by Cross-Border Mediation (EU Directive) Regulations 2011, SI 2011/1133.
[88] Inserted by Deregulation Act 2015.
[89] Repealed by Deregulation Act 2015.

(5) It must not make an order under subsection (2)(b) unless it first considers whether to act under subsection (2)(a) or (c).
(6) The amount of compensation which may be awarded under subsection (2)(b) corresponds to the amount which could be awarded by [the county court][90] or the sheriff under section 119.
(7) If a respondent fails, without reasonable excuse, to comply with an appropriate recommendation [...][91], the tribunal may—
    (a) if an order was made under subsection (2)(b), increase the amount of compensation to be paid;
    (b) if no such order was made, make one.

125 Remedies: national security

[...][92]

126 Remedies: occupational pension schemes

(1) This section applies if an employment tribunal finds that there has been a contravention of a provision referred to in section 120(1) in relation to—
    (a) the terms on which persons become members of an occupational pension scheme, or
    (b) the terms on which members of an occupational pension scheme are treated.
(2) In addition to anything which may be done by the tribunal under section 124 the tribunal may also by order declare—
    (a) if the complaint relates to the terms on which persons become members of a scheme, that the complainant has a right to be admitted to the scheme;
    (b) if the complaint relates to the terms on which members of the scheme are treated, that the complainant has a right to membership of the scheme without discrimination.
(3) The tribunal may not make an order under subsection (2)(b) of section 124 unless—
    (a) the compensation is for injured feelings, or
    (b) the order is made by virtue of subsection (7) of that section.
(4) An order under subsection (2)—
    (a) may make provision as to the terms on which or the capacity in which the claimant is to enjoy the admission or membership;
    (b) may have effect in relation to a period before the order is made.

CHAPTER 4
EQUALITY OF TERMS

127 Jurisdiction

(1) An employment tribunal has, subject to subsection (6), jurisdiction to determine a complaint relating to a breach of an equality clause or rule.
(2) The jurisdiction conferred by subsection (1) includes jurisdiction to determine a complaint arising out of a breach of an equality clause or rule; and a reference in this Chapter to a complaint relating to such a breach is to be read accordingly.

---

[90] Substituted by Crime and Courts Act 2013.
[91] Repealed by Deregulation Act 2015.
[92] Repealed by Deregulation Act 2015.

(3) An employment tribunal also has jurisdiction to determine an application by a responsible person for a declaration as to the rights of that person and a worker in relation to a dispute about the effect of an equality clause or rule.

(4) An employment tribunal also has jurisdiction to determine an application by the trustees or managers of an occupational pension scheme for a declaration as to their rights and those of a member in relation to a dispute about the effect of an equality rule.

(5) An employment tribunal also has jurisdiction to determine a question that—
   (a) relates to an equality clause or rule, and
   (b) is referred to the tribunal by virtue of section 128(2).

(6) This section does not apply to a complaint relating to an act done when the complainant was serving as a member of the armed forces unless—
   (a) the complainant has made a service complaint about the matter, and
   (b) the complaint has not been withdrawn.

(7) [Subsections (2) to (6)][93] of section 121 apply for the purposes of subsection (6) of this section as they apply for the purposes of subsection (1) of that section.

(8) In proceedings before an employment tribunal on a complaint relating to a breach of an equality rule, the employer—
   (a) is to be treated as a party, and
   (b) is accordingly entitled to appear and be heard.

(9) Nothing in this section affects such jurisdiction as the High Court, [the county court][94], the Court of Session or the sheriff has in relation to an equality clause or rule.

128 References by court to tribunal, etc.

(1) If it appears to a court in which proceedings are pending that a claim or counter-claim relating to an equality clause or rule could more conveniently be determined by an employment tribunal, the court may strike out the claim or counter-claim.

(2) If in proceedings before a court a question arises about an equality clause or rule, the court may (whether or not on an application by a party to the proceedings)—
   (a) refer the question, or direct that it be referred by a party to the proceedings, to an employment tribunal for determination, and
   (b) stay or sist the proceedings in the meantime.

129 Time limits

(1) This section applies to—
   (a) a complaint relating to a breach of an equality clause or rule;
   (b) an application for a declaration referred to in section 127(3) or (4).

(2) Proceedings on the complaint or application may not be brought in an employment tribunal after the end of the qualifying period.

(3) If the complaint or application relates to terms of work other than terms of service in the armed forces, the qualifying period is, in a case mentioned in the first column of the table, the period mentioned in the second column [, subject to [sections 140A and 140B][95]].[96]

---

[93] Substituted by Armed Forces (Service Complaints and Financial Assistance) Act 2015.
[94] Substituted by Crime and Courts Act 2013.
[95] Substituted by Enterprise and Regulatory Reform Act 2013.
[96] Inserted by Cross-Border Mediation (EU Directive) Regulations 2011, SI 2011/1133.

Case	Qualifying period
A standard case	The period of 6 months beginning with the last day of the employment or appointment.
A stable work case (but not if it is also a concealment or incapacity case (or both))	The period of 6 months beginning with the day on which the stable working relationship ended.
A concealment case (but not if it is also an incapacity case)	The period of 6 months beginning with the day on which the worker discovered (or could with reasonable diligence have discovered) the qualifying fact.
An incapacity case (but not if it is also a concealment case)	The period of 6 months beginning with the day on which the worker ceased to have the incapacity.
A case which is a concealment case and an incapacity case.	The period of 6 months beginning with the later of the days on which the period would begin if the case were merely a concealment or incapacity case.

(4) If the complaint or application relates to terms of service in the armed forces, the qualifying period is, in a case mentioned in the first column of the table, the period mentioned in the second column [, subject to section 140B][97].

Case	Qualifying period
A standard case	The period of 9 months beginning with the last day of the period of service during which the complaint arose.
A concealment case (but not if it is also an incapacity case)	The period of 9 months beginning with the day on which the worker discovered (or could with reasonable diligence have discovered) the qualifying fact.
An incapacity case (but not if it is also a concealment case)	The period of 9 months beginning with the day on which the worker ceased to have the incapacity.
A case which is a concealment case and an incapacity case.	The period of 9 months beginning with the later of the days on which the period would begin if the case were merely a concealment or incapacity case.

130 Section 129: supplementary

(1) This section applies for the purposes of section 129.

(2) A standard case is a case which is not—
(a) a stable work case,
(b) a concealment case,
(c) an incapacity case, or
(d) a concealment case and an incapacity case.

(3) A stable work case is a case where the proceedings relate to a period during which there was a stable working relationship between the worker and the responsible person (including any time after the terms of work had expired).

(4) A concealment case in proceedings relating to an equality clause is a case where—
(a) the responsible person deliberately concealed a qualifying fact from the worker, and
(b) the worker did not discover (or could not with reasonable diligence have discovered) the qualifying fact until after the relevant day.

---

[97] Inserted by Enterprise and Regulatory Reform Act 2013.

(5) A concealment case in proceedings relating to an equality rule is a case where—
  (a) the employer or the trustees or managers of the occupational pension scheme in question deliberately concealed a qualifying fact from the member, and
  (b) the member did not discover (or could not with reasonable diligence have discovered) the qualifying fact until after the relevant day.

(6) A qualifying fact for the purposes of subsection (4) or (5) is a fact—
  (a) which is relevant to the complaint, and
  (b) without knowledge of which the worker or member could not reasonably have been expected to bring the proceedings.

(7) An incapacity case in proceedings relating to an equality clause with respect to terms of work other than terms of service in the armed forces is a case where the worker had an incapacity during the period of 6 months beginning with the later of—
  (a) the relevant day, or
  (b) the day on which the worker discovered (or could with reasonable diligence have discovered) the qualifying fact deliberately concealed from the worker by the responsible person.

(8) An incapacity case in proceedings relating to an equality clause with respect to terms of service in the armed forces is a case where the worker had an incapacity during the period of 9 months beginning with the later of—
  (a) the last day of the period of service during which the complaint arose, or
  (b) the day on which the worker discovered (or could with reasonable diligence have discovered) the qualifying fact deliberately concealed from the worker by the responsible person.

(9) An incapacity case in proceedings relating to an equality rule is a case where the member of the occupational pension scheme in question had an incapacity during the period of 6 months beginning with the later of—
  (a) the relevant day, or
  (b) the day on which the member discovered (or could with reasonable diligence have discovered) the qualifying fact deliberately concealed from the member by the employer or the trustees or managers of the scheme.

(10) The relevant day for the purposes of this section is—
  (a) the last day of the employment or appointment, or
  (b) the day on which the stable working relationship between the worker and the responsible person ended.

131 Assessment of whether work is of equal value

(1) This section applies to proceedings before an employment tribunal on—
  (a) a complaint relating to a breach of an equality clause or rule, or
  (b) a question referred to the tribunal by virtue of section 128(2).

(2) Where a question arises in the proceedings as to whether one person's work is of equal value to another's, the tribunal may, before determining the question, require a member of the panel of independent experts to prepare a report on the question.

(3) The tribunal may withdraw a requirement that it makes under subsection (2); and, if it does so, it may—
  (a) request the panel member to provide it with specified documentation;
  (b) make such other requests to that member as are connected with the withdrawal of the requirement.

(4) If the tribunal requires the preparation of a report under subsection (2) (and does not withdraw the requirement), it must not determine the question unless it has received the report.

(5) Subsection (6) applies where—
  (a) a question arises in the proceedings as to whether the work of one person (A) is of equal value to the work of another (B), and
  (b) A's work and B's work have been given different values by a job evaluation study.
(6) The tribunal must determine that A's work is not of equal value to B's work unless it has reasonable grounds for suspecting that the evaluation contained in the study—
  (a) was based on a system that discriminates because of sex, or
  (b) is otherwise unreliable.
(7) For the purposes of subsection (6)(a), a system discriminates because of sex if a difference (or coincidence) between values that the system sets on different demands is not justifiable regardless of the sex of the person on whom the demands are made.
(8) A reference to a member of the panel of independent experts is a reference to a person—
  (a) who is for the time being designated as such by the Advisory, Conciliation and Arbitration Service (ACAS) for the purposes of this section, and
  (b) who is neither a member of the Council of ACAS nor one of its officers or members of staff.
(9) 'Job evaluation study' has the meaning given in section 80(5).

132 Remedies in non-pensions cases

(1) This section applies to proceedings before a court or employment tribunal on a complaint relating to a breach of an equality clause, other than a breach with respect to membership of or rights under an occupational pension scheme.
(2) If the court or tribunal finds that there has been a breach of the equality clause, it may—
  (a) make a declaration as to the rights of the parties in relation to the matters to which the proceedings relate;
  (b) order an award by way of arrears of pay or damages in relation to the complainant.
(3) The court or tribunal may not order a payment under subsection (2)(b) in respect of a time before the arrears day.
(4) In relation to proceedings in England and Wales, the arrears day is, in a case mentioned in the first column of the table, the day mentioned in the second column.
(5) In relation to proceedings in Scotland, the arrears day is the first day of—
  (a) the period of 5 years ending with the day on which the proceedings were commenced, or
  (b) if the case involves a relevant incapacity, or a relevant fraud or error, [the period determined in accordance with section 135(6) and (7)].[98]

133 Remedies in pensions cases

(1) This section applies to proceedings before a court or employment tribunal on a complaint relating to—
  (a) a breach of an equality rule, or
  (b) a breach of an equality clause with respect to membership of, or rights under, an occupational pension scheme.
(2) If the court or tribunal finds that there has been a breach as referred to in subsection (1)—
  (a) it may make a declaration as to the rights of the parties in relation to the matters to which the proceedings relate;
  (b) it must not order arrears of benefits or damages or any other amount to be paid to the complainant.

[98] Substituted by Equality Act 2010 (Consequential Amendments, Saving and Supplementary Provisions) Order 2010, SI 2010/2279.

(3) Subsection (2)(b) does not apply if the proceedings are proceedings to which section 134 applies.

(4) If the breach relates to a term on which persons become members of the scheme, the court or tribunal may declare that the complainant is entitled to be admitted to the scheme with effect from a specified date.

(5) A date specified for the purposes of subsection (4) must not be before 8 April 1976.

(6) If the breach relates to a term on which members of the scheme are treated, the court or tribunal may declare that the complainant is, in respect of a specified period, entitled to secure the rights that would have accrued if the breach had not occurred.

(7) A period specified for the purposes of subsection (6) must not begin before 17 May 1990.

(8) If the court or tribunal makes a declaration under subsection (6), the employer must provide such resources to the scheme as are necessary to secure for the complainant (without contribution or further contribution by the complainant or other members) the rights referred to in that subsection.

134 Remedies in claims for arrears brought by pensioner members

(1) This section applies to proceedings before a court or employment tribunal on a complaint by a pensioner member of an occupational pension scheme relating to a breach of an equality clause or rule with respect to a term on which the member is treated.

(2) If the court or tribunal finds that there has been a breach referred to in subsection (1), it may—
   (a) make a declaration as to the rights of the complainant and the respondent in relation to the matters to which the proceedings relate;
   (b) order an award by way of arrears of benefits or damages or of any other amount in relation to the complainant.

(3) The court or tribunal must not order an award under subsection (2)(b) in respect of a time before the arrears day.

(4) If the court or tribunal orders an award under subsection (2)(b), the employer must provide such resources to the scheme as are necessary to secure for the complainant (without contribution or further contribution by the complainant or other members) the amount of the award.

(5) In relation to proceedings in England and Wales, the arrears day is, in a case mentioned in the first column of the table, the day mentioned in the second column.

Case	Arrears day
A standard case	The day falling 6 years before the day on which the proceedings were instituted.
A concealment case or an incapacity case (or a case which is both).	The day on which the breach first occurred.

(6) In relation to proceedings in Scotland, the arrears day is the first day of—
   (a) the period of 5 years ending with the day on which the proceedings were commenced, or
   (b) if the case involves a relevant incapacity, or a relevant fraud or error, [the period determined in accordance with section 135(6) and (7)].[99]

---

[99] Substituted by Equality Act 2010 (Consequential Amendments, Saving and Supplementary Provisions) Order 2010, SI 2010/2279.

135 Supplementary

(1) This section applies for the purposes of sections 132 to 134.

(2) A standard case is a case which is not—

    (a) a concealment case,

    (b) an incapacity case, or

    (c) a concealment case and an incapacity case.

(3) A concealment case in relation to an equality clause is a case where—

    (a) the responsible person deliberately concealed a qualifying fact (as defined by section 130) from the worker, and

    (b) the worker commenced the proceedings before the end of the period of 6 years beginning with the day on which the worker discovered (or could with reasonable diligence have discovered) the qualifying fact.

(4) A concealment case in relation to an equality rule is a case where—

    (a) the employer or the trustees or managers of the occupational pension scheme in question deliberately concealed a qualifying fact (as defined by section 130) from the member, and

    (b) the member commenced the proceedings before the end of the period of 6 years beginning with the day on which the member discovered (or could with reasonable diligence have discovered) the qualifying fact.

(5) An incapacity case is a case where the worker or member—

    (a) had an incapacity when the breach first occurred, and

    (b) commenced the proceedings before the end of the period of 6 years beginning with the day on which the worker or member ceased to have the incapacity.

(6) A case involves a relevant incapacity or a relevant fraud or error if the period of 5 years referred to in section 132(5)(a) [or 134(6)(a)][100] is, as a result of subsection (7) below, reckoned as a period of more than [5 years; and—

    (a) if, as a result of subsection (7), that period is reckoned as a period of more than 5 years but no more than 20 years, the period for the purposes of section 132(5)(b) or (as the case may be) section 134(6)(b) is that extended period;

    (b) if, as a result of subsection (7), that period is reckoned as a period of more than 20 years, the period for the purposes of section 132(5)(b) or (as the case may be) section 134(6)(b) is a period of 20 years.][101]

(7) For the purposes of the reckoning referred to in subsection (6), no account is to be taken of time when the worker or member—

    (a) had an incapacity, or

    (b) was induced by a relevant fraud or error to refrain from commencing proceedings (not being a time after the worker or member could with reasonable diligence have discovered the fraud or error).

(8) For the purposes of subsection (7)—

    (a) a fraud is relevant in relation to an equality clause if it is a fraud on the part of the responsible person;

    (b) an error is relevant in relation to an equality clause if it is induced by the words or conduct of the responsible person;

    (c) a fraud is relevant in relation to an equality rule if it is a fraud on the part of the employer or the trustees or managers of the scheme;

---

[100] Inserted by Equality Act 2010 (Consequential Amendments, Saving and Supplementary Provisions) Order 2010, SI 2010/2279.

[101] Substituted by Equality Act 2010 (Consequential Amendments, Saving and Supplementary Provisions) Order 2010, SI 2010/2279.

(d) an error is relevant in relation to an equality rule if it is induced by the words or conduct of the employer or the trustees or managers of the scheme.

(9) A reference in subsection (8) to the responsible person, the employer or the trustees or managers includes a reference to a person acting on behalf of the person or persons concerned.

(10) In relation to terms of service, a reference in section 132(5) or subsection (3) or (5)(b) of this section to commencing proceedings is to be read as a reference to making a service complaint.

(11) A reference to a pensioner member of a scheme includes a reference to a person who is entitled to the present payment of pension or other benefits derived through a member.

(12) In relation to proceedings before a court—

(a) a reference to a complaint is to be read as a reference to a claim, and

(b) a reference to a complainant is to be read as a reference to a claimant.

CHAPTER 5
MISCELLANEOUS

136 Burden of proof

(1) This section applies to any proceedings relating to a contravention of this Act.

(2) If there are facts from which the court could decide, in the absence of any other explanation, that a person (A) contravened the provision concerned, the court must hold that the contravention occurred.

(3) But subsection (2) does not apply if A shows that A did not contravene the provision.

(4) The reference to a contravention of this Act includes a reference to a breach of an equality clause or rule.

(5) This section does not apply to proceedings for an offence under this Act.

(6) A reference to the court includes a reference to—

(a) an employment tribunal;

(b) the Asylum and Immigration Tribunal;

(c) the Special Immigration Appeals Commission;

(d) the First-tier Tribunal;

(e) the Special Educational Needs Tribunal for Wales;

(f) [the First-tier Tribunal for Scotland Health and Education Chamber][102].

137 Previous findings

(1) A finding in relevant proceedings in respect of an act which has become final is to be treated as conclusive in proceedings under this Act.

(2) Relevant proceedings are proceedings before a court or employment tribunal under any of the following—

(a) section 19 or 20 of the Race Relations Act 1968;

(b) the Equal Pay Act 1970;

(c) the Sex Discrimination Act 1975;

(d) the Race Relations Act 1976;

(e) section 6(4A) of the Sex Discrimination Act 1986;

(f) the Disability Discrimination Act 1995;

(g) Part 2 of the Equality Act 2006;

---

[102] Substituted by First-tier Tribunal for Scotland (Transfer of Functions of the Additional Support Needs Tribunals for Scotland) Regulations 2018, SI 2018/4.

    (h) the Employment Equality (Religion and Belief) Regulations 2003 (S.I. 2003/1660);

    (i) the Employment Equality (Sexual Orientation) Regulations 2003 (S.I. 2003/1661);

    (j) the Employment Equality (Age) Regulations 2006 (S.I. 2006/1031);

    (k) the Equality Act (Sexual Orientation) Regulations 2007 (S.I. 2007/1263).

(3) A finding becomes final—

    (a) when an appeal against the finding is dismissed, withdrawn or abandoned, or

    (b) when the time for appealing expires without an appeal having been brought.

138 Obtaining information, etc.

[...][103]

139 Interest

(1) Regulations may make provision—

    (a) for enabling an employment tribunal to include interest on an amount awarded by it in proceedings under this Act;

    (b) specifying the manner in which, and the periods and rate by reference to which, the interest is to be determined.

(2) Regulations may modify the operation of an order made under section 14 of the Employment Tribunals Act 1996 (power to make provision as to interest on awards) in so far as it relates to an award in proceedings under this Act.

[139A Equal pay audits

(1) Regulations may make provision requiring an employment tribunal to order the respondent to carry out an equal pay audit in any case where the tribunal finds that there has been an equal pay breach.

(2) An equal pay breach is—

    (a) a breach of an equality clause, or

    (b) a contravention in relation to pay of section 39(2), 49(6) or 50(6), so far as relating to sex discrimination.

(3) An equal pay audit is an audit designed to identify action to be taken to avoid equal pay breaches occurring or continuing.

(4) The regulations may make further provision about equal pay audits, including provision about—

    (a) the content of an audit;

    (b) the powers and duties of a tribunal for deciding whether its order has been complied with;

    (c) any circumstances in which an audit may be required to be published or may be disclosed to any person.

(5) The regulations must provide for an equal pay audit not to be ordered where the tribunal considers that—

    (a) an audit completed by the respondent in the previous 3 years meets requirements prescribed for this purpose,

    (b) it is clear without an audit whether any action is required to avoid equal pay breaches occurring or continuing,

    (c) the breach the tribunal has found gives no reason to think that there may be other breaches, or

    (d) the disadvantages of an equal pay audit would outweigh its benefits.

---

[103] Repealed by Enterprise and Regulatory Reform Act 2013.

(6) The regulations may provide for an employment tribunal to have power, where a person fails to comply with an order to carry out an equal pay audit, to order that person to pay a penalty to the Secretary of State of not more than an amount specified in the regulations.

(7) The regulations may provide for that power—
   (a) to be exercisable in prescribed circumstances;
   (b) to be exercisable more than once, if the failure to comply continues.

(8) The first regulations made by virtue of subsection (6) must not specify an amount of more than £5,000.

(9) Sums received by the Secretary of State under the regulations must be paid into the Consolidated Fund.

(10) The first regulations under this section must specify an exemption period during which the requirement to order an equal pay audit does not apply in the case of a business that—
   (a) had fewer than 10 employees immediately before a specified time, or
   (b) was begun as a new business in a specified period.

(11) For the purposes of subsection (10)—
   (a) 'specified' means specified in the regulations, and
   (b) the number of employees a business had or the time when a business was begun as a new business is to be determined in accordance with the regulations.

(12) Before making regulations under this section, a Minister of the Crown must consult any other Minister of the Crown with responsibility for employment tribunals.][104]

140 Conduct giving rise to separate proceedings

(1) This section applies in relation to conduct which has given rise to two or more separate proceedings under this Act, with at least one being for a contravention of section 111 (instructing, causing or inducing contraventions).

(2) A court may transfer proceedings to an employment tribunal.

(3) An employment tribunal may transfer proceedings to a court.

(4) A court or employment tribunal is to be taken for the purposes of this Part to have jurisdiction to determine a claim or complaint transferred to it under this section; accordingly—
   (a) a reference to a claim within section 114(1) includes a reference to a claim transferred to a court under this section, and
   (b) a reference to a complaint within section 120(1) includes a reference to a complaint transferred to an employment tribunal under this section.

(5) A court or employment tribunal may not make a decision that is inconsistent with an earlier decision in proceedings arising out of the conduct.

(6) 'Court' means—
   (a) in relation to proceedings in England and Wales, [the county court][105];
   (b) in relation to proceedings in Scotland, the sheriff.

[140A Extension of time limits because of mediation in certain cross-border disputes

(1) In this section—
   (a) 'Mediation Directive' means Directive 2008/52/EC of the European Parliament and of the Council of 21 May 2008 on certain aspects of mediation in civil and commercial matters,
   (b) 'mediation' has the meaning given by article 3(a) of the Mediation Directive,
   (c) 'mediator' has the meaning given by article 3(b) of the Mediation Directive, and

---

[104] Inserted by Enterprise and Regulatory Reform Act 2013.
[105] Substituted by Crime and Courts Act 2013.

    (d) 'relevant dispute' means a dispute to which article 8(1) of the Mediation Directive applies (certain cross-border disputes).

(2) Subsection (3) applies where—

    (a) a time limit is set by section 118(1)(a), 118(2) or 129(3) in relation to the whole or part of a relevant dispute,

    (b) a mediation in relation to the relevant dispute starts before the time limit expires, and

    (c) if not extended by this section, the time limit would expire before the mediation ends or less than eight weeks after it ends.

(3) The time limit expires instead at the end of eight weeks after the mediation ends (subject to subsection (4))

(4) If a time limit mentioned in subsection (2)(a) has been extended by this section, subsections (2) and (3) apply to the extended time limit as they apply to a time limit mentioned in subsection (2)(a).

(5) Subsection (6) applies where—

    (a) a time limit is set by section 123(1)(a) in relation to the whole or part of a relevant dispute,

    (b) a mediation in relation to the relevant dispute starts before the time limit expires, and

    (c) if not extended by this section the time limit would expire before the mediation ends or less than four weeks after it ends.

(6) The time limit expires instead at the end of four weeks after the mediation ends (subject to subsection (7)).

(7) If a time limit mentioned in subsection (5)(a) has been extended by this section, subsections (5) and (6) apply to the extended time limit as they apply to a time limit mentioned in subsection (5)(a).

(8) Where more than one time limit applies in relation to a relevant dispute, the extension by subsection (3) or (6) of one of those time limits does not affect the others.

(9) For the purposes of this section, a mediation starts on the date of the agreement to mediate that is entered into by the parties and the mediator.

(10) For the purposes of this section, a mediation ends on the date of the first of these to occur—

    (a) the parties reach an agreement in resolution of the relevant dispute,

    (b) a party completes the notification of the other parties that it has withdrawn from the mediation,

    (c) a party to whom a qualifying request is made fails to give a response reaching the other parties within 14 days of the request,

    (d) the parties, after being notified that the mediator's appointment has ended (by death, resignation or otherwise), fail to agree within 14 days to seek to appoint a replacement mediator,

    (e) the mediation otherwise comes to an end pursuant to the terms of the agreement to mediate.

(11) For the purpose of subsection (10), a qualifying request is a request by a party that another (A) confirm to all parties that A is continuing with the mediation.

(12) In the case of any relevant dispute, references in this section to a mediation are references to the mediation so far as it relates to that dispute, and references to a party are to be read accordingly.

(13) Where a court or tribunal has power under section 118(1)(b) or 123(1)(b) to extend a period of limitation, the power is exercisable in relation to the period of limitation as extended by this section.][106]

---

[106] Inserted by Cross-Border Mediation (EU Directive) Regulations 2011, SI 2011/1133.

[140AA Extension of time limits because of alternative dispute resolution in certain cross border or domestic contractual disputes

(1) In this section—
   (a) 'ADR Directive' means Directive 2013/11/EU of the European Parliament and of the Council of 21 May 2013 on alternative dispute resolution for consumer disputes and amending Regulation (EC) No 2006/2004 and Directive 2009/22/EC;
   (b) 'ADR entity' has the meaning given by article 4(1)(h) of the ADR Directive;
   (c) […][107]
   (d) 'ADR procedure' has the meaning given by article 4(1)(g) of the ADR Directive;
   (e) 'non-binding ADR procedure' means an ADR procedure the outcome of which is not binding on the parties;
   (f) 'relevant dispute' means a dispute to which Article 12(1) of the ADR Directive applies (certain cross-border or domestic contractual disputes brought by a consumer against a trader).
(2) Subsection (3) applies where—
   (a) a time limit is set by section 118(1)(a) and (2) in relation to the whole or part of a relevant dispute;
   (b) a non-binding ADR procedure in relation to the relevant dispute starts before the time limit expires; and
   (c) if not extended by this section, the time limit would expire before the non-binding ADR procedure ends or less than eight weeks after it ends.
(3) For the purposes of initiating judicial proceedings, the time limit expires instead at the end of eight weeks after the non-binding ADR procedure ends (subject to subsection (4)).
(4) If a time limit has been extended by this section, subsections (2) and (3) apply to the extended time limit as they apply to a time limit mentioned in subsection (2)(a).
(5) Where more than one time limit applies in relation to a relevant dispute, the extension by subsection (3) of one of those time limits does not affect the others.
(6) For the purposes of this section, a non-binding ADR procedure starts in relation to a relevant dispute on the date when the dispute is first sent or otherwise communicated to the ADR entity in accordance with the entity's rules regarding the submission of complaints.
(7) For the purposes of this section, the non-binding ADR procedure ends on the date of the first of these to occur—
   (a) the parties reach an agreement in resolution of the relevant dispute;
   (b) a party completes the notification of the other parties that it has withdrawn from the non-binding ADR procedure;
   (c) a party to whom a qualifying request is made fails to give a response reaching the other parties within 14 days of the request;
   (d) that the ADR entity notifies the party that submitted the relevant dispute to the ADR entity that, in accordance with its policy, the ADR entity refuses to deal with the relevant dispute;
   (e) after the parties are notified that the ADR entity can no longer act in relation to the relevant dispute (for whatever reason), the parties fail to agree within 14 days to submit the dispute to an alternative ADR entity;
   (f) the non-binding ADR procedure otherwise comes to an end pursuant to the rules of the ADR entity.

---

[107] Repealed by Alternative Dispute Resolution for Consumer Disputes (Amendment) (No. 2) Regulations 2015, SI 2015/1972.

(8) For the purpose of subsection (6), a qualifying request is a request by a party that another (A) confirm to all parties that A is continuing with the non-binding ADR procedure.

(9) In the case of any relevant dispute, references in this section to a non-binding ADR procedure are references to the non-binding ADR procedure so far as it relates to that dispute, and references to a party are to be read accordingly.

(10) Where a court or tribunal has power under section 118(1)(b) to extend a period of limitation, the power is exercisable in relation to the period of limitation as extended by this section.][108]

[140B Extension of time limits to facilitate conciliation before institution of proceedings

(1) This section applies where a time limit is set by section 123(1)(a) or 129(3) or (4). But it does not apply to a dispute that is (or so much of a dispute as is) a relevant dispute for the purposes of section 140A.

(2) In this section—
   (a) Day A is the day on which the complainant or applicant concerned complies with the requirement in subsection (1) of section 18A of the Employment Tribunals Act 1996 (requirement to contact ACAS before instituting proceedings) in relation to the matter in respect of which the proceedings are brought, and
   (b) Day B is the day on which the complainant or applicant concerned receives or, if earlier, is treated as receiving (by virtue of regulations made under subsection (11) of that section) the certificate issued under subsection (4) of that section.

(3) In working out when the time limit set by section 123(1)(a) or 129(3) or (4) expires the period beginning with the day after Day A and ending with Day B is not to be counted.

(4) If the time limit set by section 123(1)(a) or 129(3) or (4) would (if not extended by this subsection) expire during the period beginning with Day A and ending one month after Day B, the time limit expires instead at the end of that period.

(5) The power conferred on the employment tribunal by subsection (1)(b) of section 123 to extend the time limit set by subsection (1)(a) of that section is exercisable in relation to that time limit as extended by this section.][109]

141 Interpretation, etc.

(1) This section applies for the purposes of this Part.

(2) A reference to the responsible person, in relation to an equality clause or rule, is to be construed in accordance with Chapter 3 of Part 5.

(3) A reference to a worker is a reference to the person to the terms of whose work the proceedings in question relate; and, for the purposes of proceedings relating to an equality rule or a nondiscrimination rule, a reference to a worker includes a reference to a member of the occupational pension scheme in question.

(4) A reference to the terms of a person's work is to be construed in accordance with Chapter 3 of Part 5.

(5) A reference to a member of an occupational pension scheme includes a reference to a prospective member.

(6) In relation to proceedings in England and Wales, a person has an incapacity if the person—
   (a) has not attained the age of 18, or
   (b) lacks capacity (within the meaning of the Mental Capacity Act 2005).

---

[108] Inserted by Alternative Dispute Resolution for Consumer Disputes (Amendment) Regulations 2015, SI 2015/1392.
[109] Inserted by Enterprise and Regulatory Reform Act 2013.

(7) In relation to proceedings in Scotland, a person has an incapacity if the person—
    (a) has not attained the age of 16, or
    (b) is incapable (within the meaning of the Adults with Incapacity (Scotland) Act 2000 (asp 4)).
[(8) 'Service complaint' means a complaint made under section 340A(1) or (2) of the Armed Forces Act 2006.][110]
(9) 'Criminal matter' means—
    (a) an investigation into the commission of an alleged offence;
    (b) a decision whether to commence criminal proceedings;
    (c) criminal proceedings.

PART 10
CONTRACTS, ETC.

Contracts and other agreements

142 Unenforceable terms

(1) A term of a contract is unenforceable against a person in so far as it constitutes, promotes or provides for treatment of that or another person that is of a description prohibited by this Act.
(2) A relevant non-contractual term is unenforceable against a person in so far as it constitutes, promotes or provides for treatment of that or another person that is of a description prohibited by this Act, in so far as this Act relates to disability.
(3) A relevant non-contractual term is a term which—
    (a) is a term of an agreement that is not a contract, and
    (b) relates to the provision of an employment service within section 56(2)(a) to (e) or to the provision under a group insurance arrangement of facilities by way of insurance.
(4) A reference in subsection (1) or (2) to treatment of a description prohibited by this Act does not include—
    (a) a reference to the inclusion of a term in a contract referred to in section 70(2)(a) or 76(2), or
    (b) a reference to the failure to include a term in a contract as referred to in section 70(2)(b).
(5) Subsection (4) does not affect the application of section 148(2) to this section.

143 Removal or modification of unenforceable terms

(1) [The county court][111] or the sheriff may, on an application by a person who has an interest in a contract or other agreement which includes a term that is unenforceable as a result of section 142, make an order for the term to be removed or modified.
(2) An order under this section must not be made unless every person who would be affected by it—
    (a) has been given notice of the application (except where notice is dispensed with in accordance with rules of court), and
    (b) has been afforded an opportunity to make representations to the county court or sheriff.

---

[110] Substituted by Armed Forces (Service Complaints and Financial Assistance) Act 2015.
[111] Substituted by Crime and Courts Act 2013.

(3) An order under this section may include provision in respect of a period before the making of the order.

144 Contracting out

(1) A term of a contract is unenforceable by a person in whose favour it would operate in so far as it purports to exclude or limit a provision of or made under this Act.

(2) A relevant non-contractual term (as defined by section 142) is unenforceable by a person in whose favour it would operate in so far as it purports to exclude or limit a provision of or made under this Act, in so far as the provision relates to disability.

(3) This section does not apply to a contract which settles a claim within section 114.

(4) This section does not apply to a contract which settles a complaint within section 120 if the contract—

    (a) is made with the assistance of a conciliation officer, or

    (b) is a qualifying [settlement agreement][112].

(5) A contract within subsection (4) includes a contract which settles a complaint relating to a breach of an equality clause or rule or of a non-discrimination rule.

(6) A contract within subsection (4) includes an agreement by the parties to a dispute to submit the dispute to arbitration if—

    (a) the dispute is covered by a scheme having effect by virtue of an order under section 212A of the Trade Union and Labour Relations (Consolidation) Act 1992, and

    (b) the agreement is to submit the dispute to arbitration in accordance with the scheme.

Collective agreements and rules of undertakings

145 Void and unenforceable terms

(1) A term of a collective agreement is void in so far as it constitutes, promotes or provides for treatment of a description prohibited by this Act.

(2) A rule of an undertaking is unenforceable against a person in so far as it constitutes, promotes or provides for treatment of the person that is of a description prohibited by this Act.

146 Declaration in respect of void term, etc.

(1) A qualifying person (P) may make a complaint to an employment tribunal that a term is void, or that a rule is unenforceable, as a result of section 145.

(2) But subsection (1) applies only if—

    (a) the term or rule may in the future have effect in relation to P, and

    (b) where the complaint alleges that the term or rule provides for treatment of a description prohibited by this Act, P may in the future be subjected to treatment that would (if P were subjected to it in present circumstances) be of that description.

(3) If the tribunal finds that the complaint is well-founded, it must make an order declaring that the term is void or the rule is unenforceable.

(4) An order under this section may include provision in respect of a period before the making of the order.

(5) In the case of a complaint about a term of a collective agreement, where the term is one made by or on behalf of a person of a description specified in the first column of the table, a qualifying person is a person of a description specified in the second column.

---

[112] Substituted by Enterprise and Regulatory Reform Act 2013.

Description of person who made collective agreement	Qualifying person
Employer	A person who is, or is seeking to be, an employee of that employer
Organisation of employers	A person who is, or is seeking to be, an employee of an employer who is a member of that organisation
Association of organisations of employers	A person who is, or is seeking to be, an employee of an employer who is a member of an organisation in that association

(6) In the case of a complaint about a rule of an undertaking, where the rule is one made by or on behalf of a person of a description specified in the first column of the table, a qualifying person is a person of a description specified in the second column.

Description of person who made rule of undertaking	Qualifying person
Employer	A person who is, or is seeking to be, an employee of that employer
Trade organisation or qualifications body	A person who is, or is seeking to be, a member of the organisation or body
	A person upon whom the body has conferred a relevant qualification
	A person seeking conferment by the body of a relevant qualification

Supplementary

147 Meaning of 'qualifying [settlement agreement]'[113]

(1) This section applies for the purposes of this Part.
(2) A qualifying [settlement agreement][114] is a contract in relation to which each of the conditions in subsection (3) is met.
(3) Those conditions are that—
    (a) the contract is in writing,
    (b) the contract relates to the particular complaint,
    (c) the complainant has, before entering into the contract, received advice from an independent adviser about its terms and effect (including, in particular, its effect on the complainant's ability to pursue the complaint before an employment tribunal),
    (d) on the date of the giving of the advice, there is in force a contract of insurance, or an indemnity provided for members of a profession or professional body, covering the risk of a claim by the complainant in respect of loss arising from the advice,
    (e) the contract identifies the adviser, and
    (f) the contract states that the conditions in paragraphs (c) and (d) are met.
(4) Each of the following is an independent adviser—
    (a) a qualified lawyer;
    (b) an officer, official, employee or member of an independent trade union certified in writing by the trade union as competent to give advice and as authorised to do so on its behalf;
    (c) a worker at an advice centre (whether as an employee or a volunteer) certified in writing by the centre as competent to give advice and as authorised to do so on its behalf;
    (d) a person of such description as may be specified by order.

---

[113] Substituted by Enterprise and Regulatory Reform Act 2013.
[114] Substituted by Enterprise and Regulatory Reform Act 2013.

(5) Despite subsection (4), none of the following is an independent adviser [to the complainant][115] in relation to a qualifying [settlement agreement][116]—

    (a) a person [(other than the complainant)][117] who is a party to the contract or the complaint;

    (b) a person who is connected to a person within paragraph (a);

    (c) a person who is employed by a person within paragraph (a) or (b);

    (d) a person who is acting for a person within paragraph (a) or (b) in relation to the contract or the complaint;

    (e) a person within subsection (4)(b) or (c), if the trade union or advice centre is a person within paragraph (a) or (b);

    (f) a person within subsection (4)(c) to whom the complainant makes a payment for the advice.

(6) A 'qualified lawyer', for the purposes of subsection (4)(a), is—

    (a) in relation to England and Wales, a person who, for the purposes of the Legal Services Act 2007, is an authorised person in relation to an activity which constitutes the exercise of a right of audience or the conduct of litigation;

    (b) in relation to Scotland, an advocate (whether in practice as such or employed to give legal advice) or a solicitor who holds a practising certificate.

(7) 'Independent trade union' has the meaning given in section 5 of the Trade Union and Labour Relations (Consolidation) Act 1992.

(8) Two persons are connected for the purposes of subsection (5) if—

    (a) one is a company of which the other (directly or indirectly) has control, or

    (b) both are companies of which a third person (directly or indirectly) has control.

(9) Two persons are also connected for the purposes of subsection (5) in so far as a connection between them gives rise to a conflict of interest in relation to the contract or the complaint.

148 Interpretation

(1) This section applies for the purposes of this Part.

(2) A reference to treatment of a description prohibited by this Act does not include treatment in so far as it is treatment that would contravene—

    (a) Part 1 (public sector duty regarding socio-economic inequalities), or

    (b) Chapter 1 of Part 11 (public sector equality duty).

(3) 'Group insurance arrangement' means an arrangement between an employer and another person for the provision by that other person of facilities by way of insurance to the employer's employees (or a class of those employees).

(4) 'Collective agreement' has the meaning given in section 178 of the Trade Union and Labour Relations (Consolidation) Act 1992.

(5) A rule of an undertaking is a rule within subsection (6) or (7).

(6) A rule within this subsection is a rule made by a trade organisation or a qualifications body for application to—

    (a) its members or prospective members,

    (b) persons on whom it has conferred a relevant qualification, or

    (c) persons seeking conferment by it of a relevant qualification.

(7) A rule within this subsection is a rule made by an employer for application to—

    (a) employees,

    (b) persons who apply for employment, or

    (c) persons the employer considers for employment.

---

[115] Inserted by Equality Act 2010 (Amendment) Order 2012, SI 2012/334.

[116] Substituted by Enterprise and Regulatory Reform Act 2013.

[117] Inserted by Equality Act 2010 (Amendment) Order 2012, SI 2012/334.

(8) 'Trade organisation', 'qualifications body' and 'relevant qualification' each have the meaning given in Part 5 (work).

PART 11
ADVANCEMENT OF EQUALITY

CHAPTER 1
PUBLIC SECTOR EQUALITY DUTY

149 Public sector equality duty

(1) A public authority must, in the exercise of its functions, have due regard to the need to—
  (a) eliminate discrimination, harassment, victimisation and any other conduct that is prohibited by or under this Act;
  (b) advance equality of opportunity between persons who share a relevant protected characteristic and persons who do not share it;
  (c) foster good relations between persons who share a relevant protected characteristic and persons who do not share it.

(2) A person who is not a public authority but who exercises public functions must, in the exercise of those functions, have due regard to the matters mentioned in subsection (1).

(3) Having due regard to the need to advance equality of opportunity between persons who share a relevant protected characteristic and persons who do not share it involves having due regard, in particular, to the need to—
  (a) remove or minimise disadvantages suffered by persons who share a relevant protected characteristic that are connected to that characteristic;
  (b) take steps to meet the needs of persons who share a relevant protected characteristic that are different from the needs of persons who do not share it;
  (c) encourage persons who share a relevant protected characteristic to participate in public life or in any other activity in which participation by such persons is disproportionately low.

(4) The steps involved in meeting the needs of disabled persons that are different from the needs of persons who are not disabled include, in particular, steps to take account of disabled persons' disabilities.

(5) Having due regard to the need to foster good relations between persons who share a relevant protected characteristic and persons who do not share it involves having due regard, in particular, to the need to—
  (a) tackle prejudice, and
  (b) promote understanding.

(6) Compliance with the duties in this section may involve treating some persons more favourably than others; but that is not to be taken as permitting conduct that would otherwise be prohibited by or under this Act.

(7) The relevant protected characteristics are—
  age;
  disability;
  gender reassignment;
  pregnancy and maternity;
  race;
  religion or belief;
  sex;
  sexual orientation.

(8) A reference to conduct that is prohibited by or under this Act includes a reference to—

    (a) a breach of an equality clause or rule;

    (b) a breach of a non-discrimination rule.

(9) Schedule 18 (exceptions) has effect.

150 Public authorities and public functions

(1) A public authority is a person who is specified in Schedule 19.

(2) In that Schedule—

Part 1specifies public authorities generally;

Part 2specifies relevant Welsh authorities;

Part 3specifies relevant Scottish authorities.

(3) A public authority specified in Schedule 19 is subject to the duty imposed by section 149(1) in relation to the exercise of all of its functions unless subsection (4) applies.

(4) A public authority specified in that Schedule in respect of certain specified functions is subject to that duty only in respect of the exercise of those functions.

(5) A public function is a function that is a function of a public nature for the purposes of the Human Rights Act 1998.

151 Power to specify public authorities

(1) A Minister of the Crown may by order amend Part 1, 2 or 3 of Schedule 19.

(2) The Welsh Ministers may by order amend Part 2 of Schedule 19.

(3) The Scottish Ministers may by order amend Part 3 of Schedule 19.

(4) The power under subsection (1), (2) or (3) may not be exercised so as to—

    (a) add an entry to Part 1 relating to a relevant Welsh or Scottish authority or a cross-border Welsh or Scottish authority;

    (b) add an entry to Part 2 relating to a person who is not a relevant Welsh authority;

    (c) add an entry to Part 3 relating to a person who is not a relevant Scottish authority.

(5) A Minister of the Crown may by order amend Schedule 19 so as to make provision relating to a cross-border Welsh or Scottish authority.

(6) On the first exercise of the power under subsection (5) to add an entry relating to a cross-border Welsh or Scottish authority to Schedule 19, a Minister of the Crown must—

    (a) add a Part 4 to the Schedule for cross-border authorities, and

    (b) add the cross-border Welsh or Scottish authority to that Part.

(7) Any subsequent exercise of the power under subsection (5) to add an entry relating to a cross-border Welsh or Scottish authority to Schedule 19 must add that entry to Part 4 of the Schedule.

(8) An order may not be made under this section so as to extend the application of section 149 unless the person making it considers that the extension relates to a person by whom a public function is exercisable.

(9) An order may not be made under this section so as to extend the application of section 149 to—

    (a) the exercise of a function referred to in paragraph 3 of Schedule 18 (judicial functions, etc);

    (b) a person listed in paragraph 4(2)(a) to (e) of that Schedule (Parliament, devolved legislatures and General Synod);

    (c) the exercise of a function listed in paragraph 4(3) of that Schedule (proceedings in Parliament or devolved legislatures).

152 Power to specify public authorities: consultation […][118]

(1) Before making an order under a provision specified in the first column of the Table, a Minister of the Crown must consult the person or persons specified in the second column.

Provision	Consultees
Section 151(1)	The Commission
Section 151(1), so far as relating to a relevant Welsh authority	The Welsh Ministers
Section 151(1), so far as relating to a relevant Scottish authority	The Scottish Ministers
Section 151(5)	The Commission
Section 151(5), so far as relating to a cross-border Welsh authority	The Welsh Ministers
Section 151(5), so far as relating to a cross-border Scottish authority	The Scottish Ministers

(2) Before making an order under section 151(2), the Welsh Ministers must [consult the Commission, and after making such an order they must inform a Minister of the Crown.][119]

(3) Before making an order under section 151(3), the Scottish Ministers must [consult the Commission, and after making such an order they must inform a Minister of the Crown.][120]

153 Power to impose specific duties

(1) A Minister of the Crown may by regulations impose duties on a public authority specified in Part 1 of Schedule 19 for the purpose of enabling the better performance by the authority of the duty imposed by section 149(1).

(2) The Welsh Ministers may by regulations impose duties on a public authority specified in Part 2 of Schedule 19 for that purpose.

(3) The Scottish Ministers may by regulations impose duties on a public authority specified in Part 3 of Schedule 19 for that purpose.

(4) Before making regulations under this section, the person making them must consult the Commission.

154 Power to impose specific duties: cross-border authorities

(1) If a Minister of the Crown exercises the power in section 151(5) to add an entry for a public authority to Part 4 of Schedule 19, the Minister must include after the entry a letter specified in the first column of the Table in subsection (3).

(2) Where a letter specified in the first column of the Table in subsection (3) is included after an entry for a public authority in Part 4 of Schedule 19, the person specified in the second column of the Table—

  (a) may by regulations impose duties on the authority for the purpose of enabling the better performance by the authority of the duty imposed by section 149(1), subject to such limitations as are specified in that column;

  (b) must in making the regulations comply with the procedural requirement specified in that column.

---

[118] Repealed by Wales Act 2017.
[119] Substituted by Wales Act 2017.
[120] Substituted by Scotland Act 2016.

(3) This is the Table—

Letter	Person by whom regulations may be made and procedural requirements
A	Regulations may be made by a Minister of the Crown in relation to the authority's functions that are not devolved Welsh functions.
	The Minister of the Crown must consult the Welsh Ministers before making the regulations.
	Regulations may be made by the Welsh Ministers in relation to the authority's devolved Welsh functions.
	[The Welsh Ministers must inform a Minister of the Crown after][121] making the regulations.
B	Regulations may be made by a Minister of the Crown in relation to the authority's functions that are not devolved Scottish functions.
	The Minister of the Crown must consult the Scottish Ministers before making the regulations.
	Regulations may be made by the Scottish Ministers in relation to the authority's devolved Scottish functions.
	[The Scottish Ministers must inform a Minister of the Crown after][122] making the regulations.
C	Regulations may be made by a Minister of the Crown in relation to the authority's functions that are neither devolved Welsh functions nor devolved Scottish functions.
	The Minister of the Crown must consult the Welsh Ministers and the Scottish Ministers before making the regulations.
	Regulations may be made by the Welsh Ministers in relation to the authority's devolved Welsh functions.
	[The Welsh Ministers must inform a Minister of the Crown after][123] making the regulations.
	Regulations may be made by the Scottish Ministers in relation to the authority's devolved Scottish functions.
	[The Scottish Ministers must inform a Minister of the Crown after][124] making the regulations.
D	The regulations may be made by a Minister of the Crown.
	The Minister of the Crown must consult the Welsh Ministers before making the regulations.

(4) Before making regulations under subsection (2), the person making them must consult the Commission.

155 Power to impose specific duties: supplementary

(1) Regulations under section 153 or 154 may require a public authority to consider such matters as may be specified from time to time by—
   (a) a Minister of the Crown, where the regulations are made by a Minister of the Crown;
   (b) the Welsh Ministers, where the regulations are made by the Welsh Ministers;
   (c) the Scottish Ministers, where the regulations are made by the Scottish Ministers.
(2) Regulations under section 153 or 154 may impose duties on a public authority that is a contracting authority within the meaning of the Public Sector Directive in connection with its public procurement functions.

---

[121] Substituted by Wales Act 2017.
[122] Substituted by Scotland Act 2016.
[123] Substituted by Wales Act 2017.
[124] Substituted by Scotland Act 2016.

(3) In subsection (2)—

'public procurement functions' means functions the exercise of which is regulated by the Public Sector Directive;

['the Public Sector Directive' means Directive 2014/24/EU of the European Parliament and of the Council of 26 February 2014 on public procurement and repealing Directive 2004/18/EC, as amended from time to time.][125]

(4) Subsections (1) and (2) do not affect the generality of section 153 or 154(2)(a).

(5) A duty imposed on a public authority under section 153 or 154 may be modified or removed by regulations made by—

(a) a Minister of the Crown, where the original duty was imposed by regulations made by a Minister of the Crown;

(b) the Welsh Ministers, where the original duty was imposed by regulations made by the Welsh Ministers;

(c) the Scottish Ministers, where the original duty was imposed by regulations made by the Scottish Ministers.

156 Enforcement

A failure in respect of a performance of a duty imposed by or under this Chapter does not confer a cause of action at private law.

157 Interpretation

(1) This section applies for the purposes of this Chapter.

[(2) A relevant Welsh authority is a devolved Welsh authority (within the meaning given by section 157A of the Government of Wales Act 2006) other than the Assembly Commission.][126]

(3) A cross-border Welsh authority is a person other than a relevant Welsh authority (or the Assembly Commission) who has any function that—

(a) is exercisable in or as regards Wales, and

(b) is a devolved Welsh function.

(4) The Assembly Commission has the same meaning as in the Government of Wales Act 2006.

[(5) A function is a devolved Welsh function if—

(a) it relates to a matter in respect of which functions are exercisable by the Welsh Ministers, the First Minister for Wales or the Counsel General to the Welsh Government, or

(b) provision conferring the function would be within the legislative competence of the National Assembly for Wales.][127]

(6) A relevant Scottish authority is a public body, public office or holder of a public office—

(a) which is not a cross-border Scottish authority or the Scottish Parliamentary Corporate Body,

(b) whose functions are exercisable only in or as regards Scotland, and

(c) at least some of whose functions do not relate to reserved matters.

(7) A cross-border Scottish authority is a cross-border public authority within the meaning given by section 88(5) of the Scotland Act 1998.

---

[125] Substituted by Public Procurement (Amendments, Repeals and Revocations) Regulations 2016, SI 2016/275.

[126] Substituted by Wales Act 2017.

[127] Substituted by Wales Act 2017.

(8) A function is a devolved Scottish function if it—
  (a) is exercisable in or as regards Scotland, and
  (b) does not relate to reserved matters.
(9) Reserved matters has the same meaning as in the Scotland Act 1998.

CHAPTER 2
POSITIVE ACTION

158 Positive action: general

(1) This section applies if a person (P) reasonably thinks that—
  (a) persons who share a protected characteristic suffer a disadvantage connected to the characteristic,
  (b) persons who share a protected characteristic have needs that are different from the needs of persons who do not share it, or
  (c) participation in an activity by persons who share a protected characteristic is disproportionately low.
(2) This Act does not prohibit P from taking any action which is a proportionate means of achieving the aim of—
  (a) enabling or encouraging persons who share the protected characteristic to overcome or minimise that disadvantage,
  (b) meeting those needs, or
  (c) enabling or encouraging persons who share the protected characteristic to participate in that activity.
(3) Regulations may specify action, or descriptions of action, to which subsection (2) does not apply.
(4) This section does not apply to—
  (a) action within section 159(3), or
  (b) anything that is permitted by virtue of section 104.
(5) If section 104(7) is repealed by virtue of section 105, this section will not apply to anything that would have been so permitted but for the repeal.
(6) This section does not enable P to do anything that is prohibited by or under an enactment other than this Act.

159 Positive action: recruitment and promotion

(1) This section applies if a person (P) reasonably thinks that—
  (a) persons who share a protected characteristic suffer a disadvantage connected to the characteristic, or
  (b) participation in an activity by persons who share a protected characteristic is disproportionately low.
(2) Part 5 (work) does not prohibit P from taking action within subsection (3) with the aim of enabling or encouraging persons who share the protected characteristic to—
  (a) overcome or minimise that disadvantage, or
  (b) participate in that activity.
(3) That action is treating a person (A) more favourably in connection with recruitment or promotion than another person (B) because A has the protected characteristic but B does not.
(4) But subsection (2) applies only if—
  (a) A is as qualified as B to be recruited or promoted,

(b) P does not have a policy of treating persons who share the protected characteristic more favourably in connection with recruitment or promotion than persons who do not share it, and

(c) taking the action in question is a proportionate means of achieving the aim referred to in subsection (2).

(5) 'Recruitment' means a process for deciding whether to—

(a) offer employment to a person,

(b) make contract work available to a contract worker,

(c) offer a person a position as a partner in a firm or proposed firm,

(d) offer a person a position as a member of an LLP or proposed LLP,

(e) offer a person a pupillage or tenancy in barristers' chambers,

(f) take a person as an advocate's devil or offer a person membership of an advocate's stable,

(g) offer a person an appointment to a personal office,

(h) offer a person an appointment to a public office, recommend a person for such an appointment or approve a person's appointment to a public office, or

(i) offer a person a service for finding employment.

(6) This section does not enable P to do anything that is prohibited by or under an enactment other than this Act.

PART 12
DISABLED PERSONS: TRANSPORT

CHAPTER 1
TAXIS, ETC.

160 Taxi accessibility regulations

(1) The Secretary of State may make regulations (in this Chapter referred to as 'taxi accessibility regulations') for securing that it is possible for disabled persons—

(a) to get into and out of taxis in safety;

(b) to do so while in wheelchairs;

(c) to travel in taxis in safety and reasonable comfort;

(d) to do so while in wheelchairs.

(2) The regulations may, in particular, require a regulated taxi to conform with provision as to—

(a) the size of a door opening for the use of passengers;

(b) the floor area of the passenger compartment;

(c) the amount of headroom in the passenger compartment;

(d) the fitting of restraining devices designed to ensure the stability of a wheelchair while the taxi is moving.

(3) The regulations may also—

(a) require the driver of a regulated taxi which is plying for hire, or which has been hired, to comply with provisions as to the carrying of ramps or other devices designed to facilitate the loading and unloading of wheelchairs;

(b) require the driver of a regulated taxi in which a disabled person is being carried while in a wheelchair to comply with provisions as to the position in which the wheelchair is to be secured.

(4) The driver of a regulated taxi which is plying for hire or has been hired commits an offence—

(a) by failing to comply with a requirement of the regulations, or

(b) if the taxi fails to conform with any provision of the regulations with which it is required to conform.

(5) A person guilty of an offence under subsection (4) is liable on summary conviction to a fine not exceeding level 3 on the standard scale.

(6) In this section—

'passenger compartment' has such meaning as is specified in taxi accessibility regulations;

'regulated taxi' means a taxi to which taxi accessibility regulations are expressed to apply.

161 Control of numbers of licensed taxis: exception

(1) This section applies if—
- (a) an application for a licence in respect of a vehicle is made under section 37 of the Town Police Clauses Act 1847,
- (b) it is possible for a disabled person—
  - (i) to get into and out of the vehicle in safety,
  - (ii) to travel in the vehicle in safety and reasonable comfort, and
  - (iii) to do the things mentioned in sub-paragraphs (i) and (ii) while in a wheelchair of a size prescribed by the Secretary of State, and
- (c) the proportion of taxis licensed in respect of the area to which the licence would (if granted) apply that conform to the requirement in paragraph (b) is less than the proportion that is prescribed by the Secretary of State.

(2) Section 16 of the Transport Act 1985 (which modifies the provisions of the Town Police Clauses Act 1847 about hackney carriages to allow a licence to ply for hire to be refused in order to limit the number of licensed carriages) does not apply in relation to the vehicle; and those provisions of the Town Police Clauses Act 1847 are to have effect subject to this section.

(3) In section 16 of the Transport Act 1985, after 'shall' insert '(subject to section 161 of the Equality Act 2010)'.

162 Designated transport facilities

(1) The appropriate authority may by regulations provide for the application of any taxi provision (with or without modification) to—
- (a) vehicles used for the provision of services under a franchise agreement, or
- (b) drivers of such vehicles.

(2) A franchise agreement is a contract entered into by the operator of a designated transport facility for the provision, by the other party to the contract, of hire car services—
- (a) for members of the public using any part of the facility, and
- (b) which involve vehicles entering any part of the facility.

(3) In this section—

'appropriate authority' means—
- (a) in relation to transport facilities in England and Wales, the Secretary of State;
- (b) in relation to transport facilities in Scotland, the Scottish Ministers;

'designated' means designated by order made by the appropriate authority;

'hire car' has such meaning as is prescribed by the appropriate authority;

'operator', in relation to a transport facility, means a person who is concerned with the management or operation of the facility;

'taxi provision' means a provision of—
- (a) this Chapter, or
- (b) regulations made in pursuance of section 20(2A) of the Civic Government (Scotland) Act 1982, which applies in relation to taxis or drivers of taxis;

'transport facility' means premises which form part of a port, airport, railway station or bus station.

(4) For the purposes of section 2(2) of the European Communities Act 1972 (implementation of EU obligations), the Secretary of State may exercise a power conferred by this section on the Scottish Ministers.

163 Taxi licence conditional on compliance with taxi accessibility regulations

(1) A licence for a taxi to ply for hire must not be granted unless the vehicle conforms with the provisions of taxi accessibility regulations with which a vehicle is required to conform if it is licensed.

(2) Subsection (1) does not apply if a licence is in force in relation to the vehicle at any time during the period of 28 days immediately before the day on which the licence is granted.

(3) The Secretary of State may by order provide for subsection (2) to cease to have effect on a specified date.

(4) The power under subsection (3) may be exercised differently for different areas or localities.

164 Exemption from taxi accessibility regulations

(1) The Secretary of State may by regulations provide for a relevant licensing authority to apply for an order (an 'exemption order') exempting the authority from the requirements of section 163.

(2) Regulations under subsection (1) may, in particular, make provision requiring an authority proposing to apply for an exemption order—
(a) to carry out such consultation as is specified;
(b) to publish its proposals in the specified manner;
(c) before applying for the order, to consider representations made about the proposal;
(d) to make the application in the specified form.
In this subsection 'specified' means specified in the regulations.

(3) An authority may apply for an exemption order only if it is satisfied—
(a) that, having regard to the circumstances in its area, it is inappropriate for section 163 to apply, and
(b) that the application of that section would result in an unacceptable reduction in the number of taxis in its area.

(4) After consulting the Disabled Persons Transport Advisory Committee and such other persons as the Secretary of State thinks appropriate, the Secretary of State may—
(a) make an exemption order in the terms of the application for the order;
(b) make an exemption order in such other terms as the Secretary of State thinks appropriate;
(c) refuse to make an exemption order.

(5) The Secretary of State may by regulations make provision requiring a taxi plying for hire in an area in respect of which an exemption order is in force to conform with provisions of the regulations as to the fitting and use of swivel seats.

(6) Regulations under subsection (5) may make provision corresponding to section 163.

(7) In this section—
'relevant licensing authority' means an authority responsible for licensing taxis in any area of England and Wales other than the area to which the Metropolitan Public Carriage Act 1869 applies;
'swivel seats' has such meaning as is specified in regulations under subsection (5).

165 Passengers in wheelchairs

(1) This section imposes duties on the driver of a designated taxi which has been hired—
  (a) by or for a disabled person who is in a wheelchair, or
  (b) by another person who wishes to be accompanied by a disabled person who is in a wheelchair.

(2) This section also imposes duties on the driver of a designated private hire vehicle, if a person within paragraph (a) or (b) of subsection (1) has indicated to the driver that the person wishes to travel in the vehicle.

(3) For the purposes of this section—
  (a) a taxi or private hire vehicle is 'designated' if it appears on a list maintained under section 167;
  (b) 'the passenger' means the disabled person concerned.

(4) The duties are—
  (a) to carry the passenger while in the wheelchair;
  (b) not to make any additional charge for doing so;
  (c) if the passenger chooses to sit in a passenger seat, to carry the wheelchair;
  (d) to take such steps as are necessary to ensure that the passenger is carried in safety and reasonable comfort;
  (e) to give the passenger such mobility assistance as is reasonably required.

(5) Mobility assistance is assistance—
  (a) to enable the passenger to get into or out of the vehicle;
  (b) if the passenger wishes to remain in the wheelchair, to enable the passenger to get into and out of the vehicle while in the wheelchair;
  (c) to load the passenger's luggage into or out of the vehicle;
  (d) if the passenger does not wish to remain in the wheelchair, to load the wheelchair into or out of the vehicle.

(6) This section does not require the driver—
  (a) unless the vehicle is of a description prescribed by the Secretary of State, to carry more than one person in a wheelchair, or more than one wheelchair, on any one journey;
  (b) to carry a person in circumstances in which it would otherwise be lawful for the driver to refuse to carry the person.

(7) A driver of a designated taxi or designated private hire vehicle commits an offence by failing to comply with a duty imposed on the driver by this section.

(8) A person guilty of an offence under subsection (7) is liable on summary conviction to a fine not exceeding level 3 on the standard scale.

(9) It is a defence for a person charged with the offence to show that at the time of the alleged offence—
  (a) the vehicle conformed to the accessibility requirements which applied to it, but
  (b) it would not have been possible for the wheelchair to be carried safely in the vehicle.

(10) In this section and sections 166 and 167 'private hire vehicle' means—
  (a) a vehicle licensed under section 48 of the Local Government (Miscellaneous Provisions) Act 1976;
  (b) a vehicle licensed under section 7 of the Private Hire Vehicles (London) Act 1998;
  (c) a vehicle licensed under an equivalent provision of a local enactment;
  (d) a private hire car licensed under section 10 of the Civic Government (Scotland) Act 1982.

166 Passengers in wheelchairs: exemption certificates

(1) A licensing authority must issue a person with a certificate exempting the person from the duties imposed by section 165 (an 'exemption certificate') if satisfied that it is appropriate to do so—

    (a) on medical grounds, or

    (b) on the ground that the person's physical condition makes it impossible or unreasonably difficult for the person to comply with those duties.

(2) An exemption certificate is valid for such period as is specified in the certificate.

(3) The driver of a designated taxi is exempt from the duties imposed by section 165 if—

    (a) an exemption certificate issued to the driver is in force, and

    (b) the prescribed notice of the exemption is exhibited on the taxi in the prescribed manner.

(4) The driver of a designated private hire vehicle is exempt from the duties imposed by section 165 if—

    (a) an exemption certificate issued to the driver is in force, and

    (b) the prescribed notice of the exemption is exhibited on the vehicle in the prescribed manner.

(5) For the purposes of this section, a taxi or private hire vehicle is 'designated' if it appears on a list maintained under section 167.

(6) In this section and section 167 'licensing authority', in relation to any area, means the authority responsible for licensing taxis or, as the case may be, private hire vehicles in that area.

167 Lists of wheelchair-accessible vehicles

(1) For the purposes of section 165, a licensing authority may maintain a list of vehicles falling within subsection (2).

(2) A vehicle falls within this subsection if—

    (a) it is either a taxi or a private hire vehicle, and

    (b) it conforms to such accessibility requirements as the licensing authority thinks fit.

(3) A licensing authority may, if it thinks fit, decide that a vehicle may be included on a list maintained under this section only if it is being used, or is to be used, by the holder of a special licence under that licence.

(4) In subsection (3) 'special licence' has the meaning given by section 12 of the Transport Act 1985 (use of taxis or hire cars in providing local services).

(5) 'Accessibility requirements' are requirements for securing that it is possible for disabled persons in wheelchairs—

    (a) to get into and out of vehicles in safety, and

    (b) to travel in vehicles in safety and reasonable comfort, either staying in their wheelchairs or not (depending on which they prefer).

(6) The Secretary of State may issue guidance to licensing authorities as to—

    (a) the accessibility requirements which they should apply for the purposes of this section;

    (b) any other aspect of their functions under or by virtue of this section.

(7) A licensing authority which maintains a list under subsection (1) must have regard to any guidance issued under subsection (6).

168 Assistance dogs in taxis

(1) This section imposes duties on the driver of a taxi which has been hired—

    (a) by or for a disabled person who is accompanied by an assistance dog, or

    (b) by another person who wishes to be accompanied by a disabled person with an assistance dog.

(2) The driver must—
    (a) carry the disabled person's dog and allow it to remain with that person;
    (b) not make any additional charge for doing so.

(3) The driver of a taxi commits an offence by failing to comply with a duty imposed by this section.

(4) A person guilty of an offence under this section is liable on summary conviction to a fine not exceeding level 3 on the standard scale.

169 Assistance dogs in taxis: exemption certificates

(1) A licensing authority must issue a person with a certificate exempting the person from the duties imposed by section 168 (an 'exemption certificate') if satisfied that it is appropriate to do so on medical grounds.

(2) In deciding whether to issue an exemption certificate the authority must have regard, in particular, to the physical characteristics of the taxi which the person drives or those of any kind of taxi in relation to which the person requires the certificate.

(3) An exemption certificate is valid—
    (a) in respect of a specified taxi or a specified kind of taxi;
    (b) for such period as is specified in the certificate.

(4) The driver of a taxi is exempt from the duties imposed by section 168 if—
    (a) an exemption certificate issued to the driver is in force with respect to the taxi, and
    (b) the prescribed notice of the exemption is exhibited on the taxi in the prescribed manner.
    The power to make regulations under paragraph (b) is exercisable by the Secretary of State.

(5) In this section 'licensing authority' means—
    (a) in relation to the area to which the Metropolitan Public Carriage Act 1869 applies, Transport for London;
    (b) in relation to any other area in England and Wales, the authority responsible for licensing taxis in that area.

170 Assistance dogs in private hire vehicles

(1) The operator of a private hire vehicle commits an offence by failing or refusing to accept a booking for the vehicle—
    (a) if the booking is requested by or on behalf of a disabled person or a person who wishes to be accompanied by a disabled person, and
    (b) the reason for the failure or refusal is that the disabled person will be accompanied by an assistance dog.

(2) The operator commits an offence by making an additional charge for carrying an assistance dog which is accompanying a disabled person.

(3) The driver of a private hire vehicle commits an offence by failing or refusing to carry out a booking accepted by the operator—
    (a) if the booking is made by or on behalf of a disabled person or a person who wishes to be accompanied by a disabled person, and
    (b) the reason for the failure or refusal is that the disabled person is accompanied by an assistance dog.

(4) A person guilty of an offence under this section is liable on summary conviction to a fine not exceeding level 3 on the standard scale.

(5) In this section—
    'driver' means a person who holds a licence under—
        (a) section 13 of the Private Hire Vehicles (London) Act 1998 ('the 1998 Act'),

    (b) section 51 of the Local Government (Miscellaneous Provisions) Act 1976 ('the 1976 Act'), or

    (c) an equivalent provision of a local enactment;

'licensing authority', in relation to any area in England and Wales, means the authority responsible for licensing private hire vehicles in that area;

'operator' means a person who holds a licence under—

    (a) section 3 of the 1998 Act,

    (b) section 55 of the 1976 Act, or

    (c) an equivalent provision of a local enactment;

'private hire vehicle' means a vehicle licensed under—

    (a) section 6 of the 1998 Act,

    (b) section 48 of the 1976 Act, or

    (c) an equivalent provision of a local enactment.

171 Assistance dogs in private hire vehicles: exemption certificates

(1) A licensing authority must issue a driver with a certificate exempting the driver from the offence under section 170(3) (an 'exemption certificate') if satisfied that it is appropriate to do so on medical grounds.

(2) In deciding whether to issue an exemption certificate the authority must have regard, in particular, to the physical characteristics of the private hire vehicle which the person drives or those of any kind of private hire vehicle in relation to which the person requires the certificate.

(3) An exemption certificate is valid—

    (a) in respect of a specified private hire vehicle or a specified kind of private hire vehicle;

    (b) for such period as is specified in the certificate.

(4) A driver does not commit an offence under section 170(3) if—

    (a) an exemption certificate issued to the driver is in force with respect to the private hire vehicle, and

    (b) the prescribed notice of the exemption is exhibited on the vehicle in the prescribed manner.

The power to make regulations under paragraph (b) is exercisable by the Secretary of State.

(5) In this section 'driver', 'licensing authority' and 'private hire vehicle' have the same meaning as in section 170.

172 Appeals

(1) A person who is aggrieved by the refusal of a licensing authority in England and Wales to issue an exemption certificate under section 166, 169 or 171 may appeal to a magistrates' court before the end of the period of 28 days beginning with the date of the refusal.

(2) A person who is aggrieved by the refusal of a licensing authority in Scotland to issue an exemption certificate under section 166 may appeal to the sheriff before the end of the period of 28 days beginning with the date of the refusal.

(3) On an appeal under subsection (1) or (2), the magistrates' court or sheriff may direct the licensing authority to issue the exemption certificate to have effect for such period as is specified in the direction.

(4) A person who is aggrieved by the decision of a licensing authority to include a vehicle on a list maintained under section 167 may appeal to a magistrates' court or, in Scotland, the sheriff before the end of the period of 28 days beginning with the date of the inclusion.

173 Interpretation

(1) In this Chapter—

'accessibility requirements' has the meaning given in section 167(5);

'assistance dog' means—

    (a) a dog which has been trained to guide a blind person;

    (b) a dog which has been trained to assist a deaf person;

    (c) a dog which has been trained by a prescribed charity to assist a disabled person who has a disability that consists of epilepsy or otherwise affects the person's mobility, manual dexterity, physical co-ordination or ability to lift, carry or otherwise move everyday objects;

    (d) a dog of a prescribed category which has been trained to assist a disabled person who has a disability (other than one falling within paragraph (c)) of a prescribed kind;

'taxi'—

    (a) means a vehicle which is licensed under section 37 of the Town Police Clauses Act 1847 or section 6 of the Metropolitan Public Carriage Act 1869, and

    (b) in sections 162 and 165 to 167, also includes a taxi licensed under section 10 of the Civic Government (Scotland) Act 1982, but does not include a vehicle drawn by a horse or other animal;

'taxi accessibility regulations' has the meaning given by section 160(1).

(2) A power to make regulations under paragraph (c) or (d) of the definition of 'assistance dog' in subsection (1) is exercisable by the Secretary of State.

CHAPTER 2
PUBLIC SERVICE VEHICLES

174 PSV accessibility regulations

(1) The Secretary of State may make regulations (in this Chapter referred to as 'PSV accessibility regulations') for securing that it is possible for disabled persons—

    (a) to get on to and off regulated public service vehicles in safety and without unreasonable difficulty (and, in the case of disabled persons in wheelchairs, to do so while remaining in their wheelchairs), and

    (b) to travel in such vehicles in safety and reasonable comfort.

(2) The regulations may, in particular, make provision as to the construction, use and maintenance of regulated public service vehicles, including provision as to—

    (a) the fitting of equipment to vehicles;

    (b) equipment to be carried by vehicles;

    (c) the design of equipment to be fitted to, or carried by, vehicles;

    (d) the fitting and use of restraining devices designed to ensure the stability of wheelchairs while vehicles are moving;

    (e) the position in which wheelchairs are to be secured while vehicles are moving.

(3) In this section 'public service vehicle' means a vehicle which is—

    (a) adapted to carry more than 8 passengers, and

    (b) a public service vehicle for the purposes of the Public Passenger Vehicles Act 1981; and in this Chapter 'regulated public service vehicle' means a public service vehicle to which PSV accessibility regulations are expressed to apply.

(4) The regulations may make different provision—
   (a) as respects different classes or descriptions of vehicle;
   (b) as respects the same class or description of vehicle in different circumstances.
(5) The Secretary of State must not make regulations under this section or section 176 or 177 without consulting—
   (a) the Disabled Persons Transport Advisory Committee, and
   (b) such other representative organisations as the Secretary of State thinks fit.

175 Offence of contravening PSV accessibility regulations

(1) A person commits an offence by—
   (a) contravening a provision of PSV accessibility regulations;
   (b) using on a road a regulated public service vehicle which does not conform with a provision of the regulations with which it is required to conform;
   (c) causing or permitting such a regulated public service vehicle to be used on a road.
(2) A person guilty of an offence under this section is liable on summary conviction to a fine not exceeding level 4 on the standard scale.
(3) If an offence under this section committed by a body corporate is committed with the consent or connivance of, or is attributable to neglect on the part of, a responsible person, the responsible person as well as the body corporate is guilty of the offence.
(4) In subsection (3) a responsible person, in relation to a body corporate, is—
   (a) a director, manager, secretary or similar officer;
   (b) a person purporting to act in the capacity of a person mentioned in paragraph (a);
   (c) in the case of a body corporate whose affairs are managed by its members, a member.
(5) If, in Scotland, an offence committed by a partnership or an unincorporated association is committed with the consent or connivance of, or is attributable to neglect on the part of, a partner or person concerned in the management of the association, the partner or person as well as the partnership or association is guilty of the offence.

176 Accessibility certificates

(1) A regulated public service vehicle must not be used on a road unless—
   (a) a vehicle examiner has issued a certificate (an 'accessibility certificate') that such provisions of PSV accessibility regulations as are prescribed are satisfied in respect of the vehicle, or
   (b) an approval certificate has been issued under section 177 in respect of the vehicle.
(2) Regulations may make provision—
   (a) with respect to applications for, and the issue of, accessibility certificates;
   (b) providing for the examination of vehicles in respect of which applications have been made;
   (c) with respect to the issue of copies of accessibility certificates which have been lost or destroyed.
(3) The operator of a regulated public service vehicle commits an offence if the vehicle is used in contravention of this section.
(4) A person guilty of an offence under this section is liable on summary conviction to a fine not exceeding level 4 on the standard scale.
(5) A power to make regulations under this section is exercisable by the Secretary of State.
(6) In this section 'operator' has the same meaning as in the Public Passenger Vehicles Act 1981.

177 Approval certificates

(1) The Secretary of State may approve a vehicle for the purposes of this section if satisfied that such provisions of PSV accessibility regulations as are prescribed for the purposes of section 176 are satisfied in respect of the vehicle.

(2) A vehicle which is so approved is referred to in this section as a 'type vehicle'.

(3) Subsection (4) applies if a declaration in the prescribed form is made by an authorised person that a particular vehicle conforms in design, construction and equipment with a type vehicle.

(4) A vehicle examiner may issue a certificate in the prescribed form (an 'approval certificate') that it conforms to the type vehicle.

(5) Regulations may make provision—
    (a) with respect to applications for, and grants of, approval under subsection (1);
    (b) with respect to applications for, and the issue of, approval certificates;
    (c) providing for the examination of vehicles in respect of which applications have been made;
    (d) with respect to the issue of copies of approval certificates in place of certificates which have been lost or destroyed.

(6) The Secretary of State may at any time withdraw approval of a type vehicle.

(7) If an approval is withdrawn—
    (a) no further approval certificates are to be issued by reference to the type vehicle; but
    (b) an approval certificate issued by reference to the type vehicle before the withdrawal continues to have effect for the purposes of section 176.

(8) A power to make regulations under this section is exercisable by the Secretary of State.

(9) In subsection (3) 'authorised person' means a person authorised by the Secretary of State for the purposes of that subsection.

178 Special authorisations

(1) The Secretary of State may by order authorise the use on roads of—
    (a) a regulated public service vehicle of a class or description specified by the order, or
    (b) a regulated public service vehicle which is so specified.

(2) Nothing in sections 174 to 177 prevents the use of a vehicle in accordance with the order.

(3) The Secretary of State may by order make provision for securing that provisions of PSV accessibility regulations apply to regulated public service vehicles of a description specified by the order, subject to any modifications or exceptions specified by the order.

(4) An order under subsection (1) or (3) may make the authorisation or provision (as the case may be) subject to such restrictions and conditions as are specified by or under the order.

(5) Section 207(2) does not require an order under this section that applies only to a specified vehicle, or to vehicles of a specified person, to be made by statutory instrument; but such an order is as capable of being amended or revoked as an order made by statutory instrument.

179 Reviews and appeals

(1) Subsection (2) applies if the Secretary of State refuses an application for the approval of a vehicle under section 177(1) and, before the end of the prescribed period, the applicant—
    (a) asks the Secretary of State to review the decision, and
    (b) pays any fee fixed under section 180.

(2) The Secretary of State must—
    (a) review the decision, and
    (b) in doing so, consider any representations made in writing by the applicant before the end of the prescribed period.

(3) A person applying for an accessibility certificate or an approval certificate may appeal to the Secretary of State against the refusal of a vehicle examiner to issue the certificate.

(4) An appeal must be made within the prescribed time and in the prescribed manner.

(5) Regulations may make provision as to the procedure to be followed in connection with appeals.

(6) On the determination of an appeal, the Secretary of State may—

(a) confirm, vary or reverse the decision appealed against;

(b) give directions to the vehicle examiner for giving effect to the Secretary of State's decision.

(7) A power to make regulations under this section is exercisable by the Secretary of State.

180 Fees

(1) The Secretary of State may charge such fees, payable at such times, as are prescribed in respect of—

(a) applications for, and grants of, approval under section 177(1);

(b) applications for, and the issue of, accessibility certificates and approval certificates;

(c) copies of such certificates;

(d) reviews and appeals under section 179.

(2) Fees received by the Secretary of State must be paid into the Consolidated Fund.

(3) The power to make regulations under subsection (1) is exercisable by the Secretary of State.

(4) The regulations may make provision for the repayment of fees, in whole or in part, in such circumstances as are prescribed.

(5) Before making the regulations the Secretary of State must consult such representative organisations as the Secretary of State thinks fit.

181 Interpretation

In this Chapter—

'accessibility certificate' has the meaning given in section 176(1);

'approval certificate' has the meaning given in section 177(4);

'PSV accessibility regulations' has the meaning given in section 174(1);

'regulated public service vehicle' has the meaning given in section 174(3).

[CHAPTER 2A
BUS SERVICES

181A Information for bus passengers

(1) The Secretary of State may, for the purpose of facilitating travel by disabled persons, make regulations requiring operators of local services to make available information about a local service to persons travelling on the service.

(2) The regulations may make provision about—

(a) the descriptions of information that are to be made available;

(b) how information is to be made available.

(3) The regulations may, in particular, require an operator of a local service to make available information of a prescribed description about—

(a) the name or other designation of the local service;

(b) the direction of travel;

(c) stopping places;

(d) diversions;

(e) connecting local services.

(4) The regulations may, in particular—

   (a) specify when information of a prescribed description is to be made available;

   (b) specify how information of a prescribed description is to be made available, including requiring information to be both announced and displayed;

   (c) specify standards for the provision of information, including standards based on an announcement being audible or a display being visible to a person of a prescribed description in a prescribed location;

   (d) specify forms of communication that are not to be regarded as satisfying a requirement to make information available.

(5) Regulations under this section may make different provision—

   (a) as respects different descriptions of vehicle;

   (b) as respects the same description of vehicle in different circumstances.

(6) Before making regulations under this section, the Secretary of State must consult—

   (a) the Welsh Ministers;

   (b) the Scottish Ministers.

181B Exemptions etc

(1) The Secretary of State may by regulations make provision for securing that the provisions of regulations under section 181A do not apply or apply subject to such modifications or exceptions as the regulations may specify to—

   (a) public service vehicles of a prescribed description;

   (b) operators of a prescribed description;

   (c) local services of a prescribed description.

(2) Regulations under subsection (1)(b) may, in particular, make provision by reference to an operator's size.

(3) Regulations under this section may also make provision for securing that the provisions of regulations under section 181A do not apply or apply subject to such modifications or exceptions as the regulations may specify to—

   (a) a prescribed public service vehicle;

   (b) public service vehicles of a prescribed operator;

   (c) a prescribed local service.

(4) Regulations under subsection (1) or (3) may make the provision subject to such restrictions and conditions as are specified in the regulations.

(5) Regulations under subsection (1) or (3) may specify the period for which provisions of those regulations are to have effect.

(6) Regulations under subsection (1) may make different provision for different areas.

(7) Section 207(2) does not require regulations under this section that apply only to—

   (a) a prescribed public service vehicle,

   (b) public service vehicles of a prescribed operator, or

   (c) a prescribed local service,

   to be made by statutory instrument; but such regulations are as capable of being amended or revoked as regulations made by statutory instrument.

(8) Before making regulations under this section, the Secretary of State must consult—

   (a) the Welsh Ministers;

   (b) the Scottish Ministers.

181C Guidance

(1) The Secretary of State must issue guidance about the duties imposed on operators of local services by regulations under section 181A.

(2) The Secretary of State—

(a) must review the guidance issued under subsection (1), at intervals not exceeding five years, and

(b) may revise it.

(3) Before issuing the guidance or revising it in a way which would, in the opinion of the Secretary of State, result in a substantial change to it, the Secretary of State must consult—

(a) the Welsh Ministers,

(b) the Scottish Ministers,

(c) the Passengers' Council,

(d) such organisations representing disabled persons, including the Disabled Persons Transport Advisory Committee and the committee established under section 72 of the Transport (Scotland) Act 2001, as the Secretary of State thinks fit,

(e) such organisations representing operators of local services as the Secretary of State thinks fit, and

(f) such other persons as the Secretary of State thinks fit.

(4) The Secretary of State must arrange for any guidance issued or revised under this section to be published in a way the Secretary of State considers appropriate.

181D Interpretation

(1) In this Chapter—

'local service' has the same meaning as in the Transport Act 1985;

'public service vehicle' means a vehicle that is a public service vehicle for the purposes of the Public Passenger Vehicles Act 1981;

'stopping place' has the same meaning as in the Transport Act 1985.

(2) For the purposes of this Chapter, a local service ('service A') is a connecting local service in relation to another local service ('service B') if service A has a stopping place at, or in the vicinity of, a stopping place of service B.

(3) References in this Chapter to the operator of a passenger transport service of any description are to be construed in accordance with section 137(7) of the Transport Act 1985.][128]

CHAPTER 3
RAIL VEHICLES

182 Rail vehicle accessibility regulations

(1) The Secretary of State may make regulations (in this Chapter referred to as 'rail vehicle accessibility regulations') for securing that it is possible for disabled persons—

(a) to get on to and off regulated rail vehicles in safety and without unreasonable difficulty;

(b) to do so while in wheelchairs;

(c) to travel in such vehicles in safety and reasonable comfort;

(d) to do so while in wheelchairs.

---

[128] Inserted by Bus Services Act 2017.

(2) The regulations may, in particular, make provision as to the construction, use and maintenance of regulated rail vehicles including provision as to—
   (a) the fitting of equipment to vehicles;
   (b) equipment to be carried by vehicles;
   (c) the design of equipment to be fitted to, or carried by, vehicles;
   (d) the use of equipment fitted to, or carried by, vehicles;
   (e) the toilet facilities to be provided in vehicles;
   (f) the location and floor area of the wheelchair accommodation to be provided in vehicles;
   (g) assistance to be given to disabled persons.
(3) The regulations may contain different provision—
   (a) as respects different classes or descriptions of rail vehicle;
   (b) as respects the same class or description of rail vehicle in different circumstances;
   (c) as respects different networks.
(4) In this section—
   'network' means any permanent way or other means of guiding or supporting rail vehicles, or
   any section of it;
   'rail vehicle' means a vehicle constructed or adapted to carry passengers on a railway, tramway
   or prescribed system other than a vehicle used in the provision of a service for the carriage of
   passengers on the [trans-European rail system located in Great Britain];[129]
   'regulated rail vehicle' means a rail vehicle to which provisions of rail vehicle accessibility
   regulations are expressed to apply.
(5) In subsection (4)—
   […][130]
   'prescribed system' means a system using a mode of guided transport ('guided transport' having the same meaning as in the Transport and Works Act 1992) that is specified in rail vehicle
   accessibility regulations;
   'railway' and 'tramway' have the same meaning as in the Transport and Works Act 1992 [;]
   ['trans-European rail system' has the meaning given in regulation 2(1) of the Railways
   (Interoperability) Regulations 2011.][131]
(6) The Secretary of State must exercise the power to make rail vehicle accessibility regulations so
as to secure that on and after 1 January 2020 every rail vehicle is a regulated rail vehicle.
(7) Subsection (6) does not affect subsection (3), section 183(1) or section 207(4)(a).
(8) Before making regulations under subsection (1) or section 183, the Secretary of State must
consult—
   (a) the Disabled Persons Transport Advisory Committee, and
   (b) such other representative organisations as the Secretary of State thinks fit.

183 Exemptions from rail vehicle accessibility regulations

(1) The Secretary of State may by order (an 'exemption order')—
   (a) authorise the use for carriage of a regulated rail vehicle even though the vehicle does
   not conform with the provisions of rail vehicle accessibility regulations with which it is
   required to conform;
   (b) authorise a regulated rail vehicle to be used for carriage otherwise than in conformity
   with the provisions of rail vehicle accessibility regulations with which use of the vehicle is
   required to conform.

---

[129] Substituted by Railways (Interoperability) Regulations 2011, SI 2011/3066.
[130] Repealed by Railways (Interoperability) Regulations 2011, SI 2011/3066.
[131] Inserted by Railways (Interoperability) Regulations 2011, SI 2011/3066.

(2) Authority under subsection (1)(a) or (b) may be for—
  (a) a regulated rail vehicle that is specified or of a specified description,
  (b) use in specified circumstances of a regulated rail vehicle, or
  (c) use in specified circumstances of a regulated rail vehicle that is specified or of a specified description.
(3) [...]¹³²
(4) After consulting the Disabled Persons Transport Advisory Committee and such other persons as the Secretary of State thinks appropriate, the Secretary of State may—
  (a) make an exemption order in the terms of the application for the order;
  (b) make an exemption order in such other terms as the Secretary of State thinks appropriate;
  (c) refuse to make an exemption order.
(5) The Secretary of State may make an exemption order subject to such conditions and restrictions as are specified.
(6) 'Specified' means specified in an exemption order.
[(7) Section 207(2) does not require an exemption order to be made by statutory instrument; but such an order is as capable of being amended or revoked as an order made by statutory instrument.]¹³³

184 Procedure for making exemption orders
  [...]¹³⁴

185 Annual report on exemption orders

(1) After the end of each calendar year the Secretary of State must prepare a report on—
  (a) the exercise in that year of the power to make orders under section 183(1) [.]
  (b) [...]¹³⁵
(2) A report under subsection (1) must (in particular) contain—
  (a) details of each order made under section 183(1) in the year in question;
  (b) details of consultation carried out under [section 183(4)]¹³⁶ in connection with orders made in that year under section 183(1).
(3) The Secretary of State must lay before Parliament each report prepared under this section.

186 Rail vehicle accessibility: compliance
  [...]¹³⁷

187 Interpretation

(1) In this Chapter—
  'rail vehicle' and 'regulated rail vehicle' have the meaning given in section 182(4);
  'rail vehicle accessibility regulations' has the meaning given in section 182(1).
(2) For the purposes of this Chapter a vehicle is used 'for carriage' if it is used for the carriage of passengers.

---

¹³² Repealed by Deregulation Act 2015.
¹³³ Inserted by Deregulation Act 2015.
¹³⁴ Repealed by Deregulation Act 2015.
¹³⁵ Repealed by Deregulation Act 2015.
¹³⁶ Substituted by Deregulation Act 2015.
¹³⁷ Repealed by Equality Act 2010.

CHAPTER 4
SUPPLEMENTARY

188 Forgery, etc.

(1) In this section 'relevant document' means—
   (a) an exemption certificate issued under section 166, 169 or 171;
   (b) a notice of a kind mentioned in section 166(3)(b), 169(4)(b) or 171(4)(b);
   (c) an accessibility certificate (see section 176);
   (d) an approval certificate (see section 177).
(2) A person commits an offence if, with intent to deceive, the person—
   (a) forges, alters or uses a relevant document;
   (b) lends a relevant document to another person;
   (c) allows a relevant document to be used by another person;
   (d) makes or has possession of a document which closely resembles a relevant document.
(3) A person guilty of an offence under subsection (2) is liable—
   (a) on summary conviction, to a fine not exceeding the statutory maximum;
   (b) on conviction on indictment, to imprisonment for a term not exceeding 2 years or to a fine or to both.
(4) A person commits an offence by knowingly making a false statement for the purpose of obtaining an accessibility certificate or an approval certificate.
(5) A person guilty of an offence under subsection (4) is liable on summary conviction to a fine not exceeding level 4 on the standard scale.

PART 13
DISABILITY: MISCELLANEOUS

189 Reasonable adjustments

Schedule 21 (reasonable adjustments: supplementary) has effect.

190 Improvements to let dwelling houses

(1) This section applies in relation to a lease of a dwelling house if each of the following applies—
   (a) the tenancy is not a protected tenancy, a statutory tenancy or a secure tenancy;
   (b) the tenant or another person occupying or intending to occupy the premises is a disabled person;
   (c) the disabled person occupies or intends to occupy the premises as that person's only or main home;
   (d) the tenant is entitled, with the consent of the landlord, to make improvements to the premises;
   (e) the tenant applies to the landlord for consent to make a relevant improvement.
(2) Where the tenant applies in writing for the consent—
   (a) if the landlord refuses to give consent, the landlord must give the tenant a written statement of the reason why the consent was withheld;
   (b) if the landlord neither gives nor refuses to give consent within a reasonable time, consent must be taken to have been unreasonably withheld.

(3) If the landlord gives consent subject to a condition which is unreasonable, the consent must be taken to have been unreasonably withheld.

(4) If the landlord's consent is unreasonably withheld, it must be taken to have been given.

(5) On any question as to whether—

(a) consent was unreasonably withheld, or

(b) a condition imposed was unreasonable, it is for the landlord to show that it was not.

(6) If the tenant fails to comply with a reasonable condition imposed by the landlord on the making of a relevant improvement, the failure is to be treated as a breach by the tenant of an obligation of the tenancy.

(7) An improvement to premises is a relevant improvement if, having regard to the disabled person's disability, it is likely to facilitate that person's enjoyment of the premises.

(8) Subsections (2) to (7) apply only in so far as provision of a like nature is not made by the lease.

(9) In this section—

'improvement' means an alteration in or addition to the premises and includes—

(a) an addition to or alteration in the landlord's fittings and fixtures;

(b) an addition or alteration connected with the provision of services to the premises;

(c) the erection of a wireless or television aerial;

(d) carrying out external decoration;

'lease' includes a sub-lease or other tenancy, and 'landlord' and 'tenant' are to be construed accordingly;

'protected tenancy' has the same meaning as in section 1 of the Rent Act 1977;

'statutory tenancy' is to be construed in accordance with section 2 of that Act;

'secure tenancy' has the same meaning as in section 79 of the Housing Act 1985.

PART 14
GENERAL EXCEPTIONS

191 Statutory provisions

Schedule 22 (statutory provisions) has effect.

192 National security

A person does not contravene this Act only by doing, for the purpose of safeguarding national security, anything it is proportionate to do for that purpose.

193 Charities

(1) A person does not contravene this Act only by restricting the provision of benefits to persons who share a protected characteristic if—

(a) the person acts in pursuance of a charitable instrument, and

(b) the provision of the benefits is within subsection (2).

(2) The provision of benefits is within this subsection if it is—

(a) a proportionate means of achieving a legitimate aim, or

(b) for the purpose of preventing or compensating for a disadvantage linked to the protected characteristic.

(3) It is not a contravention of this Act for—
    (a) a person who provides supported employment to treat persons who have the same disability or a disability of a prescribed description more favourably than those who do not have that disability or a disability of such a description in providing such employment;
    (b) a Minister of the Crown to agree to arrangements for the provision of supported employment which will, or may, have that effect.

(4) If a charitable instrument enables the provision of benefits to persons of a class defined by reference to colour, it has effect for all purposes as if it enabled the provision of such benefits—
    (a) to persons of the class which results if the reference to colour is ignored, or
    (b) if the original class is defined by reference only to colour, to persons generally.

(5) It is not a contravention of this Act for a charity to require members, or persons wishing to become members, to make a statement which asserts or implies membership or acceptance of a religion or belief; and for this purpose restricting the access by members to a benefit, facility or service to those who make such a statement is to be treated as imposing such a requirement.

(6) Subsection (5) applies only if—
    (a) the charity, or an organisation of which it is part, first imposed such a requirement before 18 May 2005, and
    (b) the charity or organisation has not ceased since that date to impose such a requirement.

(7) It is not a contravention of section 29 for a person, in relation to an activity which is carried on for the purpose of promoting or supporting a charity, to restrict participation in the activity to persons of one sex.

(8) A charity regulator does not contravene this Act only by exercising a function in relation to a charity in a manner which the regulator thinks is expedient in the interests of the charity, having regard to the charitable instrument.

(9) Subsection (1) does not apply to a contravention of—
    (a) section 39;
    (b) section 40;
    (c) section 41;
    (d) section 55, so far as relating to the provision of vocational training.

(10) Subsection (9) does not apply in relation to disability.

194 Charities: supplementary

(1) This section applies for the purposes of section 193.

(2) That section does not apply to race, so far as relating to colour.

(3) 'Charity'—
    (a) in relation to England and Wales, has the meaning given by [section 1(1) of the Charities Act 2011];[138]
    (b) in relation to Scotland, means a body entered in the Scottish Charity Register.

(4) 'Charitable instrument' means an instrument establishing or governing a charity (including an instrument made or having effect before the commencement of this section).

(5) The charity regulators are—
    (a) the Charity Commission for England and Wales;
    (b) the Scottish Charity Regulator.

(6) Section 107(5) applies to references in subsection (5) of section 193 to members, or persons wishing to become members, of a charity.

---

[138] Substituted by Charities Act 2011.

(7) 'Supported employment' means facilities provided, or in respect of which payments are made, under section 15 of the Disabled Persons (Employment) Act 1944.

195 Sport

(1) A person does not contravene this Act, so far as relating to sex, only by doing anything in relation to the participation of another as a competitor in a gender-affected activity.

(2) A person does not contravene section 29, 33, 34 or 35, so far as relating to gender reassignment, only by doing anything in relation to the participation of a transsexual person as a competitor in a gender-affected activity if it is necessary to do so to secure in relation to the activity—

(a) fair competition, or

(b) the safety of competitors.

(3) A gender-affected activity is a sport, game or other activity of a competitive nature in circumstances in which the physical strength, stamina or physique of average persons of one sex would put them at a disadvantage compared to average persons of the other sex as competitors in events involving the activity.

(4) In considering whether a sport, game or other activity is gender-affected in relation to children, it is appropriate to take account of the age and stage of development of children who are likely to be competitors.

(5) A person who does anything to which subsection (6) applies does not contravene this Act only because of the nationality or place of birth of another or because of the length of time the other has been resident in a particular area or place.

(6) This subsection applies to—

(a) selecting one or more persons to represent a country, place or area or a related association, in a sport or game or other activity of a competitive nature;

(b) doing anything in pursuance of the rules of a competition so far as relating to eligibility to compete in a sport or game or other such activity.

[(7) A person does not contravene this Act, so far as relating to age discrimination, only by doing anything in relation to the participation of another as a competitor in an age-banded activity if it is necessary to do so—

(a) to secure in relation to the activity fair competition or the safety of competitors,

(b) to comply with the rules of a national or international competition, or

(c) to increase participation in that activity.

(8) For the purposes of subsection (7), an age-banded activity is a sport, game or other activity of a competitive nature in circumstances in which the physical or mental strength, agility, stamina, physique, mobility, maturity or manual dexterity of average persons of a particular age group would put them at a disadvantage compared to average persons of another age group as competitors in events involving the activity.][139]

196 General

Schedule 23 (general exceptions) has effect.

197 Age

(1) A Minister of the Crown may by order amend this Act to provide that any of the following does not contravene this Act so far as relating to age—

(a) specified conduct;

---

[139] Inserted by Equality Act 2010 (Age Exceptions) Order 2012, SI 2012/2466.

    (b) anything done for a specified purpose;

    (c) anything done in pursuance of arrangements of a specified description.

(2) Specified conduct is conduct—

    (a) of a specified description,

    (b) carried out in specified circumstances, or

    (c) by or in relation to a person of a specified description.

(3) An order under this section may—

    (a) confer on a Minister of the Crown or the Treasury a power to issue guidance about the operation of the order (including, in particular, guidance about the steps that may be taken by persons wishing to rely on an exception provided for by the order);

    (b) require the Minister or the Treasury to carry out consultation before issuing guidance under a power conferred by virtue of paragraph (a);

    (c) make provision (including provision to impose a requirement) that refers to guidance issued under a power conferred by virtue of paragraph (a).

(4) Guidance given by a Minister of the Crown or the Treasury in anticipation of the making of an order under this section is, on the making of the order, to be treated as if it has been issued in accordance with the order.

(5) For the purposes of satisfying a requirement imposed by virtue of subsection (3)(b), the Minister or the Treasury may rely on consultation carried out before the making of the order that imposes the requirement (including consultation carried out before the commencement of this section).

(6) Provision by virtue of subsection (3)(c) may, in particular, refer to provisions of the guidance that themselves refer to a document specified in the guidance.

(7) Guidance issued (or treated as issued) under a power conferred by virtue of subsection (3)(a) comes into force on such day as the person who issues the guidance may by order appoint; and an order under this subsection may include the text of the guidance or of extracts from it.

(8) This section is not affected by any provision of this Act which makes special provision in relation to age.

(9) The references to this Act in subsection (1) do not include references to—

    (a) Part 5 (work);

    (b) Chapter 2 of Part 6 (further and higher education).

PART 15

FAMILY PROPERTY

198 Abolition of husband's duty to maintain wife

The rule of common law that a husband must maintain his wife is abolished.

199 Abolition of presumption of advancement

(1) The presumption of advancement (by which, for example, a husband is presumed to be making a gift to his wife if he transfers property to her, or purchases property in her name) is abolished.

(2) The abolition by subsection (1) of the presumption of advancement does not have effect in relation to—

    (a) anything done before the commencement of this section, or

    (b) anything done pursuant to any obligation incurred before the commencement of this section.

200 Amendment of Married Women's Property Act 1964

(1) In section 1 of the Married Women's Property Act 1964 (money and property derived from housekeeping allowance made by husband to be treated as belonging to husband and wife in equal shares)—
  (a) for 'the husband for' substitute 'either of them for', and
  (b) for 'the husband and the wife' substitute 'them'.

(2) Accordingly, that Act may be cited as the Matrimonial Property Act 1964.

(3) The amendments made by this section do not have effect in relation to any allowance made before the commencement of this section.

201 Civil partners: housekeeping allowance

(1) After section 70 of the Civil Partnership Act 2004 insert—
  '70A Money and property derived from housekeeping allowance
  Section 1 of the Matrimonial Property Act 1964 (money and property derived from house-keeping allowance to be treated as belonging to husband and wife in equal shares) applies in relation to—
  (a) money derived from any allowance made by a civil partner for the expenses of the civil partnership home or for similar purposes, and
  (b) any property acquired out of such money, as it applies in relation to money derived from any allowance made by a husband or wife for the expenses of the matrimonial home or for similar purposes, and any property acquired out of such money.'

(2) The amendment made by this section does not have effect in relation to any allowance made before the commencement of this section.

PART 16
GENERAL AND MISCELLANEOUS

Civil partnerships

202 Civil partnerships on religious premises

(1) The Civil Partnership Act 2004 is amended as follows.

(2) Omit section 6(1)(b) and (2) (prohibition on use of religious premises for registration of civil partnership).

(3) In section 6A (power to approve premises for registration of civil partnership), after subsection (2), insert—
  '(2A) Regulations under this section may provide that premises approved for the registration of civil partnerships may differ from those premises approved for the registration of civil marriages.
  (2B) Provision by virtue of subsection (2)(b) may, in particular, provide that applications for approval of premises may only be made with the consent (whether general or specific) of a person specified, or a person of a description specified, in the provision.
  (2C) The power conferred by section 258(2), in its application to the power conferred by this section, includes in particular—
    (a) power to make provision in relation to religious premises that differs from provision in relation to other premises;
    (b) power to make different provision for different kinds of religious premises.'

(4) In that section, after subsection (3), insert—

'(3A) For the avoidance of doubt, nothing in this Act places an obligation on religious organisations to host civil partnerships if they do not wish to do so.

(3B) 'Civil marriage' means marriage solemnised otherwise than according to the rites of the Church of England or any other religious usages.

(3C) 'Religious premises' means premises which—

(a) are used solely or mainly for religious purposes, or

(b) have been so used and have not subsequently been used solely or mainly for other purposes.'

EU obligations

203 Harmonisation

(1) This section applies if—

(a) there is [an EU][140] obligation of the United Kingdom which a Minister of the Crown thinks relates to the subject matter of the Equality Acts,

(b) the obligation is to be implemented by the exercise of the power under section 2(2) of the European Communities Act 1972 (the implementing power), and

(c) the Minister thinks that it is appropriate to make harmonising provision in the Equality Acts.

(2) The Minister may by order make the harmonising provision.

(3) If the Minister proposes to make an order under this section, the Minister must consult persons and organisations the Minister thinks are likely to be affected by the harmonising provision.

(4) If, as a result of the consultation under subsection (3), the Minister thinks it appropriate to change the whole or part of the proposal, the Minister must carry out such further consultation with respect to the changes as the Minister thinks appropriate.

(5) The Equality Acts are the Equality Act 2006 and this Act.

(6) Harmonising provision is provision made in relation to relevant subject matter of the Equality Acts—

(a) which corresponds to the implementing provision, or

(b) which the Minister thinks is necessary or expedient in consequence of or related to provision made in pursuance of paragraph (a) or the implementing provision.

(7) The implementing provision is provision made or to be made in exercise of the implementing power in relation to so much of the subject matter of the Equality Acts as implements [an EU][141] obligation.

(8) Relevant subject matter of the Equality Acts is so much of the subject matter of those Acts as does not implement [an EU][142] obligation.

(9) A harmonising provision may amend a provision of the Equality Acts.

(10) The reference to this Act does not include a reference to this section or Schedule 24 or to a provision specified in that Schedule.

(11) A Minister of the Crown must report to Parliament on the exercise of the power under subsection (2)—

(a) at the end of the period of 2 years starting on the day this section comes into force;

(b) at the end of each succeeding period of 2 years.

---

[140] Substituted by Treaty of Lisbon (Changes in Terminology) Order 2011, SI 2011/1043.

[141] Substituted by Treaty of Lisbon (Changes in Terminology) Order 2011, SI 2011/1043.

[142] Substituted by Treaty of Lisbon (Changes in Terminology) Order 2011, SI 2011/1043.

204 Harmonisation: procedure

(1) If, after the conclusion of the consultation required under section 203, the Minister thinks it appropriate to proceed with the making of an order under that section, the Minister must lay before Parliament—
 (a) a draft of a statutory instrument containing the order, together with
 (b) an explanatory document.

(2) The explanatory document must—
 (a) introduce and give reasons for the harmonising provision;
 (b) explain why the Minister thinks that the conditions in subsection (1) of section 203 are satisfied;
 (c) give details of the consultation carried out under that section;
 (d) give details of the representations received as a result of the consultation;
 (e) give details of such changes as were made as a result of the representations.

(3) Where a person making representations in response to the consultation has requested the Minister not to disclose them, the Minister must not disclose them under subsection (2)(d) if, or to the extent that, to do so would (disregarding any connection with proceedings in Parliament) constitute an actionable breach of confidence.

(4) If information in representations made by a person in response to consultation under section 203 relates to another person, the Minister need not disclose the information under subsection (2)(d) if or to the extent that—
 (a) the Minister thinks that the disclosure of information could adversely affect the interests of that other person, and
 (b) the Minister has been unable to obtain the consent of that other person to the disclosure.

(5) The Minister may not act under subsection (1) before the end of the period of 12 weeks beginning with the day on which the consultation under section 203(3) begins.

(6) Laying a draft of a statutory instrument in accordance with subsection (1) satisfies the condition as to laying imposed by subsection (8) of section 208, in so far as that subsection applies in relation to orders under section 203.

Application

205 Crown application

(1) The following provisions of this Act bind the Crown—
 (a) Part 1 (public sector duty regarding socio-economic inequalities);
 (b) Part 3 (services and public functions), so far as relating to the exercise of public functions;
 (c) Chapter 1 of Part 11 (public sector equality duty).

(2) Part 5 (work) binds the Crown as provided for by that Part.

(3) The remainder of this Act applies to Crown acts as it applies to acts done by a private person.

(4) For the purposes of subsection (3), an act is a Crown act if (and only if) it is done—
 (a) by or on behalf of a member of the executive,
 (b) by a statutory body acting on behalf of the Crown, or
 (c) by or on behalf of the holder of a statutory office acting on behalf of the Crown.

(5) A statutory body or office is a body or office established by an enactment.

(6) The provisions of Parts 2 to 4 of the Crown Proceedings Act 1947 apply to proceedings against the Crown under this Act as they apply to proceedings in England and Wales which, as a result of section 23 of that Act, are treated for the purposes of Part 2 of that Act as civil proceedings by or against the Crown.

(7) The provisions of Part 5 of that Act apply to proceedings against the Crown under this Act as they apply to proceedings in Scotland which, as a result of that Part, are treated as civil proceedings by or against the Crown.

(8) But the proviso to section 44 of that Act (removal of proceedings from the sheriff to the Court of Session) does not apply to proceedings under this Act.

206 Information society services

Schedule 25 (information society services) has effect.

Subordinate legislation

207 Exercise of power

(1) A power to make an order or regulations under this Act is exercisable by a Minister of the Crown, unless there is express provision to the contrary.

(2) Orders, regulations or rules under this Act must be made by statutory instrument.

(3) Subsection (2) does not apply to—
   (a) a transitional exemption order under Part 1 of Schedule 11,
   (b) a transitional exemption order under Part 1 of Schedule 12, or
   (c) an order under paragraph 1(3) of Schedule 14 that does not modify an enactment.

(4) Orders or regulations under this Act—
   (a) may make different provision for different purposes;
   (b) may include consequential, incidental, supplementary, transitional, transitory or saving provision.

(5) Nothing in section 163(4), 174(4) [, 181A(5), 181B(6)][143] or 182(3) affects the generality of the power under subsection (4)(a).

(6) The power under subsection (4)(b), in its application to section 37, [139A,][144] 153, 154(2), 155(5), 197 or 216 or to paragraph 7(1) of Schedule 11 or paragraph 1(3) or 2(3) of Schedule 14, includes power to amend an enactment (including, in the case of section [139A,][145] 197 or 216, this Act).

(7) In the case of section 216 (commencement), provision by virtue of subsection (4)(b) may be included in a separate order from the order that provides for the commencement to which the provision relates; and, for that purpose, it does not matter—
   (a) whether the order providing for the commencement includes provision by virtue of subsection (4)(b);
   (b) whether the commencement has taken place.

(8) A statutory instrument containing an Order in Council under section 82 (offshore work) is subject to annulment in pursuance of a resolution of either House of Parliament.

208 Ministers of the Crown, etc.

(1) This section applies where the power to make an order or regulations under this Act is exercisable by a Minister of the Crown or the Treasury.

(2) A statutory instrument containing (whether alone or with other provision) an order or regulations that amend this Act or another Act of Parliament, or an Act of the Scottish Parliament or an Act or Measure of the National Assembly for Wales, is subject to the affirmative procedure.

(3) But a statutory instrument is not subject to the affirmative procedure by virtue of subsection (2) merely because it contains—
   (a) an order under section 59 (local authority functions);

---

[143] Inserted by Bus Services Act 2017.
[144] Inserted by Enterprise and Regulatory Reform Act 2013.
[145] Inserted by Enterprise and Regulatory Reform Act 2013.

   (b) an order under section 151 (power to amend list of public authorities for the purposes of the public sector equality duty) that provides for the omission of an entry where the authority concerned has ceased to exist or the variation of an entry where the authority concerned has changed its name;

   (c) an order under paragraph 1(3) of Schedule 14 (educational charities and endowments) that modifies an enactment.

(4) A statutory instrument containing (whether alone or with other provision) an order or regulations mentioned in subsection (5) is subject to the affirmative procedure.

(5) The orders and regulations referred to in subsection (4) are—

   (a) regulations under section 30 (services: ships and hovercraft);

   (b) regulations under section 78 (gender pay gap information);

   (c) regulations under section 81 (work: ships and hovercraft);

   (d) an order under section 105 (election candidates: expiry of provision);

   (e) regulations under section 106 (election candidates: diversity information);

   [(ea) regulations under section 139A (equal pay audits);][146]

   (f) regulations under section 153 or 154(2) (public sector equality duty: powers to impose specific duties);

   [(fa) regulations under section 181A or 181B (information for bus passengers);][147]

   (g) [...][148]

   (h) an order under section 203 (EU obligations: harmonisation);

   (i) regulations under paragraph 9(3) of Schedule 20 (rail vehicle accessibility: determination of turnover for purposes of penalties).

(6) A statutory instrument that is not subject to the affirmative procedure by virtue of subsection (2) or (4) is subject to the negative procedure.

(7) But a statutory instrument is not subject to the negative procedure by virtue of sub-section (6) merely because it contains—

   (a) [...][149]

   (b) an order under section 216 (commencement) that—

      (i) does not amend an Act of Parliament, an Act of the Scottish Parliament or an Act or Measure of the National Assembly for Wales, and

      (ii) is not made in reliance on section 207(7).

(8) If a statutory instrument is subject to the affirmative procedure, the order or regulations contained in it must not be made unless a draft of the instrument is laid before and approved by a resolution of each House of Parliament.

(9) If a statutory instrument is subject to the negative procedure, it is subject to annulment in pursuance of a resolution of either House of Parliament.

(10) If a draft of a statutory instrument containing an order or regulations under section 2, 151, 153, 154(2) or 155(5) would, apart from this subsection, be treated for the purposes of the Standing Orders of either House of Parliament as a hybrid instrument, it is to proceed in that House as if it were not a hybrid instrument.

209 The Welsh Ministers

(1) This section applies where the power to make an order or regulations under this Act is exercisable by the Welsh Ministers.

---

[146] Inserted by Enterprise and Regulatory Reform Act 2013.
[147] Inserted by Bus Services Act 2017.
[148] Repealed by Deregulation Act 2015.
[149] Repealed by Deregulation Act 2015.

(2) A statutory instrument containing (whether alone or with other provision) an order or regulations mentioned in subsection (3) is subject to the affirmative procedure.

(3) The orders and regulations referred to in subsection (2) are—

(a) regulations under section 2 (socio-economic inequalities);

(b) an order under section 151 (power to amend list of public authorities for the purposes of the public sector equality duty);

(c) regulations under section 153 or 154(2) (public sector equality duty: powers to impose specific duties);

(d) regulations under section 155(5) that amend an Act of Parliament or an Act or Measure of the National Assembly for Wales (public sector equality duty: power to modify or remove specific duties).

(4) But a statutory instrument is not subject to the affirmative procedure by virtue of subsection (2) merely because it contains an order under section 151 that provides for—

(a) the omission of an entry where the authority concerned has ceased to exist, or

(b) the variation of an entry where the authority concerned has changed its name.

(5) A statutory instrument that is not subject to the affirmative procedure by virtue of subsection (2) is subject to the negative procedure.

(6) If a statutory instrument is subject to the affirmative procedure, the order or regulations contained in it must not be made unless a draft of the instrument is laid before and approved by a resolution of the National Assembly for Wales.

(7) If a statutory instrument is subject to the negative procedure, it is subject to annulment in pursuance of a resolution of the National Assembly for Wales.

210 The Scottish Ministers

(1) This section applies where the power to make an order, regulations or rules under this Act is exercisable by the Scottish Ministers.

(2) A statutory instrument containing (whether alone or with other provision) an order or regulations mentioned in subsection (3) is subject to the affirmative procedure.

(3) The orders and regulations referred to in subsection (2) are—

(a) regulations under section 2 (socio-economic inequalities);

(b) regulations under section 37 (power to make provision about adjustments to common parts in Scotland);

(c) an order under section 151 (power to amend list of public authorities for the purposes of the public sector equality duty);

(d) regulations under section 153 or 154(2) (public sector equality duty: powers to impose specific duties);

(e) regulations under section 155(5) that amend an Act of Parliament or an Act of the Scottish Parliament (public sector equality duty: power to modify or remove specific duties).

(4) But a statutory instrument is not subject to the affirmative procedure by virtue of subsection (2) merely because it contains an order under section 151 that provides for—

(a) the omission of an entry where the authority concerned has ceased to exist, or

(b) the variation of an entry where the authority concerned has changed its name.

(5) A statutory instrument that is not subject to the affirmative procedure by virtue of subsection (2) is subject to the negative procedure.

(6) If a statutory instrument is subject to the affirmative procedure, the order or regulations contained in it must not be made unless a draft of the instrument is laid before and approved by a resolution of the Scottish Parliament.

(7) If a statutory instrument is subject to the negative procedure, it is subject to annulment in pursuance of a resolution of the Scottish Parliament.

Amendments, etc.

211 Amendments, repeals and revocations

(1) Schedule 26 (amendments) has effect.

(2) Schedule 27 (repeals and revocations) has effect.

Interpretation

212 General interpretation

(1) In this Act—

'armed forces' means any of the naval, military or air forces of the Crown;

'the Commission' means the Commission for Equality and Human Rights;

'detriment' does not, subject to subsection (5), include conduct which amounts to harassment;

'the Education Acts' has the meaning given in section 578 of the Education Act 1996;

'employment' and related expressions are (subject to subsection (11)) to be read with section 83;

'enactment' means an enactment contained in—

   (a) an Act of Parliament,

   (b) an Act of the Scottish Parliament,

   (c) an Act or Measure of the National Assembly for Wales, or

   (d) subordinate legislation;

'equality clause' means a sex equality clause or maternity equality clause;

'equality rule' means a sex equality rule or maternity equality rule;

'man' means a male of any age;

'maternity equality clause' has the meaning given in section 73;

'maternity equality rule' has the meaning given in section 75;

'non-discrimination rule' has the meaning given in section 61;

'occupational pension scheme' has the meaning given in section 1 of the Pension Schemes Act 1993;

'parent' has the same meaning as in—

   (a) the Education Act 1996 (in relation to England and Wales);

   (b) the Education (Scotland) Act 1980 (in relation to Scotland);

'prescribed' means prescribed by regulations;

'profession' includes a vocation or occupation;

'sex equality clause' has the meaning given in section 66;

'sex equality rule' has the meaning given in section 67;

'subordinate legislation' means—

   (a) subordinate legislation within the meaning of the Interpretation Act 1978, or

   (b) an instrument made under an Act of the Scottish Parliament or an Act or Measure of the National Assembly for Wales;

'substantial' means more than minor or trivial;

'trade' includes any business;

'woman' means a female of any age.

(2) A reference (however expressed) to an act includes a reference to an omission.

(3) A reference (however expressed) to an omission includes (unless there is express provision to the contrary) a reference to—

   (a) a deliberate omission to do something;

   (b) a refusal to do it;

   (c) a failure to do it.

(4) A reference (however expressed) to providing or affording access to a benefit, facility or service includes a reference to facilitating access to the benefit, facility or service.

(5) Where this Act disapplies a prohibition on harassment in relation to a specified protected characteristic, the disapplication does not prevent conduct relating to that characteristic from amounting to a detriment for the purposes of discrimination within section 13 because of that characteristic.

(6) A reference to occupation, in relation to premises, is a reference to lawful occupation.

(7) The following are members of the executive—

    (a) a Minister of the Crown;

    (b) a government department;

    (c) the Welsh Ministers, the First Minister for Wales or the Counsel General to the Welsh Assembly Government;

    (d) any part of the Scottish Administration.

(8) A reference to a breach of an equality clause or rule is a reference to a breach of a term modified by, or included by virtue of, an equality clause or rule.

(9) A reference to a contravention of this Act does not include a reference to a breach of an equality clause or rule, unless there is express provision to the contrary.

(10) 'Member', in relation to an occupational pension scheme, means an active member, a deferred member or a pensioner member (within the meaning, in each case, given by section 124 of the Pensions Act 1995).

(11) 'Employer', 'deferred member', 'pension credit member', 'pensionable service', 'pensioner member' and 'trustees or managers' each have, in relation to an occupational pension scheme, the meaning given by section 124 of the Pensions Act 1995.

(12) A reference to the accrual of rights under an occupational pension scheme is to be construed in accordance with that section.

(13) Nothing in section 28, 32, 84, 90, 95 or 100 is to be regarded as an express exception.

213 References to maternity leave, etc.

(1) This section applies for the purposes of this Act.

(2) A reference to a woman on maternity leave is a reference to a woman on—

    (a) compulsory maternity leave,

    (b) ordinary maternity leave, or

    (c) additional maternity leave.

(3) A reference to a woman on compulsory maternity leave is a reference to a woman absent from work because she satisfies the conditions prescribed for the purposes of section 72(1) of the Employment Rights Act 1996.

(4) A reference to a woman on ordinary maternity leave is a reference to a woman absent from work because she is exercising the right to ordinary maternity leave.

(5) A reference to the right to ordinary maternity leave is a reference to the right conferred by section 71(1) of the Employment Rights Act 1996.

(6) A reference to a woman on additional maternity leave is a reference to a woman absent from work because she is exercising the right to additional maternity leave.

(7) A reference to the right to additional maternity leave is a reference to the right conferred by section 73(1) of the Employment Rights Act 1996.

(8) 'Additional maternity leave period' has the meaning given in section 73(2) of that Act.

214 Index of defined expressions

Schedule 28 lists the places where expressions used in this Act are defined or otherwise explained.

Final provisions

215 Money

There is to be paid out of money provided by Parliament any increase attributable to this Act in the expenses of a Minister of the Crown.

216 Commencement

(1) The following provisions come into force on the day on which this Act is passed—

    (a) section 186(2) (rail vehicle accessibility: compliance);

    (b) this Part (except sections 202 (civil partnerships on religious premises), 206 (information society services) and 211 (amendments, etc)).

(2) Part 15 (family property) comes into force on such day as the Lord Chancellor may by order appoint.

(3) [Subject to [subsections (4) and (6)][150],][151] [t]he other provisions of this Act come into force on such day as a Minister of the Crown may by order appoint.

[(4) The following provisions of Part 1 (socio-economic inequalities) come into force on such day as the Scottish Ministers may by order appoint—

    (a) section 1, so far as it applies to a relevant authority as defined by section 2(5);

    (b) section 2, so far as it confers a power on the Scottish Ministers;

    (c) section 3, for the purposes of section 1 to the extent mentioned in paragraph (a).

(5) The following do not apply to an order under subsection (4)—

    (a) section 207(2) (see instead section 27 of the Interpretation and Legislative Reform (Scotland) Act 2010: powers exercisable by Scottish statutory instrument), and

    (b) section 210.][152]

[(6) The following provisions of Part 1 come into force on such day as the Welsh Ministers may by order appoint—

    (a) section 1, so far as it applies to a relevant authority as defined by section 2(6);

    (b) section 2, so far as it confers a power on the Welsh Ministers;

    (c) section 3, for the purposes of section 1 to the extent mentioned in paragraph (a).

(7) Section 209 does not apply to an order under subsection (6).][153]

217 Extent

(1) This Act forms part of the law of England and Wales.

(2) This Act, apart from section 190 (improvements to let dwelling houses) and Part 15 (family property), forms part of the law of Scotland.

(3) Each of the following also forms part of the law of Northern Ireland—

    (a) section 82 (offshore work);

    (b) section 105(3) and (4) (expiry of Sex Discrimination (Election Candidates) Act 2002);

    (c) section 199 (abolition of presumption of advancement).

218 Short title

This Act may be cited as the Equality Act 2010.

---

[150] Substituted by Wales Act 2017.
[151] Inserted by Scotland Act 2016.
[152] Inserted by Scotland Act 2016.
[153] Inserted by Wales Act 2017.

SCHEDULES

SCHEDULE 1   **Section 6**

DISABILITY: SUPPLEMENTARY PROVISION

PART 1
DETERMINATION OF DISABILITY

Impairment

1   Regulations may make provision for a condition of a prescribed description to be, or not to be, an impairment.

Long-term effects

2   (1) The effect of an impairment is long-term if—
         (a) it has lasted for at least 12 months,
         (b) it is likely to last for at least 12 months, or
         (c) it is likely to last for the rest of the life of the person affected.
     (2) If an impairment ceases to have a substantial adverse effect on a person's ability to carry out normal day-to-day activities, it is to be treated as continuing to have that effect if that effect is likely to recur.
     (3) For the purposes of sub-paragraph (2), the likelihood of an effect recurring is to be disregarded in such circumstances as may be prescribed.
     (4) Regulations may prescribe circumstances in which, despite sub-paragraph (1), an effect is to be treated as being, or as not being, long-term.

Severe disfigurement

3   (1) An impairment which consists of a severe disfigurement is to be treated as having a substantial adverse effect on the ability of the person concerned to carry out normal day-to-day activities.
     (2) Regulations may provide that in prescribed circumstances a severe disfigurement is not to be treated as having that effect.
     (3) The regulations may, in particular, make provision in relation to deliberately acquired disfigurement.

Substantial adverse effects

4   Regulations may make provision for an effect of a prescribed description on the ability of a person to carry out normal day-to-day activities to be treated as being, or as not being, a substantial adverse effect.

Effect of medical treatment

5   (1) An impairment is to be treated as having a substantial adverse effect on the ability of the person concerned to carry out normal day-to-day activities if—
         (a) measures are being taken to treat or correct it, and
         (b) but for that, it would be likely to have that effect.

(2) 'Measures' includes, in particular, medical treatment and the use of a prosthesis or other aid.

(3) Sub-paragraph (1) does not apply—

    (a) in relation to the impairment of a person's sight, to the extent that the impairment is, in the person's case, correctable by spectacles or contact lenses or in such other ways as may be prescribed;

    (b) in relation to such other impairments as may be prescribed, in such circumstances as are prescribed.

Certain medical conditions

6 (1) Cancer, HIV infection and multiple sclerosis are each a disability.

(2) HIV infection is infection by a virus capable of causing the Acquired Immune Deficiency Syndrome.

Deemed disability

7 (1) Regulations may provide for persons of prescribed descriptions to be treated as having disabilities.

(2) The regulations may prescribe circumstances in which a person who has a disability is to be treated as no longer having the disability.

(3) This paragraph does not affect the other provisions of this Schedule.

Progressive conditions

8 (1) This paragraph applies to a person (P) if—

    (a) P has a progressive condition,

    (b) as a result of that condition P has an impairment which has (or had) an effect on P's ability to carry out normal day-to-day activities, but

    (c) the effect is not (or was not) a substantial adverse effect.

(2) P is to be taken to have an impairment which has a substantial adverse effect if the condition is likely to result in P having such an impairment.

(3) Regulations may make provision for a condition of a prescribed description to be treated as being, or as not being, progressive.

Past disabilities

9 (1) A question as to whether a person had a disability at a particular time ('the relevant time') is to be determined, for the purposes of section 6, as if the provisions of, or made under, this Act were in force when the act complained of was done had been in force at the relevant time.

(2) The relevant time may be a time before the coming into force of the provision of this Act to which the question relates.

PART 2
GUIDANCE

Preliminary

10 This Part of this Schedule applies in relation to guidance referred to in section 6(5).

Examples

11 The guidance may give examples of—
  (a) effects which it would, or would not, be reasonable, in relation to particular activities, to regard as substantial adverse effects;
  (b) substantial adverse effects which it would, or would not, be reasonable to regard as long-term.

Adjudicating bodies

12 (1) In determining whether a person is a disabled person, an adjudicating body must take account of such guidance as it thinks is relevant.
   (2) An adjudicating body is—
     (a) a court;
     (b) a tribunal;
     (c) a person (other than a court or tribunal) who may decide a claim relating to a contravention of Part 6 (education).

Representations

13 Before issuing the guidance, the Minister must—
  (a) publish a draft of it;
  (b) consider any representations made to the Minister about the draft;
  (c) make such modifications as the Minister thinks appropriate in the light of the representations.

Parliamentary procedure

14 (1) If the Minister decides to proceed with proposed guidance, a draft of it must be laid before Parliament.
   (2) If, before the end of the 40-day period, either House resolves not to approve the draft, the Minister must take no further steps in relation to the proposed guidance.
   (3) If no such resolution is made before the end of that period, the Minister must issue the guidance in the form of the draft.
   (4) Sub-paragraph (2) does not prevent a new draft of proposed guidance being laid before Parliament.
   (5) The 40-day period—
     (a) begins on the date on which the draft is laid before both Houses (or, if laid before each House on a different date, on the later date);
     (b) does not include a period during which Parliament is prorogued or dissolved;
     (c) does not include a period during which both Houses are adjourned for more than 4 days.

Commencement

15 The guidance comes into force on the day appointed by order by the Minister.

Revision and revocation

16 (1) The Minister may—
     (a) revise the whole or part of guidance and re-issue it;
     (b) by order revoke guidance.
   (2) A reference to guidance includes a reference to guidance which has been revised and re-issued.

SCHEDULE 2 Section 31

SERVICES AND PUBLIC FUNCTIONS: REASONABLE ADJUSTMENTS

Preliminary

1   This Schedule applies where a duty to make reasonable adjustments is imposed on A by this Part.

The duty

2   (1) A must comply with the first, second and third requirements.

(2) For the purposes of this paragraph, the reference in section 20(3), (4) or (5) to a disabled person is to disabled persons generally.

(3) Section 20 has effect as if, in subsection (4), for 'to avoid the disadvantage' there were substituted—

'(a) to avoid the disadvantage, or

(b) to adopt a reasonable alternative method of providing the service or exercising the function.'

(4) In relation to each requirement, the relevant matter is the provision of the service, or the exercise of the function, by A.

(5) Being placed at a substantial disadvantage in relation to the exercise of a function means—

(a) if a benefit is or may be conferred in the exercise of the function, being placed at a substantial disadvantage in relation to the conferment of the benefit, or

(b) if a person is or may be subjected to a detriment in the exercise of the function, suffering an unreasonably adverse experience when being subjected to the detriment.

(6) In relation to the second requirement, a physical feature includes a physical feature brought by or on behalf of A, in the course of providing the service or exercising the function, on to premises other than those that A occupies (as well as including a physical feature in or on premises that A occupies).

(7) If A is a service-provider, nothing in this paragraph requires A to take a step which would fundamentally alter—

(a) the nature of the service, or

(b) the nature of A's trade or profession.

(8) If A exercises a public function, nothing in this paragraph requires A to take a step which A has no power to take.

Special provision about transport

3   (1) This paragraph applies where A is concerned with the provision of a service which involves transporting people by land, air or water.

(2) It is never reasonable for A to have to take a step which would—

(a) involve the alteration or removal of a physical feature of a vehicle used in providing the service;

(b) affect whether vehicles are provided;

(c) affect what vehicles are provided;

(d) affect what happens in the vehicle while someone is travelling in it.

(3) But, for the purpose of complying with the first or third requirement, A may not rely on sub-paragraph (2)(b), (c) or (d) if the vehicle concerned is—

(a) a hire-vehicle designed and constructed for the carriage of passengers, comprising more than 8 seats in addition to the driver's seat and having a maximum mass not exceeding 5 tonnes,

413

    (b) a hire-vehicle designed and constructed for the carriage of goods and having a maximum mass not exceeding 3.5 tonnes,

    (c) a vehicle licensed under section 48 of the Local Government (Miscellaneous Provisions) Act 1976 or section 7 of the Private Hire Vehicles (London) Act 1998 (or under a provision of a local Act corresponding to either of those provisions),

    (d) a private hire car (within the meaning of section 23 of the Civic Government (Scotland) Act 1982),

    (e) a public service vehicle (within the meaning given by section 1 of the Public Passenger Vehicles Act 1981),

    (f) a vehicle built or adapted to carry passengers on a railway or tramway (within the meaning, in each case, of the Transport and Works Act 1992),

    (g) a taxi,

    (h) a vehicle deployed to transport the driver and passengers of a vehicle that has broken down or is involved in an accident, or

    (i) a vehicle deployed on a system using a mode of guided transport (within the meaning of the Transport and Works Act 1992).

(4) In so far as the second requirement requires A to adopt a reasonable alternative method of providing the service to disabled persons, A may not, for the purpose of complying with the requirement, rely on sub-paragraph (2)(b), (c) or (d) if the vehicle is within sub-paragraph (3)(h).

(5) A may not, for the purpose of complying with the first, second or third requirement rely on sub-paragraph (2) of this paragraph if A provides the service by way of a hire-vehicle built to carry no more than 8 passengers.

(6) For the purposes of sub-paragraph (5) in its application to the second requirement, a part of a vehicle is to be regarded as a physical feature if it requires alteration in order to facilitate the provision of—

    (a) hand controls to enable a disabled person to operate braking and accelerator systems in the vehicle, or

    (b) facilities for the stowage of a wheelchair.

(7) For the purposes of sub-paragraph (6)(a), fixed seating and in-built electrical systems are not physical features; and for the purposes of sub-paragraph (6)(b), fixed seating is not a physical feature.

(8) In the case of a vehicle within sub-paragraph (3), a relevant device is not an auxiliary aid for the purposes of the third requirement.

(9) A relevant device is a device or structure, or equipment, the installation, operation or maintenance of which would necessitate making a permanent alteration to, or which would have a permanent effect on, the internal or external fabric of the vehicle.

(10) Regulations may amend this paragraph so as to provide for sub-paragraph (2) not to apply, or to apply only so far as is prescribed, in relation to vehicles of a prescribed description.

Interpretation

4   (1) This paragraph applies for the purposes of paragraph 3.

    (2) A 'hire-vehicle' is a vehicle hired (by way of a trade) under a hiring agreement to which section 66 of the Road Traffic Offenders Act 1988 applies.

    (3) A 'taxi', in England and Wales, is a vehicle—

        (a) licensed under section 37 of the Town Police Clauses Act 1847,

        (b) licensed under section 6 of the Metropolitan Public Carriage Act 1869, or

        (c) drawn by one or more persons or animals.

(4) A 'taxi', in Scotland, is—

    (a) a hire car engaged, by arrangements made in a public place between the person to be transported (or a person acting on that person's behalf) and the driver, for a journey starting there and then, or

    (b) a vehicle drawn by one or more persons or animals.

SCHEDULE 3   **Section 31**

SERVICES AND PUBLIC FUNCTIONS: EXCEPTIONS

PART 1
CONSTITUTIONAL MATTERS

Parliament

1   (1) Section 29 does not apply to the exercise of—

    (a) a function of Parliament;

    (b) a function exercisable in connection with proceedings in Parliament.

   (2) Sub-paragraph (1) does not permit anything to be done to or in relation to an individual unless it is done by or in pursuance of a resolution or other deliberation of either House or of a Committee of either House.

Legislation

2   (1) Section 29 does not apply to preparing, making or considering—

    (a) an Act of Parliament;

    (b) a Bill for an Act of Parliament;

    (c) an Act of the Scottish Parliament;

    (d) a Bill for an Act of the Scottish Parliament;

    (e) an Act of the National Assembly for Wales;

    (f) a Bill for an Act of the National Assembly for Wales.

   (2) Section 29 does not apply to preparing, making, approving or considering—

    (a) a Measure of the National Assembly for Wales;

    (b) a proposed Measure of the National Assembly for Wales.

   (3) Section 29 does not apply to preparing, making, confirming, approving or considering an instrument which is made under an enactment by—

    (a) a Minister of the Crown;

    (b) the Scottish Ministers or a member of the Scottish Executive;

    (c) the Welsh Ministers, the First Minister for Wales or the Counsel General to the Welsh Assembly Government.

   (4) Section 29 does not apply to preparing, making, confirming, approving or considering an instrument to which paragraph 6(a) of Schedule 2 to the Synodical Government Measure 1969 (1969 No. 2) (Measures, Canons, Acts of Synod, orders, etc.) applies.

   (5) Section 29 does not apply to anything done in connection with the preparation, making, consideration, approval or confirmation of an instrument made by—

    (a) Her Majesty in Council;

    (b) the Privy Council.

   (6) Section 29 does not apply to anything done in connection with the imposition of a requirement or condition which comes within Schedule 22 (statutory provisions).

Judicial functions

3   (1) Section 29 does not apply to—

    (a) a judicial function;

    (b) anything done on behalf of, or on the instructions of, a person exercising a judicial function;

    (c) a decision not to commence or continue criminal proceedings;

    (d) anything done for the purpose of reaching, or in pursuance of, a decision not to commence or continue criminal proceedings.

    (2) A reference in sub-paragraph (1) to a judicial function includes a reference to a judicial function conferred on a person other than a court or tribunal.

Armed forces

4   (1) Section 29(6), so far as relating to relevant discrimination, does not apply to anything done for the purpose of ensuring the combat effectiveness of the armed forces.

    (2) 'Relevant discrimination' is—

    (a) age discrimination;

    (b) disability discrimination;

    (c) gender reassignment discrimination;

    (d) sex discrimination.

Security services, etc.

5   Section 29 does not apply to—

    (a) the Security Service;

    (b) the Secret Intelligence Service;

    (c) the Government Communications Headquarters;

    (d) a part of the armed forces which is, in accordance with a requirement of the Secretary of State, assisting the Government Communications Headquarters.

PART 2

EDUCATION

6   In its application to a local authority in England and Wales, section 29, so far as relating to age discrimination or religious or belief-related discrimination, does not apply to—

    (a) the exercise of the authority's functions under section 14 of the Education Act 1996 (provision of schools);

    (b) the exercise of its function under section 13 of that Act in so far as it relates to a function of its under section 14 of that Act.

7   In its application to an education authority, section 29, so far as relating to age discrimination or religious or belief-related discrimination, does not apply to—

    (a) the exercise of the authority's functions under section 17 of the Education (Scotland) Act 1980 (provision of schools);

    (b) the exercise of its functions under section 1 of that Act, section 2 of the Standards in Scotland's Schools etc. Act 2000 (asp 6) or section 4 or 5 of the Education (Additional Support for Learning) (Scotland) Act 2004 (asp 4) (general responsibility for education) in so far as it relates to a matter specified in paragraph (a);

    (c) the exercise of its functions under subsection (1) of section 50 of the Education (Scotland) Act 1980 (education of pupils in exceptional circumstances) in so far as it consists of making arrangements of the description referred to in subsection (2) of that section.

8 (1) In its application to a local authority in England and Wales or an education authority, section 29, so far as relating to sex discrimination, does not apply to the exercise of the authority's functions in relation to the establishment of a school.

   (2) But nothing in sub-paragraph (1) is to be taken as disapplying section 29 in relation to the exercise of the authority's functions under section 14 of the Education Act 1996 or section 17 of the Education (Scotland) Act 1980.

9 Section 29, so far as relating to age discrimination, does not apply in relation to anything done in connection with—
   (a) the curriculum of a school,
   (b) admission to a school,
   (c) transport to or from a school, or
   (d) the establishment, alteration or closure of schools.

10 (1) Section 29, so far as relating to disability discrimination, does not require a local authority in England or Wales exercising functions under the Education Acts or an education authority exercising relevant functions to remove or alter a physical feature.

   (2) Relevant functions are functions under—
       (a) the Education (Scotland) Act 1980,
       (b) the Education (Scotland) Act 1996,
       (c) the Standards in Scotland's Schools etc. Act 2000, or
       (d) the Education (Additional Support for Learning) (Scotland) Act 2004.

11 Section 29, so far as relating to religious or belief-related discrimination, does not apply in relation to anything done in connection with—
   (a) the curriculum of a school;
   (b) admission to a school which has a religious ethos;
   (c) acts of worship or other religious observance organised by or on behalf of a school (whether or not forming part of the curriculum);
   (d) the responsible body of a school which has a religious ethos;
   (e) transport to or from a school;
   (f) the establishment, alteration or closure of schools.

12 This Part of this Schedule is to be construed in accordance with Chapter 1 of Part 6.

PART 3
HEALTH AND CARE

Blood services

13 (1) A person operating a blood service does not contravene section 29 only by refusing to accept a donation of an individual's blood if—
       (a) the refusal is because of an assessment of the risk to the public, or to the individual, based on clinical, epidemiological or other data obtained from a source on which it is reasonable to rely, and
       (b) the refusal is reasonable.

   (2) A blood service is a service for the collection and distribution of human blood for the purposes of medical services.

   (3) 'Blood' includes blood components.

Health and safety

14 (1) A service-provider (A) who refuses to provide the service to a pregnant woman does not discriminate against her in contravention of section 29 because she is pregnant if—

    (a) A reasonably believes that providing her with the service would, because she is pregnant, create a risk to her health or safety,

    (b) A refuses to provide the service to persons with other physical conditions, and

    (c) the reason for that refusal is that A reasonably believes that providing the service to such persons would create a risk to their health or safety.

  (2) A service-provider (A) who provides, or offers to provide, the service to a pregnant woman on conditions does not discriminate against her in contravention of section 29 because she is pregnant if—

    (a) the conditions are intended to remove or reduce a risk to her health or safety,

    (b) A reasonably believes that the provision of the service without the conditions would create a risk to her health or safety,

    (c) A imposes conditions on the provision of the service to persons with other physical conditions, and

    (d) the reason for the imposition of those conditions is that A reasonably believes that the provision of the service to such persons without those conditions would create a risk to their health or safety.

Care within the family

15 A person (A) does not contravene section 29 only by participating in arrangements under which (whether or not for reward) A takes into A's home, and treats as members of A's family, persons requiring particular care and attention.

PART 4
IMMIGRATION

Disability

[Age

15A.—

(1) This paragraph applies in relation to age discrimination.

(2) Section 29 does not apply to anything done by a relevant person in the exercise of functions exercisable by virtue of a relevant enactment.

(3) A relevant person is—

    (a) a Minister of the Crown acting personally, or

    (b) a person acting in accordance with a relevant authorisation.

(4) A relevant authorisation is a requirement imposed or express authorisation given—

    (a) with respect to a particular case or class of case, by a Minister of the Crown acting personally;

    (b) with respect to a particular class of case, by a relevant enactment or by an instrument made under or by virtue of a relevant enactment.

(5) The relevant enactments are—

    (a) the Immigration Acts,

    (b) the Special Immigration Appeals Commission Act 1997,

(c) a provision made under section 2(2) of the European Communities Act 1972 which relates to immigration or asylum, and

(d) a provision of EU law which relates to immigration or asylum.

(6) The reference in sub-paragraph (5)(a) to the Immigration Acts does not include a reference to—

(a) sections 28A to 28K of the Immigration Act 1971 (powers of arrest, entry and search, etc.), or

(b) section 14 of the Asylum and Immigration (Treatment of Claimants, etc.) Act 2004 (power of arrest).][154]

16 (1) This paragraph applies in relation to disability discrimination.

(2) Section 29 does not apply to—

(a) a decision within sub-paragraph (3);

(b) anything done for the purposes of or in pursuance of a decision within that sub-paragraph.

(3) A decision is within this sub-paragraph if it is a decision (whether or not taken in accordance with immigration rules) to do any of the following on the ground that doing so is necessary for the public good—

(a) to refuse entry clearance;

(b) to refuse leave to enter or remain in the United Kingdom;

(c) to cancel leave to enter or remain in the United Kingdom;

(d) to vary leave to enter or remain in the United Kingdom;

(e) to refuse an application to vary leave to enter or remain in the United Kingdom.

(4) Section 29 does not apply to—

(a) a decision taken, or guidance given, by the Secretary of State in connection with a decision within sub-paragraph (3);

(b) a decision taken in accordance with guidance given by the Secretary of State in connection with a decision within that sub-paragraph.

Nationality and ethnic or national origins

17 (1) This paragraph applies in relation to race discrimination so far as relating to—

(a) nationality, or

(b) ethnic or national origins.

(2) Section 29 does not apply to anything done by a relevant person in the exercise of functions exercisable by virtue of a relevant enactment.

(3) A relevant person is—

(a) a Minister of the Crown acting personally, or

(b) a person acting in accordance with a relevant authorisation.

(4) A relevant authorisation is a requirement imposed or express authorisation given—

(a) with respect to a particular case or class of case, by a Minister of the Crown acting personally;

(b) with respect to a particular class of case, by a relevant enactment or by an instrument made under or by virtue of a relevant enactment.

(5) The relevant enactments are—

(a) the Immigration Acts,

(b) the Special Immigration Appeals Commission Act 1997,

---

[154] Inserted by Equality Act 2010 (Age Exceptions) Order 2012, SI 2012/2466.

(c) a provision made under section 2(2) of the European Communities Act 1972 which relates to immigration or asylum, and

(d) a provision of [EU law]¹⁵⁵ which relates to immigration or asylum.

(6) The reference in sub-paragraph (5)(a) to the Immigration Acts does not include a reference to—

(a) sections 28A to 28K of the Immigration Act 1971 (powers of arrest, entry and search, etc.), or

(b) section 14 of the Asylum and Immigration (Treatment of Claimants, etc.) Act 2004 (power of arrest).

Religion or belief

18 (1) This paragraph applies in relation to religious or belief-related discrimination.

(2) Section 29 does not apply to a decision within sub-paragraph (3) or anything done for the purposes of or in pursuance of a decision within that subparagraph.

(3) A decision is within this sub-paragraph if it is a decision taken in accordance with immigration rules—

(a) to refuse entry clearance or leave to enter the United Kingdom, or to cancel leave to enter or remain in the United Kingdom, on the grounds that the exclusion of the person from the United Kingdom is conducive to the public good, or

(b) to vary leave to enter or remain in the United Kingdom, or to refuse an application to vary leave to enter or remain in the United Kingdom, on the grounds that it is undesirable to permit the person to remain in the United Kingdom.

(4) Section 29 does not apply to a decision within sub-paragraph (5), or anything done for the purposes of or in pursuance of a decision within that sub-paragraph, if the decision is taken on grounds mentioned in subparagraph (6).

(5) A decision is within this sub-paragraph if it is a decision (whether or not taken in accordance with immigration rules) in connection with an application for entry clearance or for leave to enter or remain in the United Kingdom.

(6) The grounds referred to in sub-paragraph (4) are—

(a) the grounds that a person holds an office or post in connection with a religion or belief or provides a service in connection with a religion or belief,

(b) the grounds that a religion or belief is not to be treated in the same way as certain other religions or beliefs, or

(c) the grounds that the exclusion from the United Kingdom of a person to whom paragraph (a) applies is conducive to the public good.

(7) Section 29 does not apply to—

(a) a decision taken, or guidance given, by the Secretary of State in connection with a decision within sub-paragraph (3) or (5);

(b) a decision taken in accordance with guidance given by the Secretary of State in connection with a decision within either of those subparagraphs.

Interpretation

19 A reference to entry clearance, leave to enter or remain or immigration rules is to be construed in accordance with the Immigration Act 1971.

---

¹⁵⁵ Substituted by Equality Act 2010 (Consequential Amendments, Saving and Supplementary Provisions) Order 2010, SI 2010/2279.

PART 5

[INSURANCE AND OTHER FINANCIAL SERVICES][156]

Services arranged by employer

20 (1) Section 29 does not apply to the provision of a relevant financial service if the provision is in pursuance of arrangements made by an employer for the service-provider to provide the service to the employer's employees, and other persons, as a consequence of the employment.

(2) 'Relevant financial service' means—

(a) insurance or a related financial service, or

(b) a service relating to membership of or benefits under a personal pension scheme (within the meaning given by section 1 of the Pension Schemes Act 1993).

[*Age*

20A.—

(1) A person (A) does not contravene section 29, so far as relating to age discrimination, by doing anything in connection with the provision of a financial service.

(2) Where A conducts an assessment of risk for the purposes of providing the financial service to another person (B), A may rely on sub-paragraph (1) only if the assessment of risk, so far as it involves a consideration of B's age, is carried out by reference to information which is relevant to the assessment of risk and from a source on which it is reasonable to rely.

(3) In this paragraph, 'financial service' includes a service of a banking, credit, insurance, personal pension, investment or payment nature.][157]

Disability

21 (1) It is not a contravention of section 29, so far as relating to disability discrimination, to do anything in connection with insurance business if—

(a) that thing is done by reference to information that is both relevant to the assessment of the risk to be insured and from a source on which it is reasonable to rely, and

(b) it is reasonable to do that thing.

(2) 'Insurance business' means business which consists of effecting or carrying out contracts of insurance; and that definition is to be read with—

(a) section 22 of the Financial Services and Markets Act 2000,

(b) any relevant order under that Act, and

(c) Schedule 2 to that Act.

Sex, gender reassignment, pregnancy and maternity

22 […][158]

Existing insurance policies

23 (1) It is not a contravention of section 29, so far as relating to relevant discrimination, to do anything in connection with insurance business in relation to an existing insurance policy.

---

[156] Substituted by Equality Act 2010 (Age Exceptions) Order 2012, SI 2012/2466.

[157] Inserted by Equality Act 2010 (Age Exceptions) Order 2012, SI 2012/2466.

[158] Repealed by Equality Act 2010 (Amendment) Regulations 2012, SI 2012/2992.

(2) 'Relevant discrimination' is—

    (a) age discrimination;

    (b) disability discrimination;

    (c) gender reassignment discrimination;

    (d) pregnancy and maternity discrimination;

    (e) race discrimination;

    (f) religious or belief-related discrimination;

    (g) sex discrimination;

    (h) sexual orientation discrimination.

(3) An existing insurance policy is a policy of insurance entered into before the date on which this paragraph comes into force.

(4) Sub-paragraph (1) does not apply where an existing insurance policy was renewed, or the terms of such a policy were reviewed, on or after the date on which this paragraph comes into force.

(5) A review of an existing insurance policy which was part of, or incidental to, a general reassessment by the service-provider of the pricing structure for a group of policies is not a review for the purposes of sub-paragraph (4).

(6) 'Insurance business' has the meaning given in paragraph 21.

PART 6
[MARRIAGE: GENDER REASSIGNMENT][159]

Gender reassignment: England and Wales

24 (1) A person does not contravene section 29, so far as relating to gender reassignment discrimination, only because of anything done in reliance on section 5B of the Marriage Act 1949 (solemnisation of marriages involving person of acquired gender).

    (2) A person (A) whose consent to the solemnisation of the marriage of a person (B) is required under section 44(1) of the Marriage Act 1949 (solemnisation in registered building) does not contravene section 29, so far as relating to gender reassignment discrimination, by refusing to consent if A reasonably believes that B's gender has become the acquired gender under the Gender Recognition Act 2004.

    (3) Sub-paragraph (4) applies to a person (A) who may, in a case that comes within the Marriage Act 1949 (other than the case mentioned in subparagraph (1)), solemnise marriages according to a form, rite or ceremony of a body of persons who meet for religious worship.

    (4) A does not contravene section 29, so far as relating to gender reassignment discrimination, by refusing to solemnise, in accordance with a form, rite or ceremony as described in sub-paragraph (3), the marriage of a person (B) if A reasonably believes that B's gender has become the acquired gender under the Gender Recognition Act 2004.

---

[159] Substituted by Marriage (Same Sex Couples) Act 2013.

[PART 6ZA
MARRIAGE AND CIVIL PARTNERSHIP: SCOTLAND][160]

Gender reassignment: Scotland

25 (1) An approved celebrant (A) does not contravene section 29, so far as relating to gender reassignment discrimination, only by refusing to solemnise the marriage of a person (B) if A reasonably believes that B's gender has become the acquired gender under the Gender Recognition Act 2004.

(2) In sub-paragraph (1) 'approved celebrant' has the meaning given in section 8(2)(a) of the Marriage (Scotland) Act 1977 (persons who may solemnise marriage).

[(3) An approved celebrant (A) does not contravene section 29, so far as relating to gender reassignment discrimination, only by refusing to register the civil partnership of a person (B) if A reasonably believes that B's gender has become the acquired gender under the Gender Recognition Act 2004.

(4) In sub-paragraph (3) 'approved celebrant' has the meaning given in section 94A(4)(a) of the Civil Partnership Act 2004.][161]

[PART 6A
MARRIAGE OF SAME SEX COUPLES [AND CIVIL PARTNERSHP][162]
IN ENGLAND AND WALES][163]

[Marriage according to religious rites: no compulsion to solemnize etc

25A(1) A person does not contravene section 29 only because the person—
  (a) does not conduct a relevant marriage,
  (b) is not present at, does not carry out, or does not otherwise participate in, a relevant marriage, or
  (c) does not consent to a relevant marriage being conducted, for the reason that the marriage is the marriage of a same sex couple.

(2) Expressions used in this paragraph and in section 2 of the Marriage (Same Sex Couples) Act 2013 have the same meanings in this paragraph as in that section.][164]

[No compulsion for religious organisations or persons acting on their behalf to act in relation to civil partnerships

25AA—
  (1) A protected person does not contravene section 29 only because the person—
    (a) does not allow religious premises to be used as the place at which two people register as civil partners of each other under Part 2 of the Civil Partnership Act 2004 ("the 2004 Act"), or

---

[160] Inserted by Marriage and Civil Partnership (Scotland) Act 2014 and Civil Partnership Act 2004 (Consequential Provisions and Modifications) Order 2014, SI 2014/3229.

[161] Inserted by Marriage and Civil Partnership (Scotland) Act 2014 and Civil Partnership Act 2004 (Consequential Provisions and Modifications) Order 2014, SI 2014/3229.

[162] Inserted by Civil Partnership (Opposite-sex couples) Regulations 2019, SI 2019/1458.

[163] Inserted by Marriage (Same Sex Couples) Act 2013.

[164] Inserted by Marriage (Same Sex Couples) Act 2013.

    (b) does not provide, arrange, facilitate or participate in, or is not present at—
        (i) an occasion during which two people register as civil partners of each other on religious premises under Part 2 of the 2004 Act, or
        (ii) a ceremony or event in England or Wales to mark the formation of a civil partnership,

for the reason that the person does not wish to do things of that sort in relation to civil partnerships generally, or those between two people of the same sex, or those between two people of the opposite sex.

(2) An employer or principal does not contravene section 29 only because the employer or principal is treated under section 109 as doing something that does not, by virtue of sub-paragraph (1), amount to a contravention of section 29 by the employee or agent who in fact does it.

(3) In this paragraph—
    'protected person' has the meaning given by section 30ZA(2) of the 2004 Act;
    'religious premises' has the meaning given by section 6A(3C) of the 2004 Act.][165]

[PART 6B
MARRIAGE OF SAME SEX COUPLES AND CIVIL PARTNERSHIP: SCOTLAND

25B Marriage of same sex couples and civil partnership: Scotland

(1) An approved celebrant does not contravene section 29 only by refusing to solemnise a relevant Scottish marriage for the reason that the marriage is the marriage of two persons of the same sex.

(2) An approved celebrant does not contravene section 29 only by refusing to register a relevant Scottish civil partnership for the reason that the civil partnership is between two persons of the same sex.

(3) A person does not contravene section 29 only by refusing to participate in a religious or belief ceremony forming part of, or connected with, the solemnising of a relevant Scottish marriage for the reason that the marriage is the marriage of two persons of the same sex.

(4) A person does not contravene section 29 only by refusing to participate in a religious or belief ceremony forming part of, or connected with, the registration of a relevant Scottish civil partnership for the reason that the civil partnership is between two persons of the same sex.

(5) For the purposes of this paragraph, a person is an approved celebrant for the purposes of both marriage and civil partnership whether the person is an approved celebrant within the meaning of section 8(2)(a) of the Marriage (Scotland) Act 1977 or section 94A(4)(a) of the Civil Partnership Act 2004.

(6) In this paragraph—
    'relevant Scottish civil partnership' means a religious or belief civil partnership within the meaning of section 94A(4)(b) of the Civil Partnership Act 2004;
    'relevant Scottish marriage' means a religious or belief marriage of two persons of the same sex within the meaning of section 8(2)(a) of the Marriage (Scotland) Act 1977.

---

[165] Inserted by Civil Partnership (Opposite-sex couples) Regulations 2019, SI 2019/1458.

25C **Marriage of same sex couples: Scottish forces marriages**

(1) A chaplain does not contravene section 29 only by refusing to solemnise a relevant Scottish forces marriage according to religious rites or usages for the reason that the marriage is the marriage of two persons of the same sex.

(2) In this paragraph—

'chaplain' has the meaning given by paragraph (a) of the definition of 'authorized person' in paragraph 12(2) of Schedule 6 to the Marriage (Same Sex Couples) Act 2013;

'forces marriage' has the meaning given by paragraph 12(2) of Schedule 6 to the Marriage (Same Sex Couples) Act 2013; 'relevant Scottish forces marriage' means a forces marriage of two

persons of the same sex where Scotland is the relevant part of the United Kingdom within the meaning of paragraph 12 of Schedule 6 to the Marriage (Same Sex Couples) Act 2013.][166]

PART 7
[SEPARATE, SINGLE AND CONCESSIONARY SERVICES, ETC][167]

Separate services for the sexes

26 (1) A person does not contravene section 29, so far as relating to sex discrimination, by providing separate services for persons of each sex if—

(a) a joint service for persons of both sexes would be less effective, and

(b) the limited provision is a proportionate means of achieving a legitimate aim.

(2) A person does not contravene section 29, so far as relating to sex discrimination, by providing separate services differently for persons of each sex if—

(a) a joint service for persons of both sexes would be less effective,

(b) the extent to which the service is required by one sex makes it not reasonably practicable to provide the service otherwise than as a separate service provided differently for each sex, and

(c) the limited provision is a proportionate means of achieving a legitimate aim.

(3) This paragraph applies to a person exercising a public function in relation to the provision of a service as it applies to the person providing the service.

Single-sex services

27 (1) A person does not contravene section 29, so far as relating to sex discrimination, by providing a service only to persons of one sex if—

(a) any of the conditions in sub-paragraphs (2) to (7) is satisfied, and

(b) the limited provision is a proportionate means of achieving a legitimate aim.

(2) The condition is that only persons of that sex have need of the service.

(3) The condition is that—

(a) the service is also provided jointly for persons of both sexes, and

(b) the service would be insufficiently effective were it only to be provided jointly.

---

[166] Inserted by Marriage and Civil Partnership (Scotland) Act 2014 and Civil Partnership Act 2004 (Consequential Provisions and Modifications) Order 2014, SI 2014/3229.

[167] Substituted by Equality Act 2010 (Age Exceptions) Order 2012, SI 2012/2466.

(4) The condition is that—

    (a) a joint service for persons of both sexes would be less effective, and

    (b) the extent to which the service is required by persons of each sex makes it not reasonably practicable to provide separate services.

(5) The condition is that the service is provided at a place which is, or is part of—

    (a) a hospital, or

    (b) another establishment for persons requiring special care, supervision or attention.

(6) The condition is that—

    (a) the service is provided for, or is likely to be used by, two or more persons at the same time, and

    (b) the circumstances are such that a person of one sex might reasonably object to the presence of a person of the opposite sex.

(7) The condition is that—

    (a) there is likely to be physical contact between a person (A) to whom the service is provided and another person (B), and

    (b) B might reasonably object if A were not of the same sex as B.

(8) This paragraph applies to a person exercising a public function in relation to the provision of a service as it applies to the person providing the service.

Gender reassignment

28 (1) A person does not contravene section 29, so far as relating to gender reassignment discrimination, only because of anything done in relation to a matter within sub-paragraph (2) if the conduct in question is a proportionate means of achieving a legitimate aim.

    (2) The matters are—

        (a) the provision of separate services for persons of each sex;

        (b) the provision of separate services differently for persons of each sex;

        (c) the provision of a service only to persons of one sex.

Services relating to religion

29 (1) A minister does not contravene section 29, so far as relating to sex discrimination, by providing a service only to persons of one sex or separate services for persons of each sex, if—

    (a) the service is provided for the purposes of an organised religion,

    (b) it is provided at a place which is (permanently or for the time being) occupied or used for those purposes, and

    (c) the limited provision of the service is necessary in order to comply with the doctrines of the religion or is for the purpose of avoiding conflict with the strongly held religious convictions of a significant number of the religion's followers.

    (2) The reference to a minister is a reference to a minister of religion, or other person, who—

        (a) performs functions in connection with the religion, and

        (b) holds an office or appointment in, or is accredited, approved or recognised for purposes of, a relevant organisation in relation to the religion.

    (3) An organisation is a relevant organisation in relation to a religion if its purpose is—

        (a) to practise the religion,

        (b) to advance the religion,

        (c) to teach the practice or principles of the religion,

        (d) to enable persons of the religion to receive benefits, or to engage in activities, within the framework of that religion, or

        (e) to foster or maintain good relations between persons of different religions.

(4) But an organisation is not a relevant organisation in relation to a religion if its sole or main purpose is commercial.

Services generally provided only for persons who share a protected characteristic

30 If a service is generally provided only for persons who share a protected characteristic, a person (A) who normally provides the service for persons who share that characteristic does not contravene section 29(1) or (2)—

(a) by insisting on providing the service in the way A normally provides it, or

(b) if A reasonably thinks it is impracticable to provide the service to persons who do not share that characteristic, by refusing to provide the service.

[*Concessions*

30A.—

(1) A person does not contravene section 29, so far as relating to age discrimination, by giving a concession in respect of a service to persons of a particular age group.

(2) The reference to a concession in respect of a service is a reference to a benefit, right or privilege having the effect that the manner in which the service is provided is, or the terms on which it is provided are, more favourable than the manner in which, or the terms on which, it is usually provided to the public (or, where it is provided to a section of the public, that section).][168]

[*Age related holidays*

30B.—

(1) A person (P) does not contravene section 29, so far as relating to age discrimination, by providing a relevant holiday service to persons of a particular age group.

(2) In sub-paragraph (1) 'relevant holiday service' means a service—

(a) which involves the provision of at least two of the following together for a single price—

(i) travel;

(ii) accommodation;

(iii) access to activities or services not ancillary to travel or accommodation which form a significant part of the service or its cost;

(b) the provision of which is for a period of more than 24 hours or includes the provision of overnight accommodation;

(c) which P provides only to persons of the age group in question; and

(d) an essential feature of which is the bringing together of persons of that age group with a view to facilitating their enjoyment of facilities or services designed with particular regard to persons of that age group.

(3) P may not rely on sub-paragraph (1) unless, before providing a person with a relevant holiday service, P provides the person with a written statement that the service is provided only to persons of the age group in question.

(4) For the purpose of sub-paragraph (2)(a)(i), 'travel' includes an option for an individual to make alternative travel arrangements to those included in the relevant holiday service as offered by P.][169]

---

[168] Inserted by Equality Act 2010 (Age Exceptions) Order 2012, SI 2012/2466.
[169] Inserted by Equality Act 2010 (Age Exceptions) Order 2012, SI 2012/2466.

[Age restricted services

30C.—

   (1) This paragraph applies where a person (P)—

      (a) provides a service the provision of which is prohibited by or under an enactment to persons under the age specified in or under the enactment ('the statutory age'), and

      (b) displays on the premises on which the service is provided an age warning in relation to the provision of the service.

   (2) An age warning in relation to the provision of a service is a statement to the effect that the service will not be provided to a person who—

      (a) appears to P, or an employee or agent of P's, to be under the age specified in the statement, and

      (b) on being required to do so by P or the employee or agent, fails to produce satisfactory identification.

   (3) P does not contravene section 29, so far as relating to age discrimination, by not providing the service to a person, who—

      (a) appears to P, or an employee or agent of P's, to be under the age specified in the age warning in relation to the provision of the service, and

      (b) on being required to do so by P or the employee or agent, fails to produce satisfactory identification.

   (4) In this paragraph—

      (a) a reference to the provision of a service includes a reference to provision of access to the service, and

      (b) 'satisfactory identification', in relation to a person, means a valid document which—

         (i) in the case of licensed premises where an age condition applies, meets that condition, and

         (ii) in any other case includes a photograph of the person and establishes that the person has attained the statutory age in relation to the provision of a service;

      'licensed premises' means premises in respect of which a relevant premises licence within the meaning of section 19A of the Licensing Act 2003 (mandatory conditions where alcohol sold) has effect; and

      'age condition' means a condition specified in an order under subsection (1) of section 19A of that Act requiring the age of certain persons to be verified in the manner specified in the condition before they are served alcohol in premises where the condition applies.][170]

[Residential mobile homes

30D.—

   (1) A person (A) who is the owner of a protected site does not contravene section 29, so far as relating to age discrimination, by—

      (a) entering into a mobile home agreement with a person (B) that entitles only persons who have attained a particular age to station and occupy a mobile home on land forming part of the site, or

      (b) refusing to permit assignment by B of a mobile home agreement to any person other than a person who has attained a particular age.

---

[170] Inserted by Equality Act 2010 (Age Exceptions) Order 2012, SI 2012/2466.

(2) A does not contravene section 29, so far as relating to age discrimination, by imposing a requirement in park rules that mobile homes stationed on land forming part of the site and occupied under mobile home agreements may be occupied only by persons who have attained a particular age.

(3) A does not contravene section 29, so far as relating to age discrimination, by—

(a) imposing in or under a mobile home rental agreement with a person (C) a requirement that the mobile home to which the agreement relates may be occupied only by persons who have attained a particular age, or

(b) refusing to permit assignment by C of a mobile home rental agreement to any person other than a person who has attained a particular age.

(4) But A may not rely on sub-paragraph (1) or (3) unless, before doing something mentioned in that sub-paragraph, A provides B or C, as the case may be, with a written statement to the effect that the mobile home in question may be occupied only by persons who have attained the age in question.

(5) In this paragraph,

'mobile home agreement' means an agreement to which the Mobile Homes Act 1983 [or Part 4 of the Mobile Homes (Wales) Act 2013][171] applies; and 'owner', 'protected site' and 'mobile home' have the same meaning as in that Act [or that Part of that Act][172];

'park rules' means rules applying to residents of mobile homes on the protected site and required to be observed by a term in the mobile home agreement or the mobile home rental agreement as the case may be;

'mobile home rental agreement' means an agreement (other than an arrangement to occupy a mobile home for the purposes of a holiday) under which a person ('the occupier') is entitled to occupy a mobile home on the protected site as the occupier's residence whether for a specified period or for successive periods of a specified duration subject to payment of money and the performance of other obligations.][173]

PART 8
TELEVISION, RADIO AND ON-LINE BROADCASTING AND DISTRIBUTION

31 (1) Section 29 does not apply to the provision of a content service (within the meaning given by section 32(7) of the Communications Act 2003).

(2) Sub-paragraph (1) does not apply to the provision of an electronic communications network, electronic communications service or associated facility (each of which has the same meaning as in that Act).

---

[171] Inserted by Mobile Homes (Wales) Act 2013.

[172] Inserted by Mobile Homes (Wales) Act 2013. Please note that 'or that Part of that Act' refers to the following text—'or Part 4 of the Mobile Homes (Wales) Act 2013'; inserted by Mobile Homes (Wales) Act 2013.

[173] Inserted by Equality Act 2010 (Age Exceptions) Order 2012, SI 2012/2466.

PART 9

TRANSPORT

Application to disability

32 This Part of this Schedule applies in relation to disability discrimination.

Transport by air

33 (1) Section 29 does not apply to—
 (a) transporting people by air;
 (b) a service provided on a vehicle for transporting people by air.
 (2) Section 29 does not apply to anything governed by Regulation (EC) No 1107/2006 of the European Parliament and of the Council of 5 July 2006 concerning the rights of disabled persons and persons with reduced mobility when travelling by air.

[Transport by land: road][174]

34 (1) Section 29 does not apply to transporting people by land, unless the vehicle concerned is—
 (a) a hire-vehicle designed and constructed for the carriage of passengers and comprising no more than 8 seats in addition to the driver's seat,
 (b) a hire-vehicle designed and constructed for the carriage of passengers, comprising more than 8 seats in addition to the driver's seat and having a maximum mass not exceeding 5 tonnes,
 (c) a hire-vehicle designed and constructed for the carriage of goods and having a maximum mass not exceeding 3.5 tonnes,
 (d) a vehicle licensed under section 48 of the Local Government (Miscellaneous Provisions) Act 1976 or section 7 of the Private Hire Vehicles (London) Act 1998 (or under a provision of a local Act corresponding to either of those provisions),
 (e) a private hire car (within the meaning of section 23 of the Civic Government (Scotland) Act 1982),
 (f) a public service vehicle (within the meaning given by section 1 of the Public Passenger Vehicles Act 1981),
 (g) a vehicle built or adapted to carry passengers on a railway or tramway (within the meaning, in each case, of the Transport and Works Act 1992),
 (h) a taxi,
 (i) a vehicle deployed to transport the driver and passengers of a vehicle that has broken down or is involved in an accident, or
 (j) a vehicle deployed on a system using a mode of guided transport (within the meaning of the Transport and Works Act 1992).
 [(1A) Sections 20 to 22 and section 29 do not apply to anything that is governed by Regulation (EU) No 181/2011 of the European Parliament and of the Council of 16 February 2011 concerning the rights of passengers in bus and coach transport and amending Regulation (EC) No 2006/2004.][175]

---

[174] Substituted by Equality Act 2010 (Consequential Amendments, Saving and Supplementary Provisions) Order 2010, SI 2010/2279.
[175] Inserted by Rights of Passengers in Bus and Coach Transport (Exemptions and Enforcement) Regulations 2013, SI 2013/1865.

(2) Paragraph 4 of Schedule 2 applies for the purposes of this paragraph as it applies for the purposes of paragraph 3 of that Schedule.

[Transport by land: rail

34A. Section 29 does not apply to anything governed by Regulation (EC) No 1371/2007 of the European Parliament and of the Council of 23 October 2007 on rail passengers' rights and obligations.][176]

PART 10
SUPPLEMENTARY

Power to amend

35 (1) A Minister of the Crown may by order amend this Schedule—
   (a) so as to add, vary or omit an exception to section 29, so far as relating to disability, religion or belief or sexual orientation;
   (b) so as to add, vary or omit an exception to section 29(6), so far as relating to gender reassignment, pregnancy and maternity, race or sex.
(2) But provision by virtue of sub-paragraph (1) may not amend this Schedule—
   (a) so as to omit an exception in paragraph 1, 2 or 3;
   (b) so as to reduce the extent to which an exception in paragraph 1, 2 or 3 applies.
(3) For the purposes of an order under sub-paragraph (1)(a), so far as relating to disability, which makes provision in relation to transport by air, it does not matter whether the transport is within or outside the United Kingdom.
(4) Before making an order under this paragraph the Minister must consult the Commission.
(5) Nothing in this paragraph affects the application of any other provision of this Act to conduct outside England and Wales or Scotland.

SCHEDULE 4   Section 38

PREMISES: REASONABLE ADJUSTMENTS

Preliminary

1 This Schedule applies where a duty to make reasonable adjustments is imposed on A by this Part.

The duty in relation to let premises

2 (1) This paragraph applies where A is a controller of let premises.
(2) A must comply with the first and third requirements.
(3) For the purposes of this paragraph, the reference in section 20(3) to a provision, criterion or practice of A's includes a reference to a term of the letting.

---

[176] Inserted by Equality Act 2010 (Consequential Amendments, Saving and Supplementary Provisions) Order 2010, SI 2010/2279.

(4) For those purposes, the reference in section 20(3) or (5) to a disabled person is a reference to a disabled person who—

    (a) is a tenant of the premises, or

    (b) is otherwise entitled to occupy them.

(5) In relation to each requirement, the relevant matters are—

    (a) the enjoyment of the premises;

    (b) the use of a benefit or facility, entitlement to which arises as a result of the letting.

(6) Sub-paragraph (2) applies only if A receives a request from or on behalf of the tenant or a person entitled to occupy the premises to take steps to avoid the disadvantage or provide the auxiliary aid.

(7) If a term of the letting that prohibits the tenant from making alterations puts the disabled person at the disadvantage referred to in the first requirement, A is required to change the term only so far as is necessary to enable the tenant to make alterations to the let premises so as to avoid the disadvantage.

(8) It is never reasonable for A to have to take a step which would involve the removal or alteration of a physical feature.

(9) For the purposes of this paragraph, physical features do not include furniture, furnishings, materials, equipment or other chattels in or on the premises; and none of the following is an alteration of a physical feature—

    (a) the replacement or provision of a sign or notice;

    (b) the replacement of a tap or door handle;

    (c) the replacement, provision or adaptation of a door bell or door entry system;

    (d) changes to the colour of a wall, door or any other surface.

(10) The terms of a letting include the terms of an agreement relating to it.

The duty in relation to premises to let

3   (1) This paragraph applies where A is a controller of premises to let.

    (2) A must comply with the first and third requirements.

    (3) For the purposes of this paragraph, the reference in section 20(3) or (5) to a disabled person is a reference to a disabled person who is considering taking a letting of the premises.

    (4) In relation to each requirement, the relevant matter is becoming a tenant of the premises.

    (5) Sub-paragraph (2) applies only if A receives a request by or on behalf of a disabled person within sub-paragraph (3) for A to take steps to avoid the disadvantage or provide the auxiliary aid.

    (6) Nothing in this paragraph requires A to take a step which would involve the removal or alteration of a physical feature.

    (7) Sub-paragraph (9) of paragraph 2 applies for the purposes of this paragraph as it applies for the purposes of that paragraph.

The duty in relation to commonhold units

4   (1) This paragraph applies where A is a commonhold association; and the reference to a commonhold association is a reference to the association in its capacity as the person who manages a commonhold unit.

    (2) A must comply with the first and third requirements.

(3) For the purposes of this paragraph, the reference in section 20(3) to a provision, criterion or practice of A's includes a reference to—
  (a) a term of the commonhold community statement, or
  (b) any other term applicable by virtue of the transfer of the unit to the unit-holder.

(4) For those purposes, the reference in section 20(3) or (5) to a disabled person is a reference to a disabled person who—
  (a) is the unit-holder, or
  (b) is otherwise entitled to occupy the unit.

(5) In relation to each requirement, the relevant matters are—
  (a) the enjoyment of the unit;
  (b) the use of a benefit or facility, entitlement to which arises as a result of a term within sub-paragraph (3)(a) or (b).

(6) Sub-paragraph (2) applies only if A receives a request from or on behalf of the unit-holder or a person entitled to occupy the unit to take steps to avoid the disadvantage or provide the auxiliary aid.

(7) If a term within sub-paragraph (3)(a) or (b) that prohibits the unit-holder from making alterations puts the disabled person at the disadvantage referred to in the first requirement, A is required to change the term only so far as is necessary to enable the unit-holder to make alterations to the unit so as to avoid the disadvantage.

(8) It is never reasonable for A to have to take a step which would involve the removal or alteration of a physical feature; and sub-paragraph (9) of paragraph 2 applies in relation to a commonhold unit as it applies in relation to let premises.

The duty in relation to common parts

5 (1) This paragraph applies where A is a responsible person in relation to common parts.

(2) A must comply with the second requirement.

(3) For the purposes of this paragraph, the reference in section 20(4) to a physical feature is a reference to a physical feature of the common parts.

(4) For those purposes, the reference in section 20(4) to a disabled person is a reference to a disabled person who—
  (a) is a tenant of the premises,
  (b) is a unit-holder, or
  (c) is otherwise entitled to occupy the premises, and uses or intends to use the premises as the person's only or main home.

(5) In relation to the second requirement, the relevant matter is the use of the common parts.

(6) Sub-paragraph (2) applies only if—
  (a) A receives a request by or on behalf of a disabled person within subparagraph (4) for A to take steps to avoid the disadvantage, and
  (b) the steps requested are likely to avoid or reduce the disadvantage.

Consultation on adjustments relating to common parts

6 (1) In deciding whether it is reasonable to take a step for the purposes of paragraph 5, A must consult all persons A thinks would be affected by the step.

(2) The consultation must be carried out within a reasonable period of the request being made.

(3) A is not required to have regard to a view expressed against taking a step in so far as A reasonably believes that the view is expressed because of the disabled person's disability.

(4) Nothing in this paragraph affects anything a commonhold association is required to do pursuant to Part 1 of the Commonhold and Leasehold Reform Act 2002.

Agreement on adjustments relating to common parts

7   (1) If A decides that it is reasonable to take a step for the purposes of paragraph 5, A and the disabled person must agree in writing the rights and responsibilities of each of them in relation to the step.

(2) An agreement under this paragraph must, in particular, make provision as to the responsibilities of the parties in relation to—

(a) the costs of any work to be undertaken;

(b) other costs arising from the work;

(c) the restoration of the common parts to their former condition if the relevant disabled person stops living in the premises.

(3) It is always reasonable before the agreement is made for A to insist that the agreement should require the disabled person to pay—

(a) the costs referred to in paragraphs (a) and (b) of sub-paragraph (2), and

(b) the costs of the restoration referred to in paragraph (c) of that subparagraph.

(4) If an agreement under this paragraph is made, A's obligations under the agreement become part of A's interest in the common parts and pass on subsequent disposals accordingly.

(5) Regulations may require a party to an agreement under this paragraph to provide, in prescribed circumstances, prescribed information about the agreement to persons of a prescribed description.

(6) The regulations may require the information to be provided in a prescribed form.

(7) Regulations may make provision as to circumstances in which an agreement under this paragraph is to cease to have effect, in so far as the agreement does not itself make provision for termination.

Victimisation

8   (1) This paragraph applies where the relevant disabled person comes within paragraph 2(4)(b), 4(4)(b) or 5(4)(c).

(2) A must not, because of costs incurred in connection with taking steps to comply with a requirement imposed for the purposes of paragraph 2, 4 or 5, subject to a detriment—

(a) a tenant of the premises, or

(b) the unit-holder.

Regulations

9   (1) This paragraph applies for the purposes of section 36 and this Schedule.

(2) Regulations may make provision as to—

(a) circumstances in which premises are to be treated as let, or as not let, to a person;

(b) circumstances in which premises are to be treated as being, or as not being, to let;

(c) who is to be treated as being, or as not being, a person entitled to occupy premises otherwise than as tenant or unit-holder;

(d) who is to be treated as being, or as not being, a person by whom premises are let;

(e) who is to be treated as having, or as not having, premises to let;

(f) who is to be treated as being, or as not being, a manager of premises.

(3) Provision made by virtue of this paragraph may amend this Schedule.

SCHEDULE 5   Section 38

PREMISES: EXCEPTIONS

Owner-occupier

1   (1) This paragraph applies to the private disposal of premises by an owner-occupier.
    (2) A disposal is a private disposal only if the owner-occupier does not—
        (a) use the services of an estate agent for the purpose of disposing of the premises, or
        (b) publish (or cause to be published) an advertisement in connection with their disposal.
    (3) Section 33(1) applies only in so far as it relates to race.
    (4) Section 34(1) does not apply in so far as it relates to—
        (a) religion or belief, or
        (b) sexual orientation.
    (5) In this paragraph—
        'estate agent' means a person who, by way of profession or trade, provides services for the
        purpose of—
        (a) finding premises for persons seeking them, or
        (b) assisting in the disposal of premises;
        'owner-occupier' means a person who—
        (a) owns an estate or interest in premises, and
        (b) occupies the whole of them.

2   (1) Section 36(1)(a) does not apply if—
        (a) the premises are, or have been, the only or main home of a person by whom they are
            let, and
        (b) since entering into the letting, neither that person nor any other by whom they are
            let has used a manager for managing the premises.
    (2) A manager is a person who, by profession or trade, manages let premises.
    (3) Section 36(1)(b) does not apply if—
        (a) the premises are, or have been, the only or main home of a person who has them to
            let, and
        (b) neither that person nor any other who has the premises to let uses the services of an
            estate agent for letting the premises.
    (4) 'Estate agent' has the meaning given in paragraph 1.

Small premises

3   (1) This paragraph applies to anything done by a person in relation to the disposal, occupa-
        tion or management of part of small premises if—
        (a) the person or a relative of that person resides, and intends to continue to reside, in
            another part of the premises, and
        (b) the premises include parts (other than storage areas and means of access) shared with
            residents of the premises who are not members of the same household as the resident
            mentioned in paragraph (a).
    (2) Sections 33(1), 34(1) and 35(1) apply only in so far as they relate to race.
    (3) Premises are small if—
        (a) the only other persons occupying the accommodation occupied by the resident men-
            tioned in sub-paragraph (1)(a) are members of the same household,

(b) the premises also include accommodation for at least one other household,

(c) the accommodation for each of those other households is let, or available for letting, on a separate tenancy or similar agreement, and

(d) the premises are not normally sufficient to accommodate more than two other households.

(4) Premises are also small if they are not normally sufficient to provide residential accommodation for more than six persons (in addition to the resident mentioned in sub-paragraph (1)(a) and members of the same household).

(5) In this paragraph, 'relative' means—

(a) spouse or civil partner,

(b) unmarried partner,

(c) parent or grandparent,

(d) child or grandchild (whether or not legitimate),

(e) the spouse, civil partner or unmarried partner of a child or grandchild,

(f) brother or sister (whether of full blood or half-blood), or

(g) a relative within paragraph (c), (d), (e) or (f) whose relationship arises as a result of marriage or civil partnership.

(6) In sub-paragraph (5), a reference to an unmarried partner is a reference to the other member of a couple consisting [of two people who are not married to, or civil partners of, each other but are living together as if they were a married couple or civil partners.][177]

4 (1) Section 36(1) does not apply if—

(a) the premises in question are small premises,

(b) the relevant person or a relative of that person resides, and intends to continue to reside, in another part of the premises, and

(c) the premises include parts (other than storage areas and means of access) shared with residents of the premises who are not members of the same household as the resident mentioned in paragraph (b).

(2) The relevant person is the person who, for the purposes of section 36(1), is—

(a) the controller of the premises, or

(b) the responsible person in relation to the common parts to which the premises relate.

(3) 'Small premises' and 'relative' have the same meaning as in paragraph 3.

5 A Minister of the Crown may by order amend paragraph 3 or 4.

SCHEDULE 6   Section 52

OFFICE-HOLDERS: EXCLUDED OFFICES

Work to which other provisions apply

1 (1) An office or post is not a personal or public office in so far as one or more of the provisions mentioned in sub-paragraph (2)—

(a) applies in relation to the office or post, or

(b) would apply in relation to the office or post but for the operation of some other provision of this Act.

---

[177] Substituted by Civil Partnership (Opposite-sex couples) Regulations 2019, SI 2019/1458.

(2) Those provisions are—
- (a) section 39 (employment);
- (b) section 41 (contract work);
- (c) section 44 (partnerships);
- (d) section 45 (LLPs);
- (e) section 47 (barristers);
- (f) section 48 (advocates);
- (g) section 55 (employment services) so far as applying to the provision of work experience within section 56(2)(a) or arrangements within section 56(2)(c) for such provision.

Political offices

2 (1) An office or post is not a personal or public office if it is a political office.

(2) A political office is an office or post set out in the second column of the following Table—

Political setting	*Office or post*
Houses of Parliament	An office of the House of Commons held by a member of that House
	An office of the House of Lords held by a member of that House
	A Ministerial office within the meaning of section 2 of the House of Commons Disqualification Act 1975
	The office of the Leader of the Opposition within the meaning of the Ministerial and other Salaries Act 1975
	The office of the Chief Opposition Whip, or of an Assistant Opposition Whip, within the meaning of that Act
Scottish Parliament	An office of the Scottish Parliament held by a member of the Parliament
	The office of a member of the Scottish Executive
	The office of a junior Scottish Minister
National Assembly for Wales	An office of the National Assembly for Wales held by a member of the Assembly
	The office of a member of the Welsh Assembly Government
Local government in England (outside London)	An office of a county council, district council or parish council in England held by a member of the council
	An office of the Council of the Isles of Scilly held by a member of the Council
Local government in London	An office of the Greater London Authority held by the Mayor of London or a member of the London Assembly
	An office of a London borough council held by a member of the council
	An office of the Common Council of the City of London held by a member of the Council
Local government in Wales	An office of a county council, county borough council or community council in Wales held by a member of the council
Local government in Scotland	An office of a council constituted under section 2 of the Local Government etc. (Scotland) Act 1994 held by a member of the council
	An office of a council established under section 51 of the Local Government (Scotland) Act 1973 held by a member of the council
Political parties	An office of a registered political party

(3) The reference to a registered political party is a reference to a party registered in the Great Britain register under Part 2 of the Political Parties, Elections and Referendums Act 2000.

Honours etc.

3   A life peerage (within the meaning of the Life Peerages Act 1958), or any other dignity or honour conferred by the Crown, is not a personal or public office.

[Bishops

4   The office of diocesan or suffragan bishop is not a public office.][178]

SCHEDULE 7   **Section 80**

EQUALITY OF TERMS: EXCEPTIONS

PART 1
TERMS OF WORK

Compliance with laws regulating employment of women, etc.

1   Neither a sex equality clause nor a maternity equality clause has effect in relation to terms of work affected by compliance with laws regulating—
     (a) the employment of women;
     (b) the appointment of women to personal or public offices.

Pregnancy, etc.

2   A sex equality clause does not have effect in relation to terms of work affording special treatment to women in connection with pregnancy or childbirth.

PART 2
OCCUPATIONAL PENSION SCHEMES

Preliminary

3   (1) A sex equality rule does not have effect in relation to a difference as between men and women in the effect of a relevant matter if the difference is permitted by or by virtue of this Part of this Schedule.
     (2) 'Relevant matter' has the meaning given in section 67.

State retirement pensions

4   (1) This paragraph applies where a man and a woman are eligible, in such circumstances as may be prescribed, to receive different amounts by way of pension.
     (2) The difference is permitted if, in prescribed circumstances, it is attributable only to differences between men and women in the retirement benefits to which, in prescribed circumstances, the man and woman are or would be entitled.

[178] Inserted by Bishops and Priests (Consecration and Ordination of Women) Measure 2014 (No.2).

(3) 'Retirement benefits' are benefits under sections 43 to 55 of the Social Security Contributions and Benefits Act 1992 (state retirement pensions) [or sections 2 to 12 of the Pensions Act 2014 (state pension)][179].

Actuarial factors

5 (1) A difference as between men and women is permitted if it consists of applying to the calculation of the employer's contributions to an occupational pension scheme actuarial factors which—

(a) differ for men and women, and

(b) are of such description as may be prescribed.

(2) A difference as between men and women is permitted if it consists of applying to the determination of benefits of such description as may be prescribed actuarial factors which differ for men and women.

Power to amend

6 (1) Regulations may amend this Part of this Schedule so as to add, vary or omit provision about cases where a difference as between men and women in the effect of a relevant matter is permitted.

(2) The regulations may make provision about pensionable service before the date on which they come into force (but not about pensionable service before 17 May 1990).

SCHEDULE 8   Section 83

WORK: REASONABLE ADJUSTMENTS

PART 1
INTRODUCTORY

Preliminary

1 This Schedule applies where a duty to make reasonable adjustments is imposed on A by this Part of this Act.

The duty

2 (1) A must comply with the first, second and third requirements.

(2) For the purposes of this paragraph—

(a) the reference in section 20(3) to a provision, criterion or practice is a reference to a provision, criterion or practice applied by or on behalf of A;

(b) the reference in section 20(4) to a physical feature is a reference to a physical feature of premises occupied by A;

(c) the reference in section 20(3), (4) or (5) to a disabled person is to an interested disabled person.

(3) In relation to the first and third requirements, a relevant matter is any matter specified in the first column of the applicable table in Part 2 of this Schedule.

(4) In relation to the second requirement, a relevant matter is—

---

[179] Inserted by Pensions Act 2014 (Consequential and Supplementary Amendments) Order 2016, SI 2016/224.

    (a) a matter specified in the second entry of the first column of the applicable table in Part 2 of this Schedule, or

    (b) where there is only one entry in a column, a matter specified there.

(5) If two or more persons are subject to a duty to make reasonable adjustments in relation to the same interested disabled person, each of them must comply with the duty so far as it is reasonable for each of them to do so.

3 (1) This paragraph applies if a duty to make reasonable adjustments is imposed on A by section 55 (except where the employment service which A provides is the provision of vocational training within the meaning given by section 56(6)(b)).

  (2) The reference in section 20(3), (4) and (5) to a disabled person is a reference to an interested disabled person.

  (3) In relation to each requirement, the relevant matter is the employment service which A provides.

  (4) Sub-paragraph (5) of paragraph 2 applies for the purposes of this paragraph as it applies for the purposes of that paragraph.

PART 2
INTERESTED DISABLED PERSON

Preliminary

4 An interested disabled person is a disabled person who, in relation to a relevant matter, is of a description specified in the second column of the applicable table in this Part of this Schedule.

Employers (see section 39)

5 (1) This paragraph applies where A is an employer.

Relevant matter	Description of disabled person
Deciding to whom to offer employment.	A person who is, or has notified A that the person may be, an applicant for the employment.
Employment by A.	An applicant for employment by A. An employee of A's.

  (2) Where A is the employer of a disabled contract worker (B), A must comply with the first, second and third requirements on each occasion when B is supplied to a principal to do contract work.

  (3) In relation to the first requirement (as it applies for the purposes of subparagraph (2))—

    (a) the reference in section 20(3) to a provision, criterion or practice is a reference to a provision, criterion or practice applied by or on behalf of all or most of the principals to whom B is or might be supplied,

    (b) the reference to being put at a substantial disadvantage is a reference to being likely to be put at a substantial disadvantage that is the same or similar in the case of each of the principals referred to in paragraph (a), and

    (c) the requirement imposed on A is a requirement to take such steps as it would be reasonable for A to have to take if the provision, criterion or practice were applied by or on behalf of A.

(4) In relation to the second requirement (as it applies for the purposes of subparagraph (2))—

    (a) the reference in section 20(4) to a physical feature is a reference to a physical feature of premises occupied by each of the principals referred to in sub-paragraph (3)(a),

    (b) the reference to being put at a substantial disadvantage is a reference to being likely to be put at a substantial disadvantage that is the same or similar in the case of each of those principals, and

    (c) the requirement imposed on A is a requirement to take such steps as it would be reasonable for A to have to take if the premises were occupied by A.

(5) In relation to the third requirement (as it applies for the purposes of subparagraph (2))—

    (a) the reference in section 20(5) to being put at a substantial disadvantage is a reference to being likely to be put at a substantial disadvantage that is the same or similar in the case of each of the principals referred to in sub-paragraph (3)(a), and

    (b) the requirement imposed on A is a requirement to take such steps as it would be reasonable for A to have to take if A were the person to whom B was supplied.

Principals in contract work (see section 41)

6   (1) This paragraph applies where A is a principal.

Relevant matter	Description of disabled person
Contract work that A may make available.	A person who is, or has notified A that the person may be, an applicant to do the work.
Contract work that A makes available.	A person who is supplied to do the work.

    (2) A is not required to do anything that a disabled person's employer is required to do by virtue of paragraph 5.

Partnerships (see section 44)

7   (1) This paragraph applies where A is a firm or a proposed firm.

Relevant matter	Description of disabled person
Deciding to whom to offer a position as a partner.	A person who is, or has notified A that the person may be, a candidate for the position.
A position as a partner.	A candidate for the position.
	The partner who holds the position.

    (2) Where a firm or proposed firm (A) is required by this Schedule to take a step in relation to an interested disabled person (B)—

    (a) the cost of taking the step is to be treated as an expense of A;

    (b) the extent to which B should (if B is or becomes a partner) bear the cost is not to exceed such amount as is reasonable (having regard in particular to B's entitlement to share in A's profits).

LLPs (see section 45)

8   (1) This paragraph applies where A is an LLP or a proposed LLP.

Relevant matter	Description of disabled person
Deciding to whom to offer a position as a member.	A person who is, or has notified A that the person may be, a candidate for the position.
A position as a member.	A candidate for the position.
	The member who holds the position.

(2) Where an LLP or proposed LLP (A) is required by this Schedule to take a step in relation to an interested disabled person (B)—

    (a) the cost of taking the step is to be treated as an expense of A;

    (b) the extent to which B should (if B is or becomes a member) bear the cost is not to exceed such amount as is reasonable (having regard in particular to B's entitlement to share in A's profits).

Barristers and their clerks (see section 47)

9   This paragraph applies where A is a barrister or barrister's clerk.

Relevant matter	Description of disabled person
Deciding to whom to offer a pupillage or tenancy.	A person who is, or has notified A that the person may be, an applicant for the pupillage or tenancy.
A pupillage or tenancy.	An applicant for the pupillage or tenancy.
	The pupil or tenant.

Advocates and their clerks (see section 48)

10   This paragraph applies where A is an advocate or advocate's clerk.

Relevant matter	Description of disabled person
Deciding who to offer to take as a devil or to whom to offer membership of a stable.	A person who applies, or has notified A that the person may apply, to be taken as a devil or to become a member of the stable.
The relationship with a devil or membership of a stable.	An applicant to be taken as a devil or to become a member of the stable.
	The devil or member.

Persons making appointments to offices etc. (see sections 49 to 51)

11   This paragraph applies where A is a person who has the power to make an appointment to a personal or public office.

Relevant matter	Description of disabled person
Deciding to whom to offer the appointment.	A person who is, or has notified A that the person may be, seeking the appointment.
	A person who is being considered for the appointment.
Appointment to the office.	A person who is seeking, or being considered for, appointment to the office.

12 This paragraph applies where A is a relevant person in relation to a personal or public office.

Relevant matter	Description of disabled person
Appointment to the office.	A person appointed to the office.

13 This paragraph applies where A is a person who has the power to make a recommendation for, or give approval to, an appointment to a public office.

Relevant matter	Description of disabled person
Deciding who to recommend or approve for appointment to the office.	A person who is, or has notified A that the person may be, seeking recommendation or approval for appointment to the office.
	A person who is being considered for recommendation or approval for appointment to the office.
An appointment to the office.	A person who is seeking, or being considered for, appointment to the office in question.

14 In relation to the second requirement in a case within paragraph 11, 12 or 13, the reference in paragraph 2(2)(b) to premises occupied by A is to be read as a reference to premises—
  (a) under the control of A, and
  (b) at or from which the functions of the office concerned are performed.

Qualifications bodies (see section 53)

15 (1) This paragraph applies where A is a qualifications body.

Relevant matter	Description of disabled person
Deciding upon whom to confer a relevant qualification.	A person who is, or has notified A that the person may be, an applicant for the conferment of the qualification.
Conferment by the body of a relevant qualification.	An applicant for the conferment of the qualification. A person who holds the qualification.

(2) A provision, criterion or practice does not include the application of a competence standard.

Employment service-providers (see section 55)

16 This paragraph applies where—
  (a) A is an employment service-provider, and
  (b) the employment service which A provides is vocational training within the meaning given by section 56(6)(b).

Relevant matter	Description of disabled person
Deciding to whom to offer to provide the service.	A person who is, or has notified A that the person may be, an applicant for the provision of the service.
Provision by A of the service.	A person who applies to A for the provision of the service. A person to whom A provides the service.

Trade organisations (see section 57)

17 This paragraph applies where A is a trade organisation.

Relevant matter	Description of disabled person
Deciding to whom to offer membership of the organisation.	A person who is, or has notified A that the person may be, an applicant for membership.
Membership of the organisation.	An applicant for membership. A member.

Local authorities (see section 58)

18 (1) This paragraph applies where A is a local authority.

Relevant matter	Description of disabled person
A member's carrying-out of official business.	The member.

    (2) Regulations may, for the purposes of a case within this paragraph, make provision—

        (a) as to circumstances in which a provision, criterion or practice is, or is not, to be taken to put a disabled person at the disadvantage referred to in the first requirement;

        (b) as to circumstances in which a physical feature is, or is not, to be taken to put a disabled person at the disadvantage referred to in the second requirement;

        (c) as to circumstances in which it is, or in which it is not, reasonable for a local authority to be required to take steps of a prescribed description;

        (d) as to steps which it is always, or which it is never, reasonable for a local authority to take.

Occupational pensions (see section 61)

19 This paragraph applies where A is, in relation to an occupational pension scheme, a responsible person within the meaning of section 61.

Relevant matter	Description of disabled person
Carrying out A's functions in relation to the scheme.	A person who is or may be a member of the scheme.

PART 3
LIMITATIONS ON THE DUTY

Lack of knowledge of disability, etc.

20 (1) A is not subject to a duty to make reasonable adjustments if A does not know, and could not reasonably be expected to know—

        (a) in the case of an applicant or potential applicant, that an interested disabled person is or may be an applicant for the work in question;

(b) [in any case referred to in Part 2 of this Schedule],[180] that an interested disabled person has a disability and is likely to be placed at the disadvantage referred to in the first, second or third requirement.

(2) An applicant is, in relation to the description of A specified in the first column of the table, a person of a description specified in the second column (and the reference to a potential applicant is to be construed accordingly).

Description of A	Applicant
An employer	An applicant for employment
A firm or proposed firm	A candidate for a position as a partner
An LLP or proposed LLP	A candidate for a position as a member
A barrister or barrister's clerk	An applicant for a pupillage or tenancy
An advocate or advocate's clerk	An applicant for being taken as an advocate's devil or for becoming a member of a stable
A relevant person in relation to a personal or public office	A person who is seeking appointment to, or recommendation or approval for appointment to, the office
A qualifications body	An applicant for the conferment of a relevant qualification
An employment service provider	An applicant for the provision of an employment service
A trade organisation	An applicant for membership

(3) If the duty to make reasonable adjustments is imposed on A by section 55, this paragraph applies only in so far as the employment service which A provides is vocational training within the meaning given by section 56(6)(b).

SCHEDULE 9   Section 83

WORK: EXCEPTIONS

PART 1
OCCUPATIONAL REQUIREMENTS

General

1 (1) A person (A) does not contravene a provision mentioned in sub-paragraph (2) by applying in relation to work a requirement to have a particular protected characteristic, if A shows that, having regard to the nature or context of the work—
   (a) it is an occupational requirement,
   (b) the application of the requirement is a proportionate means of achieving a legitimate aim, and
   (c) the person to whom A applies the requirement does not meet it (or A has reasonable grounds for not being satisfied that the person meets it).

---

[180] Substituted by Equality Act 2010 (Public Authorities and Consequential and Supplementary Amendments) Order 2011, SI 2011/1060.

(2) The provisions are—
- (a) section 39(1)(a) or (c) or (2)(b) or (c);
- (b) section 41(1)(b);
- (c) section 44(1)(a) or (c) or (2)(b) or (c);
- (d) section 45(1)(a) or (c) or (2)(b) or (c);
- (e) section 49(3)(a) or (c) or (6)(b) or (c);
- (f) section 50(3)(a) or (c) or (6)(b) or (c);
- (g) section 51(1).

(3) The references in sub-paragraph (1) to a requirement to have a protected characteristic are to be read—
- (a) in the case of gender reassignment, as references to a requirement not to be a transsexual person (and section 7(3) is accordingly to be ignored);
- (b) in the case of marriage and civil partnership, as references to a requirement not to be married or a civil partner (and section 8(2) is accordingly to be ignored).

(4) In the case of a requirement to be of a particular sex, sub-paragraph (1) has effect as if in paragraph (c), the words from '(or' to the end were omitted.

Religious requirements relating to sex, marriage etc., sexual orientation

2 (1) A person (A) does not contravene a provision mentioned in sub-paragraph (2) by applying in relation to employment a requirement to which subparagraph (4) applies if A shows that—
- (a) the employment is for the purposes of an organised religion,
- (b) the application of the requirement engages the compliance or nonconflict principle, and
- (c) the person to whom A applies the requirement does not meet it (or A has reasonable grounds for not being satisfied that the person meets it).

(2) The provisions are—
- (a) section 39(1)(a) or (c) or (2)(b) or (c);
- (b) section 49(3)(a) or (c) or (6)(b) or (c);
- (c) section 50(3)(a) or (c) or (6)(b) or (c);
- (d) section 51(1).

(3) A person does not contravene section 53(1) or (2)(a) or (b) by applying in relation to a relevant qualification (within the meaning of that section) a requirement to which sub-paragraph (4) applies if the person shows that—
- (a) the qualification is for the purposes of employment mentioned in sub-paragraph (1)(a), and
- (b) the application of the requirement engages the compliance or nonconflict principle.

(4) This sub-paragraph applies to—
- (a) a requirement to be of a particular sex;
- (b) a requirement not to be a transsexual person;
- (c) a requirement not to be married or a civil partner;
- [(ca) a requirement not to be married to [, or the civil partner of,][181] a person of the same sex;][182]
- [(cb) a requirement not to be the civil partner of a person of the opposite sex;][183]

[181] Inserted by Civil Partnership (Opposite-sex couples) Regulations 2019, SI 2019/1458.
[182] Inserted by Marriage (Same Sex Couples) Act 2013.
[183] Inserted by Civil Partnership (Opposite-sex couples) Regulations 2019, SI 2019/1458.

    (d) a requirement not to be married to, or the civil partner of, a person who has a living former spouse or civil partner;

    (e) a requirement relating to circumstances in which a marriage or civil partnership came to an end;

    (f) a requirement related to sexual orientation.

(5) The application of a requirement engages the compliance principle if the requirement is applied so as to comply with the doctrines of the religion.

(6) The application of a requirement engages the non-conflict principle if, because of the nature or context of the employment, the requirement is applied so as to avoid conflicting with the strongly held religious convictions of a significant number of the religion's followers.

(7) A reference to employment includes a reference to an appointment to a personal or public office.

(8) In the case of a requirement within sub-paragraph (4)(a), sub-paragraph (1) has effect as if in paragraph (c) the words from '(or' to the end were omitted.

Other requirements relating to religion or belief

3   A person (A) with an ethos based on religion or belief does not contravene a provision mentioned in paragraph 1(2) by applying in relation to work a requirement to be of a particular religion or belief if A shows that, having regard to that ethos and to the nature or context of the work—

    (a) it is an occupational requirement,

    (b) the application of the requirement is a proportionate means of achieving a legitimate aim, and

    (c) the person to whom A applies the requirement does not meet it (or A has reasonable grounds for not being satisfied that the person meets it).

Armed forces

4   (1) A person does not contravene section 39(1)(a) or (c) or (2)(b) by applying in relation to service in the armed forces a relevant requirement if the person shows that the application is a proportionate means of ensuring the combat effectiveness of the armed forces.

    (2) A relevant requirement is—

        (a) a requirement to be a man;

        (b) a requirement not to be a transsexual person.

    (3) This Part of this Act, so far as relating to age or disability, does not apply to service in the armed forces; and section 55, so far as relating to disability, does not apply to work experience in the armed forces.

Employment services

5   (1) A person (A) does not contravene section 55(1) or (2) if A shows that A's treatment of another person relates only to work the offer of which could be refused to that other person in reliance on paragraph 1, 2, 3 or 4.

    (2) A person (A) does not contravene section 55(1) or (2) if A shows that A's treatment of another person relates only to training for work of a description mentioned in sub-paragraph (1).

    (3) A person (A) does not contravene section 55(1) or (2) if A shows that—

        (a) A acted in reliance on a statement made to A by a person with the power to offer the work in question to the effect that, by virtue of subparagraph (1) or (2), A's action would be lawful, and

        (b) it was reasonable for A to rely on the statement.

(4) A person commits an offence by knowingly or recklessly making a statement such as is mentioned in sub-paragraph (3)(a) which in a material respect is false or misleading.

(5) A person guilty of an offence under sub-paragraph (4) is liable on summary conviction to a fine not exceeding level 5 on the standard scale.

Interpretation

6 (1) This paragraph applies for the purposes of this Part of this Schedule.

(2) A reference to contravening a provision of this Act is a reference to contravening that provision by virtue of section 13.

(3) A reference to work is a reference to employment, contract work, a position as a partner or as a member of an LLP, or an appointment to a personal or public office.

(4) A reference to a person includes a reference to an organisation.

(5) A reference to section 39(2)(b), 44(2)(b), 45(2)(b), 49(6)(b) or 50(6)(b) is to be read as a reference to that provision with the omission of the words 'or for receiving any other benefit, facility or service'.

(6) A reference to section 39(2)(c), 44(2)(c), 45(2)(c), 49(6)(c), 50(6)(c), 53(2)(a) or 55(2) (c) (dismissal, etc.) does not include a reference to that provision so far as relating to sex.

(7) The reference to paragraph (b) of section 41(1), so far as relating to sex, is to be read as if that paragraph read—

'(b) by not allowing the worker to do the work.'

PART 2
EXCEPTIONS RELATING TO AGE

Preliminary

7 For the purposes of this Part of this Schedule, a reference to an age contravention is a reference to a contravention of this Part of this Act, so far as relating to age.

Retirement

8 [...][184]

Application at or approaching retirement age

9 [...][185]

Benefits based on length of service

10 (1) It is not an age contravention for a person (A) to put a person (B) at a disadvantage when compared with another (C), in relation to the provision of a benefit, facility or service in so far as the disadvantage is because B has a shorter period of service than C.

(2) If B's period of service exceeds 5 years, A may rely on sub-paragraph (1) only if A reasonably believes that doing so fulfils a business need.

(3) A person's period of service is whichever of the following A chooses—

---

[184] Repealed by Employment Equality (Repeal of Retirement Age Provisions) Regulations 2011, SI 2011/1069.
[185] Repealed by Employment Equality (Repeal of Retirement Age Provisions) Regulations 2011, SI 2011/1069.

(a) the period for which the person has been working for A at or above a level (assessed by reference to the demands made on the person) that A reasonably regards as appropriate for the purposes of this paragraph, or

(b) the period for which the person has been working for A at any level.

(4) The period for which a person has been working for A must be based on the number of weeks during the whole or part of which the person has worked for A.

(5) But for that purpose A may, so far as is reasonable, discount—

(a) periods of absence;

(b) periods that A reasonably regards as related to periods of absence.

(6) For the purposes of sub-paragraph (3)(b), a person is to be treated as having worked for A during any period in which the person worked for a person other than A if—

(a) that period counts as a period of employment with A as a result of section 218 of the Employment Rights Act 1996, or

(b) if sub-paragraph (a) does not apply, that period is treated as a period of employment by an enactment pursuant to which the person's employment was transferred to A.

(7) For the purposes of this paragraph, the reference to a benefit, facility or service does not include a reference to a benefit, facility or service which may be provided only by virtue of a person's ceasing to work.

The national minimum wage: young workers

11 (1) It is not an age contravention for a person to pay a young worker (A) at a lower rate than that at which the person pays an older worker (B) if—

(a) the hourly rate for the national minimum wage for a person of A's age is lower than that for a person of B's age, and

(b) the rate at which A is paid is below the single hourly rate.

(2) A young worker is a person who qualifies for the national minimum wage at a lower rate than the single hourly rate; and an older worker is a person who qualifies for the national minimum wage at a higher rate than that at which the young worker qualifies for it.

(3) The single hourly rate is the rate prescribed under section 1(3) of the National Minimum Wage Act 1998.

The national minimum wage: apprentices

12 (1) It is not an age contravention for a person to pay an apprentice who does not qualify for the national minimum wage at a lower rate than the person pays an apprentice who does.

(2) An apprentice is a person who—

(a) is employed under a contract of apprenticeship, or

(b) as a result of provision made by virtue of section 3(2)(a) of the National Minimum Wage Act 1998 (persons not qualifying), is treated as employed under a contract of apprenticeship.

Redundancy

13 (1) It is not an age contravention for a person to give a qualifying employee an enhanced redundancy payment of an amount less than that of an enhanced redundancy payment which the person gives to another qualifying employee, if each amount is calculated on the same basis.

(2) It is not an age contravention to give enhanced redundancy payments only to those who are qualifying employees by virtue of sub-paragraph (3)(a) or (b).

(3) A person is a qualifying employee if the person—
  (a) is entitled to a redundancy payment as a result of section 135 of the Employment Rights Act 1996,
  (b) agrees to the termination of the employment in circumstances where the person would, if dismissed, have been so entitled,
  (c) would have been so entitled but for section 155 of that Act (requirement for two years' continuous employment), or
  (d) agrees to the termination of the employment in circumstances where the person would, if dismissed, have been so entitled but for that section.

(4) An enhanced redundancy payment is a payment the amount of which is, subject to sub-paragraphs (5) and (6), calculated in accordance with section 162(1) to (3) of the Employment Rights Act 1996.

(5) A person making a calculation for the purposes of sub-paragraph (4)—
  (a) may treat a week's pay as not being subject to a maximum amount;
  (b) may treat a week's pay as being subject to a maximum amount above that for the time being specified in section 227(1) of the Employment Rights Act 1996;
  (c) may multiply the appropriate amount for each year of employment by a figure of more than one.

(6) Having made a calculation for the purposes of sub-paragraph (4) (whether or not in reliance on sub-paragraph (5)), a person may multiply the amount calculated by a figure of more than one.

(7) In sub-paragraph (5), 'the appropriate amount' has the meaning given in section 162 of the Employment Rights Act 1996, and 'a week's pay' is to be read with Chapter 2 of Part 14 of that Act.

(8) For the purposes of sub-paragraphs (4) to (6), the reference to 'the relevant date' in sub-section (1)(a) of section 162 of that Act is, in the case of a person who is a qualifying employee by virtue of sub-paragraph (3)(b) or (d), to be read as reference to the date of the termination of the employment.

[Insurance etc.

14 (1) It is not an age contravention for an employer to make arrangements for, or afford access to, the provision of insurance or a related financial service to or in respect of an employee for a period ending when the employee attains whichever is the greater of—
  (a) the age of 65, and
  (b) the state pensionable age.

(2) It is not an age contravention for an employer to make arrangements for, or afford access to, the provision of insurance or a related financial service to or in respect of only such employees as have not attained whichever is the greater of—
  (a) the age of 65, and
  (b) the state pensionable age.

(3) Sub-paragraphs (1) and (2) apply only where the insurance or related financial service is, or is to be, provided to the employer's employees or a class of those employees—
  (a) in pursuance of an arrangement between the employer and another person, or
  (b) where the employer's business includes the provision of insurance or financial services of the description in question, by the employer.

(4) The state pensionable age is the pensionable age determined in accordance with the rules in paragraph 1 of Schedule 4 to the Pensions Act 1995.][186]

---

[186] Substituted by Employment Equality (Repeal of Retirement Age Provisions) Regulations 2011, SI 2011/1069.

Child care

15 (1) A person does not contravene a relevant provision, so far as relating to age, only by providing, or making arrangements for or facilitating the provision of, care for children of a particular age group.

(2) The relevant provisions are—

(a) section 39(2)(b);

(b) section 41(1)(c);

(c) section 44(2)(b);

(d) section 45(2)(b);

(e) section 47(2)(b);

(f) section 48(2)(b);

(g) section 49(6)(b);

(h) section 50(6)(b);

(i) section 57(2)(a);

(j) section 58(3)(a).

(3) Facilitating the provision of care for a child includes—

(a) paying for some or all of the cost of the provision;

(b) helping a parent of the child to find a suitable person to provide care for the child;

(c) enabling a parent of the child to spend more time providing care for the child or otherwise assisting the parent with respect to the care that the parent provides for the child.

(4) A child is a person who has not attained the age of 17.

(5) A reference to care includes a reference to supervision.

Contributions to personal pension schemes

16 (1) A Minister of the Crown may by order provide that it is not an age contravention for an employer to maintain or use, with respect to contributions to personal pension schemes, practices, actions or decisions relating to age which are of a specified description.

(2) An order authorising the use of practices, actions or decisions which are not in use before the order comes into force must not be made unless the Minister consults such persons as the Minister thinks appropriate.

(3) 'Personal pension scheme' has the meaning given in section 1 of the Pension Schemes Act 1993; and 'employer', in relation to a personal pension scheme, has the meaning given in section 318(1) of the Pensions Act 2004.

PART 3

OTHER EXCEPTIONS

Non-contractual payments to women on maternity leave

17 (1) A person does not contravene section 39(1)(b) or (2), so far as relating to pregnancy and maternity, by depriving a woman who is on maternity leave of any benefit from the terms of her employment relating to pay.

(2) The reference in sub-paragraph (1) to benefit from the terms of a woman's employment relating to pay does not include a reference to—

(a) maternity-related pay (including maternity-related pay that is increase-related),

(b) pay (including increase-related pay) in respect of times when she is not on maternity leave, or

(c) pay by way of bonus in respect of times when she is on compulsory maternity leave.

(3) For the purposes of sub-paragraph (2), pay is increase-related in so far as it is to be calculated by reference to increases in pay that the woman would have received had she not been on maternity leave.

(4) A reference to terms of her employment is a reference to terms of her employment that are not in her contract of employment, her contract of apprenticeship or her contract to do work personally.

(5) 'Pay' means benefits—

(a) that consist of the payment of money to an employee by way of wages or salary, and

(b) that are not benefits whose provision is regulated by the contract referred to in sub-paragraph (4).

(6) 'Maternity-related pay' means pay to which a woman is entitled—

(a) as a result of being pregnant, or

(b) in respect of times when she is on maternity leave.

Benefits dependent on marital status, etc.

18 (1) A person does not contravene this Part of this Act, so far as relating to sexual orientation, by doing anything which prevents or restricts a person who is not [within sub-paragraph (1A)][187] from having access to a benefit, facility or service—

(a) the right to which accrued before 5 December 2005 (the day on which section 1 of the Civil Partnership Act 2004 came into force), or

(b) which is payable in respect of periods of service before that date.

[(1A) A person is within this sub-paragraph if the person is—

(a) a man who is married to a woman, or

(b) a woman who is married to a man, or

(c) married to a person of the same sex in a relevant gender change case.

(1B) The reference in sub-paragraph (1A)(c) to a relevant gender change case is a reference to a case where—

(a) the married couple were of the opposite sex at the time of their marriage, and

(b) a full gender recognition certificate has been issued to one of the couple under the Gender Recognition Act 2004.][188]

(2) A person does not contravene this Part of this Act, so far as relating to sexual orientation, by providing married persons and civil partners (to the exclusion of all other persons) with access to a benefit, facility or service.

Provision of services etc. to the public

19 (1) A does not contravene a provision mentioned in sub-paragraph (2) in relation to the provision of a benefit, facility or service to B if A is concerned with the provision (for payment or not) of a benefit, facility or service of the same description to the public.

(2) The provisions are—

(a) section 39(2) and (4);

(b) section 41(1) and (3);

---

[187] Substituted by Marriage (Same Sex Couples) Act 2013.

[188] Inserted by Marriage (Same Sex Couples) Act 2013.

    (c) sections 44(2) and (6) and 45(2) and (6);

    (d) sections 49(6) and (8) and 50(6), (7), (9) and (10).

(3) Sub-paragraph (1) does not apply if—

    (a) the provision by A to the public differs in a material respect from the provision by A to comparable persons,

    (b) the provision to B is regulated by B's terms, or

    (c) the benefit, facility or service relates to training.

(4) 'Comparable persons' means—

    (a) in relation to section 39(2) or (4), the other employees;

    (b) in relation to section 41(1) or (3), the other contract workers supplied to the principal;

    (c) in relation to section 44(2) or (6), the other partners of the firm;

    (d) in relation to section 45(2) or (6), the other members of the LLP;

    (e) in relation to section 49(6) or (8) or 50(6), (7), (9) or (10), persons holding offices or posts not materially different from that held by B.

(5) 'B's terms' means—

    (a) the terms of B's employment,

    (b) the terms on which the principal allows B to do the contract work,

    (c) the terms on which B has the position as a partner or member, or

    (d) the terms of B's appointment to the office.

(6) A reference to the public includes a reference to a section of the public which includes B.

Insurance contracts, etc.

20 (1) It is not a contravention of this Part of this Act, so far as relating to relevant discrimination, to do anything in relation to an annuity, life insurance policy, accident insurance policy or similar matter involving the assessment of risk if—

    (a) that thing is done by reference to actuarial or other data from a source on which it is reasonable to rely, and

    (b) it is reasonable to do it.

(2) 'Relevant discrimination' is—

    (a) gender reassignment discrimination;

    (b) marriage and civil partnership discrimination;

    (c) pregnancy and maternity discrimination;

    (d) sex discrimination.

SCHEDULE 10   **Section 88**

ACCESSIBILITY FOR DISABLED PUPILS

Accessibility strategies

1 (1) A local authority in England and Wales must, in relation to schools for which it is the responsible body, prepare—

    (a) an accessibility strategy;

    (b) further such strategies at such times as may be prescribed.

(2) An accessibility strategy is a strategy for, over a prescribed period—

    (a) increasing the extent to which disabled pupils can participate in the schools' curriculums;

    (b) improving the physical environment of the schools for the purpose of increasing the extent to which disabled pupils are able to take advantage of education and benefits, facilities or services provided or offered by the schools;

      (c) improving the delivery to disabled pupils of information which is readily accessible to pupils who are not disabled.

(3) The delivery in sub-paragraph (2)(c) must be—

      (a) within a reasonable time;

      (b) in ways which are determined after taking account of the pupils' disabilities and any preferences expressed by them or their parents.

(4) An accessibility strategy must be in writing.

(5) A local authority must keep its accessibility strategy under review during the period to which it relates and, if necessary, revise it.

(6) A local authority must implement its accessibility strategy.

2   (1) In preparing its accessibility strategy, a local authority must have regard to—

      (a) the need to allocate adequate resources for implementing the strategy;

      (b) guidance as to the matters mentioned in sub-paragraph (3).

(2) The authority must also have regard to guidance as to compliance with paragraph 1(5).

(3) The matters are—

      (a) the content of an accessibility strategy;

      (b) the form in which it is to be produced;

      (c) persons to be consulted in its preparation.

(4) Guidance may be issued—

      (a) for England, by a Minister of the Crown;

      (b) for Wales, by the Welsh Ministers.

(5) A local authority must, if asked, make a copy of its accessibility strategy available for inspection at such reasonable times as it decides.

(6) A local authority in England must, if asked by a Minister of the Crown, give the Minister a copy of its accessibility strategy.

(7) A local authority in Wales must, if asked by the Welsh Ministers, give them a copy of its accessibility strategy.

Accessibility plans

3   (1) The responsible body of a school in England and Wales must prepare—

      (a) an accessibility plan;

      (b) further such plans at such times as may be prescribed.

(2) An accessibility plan is a plan for, over a prescribed period—

      (a) increasing the extent to which disabled pupils can participate in the school's curriculum,

      (b) improving the physical environment of the school for the purpose of increasing the extent to which disabled pupils are able to take advantage of education and benefits, facilities or services provided or offered by the school, and

      (c) improving the delivery to disabled pupils of information which is readily accessible to pupils who are not disabled.

(3) The delivery in sub-paragraph (2)(c) must be—

      (a) within a reasonable time;

      (b) in ways which are determined after taking account of the pupils' disabilities and any preferences expressed by them or their parents.

(4) An accessibility plan must be in writing.

(5) The responsible body must keep its accessibility plan under review during the period to which it relates and, if necessary, revise it.

(6) The responsible body must implement its accessibility plan.

(7) A relevant inspection may extend to the performance by the responsible body of its functions in relation to the preparation, publication, review, revision and implementation of its accessibility plan.

(8) A relevant inspection is an inspection under—

(a) Part 1 of the Education Act 2005, or

(b) Chapter 1 of Part 4 of the Education and Skills Act 2008 (regulation and inspection of independent education provision in England).

4 (1) In preparing an accessibility plan, the responsible body must have regard to the need to allocate adequate resources for implementing the plan.

(2) The proprietor of an independent educational institution (other than an Academy) must, if asked, make a copy of the school's accessibility plan available for inspection at such reasonable times as the proprietor decides.

(3) The proprietor of an independent educational institution in England (other than an Academy) must, if asked by a Minister of the Crown, give the Minister a copy of the school's accessibility plan.

(4) The proprietor of an independent school in Wales (other than an Academy) must, if asked by the Welsh Ministers, give them a copy of the school's accessibility plan.

Power of direction

5 (1) This sub-paragraph applies if the appropriate authority is satisfied (whether or not on a complaint) that a responsible body—

(a) has acted or is proposing to act unreasonably in the discharge of a duty under this Schedule, or

(b) has failed to discharge such a duty.

(2) This sub-paragraph applies if the appropriate authority is satisfied (whether or not on a complaint) that a responsible body of a school specified in subparagraph (3)—

(a) has acted or is proposing to act unreasonably in the discharge of a duty the body has in relation to the provision to the authority of copies of the body's accessibility plan or the inspection of that plan, or

(b) has failed to discharge the duty.

(3) The schools are—

(a) schools approved under section 342 of the Education Act 1996 (nonmaintained special schools);

[(b) Academy schools;

(c) alternative provision Academies.][189]

(4) This sub-paragraph applies if a Tribunal has made an order under paragraph 5 of Schedule 17 and the appropriate authority is satisfied (whether or not on a complaint) that the responsible body concerned—

(a) has acted or is proposing to act unreasonably in complying with the order, or

(b) has failed to comply with the order.

(5) If sub-paragraph (1), (2) or (4) applies, the appropriate authority may give a responsible body such directions as the authority thinks expedient as to—

(a) the discharge by the body of the duty, or

(b) compliance by the body with the order.

---

[189] Substituted by Education Act 2011.

(6) A direction may be given in relation to sub-paragraph (1) or (2) even if the performance of the duty is contingent on the opinion of the responsible body.

(7) A direction may not, unless sub-paragraph (8) applies, be given to the responsible body of a school in England in respect of a matter—

    (a) that has been complained about to a Local Commissioner in accordance with Chapter 2 of Part 10 of the Apprenticeships, Skills, Children and Learning Act 2009 (parental complaints against governing bodies etc.), or

    (b) that the appropriate authority thinks could have been so complained about.

(8) This sub-paragraph applies if—

    (a) the Local Commissioner has made a recommendation to the responsible body under section 211(4) of the Apprenticeships, Skills, Children and Learning Act 2009 (statement following investigation) in respect of the matter, and

    (b) the responsible body has not complied with the recommendation.

(9) A direction—

    (a) may be varied or revoked by the appropriate authority;

    (b) may be enforced, on the application of the appropriate authority, by a mandatory order obtained in accordance with section 31 of the Senior Courts Act 1981.

(10) The appropriate authority is—

    (a) in relation to the responsible body of a school in England, the Secretary of State;

    (b) in relation to the responsible body of a school in Wales, the Welsh Ministers.

Supplementary

6 (1) This paragraph applies for the purposes of this Schedule.

(2) Regulations may prescribe services which are, or are not, to be regarded as being—

    (a) education;

    (b) a benefit, facility or service.

(3) The power to make regulations is exercisable by—

    (a) in relation to England, a Minister of the Crown;

    (b) in relation to Wales, the Welsh Ministers.

(4) 'Disabled pupil' includes a disabled person who may be admitted to the school as a pupil.

(5) 'Responsible body' means—

    (a) in relation to a maintained school or a maintained nursery school, the local authority or governing body;

    (b) in relation to a pupil referral unit, the local authority;

    (c) in relation to an independent educational institution [or an alternative provision Academy that is not an independent educational institution],[190] the proprietor;

    (d) in relation to a special school not maintained by a local authority, the proprietor.

(6) 'Governing body', in relation to a maintained school, means the body corporate (constituted in accordance with regulations under section 19 of the Education Act 2002) which the school has as a result of that section.

(7) 'Maintained school' has the meaning given in section 20 of the School Standards and Framework Act 1998; and 'maintained nursery school' has the meaning given in section 22 of that Act.

---

[190] Inserted by Alternative Provision Academies (Consequential Amendments to Acts) (England) Order 2012, SI 2012/976.

SCHEDULE 11   **Section 89**

SCHOOLS: EXCEPTIONS

PART 1
SEX DISCRIMINATION

Admission to single-sex schools

1   (1)   Section 85(1), so far as relating to sex, does not apply in relation to a single-sex school.
    (2)   A single-sex school is a school which—
          (a)   admits pupils of one sex only, or
          (b)   on the basis of the assumption in sub-paragraph (3), would be taken to admit pupils of one sex only.
    (3)   That assumption is that pupils of the opposite sex are to be disregarded if—
          (a)   their admission to the school is exceptional, or
          (b)   their numbers are comparatively small and their admission is confined to particular courses or classes.
    (4)   In the case of a school which is a single-sex school by virtue of subparagraph (3)(b), section 85(2)(a) to (d), so far as relating to sex, does not prohibit confining pupils of the same sex to particular courses or classes.

Single-sex boarding at schools

2   (1)   Section 85(1), so far as relating to sex, does not apply in relation to admission as a boarder to a school to which this paragraph applies.
    (2)   Section 85(2)(a) to (d), so far as relating to sex, does not apply in relation to boarding facilities at a school to which this paragraph applies.
    (3)   This paragraph applies to a school (other than a single-sex school) which has some pupils as boarders and others as non-boarders and which—
          (a)   admits as boarders pupils of one sex only, or
          (b)   on the basis of the assumption in sub-paragraph (4), would be taken to admit as boarders pupils of one sex only.
    (4)   That assumption is that pupils of the opposite sex admitted as boarders are to be disregarded if their numbers are small compared to the numbers of other pupils admitted as boarders.

Single-sex schools turning co-educational

3   (1)   If the responsible body of a single-sex school decides to alter its admissions arrangements so that the school will cease to be a single-sex school, the body may apply for a transitional exemption order in relation to the school.
    (2)   If the responsible body of a school to which paragraph 2 applies decides to alter its admissions arrangements so that the school will cease to be one to which that paragraph applies, the body may apply for a transitional exemption order in relation to the school.
    (3)   A transitional exemption order in relation to a school is an order which, during the period specified in the order as the transitional period, authorises—
          (a)   sex discrimination by the responsible body of the school in the arrangements it makes for deciding who is offered admission as a pupil;
          (b)   the responsible body, in the circumstances specified in the order, not to admit a person as a pupil because of the person's sex.

457

    (4) Paragraph 4 applies in relation to the making of transitional exemption orders.

    (5) The responsible body of a school does not contravene this Act, so far as relating to sex discrimination, if—

        (a) in accordance with a transitional exemption order, or

        (b) pending the determination of an application for a transitional exemption order in relation to the school, it does not admit a person as a pupil because of the person's sex.

4   (1) In the case of a maintained school within the meaning given by section 32 of the Education and Inspections Act 2006, a transitional exemption order may be made in accordance with such provision as is made in regulations under section 21 of that Act (orders made by local authority or adjudicator in relation to schools in England).

    (2) In the case of a school in Wales maintained by a local authority, a transitional exemption order may be made in accordance with [section 82 of, or Part 3 of Schedule 3 to, the School Standards and Organisation (Wales) Act 2013][191] (orders made by Welsh Ministers).

    (3) In the case of a school in Scotland managed by an education authority or in respect of which the managers are for the time being receiving grants under section 73(c) or (d) of the Education (Scotland) Act 1980—

        (a) the responsible body may submit to the Scottish Ministers an application for the making of a transitional exemption order, and

        (b) the Scottish Ministers may make the order.

    (4) [...][192]

    (5) [...][193]

    (6) In the case of a school in England or Wales not coming within sub-paragraph (1), (2), (4) or (5) or an independent school in Scotland—

        (a) the responsible body may submit to the Commission an application for the making of a transitional exemption order, and

        (b) the Commission may make the order.

    (7) An application under sub-paragraph (6) must specify—

        (a) the period proposed by the responsible body as the transitional period to be specified in the order,

        (b) the stages within that period by which the body proposes to move to the position where section 85(1)(a) and (c), so far as relating to sex, is complied with, and

        (c) any other matters relevant to the terms and operation of the order applied for.

    (8) The Commission must not make an order on an application under subparagraph (6) unless satisfied that the terms of the application are reasonable, having regard to—

        (a) the nature of the school's premises,

        (b) the accommodation, equipment and facilities available, and

        (c) the responsible body's financial resources.

---

[191] Substituted by School Standards and Organisation (Wales) Act 2013.

[192] Repealed by Equality Act 2010 (Consequential Amendments, Saving and Supplementary Provisions) Order 2010, SI 2010/2279.

[193] Repealed by School Standards and Organisation (Wales) Act 2013.

PART 2
RELIGIOUS OR BELIEF-RELATED DISCRIMINATION

School with religious character etc.

5   Section 85(1) and (2)(a) to (d), so far as relating to religion or belief, does not apply in
    relation to—
    (a) a school designated under section 69(3) of the School Standards and Framework Act
         1998 (foundation or voluntary school with religious character);
    (b) a school [(other than an alternative provision Academy)][194] listed in the register of inde-
         pendent schools for England or for Wales, if the school's entry in the register records that
         the school has a religious ethos;
    (c) a school transferred to an education authority under section 16 of the Education
         (Scotland) Act 1980 (transfer of certain schools to education authorities) which is con-
         ducted in the interest of a church or denominational body;
    (d) a school provided by an education authority under section 17(2) of that Act (denomina-
         tional schools);
    (e) a grant-aided school (within the meaning of that Act) which is conducted in the interest
         of a church or denominational body;
    (f) a school registered in the register of independent schools for Scotland if the school
         admits only pupils who belong, or whose parents belong, to one or more particular
         denominations;
    (g) a school registered in that register if the school is conducted in the interest of a church or
         denominational body.

Curriculum, worship, etc.

6   Section 85(2)(a) to (d), so far as relating to religion or belief, does not apply in relation to
    anything done in connection with acts of worship or other religious observance organised by
    or on behalf of a school (whether or not forming part of the curriculum).

Power to amend

7   (1) A Minister of the Crown may by order amend this Part of this Schedule—
        (a) so as to add, vary or omit an exception to section 85;
        (b) so as to make provision about the construction or application of section 19(2)(d) in
             relation to section 85.
    (2) The power under sub-paragraph (1) is exercisable only in relation to religious or belief-
         related discrimination.
    (3) Before making an order under this paragraph the Minister must consult—
        (a) the Welsh Ministers,
        (b) the Scottish Ministers, and
        (c) such other persons as the Minister thinks appropriate.

---

[194] Inserted by Alternative Provision Academies (Consequential Amendments to Acts) (England) Order
2012, SI 2012/976.

PART 3
DISABILITY DISCRIMINATION

Permitted form of selection

8   (1) A person does not contravene section 85(1), so far as relating to disability, only by applying a permitted form of selection.

(2) In relation to England and Wales, a permitted form of selection is—

   (a) in the case of a maintained school which is not designated as a grammar school under
section 104 of the School Standards and Framework Act 1998, a form of selection
mentioned in section 99(2) or (4) of that Act;

   (b) in the case of a maintained school which is so designated, its selective admission
arrangements (within the meaning of section 104 of that Act);

   (c) in the case of an independent educational institution, arrangements which provide
for some or all of its pupils to be selected by reference to general or special ability or
aptitude, with a view to admitting only pupils of high ability or aptitude.

(3) In relation to Scotland, a permitted form of selection is—

   (a) in the case of a school managed by an education authority, arrangements approved by
the Scottish Ministers for the selection of pupils for admission;

   (b) in the case of an independent school, arrangements which provide for some or all of
its pupils to be selected by reference to general or special ability or aptitude, with a
view to admitting only pupils of high ability or aptitude.

(4) 'Maintained school' has the meaning given in section 22 of the School Standards and
Framework Act 1998.

SCHEDULE 12   **Section 94**

FURTHER AND HIGHER EDUCATION EXCEPTIONS

PART 1
SINGLE-SEX INSTITUTIONS, ETC.

Admission to single-sex institutions

1   (1) Section 91(1), so far as relating to sex, does not apply in relation to a single-sex institution.

(2) A single-sex institution is an institution to which section 91 applies, which—

   (a) admits students of one sex only, or

   (b) on the basis of the assumption in sub-paragraph (3), would be taken to admit students of one sex only.

(3) That assumption is that students of the opposite sex are to be disregarded if—

   (a) their admission to the institution is exceptional, or

   (b) their numbers are comparatively small and their admission is confined to particular
courses or classes.

(4) In the case of an institution which is a single-sex institution by virtue of subparagraph (3)
(b), section 91(2)(a) to (d), so far as relating to sex, does not prohibit confining students
of the same sex to particular courses or classes.

Single-sex institutions turning co-educational

2   (1) If the responsible body of a single-sex institution decides to alter its admissions arrangements so that the institution will cease to be a single-sex institution, the body may apply for a transitional exemption order in relation to the institution.

    (2) A transitional exemption order relating to an institution is an order which, during the period specified in the order as the transitional period, authorises—

      (a) sex discrimination by the responsible body of the institution in the arrangements it makes for deciding who is offered admission as a student;

      (b) the responsible body, in the circumstances specified in the order, not to admit a person as a student because of the person's sex.

    (3) Paragraph 3 applies in relation to the making of a transitional exemption order.

    (4) The responsible body of an institution does not contravene this Act, so far as relating to sex discrimination, if—

      (a) in accordance with a transitional exemption order, or

      (b) pending the determination of an application for a transitional exemption order in relation to the institution, it does not admit a person as a student because of the person's sex.

    (5) The responsible body of an institution does not contravene this Act, so far as relating to sex discrimination, if—

      (a) in accordance with a transitional exemption order, or

      (b) pending the determination of an application for a transitional exemption order in relation to the institution, it discriminates in the arrangements it makes for deciding who is offered admission as a student.

3   (1) In the case of a single-sex institution—

      (a) its responsible body may submit to the Commission an application for the making of a transitional exemption order, and

      (b) the Commission may make the order.

    (2) An application under sub-paragraph (1) must specify—

      (a) the period proposed by the responsible body as the transitional period to be specified in the order,

      (b) the stages, within that period, by which the body proposes to move to the position where section 91(1)(a) and (c), so far as relating to sex, is complied with, and

      (c) any other matters relevant to the terms and operation of the order applied for.

    (3) The Commission must not make an order on an application under subparagraph (1) unless satisfied that the terms of the application are reasonable, having regard to—

      (a) the nature of the institution's premises,

      (b) the accommodation, equipment and facilities available, and

      (c) the responsible body's financial resources.

PART 2
OTHER EXCEPTIONS

Occupational requirements

4   A person (P) does not contravene section 91(1) or (2) if P shows that P's treatment of another person relates only to training that would help fit that other person for work the offer of which the other person could be refused in reliance on Part 1 of Schedule 9.

Institutions with a religious ethos

5 (1) The responsible body of an institution which is designated for the purposes of this paragraph does not contravene section 91(1), so far as relating to religion or belief, if, in the admission of students to a course at the institution—

   (a) it gives preference to persons of a particular religion or belief,

   (b) it does so to preserve the institution's religious ethos, and

   (c) the course is not a course of vocational training.

   (2) A Minister of the Crown may by order designate an institution if satisfied that the institution has a religious ethos.

Benefits dependent on marital status, etc.

6 A person does not contravene section 91, so far as relating to sexual orientation, by providing married persons and civil partners (to the exclusion of all other persons) with access to a benefit, facility or service.

Child care

7 (1) A person does not contravene section 91(2)(b) or (d), so far as relating to age, only by providing, or making arrangements for or facilitating the provision of, care for children of a particular age group.

   (2) Facilitating the provision of care for a child includes—

   (a) paying for some or all of the cost of the provision;

   (b) helping a parent of the child to find a suitable person to provide care for the child;

   (c) enabling a parent of the child to spend more time providing care for the child or otherwise assisting the parent with respect to the care that the parent provides for the child.

   (3) A child is a person who has not attained the age of 17.

   (4) A reference to care includes a reference to supervision.

SCHEDULE 13   Section 98

EDUCATION: REASONABLE ADJUSTMENTS

Preliminary

1 This Schedule applies where a duty to make reasonable adjustments is imposed on A by this Part.

The duty for schools

2 (1) This paragraph applies where A is the responsible body of a school to which section 85 applies.

   (2) A must comply with the first and third requirements.

   (3) For the purposes of this paragraph—

   (a) the reference in section 20(3) to a provision, criterion or practice is a reference to a provision, criterion or practice applied by or on behalf of A;

   (b) the reference in section 20(3) or (5) to a disabled person is—

      (i) in relation to a relevant matter within sub-paragraph (4)(a), a reference to disabled persons generally;

        (ii) in relation to a relevant matter within sub-paragraph (4)(b), a reference to disabled pupils generally.

(4) In relation to each requirement, the relevant matters are—
  (a) deciding who is offered admission as a pupil;
  (b) provision of education or access to a benefit, facility or service.

The duty for further or higher education institutions

3 (1) This paragraph applies where A is the responsible body of an institution to which section 91 applies.
  (2) A must comply with the first, second and third requirements.
  (3) For the purposes of this paragraph—
    (a) the reference in section 20(3) to a provision, criterion or practice is a reference to a provision, criterion or practice applied by or on behalf of A;
    (b) the reference in section 20(4) to a physical feature is a reference to a physical feature of premises occupied by A;
    (c) the reference in section 20(3), (4) or (5) to a disabled person is—
      (i) in relation to a relevant matter within sub-paragraph (4)(a), a reference to disabled persons generally;
      (ii) in relation to a relevant matter within sub-paragraph (4)(b) or (c), a reference to disabled students generally;
      (iii) in relation to a relevant matter within sub-paragraph (4)(d) or (e) below, a reference to an interested disabled person.
  (4) In relation to each requirement, the relevant matters are—
    (a) deciding who is offered admission as a student;
    (b) provision of education;
    (c) access to a benefit, facility or service;
    (d) deciding on whom a qualification is conferred;
    (e) a qualification that A confers.

4 (1) An interested disabled person is a disabled person who, in relation to a relevant matter specified in the first column of the table, is of a description specified in the second column.

Case	Description of disabled person
Deciding upon whom to confer a qualification.	A person who is, or has notified A that the person may be, an applicant for the conferment of the qualification.
A qualification that A confers.	An applicant for the conferment by A of the qualification.
	A person on whom A confers the qualification.

  (2) A provision, criterion or practice does not include the application of a competence standard.
  (3) A competence standard is an academic, medical or other standard applied for the purpose of determining whether or not a person has a particular level of competence or ability.

The duty relating to certain other further or higher education courses

5 (1) This paragraph applies where A is the responsible body in relation to a course to which section 92 applies.
  (2) A must comply with the first, second and third requirements; but if A is the governing body of a maintained school (within the meaning given by that section), A is not required to comply with the second requirement.

(3) For the purposes of this paragraph—

    (a) the reference in section 20(3) to a provision, criterion or practice is a reference to a provision, criterion or practice applied by or on behalf of A;

    (b) the reference in section 20(4) to a physical feature is a reference to a physical feature of premises occupied by A;

    (c) the reference in section 20(3), (4) or (5) to a disabled person is—

        (i) in relation to a relevant matter within sub-paragraph (4)(a), a reference to disabled persons generally;

        (ii) in relation to a relevant matter within sub-paragraph (4)(b), a reference to disabled persons generally who are enrolled on the course.

(4) In relation to each requirement, the relevant matters are—

    (a) arrangements for enrolling persons on a course of further or higher education secured by A;

    (b) services provided by A for persons enrolled on the course.

The duty relating to recreational or training facilities

6 (1) This paragraph applies where A is the responsible body in relation to facilities to which section 93 applies.

    (2) A must comply with the first, second and third requirements.

    (3) For the purposes of this paragraph—

        (a) the reference in section 20(3) to a provision, criterion or practice is a reference to a provision, criterion or practice applied by or on behalf of A;

        (b) the reference in section 20(4) to a physical feature is a reference to a physical feature of premises occupied by A;

        (c) the reference in section 20(3), (4) or (5) to a disabled person is a reference to disabled persons generally.

    (4) In relation to each requirement, the relevant matter is A's arrangements for providing the recreational or training facilities.

Code of practice

7 In deciding whether it is reasonable for A to have to take a step for the purpose of complying with the first, second or third requirement, A must have regard to relevant provisions of a code of practice issued under section 14 of the Equality Act 2006.

Confidentiality requests

8 (1) This paragraph applies if a person has made a confidentiality request of which A is aware.

    (2) In deciding whether it is reasonable for A to have to take a step in relation to that person so as to comply with the first, second or third requirement, A must have regard to the extent to which taking the step is consistent with the request.

    (3) In a case within paragraph 2, a 'confidentiality request' is a request—

        (a) that the nature or existence of a disabled person's disability be treated as confidential, and

        (b) which satisfies either of the following conditions.

    (4) The first condition is that the request is made by the person's parent.

    (5) The second condition is that—

        (a) it is made by the person, and

        (b) A reasonably believes that the person has sufficient understanding of the nature and effect of the request.

(6) In a case within paragraph 3, a 'confidentiality request' is a request by a disabled person that the nature or existence of the person's disability be treated as confidential.

The duty for general qualifications bodies

9 (1) This paragraph applies where A is a qualifications body for the purposes of section 96.

(2) Paragraphs 3 and 4(1), so far as relating to qualifications, apply to a qualifications body as they apply to a responsible body.

(3) This paragraph is subject to section 96(7).

SCHEDULE 14   **Section 99**

EDUCATIONAL CHARITIES AND ENDOWMENTS

Educational charities

1 (1) This paragraph applies to a trust deed or other instrument—

(a) which concerns property applicable for or in connection with the provision of education in an establishment in England and Wales to which section 85 or 91 applies, and

(b) which in any way restricts the benefits available under the instrument to persons of one sex.

(2) Sub-paragraph (3) applies if, on the application of the trustees or the responsible body (within the meaning of that section), a Minister of the Crown is satisfied that the removal or modification of the restriction would be conducive to the advancement of education without sex discrimination.

(3) The Minister may by order make such modifications of the instrument as appear to the Minister expedient for removing or modifying the restriction.

(4) If the trust was created by a gift or bequest, an order must not be made until the end of the period of 25 years after the date when the gift or bequest took effect.

(5) Sub-paragraph (4) does not apply if the donor or the personal representatives of the donor or testator consent in writing to making the application for the order.

(6) The Minister must require the applicant to publish a notice—

(a) containing particulars of the proposed order;

(b) stating that representations may be made to the Minister within a period specified in the notice.

(7) The period must be not less than one month beginning with the day after the date of the notice.

(8) The applicant must publish the notice in the manner specified by the Minister.

(9) The cost of publication may be paid out of the property of the trust.

(10) Before making the order, the Minister must take account of representations made in accordance with the notice.

Educational endowments

2 (1) This paragraph applies to an educational endowment—

(a) to which section 104 of the Education (Scotland) Act 1980 applies, and

(b) which in any way restricts the benefit of the endowment to persons of one sex.

(2) Sub-paragraph (3) applies if, on the application of the governing body of an educational endowment, the Scottish Ministers are satisfied that the removal or modification of the

465

provision which restricts the benefit of the endowment to persons of one sex would be conducive to the advancement of education without sex discrimination.

(3) The Scottish Ministers may by order make such provision as they think expedient for removing or modifying the restriction.

(4) If the Scottish Ministers propose to make such an order they must publish a notice in such manner as they think sufficient for giving information to persons they think may be interested in the endowment—

   (a) containing particulars of the proposed order;

   (b) stating that representations may be made with respect to the proposal within such period as is specified in the notice.

(5) The period must be not less than one month beginning with the day after the date of publication of the notice.

(6) The cost of publication is to be paid out of the funds of the endowment to which the notice relates.

(7) Before making an order, the Scottish Ministers—

   (a) must consider representations made in accordance with the notice;

   (b) may cause a local inquiry to be held into the representations under section 67 of the Education (Scotland) Act 1980.

(8) A reference to an educational endowment includes a reference to—

   (a) a scheme made or approved for the endowment under Part 6 of the Education (Scotland) Act 1980;

   (b) in the case of an endowment the governing body of which is entered in the Scottish Charity Register, a scheme approved for the endowment under section 39 or 40 of the Charities and Trustee Investment (Scotland) Act 2005 (asp 10);

   (c) an endowment which is, by virtue of section 108(1) of the Education (Scotland) Act 1980, treated as if it were an educational endowment (or which would, but for the disapplication of that section by section 122(4) of that Act, be so treated);

   (d) a university endowment, the Carnegie Trust, a theological endowment and a new endowment.

(9) Expressions used in this paragraph and in Part 6 of the Education (Scotland) Act 1980 have the same meaning in this paragraph as in that Part.

SCHEDULE 15   Section 107

ASSOCIATIONS: REASONABLE ADJUSTMENTS

Preliminary

1   This Schedule applies where a duty to make reasonable adjustments is imposed on an association (A) by this Part.

The duty

2   (1) A must comply with the first, second and third requirements.

   (2) For the purposes of this paragraph, the reference in section 20(3), (4) or (5) to a disabled person is a reference to disabled persons who—

     (a) are, or are seeking to become or might wish to become, members,

     (b) are associates, or

     (c) are, or are likely to become, guests.

(3) Section 20 has effect as if, in subsection (4), for 'to avoid the disadvantage' there were substituted—
  '(a) to avoid the disadvantage, or
  (b) to adopt a reasonable alternative method of affording access to the benefit, facility or service or of admitting persons to membership or inviting persons as guests.'
(4) In relation to the first and third requirements, the relevant matters are—
  (a) access to a benefit, facility or service;
  (b) members' or associates' retaining their rights as such or avoiding having them varied;
  (c) being admitted to membership or invited as a guest.
(5) In relation to the second requirement, the relevant matters are—
  (a) access to a benefit, facility or service;
  (b) being admitted to membership or invited as a guest.
(6) In relation to the second requirement, a physical feature includes a physical feature brought by or on behalf of A, in the course of or for the purpose of providing a benefit, facility or service, on to premises other than those that A occupies (as well as including a physical feature in or on premises that A occupies).
(7) Nothing in this paragraph requires A to take a step which would fundamentally alter—
  (a) the nature of the benefit, facility or service concerned, or
  (b) the nature of the association.
(8) Nor does anything in this paragraph require a member or associate in whose house meetings of the association take place to make adjustments to a physical feature of the house.

SCHEDULE 16   Section 107

ASSOCIATIONS: EXCEPTIONS

Single characteristic associations

1 (1) An association does not contravene section 101(1) by restricting membership to persons who share a protected characteristic.
  (2) An association that restricts membership to persons who share a protected characteristic does not breach section 101(3) by restricting the access by associates to a benefit, facility or service to such persons as share the characteristic.
  (3) An association that restricts membership to persons who share a protected characteristic does not breach section 102(1) by inviting as guests, or by permitting to be invited as guests, only such persons as share the characteristic.
  (4) Sub-paragraphs (1) to (3), so far as relating to race, do not apply in relation to colour.
  (5) This paragraph does not apply to an association that is a registered political party.

[*Age*

1A.—
  (1) An association does not contravene section 101(1) or (2), so far as relating to age discrimination, by giving a concession on admission to membership for—
    (a) persons of a particular age group, or
    (b) persons who have been members of the association for more than a number of years specified by the association for this purpose.

(2) An association does not contravene section 101(2) or (3), so far as relating to age discrimination, by giving a concession on access to a benefit, facility or service for—

    (a) members of a particular age group, or

    (b) persons who have been members of the association for more than a number of years specified by the association for this purpose.

(3) An association does not contravene section 102(1), so far as relating to age discrimination, by giving a concession on invitations of persons of a particular age group as guests.

(4) An association does not contravene section 102(2), so far as relating to age discrimination, by giving a concession on access to a benefit, facility or service for guests of a particular age group.

(5) For the purposes of this paragraph, affording only persons of a particular age group access to a benefit, facility or service for a limited time is to be regarded as a concession.

(6) The reference to a concession in respect of something done by an association is a reference to a benefit, right or privilege having the effect that the manner in which, or the terms on which, it does it are more favourable than the manner in which, or the terms on which, it usually does the thing.][195]

Health and safety

2 (1) An association (A) does not discriminate against a pregnant woman in contravention of section 101(1)(b) because she is pregnant if—

    (a) the terms on which A is prepared to admit her to membership include a term intended to remove or reduce a risk to her health or safety,

    (b) A reasonably believes that admitting her to membership on terms which do not include that term would create a risk to her health or safety,

    (c) the terms on which A is prepared to admit persons with other physical conditions to membership include a term intended to remove or reduce a risk to their health or safety, and

    (d) A reasonably believes that admitting them to membership on terms which do not include that term would create a risk to their health or safety.

(2) Sub-paragraph (1) applies to section 102(1)(b) as it applies to section 101(1)(b); and for that purpose a reference to admitting a person to membership is to be read as a reference to inviting the person as a guest or permitting the person to be invited as a guest.

(3) An association (A) does not discriminate against a pregnant woman in contravention of section 101(2)(a) or (3)(a) or 102(2)(a) because she is pregnant if—

    (a) the way in which A affords her access to a benefit, facility or service is intended to remove or reduce a risk to her health or safety,

    (b) A reasonably believes that affording her access to the benefit, facility or service otherwise than in that way would create a risk to her health or safety,

    (c) A affords persons with other physical conditions access to the benefit, facility or service in a way that is intended to remove or reduce a risk to their health or safety, and

    (d) A reasonably believes that affording them access to the benefit, facility or service otherwise than in that way would create a risk to their health or safety.

(4) An association (A) which does not afford a pregnant woman access to a benefit, facility or service does not discriminate against her in contravention of section 101(2)(a) or (3)(a) or 102(2)(a) because she is pregnant if—

    (a) A reasonably believes that affording her access to the benefit, facility or service would, because she is pregnant, create a risk to her health or safety,

---

[195] Inserted by Equality Act 2010 (Age Exceptions) Order 2012, SI 2012/2466.

(b) A does not afford persons with other physical conditions access to the benefit, facility or service, and

(c) the reason for not doing so is that A reasonably believes that affording them access to the benefit, facility or service would create a risk to their health or safety.

(5) An association (A) does not discriminate against a pregnant woman under section 101(2) (c) or (3)(c) because she is pregnant if—

(a) the variation of A's terms of membership, or rights as an associate, is intended to remove or reduce a risk to her health or safety,

(b) A reasonably believes that not making the variation to A's terms or rights would create a risk to her health or safety,

(c) A varies the terms of membership, or rights as an associate, of persons with other physical conditions,

(d) the variation of their terms or rights is intended to remove or reduce a risk to their health or safety, and

(e) A reasonably believes that not making the variation to their terms or rights would create a risk to their health or safety.

SCHEDULE 17   **Section 116**

DISABLED PUPILS: ENFORCEMENT

PART 1
INTRODUCTORY

1   In this Schedule—
'the Tribunal' means—
(a) in relation to a school in England, the First-tier Tribunal;
(b) in relation to a school in Wales, the Special Educational Needs Tribunal for Wales;
(c) in relation to a school in Scotland, [the First-tier Tribunal for Scotland][196];
'the English Tribunal' means the First-tier Tribunal;
'the Welsh Tribunal' means the Special Educational Needs Tribunal for Wales;
'the Scottish Tribunal' means [the First-tier Tribunal for Scotland][197];
'responsible body' is to be construed in accordance with section 85.

PART 2
TRIBUNALS IN ENGLAND AND WALES

Introductory

2   This Part of this Schedule applies in relation to the English Tribunal and the Welsh Tribunal.

---

[196] Substituted by First-tier Tribunal for Scotland (Transfer of Functions of the Additional Support Needs Tribunals for Scotland) Regulations 2018, SI 2018/4.

[197] Substituted by First-tier Tribunal for Scotland (Transfer of Functions of the Additional Support Needs Tribunals for Scotland) Regulations 2018, SI 2018/4.

Jurisdiction [—England and Wales][198]

3   A claim that a responsible body has contravened Chapter 1 of Part 6 because of a person's disability may be made [—
   (a) to the English Tribunal by the person's parent or, if the person is over compulsory school age, the person;
   (b) to the Welsh Tribunal by the person's parent.][199]

[Jurisdiction—Wales

3A (1) A claim that a responsible body for a school in Wales has contravened Chapter 1 of Part 6 in relation to a person because of disability may be made to the Tribunal by that person ('the relevant person').
   (2) But this paragraph does not apply to a claim to which paragraph 13 or 14 applies.
   (3) The relevant person's right to claim is exercisable concurrently with the right of the relevant person's parent under paragraph 3.
   (4) The exercise of rights under this paragraph is subject to provision made by regulations under paragraphs 6 and 6A.][200]

Time for bringing proceedings

4   (1) Proceedings on a claim may not be brought after the end of the period of 6 months starting with the date when the conduct complained of occurred.
   (2) [...][201]
   [(2A) If, in relation to proceedings or prospective proceedings on a claim under paragraph 3 or 3A, the dispute is referred for resolution in pursuance of arrangements under paragraph 6C [...][202] before the end of the period of 6 months mentioned in subparagraph (1), that period is extended by 3 months.][203]
   (3) The Tribunal may consider a claim which is out of time.
   (4) Sub-paragraph (3) does not apply if the Tribunal has previously decided under that sub-paragraph not to consider a claim.
   (5) For the purposes of sub-paragraph (1)—
      (a) if the contravention is attributable to a term in a contract, the conduct is to be treated as extending throughout the duration of the contract;
      (b) conduct extending over a period is to be treated as occurring at the end of the period;
      (c) failure to do something is to be treated as occurring when the person in question decided on it.
   (6) In the absence of evidence to the contrary, a person (P) is to be taken to decide on failure to do something—
      (a) when P acts inconsistently with doing it, or
      (b) if P does not act inconsistently, on the expiry of the period in which P might reasonably have been expected to do it.

---

[198] Inserted by Education (Wales) Measure 2009.
[199] Substituted by Children and Families Act 2014.
[200] Inserted by Education (Wales) Measure 2009.
[201] Repealed by Enterprise and Regulatory Reform Act 2013.
[202] Repealed by Enterprise and Regulatory Reform Act 2013.
[203] Inserted by Education (Wales) Measure 2009.

Powers

5 (1) This paragraph applies if the Tribunal finds that the contravention has occurred.

(2) The Tribunal may make such order as it thinks fit.

(3) The power under sub-paragraph (2)—

(a) may, in particular, be exercised with a view to obviating or reducing the adverse effect on the person of any matter to which the claim relates;

(b) does not include power to order the payment of compensation.

Procedure

6 (1) This paragraph applies in relation to the Welsh Tribunal.

(2) The Welsh Ministers may by regulations make provision as to—

(a) the proceedings on a claim under paragraph 3 [or 3A];[204]

(b) the making of a claim.

(3) The regulations may, in particular, include provision—

(a) as to the manner in which a claim must be made;

(b) for enabling functions relating to preliminary or incidental matters (including in particular a decision under paragraph 4(3) to be performed by the President or by the person occupying the chair);

(c) enabling hearings to be conducted in the absence of a member other than the person occupying the chair;

[(ca) for adding and substituting parties;][205]

(d) as to persons who may appear on behalf of the parties;

(e) for granting such rights to disclosure or inspection of documents or to further particulars as may be granted by the county court;

(f) requiring persons to attend to give evidence and produce documents;

(g) for authorising the administration of oaths to witnesses;

(h) for deciding claims without a hearing in prescribed circumstances;

(i) as to the withdrawal of claims;

(j) for enabling the Tribunal to stay proceedings;

(k) for the award of costs or expenses;

(l) for settling costs or expenses (and, in particular, for enabling costs to be assessed in the county court);

(m) for the registration and proof of decisions and orders;

(n) for enabling prescribed decisions to be reviewed, or prescribed orders to be varied or revoked, in such circumstances as may be decided in accordance with the regulations.

(4) Proceedings must be held in private, except in prescribed circumstances.

(5) The Welsh Ministers may pay such allowances for the purpose of or in connection with the attendance of persons at the Tribunal as they may decide.

(6) Part 1 of the Arbitration Act 1996 does not apply to the proceedings, but regulations may make provision in relation to such proceedings that corresponds to a provision of that Part.

(7) The regulations may make provision for a claim to be heard, in prescribed circumstances, with an appeal under Part 4 of the Education Act 1996 (special educational needs).

---

[204] Inserted by Education (Wales) Measure 2009.
[205] Inserted by Education (Wales) Measure 2009.

(8) A person commits an offence by failing to comply with—

    (a) a requirement in respect of the disclosure or inspection of documents imposed by virtue of sub-paragraph (3)(e), or

    (b) a requirement imposed by virtue of sub-paragraph (3)(f).

(9) A person guilty of the offence is liable on summary conviction to a fine not exceeding level 3 on the standard scale.

[Case friends—Wales

6A

(1) The Welsh Ministers may by regulations provide for—

    (a) a disabled child in a local authority area in Wales to have a person to make representations on behalf of the disabled child with a view to avoiding or resolving disagreements about contraventions of Chapter 1 of Part 6; and

    (b) a relevant person (within the meaning of paragraph 3A) to have another person to exercise the relevant person's rights under that paragraph on the relevant person's behalf.

(2) A person exercising rights or making representations on behalf of a disabled child or a relevant person under sub-paragraph (1) is referred to in this Schedule as a 'case friend'.

(3) A case friend must—

    (a) make representations and exercise rights fairly and competently;

    (b) have no interest adverse to that of the disabled child or relevant person;

    (c) ensure that all steps and decisions taken by the case friend are for the benefit of the disabled child or relevant person and take account of the disabled child or relevant person's views.

(4) Regulations made under this paragraph may (among other things)—

    (a) confer functions on the Welsh Tribunal;

    (b) make provision about procedures in relation to case friends;

    (c) make provision about the appointment and removal of case friends;

    (d) specify the circumstances in which a person may or may not act as a case friend;

    (e) specify the circumstances in which a relevant person (within the meaning of paragraph 3A) must have a case friend;

    (f) specify further requirements in respect of the conduct of case friends.

(5) In this paragraph and in paragraphs 6B, 6C, 6D and 6E, 'local authority' has the meaning given in section 89(10).

(6) In this paragraph and in paragraphs 6B, 6C and 6D—

'disabled child' means any disabled person who is a pupil (or a prospective pupil) of—

    (a) a maintained school or maintained nursery school,

    (b) a pupil referral unit,

    (c) an independent school, or

    (d) a special school not maintained by a local authority;

'proprietor' has the meaning given in section 89(4);

'school' has the meanings given in section 89(5).

(7) In sub-paragraph (6)—

'independent school' has the meaning given in section 89(8);

'maintained school' has the meaning given in section 20(7) of the School Standards and Framework Act 1998;

'maintained nursery school' has the meaning given in section 22(9) of the School Standards and Framework Act 1998;

'pupil' has the meanings given in section 89(3);

'pupil referral unit' has the meaning given in section 19 of the Education Act 1996; and

'special school' has the meaning given in section 89(9)].[206]

[Advice and information—Wales

6B

(1) A local authority in Wales must arrange for any disabled child in its area and for the case friend of any such child to be provided with advice and information about matters relating to disability discrimination in schools.

(2) In making the arrangements, the local authority must have regard to any guidance given by the Welsh Ministers.

(3) The arrangements must comply with any provisions made in regulations by the Welsh Ministers that relate to the arrangements.

(4) The local authority must take such steps as it considers appropriate for making the services provided under sub-paragraph (1) known to—
 (a) disabled children in its area,
 (b) parents of disabled children in its area,
 (c) head teachers and proprietors of schools in its area, and
 (d) such other persons as it considers appropriate.][207]

[Resolution of disputes—Wales

6C

(1) A local authority in Wales must make arrangements with a view to avoiding or resolving disagreements between responsible bodies and disabled children in its area about contraventions of Chapter 1 of Part 6.

(2) The arrangements must provide for the appointment of independent persons with the functions of facilitating the avoidance or resolution of such disagreements.

(3) In making the arrangements, the local authority must have regard to any guidance given by the Welsh Ministers.

(4) The arrangements must comply with any provisions made in regulations by the Welsh Ministers that relate to the arrangements.

(5) The local authority must take such steps as it considers appropriate for making the arrangements under sub-paragraph (1) known to—
 (a) disabled children in its area,
 (b) parents of disabled children in its area,
 (c) head teachers and proprietors of schools in its area, and
 (d) such other persons as it considers appropriate.

(6) The arrangements cannot affect the entitlement of any person to make a claim to the Tribunal, and the local authority must take such steps as it considers appropriate to make that fact known to disabled children, to parents of disabled children and to case friends for disabled children in its area.][208]

---

[206] Inserted by Education (Wales) Measure 2009.

[207] Inserted by Education (Wales) Measure 2009.

[208] Inserted by Education (Wales) Measure 2009.

[Independent advocacy services—Wales

6D

(1) Every local authority in Wales must—
   (a) make arrangements for the provision of independent advocacy services in its area;
   (b) refer any disabled child in its area who requests independent advocacy services to a service provider;
   (c) refer any person who is a case friend for a disabled child in its area and who requests independent advocacy services to a service provider.

(2) In this paragraph 'independent advocacy services' are services providing advice and assistance (by way of representation or otherwise) to a disabled child who is—
   (a) making, or intending to make a claim that a responsible body has contravened Chapter 1 of Part 6 because of the child's disability; or
   (b) considering whether to make such a claim; or
   (c) taking part in or intending to take part in dispute resolution arrangements made under paragraph 6C.

(3) In making arrangements under this paragraph, every local authority must have regard to the principle that any services provided under the arrangements must be independent of any person who is—
   (a) the subject of a claim to the Tribunal, or
   (b) involved in investigating or adjudicating on such a claim.

(4) The arrangements must comply with any provisions made in regulations by the Welsh Ministers that relate to the arrangements.

(5) Every local authority in Wales must take such steps as it considers appropriate for making the arrangements under this paragraph known to—
   (a) disabled children in its area,
   (b) parents of disabled children in its area,
   (c) head teachers and proprietors of schools in its area, and
   (d) such other persons as it considers appropriate.

(6) The arrangements may include provision for payments to be made to, or in relation to, any person carrying out functions in accordance with the arrangements.

(7) A local authority must have regard to any guidance given from time to time by the Welsh Ministers.][209]

[Power of direction—Wales

6E

(1) If the Welsh Ministers are satisfied (whether on a complaint or otherwise) that a local authority—
   (a) has acted, or is proposing to act, unreasonably in the discharge of a duty imposed by or under paragraph 6B, 6C or 6D, or
   (b) has failed to discharge a duty imposed by or under any of those paragraphs,
   they may give that local authority such directions as to the discharge of the duty as appear to them to be expedient.

(2) A direction may be given under subparagraph (1) even if the performance of the duty is contingent on the opinion of the local authority.

(3) A direction—
   (a) may be varied or revoked by the Welsh Ministers;

---

[209] Inserted by Education (Wales) Measure 2009.

(b) may be enforced, on the application of the Welsh Ministers, by a mandatory order obtained in accordance with section 31 of the Senior Courts Act 1981.][210]

PART 3
TRIBUNALS IN SCOTLAND

Introductory

7   This Part of this Schedule applies in relation to the Scottish Tribunal.

Jurisdiction

8   A claim that a responsible body has contravened Chapter 1 of Part 6 because of a person's disability may be made to the Tribunal by—
   (a) the person's parent;
   (b) where the person has capacity to make the claim, the person.

Powers

9   (1) This paragraph applies if the Tribunal finds the contravention has occurred.
     (2) The Tribunal may make such order as it thinks fit.
     (3) The power under sub-paragraph (2)—
         (a) may, in particular, be exercised with a view to obviating or reducing the adverse effect on the person of any matter to which the claim relates;
         (b) does not include power to order the payment of compensation.

Procedure etc.

10   (1) The Scottish Ministers may make rules as to—
         (a) the proceedings on a claim under paragraph 8;
         (b) the making of a claim.
     (2) The rules may, in particular, include provision for or in connection with—
         (a) the form and manner in which a claim must be made;
         (b) the time within which a claim is to be made;
         (c) the withdrawal of claims;
         (d) the recovery and inspection of documents;
         (e) the persons who may appear on behalf of the parties;
         (f) the persons who may be present at proceedings alongside any party or witness to support the party or witness;
         (g) enabling specified persons other than the parties to appear or be represented in specified circumstances;
         (h) requiring specified persons to give notice to other specified persons of specified matters;
         (i) the time within which any such notice must be given;
         (j) enabling Tribunal proceedings to be conducted in the absence of any member of a Tribunal other than the convener;
         (k) enabling any matters that are preliminary or incidental to the determination of proceedings to be determined by the convenor of a Tribunal alone or with such other members of the Tribunal as may be specified;

---

[210] Inserted by Education (Wales) Measure 2009.

(l)   enabling Tribunals to be held in private;

(m) enabling a Tribunal to exclude any person from attending all or part of Tribunal proceedings;

(n)   enabling a Tribunal to impose reporting restrictions in relation to all or part of Tribunal proceedings;

(o)   enabling a Tribunal to determine specified matters without holding a hearing;

(p)   the recording and publication of decisions and orders of a Tribunal;

(q)   enabling a Tribunal to commission medical and other reports in specified circumstances;

(r)   requiring a Tribunal to take specified actions, or to determine specified proceedings, within specified periods;

(s)   enabling a Tribunal to make an award of expenses;

(t)   the taxation or assessment of such expenses;

(u)   enabling a Tribunal, in specified circumstances, to review, or to vary or revoke, any of its decisions, orders or awards;

(v)   enabling a Tribunal, in specified circumstances, to review the decisions, orders or awards of another Tribunal and take such action (including variation and revocation) in respect of those decisions, orders or awards as it thinks fit.

Appeals

11 […]²¹¹

Amendment of Education (Additional Support for Learning) (Scotland) Act 2004

12 The Education (Additional Support for Learning) (Scotland) Act 2004 (asp 4) is amended as follows—

(a)   in section 17(1), omit 'to exercise the functions which are conferred on a Tribunal by virtue of this Act';

(b)   after section 17(1), insert—

'(1A) Tribunals are to exercise the functions which are conferred on them by virtue of—

(a)   this Act, and

(b)   the Equality Act 2010';

(c)   in the definition of 'Tribunal functions' in paragraph 1 of Schedule 1, after 'Act' insert 'or the Equality Act 2010'.

PART 4

ADMISSIONS AND EXCLUSIONS

Admissions

13 (1) This paragraph applies if appeal arrangements have been made in relation to admissions decisions.

(2) A claim that a responsible body has, because of a person's disability, contravened Chapter 1 of Part 6 in respect of an admissions decision must be made under the appeal arrangements.

---

²¹¹ Repealed by First-tier Tribunal for Scotland (Transfer of Functions of the Additional Support Needs Tribunals for Scotland) Regulations 2018, SI 2018/4.

(3) The body hearing the claim has the powers it has in relation to an appeal under the appeal arrangements.

(4) Appeal arrangements are arrangements under—

    (a) section 94 of the School Standards and Framework Act 1998, or

    (b) [Academy arrangements (as defined in section 1 of the Academies Act 2010) between the responsible body for an Academy and the Secretary of State],[212] enabling an appeal to be made by the person's parent against the decision.

(5) An admissions decision is—

    (a) a decision of a kind mentioned in section 94(1) or (2) of the School Standards and Framework Act 1998;

    (b) a decision as to the admission of a person to an [Academy school or an alternative provision Academy][213] taken by the responsible body or on its behalf.

Exclusions[: Wales][214]

14 (1) This paragraph applies if appeal arrangements have been made in relation to exclusion decisions [that are made in relation to schools in Wales].[215]

(2) A claim that a responsible body has, because of a person's disability, contravened Chapter 1 of Part 6 in respect of an exclusion decision must be made under the appeal arrangements.

(3) The body hearing the claim has the powers it has in relation to an appeal under the appeal arrangements.

[(4) Appeal arrangements are arrangements under section 52(3) of the Education Act 2002 enabling an appeal to be made against an exclusion decision.][216]

(5) An exclusion decision is—

    (a) a decision of a kind mentioned in 52(3) of the Education Act 2002 [.]

    (b) […][217]

(6) 'Responsible body', in relation to a maintained school, includes the discipline committee of the governing body if that committee is required to be established as a result of regulations made under section 19 of the Education Act 2002.

(7) 'Maintained school' has the meaning given in section 20(7) of the School Standards and Framework Act 1998.

SCHEDULE 18   **Section 149**

PUBLIC SECTOR EQUALITY DUTY: EXCEPTIONS

Children

1 (1) Section 149, so far as relating to age, does not apply to the exercise of a function relating to—

    (a) the provision of education to pupils in schools;

    (b) the provision of benefits, facilities or services to pupils in schools;

---

[212] Substituted by Education Act 2011.
[213] Substituted by Education Act 2011.
[214] Inserted by Education Act 2011.
[215] Inserted by Education Act 2011.
[216] Substituted by Education Act 2011.
[217] Repealed by Education Act 2011.

      (c)   the provision of accommodation, benefits, facilities or services in community homes pursuant to section 53(1) of the Children Act 1989;

      (d)   the provision of accommodation, benefits, facilities or services pursuant to arrangements under section 82(5) of that Act (arrangements by the Secretary of State relating to the accommodation of children);

      (e)   the provision of accommodation, benefits, facilities or services in residential establishments pursuant to section 26(1)(b) of the Children (Scotland) Act 1995.

  (2) 'Pupil' and 'school' each have the same meaning as in Chapter 1 of Part 6.

Immigration

2   (1) In relation to the exercise of immigration and nationality functions, section 149 has effect as if subsection (1)(b) did not apply to the protected characteristics of age, race or religion or belief; but for that purpose 'race' means race so far as relating to—

      (a)   nationality, or

      (b)   ethnic or national origins.

  (2) 'Immigration and nationality functions' means functions exercisable by virtue of—

      (a)   the Immigration Acts (excluding sections 28A to 28K of the Immigration Act 1971 so far as they relate to criminal offences),

      (b)   the British Nationality Act 1981,

      (c)   the British Nationality (Falkland Islands) Act 1983,

      (d)   the British Nationality (Hong Kong) Act 1990,

      (e)   the Hong Kong (War Wives and Widows) Act 1996,

      (f)   the British Nationality (Hong Kong) Act 1997,

      (g)   the Special Immigration Appeals Commission Act 1997, or

      (h)   a provision made under section 2(2) of the European Communities Act 1972, or of [EU law],[218] which relates to the subject matter of an enactment within paragraphs (a) to (g).

Judicial functions, etc.

3   (1) Section 149 does not apply to the exercise of—

      (a)   a judicial function;

      (b)   a function exercised on behalf of, or on the instructions of, a person exercising a judicial function.

  (2) The references to a judicial function include a reference to a judicial function conferred on a person other than a court or tribunal.

Exceptions that are specific to section 149(2)

4   (1) Section 149(2) (application of section 149(1) to persons who are not public authorities but by whom public functions are exercisable) does not apply to—

      (a)   a person listed in sub-paragraph (2);

      (b)   the exercise of a function listed in sub-paragraph (3).

  (2) Those persons are—

      (a)   the House of Commons;

      (b)   the House of Lords;

      (c)   the Scottish Parliament;

      (d)   the National Assembly for Wales;

---

[218] Substituted by Equality Act 2010 (Consequential Amendments, Saving and Supplementary Provisions) Order 2010, SI 2010/2279.

(e) the General Synod of the Church of England;

(f) the Security Service;

(g) the Secret Intelligence Service;

(h) the Government Communications Headquarters;

(i) a part of the armed forces which is, in accordance with a requirement of the Secretary of State, assisting the Government Communications Headquarters.

(3) Those functions are—

(a) a function in connection with proceedings in the House of Commons or the House of Lords;

(b) a function in connection with proceedings in the Scottish Parliament (other than a function of the Scottish Parliamentary Corporate Body);

(c) a function in connection with proceedings in the National Assembly for Wales (other than a function of the Assembly Commission).

Power to amend Schedule

5 (1) A Minister of the Crown may by order amend this Schedule so as to add, vary or omit an exception to section 149.

(2) But provision by virtue of sub-paragraph (1) may not amend this Schedule—

(a) so as to omit an exception in paragraph 3;

(b) so as to omit an exception in paragraph 4(1) so far as applying for the purposes of paragraph 4(2)(a) to (e) or (3);

(c) so as to reduce the extent to which an exception referred to in paragraph (a) or (b) applies.

SCHEDULE 19   **Section 150**

PUBLIC AUTHORITIES

PART 1
PUBLIC AUTHORITIES: GENERAL

Ministers of the Crown and government departments

A Minister of the Crown.

A government department other than the Security Service, the Secret Intelligence Service or the Government Communications Headquarters.

Armed forces

Any of the armed forces other than any part of the armed forces which is, in accordance with a requirement of the Secretary of State, assisting the Government Communications Headquarters.

[*Broadcasting*

The British Broadcasting Corporation ('BBC'), except in respect of functions relating to the provision of a content service (within the meaning given by section 32(7) of the Communications Act 2003); and the reference to the BBC includes a reference to a body corporate which—

(a) is a wholly owned subsidiary of the BBC,

(b) is not operated with a view to generating a profit, and

(c) undertakes activities primarily in order to promote the BBC's public purposes.

The Channel Four Television Corporation, except in respect of—
(a) functions relating to the provision of a content service (within the meaning given by section 32(7) of the Communications Act 2003), and
(b) the function of carrying on the activities referred to in section 199 of that Act.

The Welsh Authority (as defined by section 56(1) of the Broadcasting Act 1990), except in respect of functions relating to the provision of a content service (within the meaning given by section 32(7) of the Communications Act 2003).][219]

[*Citizens' rights*
The Independent Monitoring Authority for the Citizens' Rights Agreements.][220]

[*Civil liberties*
The Commission for Equality and Human Rights.
The Information Commissioner.][221]

[*Court services and legal services*
The Children and Family Court Advisory and Support Service.
The Judicial Appointments Commission.
The Legal Services Board.
[...][222]][223]

[*Criminal justice*
Her Majesty's Chief Inspector of Constabulary.
Her Majesty's Chief Inspector of the Crown Prosecution Service.
Her Majesty's Chief Inspector of Prisons.
Her Majesty's Chief Inspector of Probation for England and Wales.
The Parole Board for England and Wales.
A probation trust established by an order made under section 5(1) of the Offender Management Act 2007.
The Youth Justice Board for England and Wales.][224]

[*Environment, housing and development*
The Homes and Communities Agency.
Natural England.
[...][225]
[...][226]][227]

---

[219] Inserted by Equality Act 2010 (Public Authorities and Consequential and Supplementary Amendments) Order 2011, SI 2011/1060.
[220] Inserted by European Union (Withdrawal Agreement) Act 2020.
[221] Inserted by Equality Act 2010 (Public Authorities and Consequential and Supplementary Amendments) Order 2011, SI 2011/1060.
[222] Repealed by Legal Aid, Sentencing and Punishment of Offenders Act 2012.
[223] Inserted by Equality Act 2010 (Public Authorities and Consequential and Supplementary Amendments) Order 2011, SI 2011/1060.
[224] Inserted by Equality Act 2010 (Public Authorities and Consequential and Supplementary Amendments) Order 2011, SI 2011/1060.
[225] Repealed by Localism Act 2011.
[226] Repealed by Olympic Delivery Authority (Dissolution) Order 2014, SI 2014/3184.
[227] Inserted by Equality Act 2010 (Public Authorities and Consequential and Supplementary Amendments) Order 2011, SI 2011/1060.

[*Health, social care and social security*

[The National Health Service Commissioning Board.

A clinical commissioning group established under section 14D of the National Health Service
    Act 2006.][228]

The Care Quality Commission.

[...][229]

[Health Education England.][230]

[The Health Research Authority.][231]

The Health Service Commissioner for England, in respect of—

(a)   the Commissioner's functions set out in paragraph 11 of Schedule 1 to the Health Service
      Commissioners Act 1993; and

(b)   the Commissioner's public procurement functions (as defined in section 155(3) of this Act).

[Monitor.][232]

An NHS foundation trust within the meaning given by section 30 of the National Health Service
    Act 2006.

[...][233][...][234]

A Special Health Authority established under section 28 of that Act other than NHS Blood and
    Transplant and the NHS Business Services Authority.

[...][235]

[The Health and Social Care Information Centre.][236]

[The National Data Guardian for Health and Social Care.][237]

[The National Institute for Health and Care Excellence.][238]][239]

[*Industry, business, finance etc.*

The Advisory, Conciliation and Arbitration Service.

The Bank of England [(including the Bank in its capacity as the Prudential Regulation
    Authority)][240], in respect of its public functions.

[The Board of the Pension Protection Fund.][241]

The Civil Aviation Authority.

[The Coal Authority.][242]

[...][243]

---

[228] Inserted by Health and Social Care Act 2012.

[229] Repealed by Public Bodies (Child Maintenance and Enforcement Commission: Abolition and Transfer
of Functions) Order 2012, SI 2012/2007.

[230] Inserted by Care Act 2014.

[231] Inserted by Care Act 2014.

[232] Substituted by Health and Social Care Act 2012.

[233] Repealed by Health and Social Care Act 2012.

[234] Repealed by Health and Social Care Act 2012.

[235] Repealed by Health and Social Care Act 2012.

[236] Inserted by Health and Social Care Act 2012.

[237] Inserted by Health and Social Care (National Data Guardian) Act 2018.

[238] Inserted by Health and Social Care Act 2012.

[239] Substituted by Equality Act 2010 (Public Authorities and Consequential and Supplementary
Amendments) Order 2011, SI 2011/1060.

[240] Inserted by Bank of England and Financial Services (Consequential Amendments) Regulations 2017,
SI 2017/80.

[241] Inserted by Equality Act 2010 (Specific Duties and Public Authorities) Regulations 2017, SI 2017/353.

[242] Inserted by Equality Act 2010 (Specific Duties and Public Authorities) Regulations 2017, SI 2017/353.

[243] Repealed by Enterprise and Regulatory Reform Act 2013 (Competition) (Consequential, Transitional
and Saving Provisions) Order 2014, SI 2014/892.

[...]²⁴⁴
[The Comptroller and Auditor General.]²⁴⁵
[The Construction Industry Training Board.
The Engineering Construction Industry Training Board.]²⁴⁶
[The Financial Conduct Authority.]²⁴⁷
[The Money and Pensions Service.]²⁴⁸
The National Audit Office.
[The Nuclear Decommissioning Authority.]²⁴⁹
[The Office for Budget Responsibility.]²⁵⁰
The Office of Communications.
[The Office of Tax Simplification.]²⁵¹
[The Oil and Gas Authority.]²⁵²
[The Payment Systems Regulator established under section 40 of the Financial
Services (Banking Reform) Act 2013.]²⁵³
[...]²⁵⁴
[...]²⁵⁵
[United Kingdom Research and Innovation.]²⁵⁶]²⁵⁷

Local government

A county council, district council or parish council in England.
A parish meeting constituted under section 13 of the Local Government Act 1972.
Charter trustees constituted under section 246 of that Act for an area in England.
The Greater London Authority.
A London borough council.
The Common Council of the City of London in its capacity as a local authority or port health
    authority.
The Sub-Treasurer of the Inner Temple or the Under-Treasurer of the Middle Temple, in that
    person's capacity as a local authority.
[...]²⁵⁸
[The London Fire Commissioner.]²⁵⁹

---

²⁴⁴ Repealed by Equality Act 2010 (Specific Duties and Public Authorities) Regulations 2017, SI 2017/353.
²⁴⁵ Inserted by Budget Responsibility and National Audit Act 2011.
²⁴⁶ Inserted by Equality Act 2010 (Specific Duties and Public Authorities) Regulations 2017, SI 2017/353.
²⁴⁷ Substituted by Financial Services Act 2012.
²⁴⁸ Inserted by Financial Guidance and Claims Act 2018 (Naming and Consequential Amendments)
Regulations 2019, SI 2019/383.
²⁴⁹ Inserted by Equality Act 2010 (Specific Duties and Public Authorities) Regulations 2017, SI 2017/353.
²⁵⁰ Inserted by Budget Responsibility and National Audit Act 2011.
²⁵¹ Inserted by Finance Act 2016.
²⁵² Inserted by Equality Act 2010 (Specific Duties and Public Authorities) Regulations 2017, SI 2017/353.
²⁵³ Inserted by Financial Services (Banking Reform) Act 2013.
²⁵⁴ Repealed by Financial Guidance and Claims Act 2018 (Naming and Consequential Amendments)
Regulations 2019, SI 2019/383.
²⁵⁵ Repealed by Bank of England and Financial Services (Consequential Amendments) Regulations 2017,
SI 2017/80.
²⁵⁶ Inserted by Higher Education and Research Act 2017.
²⁵⁷ Inserted by Equality Act 2010 (Public Authorities and Consequential and Supplementary Amendments)
Order 2011, SI 2011/1060.
²⁵⁸ Repealed by Localism Act 2011.
²⁵⁹ Substituted by Policing and Crime Act 2017.

Transport for London.

[A Mayoral development corporation.][260]

The Council of the Isles of Scilly.

The Broads Authority established by section 1 of the Norfolk and Suffolk Broads Act 1988.

[…][261]

A fire and rescue authority constituted by a scheme under section 2 of the Fire and Rescue Services Act 2004, or a scheme to which section 4 of that Act applies, for an area in England.

[A fire and rescue authority created by an order under section 4A of that Act.][262]

An internal drainage board which is continued in being by virtue of section 1 of the Land Drainage Act 1991 for an area in England.

A National Park authority established by an order under section 63 of the Environment Act 1995 for an area in England.

A Passenger Transport Executive for an integrated transport area in England (within the meaning of Part 2 of the Transport Act 1968).

A port health authority constituted by an order under section 2 of the Public Health (Control of Disease) Act 1984 for an area in England.

A waste disposal authority established by virtue of an order under section 10(1) of the Local Government Act 1985.

A joint authority established under Part 4 of that Act for an area in England (including, by virtue of section 77(9) of the Local Transport Act 2008, an Integrated Transport Authority established under Part 5 of that Act of 2008).

[A sub-national transport body established under section 102E of the Local Transport Act 2008.][263]

A body corporate established pursuant to an order under section 67 of the Local Government Act 1985.

A joint committee constituted in accordance with section 102(1)(b) of the Local Government Act 1972 for an area in England.

A joint board which is continued in being by virtue of section 263(1) of that Act for an area in England.

[[…][264]

A Local Commissioner in England as defined by section 23(3) of the Local Government Act 1974, in respect of—

(a) the Commissioner's functions under sections 29(6A) and 34G(6) of that Act, and section 210(5) of the Apprenticeships, Skills, Children and Learning Act 2009; and

(b) the Commissioner's public procurement functions (as defined in section 155(3) of this Act).

[…][265][266]

[A combined authority established by an order made under section 103(1) of the Local Democracy, Economic Development and Construction Act 2009.

An economic prosperity board established by an order made under section 88(1) of the Local Democracy, Economic Development and Construction Act 2009.

---

[260] Inserted by Localism Act 2011.
[261] Repealed by Public Bodies Act 2011.
[262] Inserted by Policing and Crime Act 2017.
[263] Inserted by Cities and Local Government Devolution Act 2016.
[264] Repealed by Local Audit and Accountability Act 2014.
[265] Repealed by Equality Act 2010 (Specific Duties and Public Authorities) Regulations 2017, SI 2017/353.
[266] Inserted by Equality Act 2010 (Public Authorities and Consequential and Supplementary Amendments) Order 2011, SI 2011/1060.

An urban development corporation established by an order made under section 135 of the Local Government, Planning and Land Act 1980.][267]

Other educational bodies

The governing body of an educational establishment maintained by an English local authority (within the meaning of section 162 of the Education and Inspections Act 2006).

The governing body of an institution in England within the further education sector (within the meaning of section 91(3) of the Further and Higher Education Act 1992).

The governing body of an institution in England within the higher education sector (within the meaning of section 91(5) of that Act).

[[...][268]

A local authority with respect to the pupil referral units it establishes and maintains by virtue of section 19 of the Education Act 1996.

[The National Citizen Service Trust.][269]

[The Office for Students.][270]

[The proprietor of a City Technology College, a City College for Technology of the Arts, or an Academy.][271]

][272]

[*Parliamentary and devolved bodies*

The National Assembly for Wales Commission (Comisiwn Cynulliad Cenedlaethol Cymru).

The Parliamentary Commissioner for Administration, in respect of—

(a) the Commissioner's functions set out in section 3(1) and (1A) of the Parliamentary Commissioner Act 1967; and

(b) the Commissioner's public procurement functions (as defined in section 155(3) of this Act).

The Scottish Parliamentary Corporate Body.][273]

[*Police*

The British Transport Police Force.

A chief constable of a police force maintained under section 2 of the Police Act 1996.

The Chief Inspector of the UK Border Agency.

The Civil Nuclear Police Authority.

[The College of Policing.][274]

The Commissioner of Police for the City of London.

The Commissioner of Police of the Metropolis.

The Common Council of the City of London in its capacity as a police authority.

[The Director General of the Independent Office for Police Conduct.

---

[267] Inserted by Equality Act 2010 (Specific Duties and Public Authorities) Regulations 2017, SI 2017/353.

[268] Repealed by Higher Education and Research Act 2017.

[269] Inserted by National Citizen Service Act 2017.

[270] Inserted by Higher Education and Research Act 2017.

[271] Substituted by Equality Act 2010 (Specific Duties and Public Authorities) Regulations 2017, SI 2017/353.

[272] Inserted by Equality Act 2010 (Public Authorities and Consequential and Supplementary Amendments) Order 2011, SI 2011/1060.

[273] Inserted by Equality Act 2010 (Public Authorities and Consequential and Supplementary Amendments) Order 2011, SI 2011/1060.

[274] Inserted by Anti-social Behaviour, Crime and Policing Act 2014.

The Independent Office for Police Conduct.]²⁷⁵

[...]²⁷⁶

[A police and crime commissioner established under section 1 of the Police Reform and Social Responsibility Act 2011.

The Mayor's Office for Policing and Crime established under section 3 of that Act.]²⁷⁷

A Port Police Force established under an order made under section 14 of the Harbours Act 1964.

The Port Police Force established under Part 10 of the Port of London Act 1968.

A Port Police Force established under section 79 of the Harbours, Docks and Piers Clauses Act 1847.

[...]²⁷⁸]²⁷⁹

[*Regulators*

[**England, Scotland and Wales**]

[...]²⁸⁰

[The Association of Chartered Certified Accountants, in respect of its public functions.]²⁸¹

[...]²⁸²

The Chartered Institute of Patent Attorneys, in respect of its public functions.

The Council for Licensed Conveyancers, in respect of its public functions.

[The Disclosure and Barring Service.

The Gambling Commission.

The Gangmasters and Labour Abuse Authority.]²⁸³

The General Chiropractic Council, in respect of its public functions.

The General Council of the Bar, in respect of its public functions.

The General Dental Council, in respect of its public functions.

The General Medical Council, in respect of its public functions.

[The General Optical Council, in respect of its public functions.

The General Osteopathic Council, in respect of its public functions.

The General Pharmaceutical Council, in respect of its public functions.

The Health and Care Professions Council, in respect of its public functions.]²⁸⁴

The Health and Safety Executive.

[The Office for Nuclear Regulation.]²⁸⁵

[The Independent Monitor appointed under section 119B of the Police Act 1997.]²⁸⁶

The Insolvency Practitioners Association, in respect of its public functions.

The Institute of Chartered Accountants in England and Wales, in respect of its public functions.

The Institute of Legal Executives, in respect of its public functions.

---

²⁷⁵ Inserted by Policing and Crime Act 2017.
²⁷⁶ Repealed by Policing and Crime Act 2017.
²⁷⁷ Substituted by Police Reform and Social Responsibility Act 2011.
²⁷⁸ Repealed by Crime and Courts Act 2013.
²⁷⁹ Substituted by Equality Act 2010 (Public Authorities and Consequential and Supplementary Amendments) Order 2011, SI 2011/1060.
²⁸⁰ Repealed by Equality Act 2010 (Specific Duties and Public Authorities) Regulations 2017, SI 2017/353.
²⁸¹ Substituted by Equality Act 2010 (Specific Duties and Public Authorities) Regulations 2017, SI 2017/353.
²⁸² Repealed by Equality Act 2010 (Specific Duties and Public Authorities) Regulations 2017, SI 2017/353.
²⁸³ Inserted by Equality Act 2010 (Specific Duties and Public Authorities) Regulations 2017, SI 2017/353.
²⁸⁴ Inserted by Equality Act 2010 (Specific Duties and Public Authorities) Regulations 2017, SI 2017/353.
²⁸⁵ Inserted by Energy Act 2013.
²⁸⁶ Inserted by Equality Act 2010 (Specific Duties and Public Authorities) Regulations 2017, SI 2017/353.

The Institute of Trade Mark Attorneys, in respect of its public functions.
The Law Society of England and Wales, in respect of its public functions.
The Nursing and Midwifery Council, in respect of its public functions.
The Office of the Immigration Services Commissioner.
[The Pensions Regulator.
[The Regulator of Social Housing.]²⁸⁷
The Security Industry Authority.]²⁸⁸

[England]

[Social Work England.]²⁸⁹]²⁹⁰
[*Transport*
High Speed Two (HS2) Limited.
Highways England Company Limited.
Network Rail Limited.]²⁹¹

PART 2
PUBLIC AUTHORITIES: RELEVANT WELSH AUTHORITIES

Welsh Assembly Government, etc.

The Welsh Ministers.
The First Minister for Wales.
The Counsel General to the Welsh Assembly Government.
A subsidiary of the Welsh Ministers (within the meaning given by section 134(4) of the Government of Wales Act 2006).

National Health Service

A Local Health Board established under section 11 of the National Health Service (Wales) Act 2006.
An NHS trust established under section 18 of that Act.
[...]²⁹²
A Community Health Council in Wales.
[The Board of Community Health Councils in Wales or Bwrdd Cynghorau Iechyd Cymuned Cymru.]²⁹³

Local government

[A county council or county borough council in Wales.]²⁹⁴
[...]²⁹⁵
A fire and rescue authority constituted by a scheme under section 2 of the Fire and Rescue Services Act 2004, or a scheme to which section 4 of that Act applies, for an area in Wales.

---

²⁸⁷ Inserted by Legislative Reform (Regulator of Social Housing) (England) Order 2018, SI 2018/1040.
²⁸⁸ Inserted by Equality Act 2010 (Specific Duties and Public Authorities) Regulations 2017, SI 2017/353.
²⁸⁹ Inserted by The Social Workers Regulations 2018, SI 2018/893.
²⁹⁰ Inserted by Equality Act 2010 (Public Authorities and Consequential and Supplementary Amendments) Order 2011, SI 2011/1060.
²⁹¹ Inserted by Equality Act 2010 (Specific Duties and Public Authorities) Regulations 2017, SI 2017/353.
²⁹² Repealed by Equality Act 2010 (Specification of Relevant Welsh Authorities) Order 2011, SI 2011/1063.
²⁹³ Inserted by Equality Act 2010 (Specification of Relevant Welsh Authorities) Order 2011, SI 2011/1063.
²⁹⁴ Substituted by Equality Act 2010 (Specification of Relevant Welsh Authorities) Order 2011, SI 2011/1063.
²⁹⁵ Repealed by Equality Act 2010 (Specification of Relevant Welsh Authorities) Order 2011, SI 2011/1063

[...]²⁹⁶

A National Park authority established by an order under section 63 of the Environment Act 1995 for an area in Wales.

[...]²⁹⁷

[A strategic planning panel established under section 60D of the Planning and Compulsory Purchase Act 2004.]²⁹⁸

Other educational bodies

The governing body of an educational establishment maintained by a Welsh local authority (within the meaning of section 162 of the Education and Inspections Act 2006).

The governing body of an institution in Wales within the further education sector (within the meaning of section 91(3) of the Further and Higher Education Act 1992).

The governing body of an institution in Wales within the higher education sector (within the meaning of section 91(5) of that Act).

[The Higher Education Funding Council for Wales or Cyngor Cyllido Addysg Uwch Cymru.

The General Teaching Council for Wales or Cyngor Addysgu Cyffredinol Cymru.

Her Majesty's Chief Inspector of Education and Training in Wales or Prif Arolygydd Ei Mawrhydi dros Addysg a Hyfforddiant yng Nghymru.]²⁹⁹

[Qualifications Wales.]³⁰⁰

[Other public authorities

[The Welsh Revenue Authority or Awdurdod Cyllid Cymru.]³⁰¹

The Auditor General for Wales or Archwilydd Cyffredinol Cymru.

The Public Services Ombudsman for Wales or Ombwdsmon Gwasanaethau Cyhoeddus Cymru.

[Social Care Wales or Gofal Cymdeithasol Cymru.]³⁰²

The Arts Council for Wales or Cyngor Celfyddydau Cymru.

The National Museum of Wales or Amgueddfa Genedlaethol Cymru.

The National Library of Wales or Llyfrgell Genedlaethol Cymru.

The Sports Council for Wales or Cyngor Chwaraeon Cymru.

[Comisiynydd y Gymraeg (The Welsh Language Commissioner).]³⁰³

[...]³⁰⁴

The Commissioner for Older People in Wales or Comisiynydd Pobl Hŷn Cymru.

The Children's Commissioner for Wales or Comisiynydd Plant Cymru.

[The Wales Audit Office or Swyddfa Archwilio Cymru.]³⁰⁵]³⁰⁶

---

²⁹⁶ Repealed by Equality Act 2010 (Specification of Relevant Welsh Authorities) Order 2011, SI 2011/1063.
²⁹⁷ Repealed by Equality Act 2010 (Specification of Relevant Welsh Authorities) Order 2011, SI 2011/1063.
²⁹⁸ Inserted by Planning (Wales) Act 2015.
²⁹⁹ Inserted by Equality Act 2010 (Specification of Relevant Welsh Authorities) Order 2011, SI 2011/1063.
³⁰⁰ Inserted by Qualifications Wales Act 2015.
³⁰¹ Inserted by The Tax Collection and Management (Wales) Act 2016 (Consequential and Supplemental Provisions) Regulations 2018, SI 2018/285.
³⁰² Substituted by Equality Act 2010 (Specific Duties and Public Authorities) Regulations 2017, SI 2017/353.
³⁰³ Substituted by Welsh Language (Wales) Measure 2011 (Transfer of Functions, Transitional and Consequential Provisions) Order 2012, SI 2012/990.
³⁰⁴ Repealed by Natural Resources Body for Wales (Functions) Order 2013, SI 2013/755.
³⁰⁵ Inserted by Public Audit (Wales) Act 2013.
³⁰⁶ Inserted by Equality Act 2010 (Specification of Relevant Welsh Authorities) Order 2011, SI 2011/1063.

PART 3
PUBLIC AUTHORITIES: RELEVANT SCOTTISH AUTHORITIES

Scottish Administration

An office-holder in the Scottish Administration (within the meaning given by section 126(7)(a) of the Scotland Act 1998).

National Health Service

A Health Board constituted under section 2 of the National Health Service (Scotland) Act 1978. A Special Health Board constituted under that section.

Local government

A council constituted under section 2 of the Local Government etc. (Scotland) Act 1994.

A community council established under section 51 of the Local Government (Scotland) Act 1973.

A joint board within the meaning of section 235(1) of that Act.

[...][307]

A licensing board established under section 5 of the Licensing (Scotland) Act 2005, or continued in being by virtue of that section.

A National Park authority established by a designation order made under section 6 of the National Parks (Scotland) Act 2000.

Scottish Enterprise and Highlands and Islands Enterprise, established under the Enterprise and New Towns (Scotland) Act 1990.

Other educational bodies

An education authority in Scotland (within the meaning of section 135(1) of the Education (Scotland) Act 1980).

The managers of a grant-aided school (within the meaning of that section).

The board of management of a college of further education (within the meaning of section 36(1) of the Further and Higher Education (Scotland) Act 1992).

In the case of such a college of further education not under the management of a board of management, the board of governors of the college or any person responsible for the management of the college, whether or not formally constituted as a governing body or board of governors.

The governing body of an institution within the higher education sector (within the meaning of Part 2 of the Further and Higher Education (Scotland) Act 1992).

[Police and Fire][308]

[The Scottish Police Authority.][309]

[The chief constable of the Police Service of Scotland.

---

[307] Repealed by Police and Fire Reform (Scotland) Act 2012 (Consequential Provisions and Modifications) Order 2013, SI 2013/602.

[308] Substituted by Police and Fire Reform (Scotland) Act 2012 (Consequential Provisions and Modifications) Order 2013, SI 2013/602.

[309] Substituted by Police and Fire Reform (Scotland) Act 2012 (Consequential Provisions and Modifications) Order 2013, SI 2013/602.

The Scottish Fire and Rescue Service.
The Chief Officer of the Scottish Fire and Rescue Service.][310]

[*Other bodies and offices added on 6th April 2011*

Accounts Commission for Scotland.
Audit Scotland.
Board of Trustees of the National Galleries of Scotland.
Board of Trustees of the National Museums of Scotland.
Board of Trustees of the Royal Botanic Garden, Edinburgh.
Bòrd na Gàidhlig.
[…][311]
A chief officer of a community justice authority.
[…][312]
Commissioner for Children and Young People in Scotland.
Commission for Ethical Standards in Public Life in Scotland.
The Common Services Agency for the Scottish Health Service.
A community justice authority.
Creative Scotland.
The Crofters Commission.
The General Teaching Council for Scotland.
Healthcare Improvement Scotland.
Learning and Teaching Scotland.
The Mental Welfare Commission for Scotland.
Police Complaints Commissioner for Scotland.
Quality Meat Scotland.
A regional Transport Partnership created by an order under section 1(1) of the Transport (Scotland) Act 2005.
Risk Management Authority.
Royal Commission on the Ancient and Historical Monuments of Scotland.
Scottish Children's Reporter Administration.
Scottish Commission for Human Rights.
The Scottish Criminal Cases Review Commission.
Scottish Environment Protection Agency.
Scottish Further and Higher Education Funding Council.
Scottish Futures Trust Ltd.
Scottish Information Commissioner.
The Scottish Legal Aid Board.
The Scottish Legal Complaints Commission.
Scottish Natural Heritage.
[…][313]
Scottish Public Services Ombudsman.

---

[310] Inserted by Police and Fire Reform (Scotland) Act 2012 (Consequential Provisions and Modifications) Order 2013, SI 2013/602.
[311] Repealed by Police and Fire Reform (Scotland) Act 2012 (Consequential Provisions and Modifications) Order 2013, SI 2013/602.
[312] Repealed by Police and Fire Reform (Scotland) Act 2012 (Consequential Provisions and Modifications) Order 2013, SI 2013/602.
[313] Repealed by Police and Fire Reform (Scotland) Act 2012 (Consequential Provisions and Modifications) Order 2013, SI 2013/602.

Scottish Qualifications Authority.
The Scottish Road Works Commissioner.
The Scottish Social Services Council.
The Scottish Sports Council.
Scottish Water.
Skills Development Scotland.
Social Care and Social Work Improvement Scotland.
The Standards Commission for Scotland.
[The National Library of Scotland.][314]
VisitScotland.
A Water Customer Consultation Panel.
The Water Industry Commission for Scotland.][315]

[*Other bodies and offices added on 5th March 2012*
Children's Hearings Scotland.
The National Convener of Children's Hearings Scotland.][316]

[*Other bodies added on 1st April 2015*
Historic Environment Scotland.
An integration joint board established by order under section 9(2) of the Public Bodies (Joint Working) (Scotland) Act 2014.
A regional board (within the meaning of section 35(1) of the Further and Higher Education (Scotland) Act 2005).][317]
[*Other body added on 28th June 2018*
ILF Scotland.][318]

[PART 4
PUBLIC AUTHORITIES: CROSS-BORDER AUTHORITIES

Cross-border Welsh authorities
The Environment Agency—D
[The Natural Resources Body for Wales—A][319]
NHS Blood and Transplant—D
The NHS Business Services Authority—D
The Student Loans Company Limited—D][320]

---

[314] Substituted by Equality Act 2010 (Specification of Public Authorities) (Scotland) Order 2013, SI 2013/170.

[315] Inserted by Equality Act 2010 (Specification of Public Authorities) (Scotland) Order 2011, SI 2011/233.

[316] Inserted by Equality Act 2010 (Specification of Public Authorities) (Scotland) Order 2012, SI 2012/55.

[317] Inserted by Equality Act 2010 (Specification of Public Authorities) (Scotland) Order 2015, SI 2015/83.

[318] Inserted by The ILF Scotland (Miscellaneous Listings) Order 2018, SI 2018/214.

[319] Inserted by Natural Resources Body for Wales (Functions) Order 2013, SI 2013/755.

[320] Inserted by Equality Act 2010 (Public Authorities and Consequential and Supplementary Amendments) Order 2011, SI 2011/1060.

SCHEDULE 20   Section 186

RAIL VEHICLE ACCESSIBILITY: COMPLIANCE

Rail vehicle accessibility compliance certificates

1 [...]³²¹

Regulations as to compliance certificates

2 [...]³²²

Regulations as to compliance assessments

3 [...]³²³

Fees in respect of compliance certificates

4 [...]³²⁴

Penalty for using rail vehicle that does not conform with accessibility regulations

5 [...]³²⁵

Penalty for using rail vehicle otherwise than in conformity with accessibility regulations

6 [...]³²⁶

Inspection of rail vehicles

7 [...]³²⁷

Supplementary powers

8 [...]³²⁸

Penalties: amount, due date and recovery

9 [...]³²⁹

Penalties: code of practice

10 [...]³³⁰

Penalties: procedure

11 [...]³³¹

---

³²¹ Repealed by Equality Act 2010.
³²² Repealed by Equality Act 2010.
³²³ Repealed by Equality Act 2010.
³²⁴ Repealed by Equality Act 2010.
³²⁵ Repealed by Equality Act 2010.
³²⁶ Repealed by Equality Act 2010.
³²⁷ Repealed by Equality Act 2010.
³²⁸ Repealed by Equality Act 2010.
³²⁹ Repealed by Equality Act 2010.
³³⁰ Repealed by Equality Act 2010.
³³¹ Repealed by Equality Act 2010.

Penalties: appeals

12 [...]³³²

Forgery, etc.

13 [...]³³³

Regulations

14 [...]³³⁴

Interpretation

15 [...]³³⁵

SCHEDULE 21   Section 189

REASONABLE ADJUSTMENTS: SUPPLEMENTARY

Preliminary

1   This Schedule applies for the purposes of Schedules 2, 4, 8, 13 and 15.

Binding obligations, etc.

2   (1) This paragraph applies if—
    (a) a binding obligation requires A to obtain the consent of another person to an alteration of premises which A occupies,
    (b) where A is a controller of let premises, a binding obligation requires A to obtain the consent of another person to a variation of a term of the tenancy, or
    (c) where A is a responsible person in relation to common parts, a binding obligation requires A to obtain the consent of another person to an alteration of the common parts.
    (2) For the purpose of discharging a duty to make reasonable adjustments—
    (a) it is always reasonable for A to have to take steps to obtain the consent, but
    (b) it is never reasonable for A to have to make the alteration before the consent is obtained.
    (3) In this Schedule, a binding obligation is a legally binding obligation in relation to premises, however arising; but the reference to a binding obligation in sub-paragraph (1)(a) or (c) does not include a reference to an obligation imposed by a tenancy.
    (4) The steps referred to in sub-paragraph (2)(a) do not include applying to a court or tribunal.

Landlord's consent

3   (1) This paragraph applies if—
    (a) A occupies premises under a tenancy,

---

³³² Repealed by Equality Act 2010.
³³³ Repealed by Equality Act 2010.
³³⁴ Repealed by Equality Act 2010.
³³⁵ Repealed by Equality Act 2010.

492

(b) A is proposing to make an alteration to the premises so as to comply with a duty to make reasonable adjustments, and

(c) but for this paragraph, A would not be entitled to make the alteration.

(2) This paragraph also applies if—

    (a) A is a responsible person in relation to common parts,

    (b) A is proposing to make an alteration to the common parts so as to comply with a duty to make reasonable adjustments,

    (c) A is the tenant of property which includes the common parts, and

    (d) but for this paragraph, A would not be entitled to make the alteration.

(3) The tenancy has effect as if it provided—

    (a) for A to be entitled to make the alteration with the written consent of the landlord,

    (b) for A to have to make a written application for that consent,

    (c) for the landlord not to withhold the consent unreasonably, and

    (d) for the landlord to be able to give the consent subject to reasonable conditions.

(4) If a question arises as to whether A has made the alteration (and, accordingly, complied with a duty to make reasonable adjustments), any constraint attributable to the tenancy must be ignored unless A has applied to the landlord in writing for consent to the alteration.

(5) For the purposes of sub-paragraph (1) or (2), A must be treated as not entitled to make the alteration if the tenancy—

    (a) imposes conditions which are to apply if A makes an alteration, or

    (b) entitles the landlord to attach conditions to a consent to the alteration.

Proceedings before county court or sheriff

4   (1) This paragraph applies if, in a case within Part 3, 4, 6 or 7 of this Act—

    (a) A has applied in writing to the landlord for consent to the alteration, and

    (b) the landlord has refused to give consent or has given consent subject to a condition.

(2) A (or a disabled person with an interest in the alteration being made) may refer the matter to [the county court][336] or, in Scotland, the sheriff.

(3) The county court or sheriff must determine whether the refusal or condition is unreasonable.

(4) If the county court or sheriff finds that the refusal or condition is unreasonable, the county court or sheriff—

    (a) may make such declaration as it thinks appropriate;

    (b) may make an order authorising A to make the alteration specified in the order (and requiring A to comply with such conditions as are so specified).

Joining landlord as party to proceedings

5   (1) This paragraph applies to proceedings relating to a contravention of this Act by virtue of section 20.

(2) A party to the proceedings may request the employment tribunal, county court or sheriff ('the judicial authority') to direct that the landlord is joined or sisted as a party to the proceedings.

(3) The judicial authority—

    (a) must grant the request if it is made before the hearing of the complaint or claim begins;

---

[336] Substituted by Crime and Courts Act 2013.

(b) may refuse the request if it is made after the hearing begins;

(c) must refuse the request if it is made after the complaint or claim has been determined.

(4) If the landlord is joined or sisted as a party to the proceedings, the judicial authority may determine whether—

(a) the landlord has refused to consent to the alteration;

(b) the landlord has consented subject to a condition;

(c) the refusal or condition was unreasonable.

(5) If the judicial authority finds that the refusal or condition was unreasonable, it—

(a) may make such declaration as it thinks appropriate;

(b) may make an order authorising A to make the alteration specified in the order (and requiring A to comply with such conditions as are so specified);

(c) may order the landlord to pay compensation to the complainant or claimant.

(6) An employment tribunal may act in reliance on sub-paragraph (5)(c) instead of, or in addition to, acting in reliance on section 124(2); but if it orders the landlord to pay compensation it must not do so in reliance on section 124(2).

(7) If [the county court]³³⁷ or the sheriff orders the landlord to pay compensation, it may not order A to do so.

Regulations

6 (1) Regulations may make provision as to circumstances in which a landlord is taken for the purposes of this Schedule to have—

(a) withheld consent;

(b) withheld consent reasonably;

(c) withheld consent unreasonably.

(2) Regulations may make provision as to circumstances in which a condition subject to which a landlord gives consent is taken—

(a) to be reasonable;

(b) to be unreasonable.

(3) Regulations may make provision supplementing or modifying the preceding paragraphs of this Schedule, or provision made under this paragraph, in relation to a case where A's tenancy is a sub-tenancy.

(4) Provision made by virtue of this paragraph may amend the preceding paragraphs of this Schedule.

Interpretation

7 An expression used in this Schedule and in Schedule 2, 4, 8, 13 or 15 has the same meaning in this Schedule as in that Schedule.

SCHEDULE 22   **Section 191**

STATUTORY PROVISIONS

Statutory authority

1 (1) A person (P) does not contravene a provision specified in the first column of the table, so far as relating to the protected characteristic specified in the second column in respect of

---

³³⁷ Substituted by Crime and Courts Act 2013.

that provision, if P does anything P must do pursuant to a requirement specified in the third column.

Specified provision	Protected characteristic	Requirement
Parts 3 to 7	Age	A requirement of an enactment
Parts 3 to 7 and 12	Disability	A requirement of an enactment
		A relevant requirement or condition imposed by virtue of an enactment
Parts 3 to 7	Religion or belief	A requirement of an enactment
		A relevant requirement or condition imposed by virtue of an enactment
Section 29(6) and Parts 6 and 7	Sex	A requirement of an enactment
Parts 3, 4, 6 and 7	Sexual orientation	A requirement of an enactment
		A relevant requirement or condition imposed by virtue of an enactment

(2) A reference in the table to Part 6 does not include a reference to that Part so far as relating to vocational training.

(3) In this paragraph a reference to an enactment includes a reference to—
    (a) a Measure of the General Synod of the Church of England;
    (b) an enactment passed or made on or after the date on which this Act is passed.

(4) In the table, a relevant requirement or condition is a requirement or condition imposed (whether before or after the passing of this Act) by—
    (a) a Minister of the Crown;
    (b) a member of the Scottish Executive;
    (c) the National Assembly for Wales (constituted by the Government of Wales Act 1998);
    (d) the Welsh Ministers, the First Minister for Wales or the Counsel General to the Welsh Assembly Government.

Protection of women

2   (1) A person (P) does not contravene a specified provision only by doing in relation to a woman (W) anything P is required to do to comply with—
    (a) a pre-1975 Act enactment concerning the protection of women;
    (b) a relevant statutory provision (within the meaning of Part 1 of the Health and Safety at Work etc. Act 1974) if it is done for the purpose of the protection of W (or a description of women which includes W);
    (c) a requirement of a provision specified in Schedule 1 to the Employment Act 1989 (provisions concerned with protection of women at work).

(2) The references to the protection of women are references to protecting women in relation to—
    (a) pregnancy or maternity, or
    (b) any other circumstances giving rise to risks specifically affecting women.

(3) It does not matter whether the protection is restricted to women.

(4) These are the specified provisions—
    (a) Part 5 (work);
    (b) Part 6 (education), so far as relating to vocational training.

(5) A pre-1975 Act enactment is an enactment contained in—

    (a) an Act passed before the Sex Discrimination Act 1975;

    (b) an instrument approved or made by or under such an Act (including one approved or made after the passing of the 1975 Act).

(6) If an Act repeals and re-enacts (with or without modification) a pre-1975 enactment then the provision re-enacted must be treated as being in a pre-1975 enactment.

(7) For the purposes of sub-paragraph (1)(c), a reference to a provision in Schedule 1 to the Employment Act 1989 includes a reference to a provision for the time being having effect in place of it.

(8) This paragraph applies only to the following protected characteristics—

    (a) pregnancy and maternity;

    (b) sex.

Educational appointments, etc: religious belief

3   (1) A person does not contravene Part 5 (work) only by doing a relevant act in connection with the employment of another in a relevant position.

    (2) A relevant position is—

        (a) the head teacher or principal of an educational establishment;

        (b) the head, a fellow or other member of the academic staff of a college, or institution in the nature of a college, in a university;

        (c) a professorship of a university which is a canon professorship or one to which a canonry is annexed.

    (3) A relevant act is anything it is necessary to do to comply with—

        (a) a requirement of an instrument relating to the establishment that the head teacher or principal must be a member of a particular religious order;

        (b) a requirement of an instrument relating to the college or institution that the holder of the position must be a woman;

        (c) an Act or instrument in accordance with which the professorship is a canon professorship or one to which a canonry is annexed.

    (4) Sub-paragraph (3)(b) does not apply to an instrument taking effect on or after 16 January 1990 (the day on which section 5(3) of the Employment Act 1989 came into force).

    (5) A Minister of the Crown may by order provide that anything in subparagraphs (1) to (3) does not have effect in relation to—

        (a) a specified educational establishment or university;

        (b) a specified description of educational establishments.

    (6) An educational establishment is—

        (a) a school within the meaning of the Education Act 1996 or the Education (Scotland) Act 1980;

        (b) a college, or institution in the nature of a college, in a university;

        (c) an institution designated by order made, or having effect as if made, under section 129 of the Education Reform Act 1988;

      [(ca) a registered higher education provider of a description prescribed by regulations made for the purposes of section 39(1) of the Higher Education and Research Act 2017;][338]

        (d) a college of further education within the meaning of section 36 of the Further and Higher Education (Scotland) Act 1992;

---

[338] Inserted by The Higher Education and Research Act 2017 (Further Implementation etc.) Regulations 2019, SI 2019/1027.

(e) a university in Scotland;

(f) an institution designated by order under section 28 of the Further and Higher Education Act 1992 or section 44 of the Further and Higher Education (Scotland) Act 1992.

(7) This paragraph does not affect paragraph 2 of Schedule 9.

4 A person does not contravene this Act only by doing anything which is permitted for the purposes of—

(a) section 58(6) or (7) of the School Standards and Framework Act 1998 (dismissal of teachers because of failure to give religious education efficiently);

(b) section 60(4) and (5) of that Act (religious considerations relating to certain appointments);

(c) section 124A of that Act (preference for certain teachers at independent schools of a religious character) [;]

[(d) section 124AA(5) to (7) of that Act (religious considerations relating to certain teachers at Academies with religious character).][339]

Crown employment, etc.

5 (1) A person does not contravene this Act—

(a) by making or continuing in force rules mentioned in sub-paragraph (2);

(b) by publishing, displaying or implementing such rules;

(c) by publishing the gist of such rules.

(2) The rules are rules restricting to persons of particular birth, nationality, descent or residence—

(a) employment in the service of the Crown;

(b) employment by a prescribed public body;

(c) holding a public office (within the meaning of section 50).

(3) The power to make regulations for the purpose of sub-paragraph (2)(b) is exercisable by the Minister for the Civil Service.

(4) In this paragraph 'public body' means a body (whether corporate or unincorporated) exercising public functions (within the meaning given by section 31(4)).

SCHEDULE 23   Section 196

GENERAL EXCEPTIONS

Acts authorised by statute or the executive

1 (1) This paragraph applies to anything done—

(a) in pursuance of an enactment;

(b) in pursuance of an instrument made by a member of the executive under an enactment;

(c) to comply with a requirement imposed (whether before or after the passing of this Act) by a member of the executive by virtue of an enactment;

(d) in pursuance of arrangements made (whether before or after the passing of this Act) by or with the approval of, or for the time being approved by, a Minister of the Crown;

---

[339] Inserted by Education Act 2011.

(e) to comply with a condition imposed (whether before or after the passing of this Act) by a Minister of the Crown.

(2) A person does not contravene Part 3, 4, 5 or 6 by doing anything to which this paragraph applies which discriminates against another because of the other's nationality.

(3) A person (A) does not contravene Part 3, 4, 5 or 6 if, by doing anything to which this paragraph applies, A discriminates against another (B) by applying to B a provision, criterion or practice which relates to—
(a) B's place of ordinary residence;
(b) the length of time B has been present or resident in or outside the United Kingdom or an area within it.

Organisations relating to religion or belief

2 (1) This paragraph applies to an organisation the purpose of which is—
(a) to practise a religion or belief,
(b) to advance a religion or belief,
(c) to teach the practice or principles of a religion or belief,
(d) to enable persons of a religion or belief to receive any benefit, or to engage in any activity, within the framework of that religion or belief, or
(e) to foster or maintain good relations between persons of different religions or beliefs.

(2) This paragraph does not apply to an organisation whose sole or main purpose is commercial.

(3) The organisation does not contravene Part 3, 4 or 7, so far as relating to religion or belief or sexual orientation, only by restricting—
(a) membership of the organisation;
(b) participation in activities undertaken by the organisation or on its behalf or under its auspices;
(c) the provision of goods, facilities or services in the course of activities undertaken by the organisation or on its behalf or under its auspices;
(d) the use or disposal of premises owned or controlled by the organisation.

(4) A person does not contravene Part 3, 4 or 7, so far as relating to religion or belief or sexual orientation, only by doing anything mentioned in subparagraph (3) on behalf of or under the auspices of the organisation.

(5) A minister does not contravene Part 3, 4 or 7, so far as relating to religion or belief or sexual orientation, only by restricting—
(a) participation in activities carried on in the performance of the minister's functions in connection with or in respect of the organisation;
(b) the provision of goods, facilities or services in the course of activities carried on in the performance of the minister's functions in connection with or in respect of the organisation.

(6) Sub-paragraphs (3) to (5) permit a restriction relating to religion or belief only if it is imposed—
(a) because of the purpose of the organisation, or
(b) to avoid causing offence, on grounds of the religion or belief to which the organisation relates, to persons of that religion or belief.

(7) Sub-paragraphs (3) to (5) permit a restriction relating to sexual orientation only if it is imposed—
(a) because it is necessary to comply with the doctrine of the organisation, or

(b) to avoid conflict with strongly held convictions within subparagraph (9).

(8) In sub-paragraph (5), the reference to a minister is a reference to a minister of religion, or other person, who—

(a) performs functions in connection with a religion or belief to which the organisation relates, and

(b) holds an office or appointment in, or is accredited, approved or recognised for the purposes of the organisation.

(9) The strongly held convictions are—

(a) in the case of a religion, the strongly held religious convictions of a significant number of the religion's followers;

(b) in the case of a belief, the strongly held convictions relating to the belief of a significant number of the belief's followers.

[(9A) An organisation does not contravene Part 3, 4 or 7 only by refusing to allow premises owned or controlled by the organisation to be used—

(a) to solemnise a relevant Scottish marriage for the reason that the marriage is the marriage of two persons of the same sex;

(b) to register a relevant Scottish civil partnership for the reason that the civil partnership is between two persons of the same sex.

(9B) A person (or a group of persons) does not contravene Part 3, 4 or 7 only by refusing to allow premises owned or controlled by the person (or the group) on behalf of an organisation to be used—

(a) to solemnise a relevant Scottish marriage for the reason that the marriage is the marriage of two persons of the same sex;

(b) to register a relevant Scottish civil partnership for the reason that the civil partnership is between two persons of the same sex.

(9C) An organisation does not contravene section 29 only by allowing an approved celebrant of the organisation to act as set out in sub-paragraph (1) or (2) of paragraph 25B of Schedule 3.

(9D) In sub-paragraphs (9A) to (9C), 'approved celebrant', 'relevant Scottish marriage' and 'relevant Scottish civil partnership' have the same meaning as in paragraph 25B of Schedule 3.][340]

(10) This paragraph does not permit anything which is prohibited by section 29, so far as relating to sexual orientation, if it is done—

(a) on behalf of a public authority, and

(b) under the terms of a contract between the organisation and the public authority.

(11) In the application of this paragraph in relation to sexual orientation, subparagraph (1)(e) must be ignored.

(12) In the application of this paragraph in relation to sexual orientation, in subparagraph (3) (d), 'disposal' does not include disposal of an interest in premises by way of sale if the interest being disposed of is—

(a) the entirety of the organisation's interest in the premises, or

(b) the entirety of the interest in respect of which the organisation has power of disposal.

(13) In this paragraph—

(a) 'disposal' is to be construed in accordance with section 38;

---

[340] Inserted by Marriage and Civil Partnership (Scotland) Act 2014 and Civil Partnership Act 2004 (Consequential Provisions and Modifications) Order 2014, SI 2014/3229.

(b) 'public authority' has the meaning given in section 150(1).

Communal accommodation

3   (1) A person does not contravene this Act, so far as relating to sex discrimination or gender reassignment discrimination, only because of anything done in relation to—
       (a) the admission of persons to communal accommodation;
       (b) the provision of a benefit, facility or service linked to the accommodation.
    (2) Sub-paragraph (1)(a) does not apply unless the accommodation is managed in a way which is as fair as possible to both men and women.
    (3) In applying sub-paragraph (1)(a), account must be taken of—
       (a) whether and how far it is reasonable to expect that the accommodation should be altered or extended or that further accommodation should be provided, and
       (b) the frequency of the demand or need for use of the accommodation by persons of one sex as compared with those of the other.
    (4) In applying sub-paragraph (1)(a) in relation to gender reassignment, account must also be taken of whether and how far the conduct in question is a proportionate means of achieving a legitimate aim.
    (5) Communal accommodation is residential accommodation which includes dormitories or other shared sleeping accommodation which for reasons of privacy should be used only by persons of the same sex.
    (6) Communal accommodation may include—
       (a) shared sleeping accommodation for men and for women;
       (b) ordinary sleeping accommodation;
       (c) residential accommodation all or part of which should be used only by persons of the same sex because of the nature of the sanitary facilities serving the accommodation.
    (7) A benefit, facility or service is linked to communal accommodation if—
       (a) it cannot properly and effectively be provided except for those using the accommodation, and
       (b) a person could be refused use of the accommodation in reliance on sub-paragraph (1)(a).
    (8) This paragraph does not apply for the purposes of Part 5 (work) unless such arrangements as are reasonably practicable are made to compensate for—
       (a) in a case where sub-paragraph (1)(a) applies, the refusal of use of the accommodation;
       (b) in a case where sub-paragraph (1)(b) applies, the refusal of provision of the benefit, facility or service.

Training provided to non-EEA residents, etc.

4   (1) A person (A) does not contravene this Act, so far as relating to nationality, only by providing a non-resident (B) with training, if A thinks that B does not intend to exercise in Great Britain skills B obtains as a result.
    (2) A non-resident is a person who is not ordinarily resident in an EEA state.
    (3) The reference to providing B with training is—
       (a) if A employs B in relevant employment, a reference to doing anything in or in connection with the employment;
       (b) if A as a principal allows B to do relevant contract work, a reference to doing anything in or in connection with allowing B to do the work;
       (c) in a case within paragraph (a) or (b) or any other case, a reference to affording B access to facilities for education or training or ancillary benefits.
    (4) Employment or contract work is relevant if its sole or main purpose is the provision of training in skills.

(5) In the case of training provided by the armed forces or Secretary of State for purposes relating to defence, sub-paragraph (1) has effect as if—

    (a) the reference in sub-paragraph (2) to an EEA state were a reference to Great Britain, and

    (b) in sub-paragraph (4), for 'its sole or main purpose is' there were substituted 'it is for purposes including'.

(6) 'Contract work' and 'principal' each have the meaning given in section 41.

SCHEDULE 24 Section 203

HARMONISATION: EXCEPTIONS

Part 1 (public sector duty regarding socio-economic inequalities)

Chapter 2 of Part 5 (occupational pensions)

Section 78 (gender pay gap)

Section 106 (election candidates: diversity information)

Chapters 1 to 3 and 5 of Part 9 (enforcement), except section 136

Sections 142 and 146 (unenforceable terms, declaration in respect of void terms)

Chapter 1 of Part 11 (public sector equality duty)

Part 12 (disabled persons: transport)

Part 13 (disability: miscellaneous)

Section 197 (power to specify age exceptions)

Part 15 (family property)

Part 16 (general and miscellaneous)

Schedule 1 (disability: supplementary provision)

In Schedule 3 (services and public functions: exceptions)—

    (a) in Part 3 (health and care), paragraphs 13 and 14;

    (b) Part 4 (immigration);

    (c) Part 5 (insurance);

    (d) Part 6 (marriage);

    (e) Part 7 (separate and single services), except paragraph 30;

    (f) Part 8 (television, radio and on-line broadcasting and distribution);

    (g) Part 9 (transport);

    (h) Part 10 (supplementary)

Schedule 4 (premises: reasonable adjustments)

Schedule 5 (premises: exceptions), except paragraph 1

Schedule 6 (office-holders: excluded offices), except so far as relating to colour or nationality or marriage and civil partnership

Schedule 8 (work: reasonable adjustments)

In Schedule 9 (work: exceptions)—

    (a) Part 1 (general), except so far as relating to colour or nationality;

    (b) Part 2 (exceptions relating to age);

    (c) Part 3 (other exceptions), except paragraph 19 so far as relating to colour or nationality

Schedule 10 (education: accessibility for disabled pupils)

Schedule 13 (education: reasonable adjustments), except paragraphs 2, 5, 6 and 9

Schedule 17 (education: disabled pupils: enforcement)

Schedule 18 (public sector equality duty: exceptions)

Schedule 19 (list of public authorities)

Schedule 20 (rail vehicle accessibility: compliance)

Schedule 21 (reasonable adjustments: supplementary)

In Schedule 22 (exceptions: statutory provisions), paragraphs 2 and 5

Schedule 23 (general exceptions), except paragraph 2

Schedule 25 (information society services)

SCHEDULE 25   Section 206

INFORMATION SOCIETY SERVICES

Service providers

1   (1) This paragraph applies where a person concerned with the provision of an information society service (an 'information society service provider') is established in Great Britain.

    (2) This Act applies to anything done by the person in an EEA state (other than the United Kingdom) in providing the service as this Act would apply if the act in question were done by the person in Great Britain.

2   (1) This paragraph applies where an information society service provider is established in an EEA state (other than the United Kingdom).

    (2) This Act does not apply to anything done by the person in providing the service.

Exceptions for mere conduits

3   (1) An information society service provider does not contravene this Act only by providing so much of an information society service as consists in—

      (a) the provision of access to a communication network, or

      (b) the transmission in a communication network of information provided by the recipient of the service.

    (2) But sub-paragraph (1) applies only if the service provider does not—

      (a) initiate the transmission,

      (b) select the recipient of the transmission, or

      (c) select or modify the information contained in the transmission.

    (3) For the purposes of sub-paragraph (1), the provision of access to a communication network, and the transmission of information in a communication network, includes the automatic, intermediate and transient storage of the information transmitted so far as the storage is solely for the purpose of carrying out the transmission in the network.

    (4) Sub-paragraph (3) does not apply if the information is stored for longer than is reasonably necessary for the transmission.

Exception for caching

4   (1) This paragraph applies where an information society service consists in the transmission in a communication network of information provided by a recipient of the service.

    (2) The information society service provider does not contravene this Act only by doing anything in connection with the automatic, intermediate and temporary storage of information so provided if—

      (a) the storage of the information is solely for the purpose of making more efficient the onward transmission of the information to other recipients of the service at their request, and

      (b) the condition in sub-paragraph (3) is satisfied.

(3) The condition is that the service-provider—
  (a) does not modify the information,
  (b) complies with such conditions as are attached to having access to the information, and
  (c) (where sub-paragraph (4) applies) expeditiously removes the information or disables access to it.
(4) This sub-paragraph applies if the service-provider obtains actual knowledge that—
  (a) the information at the initial source of the transmission has been removed from the network,
  (b) access to it has been disabled, or
  (c) a court or administrative authority has required the removal from the network of, or the disablement of access to, the information.

Exception for hosting

5 (1) An information society service provider does not contravene this Act only by doing anything in providing so much of an information society service as consists in the storage of information provided by a recipient of the service, if—
  (a) the service provider had no actual knowledge when the information was provided that its provision amounted to a contravention of this Act, or
  (b) on obtaining actual knowledge that the provision of the information amounted to a contravention of that section, the service provider expeditiously removed the information or disabled access to it.
(2) Sub-paragraph (1) does not apply if the recipient of the service is acting under the authority of the control of the service provider.

Monitoring obligations

6 An injunction or interdict under Part 1 of the Equality Act 2006 may not impose on a person concerned with the provision of a service of a description given in paragraph 3(1), 4(1) or 5(1)—
  (a) a liability the imposition of which would contravene Article 12, 13 or 14 of the E-Commerce Directive;
  (b) a general obligation of the description given in Article 15 of that Directive.

Interpretation

7 (1) This paragraph applies for the purposes of this Schedule.
(2) 'Information society service'—
  (a) has the meaning given in Article 2(a) of the E-Commerce Directive (which refers to Article 1(2) of Directive 98/34/EC of the European Parliament and of the Council of 22 June 1998 laying down a procedure for the provision of information in the field of technical standards and regulations), and
  (b) is summarised in recital 17 of the E-Commerce Directive as covering 'any service normally provided for remuneration, at a distance, by means of electronic equipment for the processing (including digital compression) and storage of data, and at the individual request of a recipient of a service'.
(3) 'The E-Commerce Directive' means Directive 2000/31/EC of the European Parliament and of the Council of 8 June 2000 on certain legal aspects of information society services, in particular electronic commerce, in the Internal Market (Directive on electronic commerce).

(4) 'Recipient' means a person who (whether for professional purposes or not) uses an information society service, in particular for seeking information or making it accessible.

(5) An information society service-provider is 'established' in a country or territory if the service-provider—

  (a) effectively pursues an economic activity using a fixed establishment in that country or territory for an indefinite period, and

  (b) is a national of an EEA state or a body mentioned in [Article 54 of the Treaty on the Functioning of the European Union][341].

(6) The presence or use in a particular place of equipment or other technical means of providing an information society service is not itself sufficient to constitute the establishment of a service-provider.

(7) Where it cannot be decided from which of a number of establishments an information society service is provided, the service is to be regarded as provided from the establishment at the centre of the information society service provider's activities relating to that service.

(8) Section 212(4) does not apply to references to providing a service.

SCHEDULE 26   Section 211

AMENDMENTS

Local Government Act 1988

1–4 [Paragraphs 1 to 4 (Local Government Act 1988) become paragraphs 9 to 12.][342]

Employment Act 1989

5 [Paragraph 5 (Employment Act 1989) becomes paragraph 15.][343]

Equality Act 2006

6–30 [Paragraphs 6 to 30 (Equality Act 2006) become paragraphs 61 to 85.][344]

[PART 1
ACTS OF PARLIAMENT

Disabled Persons (Employment) Act 1944

1 In section 15 of the Disabled Persons (Employment) Act 1944 (provision of employment for seriously disabled persons), in subsection (5A), for 'the Disability Discrimination Act 1995' substitute 'the Equality Act 2010'.

---

[341] Substituted by Treaty of Lisbon (Changes in Terminology or Numbering) Order 2012, SI 2012/1809.

[342] Amended by Equality Act 2010 (Consequential Amendments, Saving and Supplementary Provisions) Order 2010, SI 2010/2279.

[343] Amended by Equality Act 2010 (Consequential Amendments, Saving and Supplementary Provisions) Order 2010, SI 2010/2279.

[344] Amended by Equality Act 2010 (Consequential Amendments, Saving and Supplementary Provisions) Order 2010, SI 2010/2279.

Teaching Council (Scotland) Act 1965

2   In section 1(3) of the Teaching Council (Scotland) Act 1965, for 'Disability Discrimination Act 1995' substitute 'Equality Act 2010'.

Employment and Training Act 1973

3   In section 12(1) of the Employment and Training Act 1973 (duty of Secretary of State to give preference to ex-service men and women when exercising power to select disabled persons for employment, training, etc.), for 'has the same meaning as in the Disability Discrimination Act 1995' substitute 'has the same meaning as in the Equality Act 2010'.

Estate Agents Act 1979

4   The Estate Agents Act 1979 is amended as follows.
5   In section 5(3) (supplementary provisions about prohibition and warning orders)—
    (a) for 'section 62 of the Sex Discrimination Act 1975, section 53 of the Race Relations Act 1976' substitute 'section 113 of the Equality Act 2010 (proceedings)'; and
    (b) omit 'those Acts and'.
6   (1) Schedule 1 (provisions supplementary to section 3(1)) is amended as follows.
    (2) For paragraph 2 substitute—
    '2.—(1) A person commits discrimination for the purposes of section 3(1)(b) in the follow-
          ing cases only.
       (2) The first case is where—
          (a) the person has been found to have contravened a relevant equality provision, and
          (b) no appeal against the finding is pending or can be brought.
       (3) The second case is where—
          (a) the person has been given an unlawful act notice under section 21 of the
              Equality Act 2006,
          (b) the notice specifies a relevant equality provision as the provision by virtue of
              which the act in question is unlawful, and
          (c) no appeal against the giving of the notice is pending or can be brought.
       (4) The third case is where—
          (a) the person is the subject of an injunction, interdict or order under section 24 of
              the Equality Act 2006 (unlawful acts), and
          (b) the unlawful act in question is a contravention of a relevant equality provision.
       (5) The relevant equality provisions are—
          (a) Parts 3 and 4 of the Equality Act 2010 (services and premises) so far as relating
              to discrimination and victimisation, and
          (b) section 112 of that Act (aiding contraventions) in relation to either of those
              Parts of that Act so far as relating to discrimination and victimisation.'
    (3) In paragraph 3 for 'discrimination' substitute 'a contravention of a relevant equality
        provision'.
    (4) For paragraph 4 substitute—
       '4. For the purposes of paragraphs 2 and 3 "discrimination" and "victimisation"
           have the same meaning as in the Equality Act 2010'.

Civic Government (Scotland) Act 1982

7   (1) Section 20 of the Civic Government (Scotland) Act 1982 (regulations relating to taxis
        and private hire cars and their drivers) is amended as follows.
    (2) In subsection (2A) for 'section 1(2) of the Disability Discrimination Act 1995' substitute
        'section 6 of the Equality Act 2010'.

(3) In subsection (2AA) for 'section 1(2) of the Disability Discrimination Act 1995 (c.50)' substitute 'section 6 of the Equality Act 2010'.

Housing (Scotland) Act 1987

8 In section 338(1) of the Housing (Scotland) Act 1987 (interpretation) in the definition of 'disabled person' for 'Disability Discrimination Act 1995 (c.50),' substitute 'Equality Act 2010,'.][345]

[*Local Government Act 1988*

9 Part 2 of the Local Government Act 1988 (public supply or works contracts) is amended as follows.

10 In section 17 (local and other public authority contracts: exclusion of non-commercial considerations)—

(a) omit subsection (9), and

(b) after that subsection insert—

'(10) This section does not prevent a public authority to which it applies from exercising any function regulated by this section with reference to a non-commercial matter to the extent that the authority considers it necessary or expedient to do so to enable or facilitate compliance with—

(a) the duty imposed on it by section 149 of the Equality Act 2010 (public sector equality duty), or

(b) any duty imposed on it by regulations under section 153 or 154 of that Act (powers to impose specific duties).'

11 Omit section 18 (exceptions to section 17 relating to race relations matters).

12 In section 19 (provisions supplementary to or consequential on section 17) omit subsection (10).][346]

[*Employment Act 1989*

13 The Employment Act 1989 is amended as follows.

14 In section 8 (exemption for discrimination in favour of lone parents in connection with training), in subsection (2), for the words from 'for the purposes of the 1975 Act' to the end substitute 'for the purposes of the Equality Act 2010 as giving rise to any contravention of Part 5 of that Act, so far as relating to marriage and civil partnership discrimination (within the meaning of that Act).'.][347]

[15 (1) Section 12 [...] (Sikhs: requirements as to safety helmets) is amended as follows.

(2) In subsection (1), for 'requirement or condition', in the first three places, substitute 'provision criterion or practice'.

(3) In that subsection, for the words from 'section 1(1)(b)' to the end substitute 'section 19 of the Equality Act 2010 (indirect discrimination), the provision, criterion or practice is to be taken as one in relation to which the condition in subsection (2)(d) of that section (proportionate means of achieving a legitimate aim) is satisfied'.

---

[345] Inserted by Equality Act 2010 (Consequential Amendments, Saving and Supplementary Provisions) Order 2010, SI 2010/2279.

[346] Amended by Equality Act 2010 (Consequential Amendments, Saving and Supplementary Provisions) Order 2010, SI 2010/2279.

[347] Inserted by Equality Act 2010 (Consequential Amendments, Saving and Supplementary Provisions) Order 2010, SI 2010/2279.

(4) In subsection (2), for the words from 'the Race Relations Act' to the end substitute 'section 13 of the Equality Act 2010 as giving rise to discrimination against any other person'.][348]

[16 In section 28 (orders etc.), omit subsections (2), (3) and (4)(a).

17 In section 29(1) (interpretation), omit the definition of 'the 1975 Act'.

Local Government and Housing Act 1989

18 In section 7(2) of the Local Government and Housing Act 1989 (requirement for appointments to be on merit to be subject to discrimination law)—

(a) omit paragraphs (c), (d) and (f), and

(b) at the end insert—

'(g) sections 39, 40 and 49 to 51 of the Equality Act 2010 (employees and office-holders), so far as relating to disability, and Schedule 8 to that Act (reasonable adjustments for disabled persons) so far as it applies in relation to sections 39 and 49 to 51 of that Act;

(h) paragraph 1 of Schedule 9 to that Act (occupational requirements), so far as relating to sex, pregnancy and maternity, marriage and civil partnership, gender reassignment or race'.

Enterprise and New Towns (Scotland) Act 1990

19 The Enterprise and New Towns (Scotland) Act 1990 is amended as follows.

20 In section 2(4)(a) (functions in relation to training for employment etc.) for 'section 3(1) of the Race Relations Act 1976' substitute 'section 9 of the Equality Act 2010'.

21 In section 16(2) (courses of training etc.: duty to give preference to certain categories) for 'Disability Discrimination Act 1995' substitute 'Equality Act 2010'.

22 For section 17 (encouragement of women, members of minority racial groups and disabled persons to take advantage of opportunities for certain work etc) substitute—

'17 **Encouragement of women, members of ethnic minorities and disabled persons to take up certain employment opportunities and training**

(1) Scottish Enterprise and Highlands and Islands Enterprise shall each, in exercising its functions, promote such actings by any employer as are lawful by virtue of section 158 of the Equality Act 2010 (the "2010 Act") (positive action: general) in relation to—

(a) affording access to facilities for training, and

(b) encouraging persons to take advantage of opportunities for taking up that employer's work.

(2) This section applies to the protected characteristics of sex, race and disability within the meaning of the 2010 Act.

(3) This section is without prejudice to paragraph (a) of section 2(4) of this Act or to any provision of the 2010 Act prohibiting discrimination within the meaning of that Act.'.

Further and Higher Education Act 1992

23 In section 62(7B) of the Further and Higher Education Act 1992 (higher education funding councils) for 'Disability Discrimination Act 1995' substitute 'Equality Act 2010'.

Trade Union and Labour Relations (Consolidation) Act 1992

24 (1) Schedule A2 to the Trade Union and Labour Relations (Consolidation) Act 1992 (tribunal jurisdictions where failure by employer or employee to comply with applicable code of practice may affect the level of damages) is amended as follows.

---

[348] Amended by Equality Act 2010 (Consequential Amendments, Saving and Supplementary Provisions) Order 2010, SI 2010/2279.

(2) Omit the entries relating to—
    (a) the Equal Pay Act 1970;
    (b) the Sex Discrimination Act 1975;
    (c) the Race Relations Act 1976;
    (d) the Disability Discrimination Act 1995;
    (e) the Employment Equality (Sexual Orientation) Regulations 2003;
    (f) the Employment Equality (Religion or Belief) Regulations 2003;
    (g) the Employment Equality (Age) Regulations 2006.
(3) At the end of the entries relating to provisions of Acts, insert—
'Sections 120 and 127 of the Equality Act 2010 (discrimination etc in work cases)'.

Trade Union Reform and Employment Rights Act 1993

25 In section 39(2) of the Trade Union Reform and Employment Rights Act 1993 (agreements not to take proceedings before employment tribunal) omit 'the Sex Discrimination Act 1975, the Race Relations Act 1976, and'.
26 In Schedule 6 (compromise contracts) omit paragraphs 1 and 2.

Employment Tribunals Act 1996

27 The Employment Tribunals Act 1996 is amended as follows.
28 In section 5(2)(c) (remuneration, fees and allowances) for '2A(1)(b) of the Equal Pay Act 1970' substitute '131(2) of the Equality Act 2010'.
29 In section 7(3)(h) (employment tribunal procedure regulations) for '2A(1)(b) of the Equal Pay Act 1970' substitute '131(2) of the Equality Act 2010'.
30 In section 12(1) (restriction of publicity in disability cases) for 'section 17A or 25(8) of the Disability Discrimination Act 1995' substitute 'section 120 of the Equality Act 2010, where the complaint relates to disability'.
31 In section 18(1) (tribunal proceedings to which conciliation provisions apply)—
    (a) for paragraph (a) substitute—
'(a) under section 120 or 127 of the Equality Act 2010,'; and
    (b) omit paragraphs (c), (k), (l) and (r).
32 In section 21(1) (Jurisdiction of appeal tribunal)—
    (a) omit paragraphs (a), (b), (c), (e), (l), (m) and (s); and
    (b) at the end of the entries relating to provisions in Acts, insert—
'(ge) the Equality Act 2010,'.

Employment Rights Act 1996

33 (1) Section 126 of the Employment Rights Act 1996 (acts which are both unfair dismissal and discrimination) is amended as follows.
(2) In subsection (1) for paragraph (b) substitute—
'(b) the Equality Act 2010.'.
(3) In subsection (2)—
    (a) for 'any one of those Acts or Regulations' substitute 'either of those Acts', and
    (b) for 'any other of them' substitute 'the other'.

Housing Grants, Construction and Regeneration Act 1996

34 In section 126 of the Housing Grants, Construction and Regeneration Act 1996 (Secretary of State's power to give financial assistance etc), in subsection (3), in the definition of 'racial group', for 'the Race Relations Act 1976' substitute 'section 9 of the Equality Act 2010'.

Education Act 1996

35 The Education Act 1996 is amended as follows.

36 (1) Section 317 of the Education Act 1996 (duties of governing bodies etc in relation to pupils with special educational needs) is amended as follows.

(2) In subsection (6)(b)(iv) for 'section 28D of the Disability Discrimination Act 1995 ("the 1995 Act") ' substitute 'paragraph 3 of Schedule 10 to the Equality Act 2010 ("the 2010 Act")'.

(3) For subsection (6A) substitute—

'(6A) In subsection (6)(b) "disabled person" means a person who is a disabled person for the purposes of the 2010 Act; and section 89 (interpretation of Part 6) of, and paragraph 6 of Schedule 10 (supplementary provisions for Schedule 10) to, the 2010 Act apply for the purposes of subsection (6)(b) as they apply for the purposes of Part 6 of and Schedule 10 to that Act.'.

37 In section 336(4A) (tribunal procedure) for 'claim under Chapter 1 of Part 4 of the Disability Discrimination Act 1995' substitute 'claim in relation to a contravention of Chapter 1 of Part 6 of the Equality Act 2010 so far as relating to disability.'.

38 In section 509AC(5)(interpretation etc), in the definition of 'disabled person', for 'Disability Discrimination Act 1995' substitute 'Equality Act 2010'.

39 Omit section 583(5) (commencement etc: transitory provision relating to the Disability Discrimination Act 1995).

40 In Schedule 35B (meaning of eligible child etc), paragraph 15(4), for 'Disability Discrimination Act 1995' substitute 'Equality Act 2010'.

41 In Schedule 35C (school travel schemes), paragraph 14, in the definition of 'disabled child', for 'Disability Discrimination Act 1995' substitute 'Equality Act 2010'.

42 (1) In Schedule 36A (education functions of local authorities) the table is amended as follows.

(2) Omit the entries relating to the Sex Discrimination Act 1975 and the Disability Discrimination Act 1995.

(3) Insert at the end—
'Equality Act 2010 (c. 15)

Section 29(7) in its application to a local authority's functions under the Education Acts.	Duty to make reasonable adjustments for disabled persons.
Section 85(6)	Duty (as responsible body) to make reasonable adjustments for disabled pupils.
Section 92(6)	Duty (as responsible body) to make reasonable adjustments for disabled persons in further and higher education.
Section 93(6)	Duty (as responsible body) to make reasonable adjustments for disabled persons in the provision of recreational or training facilities.
paragraph 1 of Schedule 10	Duty to prepare and implement accessibility strategy.
paragraph 3 of Schedule 10	Duty (as responsible body) to prepare and implement an accessibility plan.'

Teaching and Higher Education Act 1998

43 In section 1(4) of the Teaching and Higher Education Act 1998 (the General Teaching Council for England) for 'Disability Discrimination Act 1995' substitute 'Equality Act 2010'.

School Standards and Framework Act 1998

44 The School Standards and Framework Act 1998 is amended as follows.

45 In Schedule 5, in paragraph 6 (adjudicators, procedure) for subparagraphs (a) to (c) substitute—

'(a) section 71 of the Race Relations Act 1976, or

(b) Parts 3 and 6 of the Equality Act 2010,'.

46 (1) In Schedule 6, Part 5 (procedures for making transitional exemption orders in Wales) paragraph 22(4) is amended as follows.

(2) For the definition of 'the 1975 Act' substitute—

'"the 2010 Act" means the Equality Act 2010,'.

(3) In the definition of 'the responsible body' for 'section 22 of the 1975 Act' substitute 'section 85 of the 2010 Act'.

(4) In the definition of 'transitional exemption order' for 'section 27 of the 1975 Act' substitute 'paragraph 3 of Schedule 11 to the 2010 Act'.

(5) For 'section 27(1) of the 1975 Act' substitute 'paragraph 3 of Schedule 11 to the 2010 Act'.

47 (1) In Schedule 7, in Part 6 (transitional exemption orders, interpretation) paragraph 16(6) is amended as follows.

(2) For the definition of the 1975 Act substitute—

'"the 2010 Act" means the Equality Act 2010,'.

(3) In the definition of 'the responsible body' for 'section 22 of the 1975 Act' substitute 'section 85 of the 2010 Act'.

(4) In the definition of 'transitional exemption order' for 'section 27 of the 1975 Act' substitute 'paragraph 3 of Schedule 11 to the 2010 Act'.

(5) For 'section 27(1) of the 1975 Act' substitute 'paragraph 3 of Schedule 11 to the 2010 Act'.

Transport Act 2000

48 In section 112(2) of the Transport Act 2000 (plans and strategies: supplementary) for 'Disability Discrimination Act 1995' substitute 'Equality Act 2010'.

Employment Act 2002

49 (1) Schedule 5 to the Employment Act 2002 (tribunal jurisdiction) is amended as follows.

(2) Omit the entries relating to—

(a) the Equal Pay Act 1970;

(b) the Sex Discrimination Act 1975;

(c) the Race Relations Act 1976;

(d) the Disability Discrimination Act 1995;

(e) the Employment Equality (Sexual Orientation) Regulations 2003;

(f) the Employment Equality (Religion or Belief) Regulations 2003;

(g) the Employment Equality (Age) Regulations 2006.

(3) At the end of the entries relating to provisions of Acts, insert—

'Sections 120 and 127 of the Equality Act 2010 (discrimination etc in work cases)'.

Income Tax (Earnings and Pensions) Act 2003

50 The Income Tax (Earnings and Pensions) Act 2003 is amended as follows.

51 In section 439(4) (chargeable events) after 'within the meaning of' insert 'the Equality Act 2010 in England and Wales and Scotland, or'.

52 In section 477(5) (chargeable events) after 'within the meaning of' insert 'the Equality Act 2010 in England and Wales and Scotland, or'.

Communications Act 2003

53 The Communications Act 2003 is amended as follows.

54 In section 27(5) (training and equality of opportunity)—

   (a) in the definition of 'disabled' after 'meaning as in' insert 'the Equality Act 2010 or, in Northern Ireland,', and

   (b) in the definition of 'racial group' for 'Race Relations Act 1976 (c 74)' substitute 'Equality Act 2010'.

55 In section 337(9) (promotion of equal opportunities and training)—

   (a) in the definition of 'disabled' after 'meaning as in' insert 'the Equality Act 2010 or, in Northern Ireland,', and

   (b) in the definition of 'racial group' for 'Race Relations Act 1976 (c 74)' substitute 'Equality Act 2010'.

56 In Schedule 12, in paragraph 23(6) (obligations of the Welsh Authority in relation to equality of opportunity)—

   (a) in the definition of 'disability' after 'meaning as in' insert 'the Equality Act 2010 or, in Northern Ireland,', and

   (b) in the definition of 'racial group' for 'Race Relations Act 1976 (c 74)' substitute 'the Equality Act 2010'.

Finance Act 2004

57 The Finance Act 2004 is amended as follows.

58 In section 172A(5)(db) (surrender of pension benefits etc) for—

   (a) 'the Employment Equality (Age) Regulations 2006 or' substitute 'Part 5 of the Equality Act 2010, so far as relating to age, or the' and

   (b) for 'them' substitute 'those Regulations.'.

59 In paragraphs 11D(2A) and (2B)(b), 12(2C)(d) and 14(3A) and (3D)(a) of Schedule 36 (pension schemes etc: transitional provisions and savings)—

   (a) for 'the Employment Equality (Age) Regulations 2006, or' substitute 'Part 5 of the Equality Act 2010, so far as relating to age, or the', and

   (b) for 'them' substitute 'those Regulations.'.

Serious Organised Crime and Police Act 2005

60 Section 56 of the Serious Organised Crime and Police Act 2005 (the title to which becomes 'Application of discrimination legislation to SOCA seconded staff: Northern Ireland') is amended as follows—

   (a) in subsection (2), omit paragraphs (a) and (b); and

   (b) in subsection (4), omit paragraphs (a), (b), (g) and (h) and the 'and' preceding each of paragraphs (g) and (h).'.][349]

[*Equality Act 2006*

61 The Equality Act 2006 is amended as follows.

62 (1) Section 8 (equality and diversity) is amended as follows.

   (2) In subsection (1)—

      (a) in paragraph (d) for 'equality enactments' substitute 'Equality Act 2010', and

      (b) in paragraph (e) for 'the equality enactments' substitute 'that Act'.

---

[349] Inserted by Equality Act 2010 (Consequential Amendments, Saving and Supplementary Provisions) Order 2010, SI 2010/2279.

(3) In subsection (4) for 'Disability Discrimination Act 1995 (c. 50)' substitute 'Equality Act 2010'.

63 In section 10(2) (meaning of group) for paragraph (d) substitute—
'(d) gender reassignment (within the meaning of section 7 of the Equality Act 2010),'.

64 For section 11(3)(c) (interpretation) substitute—
'(c) a reference to the equality and human rights enactments is a reference to the Human Rights Act 1998, this Act and the Equality Act 2010.'

65 (1) Section 14 (codes of practice) is amended as follows.

(2) For subsection (1) substitute—
'(1) The Commission may issue a code of practice in connection with any matter addressed by the Equality Act 2010.'

(3) In subsection (2)(a) for 'a provision or enactment listed in subsection (1)' substitute 'the Equality Act 2010 or an enactment made under that Act'.

(4) In subsection (3)—
(a) in paragraph (a) for 'section 49G(7) of the Disability Discrimination Act 1995 (c. 50)' substitute 'section 190(7) of the Equality Act 2010', and
(b) for paragraph (c)(iv) substitute—
'(iv) section 190 of the Equality Act 2010.'

(5) In subsection (5)(a) for 'listed in subsection (1)' substitute 'a matter addressed by the Equality Act 2010'.

(6) In subsection (9) for 'section 76A' to 'duties)' substitute 'section 149, 153 or 154 of the Equality Act 2010 (public sector equality duty)'.

66 In section 16(4) (inquiries: matters which the Commission may consider and report on) for 'equality enactments' substitute 'Equality Act 2010'.

67 In section 21(2)(b) (unlawful act notice: specification of legislative provision) for 'equality enactments' substitute 'Equality Act 2010'.

68 After section 24 insert—
'24A Enforcement powers: supplemental
(1) This section has effect in relation to—
(a) an act which is unlawful because, by virtue of any of sections 13 to 18 of the Equality Act 2010, it amounts to a contravention of any of Parts 3, 4, 5, 6 or 7 of that Act,
(b) an act which is unlawful because it amounts to a contravention of section 60(1) of that Act (or to a contravention of section 111 or 112 of that Act that relates to a contravention of section 60(1) of that Act) (enquiries about disability and health),
(c) an act which is unlawful because it amounts to a contravention of section 106 of that Act (information about diversity in range of election candidates etc.),
(d) an act which is unlawful because, by virtue of section 108(1) of that Act, it amounts to a contravention of any of Parts 3, 4, 5, 6 or 7 of that Act, or
(e) the application of a provision, criterion or practice which, by virtue of section 19 of that Act, amounts to a contravention of that Act.
(2) For the purposes of sections 20 to 24 of this Act, it is immaterial whether the Commission knows or suspects that a person has been or may be affected by the unlawful act or application.
(3) For those purposes, an unlawful act includes making arrangements to act in a particular way which would, if applied to an individual, amount to a contravention mentioned in subsection (1)(a).
(4) Nothing in this Act affects the entitlement of a person to bring proceedings under the Equality Act 2010 in respect of a contravention mentioned in subsection (1).'

69 Omit section 25 (restraint of unlawful advertising etc.).

70 Omit section 26 (supplemental).

71 (1) Section 27 (conciliation) is amended as follows.

(2) For subsection (1) (disputes in relation to which the Commission may make arrangements for the provision of conciliation services) substitute—

'(1) The Commission may make arrangements for the provision of conciliation services for disputes in respect of which proceedings have been or could be determined by virtue of section 114 of the Equality Act 2010.'

72 (1) Section 28 (legal assistance) is amended as follows.

(2) In subsection (1)—

(a) in paragraph (a) for 'equality enactments' substitute 'Equality Act 2010', and

(b) in paragraph (b) for 'the equality enactments' substitute 'that Act'.

(3) In subsection (5) for 'Part V of the Disability Discrimination Act 1995 (c. 50) (public)' substitute 'Part 12 of the Equality Act 2010 (disabled persons:)'.

(4) In subsection (6)—

(a) for 'the equality enactments', on the first occasion it appears, substitute 'the Equality Act 2010', and

(b) for 'the equality enactments', on each other occasion it appears, substitute 'that Act'.

(5) In subsection (7)—

(a) in paragraph (a) for 'equality enactments' substitute 'Equality Act 2010', and

(b) in paragraph (b) for 'the equality enactments' substitute 'that Act'.

(6) In subsection (8) for 'Part V of the Disability Discrimination Act 1995 (c. 50)' substitute 'Part 12 of the Equality Act 2010'.

(7) In subsection (9) for 'equality enactments' substitute 'Equality Act 2010'.

(8) In subsection (12)—

(a) for 'A reference in' to 'includes a reference' substitute 'This section applies', and

(b) after paragraph (b) add 'as it applies to the Equality Act 2010.'

73 For section 31(1) (duties in respect of which Commission may assess compliance) substitute—

'(1) The Commission may assess the extent to which or the manner in which a person has complied with a duty under or by virtue of section 149, 153 or 154 of the Equality Act 2010 (public sector equality duty).'

74 (1) Section 32 (public sector duties: compliance notice) is amended as follows.

(2) For subsection (1) substitute—

'(1) This section applies where the Commission thinks that a person has failed to comply with a duty under or by virtue of section 149, 153 or 154 of the Equality Act 2010 (public sector equality duty).'

(3) In subsection (4) for 'section 76A' to 'Disability Discrimination Act 1995' substitute 'section 149 of the Equality Act 2010'.

(4) In subsection (9)(a) for 'section 76A' to 'Disability Discrimination Act 1995 (c. 50)' substitute 'section 149 of the Equality Act 2010'.

(5) In subsection (9)(b) for 'in any other case' substitute 'where the notice related to a duty by virtue of section 153 or 154 of that Act'.

(6) In subsection (11) for 'section 76B' to 'Disability Discrimination Act 1995' substitute 'section 153 or 154 of the Equality Act 2010'.

75 Omit section 33 (equality and human rights enactments).

76 (1) Section 34 (meaning of unlawful) is amended as follows.

(2) In subsection (1) for 'equality enactments' substitute 'Equality Act 2010'.

(3) In subsection (2)—

(a) after 'virtue of' insert 'any of the following provisions of the Equality Act 2010', and

(b) for paragraphs (a) to (c) substitute—

'(a) section 1 (public sector duty regarding socio-economic inequalities),

(b) section 149, 153 or 154 (public sector equality duty),

    (c) Part 12 (disabled persons: transport), or

    (d) section 190 (disability: improvements to let dwelling houses).'

77 (1) Section 35 (general: definitions) is amended as follows.

    (2) In the definition of 'religion or belief', for 'Part 2 (as defined by section 44)' substitute 'section 10 of the Equality Act 2010'.

    (3) For the definition of 'sexual orientation' substitute—

' "sexual orientation" has the same meaning as in section 12 of the Equality Act 2010.'

78 In section 39(4) (orders subject to affirmative resolution procedure) for ', 27(10) or 33(3)' substitute 'or 27(10)'.

79 Omit section 43 (transitional: rented housing in Scotland).

80 Omit Part 2 (discrimination on grounds of religion or belief).

81 Omit section 81 (regulations).

82 Omit Part 4 (public functions).

83 In section 94(3) (extent: Northern Ireland)—

    (a) omit 'and 41 to 56', and

    (b) omit 'and the Disability Discrimination Act 1995 (c. 50)'.

84 (1) Schedule 1 (the Commission: constitution, etc.) is amended as follows.

    (2) In paragraph 52(3)(a) for 'Parts 1, 3, 4, 5 and 5B of the Disability Discrimination Act 1995 (c. 50)' substitute 'Parts 2, 3, 4, 6, 7, 12 and 13 of the Equality Act 2010, in so far as they relate to disability'.

    (3) In paragraph 53 for 'Part 2 of the Disability Discrimination Act 1995 (c. 50)' substitute 'Part 5 of the Equality Act 2010'.

    (4) In paragraph 54 for 'Part 2 of the Disability Discrimination Act 1995' substitute 'Part 5 of the Equality Act 2010'.

85 In Schedule 3 (consequential amendments), omit paragraphs 6 to 35 and 41 to 56.][350]

[Immigration, Asylum and Nationality Act 2006

86 In section 23(1)(a) of the Immigration Asylum and Nationality Act 2006 (discrimination: code of practice) for 'the Race Relations Act 1976 (c. 74)' substitute 'the Equality Act 2010, so far as relating to race'.

Childcare Act 2006

87 The Childcare Act 2006 is amended as follows.

88 In section 6(6) (duty to secure sufficient childcare for working parents) in the definition of 'disabled child' for 'Disability Discrimination Act 1995 (c.50)' substitute 'Equality Act 2010'.

89 In section 12(8) (duty to provide information, advice and assistance) for 'Disability Discrimination Act 1995 (c.50)' substitute 'Equality Act 2010'.

90 In section 22(6) (duty to secure sufficient childcare for working parents (Wales)) in the definition of 'disabled child' for 'Disability Discrimination Act 1995 (c.50)' substitute 'Equality Act 2010'.

91 In section 27(8) (duty to provide information, advice and assistance (Wales)) for 'Disability Discrimination Act 1995 (c.50)' substitute 'Equality Act 2010'.

Education and Inspections Act 2006

92 The Education and Inspections Act 2006 is amended as follows.

93 In section 21(5) (proposals under section 19: procedure) for 'section 27 of the Sex Discrimination Act 1975 (c. 65) (exception for single-sex establishments turning coeducational)' substitute

---

[350] Amended by Equality Act 2010 (Consequential Amendments, Saving and Supplementary Provisions) Order 2010, SI 2010/2279.

'paragraphs 3 and 4 of Schedule 11 to the Equality Act 2010 (single-sex schools turning co-educational)'.

94 In section 91(7) (enforcement of disciplinary penalties) for 'Disability Discrimination Act 1995 (c.50)' substitute 'Equality Act 2010'.

Finance Act 2007

95 In paragraph 7(7) of Schedule 18 to the Finance Act 2007 (pension schemes: abolition of relief for life insurance premium contributions etc)—
   (a) for 'Employment Equality (Age) Regulations 2006 (SI 2006/1031)' substitute 'Equality Act 2010, so far as relating to age,', and
   (b) for 'them' substitute 'those Regulations'.

UK Borders Act 2007

96 In section 48(2)(f) of the UK Borders Act 2007 (recommendations by Chief Inspector of UK Border Agency) for 'section 19D of the Race Relations Act 1976 (c.74)' substitute 'paragraph 17 of Schedule 3 to the Equality Act 2010'.

Regulatory Enforcement and Sanctions Act 2008

97 The Regulatory Enforcement and Sanctions Act 2008 is amended as follows.
98 Insert after section 38(2) (meaning of 'relevant offence')—
   '(3) The entry in Schedule 6 for Part 5 of the Disability Discrimination Act 1995 is, in relation to England and Wales and Scotland, to be read as a reference to Part 12 of the Equality Act 2010.'
99 In Schedule 3 (enactments specified for the purposes of the Part relating to LBRO) omit 'Disability Discrimination Act 1995 (c. 50)'.

Apprenticeships, Skills, Children and Learning Act 2009

100 In section 218(3)(b) of the Apprenticeships, Skills, Children and Learning Act 2009 (arrangements etc to be made by Commission) for 'section 1(1) of the Disability Discrimination Act 1995 (c.50)' substitute 'section 6 of the Equality Act 2010'.

PART 2
ACTS OF THE SCOTTISH PARLIAMENT

Education (Disability Strategies and Pupils' Educational Records) (Scotland) Act 2002

101 In section 6 of the Education (Disability Strategies and Pupils' Educational Records) (Scotland) Act 2002 (interpretation) in the definition of 'pupil with a disability' for 'Disability Discrimination Act 1995 (c.50)' substitute 'Equality Act 2010'.

Freedom of Information (Scotland) Act 2002

102 The Freedom of Information (Scotland) Act 2002 is amended as follows.
103 In section 11(5) (means of providing information) for 'provider of services has under or by virtue of section 21 of the Disability Discrimination Act 1995 (c. 50)' substitute 'person has under or by virtue of section 29 of the Equality Act 2010 (provision of services etc)'.
104 In section 12(6) (excessive cost of compliance) for 'Disability Discrimination Act 1995 (c.50)' substitute 'Equality Act 2010'.

Dog Fouling (Scotland) Act 2003

105 In section 16 of the Dog Fouling (Scotland) Act 2003 (interpretation) in the definition of 'disabled person' for 'section 1 of the Disability Discrimination Act 1995 (c.50)' substitute 'section 6 of the Equality Act 2010'.

Education (Additional Support for Learning) (Scotland) Act 2004

106 Paragraph 3(1)(e) of Schedule 2 to the Education (Additional Support for Learning) (Scotland) Act 2004 (exclusion to duty to comply with placing requests) is amended as follows—
    (a) for 'section 26 of the Sex Discrimination Act 1975 (c.65))' substitute 'paragraph 1(2) of Part 1 of Schedule 11 to the Equality Act 2010', and
    (b) for 'section', where it occurs for the second time, substitute 'paragraph'.][351]

[*Housing (Scotland) Act 2006*

106A In section 194(1) of the Housing (Scotland) Act 2006 (interpretation), in the definition of 'disabled person', for 'Disability Discrimination Act 1995 (c. 50)' substitute 'Equality Act 2010'.][352]

[*Education (Additional Support for Learning) (Scotland) Act 2009*

107 In section 9 of the Education (Additional Support for Learning) (Scotland) Act 2009 (functions of education authority in relation to certain pre-school children etc), in the amendment to section 5(3)(c) of the Education (Additional Support for Learning) (Scotland) Act 2004, for 'Disability Discrimination Act 1995 (c.50)' substitute 'Equality Act 2010'.][353]

SCHEDULE 27   **Section 211**

REPEALS AND REVOCATIONS

PART 1
REPEALS

[

Short title	Extent of repeal
The Sex Disqualification Removal Act 1919	The whole Act.
Equal Pay Act 1970	The whole Act.
Sex Discrimination Act 1975	The whole Act.
Race Relations Act 1976	The whole Act.
Estate Agents Act 1979	In section 5(3) 'those Acts and'.
Further Education Act 1985	Section 4.

[351] Inserted by Equality Act 2010 (Consequential Amendments, Saving and Supplementary Provisions) Order 2010, SI 2010/2279.
[352] Inserted by Equality Act 2010 (Public Authorities and Consequential and Supplementary Amendments) Order 2011, SI 2011/1060.
[353] Inserted by Equality Act 2010 (Consequential Amendments, Saving and Supplementary Provisions) Order 2010, SI 2010/2279.

516

Short title	Extent of repeal
Sex Discrimination Act 1986	The whole Act.
Local Government Act 1988	Section 17(9). Section 18. Section 19(10).
Employment Act 1989	Sections 1 to 7. Section 9. Section 28(2), (3) and (4)(a). In section 29(1) the definition of 'the 1975 Act'.
Local Government and Housing Act 1989	Section 7(2)(c), (d) and (f).
Social Security Act 1989	In Schedule 5— (a) in paragraph 2(4) from '; but where' to the end, and (b) paragraph 5.
Enterprise and New Towns (Scotland) Act 1990	Section 18.
Contracts (Applicable Law) Act 1990	In Schedule 4 in paragraph 1 'Section 1(11) of the Equal Pay Act 1970 and' and the crossheading referring to the Equal Pay Act 1970.
Further and Higher Education Act 1992	In Schedule 8, paragraphs 75 to 88.
Trade Union and Labour Relations (Consolidation) Act 1992	In Schedule A2 the entries for— (a) the Equal Pay Act 1970; (b) the Sex Discrimination Act 1975; (c) the Race Relations Act 1976; (d) the Disability Discrimination Act 1995; (e) the Employment Equality (Sexual Orientation) Regulations 2003; (f) the Employment Equality (Religion or Belief) Regulations 2003; (g) the Employment Equality (Age) Regulations 2006. In Schedule 2, paragraph 3(1) to (3) and the preceding cross-heading.
Trade Union Reform and Employment Rights Act 1993	In section 39(2) 'the Sex Discrimination Act 1975, the Race Relations Act 1976, and'. In Schedule 6, paragraphs 1 and 2. In Schedule 7, paragraph 8.
Race Relations (Remedies) Act 1994	The whole Act.
Disability Discrimination Act 1995	The whole Act.
Pensions Act 1995	Sections 62 to 66.
Employment Tribunals Act 1996	Section 18(1)(c), (k), (l) and (r). Section 21(1)(a), (b), (c), (e), (l), (m) and (s). In Schedule 2, paragraph 7.
Employment Rights Act 1996	In Schedule 1, paragraph 1 and the preceding cross-heading.
Armed Forces Act 1996	Sections 21, 23 and 24.

(Continued)

Short title	Extent of repeal
Education Act 1996	In Schedule 36A, in the table, the entries for the Sex Discrimination Act 1975 and the Disability Discrimination Act 1995.
	In Schedule 37, paragraphs 31, 32, 34 to 36, 37(b), 39, 40 and 43.
Employment Rights (Dispute Resolution) Act 1998	Section 8(1), (2) and (4).
	Section 9(2)(a), (b) and (d).
	Section 10(2)(a), (b) and (d).
	In Schedule 1, paragraphs 2, 3 and 11.
School Standards and Framework Act 1998	In Schedule 30, paragraphs 5, 6 and 7.
Greater London Authority Act 1999	Section 404.
Learning and Skills Act 2000	Section 150(4)(d) and the 'or' immediately preceding it.
	In Schedule 9, paragraphs 5, 6, 7 and 9 and the preceding cross-heading.
Race Relations (Amendment) Act 2000	Section 1.
	Sections 3 to 10.
	Schedule 2, except for paragraphs 17 and 31.
	Schedule 3.
Standards In Scotland's Schools etc. Act 2000	In Schedule 2, paragraph 2.
Special Educational Needs and Disability Act 2001	Sections 11 to 33.
	Section 34(4), (5), (6) and (7).
	Sections 38 to 40.
	Schedules 2 to 6.
Sex Discrimination (Election Candidates) Act 2002	Section 1.
Employment Act 2002	Section 42 and the preceding cross-heading.
	In Schedule 5, the entries for—
	(a) the Equal Pay Act 1970;
	(b) the Sex Discrimination Act 1975;
	(c) the Race Relations Act 1976;
	(d) the Disability Discrimination Act 1995;
	(e) the Employment Equality (Sexual Orientation) Regulations 2003;
	(f) the Employment Equality (Religion or Belief) Regulations 2003;
	(g) the Employment Equality (Age) Regulations 2006.
Education Act 2002	In Schedule 7, paragraph 5 and the preceding cross-heading.
	In Schedule 18, paragraphs 7 to 12.
	In Schedule 21, paragraphs 3 and 26 to 29 and the cross-headings preceding paragraphs 3 and 26.
Private Hire Vehicles (Carriage of Guide Dogs etc) Act 2002	Sections 1 and 3 to 5.

Short title	Extent of repeal
Nationality, Immigration and Asylum Act 2002	In Schedule 7, paragraphs 11, 12 and 14 and the preceding cross-heading.
Gender Recognition Act 2004	Section 19. In Schedule 6, Part 1.
Civil Partnership Act 2004	Section 6(1)(b) and (2).
Higher Education Act 2004	Section 19.
Education (Additional Support for Learning) (Scotland) Act 2004	In section 17(1) 'to exercise the functions which are conferred on a Tribunal by virtue of this Act'.
Disability Discrimination Act 2005	The whole Act except for— (a) section 3 (b) section 9 (c) Schedule 1 paragraphs 31, 33, 34(1) and (6) and Part 2
Serious Organised Crime and Police Act 2005	Section 56(2)(a) and (b) and (4)(a), (b), (g) and (h) and the 'and' preceding each of paragraphs (g) and (h).
Education Act 2005	In Schedule 9, paragraph 8 and the preceding cross-heading. In Schedule 14, paragraphs 5 and 7. In Schedule 15, paragraph 6.
Charities and Trustee Investment (Scotland) Act 2005	In Schedule 4, paragraph 3.
Equality Act 2006	Section 25. Section 26. Section 33. Section 43. Part 2. Section 81. Part 4. In Section 94(3) 'and 41 to 56' and 'and the Disability Discrimination Act 1995(c.50)'. In Schedule 3, paragraphs 6 to 35 and paragraphs 40 to 56.
Education and Inspections Act 2006	In Schedule 1, paragraph 1 and the preceding cross-heading. In Schedule 3, paragraph 3 and the preceding cross-heading.
Legal Services Act 2007	In Schedule 21, paragraphs 32, 36 to 38 and 118 and the cross-headings preceding paragraphs 32 and 118.
Greater London Authority Act 2007	Section 11(5).
Regulatory Enforcement and Sanctions Act 2008	In Schedule 3, 'Disability Discrimination Act 1995 (c.50)'. In Schedule 6, 'Disability Discrimination Act 1995 (c.50)'.

(Continued)

519

Short title	Extent of repeal
Education and Skills Act 2008	In Schedule 1, paragraphs 1 to 4 and the crossheading preceding paragraph 1.
Local Transport Act 2008	Section 55. Section 56.
Apprenticeships, Skills, Children and Learning Act 2009	Section 221(3).

]³⁵⁴

[PART 1A
REPEALS RELATING TO THE COMMENCEMENT OF THE PUBLIC
SECTOR EQUALITY DUTY ON 5TH APRIL 2011

Short Title	Extent of repeal
Race Relations (Amendment) Act 2000	Section 2. Schedule 1. In Schedule 2, paragraph 17.
Nationality, Immigration and Asylum Act 2002	Section 6(5).
Water Act 2003	In Schedule 7, paragraph 22.
Courts Act 2003	In Schedule 8, paragraph 187.
Health and Social Care (Community Health and Standards) Act 2003	In Schedule 4, paragraphs 21 and 22.
Health Protection Agency Act 2004	In Schedule 3, paragraph 8.
Energy Act 2004	In Schedule 14, paragraph 4.
Fire and Rescue Services Act 2004	In Schedule 1, paragraph 48.
Civil Contingencies Act 2004	In Schedule 2, paragraph 10(3)(a).
Disability Discrimination Act 2005	Section 3.
Serious Organised Crime and Police Act 2005	In Schedule 4, paragraphs 33 to 35.
Education Act 2005	In Schedule 14, paragraphs 6 and 8.
Gambling Act 2005	In Schedule 16, paragraph 9.
London Olympic Games and Paralympic Games Act 2006	In Schedule 1, paragraph 21
Natural Environment and Rural Communities Act 2006	In Schedule 11— (a) paragraph 61, and (b) in paragraph 175(2), 'in the Race Relations Act 1976 (c. 74), Part 2 of Schedule 1A;'.
National Health Service (Consequential Provisions) Act 2006	In Schedule 1, paragraphs 55 and 56.
Police and Justice Act 2006	In Schedule 1, paragraph 60.
Tourist Boards (Scotland) Act 2006	In Schedule 2, paragraph 3.

³⁵⁴ Substituted by Equality Act 2010 (Consequential Amendments, Saving and Supplementary Provisions) Order 2010, SI 2010/2279.

Short Title	Extent of repeal
Tribunals, Courts and Enforcement Act 2007	In Schedule 8, paragraph 7.
Offender Management Act 2007	In Schedule 3, paragraphs 1 and 7.
Legal Services Act 2007	In Schedule 21, paragraph 39.
Health and Social Care Act 2008	In Schedule 5, paragraph 59. In Schedule 10, paragraph 6.
Housing and Regeneration Act 2008	In Schedule 8, paragraph 21. In Schedule 9, paragraph 4.
Local Transport Act 2008	In Schedule 4, paragraph 49.
Climate Change Act 2008	In Schedule 1, paragraph 32.
Pensions Act 2008	In Schedule 1, paragraph 25.
Local Democracy, Economic Development and Construction Act 2009	In Schedule 6, paragraph 44.
Apprenticeships, Skills, Children and Learning Act 2009	In Schedule 6, paragraph 1. In Schedule 12, paragraph 7.
Marine and Coastal Access Act 2009	In Schedule 2, paragraph 4.
Policing and Crime Act 2009	Section 2(3).

]355

PART 2
REVOCATIONS

Title	Extent of revocation
Occupational Pension Schemes(Equal Treatment) Regulations 1995 (S.I. 1995/3183)	The whole Regulations.
Employment Equality (Religion or Belief) Regulations 2003 (S.I. 2003/1660)	The whole Regulations.
Employment Equality (Sexual Orientation) Regulations2003 (S.I. 2003/1661)	The whole Regulations.
Disability Discrimination Act 1995 (Pensions) Regulations2003 (S.I. 2003/2770)	The whole Regulations.
Occupational Pension Schemes (Equal Treatment) (Amendment) Regulations 2005 (S.I. 2005/1923)	The whole Regulations.
Employment Equality (Age) Regulations 2006 (S.I. 2006/1031)	The whole Regulations (other than Schedules 6 and 8).
Equality Act (Sexual Orientation) Regulations 2007 (S.I. 2007/1263)	The whole Regulations.
Sex Discrimination(Amendment of Legislation) Regulations 2008 (S.I. 2008/963)	The whole Regulations.

355 Inserted by Equality Act 2010 (Public Authorities and Consequential and Supplementary Amendments) Order 2011, SI 2011/1060.

[PART 3
REVOCATIONS RELATING TO THE COMMENCEMENT OF THE PUBLIC
SECTOR EQUALITY DUTY ON 5TH APRIL 2011

Title	Extent of revocation
National Health Service Reform and Health Care Professions Act 2002 (Supplementary, Consequential etc. Provisions) Regulations 2002 (S.I. 2002/2469)	In Schedule 1, paragraph 9.
Health Professions Order 2001 (Consequential Amendments) Order 2003 (S.I. 2003/1590)	In the Schedule, paragraph 4.
Further and Higher Education (Scotland) Act 2005 (Consequential Modifications) Order 2005 (S.I. 2005/2077)	Article 5.
Water Services etc. (Scotland) Act 2005 (Consequential Provisions and Modifications) Order 2005 (S.I. 2005/3172)	In the Schedule, paragraph 2.
References to Health Authorities Order 2007 (S.I. 2007/961)	In the Schedule, paragraph 12.
Tourist Boards (Scotland) Act 2006 (Consequential Modifications) Order 2007 (S.I. 2007/1103)	In the Schedule, paragraph 3.
Government of Wales Act 2006 (Consequential Modifications and Transitional Provisions) Order 2007 (S.I. 2007/1388)	In Schedule 1, paragraphs 10 to 16.
Agriculture and Horticulture Development Board Order 2008 (S.I. 2008/576)	In Schedule 5, paragraph 4.
Apprenticeships, Skills, Children and Learning Act 2009 (Consequential Amendments) (England and Wales) Order 2010 (S.I. 2010/1080)	In Schedule 1, paragraphs 9 to 11.
Local Education Authorities and Children's Services Authorities (Integration of Functions) Order 2010 (S.I. 2010/1158)	In Schedule 2, in Part 2, paragraph 30.

][356]

SCHEDULE 28   Section 214

INDEX OF DEFINED EXPRESSIONS

Expression	Provision
Accrual of rights, in relation to an occupational pension scheme	Section 212(12)
Additional maternity leave	Section 213(6) and (7)
Additional maternity leave period	Section 213(8)
Age discrimination	Section 25(1)
Age group	Section 5(2)
Armed forces	Section 212(1)

[356] Inserted by Equality Act 2010 (Public Authorities and Consequential and Supplementary Amendments) Order 2011, SI 2011/1060.

Expression	Provision
Association	Section 107(2)
Auxiliary aid	Section 20(11)
Belief	Section 10(2)
Breach of an equality clause or rule	Section 212(8)
The Commission	Section 212(1)
Commonhold	Section 38(7)
Compulsory maternity leave	Section 213(3)
Contract work	Section 41(6)
Contract worker	Section 41(7)
Contravention of this Act	Section 212(9)
Crown employment	Section 83(9)
Detriment	Section 212(1) and (5)
Disability	Section 6(1)
Disability discrimination	Section 25(2)
Disabled person	Section 6(2) and (4)
Discrimination	Sections 13 to 19, 21 and 108
Disposal, in relation to premises	Section 38(3) to (5)
Education Acts	Section 212(1)
Employer, in relation to an occupational pension scheme	Section 212(11)
Employment	Section 212(1)
Enactment	Section 212(1)
Equality clause	Section 212(1)
Equality rule	Section 212(1)
Firm	Section 46(2)
Gender reassignment	Section 7(1)
Gender reassignment discrimination	Section 25(3)
Harassment	Section 26(1)
Independent educational institution	Section 89(7)
LLP	Section 46(4)
Man	Section 212(1)
Marriage and civil partnership	Section 8
Marriage and civil partnership discrimination	Section 25(4)
Maternity equality clause	Section 212(1)
Maternity equality rule	Section 212(1)
Maternity leave	Section 213(2)
Member, in relation to an occupational pension scheme	Section 212(10)
Member of the executive	Section 212(7)

(Continued)

Expression	Provision
Non-discrimination rule	Section 212(1)
Occupation, in relation to premises	Section 212(6)
Occupational pension scheme	Section 212(1)
Offshore work	Section 82(3)
Ordinary maternity leave	Section 213(4) and (5)
Parent	Section 212(1)
Pension credit member	Section 212(11)
Pensionable service	Section 212(11)
Pensioner member	Section 212(11)
Personal office	Section 49(2)
Physical feature	Section 20(10)
Pregnancy and maternity discrimination	Section 25(5)
Premises	Section 38(2)
Prescribed	Section 212(1)
Profession	Section 212(1)
Proposed firm	Section 46(3)
Proposed LLP	Section 46(5)
Proprietor, in relation to a school	Section 89(4)
Protected characteristics	Section 4
Protected period, in relation to pregnancy	Section 18(6)
Provision of a service	Sections 31 and 212(4)
Public function	Sections 31(4) and 150(5)
Public office	Sections 50(2) and 52(4)
Pupil	Section 89(3)
Race	Section 9(1)
Race discrimination	Section 25(6)
Reasonable adjustments, duty to make	Section 20
Relevant member of the House of Commons staff	Section 83(5)
Relevant member of the House of Lords staff	Section 83(6)
Relevant person, in relation to a personal or public office	Section 52(6)
Religion	Section 10(1)
Religious or belief-related discrimination	Section 25(7)
Requirement, the first, second or third	Section 20
Responsible body, in relation to a further or higher education institution	Section 91(12)
Responsible body, in relation to a school	Section 85(9)
School	Section 89(5) and (6)
Service-provider	Section 29(1)
Sex	Section 11

Expression	Provision
Sex discrimination	Section 25(8)
Sex equality clause	Section 212(1)
Sex equality rule	Section 212(1)
Sexual orientation	Section 12(1)
Sexual orientation discrimination	Section 25(9)
Student	Section 94(3)
Subordinate legislation	Section 212(1)
Substantial	Section 212(1)
Taxi, for the purposes of Part 3 (services and public functions)	Schedule 2, paragraph 4
Taxi, for the purposes of Chapter 1 of Part 12 (disabled persons: transport)	Section 173(1)
Tenancy	Section 38(6)
Trade	Section 212(1)
Transsexual person	Section 7(2)
Trustees or managers, in relation to an occupational pension scheme	Section 212(11)
University	Section 94(4)
Victimisation	Section 27(1)
Vocational training	Section 56(6)
Woman	Section 212(1)

Index